D0705815

Modern Education Finance and Policy

JAMES W. GUTHRIE
Peabody College of Vanderbilt University

MATTHEW G. SPRINGER
Peabody College of Vanderbilt University

R. ANTHONY ROLLE
Peabody College of Vanderbilt University

ERIC A. HOUCK
Peabody College of Vanderbilt University

PEARSON

Boston   New York   San Francisco
Mexico City   Montreal   Toronto   London   Madrid   Munich   Paris
Hong Kong   Singapore   Tokyo   Cape Town   Sydney

Senior Editor: Arnis Burvikovs
Development Editor: Christien Shangraw
Editorial Assistant: Erin Reilly
Marketing Manager: Tara Kelly
Production Editor: Gregory Erb
Editorial Production Service: Nesbitt Graphics, Inc.
Composition Buyer: Linda Cox
Manufacturing Buyer: Linda Morris
Electronic Composition: Nesbitt Graphics, Inc.
Interior Design: Nesbitt Graphics, Inc.
Cover Designer: Kristina Mose-Libon

For related titles and support materials, visit our online catalog at www.ablongman.com.

Copyright © 2007 Pearson Education, Inc.

All rights reserved. No part of the material protected by this copyright notice may be reproduced or utilized in any form or by any means, electronic or mechanical, including photocopying, recording, or by any information storage and retrieval system, without written permission from the copyright owner.

To obtain permission(s) to use material from this work, please submit a written request to Allyn and Bacon, Permissions Department, 75 Arlington Street, Boston, MA 02116 or fax your request to 617-848-7320.

Between the time website information is gathered and then published, it is not unusual for some sites to have closed. Also, the transcription of URLs can result in typographical errors. The publisher would appreciate notification where these errors occur so that they may be corrected in subsequent editions.

Library of Congress Cataloging-in-Publication Data

Modern education finance and policy/James Guthrie . . . [et al.].
    p. cm. — (Peabody education leadership series)
  Includes bibliographical references and index.
  ISBN 0-205-47001-7
  1. Education—United States—Finance—Textbooks. 2. Government aid to education—United
    States—Textbooks. 3. Education and state—United States—Textbooks. I. Guthrie, James W.
  LB2825.M49 2007
  371.2'060973—dc22

                                                                              2006023284

Printed in the United States of America

10 9 8 7 6 5 4 3 2 1 RRD-VA 10 09 08 07 06

Contents

CHAPTER FIVE

Legal Complexities of Modern Education Finance   82

CHAPTER EIGHT

Distributing State Education Funds   **166**

CHAPTER ELEVEN

Managing Capital Projects and Fiscal Resources   242

PART IV Dynamics of Modern Education Finance: Challenges of Equality, Efficiency, and Liberty   263

CHAPTER TWELVE

Equality/Equity   263

Series Preface

■ THE PEABODY EDUCATION LEADERSHIP SERIES

Vanderbilt University's Peabody College is one of the world's foremost schools of education and human development. The Peabody faculty is in the vanguard of research and knowledge creation, while a long tradition of collaboration "on the ground" with learners, educators, policymakers and organizations ensures that, at Peabody, theory and practice inform each other. In addition to conferring a full range of graduate, professional, and undergraduate degrees, the College is committed to strengthening current educators and organizational leaders in their efforts to propel greater achievement and enhance human development.

This book and others in the Allyn & Bacon Peabody Education Leadership Series are published to facilitate wider understanding of the means by which human learning takes place and how greater learning can be fostered. Much of the nation's most forward thinking regarding learning and instruction emanates from Peabody. For example, the National Research Council's famous research synthesis, *How People Learn*, was undertaken with the leadership of Peabody faculty. Current faculty members are generating research and constructing the paradigms that will influence the teaching of reading, mathematics, and science well into the future.

Consistent with its mission and its own research, Peabody strives to model good instruction. In that spirit, each book in the Education Leadership Series has a number of instructional aids. These include full outlines of the volume's substantive material, complete tables of contents, indexes filled with significant concepts and citations, technical glossaries, chapter previews with summaries of what has been and is to be covered, extensive use of topical case studies, clearly understandable graphics, and discussion questions. These aids will enable readers to grasp the complexities associated with what 21st-century leaders need to know about such topics as leadership, finance, accountability, community relations, organizational dynamics, or education law.

■ TEXT SUPPLEMENTS

Each text in this series is accompanied by a **Companion Web site**. Students and instructors should visit www.ablongman.com/Peabody for test cases, simulation exercises, sample data for end-of-chapter exercises, URLs for further research and interest, added bibliographies, and other up-to-date information.

Students can find help with research projects using **Research Navigator**™, which provides access to three exclusive databases of credible and reliable source material, including

EBSCO's ContentSelect Academic Journal Database, *The New York Times* Search by Subject Archive, and the "Best of the Web" Link Library. Research Navigator™ is available through Allyn & Bacon's **MyLabSchool**, located at www.mylabschool.com.

An **Instructor's Manual** with teaching resources and test items is also available to adopting instructors through their local Allyn & Bacon representative.

■ THE PEABODY EDUCATION LEADERSHIP SERIES AND EDUCATION'S EVOLVING CONTEXT

Education today must respond as never before to a set of global economic and cultural conditions. These rapidly changing conditions, and the competition they are creating, serve as a subtext for virtually every concept covered by books in this textbook series.

For most of the nation's history, it was possible for an individual to forego formal schooling and still own land, acquire relatively well-paying employment, participate in civic life as an informed citizen, and achieve a substantial degree of personal fulfillment. For many, probably most, individuals, these comfortable circumstances have changed. Modern economies render formal education crucial for individual success, social mobility, and engagement with the demands of the workforce, the environment, and government. The eventual outcome of these relatively new challenges now matters as much for a child being raised on a family farm in South Dakota as to one from a farm family in South Africa.

What has become true for individuals also applies to nations. A people once flourished or floundered based on what they could extract from the ground. Today, a nation is more likely to survive and prosper based on what it can extract from the minds of its citizens.

Readers of this series also will have to grapple with the challenges posed by global changes. Many of the divisive questions facing society as a whole have powerful implications for the conduct of education, as well.

- How can immigrants be fully integrated into American society?
- How many languages can schools reasonably be expected to offer or to use for instruction?
- How much testing is too much?
- How much should be spent on schools to ensure that all students have an opportunity to achieve the learning standards that governments set?
- How should teachers be trained and licensed?
- Should private providers be permitted to offer public schooling?
- Should the public pay for preschool and interschool programs?
- Should high school exit examinations determine graduation?
- What should class sizes be to maximize the positive effects of instruction?

These questions illustrate the complicated and interconnected policy and practical dilemmas upon which books in this series will attempt to shed light. The goal is not so much to provide direct answers to such questions as it is to arm readers with the tools that will enable them to keep pace with, and contribute solutions to, these and future problems. Specifically, this series will:

- Harness useful concepts and evidenced-based practical understandings applicable to understanding and solving emerging policy challenges and to managing and reforming modern organizations

- Provide readers with technical understanding of important components of education resource deployment, policy development, organizational development, and institutional governance and operation
- Suggest research-based means by which education institutions and practices can be undertaken to greater effect and with greater efficiency
- Enable educators to participate better in policy-related and professional debates regarding best practice

We welcome your comments and suggestions as a reader, researcher, or other user of this book, or other books in the series.

James W. Guthrie
Series Editor
Professor of Public Policy and Education

Camilla P. Benbow
Patricia and Rodes Hart Dean of Education
and Human Development

Peabody College
Vanderbilt University
Nashville, Tennessee

Preface

▧ THIS BOOK'S PURPOSE

The purpose of this textbook is twofold. The first is to clarify complex public policy issues at the intersection of formal precollegiate education (pre-K through 12) and resource generation and deployment. Without clarifying and communicating these complexities—as well as the foundational knowledge at the heart of education policy and school finance—we would fail in our efforts to generate a textbook with practical utility.

The second purpose is to provide the next generation of teachers, principals, administrators, policymakers and education finance scholars with prerequisite knowledge of key finance concepts and practices, and the tools that thus enable them to leverage school finance matters to further advance contemporary education operations. To that end, we draw on innovative learning techniques developed by Vanderbilt University's Cognition and Technology Group and progressive assessment techniques developed by Grant Wiggins and Jay McTighe (1998).

Education Policy and Resource Generation and Deployment

To fulfill the textbook's first purpose, three related topics are explored with considerable intensity: (1) societal interactions with education, (2) means for generating and deploying financial resources for education, and (3) major public policy and education policy issues along with their resource consequences. As a result, the book is divided into four parts. Each part contains material related to one of the three, above specified fundamental themes. A final part provides summary and describes some of the political dynamics involved in reforming finance arrangements. Chapters within each part concentrate on different facets of the three topics listed above.

Since the 1983 issuance of the federal government report *A Nation at Risk*, the United States has undertaken a sustained effort to render public schools more effective. This reform effort is characterized by three major conditions, all of which have education finance issues at their core.

One noticeable and significant change in the education finance environment is an intensified reliance on litigation as a means for altering education resource distribution. The legalization of education finance policy now takes place at an unprecedented pace in the United States. As this book goes to press, education finance lawsuits are under way, either in a discovery phase, at trial, or on appeal, in 20 states. Another 20 states have already experienced one or more such suits. Whether or not this strategy renders education more effective is a matter of debate, and this book will present empirical evidence regarding the issue. Nevertheless, because of the vastly increased personal, economic, and societal significance of schooling, advocates of all kinds want to ensure fair and adequate access to it. Hence, they rely on litigation as one means available within the political system for pursuing or protecting their interests.

Another significant contextual development since the issuance of *A Nation at Risk* is a transformed perception within the policy system of education and its management. Schools were once judged by the quality, or at least the amount, of their inputs, such as expenditures per pupil, spectrum of courses and after-school activities, teacher salaries, student social and economic composition, teacher characteristics, or richness of school facilities. Today, however, schools are increasingly judged by outputs: the academic achievement of their students. Enactment in 2001 of major federal legislation, the No Child Left Behind Act, strongly symbolizes and reinforces this transformation.

A third transformation is the emergence of three rationally conceived, sometimes competitively posed, archetypical strategies for rendering schools more effective. One of these reform strategies is a so-called "systemic reform" approach (Smith and O'Day, 1991). Another is an expanded reliance on performance incentives and market forces and greater competition among providers (Chubb and Moe, 1990). A third strategy calls for intensified efforts to reinforce the out-of-school well-being of students in hopes of enabling them to perform better in school. The three strategies are not incompatible. Each will be explained in greater detail in subsequent chapters. The strategies can fit together and in a few instances, for example, in components of the above-mentioned No Child Left Behind Act, are woven together.

These three evolving conditions—legalization, performance orientation, and strategic reform considerations—have significantly altered the field of education finance. This change is so fundamental and has such far-reaching implications for the study of education finance, research on education finance issues, and the preparation of education finance scholars and education leaders, that early sections of this book work to distinguish the "new" from "early" in education finance thinking. Hence the focus of this book on "modern education finance."

These three evolving conditions are rooted in a common societal dynamic. They have emerged, or at least have been accelerated by, a remarkable change in the significance modern society accords formal education. When formal schooling played a minor role in the well-being of individuals and the future of a society, schooling was far less often the focus of litigation, outputs mattered less, and strategies for promoting school effectiveness were of lesser concern. Now that education means more, formal schooling attracts a far larger sector of interests regarding access to it, outcomes from it, and means for linking resources to outputs. It also routinely receives larger wedges of the public sector resource pie.

One can no longer hope to understand education finance by simply attending to technical mechanics; comprehension now is also rooted in understanding societal dynamics. As a result of this change, the intensified interaction between the larger society and education has altered the balance of information contained in this book. Whereas technical mechanics still count, and are covered in detail (Part 3), they also must be linked to the forces that shape them (Part 2) and the issues they are expected to address (Part 4).

Enhancing Student Learning and Performance

In the last decade, efforts to unravel what is meant by and how to assess student understanding have generated considerable dialogue among education stakeholders in general and cognitive scientists in particular. Whereas the mere recital of discrete morsels of knowledge and facts by students was once generally accepted as an appropriate indicator of student understanding, more contemporary approaches stress elements such as conceptual clarity, real-world application, critical analysis, and detached reflection to appraise student understanding. In an extension of those approaches, this textbook strives to enhance student learning and performance through combining an innovative assessment technique called *Understanding by Design*, which promotes deep understanding and meaningful application by students.

Understanding by Design. The approach to learning employed within these pages is grounded in the performance assessments developed by Grant Wiggins and Jay McTighe, two leading advocates of situating student understanding at the core of curricular, assessment, and instructional designs. In 1998, Wiggins and McTighe published the highly acclaimed *Understanding by Design*, a resource book for educators that sponsors performance assessment as a means to promote deep understanding of content by students. Wiggins and McTighe assert that an individual truly understands when he or she: (1) can explain, (2) can interpret, (3) can apply, (4) has perspective, (5) can emphasize, and (6) has self-knowledge. This textbook draws on Wiggins and McTighe's six facets of understanding through the use of discussion questions, case studies, and articles from mainstream media to enhance student understanding of the topics under consideration.

The use of this approach to student understanding yields a standard chapter outline that will guide students through the rest of this text. Each chapter begins with a short list of learning objectives. Throughout the chapter, readers will encounter material that will be used to guide discussion. Often, this material will refer readers back to one of five case studies that are presented in Part 1.[1] In addition, each chapter will have an "In the News" feature that highlights a newspaper article, journal article, press release, or similar piece of media, presenting the issues in each chapter in a real-world context. The end of each chapter contains a chapter summary, a list of discussion questions, proposed class activities, and web links to additional resources. Some activities will be case studies of individuals or abstract problems, others will consist of databases for applied study and problem solving. In addition, key terms will be boldfaced in the text and defined in the glossary at the end of the book.

■ THIS BOOK'S ORGANIZATION

This book is organized into four parts: (1) Case Challenges Illustrating Modern Education Finance; (2) Context, Contrast, Control, Complexity, and Culture: Frameworks for Understanding Modern Education Finance; (3) Mechanics of Modern Education Finance: Generating and Distributing Financial Resources; and (4) Dynamics of Modern Education Finance: Challenges of Equality, Efficiency, and Liberty.

Case Challenges Illustrating Modern Education Finance

Part 1 presents a series of challenges through case studies. These case challenges illustrate the conflicting and perplexing nature of the education finance-related issues that school and public officials face in their day-to-day leadership roles. They are intended to illustrate how broadly education finance issues now affect day-to-day operations of schools and districts, as well as the intensity of involvement on the part of public officials at all levels and branches of government in education finance matters.

Context, Contrast, Control, Complexity, and Culture: Frameworks for Understanding Modern Education Finance

Part 2 describes the evolving contemporary societal contexts, historic contrasts, organizational controls, legal complexities, and policy cultures that are continually reshaping education finance. This part provides social perspectives, historical knowledge, and social science concepts readers can use to form a basis for understanding the education finance-specific theories and applications discussed later.

Chapter 2 describes the structural and dynamic features of education in the United States and the various social forces that give form and substance to those conditions. This chapter explains the broad boundaries of a policy paradigm, summarizes demographic and economic trends that exert tremendous force on American education, and weighs five central dimensions of the American educational system: (1) enrollments, (2) personnel, (3) governmental arrangements, (4) financial costs, and (5) student outcomes.

Chapter 3 describes the history of education finance, illustrates policy issues and operating practices that support the emergence of modern education finance, and specifies what distinguishes modern education finance from past paradigms. This chapter makes clear that education financing is now a principal instrument for pursuing education policy, moving from the periphery of policymaker concern to a far more central role.

The purpose of Chapter 4 is fourfold. The chapter (1) describes the complexity of American school and school system structure and governance; (2) describes and analyzes the organization and control of American education; (3) dissects the multiple layers of statutory and legal authority that impinge on schools and school districts; and (4) displays the myriad relationships and constituencies with which school leaders are inevitably involved. All these conditions influence the manner in which resources are generated, distributed, and committed.

Chapter 5 addresses the most dominant contemporary influence in U.S. education finance policymaking—the legal system. In fact, the last quarter of the 20th century and initial years of the 21st century display a remarkable pattern of education finance litigation covering all but four states. This chapter explains the U.S. legal system, the principles and assumptions underlying it, and the ways in which judicial decisions have been reshaping the fundamentals of U.S. education finance.

The purpose of Chapter 6 is to describe the manner in which the policy system operates and, thus, to explain how modern education finance is emerging, and emerging rapidly, from major changes in society. This discussion relies heavily on the prior explanations of societal contexts, historical contrasts, organizational controls, and legal complexities and attempts a synthesis within a framework of policy systems theory. Finally, this chapter illustrates the remarkably rich manner in which policy options can be chosen and mixed to frame new models of governance and finance.

Mechanics of Modern Education Finance: Generating and Distributing Financial Resources

Part 3 concentrates on the policy challenges and practical operation of U.S. education finance.

Chapter 7 explains the magnitude of education revenues, bases of taxation, types of taxes, the tax limitation movement, structural disequilibrium between state tax structures and education demands, and revenue alternatives to taxation.

Chapter 8 explains education finance funding distribution mechanisms such as foundation plans, full state funding, flat grants, percentage equalizing, revenue recapture, and school vouchers. It assumes knowledge regarding revenue generation, covered in Chapter 7. Matters of federal government education funding and resource allocation within school districts are covered in later chapters.

Chapter 9 provides a historical understanding of the federal role in education funding and explains significant current programs such as Impact Aid, Vocational Education, the Individuals with Disabilities Education Act (IDEA), and No Child Left Behind (NCLB). Chapter 9 also takes into account actual intergovernmental operating dynamics between federal and state officials and explores current issues such as "adequate yearly progress" and assurance of "highly qualified teachers."

Chapter 10 explains resource allocation within an operating organization, with a focus on deploying and administering resources. An effective budget process can improve an organization's productivity and accountability. When used as a strategic tool, the budget process can help to focus the efforts of an organization's personnel on educational priorities in order to maximize student learning. Conversely, a poorly managed budget process can be a constant drain on educational stakeholders' time and energy, thus diverting attention from instructional activities.

Chapter 11 explains the means by which revenues are generated and overall planning undertaken for construction of school facilities, since this is a different set of processes than those responsible for generating operating revenues.

Dynamics of Modern Education Finance: The Challenges of Equality, Efficiency, and Liberty

Part 4 concentrates on linkages between modern education finance and frequently issued proposals to make American schooling more fair, effective, and attractive to users.

Chapter 12 is devoted to a historical analysis of initial efforts to achieve finance equity, statistical means for defining and measuring equity, current status of equity in the United States education finance system, and a transition for readers into the modern version of equity, adequacy.

Chapter 13 explains the history and legal evolution of education finance adequacy (also known as equity II) and a description of means for measuring and efforts to obtain "adequate" financing.

Chapter 14 explains issues in measuring efficiency in education and emerging econometric means for appraising efficiency. It also defines and evaluates policy interventions to improve efficiency in schools.

Chapter 15 explains the means by which the U.S. education system attempts to balance policy concerns for equity with practical mechanisms that permit choice (e.g., smaller school districts, open enrollment, and charter schools) and proceeds further to illustrate the intersection of choice and finance (e.g., voucher plans, tuition tax credits, and education stamps).

■ ACKNOWLEDGMENTS

A public policy book of this coverage and complexity seldom stands by itself. It is a product of much that has preceded it. At the turn of the 20th century, Elwood Patterson Cubberley,

Stanford professor and founding dean of that campus's education school, established a scholarly basis for understanding education finance. In later years, a subsequent Stanford University professor and education school dean, H. Thomas James, began to apply social science modeling to education finance issues. One of his counterparts, University of California–Berkeley professor Charles Scott Benson, began to import economic concepts into James's finance models. In the third quarter of the 20th century, Boalt Hall Law School professors John E. Coons and Stephen D. Sugarman, Wisconsin lawyer-sociologist William H. Clune, and Arthur E. Wise, then of the University of Chicago and later of RAND and chief executive of the National Council for Accreditation of Teacher Education, revolutionized the field by linking financial conditions for schools to constitutional law theories.

Modern education finance owes much to the individuals listed above. They provided a scholarly basis for future academic inquiry and expanded the field with their research publications and understanding of interactions between public finance and education economics. However, modern education finance's roots rest as much with practicing lawyers as with public finance experts, legal scholars, and academic economists. It is principally through trial court arguments, judicial decisions, and searches for judicially acceptable policy remedies that modern education finance is being shaped.

Plaintiff advocates have been remarkably successful in shaping modern education finance. Principal among those who have plowed the field in a sustained quest to root out finance inequities are long-standing civil rights attorneys David Long, Peter Roos, and John McDermott. Even though a relative newcomer, New York attorney Michael Rebell is notable for his remarkable persistence and keen understanding that law coupled with public engagement and media campaigning can sometimes be a more powerful tool for righting wrongs than the law by itself.

Defense attorneys, sometimes prevailing in equity cases and sometimes losing, also have shaped the new education finance. Neil Slotnick and Kathleen Strasbaugh of the Alaska Attorney General's Office; David Matthews of Matthews, Campbell, Rhoads McClure, Thompson & Fryauf, P.A. in Arkansas; Robin Johansen and the late Joseph Remcho of Remcho, Johansen & Purcell in California; Ralph Urban of the Connecticut Attorney General's Office; Alfred Lindseth, Rocco Testani, and John Bonds of Sutherland, Asbill & Brennan, LLP in Georgia; Mark Overstreet and Judith Villines of Stites & Harbison, PLLC in Kentucky; Juliana Rice and Deirdre Roney of the Massachusetts Attorney General's Office; Dennis O'Brien of Littler Mendelson, PLC in Minnesota; Michael Vanselow of the Minnesota Attorney General's Office; Elizabeth Gray, Bobby Stepp, and Jackson Barnes of Sowell, Gray, Stepp and Lafitte, LLC in South Carolina; Jeff Rose and Linda Halpern of the Texas Attorney General's Office; Michael O'Donnell of the Wyoming Attorney General's Office; and Jack Speight and Robert McCue of Speight, McCue and Associates, PC in Wyoming have contributed by reminding the court of the restricted role that jurisprudence can play in public policy, the limits to what schooling, by itself, can do to create a just society, and the use of modern social science in distilling evidentiary issues.

I, James W. Guthrie, senior author of this text, have been engaged during discovery and at trial by every attorney listed above. Whether in cooperation with or in opposition to these individuals, I have never failed to admire their legal knowledge, professional commitment, breadth of understanding, and comity. Additionally, I have worked with individuals who have consistently attempted to translate between social science scholars, attorneys, and the practical world of school operation. Among these have been my past and present colleagues—James A. Kelly, Gerald C. Hayward, and James R. Smith. They too have provided inspiration and know-how enabling this book to reach fruition. The latter two have been my business partners in one of the nation's most successful litigation support and education management consulting firms, Management Analysis & Planning Inc.

I have benefited from having been mentored by many of the individuals listed above. Specifically, I owe an intellectual debt to H. Thomas James, my Stanford University adviser and friend, John E. Coons, Stephen D. Sugarman, Arthur E. Wise, and others too numerous to name.

Three other individuals are worthy of special mention. Richard Rothstein, of Teachers College, Columbia University, contributed his vast understanding of interactions between education and the larger society. Michael W. Kirst of Stanford University shared his unparalleled insights into education policy issues. And RAND Corporation Senior Policy Researcher Janet S. Hansen's sustained ability to question resulted in many positive manuscript Revisions. This book also owes much to departed colleagues, particularly Charles S. Benson and Walter I. Garms.

The teachings of all the individuals listed above are reflected in this book, I hope accurately.

We also enjoyed the benefit of commentary by expert reviewers, who offered close, critical readings of our developing manuscript. They are: Frank Brown, The University of North Carolina at Chapel Hill; Daniel Gutmore, Seton Hall University; Leon Hendricks, Chicago State University; Marilyn Hirth, Purdue University; and Mary McCullough, Loyola Marymount University. Many thanks go to them for their generous professional assistance.

Now, speaking for all four authors, we wish to express appreciation for the many means by which Peabody College colleagues assisted in this effort. Specifically, we wish to thank David Frisvold and Caroline Watral, who in their roles as Ph.D. students, contributed drafts of substantive chapters of this book. Graduate students Monica Bhatt, Deborah Enright, and Christina Hart provided additional research assistance. We also wish to thank Joyce Hilley for sustained, professional, and generous help with matters such as contract arrangements, graphics, proofreading, and logistics.

Finally, we wish to express our appreciation to Peabody College Dean, Camilla P. Benbow, and to Allyn & Bacon officials, particularly Arnis Burvikovs, Senior Editor, and Christien Shangraw, Development Editor, whose encouragements rendered this project doable.

As authors, we are flattered at reader interest in this volume and welcome suggestions for improving its accuracy and utility. As should be obvious in such ventures, errors and omissions are the responsibility of authors alone.

James W. Guthrie • Matthew G. Springer • R. Anthony Rolle • Eric A. Houck

Peabody College
Vanderbilt University
Nashville, Tennessee

---

[1]Chapters 12, 14 and 15 each include additional case studies.

About the Authors

James W. Guthrie is a professor of public policy and education, chair of Leadership, Policy and Organizations, and director of the Peabody Center for Education Policy at Peabody College of Vanderbilt University. He instructs both undergraduate and graduate courses, and conducts research on education policy and finance. He also is the founder and chairman of the board of Management Analysis & Planning, Inc. (MAP), a California private sector management consulting firm specializing in public finance and litigation support.

Previously a professor at the University of California, Berkeley for 27 years, he holds a BA, MA, and PhD from Stanford University, and undertook postdoctoral study in public finance at Harvard. He also was a postdoctoral Fellow at Oxford Brookes College, Oxford, England, and the Irving R. Melbo Visiting Professor at the University of Southern California.

He is the author or co-author of ten books and more than 200 professional and scholarly articles. He was the editor-in-chief of the *Encyclopedia of American Education*, published in 2002.

Matthew G. Springer is a research assistant professor of public policy and education with Peabody College of Vanderbilt University and director of the federally funded National Center on Performance Incentives. His research interests involve educational policy issues, with a particular focus on the impact of education policy on resource allocation decisions and student outcomes. Professor Springer received a BA from Denison University and MA and PhD degrees from Peabody College of Vanderbilt University. Previously, he served as a public school teacher in central Ohio and as an administrator and teacher at a private boarding school in upstate New York.

R. Anthony Rolle has conducted K–12 education finance and policy research for over 15 years. His primary research investigates applications of relative economic efficiency measures for improving public schools, and applications of vertical equity measures for improving state education finance mechanisms. Professor Rolle received the American Educational Finance Association's Jean Flanigan Dissertation Award for his empirical work that modified budget-maximizing theory and questioned normative ideas of efficiency in education. Currently an associate professor at Texas A&M University, Professor Rolle received a BA from Santa Clara University, an MA from the University of Washington, and a PhD from Indiana University.

Eric A. Houck is an assistant professor of educational administration and policy at the University of Georgia. His research focuses on intradistrict school finance equity. He earned his BA from the University of North Carolina at Chapel Hill, his MA from the University of Wisconsin-Madison, and his PhD from Peabody College of Vanderbilt University.

A former high school English teacher, Professor Houck has served as research director of Wake Education Partnership—a community-based public education advocacy organization—and has facilitated school/business partnerships for the Wake County (NC) Public School System, the 26th largest school system in the nation.

CHAPTER ONE

Education Finance Challenges Confronting Educators

It may be easy to see the relationship between education policymaking and education finance; it may be more difficult to see and understand the connections between educational administration and education finance. This chapter will help you make immediate connections and will continue to provide a resource throughout the remaining chapters of this text.

The following "case challenges" illustrate the conflicting and perplexing nature of education finance-related issues that school and public officials face in their day-to-day leadership roles. These cases are illustrative and do not represent real persons or places. They do, however, illustrate real situations and real problems. Issues raised in these cases will be the subject of explanations and analyses throughout later chapters.

A summary is provided at the end of this chapter distilling key education finance and policy issues with which the practitioners in the five case studies have grappled.

CASE 1

River City Blues

Frank Farley was in his second year as superintendent in River City. He had previously held other school district CEO jobs in smaller communities. However, River City, the heart of a thriving 1.5 million population metropolitan area, was the biggest career apple for him so far.

Frank had come through the education ranks, having been a classroom science teacher, assistant principal, high school principal, and central office official. He held an EdD from a respected institution and he was well known nationally among public school superintendents. He was tall, athletic, handsome, well dressed, and well spoken. He had acquired a reputation in his prior positions as being both tough minded and fair. He was also known for taking on challenging assignments, and succeeding. If he had been a private sector CEO, he might well have commanded a million dollar a year salary. As a public school superintendent, he was paid just over $200,000.

More than one newspaper article speculated on a possible career for Farley as an elected or corporate official, and on several occasions he had discussed with his wife a second career in politics or as a high-level federal appointee. They had decided that it would be better to restrain their ambitions until two conditions had been achieved: one, their children were older and, two, he had turned River City's schools around. The easier part of the equation was waiting for their children to grow older. Turning River City schools around was proving more difficult than the optimistic Farley had initially imagined.

River City was in the Midsouth but it had a Midwest can-do attitude. It had several remarkable advantages as a modern U.S. city. It had a diversified employment structure, the beginnings of a high-tech sector, and it benefited from geographic centrality and easy transportation access to midwestern and eastern markets. It was also the center of a wide geographic catchment for health services as well as the state capital. These conditions protected it from economic ups and downs. Its unemployment rate was always below the national mean. It had begun to revitalize its downtown and waterfront. It had an integrated civic power structure, many members of which regularly expressed interest in having good schools. It was the home of one of the nation's great research universities and medical complexes and it was also a center for a number of smaller universities and colleges. As a result, River City had an adult education level that placed it among the nation's highest. The city's sustained population and economic growth reflected these stable and progressive conditions.

Regrettably, River City's schools were not the prospering equal of the municipality and metroplex. They had suffered from a period of heavy politicization and citizen neglect, starting over 50 years prior to Frank Farley's arrival. River City, even if in a present day progressive Midsouth setting, had historically operated in a racially segregated manner. Following the 1954 *Brown v. Board of Education* U.S. Supreme Court decision, River City was among the nation's first big districts to desegregate, and did so in a relatively peaceful manner. However, provoking remedial action had still necessitated a civil rights lawsuit. Only recently had the district been restored to "unitary status" by a federal court, signifying that it was no longer subject to court supervision in its racial desegregation efforts.

Desegregation conflicts have costs, and River City schools had previously paid dearly and were still paying a price when Frank Farley was hired. One desegregation conflict legacy had been the formation throughout the 1950s and early 1960s of private "white academies." Of course, in the 21st century, these were now partially racially integrated. However, a major problem persisted and it impeded Farley's likely success. Many "white academies," established to avoid 1950s desegregation by middle-class parents, had evolved in modern times into River City's most prestigious and highly sought after private schools.

River City, 50 years after *Brown v. Board of Education*, still had more than a quarter of its students enrolled in private schools, two and one-half times the national average. These enrollees, regardless of color, were the offspring of the city's corporate, civic, academic, and social elite. The very political power structure that could have helped Farley the most was not fully committed to public schools. Even the popular mayor's son attended a prestigious private school, a fact not routinely mentioned in River City's press or elite country club circles. These prestigious private schools were

River City's well-kept secret and closet skeleton. They were also a major impediment to Farley's political efforts to mobilize the community for school support. For example, proposed tax increases or school construction bond referenda had to survive an unusually hostile set of arguments from normally supportive middle-class parents wondering why they—as tuition paying private school parents—had to pay yet more for public schools they were not going to use.

There was a second set of downside costs from River City's historic school segregation. If "white academies" had evolved into prestigious private middle-class institutions, public schools, except for a select few located in elite neighborhood settings, had become institutions of last resort for children from low-income families. There were very few public schools acting as cultural magnets and racial "melting pots," catering to the American dream and a classless society. The raw material of schooling—students in attendance—was remarkably of a single stripe: low-income children of color.

Matters of race were not Frank's only challenge. He had come from a state in which school districts were fiscally independent. His past school boards had possessed authority to set property tax rates. To be sure, state law restricted local school board property taxing power. Power was also restricted by perceptions of economic competition with surrounding communities. None of Farley's former school boards had wanted to get too far out in front of nearby districts for fear of a negative impact on the local business environment. Still, his boards had possessed property taxing authority. When he thought more school district resources were justified—and during periods when the state's economy was suffering—he had recommended elevating local revenue contributions.

Not so in River City. Here, the school district was fiscally dependent on the mayor's annual proposal of a school district budget to a legislatively empowered city council. To make matters worse, the city council was an awkward body comprised of more than 40 elected members, most selected by geographic ward, and only a few elected at large. This arrangement rendered schools just one of several city departments competing for resources with criminal justice, public works, convention bureaus, business development, and so on. Moreover, the ward-based nature of the council majority exacerbated a selfish, zero sum, and piecemeal approach to decision making. Often a council member's first question during a debate over a proposed budget or zoning item, school or municipal, was "What is in this for my constituents?" instead of "What is in this for our city?"

River City's teachers' union was among the more active and influential political forces when it came to city council and school board election campaigns. This condition proved to be a double-edged sword. As long as Frank was asking for added resources for schools, teachers union officials could be counted on as lobbying allies. However, if he considered reallocations of existing school resources, then union officials might reconsider and be opposed. Even so, some city issues overrode school priorities by a wide margin. When the city council quickly approved financing for a new $330 million professional football stadium, but was far more reluctant to refurbish old schools, Frank was quick to see the challenge of the school reform assignment that lay ahead of him.

Frank had been the mayor's choice for the superintendent's position, and the elected school board, always dependent on the mayor's good will for sufficient resources, had quickly gone along. Still, even with the mayor's support, a political watershed Frank always worried could evaporate, gaining city council approval for the school district's annual budget took a great deal of his and his staff's energy. As long as matters went well, the mayor, school board, and city council shared the public's praises for schools. However, when something went wrong, they were quick to deflect blame themselves and to point fingers at Frank.

Frank's predecessors were well intended, but left little on which he could build. One predecessor had been a cheerleader type, from out of state, who seemed never to hear an idea he did not like. He simply could not establish priorities and, as a result, the school district was awash in ambiguity and conflict of purpose. Frank's immediate predecessor was an experienced and highly regarded insider who had certainly tidied up much of the previous mismanagement. Still, he had little training in—or mandate for—boosting and sustaining academic achievement. It seemed as if Frank were River City's first superintendent to be held responsible, not for keeping schools operating and district conflicts quiet, but for getting teachers to teach and students to learn. He had a large challenge.

Frank hit town running. He knew a great deal about organizational dynamics and he was aware of changes he could make quickly and others that would take more time. His first priority was to establish a districtwide culture of achievement and accountability. To do this, he curried favor with the media and the city's power structure, reorganized the central office, installed loyal lieutenants, and recruited high-level administrative staff from out of state. He also moved to install specific and high academic achievement goals for all school levels. He drummed home the necessity of increasing state achievement test scores. Finally, he rapidly sorted through principals for the district's schools, appointed many new ones, and then arranged to have many others retrained.

Frank understood that in his early months he had harvested the low-hanging reform fruit. He further realized that future achievement gains would require longer and harder work, such as reallocating resources and undertaking mid-course corrections when either schools or programs were not producing results. Finally, Frank understood that while his lieutenants paid attention to reform details, he would have to protect the district politically from increasing numbers of critics, individuals whose expectations for personal rewards had been unfulfilled or whose previously comfortable organizational surroundings had been disturbed.

Frank kept a list of large issues to be addressed. In many instances, however, he knew more about the problem than about possible solutions. He also knew that the primary obstacles he would likely face in addressing these challenges would be political more than technical. Here is Frank's list:

- Reallocate secondary school resources so as to reduce class sizes in lower grades
- Adjust teacher and principal pay to reward performance instead of years of service and college credits beyond the BA degree
- Shift teacher pay toward higher amounts for incoming teachers and those in high-demand subject areas and challenging schools

- Consider closure of unusually small, boutique schools, even if in prestigious neighborhoods
- Provide principals with lump sum budgets over which they could have greater discretionary authority

Discussion Questions

1. What do you think of Farley's proposed education reforms?
2. What proportion of Farley's job as superintendent seems technical in nature? What part seems political?

CASE 2

Bay Point Principal's Performance Pressures

Sandra Howard had been the principal at Bay Point High School for 3 years. She had previously taught and been an assistant principal for a total of 10 years before being accorded this, her first principal assignment. She had been an effective and popular middle school English teacher, and her administrator colleagues throughout the district held her in high regard. As a former drama coach, she had been responsible for theatrical productions for which the district had acquired a national reputation. Her superintendent, school board, parent groups, and the district's business community also held her in high regard. She was considered an ascending administrative star and the district was proud to have her services. There was frequent talk of her assuming even more important positions in the future.

Sandra knew the right things to do and she knew how to do things right. Her personal life was in order. She was happily married to a successful private sector sales director who understood and actively supported her school district career goals. It was not at all unusual to see him, and their two children, at high school athletic events and other public ceremonies. She had pursued serious advanced professional study and was well regarded by faculty members in her university graduate program. She was a master at budgeting her time. She read widely, sustaining her interests in modern American literature and drama, and had a broad spectrum of musical interests. She and her husband had a great fondness for camping with their children. They lived within a reasonable drive to the mountains, and this hobby well suited their locality and lifestyle.

Bay Point High School had an enrollment of 2,000 students. It was located in a large suburb of an even larger West Coast city. It was the only high school in the district, and as a consequence was evenly populated racially. The student body encompassed grades 10 through 12, and was composed almost equally of African American, Hispanic, Asian, and Caucasian students, representative of a wide swath of incomes.

On assuming the Bay Point principalship, Sandra faced a long list of challenges. The school had fallen into physical disrepair. Racial tensions among students were high. Parental participation had fallen to a low level. Student discipline was ragged and attendance was worse. As a result, the school looked worn, teachers were alienated, and students reflected the defeatist attitudes of the adults around them in school. The only bright lights were the school's athletic teams. Secretly, Susan resented their successes because they contributed to individual fiefdoms. Sometimes she could not tell if she or the basketball coach was in control of Bay Point High School, and she feared putting the issue to a public opinion test.

In one of her administrator training classes, Sandra had read Bella Rosenberg's *Up the Down Staircase*, a just-barely fictional piece about a dysfunctional New York City high school, hamstrung by its educator inhabitants' provincial attitudes and administrative regulations. On becoming Bay Point's principal, Sandra could not help but continually reflect on conditions and characters in that book. They seemed to be all around her, even if she was 3,000 miles away from New York City.

Sandra was scheduled in mid-semester for a morning meeting with the district's recently appointed central office director of instruction. This was the administrator to whom Sandra most directly reported. He was new and in all prior contacts had seemed to Sandra to be pleasant and informed. Sandra thought that he would be favorably impressed by the progress she was making in addressing the deficiencies she had inherited at Bay Point High School. Parent engagement was on the upswing, student discipline was noticeably better, the school had a new coat of paint and more physical improvements were to come. With a single notable exception—the union representative in her school—her teachers seemed to be pleased with the progress.

After an initial exchange of pleasantries at her morning meeting, Sandra was caught off guard by the abrupt nature of the conversation. The director of instruction was civil, but he told her bluntly that her school was failing and that she had better address problems quickly. He was forceful. Moreover, he had chart after chart, fact after fact, to buttress his position. Whereas she was proud of the school's new feel and appearance, he was concentrating critically on something else entirely, the academic achievement of Bay Point's students.

Bay Point's average student test scores in academic subjects were fine. However, when one took them apart by racial groupings and income levels, the story was different. Half the school, white and Asian students, was scoring well. The other half, black and Hispanic students, was scoring poorly. There was no denying the evidence. Still, the message was so different from what Sandra had expected that the entire meeting felt like a strong punch to her solar plexus. She was stunned.

Sandra returned to school, driving her car as if on autopilot. She made it through the day in a mechanical manner, but her mind was elsewhere. After school was out, while sitting in the privacy and welcome quiet of her office, she reflected on the morning's conversation. What was particularly troubling to her was that she knew her boss was right. Her school was failing; at least it was failing half of its students. She began to focus less on what had happened and more on what could happen.

As Sandra contemplated her new challenge, selected facets of her graduate study began to occupy a larger segment of her thinking. Course reading regarding effective schools, productive resource allocation, professional development, school climate, teacher empowerment, community engagement, leadership style, modern cognitive science principles, and organizational culture, ideas that previously were real only as a focus of graduate class discussion, now began to circle in her mind. Then the painful disjuncture between what she knew and what she was routinely permitted to do as principal became alarmingly apparent. Conditions in her district that previously had occupied her subconscious were now bubbling to the surface and she could more clearly see the paralyzed position into which she had been placed when she became principal.

The district's human resources division assigned teachers to Bay Point schools. Sandra could reject a teaching position candidate, but resistance—exercising veto power—took a great deal of energy and used a lot of organizational capital. She had to fill out multiple forms, explaining why a candidate was not precisely what was needed. Even so, she could be overruled. One could only appeal so often. In effect, her school's faculty was not of her selection. Also, on occasion, the personnel director told her it was "her turn" to baby sit a particularly incompetent teacher that the district routinely moved from school to school rather than face extraordinarily time-consuming and expensive dismissal procedures. This rotation of incompetent instructors was sufficiently common that she and other district principals referred to it as the "Bay Point Dance of the Lemons."

Bay Point had a powerful districtwide teachers' union. This was fine by Sandra; she had been a prominent member. Still, the union representative in her school was a frustrated career teacher, personally embittered with a persistent "glass half empty" attitude. He had been a competitor for the open principal position that she had won. Life had generally passed him by and he had retaliated by carving himself a niche out of protest. He saw evil in most every proposed change and insisted on filing grievance after grievance, even when there was not an individual teacher willing to be involved. Sandra knew well what teachers ought to be teaching which classes in order to maximize instructional impact for the school. However, the union representative was single-handedly enforcing outmoded contract provisions regarding reassignment, even when no one else cared. In effect, one of her 150 faculty members occupied more than half of her time and had de facto veto power over many of her decisions. When collective bargaining time came, the district central office repeatedly ducked such issues, in hopes of avoiding conflict. Indeed, conflict was avoided, but at the expense of poor school management.

Sandra contemplated another frustration, another impediment to orienting her school toward performance and away from simply striving for regulatory compliance. Sandra had only the most remote idea of the budget for her school. She routinely was accorded a per pupil amount for supplies and expenses. Her school had 150 faculty members and another 50 staff. She estimated that its annual operation had to cost in the neighborhood of $12 to $14 million. As such, it was one of the larger payrolls in town. Still, the portion of this budget over which Sandra had control was but 1%.

Sandra could order more books for the library, arrange for a few staff development days for selected teachers, or authorize an extra field trip here and there. Too much of her discretionary money came from soft drink vending machines, and she felt compromised by having the machines at every corner of her school. On balance, however, most of the budget was outside her control. She was not free to determine salaries, decide staffing ratios, move teachers to where she knew they were most needed, hire teachers herself, bring dismissal charges against a selected few teachers she knew to be slothful or incompetent, or to use any number of other tools routinely available to a private sector manager. She came to see that however publicly visible and appreciated she was in her school and in her community, she was a puppet, with most of her strings pulled by central office procedures. Often these were procedures that had evolved in a prior era, before student academic achievement mattered.

Sandra could also see that she could exercise leadership and could—if appropriately empowered—operate a school oriented toward performance. However, under the circumstances she faced in Bay Point, this was unlikely to happen. Under existing management constraints, she was far more of a cheerleader than an academic leader. The clearer this became for her, the more she contemplated a career shift. There were companies in Bay Point that had frequently wanted to talk to her about a management position. She was becoming more interested in such conversations. She knew that her employment security would be diminished in the private sector, but she could see that her management authority, and potential rewards, might be increased. She would have to think about it.

Discussion Questions

1. Would Sandra Howard have been found wanting as a principal prior to enactment of NCLB?
2. Does Sandra Howard possess sufficient decision discretion to meet her new performance expectations?

CASE 3

Trial Judge Complexities

Judge Glenda Manheim had sat on the bench for a decade. She was a circuit court judge in a poor agricultural area of a poor state. She knew most everyone of any consequence in her district. It was here that she had married her childhood sweetheart, now an elementary school teacher, and, with him, had raised two sons. She had left home for college, attending the state university and its law school. Upon completing her graduate degree she had returned to her home community to practice law. She hoped her high school-age sons would follow in her footsteps but they both seemed to pay more attention to their guitars than to their grades.

She had been a good local lawyer and a political party loyalist. Her reward had been party endorsement for a judgeship. She had run, been elected, and been re-elected each term since. She was proud of what she had done, and liked what she did day-to-day. She strove to know the law and to adapt it appropriately for the trial circumstances she encountered. She was known to be fair, patient, and thorough. She aspired to sitting on a higher bench, but that decision was in the hands of others and would have to take care of itself. Her motto was, do right today and tomorrow will be fine.

Thus, Judge Manheim was a bit perplexed when an unusual case appeared on her docket for scheduling. It was a complaint filed by the American Civil Liberties Union, represented by several of her state's most prominent civil rights attorneys. The suit was filed on behalf of children and citizens in heavily minority and low-income dominated public school districts within her circuit. The complaint named the state legislature as defendant and claimed plaintiffs were being denied equal protection on grounds that their school districts had insufficient resources to ensure satisfactory academic achievement.

The legislature, as defendant, retained one of the state's most famous law firms and its attorney team set about filing the various rejoinders that baffle laypersons but are a significant part of the legal process. Of course, Judge Manheim was obliged to read all the paperwork and rule where necessary. A procedural calendar was agreed to by which discovery alone would occupy a year prior to trial. There would be many complaints and cross-complaints asserting that one seemingly picayune evidentiary point or process after another had suddenly risen to constitutional status and called on the judge to render a ruling resolving differences.

Could the number of plaintiff districts be reduced by considering an agreed-upon sample as representative of the larger group? Could agreement be reached regarding whether or not the case involved issues of race, a constitutionally privileged classification, or merely issues of equality? Could both sides agree that the state education database was an accurate point of factual departure for trial purposes? Were school facilities part of the complaint or was the court being asked to rule merely on school district operating resource sufficiency? How many fact witnesses would plaintiffs be able to present at trial? Would defendants' experts be able to visit plaintiff district schools and, if so, when and for how long, and to whom could they direct questions while present at a school?

Most important for Judge Manheim was a sobering decision: was the issue before the court to be the availability of educational opportunity or would plaintiffs prevail in their claim that the appropriate legal test should be actual educational achievement? If the standard the court used was to be opportunity, what would be the metric of measurement that mattered? If it were achievement, what level of student accomplishment would suffice to satisfy the state constitution?

Even before the trial, Judge Manheim felt uneasy about the case. She could see publicity engines warming up. More and more articles, not simply in the local newspaper, but also in statewide dailies, began to discuss the trial and its national significance. Plaintiff district superintendents became regular fixtures on television news programs and radio talk shows lamenting the sorry schooling conditions their students regularly experienced for lack of sufficient state funding. Nationally, liberal-leaning think tanks and their websites began to trumpet the savage resource inequalities to which plaintiff district students were allegedly subjected. A long-running and widely popular Sunday television "magazine," was contemplating a special feature on the case.

Judge Manheim had no desire to be the center of attention and she was determined that her courtroom would not be a setting for a 21st-century Scopes Trial, with all the attendant histrionics issuing from a warring set of bull elephant lawyers. Still, she could see that she was about to have her hands full. This case would either propel her into a circle of substantial public visibility or plummet the remainder of her judicial career into infamy. As a country lawyer and now a country judge, she had not signed on for such attention.

Manheim scheduled a bench trial and allocated four weeks to hear arguments from each side. She knew the case would be appealed, regardless of her decision. Her older cousin had overseen a similar case as a judge in the upper Midwest, had ruled for plaintiffs and, on appeal had been overturned and roundly rebuked by that state's supreme court. Glenda Manheim was conscious of such judicial dynamics and, thus, she was committed to an absolutely fair trial and the amassing of an encyclopedic record for her appellate superiors to review. Little did she realize the trial was to occupy her over an 18-month period, involving more than 130 trial days, hundreds of experts, and thousands of pages of exhibits.

The trial began on a sultry summer day. Opening arguments portended the complexity to come. Each side drew on a phalanx of national experts. Judge Manheim had never before heard terms such as regression discontinuity models, coefficients of variation, Thiel Index, stochastic frontier analysis, hierarchical linear modeling, endogeniety, colinearity, and heteroskedasticity. What were these experts talking about? Yet on they came. Day after day her courtroom was filled with the nation's academic research and consulting elite.

At mid-trial a newspaper calculated that plaintiffs had spent $4 million and the defense at least half that amount. Where was the money coming from? Judge Manheim knew the state was directly bankrolling the defense. Plaintiff lawyers asserted they were trying the case *pro bono publico*, in the public's interests, and were not charging clients their usual fees. Judge Manheim was sure, however, that if she decided in the plaintiffs' favor she would soon thereafter receive a demand from their attorneys to be paid legal fees by the state. One did not have to be a rocket scientist to contemplate what good might have been done for schoolchildren had these trial resources, both plaintiff and defense, been diverted to educational purposes.

Plaintiffs claimed all was bad and whatever facilities, teachers, and materials their client schoolchildren had was insufficient. Plaintiff districts were claimed to have too few, ill trained, and highly transient teachers, poorly maintained schools, old textbooks, not enough computers, crowded buildings, outdated science labs, inadequate Internet access, and old library reference books predicting, "some day man will go to the moon."

For their part, defendants disputed all, even making a logical case that state teacher credentials bore no relationship to instructor ability, small classes might not necessarily be of benefit to students, plaintiff districts were openly slothful and wasted public resources, and, simultaneously, that things were getting better in plaintiff districts relative to past performance. After all, defense witnesses intimated, the legislature oversaw schools, not the courts, and plaintiffs were incorrectly bringing a legislative issue before the judicial system. Her Honor might just consider staying out of the battle.

Then, there was her own aspiration to sit on a higher bench and her fervent wish to avoid having her decision overturned on appeal. Judge Manheim had a lot to think about.

Judge Manheim listened day after day, seeing her previously agreed to trial schedule shredded, having to ask circuit court colleagues to adjust their schedules and handle her other cases. The state school finance case became ever more complicated and plaintiffs piled on a seemingly unending number of additional witnesses. The defense was almost as long-winded. For every minute a witness spent on direct testimony, almost as much time was taken on cross-examination. It seemed that there was little about which the adversarial camps could agree.

Judge Manheim was being made increasingly aware of the significant consequences of the trial outcome. A New York judge had recently handed down a verdict
calling for billons more dollars to be allocated to schools in that state. Dollar amounts of
this magnitude would bankrupt her state, a condition Rotary Club luncheon colleagues
were quick to convey to her. Meanwhile, she had grown up in this rural area of plaintiff
districts. She knew that children in plaintiff districts were seldom well educated and often spoke a *patois* that virtually guaranteed they would not participate fully in the 21st
century's material benefits. As part of their remedy, plaintiffs wanted speech therapists.
Judge Manheim, from first-hand experience, understood this argument.

Judge Manheim had sympathy for the children, but she could not be sure that
the problem was money, or the lack of it. She also knew many of the plaintiff district
administrators and was well aware of their management shortcomings. Insofar as
she was concerned, there was a pack of them that were already paid too much,
given their limited ability to manage schools and districts. She daily wondered how
much money was enough and was there a way to ensure that if more money was
needed it would actually benefit students and not middle-class education professionals? One of her more cynical neighbors had commented over the back fence that
the most likely result of the New York trial decision would be that schools would remain
the same for students while teachers moved to the suburbs and drove better cars. The
remark stuck. In her rural neighborhood, principals and teachers were already among
the few who drove nice cars.

Near the end of the trial, issues came into sharper focus. Plaintiff attorneys were
claiming that low test scores among their students was *prima facia* evidence of discrimination and lack of equal opportunity. Conversely, defendant attorneys and witnesses were claiming that to take academic achievement as a measure of opportunity
was a slippery slope. From the defense point of view, at least in a logical sense, if one
child scored well on tests, opportunity to learn was present. If plaintiff district test
scores were rising, as defense witnesses claimed they were, that must mean districts
had sufficient resources and that opportunity to learn was present. Other children, by
virtue of personal lack of will, or family and neighborhood poverty, might not do well.
However, could a school system rightly be placed in a position of having to overcome
such external factors and guarantee learning outcomes? For Judge Manheim, that
was a worrisome proposition. Too often her schoolteacher husband seemed to be
working terribly hard, but sometimes his students nevertheless did not learn.

Judge Manheim could see she had an important decision to make. The trial
was coming to a close and still it was not clear to her how she should decide.

Discussion Questions

1. On what standard, *performance* or *opportunity*, do you think Judge Manning
   should rely?
2. Do you think class size influences student academic achievement? What about
   school facilities? Do state credential rules capture the essence of effective
   teachers?

📁 CASE 4

An Elected Official's Dilemma

Walter Romero had a complicated background. He was a second-generation American, the son of Mexican immigrants. He was proud of his Mexican heritage. He was also proud to be an American. Incongruously, he loved to learn, but he did not succeed in school. He dropped out of high school, moving from place to place and job to job. He was strong and healthy. Consequently, he could always find employment as a laborer. Although this sometimes placed him with a rough element, he was seldom intimidated. Interestingly, he found that his passion for reading and learning often rubbed off on his workmates. They seemed to want to learn from him. He found himself on more than one occasion in the unexpected position of explaining complicated political issues to people receiving the short end of the economic stick who did not fully understand their personal circumstances and why they were trapped in poverty. He came to identify with the underdog, and just as assuredly he came to see that underdogs often needed both a second chance and more education.

Walter continued to move. He also continued to read, learn, and hone his knack for explaining difficult topics to undereducated people. His ability to speak Spanish as a native helped immensely. While working on a highway project in Arizona, Walt was approached by a union representative who asked him if he wanted a job as a union organizer. He accepted and quit his laboring job, but stayed close to his fellow laborers. He seemed to be a natural. His genuine concern for workers and his remarkable ability to capture complexity and communicate simplicity rapidly propelled him through union ranks. Within 5 years, he was a high-ranking regional AFL-CIO official and had moved with his new family to another state. At this juncture, his career took a remarkable turn. He entered politics.

The transition from union official to politico was easy. Walt worked in election campaigns as a local organizer, using the community action skills his union work had taught him. After three successful election campaigns, he came to see that he was the equal of other public office seekers for whom he had worked. He was as articulate, as informed, as committed, and as visionary as all others he had seen. Moreover, now that he was a husband and father, he understood even more the everyday challenges faced by working people. He was simultaneously idealistic and realistic.

Walt was also opportunistic. When a state lower house seat opened in his home district, he sought and was awarded union endorsement as a candidate. This endorsement was a big boost, but he knew it would not be sufficient by itself for a win. He was running for office in a district where voter registration heavily favored his party, but he still needed resources to turn out the vote. This meant money, campaign manpower, or both.

Walt raised the money and won his initial election. The statewide teachers' union was quick to contribute to his campaign war chest and to supply him with campaign expertise and committed precinct workers. He felt heavily in the union's debt. Once in office, his learning continued at a fast pace. He came to see that not all opposition party members were the devils he had depicted them to be while campaigning. He also came to see that a few of his party colleagues were not the saints with which he had hoped to surround himself. People, issues, situations, events, and conditions became ever more complicated. He was calling on all of his well-honed skills to make sense of the rapidly moving political reality in which he now found himself immersed at the state capital.

Walt learned fast, and within three terms ascended to become the chair of the assembly education committee. Here he became a highly visible statewide official. Learning standards, accountability provisions, teacher certification, standardized testing, and school spending were all issues that he knew to be important and about which he had to inform himself. After all, he himself had not experienced great success in school.

In his fourth assembly term, Walt found himself faced with a comfortable dilemma—a difficult decision, but one that was better than what he had encountered previously. National and state economies were escalating dramatically. Trade was up, joblessness was down, and businesses were stunningly on the rise. His state's highly progressive personal income tax was like a jet fighter with afterburners. Revenues poured into the state treasury. It seemed like an elected officials' dream. At last free of the burden of seemingly always having to cut programs, he and his party associates could now propose government actions that he thought would aid underdogs, the people with whom he identified and badly wanted to help.

Walt had learned a lot and understood the world was not black or white. Thus, he had a great many policy questions. How much should be spent on which proposed programs? What would most benefit the underdogs? By what means or by whom should new programs be administered? Was government the best agent, or were private or not-for-profit agencies the best means for ensuring that resources actually reached targets? He was sympathetic to schools, and teachers' unions had certainly befriended him. However, he understood that for many of his constituents, there were preconditions of health, housing, poverty, and community development that preceded their ability to succeed in school.

Teachers' union lobbyists continually explained the advantages of class size reductions, particularly in the lower grades. He liked this idea, liked the scientific evidence from the Tennessee STAR study, and knew parents would approve. He also knew that teachers liked to work in smaller classes; it made their job easier.

Class size reduction was one candidate, but a separate set of child advocates continually were talking to him about the Perry Preschool Project and the advantages of investing in early childhood education. Walt liked this evidence too, and he saw that big business organizations such as the Committee for Economic Development favored this means for helping the underdog.

He could invest in class size reduction, and the teachers' union would like that. He could invest in preschool, and business lobbyists and children's advocacy groups would like that. Or, perhaps he could split his options and buy a smaller amount of each. A staff member even proposed a policy experiment, but Walt could not easily imagine that randomly assigning schoolchildren to either preschools, smaller classes, or a control group would be acceptable to parents.

Walt's dilemma was not simply restricted to two options. He read a new Economic Policy Institute book suggesting that out-of-school investment in medical care, mental health, housing, income maintenance, community restoration, family counseling, prenatal care, and other out-of-school programs would eventually boost student in-school achievement more than either smaller classes or preschools.

Then too, there were conservatives, some even in his own political party, who claimed that little of long-lasting benefit would occur from investing in public schools as they currently operated. They contended that an element of competition was needed to spur professional educators to greater productivity. After all, private school proponents would say to him, for all practical purposes, public schools had a monopoly and monopolies were seldom a good thing. They reminded him that American cars had certainly improved after Asian and European imports arrived. He agreed. Indeed, his parish priest back home, Father Gonzales, sometimes said the same during after-church coffee conversations. Not that Father Gonzales was ever very political, but he did once suggest that a voucher program could contribute to greater education competition and also serve the Catholic children Walt knew well from his own childhood.

Finally, the construction industry never failed to try to persuade Walt that overcoming overcrowded schools by constructing new facilities would help children, further fuel the economy, create jobs for his union constituents, and create community symbols of an enduring and practical nature. Indeed, perhaps there someday could be a Walter Romero High School in his district.

As Walt prepared for upcoming committee hearings, reporters from the local papers dogged his moves at the capital for a hint as to which policies he would reward with the state's newfound income. Walt always hesitated, and it seemed to some that his carefully crafted confidence was beginning to wear around the edges.

Discussion Questions

1. Should Walter Romero use added funds for class size reduction or, instead, for teacher salary increases?
2. Should Walter Romero listen to his parish priest? What about the separation of church and state?
3. Should private school parents have to pay both property taxes and their children's school tuition?

CASE 5

A Creative and Frustrated Teacher

Johnny Upshaw had been a high school science teacher for 5 years. He first taught in a small rural district. Then, after getting married, he moved to a big city. He wanted to start a family and he needed the higher salary. He liked teaching, and, according to his peers, pupils, and parents, he was good at it. He was a member of his teachers' union and proud of it. He liked his school and saw no conflict between being supportive both of union principles and his school principal. He wished he made more money, but he would not trade more salary for having his weekends and summers filled with work like those of his lawyer and accountant friends from college.

Johnny believed deeply in discovery methods of instructing in science. This meant that he had to arrange laboratory experiments. He spent a lot of time in the school's science workroom preparing for major experiments that his students conducted each week. Johnny hoped that these laboratory experiments would instill a keen understanding of science in his students, or at least in an interested subset of students. Further, he did not begrudge spending even more time with particularly interested students as they prepared to compete in science fairs and other kinds of state and national competitions.

Johnny's district had negotiated a pay-for-performance arrangement with the teachers' union. Under this plan, if students scored higher on state academic achievement examinations, there was a financial award that could be distributed equally to all teachers in the school. Johnny went along with the plan. It did not seem like much money, a potential $2,000 annual bonus, and it did not change his behavior. He was a good teacher before the plan was put into place and he strove just as hard to be a good teacher after it was in place. His school was routinely accorded a collective bonus and Johnny and his fellow teachers divided the prize equally.

Whereas this performance pay did not alter Johnny's teaching behavior, it did cause him to observe the actions of many of his colleagues more closely. As bonus payments were distributed by the principal at a high-spirited June faculty meeting, Johnny could not help but wonder how his teaching neighbor, Bill Frazer, whose chemistry classroom connected to his through the shared laboratory preparation room, could blithely walk up and publicly accept his performance bonus check. Frazer's teaching was a joke. Johnny knew it and his other hard-working colleagues knew it. After 20 years of being a teacher, Frazer was at the top of the district salary schedule. Because of his seniority he was paid almost twice annually what Johnny received. Frazer may have once tried to teach, but he seemed to have given up long ago. Frazer showed films three or four times a week. Good students did all they could to avoid his classes and lazy or uncaring students did all they could to get into his classes. Frazer was known not to work hard and to grade easy. Johnny wished that the school administrative staff would do their job, evaluate Frazer, and get rid of him.

Johnny thought of his slothful colleague one day as he was working after school with students on science fair projects. He glanced out his third floor biology laboratory window in time to see Frazer's new Pontiac pull out of the teacher parking lot, headed home almost as soon as the afternoon closing bell had rung.

A feeling that Johnny had suppressed on prior occasions welled up within him. It just did not seem fair that the efforts to which Johnny and other hard-working colleagues routinely went also resulted in rewards for a few other lazy and uncaring teachers such as Frazer.

Johnny wondered what to do. The easy way out was to do nothing. His school's administrators were as aware of the problem as he was, and they did not seem to care enough to take action. Why was it his professional duty to care?

Over the summer, Johnny spoke with several other science teachers and was pleased to see that Frazer's freeloading bothered them too. They discussed various ways to expose Frazer's inadequacies, including hiding the films that daily arrived for his use from the district central office film library. They knew, however, that if there were no movies, Frazer would just have students read in class. He would not try to teach. Besides, the National Geographic, Nova, NASA and other science films were of a high quality and students probably gleaned something from them, even if they were not having a hands-on science experience.

Another idea began to evolve. If Frazer did not want to change, and the school's administrators were not going to monitor him, that was somebody's else's problem. Johnny and his colleagues, however, did have control over parts of their own destiny. They proposed a different way of operating—a means by which students' science and mathematics knowledge could be independently measured before beginning and after completing their specialized courses. If knowledge gains in a class met predetermined targets, then participating teachers would individually receive bonuses consistent with their students' gains. No gain for students, no added rewards for a teacher. If a teacher did not want to participate, he or she did not have to. However, if a teacher signed on to engage, then he or she could earn up to a $10,000 annual bonus. This struck Johnny as worth working for. Johnny and his colleagues set this up within the math and science departments of the schools and began to brainstorm about proposed budgets and an implementation timeline. It was empowering to move beyond the school administration and work on crafting new policies with like-minded colleagues.

Johnny and his colleagues continued to discuss their ideas and to sandpaper the sharp corners where they could anticipate problems, both technical and political. When they thought they were ready, they approached their principal. She was supportive, and assisted them in gaining an audience at the central office. They received a hearing, and an endorsement from the superintendent and his cabinet. The administration agreed to undertake student achievement analyses to determine what the likely probability was of teachers' achieving goals and budgeting whatever bonus pool might be justified by such predictions. Frankly, it had all gone better than Johnny had ever imagined. It appeared that his district was more open to innovation than he had previously realized.

However, as Johnny and his colleagues were leaving the central office after their performance pay presentation, the superintendent mentioned that, even if a perfunctory detail, the proposed performance pay plan fell within the purview of the district teachers' union contract, and thus would be subject to a bargaining meeting before final presentation to the school board. The superintendent asked that Johnny and his colleagues prepare for such a meeting. He would be depending on them to present and defend their ideas. He was in their corner and would help wherever he could.

Johnny knew the district's union leaders. He thought them to be professional and progressive. He was confident they would see the logic in their performance pay plan, and, after all, it was optional within only two departments of one high school. No teacher had to participate who did not want to. He and his colleagues went home confident that they might not have harnessed Frazer and his ilk, but at least they had disassociated themselves from such sloth.

On the evening when the district's administrators and union bargaining team met to discuss the proposed pay-for-performance option, Johnny and colleagues were hopeful. Therefore, they were totally unprepared for the tongue-lashing they received from their teaching colleagues. The brunt of the criticism was about how unfair it was that some teachers had a chance to earn substantial bonuses that would not be available to all teachers. Johnny and his colleagues were told that they had abandoned the principles of their profession. It was made clear that if the school board moved to adopt this plan, or a variant of it, it would be taken as an abrogation of the union contract and would be cause for a teacher strike.

Johnny could see the anger in the faces of the union officials at the table and he just as easily could see the fear, once the strike word had been mentioned, in the superintendent's face. Perhaps Johnny had previously sized up the situation incorrectly. He was surprised by both the intensity and direction of the opposition. He had been socialized to believe that the administration was the enemy of change, not the union. Maybe his teacher colleagues really wanted to defend the do-nothing Frazer. Maybe his district was not open to innovation. Johnny was shaken by the experience. He saw himself as a champion of classroom teachers, not an enemy.

Johnny attempted to explain that the proposed plan was fair. First, it measured students' value-added performance. Having bright students unfairly advantaged no teacher and having slow students handicapped no teacher. Second, it was entirely voluntary. No teacher was being forced to participate. Third, the size of the bonus was proportionate to gains in student knowledge.

One criticism of the proposal was that elementary teachers were not included. Also, Johnny and his colleagues were asked how an English teacher would be eligible for such a bonus. Moreover, did he not think that the efforts of middle school science and mathematics teachers were assisting him as they prepared students with a base of scientific knowledge on which he could build in high school? Did he and others think it fair, therefore, to neglect middle school science teachers as bonuses were awarded? Did they not understand that their proposed plan would trigger dysfunctional competition, not cooperation, between teachers? Could they not see that a good teacher would be reluctant to share instructional strategies for fear of helping competitors who might reduce his bonus as a result? Johnny was tempted to ask them how much cooperation they thought went on now between teachers in their egg crate classrooms, but he bit his tongue.

The district administrators were useless in the discussion. They had been teachers, and they disliked conflict. This, after all, was not their initiative. It was not their fight.

Teacher officials subsequently went to the press and to the local TV stations exposing what they claimed was a harebrained and unfair scheme that would disrupt the cooperative spirit that had long characterized labor management relations in the district. The superintendent responded in press and on the air that the pay-for-performance proposal was only a trial balloon and it would not be adopted, given the high level of teacher opposition. Johnny and his colleagues felt thoroughly defeated. From their standpoint, Frazer had won, and he had not even been in the battle.

Johnny and his colleagues found themselves embittered and betrayed. They were fearful that they would lose their sense of excitement regarding teaching. They further feared that they might start working to the rules and end up more like Frazer than they had ever wanted to be.

The following fall, Johnny left public school teaching. He joined a software company that designed and sold science instruction programs to school districts. He was a gifted salesperson. He rapidly was earning commissions in excess of $100,000 per year. He, his wife, and their young son moved to a nicer house. Once he passed Frazer in his Pontiac, and simply waved out the window. Still, whenever Johnny reflected on events, his happiest days were teaching science to high school students and nothing in his subsequent material life, however comfortable, compensated for his longing in this regard.

Discussion Questions

1. Do professions other than teaching police the performance of failing members such as Bill Frazer?
2. Can you imagine any teacher performance pay proposal that might be acceptable to teacher union leaders?

Summary Questions

Below is a distillation of resource-related conditions and issues with which the five preceding case study protagonists wrestled. Each issue is addressed in one or more subsequent chapters. For now, however, consider and discuss the following:

1. What is a proper or productive link between the larger political system and school or the decision mechanisms for according resources to schools? How politicized is (should be) school finance?
2. How much money is needed to operate a school effectively, to ensure students have access to what they need to learn what they are expected to know? Can a school receive too much money? Are some schools inefficient and should the public have to pay for this inefficiency?
3. By what means can the achievement gap between low- and middle-income schoolchildren most effectively be narrowed? Can this gap ever be eliminated?
4. What should the balance be between schools and other institutions on which society relies in its efforts to elevate academic achievement of low-income students? To what degree should policymakers attend to out-of-school-strategies such as health and housing contrasted with heavier investments in instruction in schools?
5. At what juncture in an organization should resource allocation decisions be made? How much, if any, resource allocation authority should reside with a principal?
6. How and how much should teachers and administrators be paid? Does paying teachers and principals for students' performance entail unsolvable technical problems and unacceptable risks to the integrity of schools?

CHAPTER TWO

Evolving Societal Contexts Shaping Modern Education Finance

▉ INTRODUCTION

Education finance policy is not created and does not function in a vacuum. The policies by which we fund our schools are designed to function within a web of demographic, economic, and governmental forces. Understanding these forces, and the manner in which they are likely to change in the future, provides an important intellectual foundation for administrators and policymakers.

LEARNING OBJECTIVES

By the end of this chapter you should be able to:

- Discuss the manner in which demographic and population shifts have altered enrollment and achievement patterns across the nation.
- Describe the United States' standing in the world economy with reference to productivity and debt.
- Describe the United States' academic performance relative to international competition.
- Conjecture about the implications of all of the above on education policy and education finance.

The purpose of this book is to explain and analyze (1) the way the United States finances public schools, (2) the relationship between school finance and educational policy, and (3) the link between school finance and educational practice. To do justice to these diverse commitments, we must describe the structural and dynamic features of education in the United States and the various social forces that give form and substance to those conditions. This chapter explains the broad boundaries of a policy paradigm, summarizes demographic and economic trends that exert tremendous force on American education, and weighs five central dimensions of the American educational system: (1) enrollments, (2) personnel, (3) governmental arrangements, (4) financial costs, and (5) student outcomes.

In the News

Stephen Hochman, vice-president of sales at athletic shoemaker New Balance North America, once observed that, "Success is a function of an organization's capacity to absorb change as its own." That's a great way to think about the type of corporate culture you need to deal with rapid change.

Things are certainly changing fast. Think about these trends that have impacted almost every industry in the last few years:

Customers are more challenging, empowered by information, compelled by choice and driven by disloyalty;

Prices are becoming commoditized, as the "China price" means that cost alone drives purchasing decisions in many markets;

Costs are increasing continually, as a seemingly endless rise in uncontrollable costs squeezes margins;

Business models are shifting as new competitors emerge literally overnight.

These trends make it clear why agility, innovation and execution are critical. So, how can you develop a culture that will help you respond to the rapid rate of change?

Focus on collaborative relationships. Paul Moss, divisional marketing director at British Bakeries, put this trend in a nutshell when explaining why his firm was seeking a new relationship with retailers: "We have more to talk about than price." For a long time, food companies developed new products with little input from retailers and packaging companies. But today, throughout the world of retail and food products, there's a lot of collaboration among packaging firms, consumer product manufacturers and retailers, all of them working together to come up with innovative product solutions.

Respond to hyper-innovation. We're witnessing faster times to market in almost every industry. The concept of a product life cycle is disappearing as products come to market and thrive only for micro-bursts of time. Make sure your team has the agility to cope with this reality and you might survive. This means understanding the vast range of new products or services you might be responsible for in the next year to 18 months—in particular any unique and emerging sales, marketing or support issues around them.

Get used to contentious consumers. Desires, needs and demands will continue to change at an ever more furious pace, often in ways that won't make sense to you. Don't despair; rather, learn from it. For example, take the sudden birth and equally sudden death of the low-carb fad. Sure, it was a disaster simply because it was a fad, and companies that rushed into the market should have known better. Yet, rather than beating themselves up, the smart ones are using the experience to learn how agile they are, particularly how quickly they can get a new product to market. Did they respond fast enough to a rapidly changing market? What blocked their ability to do so? How can they fix that?

Capture the insight of creative new competitors—constantly. Face it: there will be folks out there who are more creative than you are. They'll beat the pants off you with short, quick bursts of tactical success, while you're still busy marshalling your forces. Rather than losing sleep over that, learn from them. Then do what they do—only better.

Ride the wave of continuous innovation in business models. Retailers, for example, are constantly experimenting with store formats, brand partnering, in-store displays, logistics and tracking studies, and countless other new ways of doing things. Get on board the tornado of change and ride it for all it is worth. How? Develop a team that has a well-tuned radar for unique trends, experiments, success stories and innovations.

The bottom line is this: the business world today is one of relentless, continuous change. Agility is your ability to respond to this change; if you lack that,

you'll miss out on big opportunities and find that challenges become barriers to success. Innovation is critical. And that's not just a matter of developing new products; it's about examining how you operate, your business model, the markets you're in, the partners you seek and how you challenge yourself to do something different every day. Execution is paramount, because these days you can't afford to be anything but your best.

From Carroll, J. (2006). *Get on top of rapid change: If your company culture doesn't embrace agility, innovation and flawless execution, you could be headed for trouble.* Posted March 27, 2006, on http://profitguide.com

■ A PRELIMINARY POLICY PARADIGM

A **policy** is a uniform rule that guides action. Social policy, which includes educational policy, encompasses those decision rules that apply to members of a society or its important subgroups. All societies have policies on common dimensions such as health, marriage, commerce, political participation, and criminal justice. All of these policies prescribe how members of the society will act toward or be treated by others. If a policy is governmentally enacted and codified, it is typically known as a **statute** or **law**. Informal, uncodified policies exist in every society, and may be every bit as prescriptive as statutes. Anyone doubting this should attempt to cut into a queue in England and experience the consequences.

Social policies are strongly influenced by three fundamental considerations which are respectively technical, cultural, and political: (1) demographic and economic dynamics; (2) preferences among three values—equality (including adequacy, sometimes termed "equity II"), efficiency, and liberty; and (3) political arrangements. The flow of influence among these three conditions is substantial and multidirectional. For example, demographic or economic circumstances can trigger political system changes, and vice versa. Thus, this paradigm provides no mechanical model for precisely predicting which policies will emerge from which conditions at which time. Public policy is continually influenced by variables outside this paradigm, such as human determination, acts of God, and elements of caprice. Simply knowing pertinent "facts" will not necessarily permit policy predictions. For example, it would have been difficult to predict from their past performance that President Lyndon B. Johnson would be an ardent advocate of civil rights, President Jimmy Carter a proponent of governmental deregulation, or President Ronald Reagan the administrator of a vastly unbalanced federal budget.

The complex social world of human interactions constitutes a vast primordial policy ooze out of which technical, cultural, and political conditions periodically coalesce to create policy predispositions. An individual or an idea may, however, spark actual policy changes. Components of the policy paradigm, while not lending themselves to precise prediction,

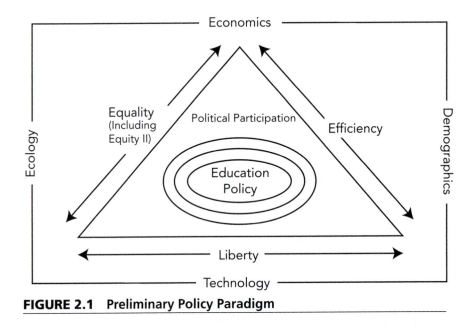

FIGURE 2.1   Preliminary Policy Paradigm

nevertheless alert one to the broader patterns of policy emergence and influence. Figure 2.1 illustrates these three predispositions. The remainder of this chapter is oriented toward the technical influences on policy—demographic and economic.

■ DEMOGRAPHIC AND ECONOMIC DYNAMICS

Throughout the world, educational policy, and its eventual expression in schooling, is driven by two variable conditions, **demography** and **economics**. These conditions are themselves related, though the nature of the relationship at any point in time depends on many additional conditions, such as society's level of technical development and its climate. For example, in a technologically undeveloped society, an explosion in the birthrate may trigger famine, poverty, and great human hardship. Conversely, in a technologically sophisticated, commercially oriented society, a dramatic upsurge in births may spur economic expansion and an increase in living standards.

Two economic dimensions exert important influence on policy: (1) level of overall economic development and (2) rate of economic growth. Obviously, a technologically sophisticated industrialized or information-oriented economy will have different policy concerns and predispositions than an agrarian or preindustrial society. Similarly, low productivity and the absence of economic growth may create conflict between elites and the poor and, depending on a society's political dynamics, may focus policy discussions obsessively on issues of economic redistribution.

Demography also has a two-dimensional influence. A society's policy predispositions are influenced not only by overall population size, but also by the geographic, racial/ethnic, and age distribution of the population. A society in which the median age is relatively low might invest a disproportionate share of its social resources in children and youth. Conversely, when the median age rises, as is currently the case in the United States, senior citizens may begin to attract a disproportionate share of social and government resources. Also, a geographically compact and racially heterogeneous society may have different domestic policy concerns than a sparsely settled or racially homogenous people. See Table 2.1 for additional information on conditions influencing the 21st century workforce.

TABLE 2.1   Forces Shaping the Future Workforce and Workplace in the United States: A Summary of Future Trends

Demographic Trends
• Workforce will continue to increase in size, but at a considerably slower rate • Composition of the workforce will be more balanced by age, sex, and ethnicity • Slower workforce growth may make it more difficult for firms to recruit workers during periods of strong economic growth • Many overseas trading partners of the U.S. are undergoing slower workforce growth, offering a new competitive advantage to the U.S.

Technological Change
• Pace of technological change will accelerate in the next 10 to 15 years • Synergies across technologies and disciplines will generate advances in research and development, production processes, and the nature of products and services • Further technological advances are expected to continue to increase demand for a highly skilled workforce, to support higher productivity growth, and to change the organization of business and the nature of employment relationships

Economic Globalization
• The reach of economic globalization will be even more expansive than before, affecting industries and segments of the workforce relatively insulated from trade-related competition in the past • The new era of globalization is partly the result of inexpensive, rapid communications and information transmission enabled by the IT revolution • Jobs will be lost in some sectors and will be counterbalanced by employment gains in other sectors

Workforce Implications
• Rapid technological change and increased international competition place the spotlight on the skills and preparation of the workforce, particularly the ability to adapt to changing technologies and shifting product demand • Growing importance of knowledge-based work also favors strong nonroutine cognitive skills, such as abstract reasoning, problem-solving, communication, and collaboration • Education and training become a continuous process throughout life, involving training and retraining • Technology-mediated learning offers potential to support lifelong learning both on the job and through traditional public and private education and training institutions • Shift away from more permanent, lifetime jobs toward nonstandard employment relationships such as "e-lancers" or self-employed workers

Karoly, L. & Panis, C. (2004). *The 21st Century at Work: Forces Shaping the Future Workforce and Workplace in the United States.* RAND Labor and Population.

Demographic Developments

On August 19, 2005 at approximately 11:10 p.m. EST, the United States Census Bureau's POPClock estimated the United States population to be 296,936,216 million people. This real-time population count can be translated into:

- one birth every 8 seconds;
- one death every 14 seconds; and
- one international migrant (net) every 26 seconds.

Ultimately, this is equivalent to a net gain of one person every 11 seconds (Census, 2005).

Geographic Location. For the last quarter century the most significant geographic trend in population growth is in the so-called Sun Belt states in the South and West. Figure 2.2 shows these changes by region from 1900–2000, while Table 2.2 displays the rate of population change between 1970–1980, 1980–1990, and 1990–2000 in the five fastest-growing and slowest-growing states within these individual time frames. This shift is occasioned by the increasing number of retired citizens seeking warmer climates, displaced Frost Belt workers seeking jobs in technologically more advanced industrial and informational fields located in the Sun Belt, and recent patterns of immigration, which is discussed in greater detail later.

These population changes have been accompanied by significant alterations in economic and political patterns. The most obvious is the shift of greater political influence to

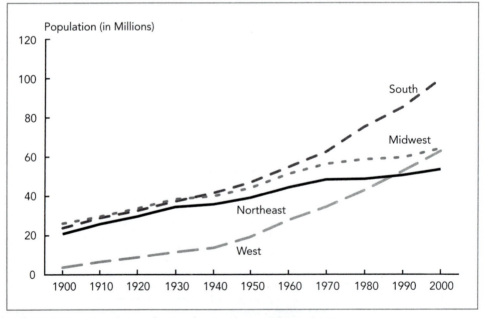

FIGURE 2.2   Total Population by Region: 1990 to 2000

Source: U.S. Census Bureau, deccennial census of population, 1900 to 2000.

TABLE 2.2   Change in Population and Per-Pupil Expenditure for the Five Fastest- and Slowest-Growing States, 1970–2000

	1970		1980		1970–1980	
	Population	Student Enrollment	Population	Student Enrollment	Change in Population	Change in Student Enrollment
Fastest-Growing States						
Nevada	488,738	113,421	800,493	134,995	63.8	19.0
Arizona	1,775,399	391,526	2,718,215	481,905	53.1	23.1
Florida	6,791,418	1,312,693	9,746,324	1,464,461	43.5	11.6
Wyoming	332,416	81,293	469,557	89,471	41.3	10.1
Utah	1,059,273	287,405	1,461,037	312,813	37.9	8.8
Slowest-Growing States						
New York	18,241,391	3,099,192	17,558,072	2,530,289	−3.7	−18.4
Rhode Island	949,723	163,205	947,154	139,195	−0.3	−14.7
Pennsylvania	11,800,766	2,169,225	11,863,895	1,808,630	0.5	−16.6
Massachusetts	5,689,170	1,056,207	5,737,037	935,960	0.8	−11.4
Ohio	10,657,423	2,246,282	10,797,630	1,849,283	1.3	−17.7

	1980		1990		1980–1990	
	Population	Student Enrollment	Population	Student Enrollment	Change in Population	Change in Student Enrollment
Fastest-Growing States						
Nevada	800,493	134,995	1,201,833	173,149	50.1	28.3
Alaska	401,851	79,945	550,043	98,213	36.9	22.9
Arizona	2,718,215	481,905	3,665,228	557,251	34.8	15.6
Florida	9,746,324	1,464,461	12,937,926	1,646,583	32.7	12.4
California	23,667,902	4,044,736	29,760,021	4,893,341	25.7	21.0
Slowest-Growing States						
West Virginia	1,949,644	353,264	1,793,477	301,947	−8.0	−14.5
Iowa	2,913,808	510,081	2,776,755	450,224	−4.7	−11.7
Wyoming	469,557	89,471	453,588	91,277	−3.4	2.0
North Dakota	652,717	118,986	638,800	109,659	−2.1	−7.8
Illinois	11,426,518	1,770,435	11,430,602	1,587,733	0.0	−10.3

	1990		2000		1990–2000	
	Population	Student Enrollment	Population	Student Enrollment	Change in Population	Change in Student Enrollment
Fastest-Growing States						
Nevada	1,201,833	173,149	1,998,257	305,067	66.3	76.2
Arizona	3,665,228	557,251	5,130,632	782,851	40.0	40.5
Colorado	3,294,394	519,419	4,301,261	656,700	30.6	26.4
Utah	1,722,850	408,917	2,233,169	448,096	29.6	9.6
Idaho	1,006,749	203,987	1,293,953	230,828	28.5	13.2
Slowest-Growing States						
North Dakota	638,800	109,659	642,200	105,123	0.5	−4.1

continued

continued

West Virginia	1,793,477	301,947	1,808,344	273,277	0.8	−9.5
Pennsylvania	11,881,643	1,524,077	12,281,054	1,684,913	3.4	10.6
Connecticut	3,287,116	439,524	3,405,565	533,779	3.6	21.4
Maine	1,227,928	195,089	1,274,923	194,554	3.8	−0.3

Source: U.S. Census Bureau

Sun Belt states (e.g., California, Texas, Florida, Arizona, and Georgia). For example, because of its population growth, California has replaced New York as the state with the largest delegation in the U.S. Congress. The Sun Belt has taken on added economic significance as well. Some changes are obvious: new job openings have reduced unemployment in the South and West to below that in many midwestern industrial states.

Other economic changes are more stable. For example, Sun Belt states derive the economic advantage of retiree spending from pension income earned earlier in the North and Midwest. Also, something of a "brain drain" has occurred. Sun Belt states benefit from educational investments made earlier in the school lives of recent arrivals from the North and Midwest.

Initially, Sun Belt states had difficulty adjusting to the new growth patterns. From 1970 to 1980, for example, they only averaged a 32% increase in per-pupil expenditures, while per-pupil expenditures in Frost Belt states increased by more than 44%. In the more dynamic economy post-1980, however, the Sun Belt states began to spend more money per pupil. They not only generated new revenues to cover pupil population growth, but also to cover added demand for education services. These Sun Belt states were often among the leaders in the educational excellence movement of the 1980s and 1990s.

Racial and Ethnic Composition. Following the colonial period of national development, the United States experienced six major population migrations. The first was the 18th- and 19th-century "manifest destiny" expansion in western lands. The second was the massive immigration from Europe during the 19th century resulting from economic dislocation and famines in southern and eastern Europe. The third was the shift of rural blacks from the South to the cities beginning in the late 1930s and escalating greatly during World War II and immediately after. The fourth was the flow of middle class families from cities to the urban periphery during and shortly after the black migration. The fifth, an ongoing phenomenon, is the large wave of immigration from Latin America and Asia that accounts for more than 75% of all immigrations from 1990–2000. The sixth is the current movement from northern to southern states.

Each of these migrations has affected education policy. The massive 19th century migrations from southern and eastern Europe intensified the assimilation functions of public schools. Many immigrants could not speak English and were not familiar with American forms of government. Also, many of these new citizens were Catholic and found public schools of that day far more religiously neutral. Reacting to the Protestant orientation of public schools, and probably desiring institutions over which they could have more influence, the new immigrants greatly expanded and participated in the nation's Catholic school system.

The 20th-century migrations of blacks to cities and middle-class families to suburbs also precipitated educational policy changes. The segregated school systems of the agricultural South did little to provide new city dwellers with the educational skills necessary to succeed in an industrial and commercial environment. The migration of middle-class families to the suburbs (i.e., "white flight") deprived city schools of much needed human, political, and economic capital. The 1965 enactment of the Elementary and Secondary Education Act (ESEA) was in large measure a response to these conditions.

Mass immigration starting in the 1980s and continuing to the present has also challenged school systems. It is estimated that the immigrant population is growing 6.5 times faster than the native-born population. The U.S. Department of Education reports that "between 1979 and 2003, the number of school-aged children who spoke a language other than English at home grew from 3.8 million to 9.9 million, or from 9 percent to 19 percent of all children. The number of those children who spoke English with difficulty also grew, from 1.3 million (or 3 percent of all school-aged children) in 1979 to 2.9 million (or 5 percent) in 2003" (U.S. Department of Education, 2003). While language is not a direct correlate of immigrant status, it does provide a rough approximation for an increasingly diverse student population that has resulted from this movement.

Age Distribution. The age distribution of the American population is undergoing dramatic changes that have major policy implications. The population is aging rapidly. The median age in 1950 was 30.2, which means that half the U.S. population was younger than 30.2 years of age. In 2000, the United States Census reported the median age to be 35.3. This not only represents a 2.5 year increase since 1990, but also the highest median age in American history. This evolving condition is a consequence of decreases in birth rates and medical advances that have significantly extended longevity for both women and men.

The aging of the American population will continue to have important policy implications, education included. The larger number of older people may entail changes in the composition of government services. The elderly may well be more interested in a different mix of economic, energy, transportation, income, and criminal justice policies than would a younger society. The distribution of government spending and public debt might be significantly altered.

Education is no exception to the possible policy changes. Older individuals may not be as directly concerned about schooling. Moreover, public school students and their parents now constitute a smaller percentage of the electorate. This may have important implications for school-related politics. For example, states or localities with particularly large concentrations of retirees may not be able to generate conventional levels of political support for public schooling. Alternatively, senior citizens may want a larger portion of the school budget devoted to adult education. Their numbers among local voters may enable them to express this preference forcefully through the electoral process.

Economic Developments

Despite a gross domestic product (GDP) second to none (approximately $10.75 trillion in 2004), United States' hegemony over the world's economy had greatly diminished during the early to mid-1980s. In November 1986, Japan's per-capita GDP matched that of the United States. By 1987, average workers' compensation in Germany, Sweden, and other European nations exceeded that of U.S. Workers. This change is illustrated practically by the remarkable spectrum of foreign-produced consumer goods widely purchased throughout the nation, intense foreign investment in fundamental financial and manufacturing technologies, and the diluted standard of living experienced by many Americans during this time.

If the United States' declining economic supremacy were simply a function of growing international interdependency, it might have been of less concern to policymakers and the informed public. However, such was not the case. Two decades of declining or stagnant productivity, unmatched federal government deficits, mounting international trade imbalances, unprecedented reversals in foreign indebtedness, growing personal debt, and roller-coaster ups and downs in currency values, unemployment, and interest rates have had their own unsettling effects. These uncertain economic conditions were summarized, at least symbolically, by the dramatic stock market drop of Monday, October 1987, when the market lost more than 20% of its value.

The U.S. economy would soon prove fundamentally vital, largely due to technological information-based advancements. Following the 1980s mini-recessionary cycles, the nation's economy had the single longest period of economic growth in its history. The United States' compound annual growth was 9.3% greater than Japan's and 22% greater than France's realized growth during this period. Studies of industrial productivity further indicate that growth in capital investment, technology, and organization efficiency, in addition to improved skill levels of the workforce far outpaced past decades. Moreover, by the arrival of the 21st century, France, Germany, and Japan were in sustained economic slumps, running high rates of unemployment and generally dependent on exports to the United States to bolster their economies.

Here are three examples of the United States' altered economic condition:

A Tale of Modern Service

The October 31, 2002 *Wall Street Journal* contained an article describing efforts of two reporters who attempted to travel 2,500 miles via airplane from Dallas, TX to Washington, DC, without benefit of human service intervention. With online ticket purchases, automated baggage check in, electronic package scanning, explosive detection machines, video surveillance, agentless boarding pass kiosks, online rental car reservations and vehicle assignment, and automated hotel reservation and room registration, they almost fulfilled their quest. They were foiled only at a rental car parking lot exit gate by a zealous employee who took an opportunity to offer them upgraded rental insurance, and a security worker who questioned the travelers about contraband eyebrow tweezers. Otherwise, from the time they departed their Dallas garage with their infrared door closing device until they used their plasticized hotel room entry key in Washington, DC, they experienced no human contact for reasons of service or information (Stringer, 2002).

A Tale of Modern Business

"Big Box" retailers (discount stores operating in warehouses such as Wal-Mart, Target, Costco, and Toys R Us), account for approximately one out of every five retail sale dollars in America. It is estimated that 40% of American women between 18 and 70 shop at Wal-Mart at least once a week (Kelly, forthcoming).

As a result of their gigantic sales volume, "Big Box" retailers have enormous leverage with suppliers. Modern electronic inventory systems, linked to point-of-sale checkout register data, enable retailers to order and replace inventory only when they need it. In fact, with just-in-time (JIT) delivery strategies, retailers are forcing suppliers to bear carrying costs and sales risks of inventory. Now most goods are not credited to a producer until they are sold over the retail counter. Even when they are on the shelf, a retailer may not have accepted formal financial delivery from a wholesaler or producer. Until they are sold, the goods are still owned by and are the financial responsibility of suppliers. Strong-armed accounting procedures such as "damage discounts," often confront suppliers with either the unanticipated choice of losing a huge customer or even lower profit margins for themselves.

A Tale of Modern Medicine

Whirr, glide, clunk; glide whirr, plop. This is an automated pharmacy in operation in Los Angeles. It is filling prescriptions from banks of pharmaceuticals faster, more accurately, and at far less cost, even after having paid off its $250,000 purchase price, than human pharmacists can. In addition, it contributes to inventory information, controlled substance security, patient billing, and insurance regulation. A supervisor oversees the machine. There is no pharmacist present.

One floor above the automated pharmacy is the robotic surgery. Here an orderly is precisely placing a patient under the electric "scalpel and suturing machine's" three-dimensional grid coordinates. A trained electronic technician is overseeing testing of the remote cameras and computerized surgery controls. A nurse anesthetist is present and monitoring the patient. The surgeon, wearing his virtual sight magnifying goggles is sitting at the robot's computerized controls, 2,000 miles away in Nashville. The surgeon has never seen the patient in person. He did talk with her yesterday on a videophone.

What is going on here? These examples are from modern transportation, retailing, and health care. One could just as easily have described Internet banking; remote control military attack vehicles, ships, and aircraft; online university degree programs; electronic monitoring of indicted criminals; online book sales, catalogue ordering, and antique auctions; church attendance through television, and so on. Modern economic imperatives represent an advanced stage of a global transition from a manufacturing and trade era to a technological information-based economy. As the article from the "In the News" box indicates, change and innovation are now the natural states of business, instead of events that occur every so often.

It is nevertheless important for readers to understand that a few features of economic depressions are amenable to short- and medium-range corrections through manipulations of government monetary and fiscal policy. For example, by altering the discount rate—the cost to commercial banks of borrowed money—the United States Federal Reserve Board can exercise short-run influence over interest rates on items such as consumer loans. There are, however, several secular trends that cannot be altered so easily and that portend longer-run economic distress for the United States. We will discuss three of these— economic productivity, debt, and international competition. There is substantial interaction among the three, but we treat each independently.

Productivity. **Productivity** is a ratio relating output to one or more of the inputs associated with producing that output. This index is crucial to a nation's well-being. It is an economist's measure of a nation's ability to produce goods and services. Productivity

Research
Navigator.com
Productivity

can be measured for an entire nation in aggregate terms, for example, of total national income or total hours at work. It can also be measured on a unit basis, such as national income per capita, output per hour at work, or output per employee. If productivity is high, a nation's standard of living can increase. If productivity is low or falling, the standard of living cannot increase and may decline. A nation's policies can encourage or discourage long-term economic growth. Thus, it is easy to envision the connection between a nation's economy and its political environment.

The quarter century following World War II was a robust period. Between 1948 and 1973, U.S. productivity increased by every measure. National income, for example, increased 3.7%, national income per employed person increased 2.16%, and national income per capita increased 2.21%. Over the following 7 years, productivity grew much less rapidly. National income increased by only 2.61%, national income per employed person by only .036%, and national income per capita by only 1.59%. The next 3 years were particularly dismal. Aggregate national income and national income per employed person decreased 0.54%; national income per capita declined 1.55%. The United States now has the highest Gross National Income (GNI) in the world, followed by Japan, whose GNI is less than half that of the United States' aggregate national income.

Year-to-year variations in productivity are too great to permit easy generalizations. Thus, determination of valid trends is best done through extrapolation over an extended period. The United States experienced economic growth rates averaging 3.2% in the 1950s, 4.2% in the 1960s, 3.2% in the 1970s, 3% in the 1980s and just 2.8% in the 1990s. In the latter half of the 1990s, economic growth rates accelerated, apparently driven by rising productivity attributed to the impact of the expansion of information technology throughout the economy. From 1995 to 2000, the economic growth rate reached 4%, a high rate by historical standards. But the nation's longest economic expansion—from 1991 to 2000—ended in 2001 when the economy began declining. At the same time, the world economy also began to slow dramatically, making 2001 the first year of global synchronization of recession since the mid-1970s. The September 11, 2001, terrorist attacks on the United States appeared at first to dramatically slow the economy. The immediate impacts were in the stock market and in the airline, travel, and tourism industries. At the beginning of 2002, signs of recovery were evident in the United States.

One can also examine productivity from another standpoint—a comparison of the manufacturing and service sectors. It is evident that productivity in the manufacturing sector has been improving. It is in the service sector that productivity lags badly. Since 1987, U.S. productivity as measured by output in the manufacturing sector has increased, though number of hours worked and employment in this sector have decreased. Productivity in the business sector has increased by all measures (output, hours worked, and employment) since 1983. On the whole, the U.S. productivity growth rate has been steadily rising since 1995 and continues to be strong at just under 3%.

If productivity per worker, particularly per service worker, or productivity per capita does not continue to increase, then the United States will face many difficult choices. For example, the nation will not be able to pay off its rising national and international debt without either reducing private standards of living or cutting back significantly on public service. In short, the nation must continue to increase its productivity or forego some items and services that many members of the public have felt to be important to this point.

Productivity is a function of several conditions, such as capital investment, managerial effectiveness, and education. A calculation of the factors spurring productivity growth from 1929 to 1982 suggests that education is exceeded in significance only by advances in knowledge—themselves products in large measure of research in higher education institutions. Education accounted for 26% of productivity growth in this period. The sagging U.S. productivity from the mid-1980s to mid-1990s was likewise a function of many conditions, among them poor management in America's industrial sector and poor government leadership. Since the 1980s, U.S. productivity in education has increased slightly, though disparity in school performance has also increased. Maintenance of current productivity rates probably will depend heavily on an effective system of schooling. This explains, at least partially, the enthusiasm for education reform that captured the American policy agenda following publication of *A Nation at Risk* in 1983.

Debt. In August 2005, the United States' federal government debt exceeded $7.8 trillion. This is an amount so large as to lose meaning for most individuals. It can be understood only in relative terms. During the nation's first 100 years, cumulative national debt was $1 billion. Total federal debt reached $1 trillion by 1950 and remained relatively constant for the next quarter century. Then it began to escalate precipitously. By the mid- to late 1980s, the federal debt was growing six times faster than the GDP and equaled half the GDP. Borrowing by the general fund has reached such proportions that accumulated debt is increasing by nearly $1.3 million dollars every 60 seconds.

Moreover, United States borrowing is not simply domestic. Between 1982 and 1985, the United States experienced a dramatic lending reversal. In 1982, the United States was the world's leading foreign investor, with more than $147 billion in net overseas assets; it ended 1985 as the world's largest net debtor, owing other nations over $100 billion. By contrast, as late as 1980, Japan's net overseas holdings were only $12 billion. This figure had increased tenfold by 1986. In the United States, political rhetoric regarding the need for national deficit reduction was intense. Reality was less impressive. The United States today is still one of the world's leading net debtors, with an external debt of $1.4 trillion placing it just behind the United Kingdom. Even so, external debt per capita in the United States is much lower than in other competing countries.

Nevertheless, the current debt situation affects education in several ways. The most obvious is that if money is needed to pay national debt interest and reduce principal, then the share of the public sector's fiscal pie available to fund schools is reduced, or at least subjected to even more intense competition. If money becomes more scarce, interest rates increase and taxes must be elevated to generate the added public funds necessary to service the debt. Voters subjected to a greater federal revenue burden are reluctant to have state and local taxes increased to pay for school. If the federal government counteracts the short money supply situation by creating more money, increased inflation is possible, and that can prove to be the cruelest tax of all, particularly for low-fixed-income individuals. The least painful solution to a burdensome debt situation is increased national productivity. Education can help.

International Competition. In June 2005, United States' annual international trade deficit reached a record high of $58.82 billion and is expected to reach $800 billion by end of 2005 if oil prices continue to be over $70 per barrel. By the middle of 1987, the United States had an annual international trade deficit approaching $200 billion. Lower oil prices and a vastly devalued dollar throughout 1986 and 1987 failed to correct the imbalance. Low productivity continued to price U.S. goods out of many markets. This was true even of agricultural products, previously an export mainstay. Not only was manufacturing a problem, but so were services. The United States was surprised to learn that by 1987 the value of its imported services exceeded that of its exported services. The U.S. annual international trade deficit increased by \$6.7 billion to \$195.1 billion in the first quarter of 2005. U.S. imports have continued to increase considerably as the manufacturing sector has diminished in strength.

Availability of lower-priced foreign goods and services has the advantage of dampening inflation. However, there is a tradeoff in jobs. The flow of manufacturing to other nations results in loss of many millions of jobs, though these jobs are replaced by employment in other emerging sectors. U.S. unemployment exceeded 10% in the early 1980s. By the mid 1980s, it had settled in the 5–7% range. The economic boom of the Internet era, beginning in the 1990s, created an unemployment low of less than 4% in 2000. The unemployment rate spiked afterward, but had settled at 4.7% as of March 2006, as reported by the Bureau of Labor Statistics. The number of youths entering the labor market has been declining since 1985, as more graduates opt to obtain higher education degrees in order to gain the advanced skills needed for emerging sector jobs in the United States. The precipitous 1987 drop in the value of the U.S. dollar against selected Asian and western European currencies stimulated U.S. exports, but still did not balance the trade deficit.

The international trade situation has consequences for education and education policy. During the 1970s and 1980s, the U.S. economy created millions of new jobs. Many, though not most, of these jobs were part-time, low-paid service positions requiring low skills. The public's view that Japan and other nations are able to sustain high productivity because of their rigorous schooling prompted the United States in the early 1980s to allocate more resources and greater attention to education. The employment sector changed in the mid-1990s, as Internet companies led the economic boom that brought unemployment down to one of the lowest percentages in the nation's history. Consequently, more youths are obtaining college degrees, seeing the correlation of education, high-skilled jobs, and salary increases.

As emphasized earlier, productivity is at the heart of American economic problems and is simultaneously the key to many solutions. Education can be a major stimulus to productivity, and subsequent parts of this book explain how. First, however, it is necessary to understand the magnitude and complexity of the difficulties involved in reforming America's schools and thus placing them in a better position not only to assist the nation's economy but also to fulfill the aspirations of individual citizens.

■ EDUCATION IN THE UNITED STATES

Demand for Schooling: Enrollments

United States enrollment in kindergarten through 12th grade peaked at 51 million in 1971. Enrollments had grown dramatically following World War II. Indeed, at the peak of the "baby boom," one out of every four Americans was enrolled in school. More than half the adult electorate had children in public schools.

Annual birthrates began to decline in the mid-1960s, a trend that persisted until a mid-1970s low point. First-grade enrollment generally lags birth by approximately five years. Thus, the overall pupil population in public and private schools declined to a 1983 low point of approximately 39 million. This shrinkage marked a period of unprecedented contraction for many U.S. school districts, particularly in the Northeast and Midwest. School closings and teacher layoffs provoked controversy and distress for many communities and individuals.

Since the early 1980s, enrollments have been increasing nationwide (see Figure 2.3). This is a consequence both of more live births and increased immigration. By 2004,

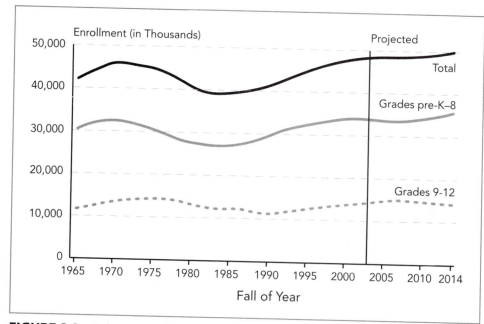

FIGURE 2.3   School Enrollment

Public Elementary and Secondary Enrollment in Pre-Kindergarten through Grade 12, by Grade Level, with Projections: Fall 1965–2014

Source: National Center for Education Statistics (NCES).

enrollment reached an all-time high of approximately 48.3 million. Figure 2.3 displays the historic and projected path of total pupil enrollments. This figure indicates that enrollments are projected to continue to increase and reach approximately 50 million in 2014. However, enrollment patterns have not been consistent across grade levels. Grades pre-K–8, for example, have been increasing at a much more rapid pace than grades 9–12.

Nonpublic Schools. On the basis of percentages, public schools in the United States have a virtual monopoly on education. Private school enrollments account for approximately only 10% of the total school-age population. However, this percentage represents a large number—approximately 5.3 million pupils in 2001. Moreover, there is substantial geographic variation in private school attendance patterns. In the Northeast, approximately 13.8% of children attend nonpublic schools. The overwhelming proportion of nonpublic schools are affiliated with the Catholic church. However, the fastest-growing segment comprises evangelical Christian schools and other religious and nonsectarian schools.

Home Schools. The National Center for Education Statistics reports that approximately 1.1 million students, or 2.2% of the total student population, were homeschooled during the 2002–2003 academic year. While more than 8 out of every 10 homeschooled students are exclusively educated outside of the traditional public school model, some homeschoolers do attend public schools for part of the academic week. For example, the National Center for Education Statistics reported that 12% of homeschooled students were enrolled in school less than 9 hours per week, and 6% were enrolled between 9 and 25 hours per week.

Research Navigator.com
home schools

Geographic Variation. Although K–12 enrollments have been increasing since the early 1980s, they have not been doing so at an even pace across regions. The vast migration to Sun Belt states has meant a corresponding increase in school enrollment. Enrollments have remained stable, or have continued to decline, in a few northern and midwestern areas. Conversely, Sun Belt states such as Florida, Georgia, Arizona, and California are having difficulty constructing schools fast enough and finding enough qualified teachers to meet burgeoning demands.

Migrants from other nations did not distribute themselves evenly across the United States. In 2003, 37% of all new immigrants to the United States settled in the West, particularly in California where approximately 26% of the state's population is foreign born. School systems in California were faced with enormous problems simply in finding teachers who spoke the 80 different languages of the new students. South Florida, New Mexico, Texas, New York, and Illinois also experienced intense enrollment spurts because of migration from other nations.

Supplier of School Services: Personnel

Education in the United States is big business. Schools employ approximately 4 million individuals. There are more school employees than uniformed military personnel, more K–12 teachers than physicians and attorneys combined. The number of K–12 teachers, both in public and private schools, was an estimated 3.4 million in 2003. The overwhelming proportion (87%) of these teachers work in public schools. The remainder, some 425,000 individuals, are employed in a wide variety of religiously affiliated and nondenominational private institutions. Catholic schools employ the largest number, approximately 155,000.

The number of teachers has been growing steadily. During the previously mentioned enrollment decline of the 1970s and early 1980s, states such as Ohio, Michigan, and New York experienced attrition and layoffs. During the same period, teacher hires increased 3% nationwide. Education makes intensive use of labor, and there appears to be little prospect in the near future of substituting capital—such as computers or other educational technology—for labor. Subsequently, current estimates indicate the number of employed teachers is predicted to increase by anywhere from 8 to 10% by 2013.

Schools also employ a substantial number of other professionals (an estimated 600,000) such as administrators, counselors, psychologists, librarians, and nurses. Approximately 1 million additional employees serve as custodians, clerks, bus drivers, cafeteria workers, and so on. These latter are typically known as classified employees. Their employment is more like civil service employment and typically does not require state licensure.

📁 CASE 2 REVISITED

Bay Point Principal's Performance Pressures

Recall the difficulty faced by Sandra Howard in Bay City as she confronted an abrupt shift in her district's priorities toward student outcomes and away from social and input markers of success. Take a moment to reflect on the impact of demographic changes on Sandra's school. Further, reflect on the ways in which a new student performance emphasis might interact with those demographic changes. What do these reflections add to your understanding of the relationships between demographics, economics, and school finance policy?

The current teacher workforce is composed overwhelmingly of women. Female teachers outnumber men two to one. Secondary school staffs are almost balanced with regard to gender. However, almost 80% of elementary teachers are women. This has been the historic pattern among American teachers. Teaching in the United States is a female-dominated occupation.

The teacher workforce has been aging. In 2003, half the public school teachers in the United States were 43 years of age or older and 29% were 50 or older. Almost 30% have taught for 20 years or longer. These statistics have important implications for future employment demand, a topic covered in detail later. America's teachers are predominently white. Less than 12% are nonwhite. These racial proportions have changed little in the last two decades. More than 99% of teachers hold a Bachelor of Arts degree or higher. More than 47% hold a master's degree or have had at least 6 years of college. In contrast, in the early 1960s almost 15% of America's teachers had not even graduated from college. Less than a quarter had any graduate preparation. Thus, if education level is associated with workforce improvement, there have been significant gains for teachers over the last quarter century.

Another dramatic change over the last quarter century has been the unionization and politicization of teachers. The National Education Association (NEA) is the largest union, with almost 1.5 million members. The American Federation of Teachers (AFT), affiliated with the national labor organization the AFL-CIO, has more than 600,000 members. The AFT's membership tends to be concentrated in large city districts. The NEA membership is more representative of suburban and rural districts. Both unions contribute money and member time to state, federal, and sometimes local political campaigns.

Projecting the Future. Expanding enrollments and increasing teacher attrition are creating an intensely renewed demand for educators. According to prediction, the United States is estimated to need approximately 2.4 million additional public school teachers between 1998 to 2008. Private schools will need approximately 560,00 additional teachers over the same period. Because private schools are not required by law to hire credentialed personnel, the precise nature of the labor market competition between them and public schools is not known. Nevertheless, it stands to reason that there is some market overlap for new instructors. Adding these two sets of figures may not yield an absolutely accurate picture of the competitive bidding for licensed teachers. Nevertheless, the sum of the two suggests the magnitude of the market demand for teachers.

The coming demand for new teachers will amount annually to approximately 20% of all U.S. college graduates. This is an impressive figure; if it is accurate for each year from 1998 to 2008, and perhaps thereafter, one out of every five U.S. college graduates will be needed to staff the nation's schools. This situation can be mitigated to the degree to which the "reserve pool" of already credentialed but nonteaching teachers can be induced to work or to work again in schools. Mathematics, science, bilingual education, and special education are identified as the subjects experiencing the largest shortage of teachers. This precipitates a race for talent. Can the schools compete? Seldom there has been an absolute shortage of teachers in the nation's history. Generally, legislative bodies resolve the problem by lowering entry qualifications. Thus, the problem becomes one of *quality*, not quantity.

Governmental Arrangements

In the United States it is government that acts overwhelmingly as a broker between those demanding school services and those willing to supply instruction. This government role is analyzed in detail in Chapter 4. Our purpose here is to describe the governmental structures involved.

The most significant structural characteristic of the governance of American education is its decentralized nature. The United States is one of the few major nations in the world that does not have a nationally operated system of schools. History accounts greatly for the decentralized American arrangement. The framers of the U.S. Constitution distrusted the central authority of the British Crown. They desired to distribute power widely in hopes of diluting the discretion of government generally, and the national government particularly. One of their interventions was the separation of power into three branches of government—*executive*, *legislative*, and *judicial*. Another intervention was the dispersal of decision-making power over three levels of government—*national, state,* and *local.*

During the colonial period, education developed as a state and local function. The majority of participants in the Constitutional Convention of 1787 did not believe this practice ought to be altered. Consequently, the document they drafted contains no explicit mention of *education* or *schooling*. The Tenth Amendment, subsequently drafted, expressed the **social contract theory** of government and made explicit the framers' intent regarding power:

Research
Navigator.com
social
contract
theory

> The powers not delegated to the United States by the Constitution, nor prohibited by it to the states, are reversed to the states respectively, or to the people.

The omission of schooling and education, when viewed in tandem with the Tenth Amendment, explains the absence of a central role for the national government in providing instruction. Also, each of the 50 states has an education provision in its constitution. Consequently, the plenary role of states in education is triply reinforced, and for many practical purposes the United States has 50 systems of education.

During the colonial and early federal periods, the primitive nature of transportation and communication constrained an active state government role in the provision of schooling. States relied on local school districts to deliver educational services, and state statutes facilitated the wide discretion of local authorities. This set of arrangements promoted the perception and reality of *local control*. While never having strong standing as a legal concept, local control nevertheless played a major ideological and practical role in early American school governance. Even today, the majority of day-to-day decisions regarding school operation are made by locally selected policymakers and professional educators.

At the peak of local control there were approximately 128,000 individual school districts in the United States. Since this high point in the 1920s, state-issued incentives and mandates have reduced the number of districts ninefold. By the mid-1980s, the number of local school districts had been reduced to less than 15,000. Even this number is deceptive, because a fifth of these districts are concentrated in five states alone—California, Texas, New York, Illinois, and Nebraska. Southern states have historically aligned school districts with counties. As a consequence, there are many fewer districts in the South than in other regions of the nation.

The movement to consolidate school districts occurred during the great population increases. Consequently, school districts, on average, have come to contain more pupils and adult residents. Near the beginning of the 20th century, each school board member represented fewer than 200 citizens. Today, the comparable figure is approximately 3,000 citizens. There are still small rural districts, some with one school or a one-room school. However, what used to be local control of education is increasingly a rhetorical myth. Local school district are larger, more bureaucratized, more subject to influence by professional educators, and more dominated by state government than at any time in American history. Be that as it may, educational governance is still less centralized in the United States than in almost any other nation in the world. It simply is not as decentralized as before and local control is probably nowhere as strong as many laypersons continue to believe it is.

Financial Costs

The financial magnitude of schooling is seldom well understood. An undertaking directly serving more than 20% of the population, operating throughout every state and most localities, and employing 4 million persons could reasonably be expected to involve a great deal of money, and it does. According to the U.S. Department of Education, total 2007 spending on elementary and secondary education was expected to reach $555 billion, with federal investment of $85 billion for student loans and higher education programs. Postsecondary schooling would add an additional $138 billion. This is approximately 5% of the GDP, the total value of all goods and services produced annually in the United States. The nation spends more only on defense and annual interest payments on the national debt.

The amount of money spent per pupil is also impressive. Expenditure per pupil for the 2001–2002 academic year was estimated at $9,139, a 24% increase from 1990. The comparable figure in 1940 was $100. The nation has increased school spending per pupil by more than 900% over the last 60 years. For proponents of education, this may be insufficient. Nevertheless, it is an impressive accomplishment.

New Jersey currently spends more than $12,000 per pupil, Arizona only has half as much. Sources of spending also differ greatly among states, and national averages are deceptive. Throughout the entire United States, locally generated school revenues constitute approximately 42.8% of the total, state funds make up approximately 48.7%, and federal funds provide the remainder. There is wide variation, however. At one extreme is Hawaii, where the overwhelming proportion of school costs, typically 90%, is borne directly by the state; the remainder results from federal funding. At the other extreme is Nevada, where local revenues make up more than $6 out of every $10 education dollars. Less than a decade ago the extreme was much more pronounced. In New Hampshire, for example, the local government contributes almost 90% of school revenues through the property tax, the state 8%, and federal revenues the remainder.

However broad the variation among states, the diversity of patterns within many states is wider yet. Some wealthy local school districts spend 15 or 20 times as much per pupil as other districts. These expenditure disparities have provoked repeated efforts at school finance reform and will be explored in greater detail in Chapters 12 and 13. While progress has been made, Figure 2.4 reveals that low poverty districts are spending significantly more than their less affluent counterparts.

Student Outcomes

The **No Child Left Behind Act of 2001** (NCLB) has created new standards of accountability that seek to increase student performance. These changes have implications for education policy. NCLB requires that students must demonstrate improvement over time and proficiency in reading and mathematics. Mechanisms of accountability vary, but generally include the establishment of a target level of student performance accompanied by fiscal consequences for the school if the student performance targets are not met. Across the nation, states are instituting student performance tests as the cornerstone of accountability systems in the wake of NCLB.

Research
Navigator.com
No Child
Left Behind
Act of 2001

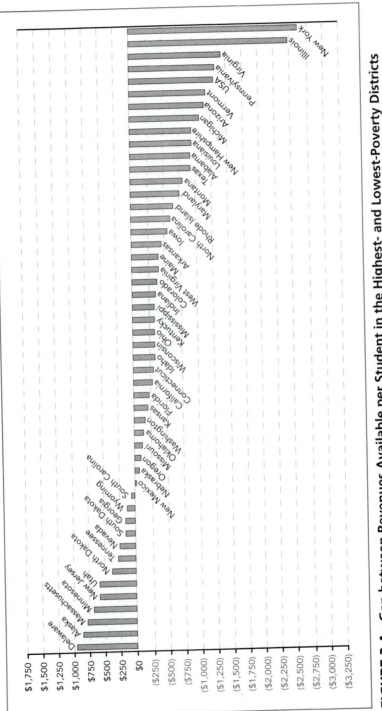

FIGURE 2.4   Gap between Revenues Available per Student in the Highest- and Lowest-Poverty Districts (Cost Adjusted Dollars, 40% Adjustment for Low-Income Students)

Source: NAEP.

> ☐ CASE 5 REVISITED ————————————————————————
>
> ## A Creative and Frustrated Teacher
>
> Recall Johnny Upshaw's frustration at the seeming intractability of his peers and union in supporting a policy innovation—pay for performance. Although political in nature, Johnny's story can also be viewed through the lens of changing economies and cultures. Take a moment to consider the ways in which demographic, social, and cultural changes work within schools to create the kinds of tensions Johnny faced. In what way does Johnny represent a new paradigm in education policy?

Research
Navigator.com

National
Assessment
of
Educational
Progress

The most widely used assessment of student performance is the **National Assessment of Educational Progress** (NAEP), otherwise known as the Nation's Report Card. Since 1969, NAEP has tested a nationally representative sample of public and nonpublic students to assess their knowledge and skills in major subject areas. Test items include both multiple-choice responses and more complex written responses to assess both basic skills and critical thinking skills. The NAEP tests, designed at the federal level, are highly regarded by many educational analysts as a reasonable measure of what students have been learning over time.

One of the primary objectives of NAEP is to track trends in student performance over time. The NAEP long-term trend analysis is conducted every 4 years in math and reading for students ages 9, 13, and 17. Every two years the NAEP is administered to students in grades 4, 8, and 12 in reading, mathematics, science, and other subject areas. Beginning in 1990, NAEP assessments have also been conducted at the state level and states choosing to participate are provided with results of student performance in that state.

Long-Term Trends. NAEP reading and mathematics scores since 1970 indicate that overall the long-term trend in student performance is mixed (see Figures 2.5 and 2.6). Results from NAEP assessments of mathematics proficiency indicate that the scores of 9-, 13-, and 17-year-old students were higher in 2004 than in 1973. Since the early 1970s, younger students have made greater strides on the math portion of the NAEP test than have teenagers, whose scores have remained relatively stagnant. For example between 1999 and 2004, average mathematics scores for 9- and 13-year-olds increased, however no measurable changes in average scores were found for 17-year-olds. This trend continued in 2004—the average score in mathematics for 9-year-olds was 9 points higher than in 1999, and for 13-year-olds the increase was 5 points—the largest single gains for these age groups since 1973.

Reading performance scores for 9-year-olds were higher in 2004 than in any previous assessment year. However, there were no detectable differences between 1999 and 1984 scores. The average score for 13-year-olds in 2004 was higher than the average score in 1971, but no difference was found from the average score in 1999. There was no detectable difference in the reading performance of 17-year-olds in 2004 compared with 1971.

The results from the 2004 long-term trend NAEP offer interesting highlights:

- Students ages 9 and 13 from the southeastern states posted the highest gains in both reading and mathematics. When the tests were first administered in the early 1970s, the southeast states were the lowest performers, with scores well below the national

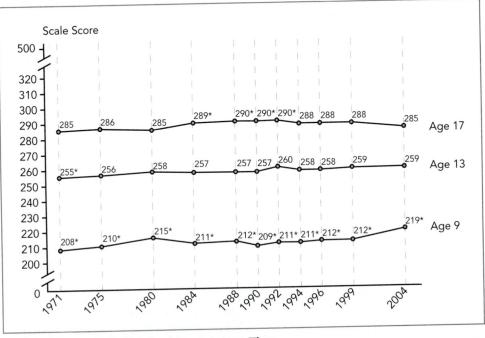

FIGURE 2.5   NAEP Reading Scores over Time

*Significantly different from 2004.

Source: U.S. Department of Education, Institute of Education Sciences, National Center for Education Statistics, National Assessment of Educational Progress (NAEP), selected years, 1971–2004 Long-Term Trend Reading Assessments.

average. The showing of the Southeast likely played a large role in the overall gains of the nation's 9-year-olds, who achieved their highest scores ever in the three-decade history of the tests.

- While the average performance of all students in the Northeast and Central regions has remained relatively flat over the life of the reading test with only modest gains in improvements for mathematics, states in the West registered gains on the 2004 NAEP.
- Hispanic and black students ages 9 and 13 made their greatest ever gains on the NAEP in math and reached their highest scores since the test's inception in 1973. Although white students continue to outscore black students in reading and math, the white–black score gap in mathematics narrowed from 1977 to 2000 for all three age groups (Figure 2.7).

The results of the 2004 NAEP longitudinal analysis suggest that concentrated efforts to provide intensive instruction for students can gradually make progress in narrowing the achievement gap and enhancing overall student performance.

International Comparisons. National level data on the performance of students in the United States also comes from international tests comparing student performance. The

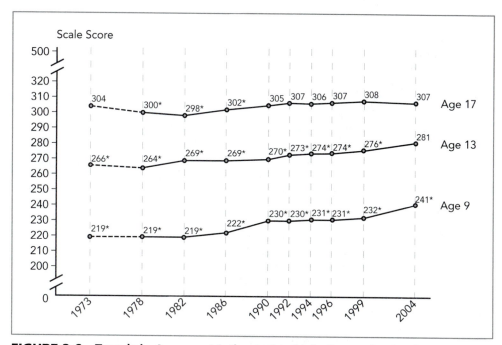

FIGURE 2.6   Trends in Average Mathematics Scale Scores for Students Ages 9, 13, and 17: 1973–2004

*Significantly different from 2004.

Note: Dashed lines represent extrapolated data.

Source: U.S. Department of Education, Institute of Education Sciences, National Center for Education Statistics, National Assessment of Educational Progress (NAEP), selected years, 1973–2004 Long-Term Trend Mathematics Assessments.

Trends in International Mathematics and Science Study (TIMSS) compares the student performance of fourth and eighth graders and the **Program for International Student Assessment** (PISA) compares the student performance of 15-year-olds in math and science literacy. Both tests are well subscribed with 46 countries participating in TIMSS 2003 and 41 participating in PISA 2003.

Results from the 2003 TIMSS showed the test-takers from United States performed above the international average in mathematics and science for all the participating countries. In mathematics, U.S. fourth graders outperformed their peers in 13 of the other 24 participating countries, and, in science, outperformed their peers in 16 countries. Three countries—Chinese Taipei, Japan, and Singapore—continued to outperform test-takers from the United States in both mathematics and science. Statistically there is no change in the fourth-grade students' average mathematics scores between 1995 and 2003. This contrasts with NAEP results, which show an improvement in the fourth-grade students' average during approximately the same time period. At the eighth-grade level, both TIMSS and NAEP indicate an improvement in the mathematics performance of students over the same time period.

Research Navigator.com
Trends in International Mathematics and Science Study

Research Navigator.com
Program for International Student Assessment

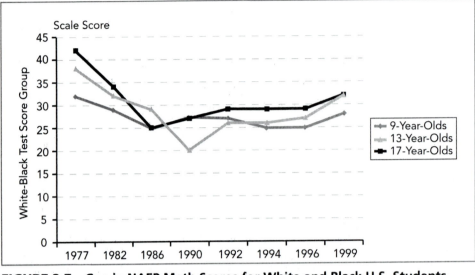

FIGURE 2.7   Gap in NAEP Math Scores for White and Black U.S. Students

Source: NAEP.

The results of the 2003 PISA showed that the 15-year-old test-takers from the United States performed below the international (Organization for Economic Cooperation and Development [OECD]) average in both mathematics and science literacy. Though the PISA results differ from the TIMSS and NAEP one cannot characterize the PISA standings as a decline from the TIMSS and NAEP performance without considering the inherent differences of each test. Given the uniqueness of the purpose of the three tests, in addition to the unique sets of test items and varying test content, it is not surprising to find differences for a given trend estimate of the performance of U.S. students.

Summary

Modern societies are engaged in a multigenerational transformation involving economic models and worldviews. Many fundamental human institutions and everyday actions are caught in the transition and are being reshaped or constrained as a result.

A global imperative for economic efficiency, facilitated by heretofore unimagined technological genius, is dramatically altering science, manufacturing, wholesale and retail business, professional endeavors, government actions and policy processes, individuals' relationship to society generally, and expectations for education specifically.

Education finance escapes none of this complexity. Modern arrangements surrounding financing of schools lead to a tangled web of interaction with virtually all of government and all of society. Hence, seeking means to render schools more efficient, more productive, more equitable, or more successful almost immediately leads to larger policy issues. It is not a leap, for example, from a school reform issue to civil rights, human rights, property rights, employment rights, civil liberties, and dozens of other controversial societal dimensions. Any proposal to significantly alter financial arrangements for schools of necessity means achieving a new political equilibrium on dozens of other dimensions. In effect, understanding modern school finance now compels one to understand almost all of government and politics.

Failure to understand this complexity—the tangled web of value judgments and political interactions surrounding school finance—virtually guarantees inability to reform American education. It is difficult to argue that school finance is the only lever for changing schools. However, it is not difficult to contend that it is one of the most important levers connected with renewing or reforming the system.

In a way far different than ever before in human history, the quality of an individual's material well-being, and possibly his or her spiritual or psychological fulfillment, is crucially linked to obtaining and continually renewing a thorough education. Similarly, societies once flourished or foundered based on what their citizens could harvest from the ground. Today's societies survive and flourish based on what they can harvest from the minds of their citizenry.

Education now matters in a way that is being felt not only throughout a household's daily life and the practical operation of the nation's overall economy, but throughout the dynamics of the policy system as well. Public officials have received the citizenry's forceful message and are striving mightily for means by which schools can be rendered more effective and more productive.

This is a transition from a time when one could have little schooling and still receive relatively high wages to the condition today where insufficient schooling virtually condemns one to a low level of material comfort and restricted opportunity for personal fulfillment.

This is the new need for education and it has triggered a "new" kind of education finance.

Discussion Questions

1. From the data and information provided in the chapter, conjecture about what a public school will look like in your neighborhood 30 years from now. Who will be attending? How will schools be funded? How will success be measured?
2. Having read excerpts from the Tenth Amendment, explain why there even exists a federal education law such as No Child Left Behind.
3. What impact might the changing age distributions in the United States have on public support for increased educational spending?

Web Resources

United States Department of Education's No Child Left Behind Resource Center: http://www.ed.gov/nclb/landing.jhtml?src=pb

TIMMS data and reports: http://nces.ed.gov/timss

PISA data and reports: http://nces.ed.gov/surveys/pisa

NCES: http://nces.ed.gov

U.S. Department of Labor Bureau of Labor Statistics: http://www.bls.gov

CHAPTER THREE

United States Education Finance History: Classic and Modern Paradigms

■ INTRODUCTION

The purposes of this chapter are to describe the history of education finance, illustrate policy issues and operating practices that support the emergence of modern education finance, and specify what distinguishes modern education finance from past paradigms.

LEARNING OBJECTIVES

By the end of this chapter you should be able to:

- Describe the three historic phases of education finance research.
- Explain the historical roles and relationships between federal, state and local levels of government in allocating educational funds.
- Describe the shift from an input-focused understanding of school finance to an outcomes-based understanding of school finance.

Modern education finance has not sprung fully formed from the brow of Zeus nor is it simply the latest incremental phase in an evolutionary sequence of technical public finance developments. Rather, what has happened in the latter quarter of the 20th century is a qualitative alteration. One can best appreciate the dramatic policy and practical differences that have occurred since the change to "modern" by first grasping the essential characteristics of past paradigms.

Classic education finance, at least the 20th-century version of it, was the province of a few accountants who were consigned to a remote alcove of state education departments and who were generally invisible except when answering regulatory questions from local school district business managers. Their moment of maximum visibility likely came during annual legislative budget hearings when finance experts were called on to construct the mechanical distribution formulae necessary to allocate to local districts whatever annual revenue increment had been decided on by a governor and legislative leaders. The usual legislative and gubernatorial strategy was to determine publicly acceptable tax rates first and then to permit revenues to be a calculable consequence. Education was routinely expected to fit, Cinderella style, into whatever revenue slipper was politically determined for it.

Under early education finance, the challenge for experts was not to decide how much funding was to be distributed, but to generate a rational basis for whatever the predetermined revenue quantum was to be. To be sure, matters of distributional equity entered into their calculations. However, additional issues such as those dominating the contemporary policy stage—matters of how much money is "adequate" for students to achieve state learning standards and how districts can be induced to spend resources more wisely to generate academic achievement—were seldom a part of their considerations.

Despite their mechanical function and the lack of linkage to instructional practice and academic achievement, practitioners of early education finance succeeded in constructing a corpus of concepts that still productively serves school administrators, policy officials, and education finance experts. What follows is a summary explanation of the evolution of early education finance as well as useful concepts that emerged from its practice.

▌ EDUCATION FINANCE'S THREE HISTORIC PHASES

Phase 1: Building a System of Schooling

By the mid-1700s, the role of education had taken on different emphases in different geographical regions of the original 13 colonies. As a result, the relationship between government and education differed as well. Overall, education was seen as a family responsibility, as were many of the other "social" sectors currently assigned to government (e.g., welfare, income maintenance, retirement security, and health care).[1] Institutional developments described below must be viewed within this context of the primary role of the family in developing literate, productive, and moral citizens.

In the New England colonies, schooling—with a focus on literacy—was deemed crucial, mostly for comprehension and interpretation of biblical scripture. As a result, New England colonies developed a system and tradition of public maintenance for educational institutions. A well-educated populace, it was thought, was a benefit to all citizens. A classic example of this impulse was Massachusetts' Ye Olde Deluder Satan Act of 1642, requiring all settlements of over 50 households to hire a reading teacher, and all settlements of over 100 households to establish and support a grammar school. This colonial statute ruled education as both compulsory and lay controlled, and authorized local townships to levy taxes for schooling. Throughout this pivotal period, schooling began to be seen as a primary medium through which to preserve law and order in the new republic, benefit business and industry, and further the Declaration of Independence's call that all men are created equal and have an inalienable right to life, liberty, and pursuit of happiness. By the 19th century, a significant exploration into universal, free, tax-supported state school systems spread throughout most geographic regions, while new forms of education finance were developed by local, state, and federal entities and slowly spread throughout the country.

In the Middle colonies, education was considered important to development of a leadership class. As a result, Middle colony education focused on parochial schools which provided basic instruction and identified gifted students for further education and training, often in Europe. Although never fully implemented, Thomas Jefferson's plans for a comprehensive Virginia public school system provide an illustration of this approach of developing intellectual leadership. Jefferson's Bill for the More General Diffusion of

Knowledge—introduced in the Virginia legislature in 1779—provided for publicly supported elementary schools, secondary schools, and colleges. Jefferson's plan was meritocratic; a small number of gifted elementary school students would advance, at public expense, to secondary schools. Similarly, a small number of gifted secondary school students would advance to the publicly supported state college. Jefferson's plan was the foundation for the 1819 formation of the University of Virginia.

Southern colonies were the most rural and agrarian of the new republic. As a result, the emphasis on education was negligible. The plantation system placed a leadership emphasis on lineage over merit for the wealthy. The family provided education—elite education was "outsourced" to England or elite academies—and received much less governmental interest from either the federal or the local levels.

Within these geographic differences in approach to the support of educational institutions, there lay similar strata of government funding. Although federal, state, and local governments were all involved in the provision of education to greater or lesser degrees, these political impulses often served to support or modify the regional approaches described above.

Federal Role. Land grants not only proved a cornerstone for federal involvement in education for more than a century, but also provided a working model for local and state schooling initiatives. As early as 1783, when England's King George III issued his Proclamation of Cessation of Hostilities, culminating in the Paris Peace Treaty (1783), there was statutory reference to the use of public lands to support schools (Barr et al., 1970). Even though it was not until the Ordinance of 1785 (later known as the Northwest Ordinance of 1787) that the Continental Congress appropriated public lands to establish schools, these conceptualizations set precedent for federal land inducements establishing educational institutions.

Such successive "common interests" initiatives as the Ordinance of 1802, appropriating land grants specifically for a burgeoning common school movement, and the Morrill Act of 1862 extending similar grants to higher education to support college-level studies relating to the "mechanic arts," further infused public education in post-Revolutionary America (Goldin & Katz, 2003; Pemberton, 1981). By the late 1800s, the United States Commissioner of Education described the Northwest Ordinance of 1787, and succeeding waves of common interest initiatives that followed, as "the ideal of Republican institutions, the gospel of American Democracy . . . set up like a beacon light for the guidance of the nation through the stormy passage yet before it in the long years to come" (Report of the United States Commissioner of Education 1894 as cited in Barr et al., 1970).

While these federal incentive grants provided land for states to establish public education systems, federal grants did not provide direct financial means for schools to subsist from year to year. Nor was it then considered a federal government responsibility to provide such support. Strict constructionists relied on the United States Constitution's omission of the words "education" or "schooling" to justify a minimal federal role.[2]

State Role. By the early 1800s, a handful of states—North Carolina (1776), Georgia (1777), Pennsylvania (1776), Vermont, (1777), Ohio (1802), and Indiana (1816)—drafted constitutional provisions for legislatures to establish permanent endowments for K–12 education (Cubberley, 1905). Interestingly, federal land grants boded particularly well for this cause since many states used proceeds from leasing or selling portions of land to establish state school funds (Mort, 1932). According to Cubberley, revenue generated for public education from permanent local and state funds and unsold lands amounted to more than $51 million by the late 1800s.

Concomitantly, states copied federal government use of financial inducements to propel localities to establish schools. New York Governor George Clinton, for example, who later served as Vice President under both Thomas Jefferson and James Madison, took great interest in public education. In 1795, Clinton made establishment of a public education system one of his chief priorities at the opening session of the legislature and appropriated 2,000 pounds as an incentive for New York townships to build and operate schools (Ramirez, 2003).

In addition to strategic use of incentives, states also explored various types of taxation to raise additional revenue for education. For example, Ohio levied a fuel tax, Connecticut collected fees on liquor licenses, and North Dakota used a poll tax. Though other revenue-generating schemes were defeated at the polls, such as Indiana's proposed insurance premium tax, use of state-authorized taxes to support education proliferated (Cubberley, 1905; Hazlett, 1971; Mort, Reusser, & Polley, 1960).

Local Role. While federal and state involvement undoubtedly shaped early education policy, colonial era schooling resulting from the Ye Olde Deluder Satan Act was largely considered a local, private endeavor principally supported by philanthropic contributions, subscriptions accepted by church and school societies, or tuition fees (known as rate bills) assessed in proportion to the number of wealthy children and merchant families sent to school (Cremin, 1980; Johns, Morphet, & Alexander, 1983). Local townships and communities bore principal responsibility for developing means to generate revenue. For example, Hazlett (1971, p. 33), in his historical recounting of financial support of schools, noted that, Providence and Newport in Rhode Island; Philadelphia, Harrisburg, Pittsburgh, and Lancaster in Pennsylvania; Baltimore, Maryland; Charleston, South Carolina; and Mobile, Alabama, were some of the first cities to successfully garner state support to levy local property taxes in support of education—a tax that comprised the greatest proportion of total school revenue generation well past the mid-1900s.

Support for public education through taxation was a heated issue and countless initiatives failed to gain legislative and voter approval. For example, Cubberley's (1905) overview of general taxation for education recounts a story of opposition encountered by Henry Barnard, when he was appointed Rhode Island's State Superintendent of Education in 1843, to a tax policy proposal.[3] Cubberley wrote, "A member of the Legislature declared that 'the school act cannot be executed at the point of a bayonet,' and Rhode Island citizens declared that 'he might as well take a man's ox to plough his neighbor's field as to take a man's money to educate his neighbor's children'" (pp.71–73).

Barnard's experience was not an anomaly. Indeed, debates on means to realize a financially stable, free, public education roared to a feverish pitch between Federalists and Whigs, and by the mid- to late 1850s, education had become one of the greatest public interests for the people of the United States (Cremin, 1980; Cubberley, 1919a; Goldin & Katz, 2003).

In 1872, education tax policy debates were elevated to judicial review when citizens of Kalamazoo, Michigan, challenged tax collection's legal basis for supporting a public high school (Goldin & Katz, 2003; Mort & Reusser, 1941; Mort, Reusser, & Polley, 1960). The case, *Stuart v. School District No. 1 of Village of Kalamazoo* (1874), was decided by the Michigan Supreme Court in 1874 and established precedent as pivotal as contemporary decisions such as *Serrano v. Priest's* (1971) on equity in California or *Rose v. Council for Better Education's* (1989) on adequacy in Kentucky. The Court decided the state had a right to levy taxes in support of a complete system of public education, including high schools and universities.

Michigan was not the only state facing such challenges. In Kansas, in 1885, *Robinson v. Schenk* ruled it was permissible for a state to levy a statewide tax in support of education, while in 1899, another Kansas case, *State v. Board of Commissioners of Elk County*, ruled county systems can be compelled by the state to levy taxes in support of schools (Johns, 1971; Mort, Reusser, & Polley, 1960). The legal authority of states to levy taxes remained a contentious issue, and it was not until the 1920s that the United States Supreme Court, in *Shaffer v. Carter*, ruled that, "unless restrained by provisions of the Federal Constitution, the power of the state as to the mode, form and extent of taxation is unlimited, where the subjects to which it applies are within her jurisdiction" (as cited in Johns, 1971).

Phase 1 education financing was initiated following the American Revolution and drafting of the Declaration of Independence (1776) and persisted into the post-Civil War Reconstruction era. Nevertheless, growth was slow during this period. While public theorists shaped most American social policies and developments, the fiscal side of schooling had only a few notable philosophic, scholarly, or technical champions (Johns, 1971). Indeed, education finance's beginnings were predicated on laypersons and social, political, economic, and religious influences. As a result, critical issues of instructional quality, financial parity, and school effectiveness were seldom a component of territorial and state officials' formal policy agenda.

Phase 2: Building a Scholarly Base

Phase 2 emerged near the end of the 19th and beginning of the 20th centuries, when states began to rigorously enforce free public education. It was during this time that a systematic literature regarding education finance emerged. For example, in 1905, Elwood Patterson Cubberley's seminal doctoral dissertation, School Funds and Their Apportionment, was published.

Cubberley, a school administrator and professor, who subsequently served as dean of Stanford University's education school, is widely considered the scholarly "father" of education finance. His professional interests initially concentrated on developing means by which states could effectively use intergovernmental fiscal arrangements to induce local districts to expand schooling opportunities for residents, which he called "reward for effort" (Cubberley, 1905, 1912). He later became concerned with means by which states could use revenue distribution criteria to compensate communities for differences in local property wealth (Cubberley, 1908, 1915, 1919b; Cubberely & Sears, 1924; Cubberley & Strayer, 1913).

Cubberley's impact on education is apparent by the sheer magnitude of publications he produced and the significant attention they garnered. He published more than 29 books, monographs, or reports and over 100 articles, addresses, editorials, reviews, and special papers. Equally impressive are the more than 90 known articles and addresses commemorating Cubberley's contributions and nearly 50 published reviews of Cubberley's books. Moreover, Stanford University's library contains a bound copy of over 400 letters received by the University upon his retirement.[4]

Several years after Cubberley's initial writing on education finance, a group of academics began to further shape education finance as a field of study. Most notable among these first-generation education finance academics are Arthur B. Moehlman of the University of Michigan, Henry C. Morrison of the University of Chicago, Harlan Updegraff of the University of Pennsylvania, and George D. Strayer, Robert Murray Haig, and Paul R. Mort of Teachers College. Under the auspices of the Educational Finance Inquiry Commission,[5] Strayer and Haig (1923), for example, developed a financial conceptualization of equalization of educational opportunity (EEO), marking part of the historical antecedents for today's search for costs in general and giving rise to the normative underpinnings of modern-day education revenue distribution.[6] As a whole, these individuals not only contributed to an expansion of scholarship, but also had substantial practical influence on the means by which states generated and distributed revenues to local school districts (Johns, 1938; Moehlman, 1922, 1927; Morrison, 1924, 1930, 1932; Mort, 1924, 1926, 1932; Updegraff, 1922; Updegraff & King, 1922).

Phase 3: Seeking Equality

Phase 3 of the early education finance paradigm was an offshoot of the broader post-World War II Civil Rights movement. It was during this time that a second cohort of scholars such as H. Thomas James of Stanford University, Roe L. Johns of the University of Florida, J. Alan Thomas of the University of Chicago, and Edgar L. Morphet and Charles Scott Benson of the University of California emerged and joined forces with first-generation scholars to collectively shape early education finance paradigms because of their concern for formulaic means by which revenues could be equitably generated and distributed.[7]

Still, during this period every state relied on local school districts as the organizational base of education and had statutory arrangements for directing state-supported subsidies (called **flat grants**) to local districts in inverse proportion to property wealth. Early equalization provisions did not strive for resource parity and, in fact, enabled local wealth variations to penetrate a finance system once a district reached a so-called **"foundation level"** in per pupil revenues.[8] In many states, interdistrict per-pupil spending disparities were substantial. Texas, for example, formerly had high-wealth districts capable of spending more than 20 times per-pupil amounts received by low-wealth districts (*Edgewood Independent School District v. Kirby*, 1989).

Research Navigator.com

foundation level

Two scholarly publications directed at these disparities signaled the beginning of Phase 3. *Private Wealth and Public Education*, by John E. Coons, William H. Clune, and Stephen D. Sugarman (1970), and *Rich Schools: Poor Schools*, by Arthur Wise (1968), were path-breaking volumes. Though initially written in isolation from one another, each book targeted property-related resource disparities within states as an injustice. Each constructed a Constitutional argument around the 14th Amendment's equal protection clause by which identified resource disparities could become a province for adjudication. They also contributed to school finance's **Proposition One**. *The quality of a child's schooling should not be a function of wealth, other than the wealth of the state as a whole.* It is this formulation that has provided the judicial system with a purchase on remedy, a criterion by which equity reforms can be judged. Prior to this formulation, courts avoided education finance litigation for fear there were no judicially manageable solutions.

Research Navigator.com

Proposition One

> ☐ CASE 3 REVISITED
>
> ## Trial Judge Complexities
>
> Recall Judge Glenda Manheim's struggles in determining the appropriate level of education spending, and how that spending was to be distributed. As you read this chapter, reflect on these issues as well as this larger question: What level of education ought to be provided to our nation's youth? Should students simply be provided with an opportunity to learn, or does the state have a greater obligation to ensure that learning occurs?

■ THE EMERGENCE OF MODERN EDUCATION FINANCE INTO POLICY PRIME TIME

This section presents a brief overview of significant policy conditions that drive modern education finance and describes two principal school improvement reform strategies that have influenced the emergence of modern education finance in the past decades.

Significant Policy Conditions Supporting Modern Education Finance

This 1983 release of *A Nation at Risk* triggered a sustained period of public concern for and policymaker attention to higher levels of performance for United States' public schools. Bill Honig's election in 1984 as California's highly visible Superintendent of Public Instruction, for example, sent an electoral signal regarding the significance of this policy shift. Honig's campaign platform claimed his incumbent opponent had concentrated on access and equity at the price of excellence and higher pupil performance. Honig stayed true to his campaign promises on election to office and advocated enactment of elevated pupil performance standards.

Five years thereafter, a highly publicized 1989 "Summit" conference of America's governors in Charlottesville, Virginia, organized by President George H. W. Bush, resulted in a host of new national- and state-level policies. For example, a set of six National Goals for educational improvement, later expanded to eight goals during the Clinton Administration, were incorporated into legislation by Congress, while heightened performance expectations for students, accompanied by accountability provisions for schools and districts, and state student achievement testing programs proliferated at the state level.[9]

Post–*A Nation at Risk* reforms were generally of two kinds. One was heightened performance expectations. This included intensified high school graduation requirements, reduced high school electives, and more stringent college admission standards. This was an era of student motivation efforts such as "No Pass–No Play" and "No Graduate–No Drive" state statues. In addition, more money was directed toward raising teachers' salaries.

The aftermath of the 1989 Charlottesville Summit marked a second post–*A Nation at Risk* education reform phase. Initial efforts at heightened rigor and spending had resulted in only minimal achievement gains as indicated by trends in average scores on the National Assessment of Educational Progress (NAEP) for the nation in reading, mathematics, and science. Emergence of systemic reform, sometimes referred to as standards-based reform, outlined in a seminal 1991 article by Marshall Smith and Jennifer O'Day, signaled a second phase.

Smith and O'Day's ideas further advanced policy proposals for aligning components of the educational system: linking standards, statewide standardized student achievement tests, teacher licensing requirements, instructional materials, professional development, state capacity-building subsidies, performance ratings and school report cards, and providing positive and negative sanctions for achievement progress. These initiatives not only became the hallmark of the Clinton administration's educational policies, but they also facilitated a new understanding that school revenue generation and distribution arrangements were something of an operating precondition, separated from the purposes of schooling under the "old" education finance paradigm. The emerging understanding of school performance emphasized the need to forge a link between these revenue matters and schooling outcomes.

Enactment in 2001 of the federal government's No Child Left Behind Act (NCLB) prioritized concerns for schooling outcomes contrasted with the prior era's concern with resource inputs. NCLB is a reauthorization by Congress of the 1965 Elementary and Secondary Education Act (ESEA; technically Public Law 89-10) and provides the federal government leverage on states, and through states on local school districts and schools, on two fronts. First, the American electorate heavily endorses the purposes for which NCLB stands. Second, the Act, though proposed by Republican President George W. Bush, won wide bipartisan support and was enacted in the Senate by a vote of 87 to 10 and in the House by 381 to 41.

NCLB poignantly signifies the outcome-oriented production model underpinning modern education finance. By 2014, for instance, states must display sufficient improvements to ensure students are performing at high levels of proficiency on achievement tests and that schools are closing achievement gaps between advantaged and disadvantaged students. If a school fails to comply with the Act's requirements and to make "adequate yearly progress" toward the prescribed goal, formidable consequences are triggered. These consequences can include permitting parents of persistently low-performing schools to claim public resources and to opt for the placement of their children at other instructional institutions, including private schools.

Significant Reform Dynamics Supporting Modern Education Finance

Education financing is now a principal instrument for mediating pursuit of educational policy and has moved from the periphery of policymaker concern to a far more central role. This section describes the two principal school improvement or education reform strategies—*systemic reform* and *economic dynamics*—that explain how modern education finance has begun to conceptualize linking resources to elevated student academic performance.

Systemic Reform. One major reform strategy hinges on the presence of measurable academic expectations or curriculum standards and an assortment of instructional and accountability components aligned in pursuit of these standards. The "production" components in this model involve dimensions such as educator time, class size (a dimension of teacher time spent with students), instructional materials and textbooks, student achievement testing, time on learning tasks, pre-service teacher training, parent and community engagement, leadership training, personnel and institutional performance reports, professional development, in-school peer group characteristics, and in-school and out-of-school extracurricular activities for students.

System reform presumes that much regarding good instruction is already known and that appropriate coherence between various instructional components can result in higher levels of student academic learning. Also, components of this strategy can be operationalized into an instructional alignment measure that can be considered either as a dependent variable, in an effort to discern policy system conditions providing the greatest or best alignment, or an independent variable to determine alignment consequences for pupil performance.[10]

Economic Dynamics. The other principal reform model takes schooling and instruction to be a "black box," perhaps a currently impenetrable or unknowable black box. Market and economic incentive advocates contend that a specification of expected outcomes and an appropriate system for measuring and sanctioning school success in producing desired student outcomes will productively guide the actions of those inside the black box. Under such assumptions it is less necessary than in a systemic alignment strategy to understand the nature of "throughputs." However, it is still crucial to understand the nature of outputs. It is also important to understand interactions of various market components, (e.g., supply; consumer information; performance incentives for students, teachers, schools, and districts; competition effects; and market regulation) than in the systems alignment model.

Competition is often posed in policy circles as an alternative reform strategy since market dependence is seen as a major incentive. The ability of clients to seek different schools, presumably schools more consistent with personal preferences, is taken to be a market incentive to motivate instructional providers. In essence, providers either perform to clients' expectations, or lose market share and accompanying resources.

While it is important to distinguish between these two intervention models and while each implies a partially different set of tools to determine its effectiveness, the two models are not mutually exclusive. There are ways in which they can be combined. For example, an operator of a private school is presumably interested in having instructional components aligned, in order to be effective. Although a systemic alignment strategy does not preclude reliance on client choice systems or performance awards and punishments for teachers or schools in the public sector, it does advocate seldom recommended performance incentives for students, teachers, schools, or school districts.

■ MODERN EDUCATION FINANCE: WHAT IS "NEW" AND HOW THAT DIFFERS FROM PAST PARADIGMS

Table 3.1 identifies 14 dimensions that can be used to contrast early and modern education finance paradigms. The table was generated following a 2-year study conducted by researchers with Vanderbilt University's Peabody Center for Education Policy, which traced the impetus for modern education finance. This section provides two illustrative examples that characterize the shift from early to modern education finance. Changing paradigms of education finance also change policy questions and issues.

◿ CASE 4 REVISITED ────────────────────

An Elected Official's Dilemma

Recall the pressures facing Walter Romero in his legislative session. In what way does Walter represent the transition from classic conceptions of education finance to modern ones?

TABLE 3.1   Summary Comparison of Classic and Modern Education Finance

Orientation / Dimension	Classic Education Finance	Modern Education Finance
Value Orientation	Equity	Efficiency and Productivity
Data Orientation	State and District Level Data	Student, Classroom, School, District, State, National Level Data
Resource Distribution Orientation	Per-Pupil Parity	Per-Pupil Sufficiency and Performance Focused
Analytic Orientation	Fiscal Neutrality, Horizontal Equity Measures, Income Elasticity, and so on	Multivariate Regression; Budget-Output Functions; Hierarchical Linear Modeling, and so on
Decision-Making Orientation	Mostly Arbitrary	Research Based and Data Driven
Policy System Oversight	Local Control	Federal, State, and Local Control
Governance	Decentralized	Integrated Governance
Incentive	Maximize Operating Budget via Input Manipulation (enrollment census and student classification)	Maximize Effectiveness of Operating Budget via Input Manipulation and Outcome Maximization
Relative Concern For . . .		
Quality, Excellence, and Academic Competency	Minimal	High
Economic Theory	Moderate	High
Application of Finance Concepts	Minimal	High
Input-Output	Minimal/Moderate	High
Evidentiary Basis	Minimal	High
Linkage to Instructional Components	Minimal	High

Example 1: Defining Education Finance

Thomas Kuhn, a professor of philosophy and historian of science, once reasoned that textbooks are integral to establishing and defining a scientific field's knowledge base. Kuhn (1962, p. 16) wrote, "no natural history can be interpreted in the absence of at least some implicit body of intertwined theoretical and methodological belief." He explained further that scientific fields are best understood by way of textbooks since textbooks are a default, an authoritative source of the history of science, and provide foundational knowledge for their respective domains. In light of Kuhn's universal observation, this example draws on two education finance textbooks spanning two distinct time periods to illustrate how the definition of education finance has changed over time.

Arthur B. Moehlman, a professor of educational administration and supervision at the University of Michigan and past president of the American Education Research Association, published an education finance textbook, *Public School Finance*, in 1927. Moehlman's textbook was described as setting the "standard for its time" which "advised superintendents to leverage their social contacts." Moehlman defines school finance as a "branch of public finance which is concerned with the money-getting and money-spending activities of public education and the organization and techniques incident thereto" (p. 3).

A much more recent education finance textbook—*School Finance: A Policy Perspective*—published by Alan Odden and Lawrence O. Picus nicely illustrates how the definition of education finance has shifted over time. Odden and Picus define school finance as concerning "the distribution and use of money for the purpose of providing educational services and producing student achievement" (p. 1). While both Moehlman and Odden and Picus reference "money-getting and money-spending," Odden and Picus explicitly link educational services and student achievement—a clear indication of modern education finance's augmented focus on educational outcomes.

Example 2: Conceptualizing Educational Adequacy

Journal articles, like textbooks, provide a documentary measure to evaluate the progress of a scholarly field, thus revealing changes in core concerns (Buboltz & Savickas, 1994). The *Journal of Education Finance (JEF)*, a peer-reviewed scholarly journal published on a quarterly basis for three decades, has been closely affiliated with the American Education Finance Association, the largest professional organization specifically concerned with education finance matters. For this reason, treatment of finance adequacy in both early and recent issues provides another valid medium with which to illustrate a paradigm shift from early to modern education finance.

In 1976, *JEF* published an article by Arthur Wise entitled, "Minimum Educational Adequacy: Beyond School Finance Reform."[11] Wise provided evidence of how education litigation had alluded to minimum educational adequacy concepts, while making his concern over "whether the minimum educational adequacy approach will result in serious educational progress" readily apparent (p. 482). Wise noted, more specifically, that "adequacy presupposes a 'hyperrationalized' view of education" on three fronts:

- it presumes that the policymaking process can settle upon a definition of adequacy which meets the legal obligation and is educationally meaningful;
- it further presumes that this definition can be translated into educational objectives, that an instructional system can be established which will attain these objectives, and that tests can be devised to ascertain whether the objectives have been achieved; and
- it requires a management, budgeting, and accounting scheme which will render the local school system accountable to the state. (p. 480)

While the effectiveness of adequacy arguments was indeterminate nearly three decades ago, it becomes quite clear that the utility of such claims are no longer dubious when juxtaposing Wise's article with recent *JEF* adequacy-related articles. As "In the News" indicates, judges are using adequacy arguments to expand the reach of publicly provided education into the realms of pre-kindergarten.

First, contemporary, state-promulgated learning standards resulting from the standards-based reform movement have permitted departure from early education finance paradigms. Learning standards, curriculum guidelines, subject matter benchmarks, and academic achievement performance targets, for example, can all be used to help define adequacy. In fact, adequacy is consistently defined in recent *Journal of Education Finance* articles (Addonizio, 2003; Alexander, 2003; Baker, 2005; Imazeki & Reschovsky, 2003; Mathis, 2003;

In the News

House Speaker Bobby Harrell and Senate leader Glenn McConnell say that an appeal from the state would be very unlikely in the December ruling of an education-equity lawsuit unless the school districts that sued decide to proceed further.

After 12 years of litigation between the state and its poorest school districts in the *Abbeville County School District vs. The State of South Carolina* case, Judge Thomas W. Cooper Jr. ruled on Dec. 29 that the state does not provide a minimally adequate education because it does not adequately fund early childhood education.

"I am inclined not to have the Senate appeal the decision," McConnell, a Charleston Republican, said Friday. "However, I am reserving all the options. I don't want to close the door on it."

Harrell, also a Charleston Republican, echoed the stance on behalf of the House.

"We do not plan on filing an appeal, but if the plaintiffs do, we will be forced to file one," Harrell said through a spokesman.

Both sides have until Jan. 29 to file an appeal, but the school districts might be able to buy more time as they consider whether further court action would be in their best interest.

"There are parts of the order that we disagree with, and parts we agree with," said Laura Hart, a partner with Nelson Mullins Riley & Scarborough, which represented the eight rural school districts named in the suit.

. . .

"Clearly, the order was not what we had hoped for, but the judge made a major finding," she said. "He said the state has failed poor children in poor districts."

From Wenger, Yvonne. "State appeal called unlikely; School districts ultimately will decide in education-equity case." The (SC) *Post and Courier.* January 9, 2006. p. B1.

Odden, 2000; Reschovsky & Imazeki, 2001; Verstegan, 2002); that is, adequacy maintains that state-provided education must make available a sufficient level of resources to all students to prevent denial of opportunity to at least reach a level of proficiency defined by state standards, regulations, or educational goals.

Second, the desire of modern policymakers to gather information regarding the costs of offering services geared toward elevated performance has further propelled researchers to develop methods to operationalize or cost-out educational adequacy. Baker (2005) delineates adequacy cost studies into two factions—education cost function and resource cost model studies. Wise's predilection for establishing an instructional system to attain learning objectives would probably find him in favor of resource cost models. Baker (2005) noted that more than 30 cost studies have been conducted and that the majority of these studies were commissioned by state legislatures seeking counsel about state aid formula design.[12] While Baker does acknowledge "scrutiny over the reliability of current methods for estimating the absolute or relative costs of education" (p. 286), it is evident that researchers have developed, and are continuing to improve, methods for operationalizing educational adequacy.

Third, education finance and organizational governance and management reform in public education have resulted in a vastly different accountability structure when compared to the 1970s. Several early *Journal of Education Finance* articles, for example, noted that while normative principles of fiscal federalism suggest that the most appropriate level of government to finance education is the state or even the federal government, history has produced a financial structure that is primarily local in nature (Goertz & Hannigan, 1978; Menz & Raphaelson, 1976). The trend in percent distribution of revenue by source from 1972 to 2002, however, reflects state governments' increasing financial involvement in support of public education. Not only did local revenue as a percentage of total revenue generated decrease by almost one-quarter, but the dispersion among states was reduced by one-third (Springer & Liu, 2005). Furthermore, NCLB reflects a major shift in thinking about organizational governance and management by concocting a unique blend of federal government oversight, state-driven reform, and increased accountability for states, districts, and schools. In essence, local school systems are not only accountable to states, but also, along with state entities, are accountable to the federal government—a vast change of events since Wise expressed skepticism about local education agencies becoming accountable to the state.

This is not to say that education policy in general and education finance in particular have completely addressed Wise's adequacy concerns. Many finance scholars contend that adequacy is in its infancy, conceptually; is only beginning to be understood by courts; is primitive in terms of social science support; is still awkward to implement (even when there is a judicial mandate); and is far from reliably or accurately measurable (Guthrie, 2004; Ladd, Chalk, & Hansen, 1999). Chapter 13 will explore these issues in more detail. Here, we are simply highlighting the considerable progress education finance as a field of scholarly study has made.

The aforementioned examples by no means encompass all of the 14 dimensions identified in Table 3.1. We encourage readers to revisit this table throughout their study of education finance.

Summary

Education financing is now a principal instrument for pursuing educational policy and has moved from the periphery of policymaker concern to a far more central role. The policy system needs more precise information regarding (1) how education resources can be deployed with greater student performance returns and (2) how much money is actually needed to guarantee students an opportunity to learn what is expected. Fulfilling the paradigm's promise will depend on successful pursuit of conceptual, technical, and informational quests. Table 3.1 summarizes the paradigm shift in school finance.

Concepts of Learning. The field of "modern" education finance presently lacks a sufficiently specified model of academic achievement production. Researchers seek more precise correlates of higher student performance and strive to determine their costs. However, this is often a blind search, absent a sufficiently comprehensive concept of what it is that effectively enables students to learn. Present-day searches for correlates of higher student achievement are limited by existing production concepts and existing information. In that class size consequences and instructional and administrator salaries comprise the overwhelming costs of contemporary public school instruction, and these data are most readily available to education finance analysts, these then are the data they continue to mine. Most searches in this regard result in incomplete explanations of academic achievement variation.

Few systematic or sustained findings suggest that class size, instructor salary, teacher qualification, or similar variables are related to variation in student achievement. Even the vaunted Tennessee STAR study appears to have flaws inviting alternative hypotheses regarding higher levels of student academic achievement. Researchers and analysts, even with the most rigorous student controls presently possible for background, race and socioeconomic status, continue to identify similar resource allocation patterns associated with widely varying levels of student performance.

Something or some things more fundamental, or in addition to, class size, school size, teacher pay, and teacher characteristics is or are in operation here. A far wider stream of variables needs to be added to the model, and data regarding these variables need to be collected. When two districts, two schools, two classrooms, or two students continually benefit from similar resource patterns but exhibit varying levels of student achievement, after controlling statistically for student, household, and community characteristics, then it is time to generate alternative explanations including matters such as the amount and allocation of teacher time, use of pedagogical techniques, school leadership, teacher and student incentive systems, and interaction effects among resources, student characteristics, and instructional contexts.

Currently fashionable (and controversial) research paradigms involving randomized field trials may result in added knowledge and an expansion of the prevailing production function knowledge storehouse. However, to do so, researchers must test different production elements than are now typically employed and they must realize that instructional, organizational, and social contexts may be powerful explanations that cannot be sorted out through randomized assignment of respondents to experimental conditions.

Technical Breakthroughs. Virtually no one believes currently configured standardized achievement tests sufficiently capture the complexity of desired schooling outcomes. Nevertheless, one finance study after another offers an initial caveat regarding the narrowness of existing student performance or school outcome measures and then relentlessly plows forward to rely exclusively on these same measures. A far more comprehensive set of measures of student achievement is necessary to fully comprehend what schools do and the resource levels needed to enable them to do it. In part, this is a technical challenge needing substantially greater time and attention from measurement specialists. Regrettably, current state and federal government-imposed narrow achievement measures restrict the likelihood of gaining greater outcome measurement breadth in the short run.

Informational Challenges. Among the frustrations involved in conducting modern education finance research is the paucity of correctly specified information, even when what is needed is well known. For example, to fully understand the consequences of resource allocation for student achievement requires accurate portrayals of what resources are actually distributed to any specified set of students. However, most spending data are aggregated to the district level, and are seldom provided for the school, classroom, or individual student level. The same is true for teacher or administrator salary data. Mean salaries disguise important variations across a district or even a state. The good news is that that modern school accounting systems permit far more accurate reporting of resource allocation patterns. The bad news is that few government agencies are willing to undertake the added effort to ensure that such precise data are distributed.

Until the finance profession can successfully pursue conceptual, technical, and informational research with greater precision and confidence, deriving the full benefit from a modern education finance paradigm is unlikely.

Discussion Questions

1. What have each of the three phases of education finance research contributed to our understanding of the relationships among spending, education, and achievement?
2. Explain how the concept of adequacy modifies or improves our understanding of school finance.
3. Under what conditions do you believe that children learn the most? Discuss how many of these conditions can be altered or improved by additional financial inputs.
4. The "In the News" item is about a judge's ruling in South Carolina that school systems weren't providing an adequate education because they did not provide early childhood education. Yet, early childhood education has not been a traditional part of the education system. Is this a progressive development? Or is there some danger in allowing definitions of adequacy to outplace the education services that government currently provides?

Web Resources

The National Conference of State Legislators webpage on school finance litigation: http://www.ncsl.org/programs/educ/LitigationCon.htm
American Education Finance Association: http://www.aefa.ca

Notes

1. As you will see, community responsibility for supporting public education came to be through a colonial understanding of the community as a "collection of families" rather than as a government entity (Demos, 1971).
2. Conventional wisdom holds that in the absence of an expressed responsibility for education, the Constitution's 10th Amendment diverts plenary authority to local and state government, and that financial support for schooling principally rests on local and state revenue-raising initiatives as a consequence.
3. Horace Mann's *Twelfth Annual Report of the Secretary of Massachusetts Board of Education* provides further examples of taxation arguments to fund public education.
4. Jesse B. Sears and Adin D. Henderson's *Cubberley of Stanford: And His Contributions to American Education* contains bibliographic references for these topics.
5. The Education Finance Inquiry Commission was formed following the Citizens' Conference on Education, called by the United States Commissioner of Education in May, 1920. The Commission was the nation's first systematic inquiry into public school finance.
6. Specifically, modern-day foundation aid programs and pupil weighting procedures owe much to these leaders' work.
7. Even though their focus was generally on resource inputs to schooling and they seldom allocated significant attention to the means by which inputs could be linked to or used to influence schooling outcomes, there were exceptions to this generalization.

Paul R. Mort and his Teachers College colleagues sustained a career-long pursuit of effectiveness in their studies of "Lighthouse School Districts" (Mort, 1957). Roe L. Johns created finance incentive systems throughout southern states by which local school districts received added revenues if they employed teachers with what were thought at the time to be higher qualifications (Johns, 1971, 1972; Johns & Kimbrough, 1968; Johns & Morphet, 1972, 1975). H. Thomas James put forth a preliminary economic model for education finance by formulating operational supply and demand measures and governmental arrangements that served as a market bridging the two (James, 1958, 1961, 1969; James, Kelly, & Garms, 1966; James, Thomas, & Dyck, 1963). J. Alan Thomas examined selected inputs and test scores in search of means by which greater efficiency could be achieved in high schools (Thomas, 1961, 1962). Charles S. Benson's *The Cheerful Prospect: A Statement of the Future of American Education* (1965) proposed integrating vocational and academic track education in an effort to eliminate educational disparity and improve efficiency. Though his writing did not initially leverage reform, it was acknowledged as pivotal in the federal enactment of the Carl D. Perkins Vocational and Applied Technology Education Act (1990) and the School-to-Work Opportunities Act (1994).

8. In this parlance, "foundation" implied an amount providing sufficient opportunity for students or an amount below which a state would not tolerate less per pupil spending. It was also a "foundation" on which a local district could add more revenue from its own sources. Whatever the meaning, however, it seldom if ever was a rationally derived dollar amount sufficient to meet some state-determined standard of student achievement.

9. For a treatment of the intersection of history and educational goals, see Ravitch and Vinovskis (1995).

10. For more information on means for measuring "alignment" and the metrics involved, see Porter (2002).

11. Two other early *JEF* articles contained adequacy criterion: Goertz and Hannigan (1978) and Brown (1978).

12. These numbers were generated from Baker, Taylor, and Vedlitz (2004).

CHAPTER FOUR

Control and Organization of American Education

■ INTRODUCTION

The purpose of this chapter is to explain the complexity of American school and school system structure and governance, to describe and analyze the organization and control of American education, to dissect analytically the multiple layers of statutory and legal authority that impinge on schools and school districts, and to display the myriad relationships and constituencies with which school leaders are inevitably involved. All these conditions influence the manner in which resources are generated, distributed, and committed.

LEARNING OBJECTIVES

By the end of this chapter, you should be able to:

- Articulate paradigms used to understand how school districts function.
- Describe the manner in which issues of control and commitment influence school district governance.
- Describe the governance structures of federal, state, and local authorities and their control over public schools and public school finance.
- Describe your local school district in terms of governance, scope, and control over resources.
- Describe external factors influencing the manner in which school districts operate.

Organizational structure, as well as governance mechanisms and other control features, are relatively static components of American education. To be sure, the number of school districts and individual schools is large and changes over time. Historically, there has been a persistent increase in the range of services schools offered, for example, preschool, meals, transportation, after-school care, and summer tutorials.

Still, the fundamental organizational scaffolding of American education has been in place for more than a century and is unlikely to change dramatically during your professional lifetime. However, because education's organizational architecture is relatively immutable does not automatically imply that the policy contexts of schooling and school financing are also static. Indeed, education finance is subject to an ever-moving set of altered societal conditions, expectations, and regulations.

■ COMPETING PARADIGMS OF SCHOOL ORGANIZATION

Researchers and organizational theorists take two perspectives when asking questions about the organization, operation, and effectiveness of public schools. One paradigm of research treats schools as firms or corporations. Another perspective acknowledges schools as bureaucracies. Within both paradigms exist considerations of **control** and **commitment**.

Schools as Firms

Some social scientists and economists operate with assumptions that schools function as other firms or corporations do. In the economic literature, **firms** exist to maximize profits. They accomplish this by decreasing costs and increasing efficiency. In this paradigm, schools exist to maximize student outcomes at value to taxpayers. Analysis that stems from this paradigm focuses on the manner in which schools "create" or maximize outcomes. The use of statistical education production functions and education cost functions allows researchers to explain the contribution of school characteristics to student performance, controlling for student and community influences.

Critics of this perspective note that schools are charged with maximizing multiple outcomes (not just academic ones), some of which are unstated, and that schools practice **allocative efficiency** (getting as much production as possible from a given set of inputs) rather than **technical efficiency** (getting more production out of fewer inputs). Critics further charge that any statistical models made with the assumptions of schools as firms misses the reality of what schools do and how they operate.

Schools as Bureaucracies

A competing perspective on school organization describes schools as **bureaucracies**. According to this perspective, schools operate more like political departments than like private firms. As a consequence, schools as organizations are slow to change, politically motivated, and ultimately more concerned with their organizational survival than with student performance. Analysis that stems from this perspective is usually concerned with issues of the application and mediation of power to implement curriculum and prevent reform. Analysis of performance tends to focus on more relative methods of measurement such as data envelopment analysis (DEA) or stochastic frontier analysis (SFA) to more carefully control for the specific sociopolitical context of any given project.

Critics of the bureaucratic model tend to be concerned with the inability to account for the myriad political variables within models and the inability of research methods to generalize to larger populations and contexts.

While there is no consensus among scholars as to which paradigm is closest to the truth, researchers working out of both paradigms and methods have contributed to a greater understanding of the role and functions of schools in our society.

Research
Navigator.com
control

Research
Navigator.com
commitment

■ CONTROL AND COMMITMENT IN PUBLIC EDUCATION

Within each of the two paradigms, researchers are concerned with issues of **control** of public education as well as with issues of **commitment** to public education.

When examining issues of control, researchers are most interested in the manner in which policies become enacted at the classroom level. Some researchers have observed that schools are "loosely coupled" (Weick, 1976) or that teachers are "street level bureaucrats" (Weatherly & Lipsky, 1997). Both of these descriptions imply that there is little connection between the policies enacted at the state or district level and the actions of teachers within classrooms once they shut the door. Control issues become leadership issues, and control-oriented questions often involve examining the capacity of state, district, and school leaders to effectively manage schools to maximize student academic performance. From a school finance perspective, questions about the use of financial resources to develop and sustain this capacity become important.

When examining issues of commitment, researchers are particularly interested in human resource questions. Specifically: How and under what conditions are teachers maximally effective? What conditions contribute to teachers staying in their jobs? How do teachers come to buy in to a leadership style or a particular policy? What factors contribute to teachers' continual improvement? From a school finance perspective, the role of resources in the form of salaries, bonuses, and professional development opportunities become important. Case 5 deals with issues of both control and commitment, as the text box describes.

⌂ CASE 5 REVISITED

A Creative and Frustrated Teacher

Johnny Upshaw's idea for pay for peformance meets with considerable resistance at the school and district level. In what ways does this resistance reflect issues of control in American education? What effect might this dynamic have on Johnny's commitment to stay in the profession? Does the organization of schools run teachers off? Would organizational changes necessarily bring in better teachers?

These paradigms and topics of interest from organizational theory are helpful in creating a framework for understanding the complex environment of public education. Schools are beset by an endless variety of demands from an endless variety of stakeholders while being bounded by the policies of multiple governments: federal, state, and local. The following sections outline this complexity in greater detail.

■ THE SEEMINGLY INFINITE SPECTRUM OF SCHOOLING STAKEHOLDERS

Almost no school leader, principal, superintendent, headmaster, teachers' union president, or other school official has the luxury of administrative autonomy. Schools serve a clientele. They are instruments of a larger society. Thus, they and their leaders have multiple masters. Moreover, an individual school—often even an independent, proprietary, or religious school—nests within multiple tiers of formal authority: local, state, federal, or national. This chapter explains this complex formal and informal governance and control network to which schools are subject. Before beginning, it is important to be aware of the following audiences to which schools are expected to pay attention.

Students and parents are obvious school stakeholders. However, there are many others. School district administrative authorities; teachers' unions; county offices of education or other intermediate authorities; state officials, including governors and legislators; state and federal administrative agencies; the entire judicial system, including the criminal justice system; and various municipal and other civic, state, and federal officials responsible for enforcing rules regarding health, safety, and building codes all come into play.

This list becomes more complicated when less formal influences such as athletic leagues, religious or ideological interest groups, philanthropic foundations, private sector financial lending institutions and investment banks, bond rating firms, and civic booster and charitable agencies are taken into account.

The examples can be extended, but the point is the same. Schools are the target of numerous expectations, influences, and interventions. Some of these influences are formal and stem from substantial structural or chartered authority such as superintendents, school boards, and state and federal government education departments. Others may have little formal authority, but may nevertheless exert substantial influence by virtue of resources they distribute or withhold (philanthropic foundations) or political capital.

While complicated, these interactions are not necessarily overwhelming. An adroit school leader can often harness external forces, shape them toward a collective purpose, and take advantage of their financial capital, organizational energy, and political momentum to gain significant improvements for his or her school.

■ THE SCALE AND SCOPE OF UNITED STATES EDUCATION

When viewed from an overseas or global perspective, schooling in the United States has three unusual governance and organizational features. First is the degree to which decision making is multilayered and compounded. Schools are the focus of governance and political forces that are simultaneously centrifugal and centripetal, centralized and decentralized, all described in a subsequent section of this chapter.

A second unique organizational feature is American education's magnitude. This is true regardless of the dimension under consideration—pupils, districts, schools, teachers, decision makers, size of administrative units, or financial resources.

A third unique feature is the diversity that characterizes the system. The United States seems to have the largest and smallest, the best, and worst, high- and low-spending districts, all of which encompass the range of school experience provided to millions of schoolchildren every day.

◻ CASE 1 REVISITED

River City Blues

Recall Superintendent Frank Farley in River City, as he faced the challenge of rebuilding a high-performing school district. As you read this chapter, consider the relationships that Frank would have with federal, state, and local officials as well as interest groups. Consider how you would design a comprehensive strategy for good relations with these actors. Further, consider how Frank's policy initiatives would serve to isolate these actors in the policy process.

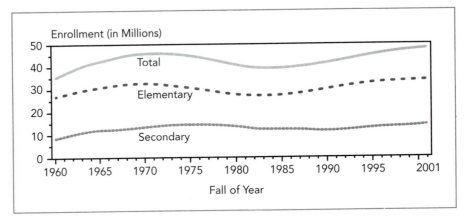

FIGURE 4.1 **Public K–12 Enrollment Trends, 1960–2002**

Source: U.S. Department of Education. National Center for Education Statistics. Statistics of State School Systems, 1959–60 through 1989–70; Statistics of Public Elementary and Secondary School Systems, 1970 through 1980. Revenues and Expenditures for Public Elementary and Secondary Education, 1970–71 through 1990–91; and The NCES Common Core of Data [CCD]. "State Nominated Survey of Public Elementary and Secondary Education." 1981–82 through 2001–02 and "National Public Education Financial Survey," 1909–90 through 2000–01; and unpublished data.

Scale

Figure 4.1 illustrates trends in enrollment over the last 40 years. One can easily see the dip in enrollment in the 1980s and the subsequent upward trend in enrollment since the 1990s. Figure 4.2 illustrates the number of teachers involved in public education, as well as the pupil/teacher ratio over the same period of time. Notice that the pupil/teacher ratio declines steadily over time and that the number of teachers employed increases steadily over time.

For higher education, Figure 4.3 demonstrates the boom in public and private college enrollment. Notice that a great deal of this growth occurs in the private sector. Figure 4.4 illustrates the boom in degree earning over the last 40 years.

These recent trends in education point to the issue of the tremendous scale and scope of the educational enterprise. Any enterprise of this scope would create a varity of interest groups and stakeholders, and education is no exception. In fact, the nature of education engenders greater commitment amongst the public and, potentially, greater interest with greater degrees of commitment to their respective causes.

Demography and Migration. Figures 4.1 through 4.4 illustrate both the current magnitude of the U.S. education system and its explosive post-World War II growth. Enrollments skyrocketed for two decades immediately following the war. Local school districts were hard pressed to keep pace with the growth. Indeed one of the more costly items for districts today is paying for physically maintaining many hurriedly constructed post-World War II buildings. In the 1970s, and for two decades thereafter, enrollments declined. By the 1990s, enrollments again began to zoom. This latter increase is instructive because it shows the cyclical effects of demography on schools.

The 1990s enrollment spurt is a function of what demographers label the "baby boom echo." These children are the offspring of post-World War II baby boomers. These

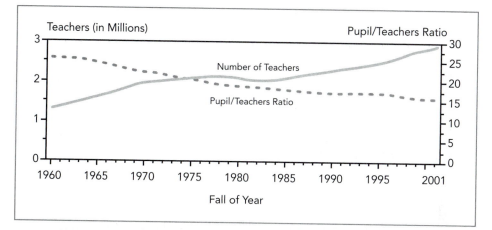

FIGURE 4.2   Number of Teachers and Pupil/Teacher Ratios for Public Schools, 1960–2002

Source: U.S. Department of Education. National Center for Education Statistics. Statistics of State School Systems. 1959–60 through 1989–70; Statistics of Public Elementary and Secondary School Systems, 1970 through 1980. Revenues and Expenditures for Public Elementary and Secondary Education, 1970–71 through 1980–81; and The NCES Common Core of Data [CCD]. "State Nominated Survey of Public Elementary and Secondary Education." 1981–82 through 2001–02 and "National Public Education Financial Survey," 1989–90 through 2000–01; and unpublished data.

younger mothers are not themselves having many children each. Indeed, their families average fewer than two children (2.1 children per each adult female is population balance, assuming no in or out migration). However, because there is such a large bulge of baby boomers themselves, their offspring still account for a sizeable portion of the current enrollment increase, even though they do not have large families.

However, turn-of-the-21st-century enrollment increases are only partially a consequence of baby boom echo children. They are also a result of one of the nation's largest ever in-migration waves. Many newcomer students are Hispanic in origin, their families coming to the United States from Mexico and other Latin American locations. In addition, there are millions of Asian immigrants. Also, the late 20th-century collapse of the Soviet Union triggered an exodus of Eastern Europeans and Middle Eastern immigrants, attracted by greater opportunities afforded by U.S. employment and citizenship. This in-migration has fueled the traditional American melting pot of immigrant energy and talent. However, it has also presented U.S. schools with multiple challenges.

There is a third immigration dynamic in operation that also shapes education resource distribution. Beginning in the latter decade of the 20th-century, U.S. residents have begun another mass migration; they are moving to southern states in huge numbers. In part, this north-to-south migration consists of baby boomers retiring. In part, also, it is a reflection of the availability of lower-priced land and better employment opportunities.

These migrations have implications for schools beyond a need for added buildings. The United States has been experiencing a vastly expanded need for teachers who know foreign languages and who are qualified to instruct. When it comes to a language as widespread as Spanish, there is a reasonably available pool of bilingual instructors. However, there are many less widely

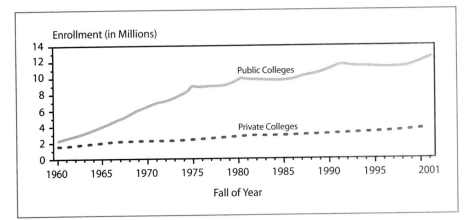

Figure 4.3　Public and Private Post-Secondary Enrollment, 1960–2002

Note: Public finance data for 2001–02 and private finance data for 1996–97 through 2001–02 are estimated.

Source: U.S. Department of Education, National Center for Education Statistics, Opening Fall Enrollment in Higher Education, 1960 through 1965; Financial Statistics of Institutions of Higher Education, 1959–60 through 1964–65; Earned Degrees Conferred, 1959–60 through 1965–66; Higher Education General Information Survey (HEGIS). "Fall Enrollment in Institutions of Higher Education," 1966 through 1985, "Degrees and Other Formal Awards Conferred," 1966–67 through 1985–86; and "Financial Statistics of Institutions of Higher Education," 1966–67 through 1985–86; and Integrated Postsecondary Education Data System (IPEDS), "Fall Enrollment," surveys, 1986 through 1999, and Spring 2001 and 2002, "Completions," 1985–87 through 1958–99 and Fall 2000 through Fall 2002, and "Finance" surveys, 1985–87 through 1999–2000, and Spring 2002.

spoken languages (e.g., Hmong, Tongan, and Hindi) that pose a far greater challenge to local superintendents and principals. Moreover, federal and state accountability regulations permit a transition period for non-English-speaking students. Eventually, however, these students, too, are expected to exhibit adequate yearly progress in tier academic performance.

Private Schools. Most American elementary and secondary enrollees attend public school. Only 10% attend private or independent schools. This percent is remarkably stable. After the *Brown v. Board of Education* decision, when many southern states were reluctant to desegregate previously racially divided school systems, segregated private schools (so-called "White Academies") flourished and nonpublic school enrollments zoomed to 14% of the school-age population. However, by the end of the 1960s, this reactionary phenomenon had dampened, private school enrollments dropped to their contemporary percentages, and public school districts—and sometimes even individual schools—began to be racially desegregated.[1] Ironically, the region of the nation that presently displays the most racially integrated school populations is the South.

However, for the moment discounting the post-*Brown* era, private school enrollments do not account for much of the U.S. enrollment, and their share of the market appears stable. The 90% of enrollments they control, for many practical purposes, positions U.S. public schools as a monopoly. The consequences of this condition, both positive and negative, are topics to which we will return in the finance and resource allocation chapters.

Research Navigator.com

private schools

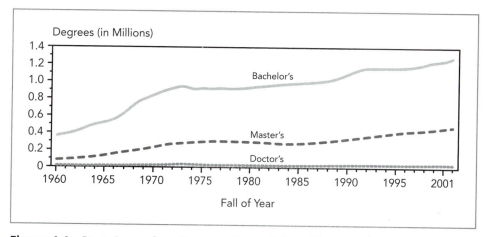

Figure 4.4   Post-Secondary Degrees Earned, in Millions, 1960–2002

Note: Public finance data for 2001–02 and private finance data for 1996–97 through 2001–02 are estimated.

Source: U.S. Department of Education, National Center for Education Statistics, Opening Fall Enrollment in Higher Education, 1960 through 1965; Financial Statistics of Institutions of Higher Education, 1959–60 through 1964–65; Earned Degrees Conferred, 1959–60 through 1965–66; Higher Education General Information Survey (HEGIS). "Fall Enrollment in Institutions of Higher Education," 1966 through 1985, "Degrees and Other Formal Awards Conferred," 1966–67 through 1985–86; and "Financial Statistics of Institutions of Higher Education," 1966–67 through 1985–86; and Integrated Postsecondary Education Data System (IPEDS), "Fall Enrollment," surveys, 1986 through 1999, and Spring 2001 and 2002, "Completions," 1985–87 through 1958–99 and Fall 2000 through Fall 2002, and "Finance" surveys, 1985–87 through 1999–2000, and Spring 2002.

Rising Academic Expectations. School enrollments are growing both horizontally and vertically. There is not just an expanding population that affects enrollments. The United States has also expanded its expectations for going to school. This applies at an early age through the availability and expansion of enrollments in kindergarten and in preschools (see Figure 4.1.) It also applies to students staying in school longer. Whereas an eighth-grade expectation was the norm, and later even some high school, most contemporary America families expect high school graduation and college attendance for their children. Figure 4.2 depicts this societal change in schooling expectations.

Figures 4.3 and 4.4 make it clear that the United States has expanded its capacity to offer instruction, in response to enrollment and expectation increases. The United States now employs over 4 million teachers. There are more individuals in the teaching force than there are immediately engaged in agriculture. There are also millions of other school employees, administrators, specialists of various kinds and so-called "classified" employees—those who perform crucial tasks as custodians, cafeteria workers, bus drivers, and so forth.

Scope and Diversity. Not only is the magnitude of America's education system daunting, but its scope and diversity is as well. At any one time, approximately 20% of the U.S. population is formally enrolled in or employed by an educational institution pre-K

Research
Navigator.com

diversity

through post-secondary. Public and private institutions, K–12 and postsecondary, serve children as young as 3 years of age and adults ten and twenty times older. Elementary and secondary instruction is delivered by districts as large as New York City with more than 1.1 million students enrolled in 1,000 schools, or Los Angeles with approximately 700,000 students in 650 schools. At the opposite end of the district size spectrum are rural school districts in the contiguous 48 states that have almost as many school board members as students, often offering instruction across all grade levels in a single building to a dozen or fewer students in total. The Alaskan "bush" offers a particularly dramatic example of such small and remote schools. Often air travel is the only connection between these unusually small and remote settlements and the larger outside world.

Small rural districts aside, most U.S. public school students are schooled in concentrations of urban and suburban districts. Fifty percent of all public school students are enrolled in only 5% (approximately 750) of the nation's largest school districts. Population-dense big city districts often operate large schools—elementary schools of 1,000 or 2,000 students, and high schools of equal or larger size. Suburban districts seldom approach such large school sizes. Indeed, one of the conditions that middle-class households seek for their children when they leave the city for suburbia is smaller, presumably more personable, schools and smaller classes. Much the same can be said of households that rely on private and independent schools. In part, they are paying tuition on top of their public school taxes to obtain smaller schools and smaller classes that they believe are advantageous to their children's learning.

Of the nation's slightly more than 14,000 public school districts, most (75%) serve fewer than 500 students. Whereas big city districts often suffer from diseconomies of scale in their operations (they are too large to be economically or instructionally efficient), rural districts often suffer from diseconomies because of their small size. They cannot easily afford to offer specialized courses to secondary students, unless they creatively rely on distance learning. Rural district costs of providing specialized teachers (e.g., calculus or advanced placement courses) may exceed available revenues.

Diversity does not adhere to organizational size alone. Student academic achievement also runs the gamut from unusually high performance in big city academic specialty high schools, residentially exclusive suburban schools, and costly private independent schools, to abysmally low standardized test scores in big cities and rural areas characterized by high levels of household poverty. Table 4.1 lists state-by-state scores in reading and mathematics on the 2003 National Assessment of Educational Progress (NAEP) exam, showing the range of performance differences among states. The range among individual school districts is wider yet.

Finally, school spending also varies enormously from a nationwide low in Mississippi of $5,534 per pupil to New Jersey's $11,793 (NCES, 2005). Even when these figures are adjusted for regional purchasing power differences, Mississippi students are disadvantaged. Upcoming revenue generation and resource distribution chapters, Chapters 7 and 8, explore these and related spending differences in greater depth.

■ CONSTITUTIONAL UNDERPINNINGS OF EDUCATION'S COMPLEXITY AND DIVERSITY

How did such enormous scope evolve? What could trigger such massive diversity? These are good questions. Answers reside in large measure within the frame of mind of Constitutional Convention participants and the federal government charter they constructed.

TABLE 4.1 Average Mathematics and Reading Score for Public School 8th-Graders, 2003

State or Jurisdiction	Math Average Scale Score in 2003	Reading Average Scale Score in 2003
Nation	276	261
Alabama	262	253
Alaska	279	256
Arizona	271	255
Arkansas	266	258
California	267	251
Colorado	283	268
Connecticut	284	267
Delaware	277	265
Florida	271	257
Georgia	270	258
Hawaii	266	251
Idaho	280	264
Illinois	277	266
Indiana	281	265
Iowa	284	268
Kansas	284	266
Kentucky	274	266
Louisiana	266	253
Maine	282	268
Maryland	278	262
Massachusetts	287	273
Michigan	276	264
Minnesota	291	268
Mississippi	261	255
Missouri	279	267
Montana	286	270
Nebraska	282	266
Nevada	268	252
New Hampshire	286	271
New Jersey	281	268
New Mexico	263	252
New York	280	265
North Carolina	281	262
North Dakota	287	270
Ohio	282	267
Oklahoma	272	262
Oregon	281	264
Pennsylvania	279	264
Rhode Island	272	261
South Carolina	277	258
South Dakota	285	270
Tennessee	268	258
Texas	277	259
Utah	281	264
Vermont	286	271
Virginia	282	268
Washington	281	264
West Virginia	271	260
Wisconsin	284	266
Wyoming	284	267

Source: U.S. Department of Education, National Center for Education Statistics, National Assessment of Educational Progress, NAEP 2002 and 2003 Reading Report Cards for the Nation and the States, prepared by Educational Testing Service.

By spreading authority, protecting individuality and liberty, permitting multiple political voices, and eschewing uniformity, this founding charter facilitated today's diversity and growth. Although more specific federal roles will be discussed in Chapter 9, the following themes and trends have had an important impact on the organization of American education.

Among the historic Constitutional conditions important for understanding U.S. education was a fear of large formal government and a strong distaste for concentrating power in the hands of those connected with government. To counter these anxieties, Constitutional framers (1) honed a set of philosophical abstractions regarding human nature into a new, applied, and anti-monarchial "Social Contract Theory of the State"; (2) limited central government to the role of facilitating commerce and sustaining personal freedom; and, (3) diluted what little government power they were willing to authorize by distributing formal authority in almost every possible direction to avoid concentration.

The historical development of greater federal involvement in education matters, as well as the authority, nature, and distribution of that aid, is discussed in Chapter 9. The following sections dig more deeply into the organizational governance of education in America by examining the state, local, and district roles successively.

▪ EDUCATION GOVERNANCE: STATE PLENARY AUTHORITY

The 10th Amendment's reservation of authority to states and the people and the absence, deliberate or not, of education as an enumerated federal government power leaves authority for education policy to states. These default conditions, when coupled with the affirmative acceptance of responsibility for education by state constitutions, render states the most responsible actors when it comes to education in the United States. States are said to have *plenary* authority ("plenary" is Latin for ultimate).

Such state responsibility accounts for the lack of a national system of education in the United States. In effect, there are 50 systems (even more if one considers the District of Columbia and the various federally overseen trust Territories and the Department of Defense schools, both domestic and overseas). Add to this the many private religious and independent schools and one can see the remarkable complexity to which this chapter has continually referred. It is a complicated mosaic indeed, one unlike that of any other nation in the world.

▪ THE STRUCTURE OF STATES FOR GOVERNING EDUCATION

Simply specifying that states have plenary authority over education insufficiently describes the situation. State governance and control of U.S. education is itself an enormously layered phenomenon. State constitutions, as a condition of acceptance into the Union, accept education as a state responsibility. State constitutions routinely specify that the state is responsibility for ensuring a "thorough and efficient" or "general and uniform" system of schools. Table 4.2 offers a summary classification of state constitutional education provisions.

A major portion of state control is undertaken through "general government." These are the constitutional officers and agencies that make and administer policy generally. A complementary set of specialist agencies and officers will be discussed later.

TABLE 4.2 Sample State Education Clause Language

Language	Sample States
Thorough and efficient system	WV, NJ, OH
Efficient system	KY, TX
Liberal system	AL
General and uniform system	AZ, NC
Complete and uniform system	WY
System of [free public schools]	NY, CT, SC
Equal educational opportunity	MT
Paramount state duty	WA
Legislature must "cherish" education	MA, NH

General Government and Education

At the highest formal levels of state government are three primary actors, the most prominent of which are state legislative bodies. Here is lodged constitutional authority to enact policy. However, as education has ascended as a priority issue for the American people, increasing numbers of governors have taken education reform as a major element of their policy portfolio. For example, Jimmy Carter and William Clinton, prior to becoming presidents of the United States, were forceful education reform champions in their respective states. Indeed, Jimmy Carter served as a local school board member in Plains, Georgia. Then, too, state courts are increasingly active in overseeing education matters within a state, particularly matters of education finance and equality of opportunity.

These formal bodies, legislative and executive, depend heavily on the expertise and energy of staff members. It is typical for a governor, particularly in a large state, to have an aide who specializes in education policy and acts as a liaison to state education agencies and to education interest groups. Such informal officials are often highly influential on policy and a few are even influential on administrative matters.

Similarly, legislatures rely on both personal and committee staff. The latter can be comprised of remarkably expert individuals. Moreover, as selected states have adopted term limits for elected officials, these staff members have ascended in importance, serving as an institution's memory and maintaining policy continuity between what is often otherwise a very fluid situation with elected policymakers frequently moving in and out of office.

State Education Officials

There is another tier of more specialized state education officials, drawing their authority more from statute and less from a state constitution. These are **chief state school officers** (CSSOs)[2] and state boards of education. In selected states, the CSSO is an elected official, often exhibiting a level of media prominence equal to that of other statewide elected officials, even the governor. In other states, the CSSO is selected by and more beholden to a state board of education.

Every state has a board of education; however, the manner in which members are selected varies. In some instances, such as in New York, state board members are elected from congressional districts or geographic regions throughout a state. In other settings,

Research
Navigator.com

chief state
school
officers

such as Alaska or California, state board members are appointed by the governor, or appointed by the governor and approved by legislative bodies.

In many states, serving as a member of the board of education is a prestigious position. For example, Florida has a small but influential gubernatorially appointed state board of education and governors have ensured that appointees are prominent members of their political party. New York State has what may be the most prestigious state board of education in the nation. This is the New York Board of Regents. Appointment to this body is by legislative district, and requires legislative approval. Its members serve for a long time and have often become quite prominent in setting education policy for the state, even becoming nationally visible.

These complicated and sometimes conflicting mechanisms for selecting education officials blur accountability. Presumably, the CSSO is the administrative officer for the State Education Department. If he or she is a statewide elected official, as in South Carolina, he or she may rely on State Education Department resources to further an expanded political career. Also, if elected from a statewide constituent base, a CSSO may not easily acquiesce to the policy-making authority of a gubernatorially appointed state board of education. The situation can be fraught with conflict and lacking in accountability. Education professionals are often befuddled regarding lines of state authority and the public can be excused if it is baffled also. Finding recourse in state constitutions is sometimes difficult.

State Education Departments

Every state has a department of education. Its functions are broad, for example, overseeing distribution of finances to local districts; monitoring quality of local district performance; overseeing statewide achievement examinations; licensing teachers; accrediting teacher training institutions; ordering textbooks, in some states; and providing advice on matters such as school facilities and buses. State education departments in California, New York, Texas, Illinois, and Florida, for example, are large institutions staffed with hundreds of professionals. These individuals are often expert in their areas of specialization.

Despite the significance of these agencies, and these officials, for the operation of education in a state, the resources of state education departments are conventionally thin and seldom sufficient to perform their many responsibilities to a high standard. They often have restricted pay scales for their executives and, thus, experience intense difficulty recruiting high-quality personnel. They cannot easily compete with local school districts when it comes to professional salaries. State education departments are routinely supported (up to 50% or more of budgeted revenues) by federal funds. These federal funds are present to assist states in monitoring local district and school compliance with federal programs such as the Education for All Handicapped Children Act and the No Child Left Behind Act. These are examples of federally funded national school programs which will be discussed in greater detail later.

Other State Agencies

There are additional state officials and agencies that have responsibility for education matters. However, these are usually tangential to instruction and to school operation. For example, it is usual for a state architect's office to collaborate in the approval of plans for new school facilities. A state treasurer may be active in the approval and sale of local district facility construction bonds. The state highway patrol may be active in overseeing school bus safety and bus driver training. A state agriculture department may act as a broker between federal and local school officials to facilitate school breakfast and lunch programs. State welfare or child protection agencies may assist in the development and oversight of daycare and preschool programs in districts. Interacting with these state agencies usually becomes a responsibility of school district officials. A principal may seldom sense their immediate presence.

■ INTERMEDIATE UNITS

Most states rely on some sort of intermediate government unit, midway between the state and local school districts. These intermediate agencies principally perform administrative and service tasks, particularly those for which scale economies exist. They are seldom responsible for the delivery of instruction, except in specialized circumstances such as Alaska Rural Education Administrative Areas (REAA). They are important, but are not a dominant feature of American education's organizational landscape. A few state examples suffice to convey their purposes and operation. These agencies assume a wide variety of forms, and one has to be careful not to overgeneralize about them.

For example, California relies on statutorily authorized County Offices of Education, some with elected County Superintendents. These agencies can generate revenues from property taxation. They are important in that they conduct budget reviews of local school districts and offer a wide variety of scale economy support services to local districts.

In Texas, by contrast, there are statutorily authorized Regional Service Centers whose state-provided operating revenues are remarkably small. The existence of these organizations depends on the entrepreneurial capacities of their staff. Still, several Texas Regional Offices are nationally famous for the quality of their administrative advice and operational service to local districts, as well as their ability to broker bulk purchases, evoke administrative efficiencies, and elevate the quality of their personnel development for teachers and others.

New York State relies on Boards of Cooperative Education Services. Here, local districts cooperate to secure provision of specialized services the high unit cost of which would virtually prohibit any one of them from acquiring individually.

Many southern states organize their local school systems along county lines, as described next. In these instances, county offices of education would be superfluous. As the In the News article indicates, executive decisions on school operations (in this case, the "65 percent Solution"), placed within this structure, can create confusion and controversy.

In the News

Everybody wants more money in the classroom. No one wants a tax increase.

The solution? Distribute education dollars differently, pouring money into classrooms without raising taxes.

The idea is the basis of the 65 Percent Solution, a proposal that would require school districts to spend at least 65 percent of their budgets on classroom expenses. Proponents want to see all 50 states and the District of Columbia impose the requirement by 2008.

The notion has at least one deep-pocketed backer: Patrick Byrne, the president of Overstock.com, Inc., who has pledged $1 million to the cause. At least 12 states are considering the idea, with one—Texas—already implementing it. California voters may see the idea on a ballot as early as 2008.

Proponents of the plan say it will make school districts spend money more efficiently. They say it also will improve student achievement by funneling dollars—$14 billion nationally and $1.5 billion in California—away from administration and toward student learning.

Districts nationwide spent an average of 61.3 percent of their budgets on in-class expenses in 2002–2003, the last year for which figures are available from the National Center for Education Statistics. California spent 60.8 percent. Only two states—New York and Maine—exceeded the 65 percent mark.

"Before every dollar is spent outside the classroom, we want asked, could this dollar be spent inside the classroom?" Republican political consultant Tim Mooney said. Mooney runs First Class Education, the nonprofit group dedicated to advancing the proposal. "Right now, it seems like the default is outside the classroom," he said.

Lawmakers in Kansas and Louisiana already have set the 65 percent mark as a goal. Proponents plan to propose legislation—or have already done so—

in Minnesota, Illinois, Georgia, Missouri and Florida. Mooney's group hopes to carry voter referendums in Ohio, Oregon, Colorado, Washington and Arizona this year.

Critics here recognize the plan's strength is its simplicity. That's also its weakness, they say.

"It's a terrible idea," said Bob Wells, executive director of the Association of California School Administrators. "There is no free money out there where this would magically get more money into classrooms. . . . The one-size-fits-all solution doesn't work for a state this size."

Part of the problem, critics say, is the plan's definition of classroom expenses. The 65 percent includes teacher salaries and benefits, supplies, classroom aides, and sports and arts programs. But it doesn't include key items such as transportation, food service, maintenance, librarians, and teacher training.

"It's an arbitrary standard," said Rick Pratt, executive director of the California School Boards Association. "Schools are expected to feed kids, provide after-school programs, provide transportation. . . . Will we have to scale back on these things? These are decisions you don't make with formulas."

From: Ranganathan, D. "65% solution touted for classroom funding." *Sacramento Bee.* January 26, 2006, B4.

■ SCHOOL DISTRICT ORGANIZATION

The United States is characterized by two dominant patterns of school district organization, a "New England Model" and a "Mid-Atlantic" or "Southern Model." There are states where these are blended. Following is a description of the pure prototypes.

New England School District Organization Model

America's school organizational roots are deep, extending back in time four centuries. As mentioned in Chapter 3, in 1647, the Massachusetts Commonwealth enacted Ye Olde

Deluder Satan Act, the title of which all by itself suggested education's major purpose at the time. This statute has had long-term ramifications for school organization. It specified each township would have a school. In effect, here is the origin of America's local schools. Further, it specified that the township would form a special governmental body, a local school board in effect, to oversee operation of the school. Finally, the school board was to be made up not of religious, military, or education professionals, but of laypersons. Here are the foundations of America's long-standing tradition of local control over schools, through a specially selected government body, separate from municipal or county government, and overseen by laypersons, not clerics or professional educators.

The New England model of schooling spread westward through federally promulgated late 18th-century land ordinances. Most western territories, including most states added by the Louisiana Purchase, as far as California, Oregon, and Washington adopted this model. It is still the dominant model today.[3]

Mid-Atlantic or Southern Model

A minority of states pursued a different organizational path. In mid-Atlantic and southern colonies, religious organizations—the Church of England generally, and the Catholic Church in the instance of Louisiana—were dominant institutions. Thus, when lay government evolved, it tended to emerge consistent with church parish lines. Today, much of the South's education is still organized on county lines, or may have both county and municipally aligned school districts with a larger county system.

School District Numbers and Consolidation

Regardless of New England or southern roots, the United States has many local school districts, slightly in excess of 14,000. Five states—Texas, California, Illinois, Nebraska, and New York—account for one-third of these districts. The remaining 9,000 districts are distributed over 45 states. As mentioned previously, southern states tend to be organized along county lines. Consequently, they typically have geographically larger and numerically fewer districts. Florida, for example, the nation's fourth most populous state, has only 67 county-organized districts. Maryland has only 24 county-aligned districts. Hawaii is a particular exception to all other patterns. It is a statewide system with no conventional local government school districts.[4]

Once, a century ago, the United States had almost ten times as many local school districts. In 1920, there were 127,000 local districts. Most of these were rural. Many had only one school, and a one-room school at that. In a bizarre way, some of these districts operated no schools. They were tax havens formed by large landholders who relied on puppet school boards to dampen the prospect of having to pay significant school taxes.

By the first quarter of the 20th century, a coalition of business leaders and university officials began a political campaign to consolidate these rural agencies into larger districts. They lobbied legislatures, arguing that small districts offered inferior education and were economically inefficient. It was a remarkably successful reform effort. It also had unanticipated and possibly deleterious and long-lasting effects. It created larger, sometimes inefficiently large, school districts; separated schools from the communities they served; and did not demonstrably produce cost savings.

Fiscal Dependence and Independence

When school districts are statutorily granted taxing authority—almost always property taxing authority—they are said to possess "fiscal independence." This is something of a misnomer because state legislatures seldom empower local districts with unfettered taxing authority. It is usually bounded. Still, about 75% of U.S. school districts, through their elected school boards or through direct citizen vote, have authority to levy property taxes.[5]

Districts that submit annual spending plans or budgets to other governmental bodies for approval and revenue generation are said to be **fiscally dependent**. This usually involves large cities (e.g., New York) and southern districts that have to submit their proposed budgets to mayors, city councils, or county boards of supervisors.

Washington, D.C., schools and the Defense Department schools are a special case because they receive funding directly from Congress.

School Boards

School boards draw formal authority from legislative statutes. Their principal, but not exclusive, function is employing and evaluating a chief executive officer—a superintendent of schools. In addition, they have authority over individual school attendance boundaries, budgetary approval, and curriculum authority, within the boundaries of state specifications regarding what is to be taught.

Boards vary in their membership size. Most have 5 members, a few have only 3, and some have more, as many as 15 in several large cities. Generally, 80% of the time, these are elected positions. Where boards are appointed, it is generally by mayors, sometimes requiring City Council advice and consent. A few unusual circumstances exist. In Pennsylvania, for example, justices of the Court of Common Pleas appoint large city board members.

Superintendents

Occupants of this position serve as the chief executive for local school districts. A few experiments have been undertaken in which districts had both a superintendent for instruction and an organizationally parallel business manger. Such bifurcation almost always leads to a lack of accountability. Superintendents sometimes serve more than a single district in the instance of sparsely populated rural areas. However, usually, each district has its own executive, selected by the school board.

The position carries a great deal of authority, perhaps the most important aspects of which are selecting and evaluating school principals and recommending an annual spending plan—a district budget. The superintendency is a difficult task. Occupants find themselves simultaneously pincered by school board member expectations and the expectations of subordinates, principals, and teachers. This may be one reason why superintendents' tenure in a district is notoriously short-lived.

■ INDIVIDUAL SCHOOL ORGANIZATION

In contrast to entire states and school districts, schools themselves are usually relatively simple organizations. This is particularly true of elementary schools. Middle and senior high schools may organize around subject matter departments such as history, mathematics, and physical education. However, elementary schools, unless unusually large, are typically operated by a principal, an (all-important) school clerk, classroom teachers, and a custodial staff. Also, depending on the district, there will be various licensed specialists such as counselors, department chairs, and school psychologists. The presence of additional administrators in a school—assistant principals, for example—is almost always a function of enrollment size. When elementary enrollments are in excess of 500 or 600 students, districts will frequently assign an assistant principal, or some variant to support the principal. Middle and senior high schools, being larger in almost every instance, will be assigned one or more additional administrators to assist the principal.

Whatever the particulars of the school administrative staff, the school generally draws its authority and operates within policy parameters specified by district, state, federal, and judicial officials. Schools are seldom otherwise empowered, beyond matters regarding student discipline. Indeed, school-level governance and its implications for school finance is one of the issues we will address later in this book. Selected reformers believe that schools would be more effective organizations if principals, perhaps teachers, and others that operated them were more fully empowered to make decisions regarding personnel and performance incentives.

■ PRIVATE AND INDEPENDENT SCHOOLS

As previously mentioned, approximately 10% of America's K–12 children attend nonpublic schools. These may include private, even proprietary, profit-seeking schools. They may be independent, having their own board of directors, financial assets, and so on. They may be religiously affiliated, for example, Catholic, Methodist, Jewish, or generically Christian.

Sometimes, as in large city Catholic systems, these schools may themselves be part of a hierarchy which, while almost always much smaller, is fashioned after a public school bureaucracy. The New York City and Chicago Diocesan schools are huge. Sometimes, a religious order or a regional or nationwide system oversees the schools' general operation. Usually, however, private and independent schools are operated with a substantial degree of autonomy.

While there are many operating similarities between public and nonpublic schools, here we will emphasize distinctions. First, the former do not have to accept or retain as students anyone who shows up at their door and is interested in attending. Private and independent schools have flexibility in which applicants they accept and retain. (Public school advocates make much of this, claiming that in a competitive free market setting, discretion over admission and continued enrollment provides an unfair advantage to nonpublic schools.) Second, private school budgets are closely tied to enrollment levels: if there are few students, the school may have to close. Public schools are also sensitive to enrollment ebb and flow. However, financial effects are seldom as immediate as they are for nonpublic schools losing students. Third, a headmaster or headmistress has more discretion over how to spend money and who to hire and fire than does the archetypal public school principal.

■ FEDERAL GOVERNMENT EDUCATION STRUCTURES

Given that it has little explicit authority for education, it is remarkable how much influence the federal government has over American K–12 schooling. Since adoption of the federal Constitution, courts have concurred that the "general welfare" clause[6] empowers

Congress to undertake actions and activities that, presumably, are in the public's interest. This is the justification for literally dozens of federal programs, and billions of federal dollars directed at public education support. (A small portion of federal funding does support private and religious school activity.)

The federal government's apparatus for overseeing education programs is similar to that of states. There are executive and legislative branch components. The President, like a governor, can initiate or vitiate (through veto) policy proposals. Congress can do the same. Generally, both must agree for a proposal to become law. Within the executive branch, there is a U.S. Department of Education. The Secretary of this agency, appointed by the President with the advice and consent of the U.S. Senate, is a cabinet-level official.

Congress, both the House and the Senate, rely heavily on a committee system for initial deliberation over legislative proposals and for program oversight. These committees have expert staff. Also, committee chairs, usually of the majority party, are themselves often knowledgeable regarding legislative programs the committee oversees.

The U.S. Department of Education has regional offices located throughout the United States. However, most federal education programs are overseen through state education departments and operated by local school districts. Federal officials certainly exercise oversight, but they seldom engage in actual organizational operations.

Any discussion of Federal government organization matters in education would be remiss without mention of the United States Supreme Court. Chapter 5 focuses on influential Supreme Court decisions such as *Brown v. Board of Education.* Suffice it to say here that this third branch of government, while not having enumerated educational responsibilities, has nevertheless exerted remarkable influence on the operation of America's schools.

■ RESIDUAL ISSUES OF CONTROL

The preceding description of structure and control is merely a summary. Regardless of the level or branch of government, describing control of American education is much like peeling an onion: there is always another layer. Many of these governance and organizational subtleties will be specified in greater detail in subsequent chapters.

■ THE EVOLVING ORGANIZATIONAL AND CONTROL CONTEXT OF EDUCATION FINANCE

The likely most powerful policy stimulus for organizational and control changes, at least for the foreseeable future, is that the judicial system is beginning to take state constitutions at their word.

Judges are no longer simply asserting that education funding must be equitable and sufficient. Increasingly, they claim that it is a state's responsibility to ensure that school services are of a specified quality sufficient to ensure that a student is capable of good citizenship, empowered to participate productively in the economy, and personally fulfilled.

Formerly, legislators and governors met state constitutional requirements by compelling school attendance, ensuring free schooling, and inducing formation of districts. From such restricted policy beginnings sprang a minor branch of educational governance, adhered to with the fervency of theology that came to be known as "local control." It is this mantra, more than any other that provided a framework for education policy choices and judicial remedies in the 19th and 20th centuries. Now, however, it is this time-honored mantra that is most at risk of succumbing to other values in the 21st century. The old equity issues have not disappeared. It is simply that emerging adequacy and efficiency considerations must now be addressed as well.

Twenty-first century court decisions in Massachusetts, Wyoming, Alabama, Arkansas, Wisconsin, New York, and North Carolina have held the state responsible not simply for ensuring that local schools are funded equitably or even sufficiently. In addition, they have held the state responsible for (1) ensuring that schools pursue higher than heretofore codified standards; (2) providing disproportionate resources to disadvantaged students; and (3) perhaps through direct provision or intense oversight, guaranteeing that instruction is of a high quality.

A Wisconsin Supreme Court's decision holds the state accountable for ensuring that schooling: ". . . will equip students for their roles as citizens and enable them to succeed economically and personally." The Court specifies that the purpose of an adequacy criterion is to ". . . adopt a standard that will equalize outcomes, not merely inputs."

In a January 2001 decision, New York trial judge Leland DeGrasse rejected as insufficient for the 21st century a conventional state constitutional standard of "basic literacy" and specified instead the necessity of schooling for civic engagement, meaning ". . . productive citizenship—not just voting or sitting on a jury—but doing so capably and knowledgeably." He proceeds to charge schools with closing, ". . . the disconnect between the skills of the State's and City's labor force and the skills of the high technology sector."

In the *Leandro* case in North Carolina, trial judge Manning rejected the state defense that passage of a standardized test at the eighth grade met constitutional requirements. Instead, Judge Manning's opinion insists that performance "at grade level" on state-specified curriculum standards is the minimum now acceptable. The Leandro decision proceeds further to insist that ". . . economically disadvantaged students need services and opportunities above those provided to the general student population."

The Wyoming Supreme Court, in its 2002 Campbell II decision, makes clear that it is the state's responsibility not simply to ensure funding is sufficient to provide Wyoming with a "proper" and "unsurpassed" education system, but also that the state must itself take responsibility for ensuring the best educational opportunities are made available to disadvantaged students, be they poor, non-English-speaking, or disabled.

In short, the judicial system, unencumbered by the narrow political constraints often felt by more directly elected public officials, is taking state constitutions literally. If a constitution charges the state with provision of schooling, then the state must ensure that such schooling is of a quality tailored to 21st-century needs.

If states are to be held accountable to new and higher education standards, then states must take more direct actions concerning the actual provision of schooling. What once was the clear and protected domain of local school board members and superintendents is now increasingly, also, the responsibility of state officials.

Thus, here is the challenge facing policy system participants in the early part of the 21st century: *How can new mechanisms of centralized authority over resources and quality be meshed with long-standing American political expectations for community responsiveness and locally overseen economic efficiency?*

Summary

Myriad parties have vested interests in public education systems. These parties exist at the local, state, and federal levels of governance; in the private sector; and in the nonprofit sector. Each level of governance can be further dissected into legislative bodies—such as legislatures at the state level and school boards at the local level—and executive authority—such as chief state school officers or superintendents. These parties offer competing paradigms for the manner in which schools operates, with the firm and the bureaucracy being the two dominant paradigms for understanding and reforming schools. Within these paradigms, those parties interested in maintaining and improving schools must grapple with issues of commitment and control. Control issues are governance and power issues, and commitment issues revolve around the workings of schools' most costly investment—human capital.

Recently, state judiciaries have become increasingly invested in interpreting state constitutional language for the provision of education to students. This increased judicial interest removes schools from discussion of paradigms and issues of control and commitment, and moves the education finance discussion into the realm of evidence and results.

Discussion Questions

1. Consider the number of layers of governance and influence that seek to affect the work of a high school or middle school principal. Chart these influences from federal, state, and local governance structures.
2. Discuss the manner in which policies designed to bring greater control to a school district may hamper teacher and administrator commitment. How will leaders find a middle ground between these two issues?
3. What does your state constitution say regarding the provision of public education? Can you think of ways in which your state's constitutional language could be used to bring suit against the state?
4. Describe the manner in which a state may defend itself against charges of not obeying the state constitution. How would you begin to formulate a defense?

Web Resources

Council of Chief State School Officers: http://www.ccsso.org/

National School Board Association: http://www.nsba.org/

Institute for Educational Leadership: http://www.iel.org/

American Association of School Administrators: http://www.aasa.org/

Urban Superintendent's Association of America: http://www.usaa.org/

Council of the Great City Schools: http://www.cgcs.org/

United States Department of Education: http://www.ed.gov

Campaign for Educational Equity: http://www.schoolfunding.info/

United States Senate Committee on Health, Education, Labor and Pensions:
   http://help.senate.gov/

United States House of Representatives Committee on Education and the Workforce:
   http://edworkforce.house.gov/

National Association of Independent Schools: http://www.nais.org

National Association of State Boards of Education: http://www.nasbe.org/

Notes

1. For a review of private schools and segregation in the South, see Clotfelter (2004).
2. Also known as Superintendent of Public Instruction in many states.
3. Nevada's county system of school organization is a western state anomaly resulting from a post-World War II consulting report submitted by a team of southern model-oriented faculty from Peabody College, Vanderbilt University.
4. Hawaii entered statehood in 1959, having previously been a monarchy consolidated under King Kamehameha. It had no continental tradition of municipal or county government around which to organize schools. The school system is highly centralized, operated by a state board of education, a chief state school officer, and a state education department.
5. California is an interesting outlier. Each of the state's almost 1,000 school districts has nominal property taxing authority. However, the overwhelming majority of districts are prevented from exercising this authority by virtue of the 1978 enacted "Proposition Thirteen," the nation's leading tax limitation initiative that restricts property taxation to 1% of a property's purchase price.
6. We the People of the United States, in Order to form a more perfect Union, establish Justice, insure domestic Tranquility, provide for the common defense, *promote the general Welfare*, and secure the Blessings of Liberty to ourselves and our Posterity, do ordain and establish this Constitution for the United States of America. (Emphasis added.)

CHAPTER FIVE

Legal Complexities and Modern Education Finance

■ INTRODUCTION

The most dominant contemporary influence in United States education finance policy making is the judicial system. In fact, the last quarter of the 20th century and the initial years of the 21st century display a remarkable pattern of education finance litigation covering all but five states (see Tables 5.1 and 5.2). The breadth of judicial involvement is new. However, courts have long played a role, even if previously nowhere near as extensive, in American education financing.

LEARNING OBJECTIVES

By the end of this chapter, you should be able to:

- Articulate key legal concepts used in school finance litigation such as suspect classification, strict scrutiny, and rational basis.
- Recount defining features of each of the three waves of school finance litigation.
- List key cases in the history of school finance litigation.

■ HISTORY AND CONTEXT—SEMINAL EDUCATION FINANCE COURT CASES

The judicial branch is now and long has been a partner in shaping U.S. education finance reform. As early as 1859, in *Springfield Township v. Quick et al.*, the United States Supreme Court was involved in school finance and determined the role of the court in education finance issues. The Court upheld a state school finance law as "a perfectly just one" and ruled that plaintiffs have "no right to call on this court to interfere with powers exercised by the state legislature in laying and collecting taxes and in appropriating them for educational purposes, at its discretion."

Sawyer v. Gilmore, decided by the Supreme Judicial Court of Maine in 1912, is the first known challenge of a state education finance distribution formula. Plaintiffs alleged violations of the U.S. Constitution's 14th Amendment **equal protection clause**, as well as unequal taxation and unequal educational opportunities. The court ruled that the state legislature had treated all residents in a similar manner and the finance system could not be unconstitutional as long as the state's distribution scheme was not explicitly prohibited within the state constitution.

Brown v. Board of Education of 1954 closed the door on the then widespread policy of allowing racially identifiable "separate but equal" facilities and resources; subsequently, greater opportunities for minority students resulted from declaring the "separate but equal" doctrine unconstitutional. The *Serrano* decision by the California Supreme Court in 1971 required the state legislature to alter its funding formula to alleviate inequitable distribution of funding across districts within the state. Although the *Serrano* decision influenced state legislatures and courts across the United States, the most influential court decision in education finance is arguably *San Antonio Independent School District v. Rodriguez.*

In its *Rodriguez* opinion, the U.S. Supreme Court specified that even "though education is one of the most important services performed by the state, it is not within the limited category of rights recognized by this Court as guaranteed by the Constitution." The *Rodriguez* decision is discussed in greater detail later in the chapter. However, it should be noted that, at least for now, *Rodriguez* ensures that subsequent school finance litigation will be addressed by state courts and thus, until and unless it is overturned, it limits the possibility of school finance reform at the federal level. If it were not for the *Rodriguez* decision, U.S. education fiscal policies might have evolved into quite a different system than that in existence today.

This historical context calls for closer scrutiny of the development and content of school finance cases. Specifically, this chapter is designed to clarify the following questions:

- What issues motivate school finance litigation?
- What is the role of courts in school finance litigation cases?
- What political and legal elements are involved in an education finance suit?
- What constitutional challenges are raised in school finance litigation?
- How are school finance cases classified?
- What are seminal cases in the history of school finance litigation and the courts' holdings?
- What does the future hold for school finance litigation?

Public education finance has a long history of societal tension. This tension coalesces around issues of education finance methodology as well as the adjudication of these methodologies relative to various equity and adequacy agendas (Wood & Thompson, 1996). Compared to legislative initiatives, reform through school finance litigation may be a slow, tedious process since the effectiveness of a court ruling may not be apparent until years after litigation has ended, if ever (Murray, Evans, & Schwab, 1998).

The following sections specify the elements that must be present to bring an education finance suit, the legal issues involved in such litigation, and a brief history of some of the seminal education finance litigation cases.[1]

▪ ROLE OF COURTS

Courts ensure that education finance policies satisfy constitutional provisions calling for efficiency, equity, and adequacy and stimulate appropriate policy changes (Swanson & King, 1991). Specifically, courts are called on to decide whether finance policies and state

Research
Navigator.com

equal
protection
clause

TABLE 5.1 Litigation Challenging Constitutionality of K–12 Funding

In Process* (23)	No Current Lawsuit (22)	Never Had a Lawsuit (5)
Alaska	Alabama	Delaware
Arizona	Arkansas	Hawaii
Connecticut	California	Nevada
Georgia	Colorado	Utah
Idaho	Florida	
Indiana	Illinois	
Iowa	Maine	
Kansas	Massachusetts	
Kentucky	Michigan	
Louisiana	Minnesota	
Maryland	Mississippi	
Missouri	Ohio	
Montana	Oklahoma	
Nebraska	Oregon	
New Hampshire	Pennsylvania	
New Jersey	Rhode Island	
New Mexico	South Dakota	
New York	Vermont	
North Carolina	Virginia	
North Dakota	Washington	
South Carolina	Wisconsin	
Tennessee		
Texas		
West Virginia		
Wyoming		

*"In Process" refers to a wide range of progress including both recently filed cases and cases where full implementation of the remedy seems close at hand.

Source: Molly A. Hunter, Litigations Challenging Constitutionality of K–12 Funding in the 50 States (Campaign for Fiscal Equity, Inc. 2005). Retrieved March 10, 2005 from http://www.accessednetwork.org/litigation/In-ProcessLitigations-01-2004.pdf

revenue distributions satisfy federal or state constitutions. Courts do not, however, typically initiate policy issues for judicial review; courts only react to challenges brought forth by affected citizens or jurisdictions. Table 5.1 highlights the states in which school finance litigation has taken place.

▪ LEGAL CONCEPTS IN SCHOOL FINANCE LITIGATION

Judicial intervention into education finance matters is frequently entangled in matters of education governance. With the exception of Hawaii, all states fund public schools with an amount of local taxes assessed on property values within local school districts. However, states' financing methods aim to achieve a greater equality in resources than that which would occur if schools were funded only by local property taxes (Thomas, 1979).

Concurrently, state plans aim at retaining locally control of schools through retaining locally imposed property taxes.

Maintaining **local control** is often at the center of judicial decisions that uphold state school finance systems. If all school funds were distributed by states, local school boards might be at risk of sacrificing a degree of control currently held over neighborhood schools. Not only does the issue of local control involve decision making, but also "freedom to devote more money to the education of one's children" (San Antonio *v*. Rodriquez, 1973). Some state constitutions have specific clauses that cite, and thus preserve, the value of local control. Therefore, balancing a mix of local and state revenues regularly results in funding inequalities and, subsequently, litigation. The following concepts provide an outline of the issues involved in a standard school finance litigation case. Subsequent sections will address the historical development of school finance litigation as well as the success or failure of differing approaches to litigation.

Research
Navigator.com
local
control

Standards for Judicial Reviews

There are two principal standards (or arguments) that school finance challenges rely on in education finance litigation. The first line of argument is a suit that seeks to establish education as a **fundamental right** because of public education's individual and collective impact on social and economic structures in society. Education articles of state constitutions must be used to demonstrate that education is a fundamental right.

Research
Navigator.com
fundamental
right

The other main argument is a suit that seeks to show how funding disparities result in **unequal opportunities** by treating students in low-wealth or low-spending school districts differently from students with access to greater fiscal resources (Wood & Thompson, 1996). In other words, legal challenges rely on standards created in the equal protection clauses of federal and state constitutions.

Equal Protection Analysis

According to equal protection guarantees, individuals in similar situations must be treated the same. Therefore, differential treatment of individuals will only be upheld if such treatment is not arbitrary or irrational according to the law. Typically, the courts have used a two-tiered test for equal protection claims. The possible levels of the test in descending order of rigor are **strict scrutiny** and **rational basis** (Swanson & King, 1991; Underwood, 1989).

Strict Scrutiny. This heightened level of review is employed to determine violations of equal protection when a policy treats some people differently solely because they belong to a suspect classification or when a fundamental right guaranteed by the constitution is violated. In order to survive the critical analysis of strict scrutiny, the classification or denial of a fundamental right must be necessary to further a compelling objective of the state or federal government. Moreover, government has the burden of showing that there is no less discriminatory method to achieve the government's purpose.

Rational Basis. Under a rational basis test, the court examines whether or not the classification is related to a legitimate or reasonable governmental objective. Therefore, to uphold the challenged policy, the government must merely show that a rational relationship exists between the classification and the governmental purpose of the law. The rational basis test has been chosen as the appropriate test by many courts, including the United States Supreme Court, in school finance challenges. Although school finance policies may permit significant fiscal disparities among districts, several courts have reasoned that policies were reasonably related to the states' interests in maintaining local control of education; therefore, financial policies are constitutional since they further the interest of liberty through local control.

The level of scrutiny used by courts will determine the outcome of litigation (Sparkman, 1990). The following describes the properties of strict scrutiny as it relates to suspect classifications and fundamental rights.

Suspect Classification

In education finance litigation, plaintiffs often maintain that a school financing system classifies districts, taxpayers, or students according to the value of the local property wealth, which may result in a **suspect classification.** Wide variations in property wealth among school districts across a state can result in disparities that are inadequately rectified by state aid. Therefore, arguably, available revenues per student and educational opportunities may vary among the school districts in each state. Plaintiffs contend that a classification system predicated on wealth, resulting in significant wealth-related revenue disparities, constitutes illegal discrimination against students and taxpayers in property-poor districts.

Courts have the ultimate responsibility for deciding what constitutes a suspect classification. However, plaintiffs often encounter difficulties in convincing courts that low-wealth district students constitute a class for equal protection purposes. The cases of *San Antonio v. Rodriguez* and *Serrano v. Priest*, which will be described in greater detail later in the chapter, illustrate this variation in the courts' recognition of wealth-based discrimination as a suspect classification.

Fundamental Right

Similar to the disagreement of the status of wealth discrimination as a suspect classification, is the courts' disagreement as to whether education is a **fundamental right.** The U.S. Supreme Court defines a fundamental right as one "explicitly or implicitly guaranteed by the Constitution." In the *Rodriquez* case, the U.S. Supreme Court, on examining the Constitution, did not determine that education is a fundamental right.

State Constitution Education Clauses

Forty-nine of fifty states have constitution clauses requiring the state to maintain a public school system.[2] Some scholars maintain that education clauses can be classified, based on particular language, into four categories in ascending order of the duty placed on the state (Ratner, 1985). Category I clauses are the weakest, insofar as the language employed in those clauses appears to impose only a minimal duty on the states. Category I education clauses only require that the state provide a system of public schools and do not elaborate on the scope of the requirement. For example, Connecticut's constitution states, "There shall always be free public elementary and secondary schools in the state."

Category II clauses exceed Category I requirements by requiring an explicit commitment to public education. Category II clauses often require that the public education system be "thorough," "efficient," or both. Essentially, the Category II clauses require that a state meet a minimal level of quality in the public education system.

A more specific education mandate is contained within Category III clauses while Category IV clauses impose the strongest requirements on states (Ratner, 1985). Category IV clauses are buttressed by language such as "primary," "fundamental," or "paramount."

Essentially, Category IV clauses impose an explicit and affirmative duty on the state to support public education. For example, the Washington constitution states, "It is the paramount duty of the state to make ample provision for the education of all children residing within its borders."

Presumably, strong education clauses should aid both equity and adequacy legal challenges. The court may more easily interpret a state constitution to find that education is a fundamental right in equity challenges and the language for higher quality standards is stronger for adequacy challenges. Essentially, if the language of the clause is stronger, the magnitude of the state's duty to support educational rights should be greater. However, evidence suggests that there is little correlation between the strength of education clauses and decisions by courts (Patt, 1999).

Arguments using equal protection clauses or education articles may be used separately or together in an education finance challenge. The following discussion of education finance litigation history illustrates differing interpretations of equity and adequacy standards as courts test whether finance statutes violate state guarantees within education articles or equal protection clauses.

■ THREE WAVES OF EDUCATION FINANCE LITIGATION

Research
Navigator.com
litigation

The progression of school finance litigation has generally been divided into three phases or "waves." The first two waves were conducted under an equity theory, while the third wave is primarily under an adequacy theory. The first wave ran from the late 1960s until 1973. These challenges were mainly based on the federal equal protection clause of the U.S. Constitution's 14th Amendment. Only *Serrano v. Priest* was decided before *Rodriguez* effectively shut down education finance challenges based on the U.S. Constitution in 1973. Table 5.2 lists school finance litigation cases by names, organized by result of the litigation. Note that many states have witnessed multiple challenges to their state school finance systems.

The beginning of the second wave was marked by *Robinson v. Cahill* and contained challenges relying on state constitutions' equal protection education clauses. Between 1973 and 1989, state supreme courts issued 22 rulings on school finance matters. At issue was equitable distribution of resources. Plaintiffs prevailed in only 7 of the 22 cases, or approximately 32% of the time (Koski, 2003).

The third wave began in 1989 and consisted of complex adequacy (or Equity II) challenges that continue to the present day. From 1989 to 2000, state supreme courts issued 24 decisions on school finance matters. Adequacy challenges claim that education provided by the state does not sufficiently fulfill requirements under state education clauses. Although third-wave challenges are judged on issues similar to those in previous waves of litigation, adequacy challenges have had greater success in the courts and courts have ruled in favor of plaintiffs in the 24 adequacy challenges approximately 50% of the time. This wave of victories coincides with state enactment and pursuit of systemic reform efforts, resulting in statutory specification of what a student is expected to know and be able to do as well as assessments to measure that progress. Once learning standards are in place, courts have an easier time determining the extent to which a state may have met its financing obligations (Patt, 1999).

Although shifts in the legal and educational underpinnings of school finance litigation throughout the waves may be discernable, an examination of judicial decisions of second- and

TABLE 5.2   Status of School Finance Constitutional Litigation

Plaintiffs Won at the State Supreme Court Level or the State Supreme Court Approved a Trial Court Decision for the Plaintiffs	
State	Case
Alabama	*Opinion of the Justice*, 1993
	Ex Parte James, 1997
Alaska	*Kasayulie v. State*, 1997, 2001[1]
Arizona	*Shofstall v. Hollins*, 1973
	Roosevelt Elementary School District 66 v. Bishop, 1994
	Hull v. Albrecht, 1997, 1998
Arkansas	*Dupree v. Alma School District*, 1985
	Tucker v. Lake View School District No. 25, 1996
	Lake View School District No. 25 v. Huckabee, 2002
California	*Serrano v. Priest*, 1971, 1976
Connecticut	*Horton v. Meskill*, 1977, 1985
	Sheff v. O'Neill, 1995, 2003 (settlement reached)
	Johnson v. Rowland, filed 1998 (withdrawn in 2003)
Kansas	*Montoy v. State*, 2003
Kentucky	*Rose v. Council for Better Education*, 1989
	Council for Better Education v. Williams (Young v. Williams), filed 2003
Massachusetts	*McDuffy v. Secretary of Education*, 1993
	Hancock v. Driscoll, 2004
Montana	*State ex. rel. Woodahl v. Straub*, 1974
	Helena Elementary School District No. 1 v. State, 1989, 1990
New Hampshire	*Claremont School District v. Governor*, 1993, 1997, 1999, 2002
New Jersey	*Robinson v. Cahill*, 1973
	Abbott v. Burke, 1985, 1990, 1994, 1997, 1998, 2000, 2002
New York	*Board of Education v. Nyquist*, 1982
	Reform Educational Financing Inequities Today v. State, 1995
	Campaign for Fiscal Equity Inc. v. State of New York, 1995, 2003, 2005
North Carolina	*Leandro v. State*, 1997
	Hoke County v. State, 2000, 2002, 2004
Ohio	*Board of Education v. Walter*, 1979
	DeRolph v. State, 2000, 2003
Tennessee	*Tennessee Small School Systems v. McWherter*, 1993, 1995, 2002
Texas	*Edgewood v. Kirby*, 1989, 1991, 1995
Vermont	*Brigham v. State*, 1997
Washington	*Northshore School District No. 417 v. Kinnear*, 1974
	Seattle School District No. 1 v. State, 1978
West Virginia	*Pauley v. Kelly*, 1979, 1984
	State ex rel. Boards of Education v. Chafin, 1988
	Tomblin v. Gainer, 1997, 2000
Wyoming	*Washakie v. Herchler*, 1980
	Campbell v. State, 1995, 2001[2]

Plaintiffs Lost at State Supreme Court Level and No Later Case Is Pending	
State	Case
Georgia	*McDaniel v. Thomas,* 1981
Illinois	*Committee for Educational Rights v. Edgar,* 1996
Louisiana	*Charlet v. Legislature of State of Louisiana,* 1998 (consolidated with)
	Minimum Foundation Commission v. State, 1998
Maine	*School Administrative District No. 1 v. Commissioner,* 1995
Michigan	*Milliken v. Green,* 1972, 1973
	East Jackson Public Schools v. State, 1984
Nebraska	*Gould v. Orr,* 1993
North Dakota	*Bismark Public Schools v. North Dakota,* 1993
Oklahoma	*Fair School Finance Council of Oklahoma, Inc. v. State,* 1987
Oregon	*Coalition for Equitable School Funding, Inc. v. State,* 1991
Rhode Island	*City of Pawtucket v. Sundlun,* 1995
Virginia	*Scott v. Virginia,* 1994
Wisconsin	*Kukor v. Grover,* 1989
	Vincent v. Voight, 2000

Plaintiffs Lost at the State Supreme Court Level, but Further Complaints Are Either Pending or Were Sustained without a Final Determination or Settled	
State	Case
Alaska	*Matanuska-Susitna Borough v. Alaska,* 1997
Colorado	*Lujan v. State Board of Education,* 1982
	Giardino v. Colorado State Board of Education, settled 2000
Florida	*Coalition for Adequacy and Fairness in School Funding v. Chiles,* 1996
	Honore v. Florida State Board of Education, filed 2000
Idaho	*Thompson v. Engelking,* 1975
	Idaho Schools for Equal Educational Opportunity v. Evans, 1993
Kansas	*Knowles v. State Board of Education Unified School District No. 229 v. State,* 1994
	Robinson v. State, filed 1999, 2002[3]
Maryland	*Hornbeck v. Somerset County,* 1983
	Bradford v. Maryland State Board of Education, consent decree 1996
Minnesota	*Skeen v. Minnesota,* 1993
	Minneapolis Branch, NAACP v. State, filed 1995, settled 2000
	Independent School District No. 625 v. State, 1999
	Xiong v. State, filed 1998, settled 2000
North Carolina	*North Carolina Britt v. North Carolina State Board of Education,* 1987
Pennsylvania	*Dansen v. Casey,* 1979
	Marrero v. Commonwealth of Pennsylvania, 1998
	Pennsylvania Association of Rural and Small Schools v. Casey, 1998
South Carolina	*Richland County v. Campbell,* 1988
	Abbeville County School District v. State of South Carolina, 1999

continued

continued

Other Outcomes		
State Case		Outcome
Alabama	*Alabama Coalition for Equity v. Siegelman*[4]	Supreme Court reopened and dismissed case
Arizona	*Roosevelt Elementary School Dist. No. 66 v. State*[5]	Funding cuts did not violate constitution—2003
California	*Williams et al. v. State of California et al.*[6]	Settlement—2004
Colorado	*Haley v. Colorado Department of Education*[7]	Complaint filed—2004
Iowa	*Coalition for a Common Cents Solution*[8]	Settlement—2004
Louisiana	*Jones v. BESE*[9]	Complaint filed—2003
Missouri	*Committee for Educational Equality v. State*[10]	Complaint filed—2004
Montana	*Columbia Falls Elementary School District No. 6 v. State of Montana*[11]	Ruling for plaintiffs—2004
Nebraska	*Douglas County v. Johanns*	Complaint filed—2003
North Dakota	Williston Public School District v. State	Complaint filed—2003
Pennsylvania	*Powell v. Ridge*	Decisions rendered 1999,[12] 2001[13] on procedural issues

Sources: Overview and Inventory of State Education Reforms: 1990 to 2000 (NCES 2003020). Access via www.accessednetwork.com, and Westlaw. Updated March 22, 2005.

1. A motion from the state to reopen the Kasayulie decision was denied by the Superior Court in March of 2001.

2. In the second *Campbell* (2001) decision, the Wyoming Supreme Court affirmed in part and reversed in part. The new funding system passed constitutional muster for the most part, but a few aspects of the funding system were deemed inadequate (e.g., capital construction, various cost adjustments, etc.).

3. The appeals court affirmed the lower court's rejection of a motion to dismiss.

4. The Alabama Supreme Court, on its own initiative, reopened the case. The court had previously ruled in favor of the plaintiffs on four occasions; however, in 2002, the court stated "[i]n Alabama, separation of powers is not merely an implicit 'doctrine,' but rather an express command; a command stated with a forcefulness rivaled by few, if any, similar provisions in constitutions of other sovereigns." The case was effectively dismissed.

5. School districts brought action against the state for not funding the Building Renewal Fund (BRF) according to the statutory formula for 1999–2003. The Superior Court, Maricopa County, entered judgment in favor of districts. The State appealed, and appeals were consolidated. The Court of Appeals held that the funding cuts did not violate the constitutional obligation to provide for the establishment and maintenance of a general and uniform public school system.

6. Statewide class action lawsuit.

7. Lawsuit concerning adequacy of special education funding, filed in district court.

8. Iowa is one of only seven states where no court has decided a legal challenge claiming the state's school funding system violates the state constitution. After legislative changes were made to the funding statutes, the case was settled and withdrawn without prejudice.

9. Filed in district court.

10. A trial court in Missouri originally found for the plaintiffs in *Committee for Educational Equality v. State* (1993). This is a reconstituted *CEE* bringing forth an adequacy and equity suit in a district court.

11. District court ruling; an appeal to the Montana Supreme Court is expected.

12. The appellate court reversed and remanded the trial court's decision to dismiss *Powell v. Ridge*, in which plaintiffs allege that the school finance system in Philadelphia and other predominately minority districts results in racially discriminatory effects.

13. Appellate court decision regarding legislative immunity.

third-wave litigation reveals the presence both of equity and adequacy arguments, as well as a focus on educational outputs and inputs. Therefore, judicial opinions characterized as belonging to a particular wave of litigation may contain arguments including equality, equity, or adequacy issues.

The following sections describe key cases associated with each wave of litigation. This review has been restricted to cases involving school district operating revenues. This time line can be used to chart the development of the legal strategies employed in the three waves of school finance litigation.[3]

First Wave: Federal Equal Protection

McInnis v. Ogilvie (1969) is one of the earliest cases involving an equal protection suit applied to school finance. Plaintiffs—children from a property-poor Illinois school district—requested, as a remedy for alleged inequity, that public school revenues be reallocated in proportion to student "needs." They contended, "only a financing system that apportions public funds according to students' educational needs satisfies the Fourteenth Amendment." Plaintiffs' position was ultimately denied; a three judge federal district court in *McInnis* concluded that the complaint stated no cause of action "for two principal reasons: (1) the Fourteenth Amendment does not require that public school expenditures be made only on the basis of pupils' educational needs, and (2) the lack of judicially manageable standards makes this controversy nonjusticiable." The court did not construct a sufficiently objective measure of a child's or group of children's educational "needs." In effect, the court affirmed equality as an abstract value but refused to accept equal treatment or equal outcomes as definitions of educational equality.

Counsel for plaintiffs in subsequent equal protection cases modified their position on remedy in order to avoid the *McInnis* problem of unmanageable standards. They sought to persuade courts to adopt the "principle of fiscal neutrality." This standard, referred to as Proposition I by Coons, Clune, and Sugarman (1970) and suggested also by Arthur Wise (1970) holds that *the quality of a child's schooling shall not be a function of wealth, other than the wealth of the state as a whole.* This is a negative yardstick; the proposition does not prescribe what a state school finance system should be; rather, it specifies what it should *not* be. Where courts have invoked fiscal neutrality, legislatures are free to redesign school finance arrangements in whatever manner appears reasonable. The only judicially imposed constraint is that the reform system not exhibit disparities related to school district and, presumably, household wealth. Coons and colleagues and Wise attempted to design a judicially manageable principle that, while furthering the value of equality, would not unduly infringe on liberty.

In *Serrano v. Priest* (1971), California was the first during the modern era to strike down a state's education finance formula.[4] In *Serrano I,* plaintiffs presented evidence of disparities across the state that resulted from the property-tax method of financing public schools. The issue the courts were requested to address was whether the finance plan significantly discriminated among districts on the basis of wealth. The court examined disparities in per-pupil expenditures resulting from differing property wealth and tax burdens within the school system. The *Serrano I* court found that plaintiffs' contention that the "school financing system classifies on the basis of wealth" irrefutable.

The California court initially triggered the strict scrutiny test by finding that the legal challenge dealt with a "suspect classification" and that education, which is essential in maintaining a democratic citizenry, is a fundamental right. The court maintained that wealth was a suspect class based on Supreme Court equal protection precedents. The court contended that the current financing system allowed wealthy districts to "have their cake and eat it too" by getting quality education at low tax rates.

Since the strict scrutiny test was applied, the burden was placed on the state to demonstrate a compelling reason for sustaining fiscal inequities. The court found that even the interests of local control were insufficiently compelling to justify finance disparities. According to the court, "no matter how the state decides to finance its system of public education, it can still leave this decision-making power in the hands of local districts." In sum, the California court found that the fiscal policy violated both the state and federal equal protection clauses.

Research
Navigator.com

wealth
neutrality

The *Serrano I* court adopted Coons, Clune, and Sugarman's concept of **wealth neutrality** as an ideal for the school finance system (1970). Justice Sullivan stated in the opinion that "in a democratic society, free public schools shall make available to all children equally the abundant gifts of learning." Consequently, "the quality of public education may not be a function of wealth other than the wealth of the state as a whole."

Issues raised in *Serrano I* were revisited by the California Supreme Court in 1976 due to charges that the legislature had not resolved issues from the initial litigation. In *Serrano II*,[5] the court delineated a manageable standard and ruled "equality of educational opportunity requires all school districts possess an equal ability in terms of revenue to provide students with substantially equal opportunities for learning." In 1977, the California Supreme Court focused on vertical equity in *Serrano III*[6] and refined its previous decision so that the state distribution formula could legitimately fund special categories (i.e., special needs programs) at varying levels (Wood & Thompson, 1996).[7]

Parker v. Mandel (1972), an education finance challenge in Maryland, deviated from the logic of the California courts. The Maryland trial court claimed that the state's supreme court did not set sufficiently clear guidelines for deciding which test to apply in an equal protection claim and therefore rejected the equal protection challenge. According to the court, "a high degree of subjectivity would appear to be involved in determining whether a subject is to be termed a fundamental interest or whether the classification is to be called suspect."

The Maryland court also rejected the idea that education was a fundamental right protected under the equal protection clause of the 14th Amendment. The *Parker* court maintained that "if the test which plaintiffs seek to apply is the appropriate standard here, then a state, on each occasion that a similar Fourteenth Amendment attack were made against a statute dealing with health, education or welfare, would be required to bear the burden of proving the existence of a compelling state interest." In sum, courts hesitated to rule that local school district wealth could not determine quality of public education since other tax-supported public services and welfare programs might then be subject to the same strict scrutiny.

In 1973, a class of Mexican American parents in San Antonio's Edgewood school district—a property-poor school district—questioned the legality of the Texas school finance system in *San Antonio v. Rodriguez*. Plaintiffs also cited state school officials for violating the U.S. Constitution's equal protection clause. However, in a five to four decision, the U.S. Supreme Court failed to concur and upheld Texas's funding system. The Supreme Court majority concluded that education was not a "fundamental right." Thus, the state of Texas was not obligated to demonstrate a "compelling interest" in defense of the fiscal disparities that accompanied its school finance plan. The U.S. Supreme Court held that Texas's distribution plan was legal as long as it complied with a "rational basis" test.

In applying the rational basis test, the U.S. Supreme Court stated that existing interdistrict expenditure disparities were balanced against state interests in maintaining local control. Although acknowledging the possibility of unjust arrangements of the school finance system in Texas, the Court concluded that they did not offend the Constitution. A measure of inequality, even though distasteful, was permitted in order to protect a measure of efficiency and liberty.

Plaintiffs' position in *Rodriguez* was found wanting on two other grounds. The Court held that students of property-poor districts were insufficiently homogenous to constitute a *suspect classification*. In other words, students were not uniformly from low-income households, nor were they largely from any particular racial or ethnic group. Moreover, the Supreme Court was not persuaded that expenditure disparities resulted in damage to students. According to the Court, the evidence was insufficient to conclude that state-imposed minimum expenditure levels throughout Texas had failed to assure children an adequate level of schooling. In effect, the Supreme Court accepted "equal access to minimally adequate resources" as a definition of equal educational opportunity.

In 2004, a Texas trial court, in *West Orange Cove Independent School District v. Nelson*, concluded that Texas's system was unconstitutional. There were a number of technical issues, including the legality of a local property-tax recapture provision, but the principal reason was that operational funding was found to be insufficient to enable local districts to offer instruction of a quality sufficient to ensure students' acquisition of heightened state learning standards. This argument—financial "adequacy"—will be treated in detail later in this chapter. Suffice it to say that, while *Rodriquez* ended aspirations for reform on a national level, it did not end state-based efforts, including litigation in Texas itself.

In a 1986 Mississippi case, the Supreme Court issued a decision in *Papasan v. Allain* that curtailed the scope of *Rodriguez*. In this case, the Court ruled that although there was no equal protection mandate to redistribute local property-tax revenues to gain spending parity, such logic did not necessarily apply to state education funds. If certain facts are held to be present, then states may have to distribute their contributions in an equitable manner.

Despite the judicial clarification in *Papasan*, the *Rodriguez* decision effectively forced education reformers to abandon federal equal protection challenges and turn to challenges based on state constitutions to address education finance disparities. Essentially, states are the agents responsible for balancing the values of local control and equality of educational opportunities.

📁 CASE 3 REVISITED

Trial Judge Complexities

Recall the flood of information and testimony to be processed by Glenda Manheim as she presided over a school finance litigation case. From previous chapters, consider the governmental and advocacy groups who would have an interest in the outcomes of such a case. How would you begin to apply a legal framework to school finance questions? Describe the forces that would be arrayed in support of or opposition to your work.

The Second Wave: State Equal Protection

Five weeks following the United States Supreme Court's decision in *Rodriguez*, hopes of school finance reformers received a boost from the New Jersey Supreme Court ruling in *Robinson v. Cahill* (1973). This decision, the most pervasive school finance reform ruling up to that time, declared New Jersey's distribution formula to be in violation of the state constitution's education clause. That clause charges the legislature with providing a "thorough and efficient" system of education. When provided with testimony regarding funding and school service disparities then present throughout the state's local school districts, the New Jersey Supreme Court found that the state education clause was being violated and mandated that the legislature redefine and comply with the constitutional directive to be "thorough and efficient."

Robinson is significant for two reasons. First, the case illustrated that school finance reform could take place on state constitutional grounds, even though the federal judicial avenue to a more uniform and possibly rapid nationwide reform had been closed by the *Rodriguez* decision.

Second, the *Robinson* ruling also demonstrated that a court mandate is not always sufficient: the New Jersey legislature did not quickly comply with the judicial edict. Legislative action would have inevitably raised taxes, lowered expenditures in high-spending school districts, or both. These alternatives were judged politically more costly than whatever gains would have accrued from greater revenue distributional equality. Eventually the state Supreme Court closed New Jersey's public schools, during a summer session, in order to force legislative compliance with its ruling (Lehne, 1978).[8] The matter was sufficiently unresolved that by 1986 plaintiffs had returned to the court and were again challenging state compliance efforts.

In 1978, the Supreme Court of Washington in *Seattle School District v. State* partially reversed its ruling in an earlier decision, *Northshore School District v. Kinnear*. In *Northshore*, the court ruled that uniformity in size and property values was not necessary to meet the requirements of the 14th Amendment. However, in *Seattle v. State* the court maintained that sufficient funding must be derived from regular and dependable tax sources. Special excess levies, then used by many Washington districts, could no longer be relied on to fund basic educational programs; accordingly, the special excess levies could only be used to fund additional enrichment programs. The court further emphasized that the state legislature must provide for all children of the state.

Buse v. Smith (1976) in Wisconsin is unique since the case challenged the state's locally generated revenue recapture provision. The Wisconsin Supreme Court found that the state constitutional requirement for uniform taxation was violated by the recapture clause. Although education was found to be a fundamental right, equalization of revenue-raising ability among school districts was not required. Twenty years later, in *Vincent v. Voight* (1996), plaintiffs questioned interdistrict spending differences, but the case was dismissed on a summary judgment.

Connecticut's school funding system experienced ongoing equity litigation beginning in 1977. *Horton v. Meskill* alleged the state's distribution formula violated the federal and state equal protection clauses as well as the state education clause. The Connecticut Superior Court ruled that the state distribution system violated the state equal protection clause. The court rationalized that education is so basic or fundamental a right as to trigger the strict scrutiny test. In 1979, the Connecticut Supreme Court upheld the trial court's decision in *Horton II*.[9] In response to the court's ruling and litigation, the Connecticut legislature enacted various amendments to the funding formula for state aid. However, the issue returned to the court in *Horton III*[10] and the Connecticut Supreme Court upheld the original court decision, ruling that various amendments passed since 1979 were insufficient in bringing equity to the state system of school finance.

New York, Arkansas, and West Virginia experienced challenges to their education finance systems during the mid-1970s to mid-1980s with varying success for plaintiffs.

Beginning in 1978, plaintiffs in *Levittown v. Nyquist* argued that the New York formula violated the equal protection clause and education article of the state's constitution. Plaintiffs presented data demonstrating vast disparities of wealth among the state's school districts. Property-poor districts were shown to have significantly higher tax rates than wealthy districts but were unable to offer comparable educational services despite their increased tax effort. Moreover, data illustrated that disparities in per-pupil operating expenditures from the wealthiest to the poorest school district ranged from a ratio of 4.5 to 1 during 1974–1975 and there was a direct correlation between local property wealth and expenditures. In response, the state maintained that its funding formula was a policy rationally related to state interests in education. Although a county court ruled in favor of plaintiffs, the ruling was ultimately reversed by the New York Court of Appeals. The appeals court noted the data-based arguments, but maintained that plaintiffs failed to argue or show that their schools did not meet a minimum standard as prescribed by the Board of Regents. In response to the claim of violation of the education clause, the appeals court stated that nowhere in the language of the state constitution is there a requirement that public education must be substantially equivalent in every school district.

In *Dupree v. Alma* (1983) a court ruled that Arkansas' distribution formula violated the state's equal protection clause on a rational relationship examination. Education was found not to be a fundamental right under the Arkansas Constitution; therefore, the education distribution formula was not subject to strict scrutiny, triggering the rational relationship test. Plaintiffs showed that 7% of the students resided in districts with over $1,500 per-pupil total revenues in contrast to 21% of students residing in districts with less than $1,100 per-pupil revenues. Ultimately, the court found the system inequitable and ruled that students were substantially harmed by access to minimum funds and heavy reliance on local taxes; thus, the distribution formula was not found to be rationally related to a legitimate state purpose. Two decades later, the Arkansas court revisited state financing in *Lakeview v. Huckabee* (2001) and found that Arkansas' system was not only inequitable but also inadequate.

In *Pauley v. Kelly* (1979), plaintiffs, parents of five children in West Virginia's Lincoln County, alleged that the state aid formula was in violation of both the "thorough and efficient" and equal protection clauses of the state constitution. The case was dismissed by the circuit court and appealed to the state supreme court. The West Virginia Supreme Court ruled in favor of the plaintiffs and required the circuit court to oversee formulation of a master plan to ensure equity, which included distribution of personnel, facilities, curriculum, and other educational resources. In 1984, *Pauley v. Bailey* was brought before the courts to force compliance with the previous state supreme court decision.

The Third Wave: State Adequacy Claims (Equity II)[11]

Although most second-wave claims continued to focus on equity, some of the litigation also dealt with state constitutional provisions requiring "thorough" and "adequate" systems of education. As more plaintiffs realized the problems associated with equity claims, "adequacy" claims became more prevalent.

Opponents to the equity approach argued that achieving *equitable* opportunity necessitated the *inequitable* distribution of resources, resulting in "Robin Hood" provisions that robbed wealthier districts to support poorer ones. Additionally, states could pursue equity at the cost of sufficiency, resulting in states where all districts were equally underfunded. This problem became highly visible in California when, as a result of *Serrano*, policies minimized interdistrict spending differences, but statewide per-pupil spending began to drop below national per-pupil averages. By focusing on a minimum level (adequacy) of educational opportunity required by a constitution instead of a relative level (equity), the standard may be more appealing both politically and economically.

The publication of *A Nation at Risk* in 1983 was a catalyst, drawing attention to U.S. education shortcomings. Legislators, governors, and the public responded to the publication by focusing on "achieving excellence in education." The practical consequences of focusing on excellence in education was changing educational achievement standards, teacher certification requirements, and funding reforms.

The third wave of litigation was presaged by the 1979 West Virginia decision in *Pauley*, but began forcefully with important plaintiff victories in Kentucky in 1989. In these adequacy cases, plaintiffs mainly relied on state education clauses to argue that all children are entitled to a minimal level of education quality. Funding disparities are not at issue per se in the third-wave cases; instead, the focus is on funding sufficiency. Like results in equity suits, adequacy suit results have been mixed. However, between 1990 and 1999, over a dozen states recognized a plaintiff's cause of action against the state for failure to provide an adequate education (Cochran, 2000). It should be noted that the shift to adequacy cases has not been complete or immediate.

In *Rose v. Council for Better Education* (1989), the Kentucky Supreme Court examined what was meant by an *efficient* system of education as guaranteed by the state's constitution. The court acknowledged that property-poor districts are at a marked disadvantage relative to property-wealthy districts. The court noted that 35% of Kentucky's adult population did not complete high school. Moreover, Kentucky ranked nationally in the lower 20 to 25 percentile in almost every educational category dealing with achievement; therefore, the court found that inadequate performance was a reality in almost every district.

Kentucky's supreme court ultimately called for a complete overhaul of the entire public elementary and secondary systems of education across the state and the court also prescribed selected educational requirements for the legislature's consideration. In 2003, *Young v. Williams* was filed, in which plaintiffs declared that *Rose* has not yet solved the state's unconstitutional funding system.

In *Edgewood v. Kirby* (1989) the Texas Supreme Court found the state's educational finance system to be in violation of the efficiency clause of the state constitution. The state constitution explicitly mandates an "efficient system of public schools." The state argued that the word *efficient* ought to be interpreted to refer to a simple and inexpensive system. However, plaintiffs contended that *efficient*, in the Texas state constitution, referred to an effective and productive system of education.

The facts in the case were not in dispute. The district spending per student varied from a low of $2,112 in property-poor districts to $19,333 and there was a 700 to 1 ratio between taxable property value in wealthy and poor districts. The Texas Supreme Court agreed with plaintiffs and ruled that constitutional framers and ratifiers did not intend for an efficient educational system to allow fiscal disparities of such magnitude. This decision triggered decades of education finance reform in Texas, culminating most recently in the previously referenced adequacy case decision *West Orange Cove ISD*. The trial court threw out the Texas financing system. However, in 2006 the Texas Supreme Court found spending to be sufficient.

Also using the adequacy framework, the state's distribution formula was ruled unconstitutional by the Montana Supreme Court. In *Helena Elementary School District v. State of Montana* (1990), the court maintained that wide fiscal disparities throughout the state resulted in unequal educational opportunity.

The challenge of Tennessee's system for funding public education was brought before the Tennessee Court of Appeals in 1992. Plaintiffs maintained that unequal distribution of funds resulted in substandard educational services and opportunities for plaintiffs' school districts. According to fact finding, the highest per-capita county sales tax base was 10 times that of the lowest in the 1986–1987 fiscal year. Due to lack of fiscal capacity, plaintiffs contended that poor school districts were unable to raise sufficient funds to provide adequate education. Plaintiffs offered evidence regarding differences in education provided by wealthy and poor districts such as teacher retention, school facilities, course offerings, textbooks, advanced placement offerings, and funding for sufficient administration. However, the court did not find that plaintiffs met the burden of proving a deprivation of any constitutional right and dismissed the suit.

In 1993, the Tennessee Supreme Court reversed the appellate court's decision and thus found the state distributional formula to be unconstitutional. The court held:

> In describing the constitutional relationship between the state and local government and their respective powers, the defendants have stated well the reason local control is no justification for a system that discriminates on the happenstance of residence. But, as we have previously noted, the legislative flexibility mentioned in the defendants' rationale does not extend to using the inability or indifference of local government to excuse a duty specifically imposed upon the General Assembly by the constitution.

Although the Wyoming Supreme Court had found the state's funding system unconstitutional in 1980, the court revisited funding issues through an adequacy framework in 1995 in *Campbell County School District v. State*.[12] Plaintiff districts alleged that the Wyoming public school finance system violated the equal protection section and the education article of the Wyoming Constitution. According to the court, "the local effort directed at improving the quality of education varied throughout the state, yielding divergent educational opportunity dependent upon the progressiveness and wealth of the local school district and community." The court again ruled in favor of the plaintiffs and found the school funding system unconstitutional on equity and adequacy grounds. The court directed the legislature to "design the best educational system by identifying the 'proper' educational package each Wyoming student is entitled to have." The Wyoming Supreme Court opined that "education is one of the state's most important functions . . . all other financial considerations must yield until education is funded."

Even though the legislature took action in response to the court's 1995 ruling, the challenger school districts continued the action and the Wyoming Supreme Court issued its second *Campbell* decision. On February 23, 2001, the court found that the state's new cost-based funding system passed the constitutional test with a few exceptions. The court ruled that the capital portion of the new funding system was inadequate; thus, the legislature was ordered to remedy the facilities deficiencies.

As of 2003, New Jersey has experienced some form of education finance litigation for 30 years. Approximately 16 years after *Robinson v. Cahill*, the New Jersey Supreme Court was again confronted with a challenge to the educational finance system. In *Abbott v. Burke*, 29 of the state's poorest urban districts filed a lawsuit claiming that the state had not yet equalized funding among the plaintiffs' and the wealthiest districts. Moreover, plaintiffs alleged that the state had failed to provide for their children's needs as required by the *Robinson* ruling. The court responded by ordering the legislature to elevate poor-district spending to equal wealthy districts and to provide additional supplemental services and resources to address the educational needs of urban children from disadvantaged backgrounds.

The *Abbott* cases are significant because they illustrate the difficulties states encounter in designing remedies and meeting court had mandates. In 1997, the New Jersey Supreme Court ruled for the fourth time in 15 years that the state finance system was unconstitutional. As of the year 2000, the court had issued approximately seven orders regarding *Abbott* cases and the legislature's lack of sufficient compliance with the orders. In 2003, the *Abbott* saga continued when an appellate court ruled that the funds due to schools during the year were improperly calculated.

In *McDuffy v. Secretary of the Executive Office of Education* (1993), 16 students in 16 different towns and cities in Massachusetts alleged that the commonwealth of Massachusetts failed to fulfill the duty of providing for an adequate education to the students in their respective communities. Plaintiffs claimed that the Massachusetts Constitution's declaration of rights requires the state to provide an adequate educational opportunity to children in the public schools.

In order to evaluate the education finance system's constitutionality and to determine the extent of the duty placed on the state, the court undertook an extensive analysis of the language and structure of constitutional provisions and Massachusetts' public education history. An example of a relevant educational provision of the Massachusetts Constitution is as follows:

> Wisdom and knowledge, as well as virtue, diffused generally among the body of the people, being necessary for the preservation of their rights and liberties; and as these depend on spreading the opportunities and advantages of education in the various parts of the country, and among the different orders of the people, it shall be the duty of legislatures and magistrates, in all future periods of this Commonwealth, to cherish the interests of literature and the sciences, and all seminaries of them; especially the university at Cambridge, public schools and grammar schools in the towns.

Through extensive analysis of such provisions, the court aimed to determine the "natural and obvious sense" of the terms (i.e., "duty," "education," "cherish," etc.) in accordance with the framers' intended meaning. In other words, the court's purpose was to determine whether the constitutional language was "merely hortatory," "aspirational," or obligatory—imposing a constitutional duty on the state in accordance with the plaintiffs' contentions.

In sum, the *McDuffy* decision is unique since the court relied on little empirical evidence and mainly used testimony (i.e., opinion testimony and affidavits) and textual analysis. This is not to say that the court had little material on which to rely; the case's record contained approximately 546 stipulations and six volumes of documentary materials. In 1993, the court ruled the distribution formula inadequate and instructed the legislature to devise a plan and fiscal system sufficient to meet the constitutional mandate. This decision is also unique since Massachusetts was the first state, following *Rose* in Kentucky, to strike down its public education funding system and adopt the *Rose* adequacy standard, a standard constructed in another state.

Massachusetts plaintiffs returned to court, questioning the sufficiency of resources under the *McDuffy* remedy. The new case, *Hancock v. Driscoll*, was tried in 2004 and 2006 appellate ruling overturned an initial trial victory for the plaintiffs.

In 1997, the New Hampshire Supreme Court reversed and remanded on appeal from the trial court in *Claremont v. Governor* a ruling that the state had a duty to provide an adequate education to all students throughout the state. Within approximately 9 years since the *Claremont I* decision, the court had rendered eight subsequent opinions regarding the case and the state's progress in providing a constitutionally adequate education. The majority in *Claremont III* maintained that the state must provide a definition of an adequate education and define appropriate standards subject to meaningful application so that it would be possible to determine whether the state had fulfilled its duty. The court ultimately concluded that a constitutionally adequate education had not been provided since the inception of the litigation and thus mandated the state to not only provide the adequate education, but also to incorporate a meaningful accountability system in the education system.

In a three to two decision, the Arizona Supreme Court ruled the state's distributional formula unconstitutional in *Roosevelt v. Bishop* (1994). The court found that a statutory financing scheme was a principal cause of gross disparities and in violation of the general and uniform requirements of the state constitution. According to the court, "if they produce a school system that cannot be said to be general and uniform throughout the state, then the laws chosen by the legislature to implement its constitutional obligation . . . fail in their purpose."

The Ohio Supreme Court ruled that the state education funding system was unconstitutional and ordered the state to make changes to the foundation program in *DeRolph v. State* (2000). The state responded to the court order by increasing funding for public education; however, the Ohio Supreme Court again found the system unconstitutional in 2000.

The *DeRolph* cases are particularly interesting because they illustrate classic tensions between judicial rulings and legislative remedies. An appropriate resolution was not developed, and consequently, in 2003, the Ohio Supreme Court ruled again that the state's school finance system was unconstitutional. The court did not provide fiscal relief in its order but instead specified that responsibility for developing a fiscal plan rested with the legislature. Moreover, the court did not retain jurisdiction over the 11-year-old case. Effectively, the court threw up its hands, specifying that it no longer knew how to evoke a legislative remedy. Ohio plaintiffs petitioned the U.S. Supreme Court to hear the case, but the U.S. Supreme Court declined without comment.

A series of cases in New York that have challenged the financing of public education may influence future education finance litigation. In *Campaign for Fiscal Equity v. State* (1994), one of the New York trial courts ruled that the school districts lacked standing to sue the state over an alleged unconstitutionality of the distribution formula. The trial court also noted that despite the fact that minority children comprised approximately 81% of the city's public school students, the burden required by the strict scrutiny standard could not be met because there were no claims that the alleged inequality in funding was the result of deliberate discrimination; accordingly, *de facto* discrimination is not sufficient for strict scrutiny. In 2001, the court found that the state education funding system violates the plaintiff's rights under the education articles of the New York Constitution and the regulations passed by the U.S. Department of Education pursuant to Title VI of the Civil Rights Act of 1964.

In 2003, the state's highest court, New York Court of Appeals, found in favor of the plaintiffs and ordered the state to remedy the situation. *Campaign for Fiscal Equity v. New York* illustrates at least two facets of the adequacy issue. First, it was difficult to design a politically acceptable remedy. The governor and legislature, as with New Jersey, did not immediately strive to comply with the court's decision. Second, the state's highest court had remanded the case to the trial judge for remedy oversight. The trial judge found himself enmeshed in a quagmire of technical matters and appointed a three-person panel of masters to assist in sorting the issues. The masters, in effect, concurred that substantially elevated amounts of money were needed, on the order of magnitude of $6 billion. Again, as of 2006, neither the governor nor the legislature had offered anything close to this amount of money. This was for a case that had its roots in the 1980s in *Levittown v. Nyquist* and which had gone to trial in 2002.

As the In the News box indicates, there has been some push against the adequacy approach.

In the News

To the backers of adequacy lawsuits, the benefits are obvious. They argue that increased funding will lead to more and better-qualified teachers, smaller classes, better facilities, and a host of programs designed to raise achievement of poor and minority students. However, adequacy lawsuits have other, more disturbing ramifications that courts, policymakers, and the public should also be aware of and consider. Otherwise, as discussed below, the billions of taxpayer dollars spent to achieve "adequacy" may be for naught.

More money, without fundamental changes in how it is spent, will not improve student performance. The underlying premise of the adequacy movement is that increased education spending will lead to improved student performance. Unfortunately, there is little evidence that this has occurred. Since the early 1960s, inflation-adjusted spending for K–12 education in the nation has almost tripled, but there has been little or no improvement in student achievement. New Jersey, which has been in the throes of adequacy litigation longer than any other state, has dramatically increased its education spending, particularly in poor districts, but has little to show for it in terms of improved student performance.

This is not to say that money well spent in the future could not have a more positive effect. However, it seems painfully obvious that fundamental changes will have to be made in the way education dollars are spent if we are to expect significant improvement in student achievement. Otherwise, there is no logical reason to expect any different outcomes from what we have seen in the past 40 years, when education spending has soared with little or no improvement in student achievement.

Unfortunately, the very organizations that are solidly behind adequacy litigation (and that also stand to benefit from increased education spending) are also the most resistant to change when it comes to how education monies should be spent. For example, teachers' unions generally support increasing teacher pay and hiring more teachers, but most oppose changes, such as incentive or merit pay, that might make such increased spending more effective at improving student performance. They generally favor provisions in collective bargaining agreements that make it difficult to retain experienced teachers in inner-city schools. Instead, they continue to insist that teachers be compensated based on years of experience and number of education units, factors which most agree have little impact on student performance.

Alternative means of education reform will be shifted to the back burner. Once a court has struck down a school finance system, the discussion in the legislature becomes focused almost entirely on money. Other education reform measures, such as stronger accountability, increased efficiency, and expanded school choice, get short shrift. First, plaintiffs and their supporters, who gain tremendous leverage in the legislative process as a result of their court victory, are almost always opposed to such alternative reform measures. Second, any consideration of other means of education reform is likely to be lost in the shuffle, as the legislature struggles to meet the financial demands of the court decision. Instead of focusing on effective means of education reform, the legislature will be preoccupied with such issues as: Where is the money going to come from? Is it going to be taken from other school districts? If so, which ones? What noneducation programs will have to be cut? What portion of the increased costs will be borne by local taxpayers? During this debate, which may last for years, fundamental at the local level often continue to be ignored.

More resources, rather than the effective use of existing resources, becomes the rule. Although many state constitutions use the word "efficient" to describe the constitutionally mandated education system, efficient use of public tax dollars is the last thing most courts consider in adequacy cases. Most courts have ducked this issue by simply ruling that, if such problems are present at the local level, the state is also liable for them. A good example is the case of *Campaign for Fiscal Equity* v. *State of New York*, where the state introduced extensive evidence of waste, fraud, and mismanagement in the New York City public schools, including a teachers' contract that (incredibly) limited the time a teacher could spend teaching classes to three hours and 45 minutes a day. Despite this powerful evidence, the court did not rule on whether local waste and mismanagement constituted a significant cause of inadequacies in the city's public schools. Instead, it ruled that, if such problems existed, they were also the state's to fix. The court totally ignored what should have been the critical issue in the case: whether then-current funding (approximately $10,400 per student at the time, or over $250,000 per classroom) would be adequate if waste and mismanagement at the local level were eliminated.

Local control of schools will be seriously eroded. As the U.S. Supreme Court has noted on several occasions, "local autonomy of school districts is a vital national tradition." Unfortunately, this tradition has been largely ignored in adequacy cases. Decisions holding states financially liable for the spending decisions of local school districts have eroded local control, and with it, responsibility. If this trend continues, more state supervision and less local autonomy will be the obvious outcome. Some will see this as a positive outcome, especially where the local school systems have proven to be inept. But for those who view local control of schools as a time-honored American tradition, the increase in state control will be anathema.

Standards will be lowered. Ultimately, the standards movement may be another casualty of adequacy litigation. Proponents of adequacy litigation have embraced the high academic standards set by most states because such standards provide specific benchmarks by which to measure whether an adequate education is being offered in the state. But if states continue to be held financially liable when significant numbers of students fail to meet these often-aspirational standards, it is a very real possibility that such standards will be lowered or indefinitely deferred. At some point, the rubber has to meet the road.

Our democratic institutions will be weakened. The separation of powers among the legislative, executive, and judicial branches of government is the foundation of our federal and state constitutions. Adequacy cases can strain the traditional relationship between the judicial and legislative branches of government to the breaking point. For example, in Kansas, a local court recently prohibited any further spending on the state's schools until the legislature complied with its order. A crisis has been averted for the time being by an order of the Kansas Supreme Court staying the lower court's order, but the Kansas situation illustrates what can happen when the courts seize control of traditional legislative prerogatives.

continued

Historically, deciding how much money to spend on education (typically one-third to one-half of most state budgets), as compared to other state needs (for example, health care, foster-child care, or family protective services), has been the province of the state legislature. However, in a state that is under a court order in an adequacy case, these normally legislative decisions are subject to being second-guessed by the plaintiffs and vetoed by the courts. This abnormal situation can go on for years and even decades. In New Jersey, school finance litigation has been ongoing for over 30 years, and the end is still nowhere in sight.

While adequacy cases may benefit adults in the educational establishment, the important question is whether they are good for schoolchildren. Until this question is addressed, there is little hope that the future will be any different from the past, regardless of how much spending on education is increased.

From Lindseth, A. "Adequacy Lawsuits: The Wrong Answer for Our Kids." *Education Week*, June 9, 2004.

Summary

Many school finance decisions and policies are driven by litigation through state courts. Federal action on finance litigation has been precluded by the *San Antonio v. Rodriguez* decision of the U.S. Supreme Court. Litigation has occurred in three waves—one that focused on equal protection arguments, one that focused on equity-based arguments, and one that focused on adequacy arguments. The first "big" school finance case, *Serrano v. Priest*, was decided in California on equal protection grounds. In equal protection cases, decisions hang on the status of education as a fundamental right and on groups of students as a suspect class. More states have been successfully sued under adequacy cases.

Discussion Questions

1. Much legal talk is about differences between the ideas of equal protection, equity, and adequacy. Take a moment to reflect on what these concepts have in common. Is it possible to design a finance system that addresses all three issues?
2. Revisit Coons, Clune, and Sugarman's Proposition I. Do our current systems of education meet these criteria? Should they?
3. Some have argued that state-level finance reform will have little impact on resource disparities among schools. Can you envision how a state system may be equitable and yet perpetuate resource inequities within schools and classrooms?
4. After reading the In the News article, assess the adequacy argument. Is this legal argument compatible with educational policy?

Web Resources

Adequacy Lawsuits: Their Growing Impact on American Education, a conference hosted by the Kennedy School of Government, Harvard University on October 13–14, 2005: http://www.ksg.harvard.edu/pepg/conferences/adequacy.htm

Campaign for Educational Equity updated school finance scorecard:
http://www.schoolfunding.info/litigation/In-Process%20Litigations-09-2004.pdf

National Council of State Legislatures School Finance Litigation page:
http://www.ncsl.org/programs/educ/LitigationMain.htm

National Center for Education Statistics' Education Finance Statistics Center Litigation
page: http://nces.ed.gov/edfin/litigation/

Public Education Network's Guide to Public Engagement and School Finance Litigation:
http://www.publiceducation.org/pdf/publications/public_engagement/
litigation_guide.pdf

Notes

1. The purpose of this chapter is to provide an overview of the education finance cases that have influenced education finance theory and frameworks. No attempt is made to cover and describe all education finance litigation that has occurred within the courts over the years.

2. Only Mississippi does not have an education clause, although there is disagreement regarding this point. The constitution does contain language about schools; however, some experts maintain that this language does not impose an obligation on the state and should not be considered an education clause. See McUsic (1991) and Thro (1989).

3. Cases involving facilities funding are discussed in Chapter 10.

4. *Serrano v. Priest*, 487 P. 2d 1241 (Cal. 1971). Hereinafter *Serrano I*.

5. *Serrano v. Priest*, 557 P. 2d 929 (Cal. 1976). Hereinafter *Serrano II*.

6. *Serrano v. Priest*, 569 P. 2d 1303 (1977). Hereinafter *Serrano III*.

7. A similar constitutional challenge was brought forth in Minnesota federal district court in 1971. *Van Dusartz v. Hatfield*, the first education distribution case in Minnesota, used a similar rationale as applied in *Serrano I* to find that education is a fundamental right and thus ruled the school finance system unconstitutional. Of interest, in a subsequent Minnesota case, that state's Supreme Court ruled that absolute per-pupil dollar parity was not a constitutional requirement.

8. It should be noted that the schools were closed in the summer—hardly a Draconian measure!

9. *Horton v. Meskill*, 376 A. 2d 359 (Conn. 1977) Hereinafter *Horton II*.

10. *Horton v. Meskill*, 486 A. 2d 1099 (Conn. 1985). Hereinafter *Horton III*.

11. The National Research Council report on education finance, *Making Money Matter*, authored by Helen Ladd and Janet S. Hansen, traced the legal logic of equal protection suits, displaying the transition in thought from equity to adequacy. It is this report that assigns "Adequacy" the label "Equity II."

12. *Campbell County School District v. State*, 907 P. 2d 1238 (Wyo. 1995). Hereinafter *Campbell I*.

CHAPTER SIX

Policy Cultures and Paradigms Shaping Modern Education Finance

■ INTRODUCTION

The purpose of this chapter is to describe the manner in which the policy system operates and, thus, to explain how modern education finance is emerging, and emerging rapidly, from major changes in society. This discussion relies heavily on the prior explanations of societal contexts, historical contrasts, organizations controls, and legal complexities and attempts a synthesis within a framework of policy systems theory. Finally, this chapter illustrates the remarkably rich manner in which policy options can be selected and mixed to frame new models of governance and finance.

LEARNING OBJECTIVES

By the end of this chapter, you should be able to:

- Describe five distinct policy cultures and their implications for educational policy making.
- Describe three distinct policy processes and their implications for educational policy making.
- Articulate and critique alternate visions for education policy frameworks.

The transition from prior policy preoccupation with taxpayer and per-pupil spending equity to a new predisposition toward resource sufficiency and system efficiency has not always been smooth. Court opinions and legislative expectations often outstrip the capacity of social science research to deliver legislatively or judicially satisfying responses to complicated policy questions. Furthermore, whereas education finance experts once only needed to know about taxation impact and distribution formulas, they are now expected to be conversant regarding matters as diverse as achievement testing, teacher qualification, student disabilities, links between poverty and academic performance, historical evolution of education and education finance, remedial instruction, class size effects, school organization, instructional strategies, performance incentives, privatization and outsourcing, economies of scale, cost function analysis, school governance, program evaluation, leadership effectiveness, and personnel deployment.

How did this change occur? Understanding the transition requires familiarity with policy system culture, institutions, and operations.

▪ THE "COMPLEXITY" OF POLICY

Policy making and implementation have become enormously complicated in post-industrial democracies. Policy making in the United States in particular, perhaps because of the nation's heretofore unmatched wealth, the increasing importance of education in the modern world, and the vast openness and pluralistic nature of the American political system, may be the most complicated of any nation in the world.

Complexity abounds. For example, even defining a policy problem depends on the perspective applied. Examine the data presented in Tables 6.1 and 6.2. Then return to the questions posed below.

International contrasts enable one to view one's own policy system in bolder relief. For example, in Table 6.1, one can compare a typical U.S. student's instructional time

TABLE 6.1 Average Number of Instructional Hours per Year Spent in Public School

Country	Hours
Greece	790
Iceland	840
Finland	860
Hungary	870
Poland	870
Portugal	900
Sweden	900
Denmark	910
Germany	910
Czech Republic	950
Ireland	950
United Kingdom	950
New Zealand	970
Spain	970
Belgium	980
Switzerland	980
Korea	990
United States	990
France	1,020
Italy	1,020
Japan	1,020
Austria	1,120

Source: U.S. Department of Education, National Center for Education Statistics, 2000 Program for International Student Assessment (PISA), "School Administrator Questionnaire" and 2001 Progress in International Reading Literacy Study (PIRLS).

TABLE 6.2 Trends in Educational Attainment of the 25- to 64-Year-Old Population (2001–2002)

OECD Countries		Educational Attainment by Percent	
		2001	2002
Australia	Below upper secondary	41	39
	Upper secondary and post secondary non tertiary	30	30
	Tertiary education	29	31
Austria	Below upper secondary	23	22
	Upper secondary and post secondary non tertiary	63	63
	Tertiary education	14	14
Belgium	Below upper secondary	41	39
	Upper secondary and post secondary non tertiary	32	33
	Tertiary education	28	28
Canada	Below upper secondary	18	17
	Upper secondary and post secondary non tertiary	40	40
	Tertiary education	42	43
Czech Republic	Below upper secondary	14	12
	Upper secondary and post secondary non tertiary	75	76
	Tertiary education	11	12
Denmark	Below upper secondary	20	20
	Upper secondary and post secondary non tertiary	54	53
	Tertiary education	26	27
Finland	Below upper secondary	26	25
	Upper secondary and post secondary non tertiary	42	42
	Tertiary education	32	33
France	Below upper secondary	36	35
	Upper secondary and post secondary non tertiary	41	41
	Tertiary education	23	24
Germany	Below upper secondary	17	17
	Upper secondary and post secondary non tertiary	59	60
	Tertiary education	23	23
Greece	Below upper secondary	49	47
	Upper secondary and post secondary non tertiary	34	34
	Tertiary education	18	18
Hungary	Below upper secondary	30	29
	Upper secondary and post secondary non tertiary	56	57
	Tertiary education	14	14
Iceland	Below upper secondary	36	34
	Upper secondary and post secondary non tertiary	39	39
	Tertiary education	25	26
Ireland	Below upper secondary	41	40
	Upper secondary and post secondary non tertiary	35	35
	Tertiary education	24	25
Italy	Below upper secondary	55	54
	Upper secondary and post secondary non tertiary	35	36
	Tertiary education	10	10
Japan	Below upper secondary	17	16
	Upper secondary and post secondary non tertiary	49	47
	Tertiary education	34	36

Korea	Below upper secondary	30	29
	Upper secondary and post secondary non tertiary	45	45
	Tertiary education	25	26
Luxembourg	Below upper secondary	41	38
	Upper secondary and post secondary non tertiary	41	43
	Tertiary education	18	19
Mexico	Below upper secondary	88	87
	Upper secondary and post secondary non tertiary	7	7
	Tertiary education	5	6
Netherlands	Below upper secondary	35	34
	Upper secondary and post secondary non tertiary	42	42
	Tertiary education	23	24
New Zealand	Below upper secondary	24	24
	Upper secondary and post secondary non tertiary	46	46
	Tertiary education	29	30
Norway	Below upper secondary	14	14
	Upper secondary and post secondary non tertiary	55	55
	Tertiary education	30	31
Poland	Below upper secondary	19	18
	Upper secondary and post secondary non tertiary	69	69
	Tertiary education	12	12
Portugal	Below upper secondary	80	80
	Upper secondary and post secondary non tertiary	11	11
	Tertiary education	9	9
Slovak Republic	Below upper secondary	15	14
	Upper secondary and post secondary non tertiary	74	75
	Tertiary education	11	11
Spain	Below upper secondary	60	58
	Upper secondary and post secondary non tertiary	17	17
	Tertiary education	24	24
Sweden	Below upper secondary	19	18
	Upper secondary and post secondary non tertiary	49	49
	Tertiary education	32	33
Switzerland	Below upper secondary	13	15
	Upper secondary and post secondary non tertiary	62	59
	Tertiary education	25	25
Turkey	Below upper secondary	76	75
	Upper secondary and post secondary non tertiary	15	16
	Tertiary education	9	9
United Kingdom	Below upper secondary	17	16
	Upper secondary and post secondary non tertiary	57	57
	Tertiary education	26	27
United States	Below upper secondary	12	13
	Upper secondary and post secondary non tertiary	50	49
	Tertiary education	37	38
Country mean	Below upper secondary	34	33
	Upper secondary and post secondary non tertiary	44	44
	Tertiary education	22	23

Source: OECD. See Annex 3 for notes (www.oecd.org/edu/eag2004).

during a school year relative to that of his or her counterparts in other nations. What can be deduced from these figures? Is the United States simply flaccid, indifferent, undisciplined, anti-intellectual, and lazy? In the interest of international commercial competition, should the U.S. school year be expanded and instructional days stretched in order to provide America's youth and the nation as a whole with a fighting chance for economic survival?

Conversely, are overseas youth simply burning out on overly intense doses of education and failing even to finish secondary school in the process? (See Table 6.2 on educational attainment.) Perhaps it is not the quantity of education that is important, but the quality of education. Do all societies value the ability to think creatively and critically, or are some school systems more focused on rote learning than on developing a critical dimension?

Is there a problem here? If so, what is it? What solution is appropriate? What agent or agency should address the problem? What perspective is appropriate? Is this a matter about which the U.S. public should simply be informed and thereafter seek its own answers through the marketplace? Should America's teachers and other professional educators mobilize and attempt to operate schools for a longer day and year? If they do, should they be paid more? Should elected officials act quickly on this situation and enact new policies about time on task and length of time spent in instruction? Are there systematic patterns of discrimination in instructional time? Do we find that the U.S. national average is merely a statistical artifact or unreal composite in which youngsters in high-wealth school districts receive ample amounts of instruction whereas their counterparts from low-income households are subjected to shorter school days and instructional years?

We will address all of these questions in later sections. For the moment, however, suffice it to say that policy should be seen as emanating from and being shaped by multiple sources, multiple ideologies and values, and multiple perceptions of how the world operates. Conversely, policy should not be conceived of as having a single source or being derived from a single set of circumstances. Indeed, there is a spectrum of lenses through which policy can be viewed; often, more than one lens is appropriate.

■ DEFINING POLICY

A policy is a uniform decision rule, intended to guide an organization's internal actions or agency practice. Policy can be formalized as a written rule or distributed action guidelines. It can also be informal, a social or organizational norm that is generally followed even if it is not codified.

Policy exists in both public and private settings. Even a family can have a "policy" regarding children's bedtime or rules for earning a child's weekly allowance. Private sector corporations have policies regarding conflicts of interest, work rules, workplace behavior and attire, and so on. Of course, governments have policies too.

Public Policy

When a policy is a product of government, and draws on public resources for its implementation, operation, or oversight, it is said to be a "public policy." Here, the range of actions and activities is enormous, as shown in Figure 6.1. Public policy encompasses all manner of activities—regulatory, symbolic, and operational. Indeed, every session of the

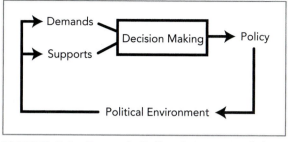

FIGURE 6.1   **Easton's Policy System Model**

U.S. Congress is marked by submission, though not necessarily deliberation about or enactment of, literally tens of thousands of bills—proposed alterations or additions to policy. Though the scale may be smaller, state legislatures, county boards, city councils, school boards, and other deliberative bodies are no different.

Education Policy

An "education policy" is presumed to be such a decision rule, one especially affecting education, schooling, instruction, or something related to these activities. For historic constitutional reasons described in Chapter 4, the United States has chosen to offer education principally through the public sector. Thus, education policy is more often than not a subset of public policy. To understand how these decision rules are derived and how they affect education finance, it is necessary to comprehend the dynamics of the public policy system and the way these political and governmental actions particularly influence education.

Research
Navigator.com

education
policy

▪ POLICY SYSTEMS

Policy system components are depicted in Figure 6.1. A policy system nests within and interacts with the larger environment, the polity. The policy system is dependent on the polity—the larger society—for supporting resources. It is also from the external environment that the policy system periodically receives stimuli. External stimuli—policy system shocks—can cause internal imbalance and trigger a search for a new systemwide homeostasis.

▪ VALUE SHIFTS AND POLICY CHANGE

Imbalance among core values can trigger a policy change. Figure 6.2 depicts a triangle within a square. Each side of the triangle represents a core value crucial to democracy: equality, efficiency, and liberty. These three values are deeply embedded in U.S. public ideology and political ecology and each is continually and collectively reinforced in the nation's symbols and political rhetoric.

In reality, the three values can be in conflict. For example, to pursue equality to its absolute metaphysical limit is to violently restrict liberty. Similarly, to eschew equality and pursue only choice, or liberty, runs the risk of creating such wealth and social class

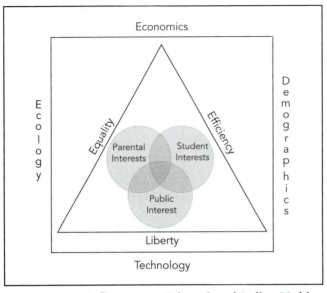

FIGURE 6.2   Influence on Educational Policy Making

extremes as to jeopardize stability of the polity. Finally, efficiency may well be furthered by choice and liberty. However, unfettered efficiency may jeopardize equality.

Liberty is often seen as the higher goal. Equality for its own sake can be empty. To be sure, a democracy must strive to achieve and maintain equality of opportunity. However, few contend that absolute material equality, with all of its trappings of drab sameness, is an end in itself. If everyone had the same clothes, cars, houses, and food, there would be material equality, but tedium might well be the order of the day. Absolute equality, or at least the pretense of it, was the hallmark of the former Soviet Union. Its ultimate downfall was a function of an inept system of individual and collective performance incentives, distance between ideological aspirations and the material corruption of its leaders, and its inability to provide consumers with choice.

Similarly, efficiency is usually taken to be an instrumental or mediating goal. For its own sake it has little value. Conversely, conserving resources so as to have more of something, be it material or psychic, would seem to be a useful means toward enhanced choice or liberty.

▪ EQUILIBRIUM THEORY

A major function of the policy system is to maintain balance among core values. Too much emphasis, for example, on equality, and perhaps an erosion of liberty, may provoke a pendulum swing. Similarly, too great a concern for liberty may alienate those who perceive that an unfettered array of choice puts them at a disadvantage and they push politically for a restoration of concern for equality.

There exists a set of dynamics that can upset the value balance, a set of dynamics that can shift the emphasis of a political system, resulting in new or altered policies. Each side of the rectangle in Figure 6.2 represents a change vector—technology, economics, demographics, and ecology. A significant change on any particular dimension can distort the public value balance, triggering altered policies, and, eventually, provoking a search for renewed policy equilibrium. Here are illustrations of this process at work.

Technological innovation is a major source of system imbalance, and, hence, a principal trigger of new policies. Here is a dramatic example. Reliable birth control pills for women were invented in the 1950s by Stanford biochemical researcher Carl DeJerassi. Few could have predicted the eventual consequences, including a decline in the national birthrate, vastly expanded workforce participation by women, increased demand for out-of-home child care services, reliance on television for occupying the time of children and youth, possible erosion of the two-parent nuclear family (or at least a diminution in the proportion of such units), widespread relaxation of prior prohibitions regarding premarital and extramarital sex, and a reduction of the ratio of children to adults in society. These changes themselves contributed to policy demands for publicly subsidized child care, extension of public school kindergarten and preschool programs, new child welfare laws, added reliance on laws to ensure women equal treatment in the workplace, increased regulation of television offerings, and a greater openness to overseas immigration to enable the workforce to keep up with the labor force demands of a vastly expanding economy resulting from two-income earners in many households.

Examples abound of the reciprocal effects of technological innovation and economic change, and the combined effect of the two on policy demands. The acceleration of a global economy in the 1990s resulted from the convergence of a number of electronic innovations leading to the formation of the World Wide Web and the Internet. These new communication and information transfer technologies disconnected capital, creative ideas, and talent from national boundaries. Companies and other organizations could now draw on ideas and recruits from overseas, in a never ceasing quest for ways to lower manufacturing and production costs. The outsourcing of jobs itself reverberated through the U.S. policy system as electoral candidates and government officials debated and sought means for regulating or limiting the flow of jobs overseas.

■ POLICY SYSTEM PARADIGMS

Political scientists are concerned with learning about both systems and processes in policy making; in other words, the *what* and *how* of public policy development. When examining systems of policy making, researchers examine the development, structure, organization, and culture of policy making bodies. When examining processes of policy making, researchers are interested in the mechanisms by which people within organizations come to understand issues and make decisions about them. Although we will review these concepts in turn, keep in mind that there are parallels between policy systems and processes that lead educational policymakers to come to radical conclusions about the best manner of education reform.

Figure 6.1 depicts a policy system paradigm initially developed by University of Chicago political scientist, David Easton. The system depicted in Figure 6.1 is a static one. Complexity is introduced into the system by the political culture that each actor in the system brings to the process. Just as beauty lay in the eye of the beholder, the key issues and roadblocks in policy development and implantation are shaped by the political culture from which policy actors view the process. The following section will outline five key cultural lenses that shape actors' views of the policy system.

Policy Cultures

Policy culture is the context or substrate in which a political system, as depicted in Figure 6.1, operates. The policy system has five identifiable cultural components—five ways of viewing reality and attempting to shape it. These policy cultures influence the manner in which advocates for a particular change will define a problem or design solutions. The unique components of each culture also shape the instruments and processes by which participants attempt to implement and oversee policy. The five policy cultures are as follows:

Political. This is the culture conventionally associated with policy making. Deliberative bodies such as legislatures, city councils, and school boards confer about issues and render recorded decisions. These politically made rules may have been the focus of intense controversy, of complicated and protracted lobbying by various parties at interests. The activity may have been partisan, linked to identifiable political parties. The newly enacted policy may alter some existing circumstance, add new service, elevate taxes, or acknowledge some important symbolic issue. Its construction is characterized by the principal components of the political process, *coalition building* and *bargaining*.

Regulative. This too is a widely perceived component of policy. However, many people misperceive regulation. They believe that regulations derive singularly from enactments by deliberative bodies. In short, they think of "regulations" as detailed rules authorized by and emanating from relatively abstract policy enactments, something of a bureaucratic follow-on to politics. There is some accuracy to this perception. However, by itself, it is insufficient.

Bureaucracies—executive branch operating agencies—also have a momentum of their own. Some of the rules they develop and promulgate stem solely from the momentum of bureaucratic practices, and only remotely from political enactments. A large organizational imperative specifies that, if there is to be a hierarchy of authority, with some individuals in greater positions of decision-making power than others, a division of labor, specialization of tasks, and an expectation that all similarly situated clients will be treated similarly, then there must be rules to enforce all of this.

The distinguishing characteristics of the regulatory policy culture are codification, rationality, rigidity, specialization, hierarchy, standardization, efforts to appear objective, and independence. Anyone with military experience will have encountered a regulatory policy culture. Military procedures may eventually be linked to statutory authority, but often one must follow the policy "food chain" to very high levels to identify the overarching authority.

Like the military, public universities and school districts have many sets of rules that, however well intentioned and effective, are a product of bureaucratic, not openly political, processes.

Legal. Courts and legal procedures comprise a third major cultural component of the policy system. The identifying features are an ability to frame an issue in keeping with long standing, judicially sanctioned doctrines, a resort to adversarial techniques, adherence to precedent, appeals to higher authority, and prescribed sets of procedural activities known only to a restricted cadre of certified technicians—lawyers.

Professional. This is the policy culture that may be least visible to the general public. From this culture stem procedures and decisions derived from self-reinforcing sets of professional participants' beliefs, not necessarily from court decisions, bureaucratic rules, or political enactments. Distinguishing characteristics are actions taken to protect clients, enhance standards, advance knowledge in a field, and insulate the profession from partisan or selfish interests. Examples include peer evaluation procedures for assessing performance of university professors, peer review among research organizations to determine a manuscript's "publishability," peer and organizational review to determine a proposed project's fundability, or grading policies for student performance in an institution of higher education or a secondary school.

Markets. This policy culture is distinguished by a fundamental belief that clients are sufficiently informed and motivated to operate in their own self interests and that, in the process of doing so, they will promote the public's long-term interests as well. Market-oriented policy culture certainly has room for rules generated in other spheres. For example, few who believe in deregulating the airline industry would also completely eliminate Federal Aviation Administration rules regarding pilot training. However, the weight of an argument from a marketplace advocate's point of view must be heavily in favor of regulation. Otherwise, the presumption should be freedom—facilitating philosopher and economist Adam Smith's metaphorical "invisible hand of the market" as the best means for ultimately shaping policy. Open choice among services or products, open competition for consumers' resources, access to capital, and a free flow of information are seen as essential in shaping policy.

◰ CASE 1 REVISITED ─────────────────────────────

River City Blues

Frank Farley is challenged to lead a major urban school system through a process of change, restructuring, and improvement. Use Easton's five political cultures to describe the challenges Frank faces in moving forward. Each culture provides a pathway to possible solutions as well as a way to understand the problems confronting Frank. Additionally, you can use Easton's political model to analyze the supports and demands made on Frank by the public.

Policy Processes

Although there are myriad theories for the ways in which policymakers come to make the decisions they do, educational finance is usually concerned with the manner in which policymakers access and interpret this information. Three perspectives on this issue are the rational actor theory from economics and the ideas of bounded rationality and irrational decision making from organizational theory.

Rational Actors. Much of economic theory is based on rational actor or rational comprehensive models of policy decision making. In these models, actors in the policy process are driven to organize, assess, and evaluate multiple streams of data and information in order to make the best decision in any given policy situation. As the dominant decision-making paradigm, rational actor theory serves as a foundation for many political science theories.

Critics of the rational actor model focus on the impossibility of obtaining all of the information required to address almost any given topic; political science theories that are based on rational actor theory are, therefore, flawed in their very concept. Defenders of the rational actor model hold that rationality should be a goal of any policy development paradigm.

Bounded Rationality. Also called incrementalism, bounded rationality theory adopts a more pragmatic stance toward information gathering and decision making in the policy process. Bounded rationality comprises two main concepts. The first is that actors make decisions with all of the information they have, not all of the information in total. That is, decision makers do not go far in gathering information to make decisions (March & Simon, 1958; Lindblom, 1959). Second, bounded rationality holds that decision makers act incrementally by gathering information from different sources across time, thus arriving at a decision at the arbitrary end of a convoluted process rather than all at once.

Irrationality and Garbage Cans. Another approach to policy decision making acknowledges that decision making may not be based on any rational activity at all, and is simply a confluence of chance, circumstance, and politics. First developed to explain the administration of colleges and universities, the term *garbage can model* was used to describe the organized anarchy that attended these types of decisions (Cohen, March, & Olsen, 1972).

📁 CASE 2 REVISITED ─────────────────────────

Bay Point Principal's Performance Pressures

Sandra Howard has been charged with making a policy shift within her school. Which framework best describes her context as she goes about making decisions about personnel, budgeting, and instructional leadership within a new student performance paradigm?

Policy Development

Each of the policy processes described above dovetails with a theory of policy development. Policy development occurs at all levels of school governance, and involves the manner in which ideas, issues, and programs find a place on the legislative agenda. Traditional policy development theory views policy development as a series of measured steps in which fully informed rational actors process information to arrive at a decision. Newer theories of policy development stress the work of "policy entrepreneurs" whose job is not to provide information but rather to bring policy ideas in line with political and circumstantial realities (Kingdon, 1984). Finally, more recent scholarship on policy development stresses the irrational and nonlinear manner in which policies develop, borrowing the terminology *punctuated equilibrium theory* from evolutionary biology (Baumgartner, 1999).

The Confluence and Confusion of Policy Reality

Those affected by policy, and almost everyone is, can benefit from understanding each of the five separate policy cultures and their identifying components, as well as the three paradigms of decision making. In reality, however, parents, students, school administrators, teacher leaders, education reformers, public officials, and interested laypersons may become engaged in an actual educational policy matter and, thus, find themselves caught in a whirling vortex of perceptions and predetermined processes from more than one policy culture. There are many intersections at which two or more of the policy and decision-making cultures collide or combine, each imparting its flavor to the whole, with the whole itself being identifiably different than any one of its parts.

For example, legalistically defined policy problems may eventually be addressed through reform legislation that, in turn, may be implemented through bureaucratically shaped rules. These new rules may subsequently serve as the basis for additional litigation, or even market-oriented solutions. The logjam of *de jure* racial segregation was broken in 1954 by a United States Supreme Court decision in *Brown v. Board of Education*. However, the court's admonition that the nation's system of dual school systems be eliminated with "all deliberate speed" ultimately contributed to federal legislation and that, in turn, ultimately led to a set of executive branch regulations regarding school desegregation. These agency rules have themselves served as bases for litigation and appeals, and in other settings have shaped the formation of organizational rules in school districts.

Thus, only rarely will one see a "pure" policy representing only one culture. Nevertheless, each individual archetype explained and explored in this book has a quintessential core of assumptions, beliefs, tenets, and historical roots which, if understood, will enable a reader, an analyst, a policymaker, or an activist to better comprehend the policy reality in both their private and professional worlds.

☐ CASE 5 REVISITED ───────────────────────

A Creative and Frustrated Teacher

Johnny Upshaw faces a difficult task in making policy change from inside the system as a science teacher. Using the bureaucratic culture as a framework, make a list of Johnny's immediate next steps.

▌ POLICY ALTERNATIVES FOR RECALIBRATING EQUITY, EFFICIENCY, AND LIBERTY

This section illustrates the manner in which issues of societal context, historical consequence, organizational control, and legal complexity merge within a policy culture paradigm to create alternative scenarios.

There is almost an infinite variety of means by which elected officials can redesign and rebalance existing educational governance and finance frameworks in order to grapple with emerging equity, adequacy, and efficiency challenges. From the spectrum of available

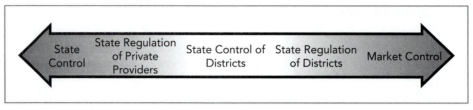

FIGURE 6.3   Control Centralization Continuum

alternatives, five archetypes have been distilled and are illustrated in Figure 6.3. In fact, components of these five models can be mixed and matched in an almost infinite matrix of decision-making models and resource recipients.

An assumption underlying each of the five illustrative governance and finance models is that the state would have responsibility for funding schooling, regardless of revenue sources. However, depending on the model selected, the recipient of financial resources might be a state agency, a local school district, a private or public contract vendor, or an individual household.

If one imagines a decision or authority spectrum anchored at one end by heavily centralized decision making and at the other end by individualized household (heavily decentralized) decision making, then what follows illustrates different points on that continuum. This practical spectrum places a powerful state education agency on one end, conventional local school districts in the middle, and household empowerment or consumer-controlled voucher plans on the other end.

Illustrative alternative governance and finance arrangements begin with a centralized alternative, one in which state government funds and operates individual local schools. This is a public control and public provision model.

The second policy alternative continues the idea of state regulation of education but allows for vendors or private providers to deliver instruction under a charter from the state. This is a public financing and private provider model.

The third alternative places heavier than is presently typical decision-making authority with the state, but enables local districts to continue to make operating decisions, such as hiring teachers. This is a mixed model of central and local public control. It might also involve, as is now the convention in the United States, a mixture of state and local financing sources.

The fourth alternative retains many current local school district functions intact, but accords the state a higher oversight role. This tool is a mixed governance model with a shift in state authority through oversight and monitoring.

A fifth alternative, vouchers, dramatically alters relationships between public schools and clients. This is a mixed model of public funding but private decision making and the possibility of both public and private service provision.

It is important to note that what follows is description and analysis, not advocacy, and little appraisal is offered regarding the political feasibility of any alternative.

A Statewide Education System

A single and uniform state system would no longer involve local schools or district authorities in activities such as setting the school curriculum, hiring teachers and administrators, selecting course grading criteria or report card formats, or purchasing textbooks.

Rather, a statewide education system would be a component of the executive branch. It might have a statewide school board such as presently exists in most states. Such a board could either be elected or appointed. If appointed, then decisions would have to be made as to the nature of the appointing authority, the governor or some other authority. Alternatively, education could simply be one component among others—for example, the attorney general, health department, or highway department—of the executive branch and have a chief executive who reported directly to the office of the governor.

Under either scenario, either with or without a state board of education, be that state board elected or appointed, the state's education administration agency would need a chief executive officer. It would not be sensible, and would badly dilute accountability, to have the chief executive officer elected statewide, as now occurs in approximately 15 states. Rather, the chief executive should be appointed, either by the state board or by the governor. If the latter, then the education chief executive, presumably, would become a member of the governor's cabinet.

A reconstituted state education department would oversee and operate a statewide education system. It would have two broad kinds of functions. One function would be an operating component performing many of the activities now undertaken by local school district central offices, and the other would be interpreting state-level policies for local implementation.

The state's operating arm for schools would recruit, employ, and induct classroom teachers and other professional educators and assign them to schools, or at least to regional offices, throughout a state. It would regularly pay teachers and other employees. It would also select and purchase items such as school buses, supplies, petroleum, food, textbooks, and all the other goods and services that schools consume. It would directly determine or assign to regional offices the responsibility for determining student attendance boundaries and the location of new school buildings.

In addition to this operating arm, a newly empowered state education department would continue in its current role of interpreting policies made by the legislature, and possibly by the state board of education, and move to implement them via directives to local schools. The state education department would also have responsibility for directly overseeing the administration of federally funded education programs.

Teacher licensure provides a good example of how the state would have a dual role in a single state school system. The new state education department would be responsible for interpreting and implementing legislation regarding teaching training and other qualifications, for licensing, and for ensuring that the teachers it hired and assigned to local schools possessed appropriate credentials. This latter function would formerly have been undertaken by a local school district.

School principals, teachers, and other school employees would be employees of the state. They might be supervised directly by state officials, either centrally or out of regional state education department offices. A state agency would be responsible for setting salaries of teachers and administrators, using a process similar to that now used to establish salaries for other state employees.

Equity, or at least equal treatment of students in similar situations, would be maximized through state control of education's mission, money, and measurement. Taxation would be statewide for education support. Local districts and local district taxing authority would be abandoned. Educators would be state employees paid consistent with a statewide salary schedule. A state agency would be responsible for constructing student performance standards, tests, and measurements; for teacher training criteria, hiring, and compensation; and for administrator standards, transportation standards, and so on.

Financial resources, in a single state system, would flow from a state agency to individual schools, not to a school district. The state would assume all existing local school debt service obligations. A school's financial and personnel resource level would be a function of state formulas. School construction—its financing, planning, and oversight—would become the responsibility of a state agency.

By moving to a single, uniform state system, a state could save money from numerous consolidations. There would no longer be a need for school boards and local school board elections. There would be no more local school district bond and debt service elections. School district superintendents and all central office staff would be eliminated. School district offices would be closed and utility bills would be reduced. There would be no such entity as a "small school district," and as a consequence, no need for a distribution formula adjustment for such districts.

The tradeoff involved in a full state system would be in citizen participation and responsiveness to local preferences and conditions. In order to compensate, at least partially, for such deficiencies, the state might well choose to have local parent advisory boards at each school to assist principals in the design and conduct of the school's programs. Additionally, consideration could be given to permitting schools to make trades between budgetary categories.

Regardless of how wrenching such a change might be, it would not be without operational counterparts. Most of America's children attend school in large systems. In fact, 25% of students attend school in only 1% of the nation's districts. In these settings, there is a direct link between local schools and a remote central management and decision-making apparatus.

A Single State Education System with a Capacity for Charters or Contracts[1]

This policy alternative places the state (through an education agency) strongly in control of education's mission, money, and measurement and leaves instructional methods and school operation and management to individual vendors or "contractors."

Under this scenario, there would again be no local school districts. There might be regional state offices. The state education agency might have a governance arrangement paralleling that outlined in the prior description of a uniform state system. Here, there might or might not be a state board of education. It could be elected or appointed. These matters are at the legislature's discretion. If there is no state education board, however constituted, then education might be an agency in the executive branch under the direct administration of the governor. Presumably, the governor would appoint the chief state school officer in circumstances where there was no state board of education to undertake such an appointment.

In this policy alternative, unlike the previously described model, the state education department would not have an operating arm. It would still have a regulatory arm, but would not itself manage schools, employ educators, issue pay checks, purchase textbooks, buy or operate buses, and so on.

Instead, in effect, the state education department would outsource the operation of local schools. Contractors would respond to Requests for Proposals (RFPs) issued by the state.[2] They would bid to operate state schools. In effect, each school or group of schools would be charter schools. The nature of the charter would be at the discretion of the state education agency.

The purpose of an individual school, its expected standards of performance for pupils, its generalized mode(s) of instruction, its spending level, and the means by which its performance would be judged could all be part of a bidding and contracting system.

Local school districts, at least as known now, would disappear. A state-issued RFP would describe the student population to be served and the outcomes required and bidders would agree to produce stated outcomes for an agreed on fee. Vendors failing to produce desired outcomes would lose their contracts. Arrangements could be made for vendors to lease and pay existing debt service on school facilities. Statewide arrangements could be made to assist in a transition of teachers from a state retirement system to a system of individual employment retirement accounts.

Who might bid to operate a school or several schools for the state? Not-for-profit organizations, such as the YMCA, might bid. Perhaps a state's teachers' union would bid to operate a school. Perhaps administrators and teachers who would like to bid to continue operating their present public school would make a joint venture submission. Perhaps a private profit-seeking firm such as Edison or Sylvan Learning Systems would bid.

The principal differences between such a statewide system of charters and the status quo are (1) that teachers, classified employees such as custodians and bus drivers, and administrators would no longer be public employees;[3] (2) there would be no local school districts; and (3) more decisions regarding the strategic direction of schools would be made by the state through issuance of contracts to vendors. Few decisions regarding the operation of schools would be made at the state level. The state would provide mission, money, and measurement. Independent vendors would provide management. Presumably, as long as vendors produced expected outcomes, the state would not interfere.

A statewide charter system could ensure compliance with many adequacy suits. For example, by specifying levels of service or outcomes for at-risk students, the state would set a standard and maintain oversight. If vendors failed to bid on such a contract, claiming that there was insufficient financing to comply with the at-risk service specification, the state would know that resources were inadequate and would have to elevate them. Simultaneously, by issuing RFPs and thereafter contracting for services, the state would retain control over costs. Market competition would set the actual cost. The state would know precisely what it cost to deliver a "basket of expectations" established either by a legislature or a court.

The state could enhance citizen participation by enlisting parental and citizen assistance in designing the Requests for Proposals for a community's school. Thereafter, the state could let parents interview bidders. Finally, by enabling parents in sufficiently populated settings to choose their child's charter school from among a range of geographically clustered schools, an element of competition would be inserted into what is now a monopoly situation. Vendors could not survive if parents did not choose to attend their schools, at least where household choice of schools was practical. This would elevate accountability.

Many questions are raised by such a vastly different approach to the operation of local schools. Would such a plan require a constitutional amendment? How would the state make a transition to such a plan? Is it not unlikely that all public schools could be converted quickly? What would happen if an insufficient number of suppliers came to the market? Would the state have to continue to operate small schools in rural areas? What would be the role of the state if a vendor defaulted on the operation of a school?

Answers to many such questions have been generated in other contexts, and could be constructed for a particular state. However, it is sufficient here to explain that the design of a statewide charter system is complicated and would take time and patience.

A Local District Operating System with Multiple State Categorical Aid Programs

This policy variant retains local school districts, but substantially constrains their decision authority.

"Categorical" in this context refers to the manner in which local officials can use a state's funds. If the state constructed "categorical" programs—for example, for vocational education, special education services for disabled students, instruction for at-risk students, and programs for limited-English-proficient students—then the state would want to ensure that specified funds were in fact spent either on target groups, on the goods and services specified in the formula, or both as intended.

School districts would retain locally elected officials and appointed chief executives. A local district, as now is true, would determine the major portion of its curriculum, employ and pay teachers, determine attendance boundaries and policies, hire administrators, and arrange student activities and programs.

However—and here is where this policy alternative would differ most dramatically with the status quo—school districts would be obligated to spend eligible funds in the manner specified by a state-defined allocation formula. Under this alternative, in addition to the possibility of a "core" operating grant, the state would make "categorical" funding available to the district and its schools. These funds would be targeted for provision of a variety of additional programs for students with special needs and interests. A district or school could spend categorical funds only in keeping with state-specified purposes for their use. A district would likely be subject to heavy fiscal accountability for such specialized funding.

The enforcement of categorical funding can occur in either of two ways. "Categorical" can mean either that funding is spent for a target group of students, say, disabled students, or is spent on a set of goods and services specified by the state. It can also be interpreted in both these ways.

For example, if a state's elementary school distribution formula generated a teacher aide for every five low-income students, then a local district would have to ensure through accounting procedures that it had so complied. The fact that the superintendent or principal might decide such funds were better spent reducing class size would be of little consequence.

The state could decide that as long as revenues were spent on the targeted category of student, how they were spent was left to local operating officials. Or, the state could determine funds had to be spent for state-specified items such as aides, supplies, or computers. Finally, the state could decide to enforce spending on both the target clientele and the specified goods and services.

Thirty years of federal government experience with this strategy has revealed its dele-terious effects. Each categorical program promotes formation of a political constituency that then seeks to protect its interests, at the risk of interrupting the operating integrity of the overall school program. However, the possible advantage of such a categorical program would be to simultaneously comply with adequacy rulings and preserve local school districts.

A Local District Operating System with a Heavily Monitored Cost-Based Block Grant

This variant also permits local districts to remain. They would have many of the conven-tional functions. They would design their curricula, hire teachers and custodians, design bus routes, purchase textbooks, and so on. However, this alternative implies an increased state presence in local school districts through significantly enhanced state oversight and auditing necessary to comply with court rulings.

To ensure that special needs and special interest students were served adequately and to ensure that the state was not unduly exposed to local districts spending funds in a way that was less than cost-effective, the state would have to engage in significantly more over-sight of local decision making. In effect, each local school district would have one or more state department officials (program monitors and auditors) responsible for approving its intended expenditures and, periodically, inspecting its actual practices.

Among the functions these state inspectors would perform is continually collecting information on the design, costs, and student performance outcomes of programs for spe-cial needs and at-risk students. This sustained information gathering would create a useful feedback loop enabling the state to continually refine the provision and its funding of spe-cial programs.

Under this more heavily monitored or regulated block grant model, districts would continue to be provided with decision discretion to trade funds from one spending cate-gory to another, at least for conventional students. However, they might be obligated to prove that deviations from state funding formula norms in certain areas were justified. District spending discretion might be substantially curtailed.

Such a policy system leaves local school districts in place. Presumably, this would continue the practice of substantial local citizen influence over many school activities. Cit-izens would have access to a local elected group of decision makers and would not have to prevail on state officials to try and shape school decisions.

However, this policy alternative would substantially constrain local decisions, at least in areas of special programming. The state could not afford to permit local decision to jeopardize the declared "adequacy" of a program for a protected class of students or a protected activity, such as instruction for limited-English-proficient students or voca-tional education. In order to protect students and programs, and to protect itself against claims of inadequacy of instruction, the state would be forced to engage in greater over-sight than it does now. Such monitoring would require expansion of most state educa-tion departments.

Still, regardless of whatever additions may be necessary for a state's department of ed-ucation to operate, this scenario seems to require fewer changes to what exists than any other described here.

Rendering the Household as the Primary Decision Unit

Voucher plans formally empower households as education decision units. As such, they represent bold departures from the convention of local school district control. However, they do offer a vehicle through which states could simultaneously comply with judicial decisions to ensure adequate schooling and political preferences for client responsiveness.

Coons and Sugarman (1978) identified the elements of vouchers operating in 19th-century England. John Stuart Mill wrote on the topic. However, modern consideration of vouchers began in earnest with the 1956 publication of *Capitalism and Freedom* by Milton and Rose Friedman. Here they argued for what today are known as unregulated vouchers. Under their plan, states would distribute warrants to households which would then be free to redeem them at schools of their choice, be they private, public, or something in between.

In the period since the appearance of the Friedmans' book, vouchers have alternatively been embraced by ideologues of the left and right. Opinion polls often reveal substantial public enthusiasm for the idea, particularly among big city parents. However, the idea has attracted little practical support. Only in Milwaukee, Cleveland, and San Antonio have public voucher plans been implemented on any recognizable scale.[4] In each instance, they are accompanied by sustained and heated controversy. These operational plans draw mixed reviews regarding their effects on student achievement. In that they enable parents to selected religiously affiliated schools, they also provoke questions of constitutional acceptability.

Whether or not vouchers will ever become politically acceptable in America or whether providers of instruction will be willing to submit to the degree of market regulation likely necessary to ensure judicial compliance with standards of quality is another set of questions.

Summary

Layers of policy enfold educational decision making at all levels. The most comprehensive understanding of the policy-making process in education is Easton's model, which provides for five cultures within which to assess the educational policy-making enterprise: political, regulative, legal, professional, and market. Each of these cultures provides insight into the workings and development of educational policies. Although the current policy climate can sometimes seem the "received wisdom" and immutable to change, there are policy alternatives to organizing a society's education function. These options range along a scale from greatest to least state control and include state public provision, state regulation, state oversight, mixed governance, and voucher oriented systems. Table 6.3 provides an evaluation of such plans.

Discussion Questions

1. Describe which of the five governance alternatives you would find most empowering and beneficial if you were: a public school principal, the mayor of a large city, the school board chair, or the local teachers' union leader.

TABLE 6.3 Comparing Policy Alternatives

Value/Policy Alternative	State System of Individual Local Schools	State System with Contract Schools	Local Districts and Categorical Aid Programs	State Oversight of Local Districts Receiving Block Grants	Vouchers
Equality of opportunity for students	All similarly situated students mandated to be treated the same	State-issued contracts specifying equal treatment	Categorical programs designed to augment regular schooling	State auditors or "inspectors" oversee provision of special services	All similarly situated students funded equally
Pursuit of excellence	State responsibility exercised through direct operation	State responsibility through legal contracts with vendors	Local responsibility, state enforcement	Local responsibility, state oversight	Parent responsibility
Responsive to parents' and policymakers' preferences	Only remotely sensitive to local preferences	Locals shape RFPs and choose schools through attendance	Remains limited by state oversight of categorical programs	Remains subject to heavier state oversight	Best feature
Efficient and innovative use of tax revenues	Diminished by absence of local participation in revenue generation	Enhanced through vendor competition	Diminished by absence of local participation in revenue generation	Diminished by absence of local participation in revenue generation. Still, modest innovation possible	Could be quite efficient
Personnel employer	State	Vendor	Local district	Local district	Vendor
Control of waste and fraud	State via direct operation of local schools	State via market	State via regulation	State via inspection and audit	Market

The above described policy alternatives can be placed on the horizontal axis in a matrix that contains values on a vertical dimension. The resulting template facilitates comparisons and evaluations.

2. Discuss the implications of assuming a rational actor or bounded rational actor in the role of educational policymaker. Observe a local school board on television and assess the manner in which these educational leaders make policy decisions.
3. The use of market-based policy reforms in education has always been contentious. Reflect on the state of education and the implications of market reform models. Describe how you think market-oriented reforms would affect the provisions of education in the United States.
4. Review the In the News article on the Florida voucher decision, using the policy cultures described in this chapter as a framework. Where do you see the market culture? Politics? Describe how the use of different policy cultures contributes to conflicts about education policy.

In the News

The Florida Supreme Court struck down the state's original school-voucher program Thursday, ruling that using taxpayer-funded scholarships to send children to private schools violates the state constitution.

The 5–2 ruling overturns a centerpiece of Gov. Jeb Bush's education-reform plans: a 1999 law that created the nation's first statewide voucher program and let children at failing public schools use state scholarships, or tuition vouchers, to go to private schools.

It also raised questions of whether two larger voucher programs created later during Bush's tenure could now be open to legal attack. More than 700 children benefit from Opportunity Scholarships, but the two other programs combined pay private-school tuition for more than 30,000 children.

Many lawyers had expected Thursday's ruling to hinge on the legality of spending public money on religious schools. Instead, the state's top court said the scholarships violated a constitutional amendment approved by voters in 1998.

That amendment declared education a "fundamental value" and required the state to maintain "uniform, efficient, safe, secure and high quality" public schools.

Diverting public money to private schools "not only reduces money available to free schools, but also funds private schools that are not "uniform" when compared with each other or other public systems," Chief Justice Barbara Pariente wrote in the majority opinion released in Tallahassee. Children using vouchers can stay at their private schools for the rest of this school year, but the program must end after that, justices said.

The 34-page opinion was a victory for those who challenged the program in court the day after Bush signed it into law. They include the Florida PTA and the Florida Education Association, the state's largest teachers union.

"It means that Florida's taxpayers will not have to pay for schools that are unaccountable," said Ron Meyer, lead attorney for the groups that sued.

For Bush, the ruling represented one of the most profound setbacks of his political career. He had championed vouchers in every run for governor, going back to his first, unsuccessful race in 1994.

The governor said he was disappointed by the decision but promised to work on a way to keep the program alive. He said he would explore "legislative fixes" or an effort to amend the constitution.

Clark Neily, an attorney representing parents who sided with Bush in the case, said his group, the Institute for Justice, also would continue its battle for school choice.

"Every parent ought to have the ability to choose where their child goes to school, and it shouldn't depend on how much money they have," Neily said.

Bush and his allies acknowledged that they were unsure how Thursday's ruling could affect Florida's other voucher programs: the McKay Scholarships designed for students with disabilities and the Corporate Tax Credit Scholarships that give businesses credit on state taxes when they give money to educate poor children.

In its ruling, the Supreme Court said attempting to read its decision as having any impact on those other programs would be "mere speculation."

Meyer said the other programs are open to legal challenges, however. He said he hoped Bush and legislative leaders would abandon their attempts to create "unconstitutional voucher programs."

Under the "Opportunity Scholarship" law, students can apply for the vouchers if their public schools earned two F's in four years on Florida's annual school report card. Students also have the option of transferring to better-performing public schools—a choice Thursday's ruling left untouched.

The voucher is worth what the state pays to educate a child at a public school. Last year, private schools got $3,400 to $5,000 for students in kindergarten through third grade.

Nearly 100 of the scholarship recipients are in Orange County. Elizabeth Walker used the vouchers to get her sons out of Mollie Ray Elementary, which got its second F in 2002, and send them to Lake Rose Christian Academy west of Orlando.

Although Mollie Ray has earned better grades since then, even getting an A last year, students who first took the vouchers are still eligible for them.

Vouchers are a "blessing," Walker said. "We pay taxes as well, and we should be able to choose the schools we want."

From Postal, L., and Kennedy, J. "Florida's top court bars vouchers for F schools." *Orlando Sentinel*, January 6, 2006.

Web Resources

The Politics of Education Association: http://www.fsu.edu/~pea/index.html

The Thomas B. Fordham Foundation:
http://www.edexcellence.net/foundation/global/index.cfm

Progressive Policy Institute Education Homepage:
http://www.ppionline.org/ppi_ka.cfm?knlgAreaID=110

Center on Education Policy: http://www.ctredpol.org/

Notes

1. The logic of statewide charter or contract competition can be extended to empowering households to become the principal education decision-making unit by providing them with vouchers redeemable only for schooling. Under such a system, private vendors presumably would be induced to come to market to offer school services and families would choose from among an array of school offerings. This arrangement is discussed in greater detail in Chapter 15.

2. The state might specify, in an RFP, that it was seeking a particular instructional strategy such as a Montessori School, A Waldorf School, and so on. However, one would expect that, generally, it would be left to vendors to describe their instructional strategies and for the state to decide what was best for the local setting involved.

3. They would be the employees of whatever company or organization held the contract with the state to operate a school.
4. Florida has enacted a voucher plan for which parents of persistently poor-performing schools are eligible, which was ruled unconstitutional by the state supreme court in December of 2005. At the time of the court decision, few schools performed poorly enough to qualify for tuition vouchers.

C H A P T E R   S E V E N

Education Revenue: Sources and Characteristics

■ INTRODUCTION

The fiscal side of school finance can be divided into three stages: (1) generating, (2) distributing, and (3) spending money. This chapter is concerned with the first phase, generating money for public education, primarily through taxation.

Education is supported chiefly by broad-based taxes (taxes based on a widespread condition), but other methods of financing are conceivable. User charges (known as tuition when applied to education) come to mind. If education were primarily a personal investment or consumption good—that is, if it did not have a preponderance of favorable social consequences—it would appear that students or their families should bear the major burden. If, however, schooling benefits accrue mainly to society rather than to the individual, society should pay costs through taxes. At present, public elementary and secondary schools of all states are tuition-free, supported primarily by local and state taxation. Thus, this chapter concentrates on taxation.

A number of states have dedicated a particular tax to education. However, these narrowly based tax sources have been found insufficient to meet revenue needs of this largest single object of state and local governmental expenditure. As a result, education finance has rested primarily on broad-based taxes such as income, sales, and property taxes.

This chapter provides detail regarding taxes' bases; equity; liberty; efficiency; impact and incidence; yield; administration and compliance costs; and economic, social, and political effects. This chapter first defines general characteristics of taxes and then describes how they apply to each of the three most general taxes. Next, the tax limitation movement of the late 20th century is discussed along with illustrations of alternatives to taxation for funding education. The chapter concludes with a comparison of the United States' revenue generation schemes and those of other industrialized nations.

LEARNING OBJECTIVES

By the end of this chapter you should be able to:

- Define the following characteristics of taxes: basis, equity, liberty, efficiency, impact and incidence, yield, cost of administration and compliance, economic and social effects, and political effects.
- Discuss the merits and drawbacks of income, sales, and property taxes.
- Define tax limitations, using the enactment of California's Proposition 13 as an example.

■ CHARACTERISTICS OF TAXES

For the 2001–2002 school year, general revenues of public elementary and secondary school in the United States amounted to $420 billion. Local, state, and federal sources contributed $180 billion, $207 billion, and $33 billion, respectively. Sixty-four percent of the revenue provided by local governments was raised through property taxes. Sixty-eight percent of the revenue provided by state governments resulted from general formula assistance, which includes revenue from state income and sales taxes (U.S. Bureau of the Census, 2002). Where does all of this money come from? How is it raised? What are the concerns about the process of taxation? These questions frame the rest of this chapter.

Basis

There are four bases, or criteria, for levying a tax: wealth, income, consumption, and privilege. These all involve money—the first three directly, the fourth indirectly.

Wealth. A tax on **wealth** is based on the ownership of property. The most common example is the property tax, the amount of which is based on the value of property owned. Another example is the federal estate tax, which is based on the size of a deceased person's estate. Note that the size of the tax bears no relation to the income generated by the property owned, but is based only on the value of the property.

Income. A tax on **income** is based on the taxable income of individuals (or corporations). Taxable income is income after allowable expenses and deductions. One of the virtues of an income tax is that the amount of the tax is related to the income used to pay it.

Research
Navigator.c⬤m

excise tax

Consumption. A tax on **consumption** is usually called a sales tax, particularly if it applies to all or most sales. If it applies only to purchase of a particular class of items (such as sin taxes or taxes on goods such as alcohol and tobacco), it is called an **excise tax**.[1] Import duties on particular goods are also excise taxes. Many states have enacted lottery statutes. A lottery can best be viewed as a product sold by the state and an excise tax on that product. (The proportion of lottery revenues paid in prizes is the product, and the difference between total revenues and prizes plus operating expenses is the tax, which is conveyed to the state.)[2]

Research
Navigator.c⬤m

license fees

Privilege. A tax on **privilege** is a tax levied on the right to engage in some sort of conduct regulated by government. It usually takes the form of **license fees**. These fees may be related directly to commercial gain, as in the case of a retail store license, a medical license, or a license to operate a taxicab. On the other hand, they may have no direct relation to money, as with a dog license, a driver's license, or a hunting license. The number of licenses required by state and local governments is large, and the money collected in fees is substantial.[3] Imposition of license fees is usually defended as being a regulatory function of government rather than a tax, with the license fees paying costs of regulation. This is only partially true: fees are often much greater than costs. Governments also sell exclusive or semi-exclusive rights to engage in certain commercial activities within city or regional boundaries. These are called **franchises** or **concessions**. An example is a franchise granted to a utility company.

Research
Navigator.com

concessions

Governments raise money by other methods that cannot strictly be called taxation. Higher levels of government transmit **intergovernmental aid** to lower levels. For example, both the federal government and state governments grant financial aid to local school districts. Governments charge **fees for service**. For example, a municipal government may operate an electric utility and sell power. Since a fee for service is a charge for a specific product, it cannot strictly be called taxation.

Equity

Since taxes are a burden imposed on all by the will of a political majority, they should treat all in an equitable manner. This may conflict with other considerations, as indicated later, but it is a worthwhile goal. What should determine whether a tax is equitable?

Horizontal Equity. In economics, horizontal equity implies that a tax should treat equals equally. For example, two individuals with the same amount of taxable income should pay the same amount of income tax. Two persons who own property of equal value in the same neighborhood should pay the same amount of property tax. This is a relatively simple criterion, and easy to judge. Most taxes are relatively equitable on this criterion; exceptions regarding the property tax will be discussed later. Unfortunately for those establishing tax criteria, not all persons are equal. It is thus necessary to establish rules for tax treatment of unequals—a more difficult task. Striving to treat unequals fairly (and perhaps equally) is known as **vertical equity**.

Research
Navigator.com

vertical
equity

The Benefit Principle. An obvious criterion for examining the fairness of a tax system is that persons should pay in proportion to benefits received, or in proportion to their contribution to the cost of whatever is supported by the tax. A prime example of a tax based on the benefit principle is the Federal Highway Trust Fund, supported by gasoline taxes. The money in the fund is used to construct and maintain federally aided highways, and the amount contributed by each person, which is a fixed amount per gallon of gas, is related to an individual's use of those highways. The benefit principle is difficult to apply in education, however. At first blush, it would appear as if only parents benefit from the public provision of education. However, public school advocates argue that entire communities benefit from strong schools—in business recruitment, in trained workers who pay taxes, and in general increased productivity.

Measurement. Taxes based on the benefit received or on the contribution to cost seem so eminently reasonable that there is a temptation to endorse this principle as a basis for all taxation. However, it is often difficult to assess either benefits received or contribution to cost. For example, should police costs be charged to the person saved from robbery or murder, on the basis of benefit received, or to the felon, on the basis of contribution to the cost of the department? Or are there benefits to an average citizen from safer streets and homes that cannot be allocated on any strict accounting basis? There is general agreement that police expenses cannot be allocated on a benefit or cost basis.

Measuring Education Benefits. Taxation based on the benefit principle for public education presents a problem. As previously discussed, if schooling benefits accrue mainly to society and not the individual, then society should pay schooling costs through taxes. But then how are benefits received or contributions to cost to be measured and how are taxes to be implemented? If education is primarily a personal investment or consumption good, then schooling benefits can more easily be measured and taxation can be based on the benefit principle. But in this case, it is students or their families that should pay schooling costs, not society, and taxation is not necessary.

> ◸ CASE 1 REVISITED
>
> ## River City Blues
>
> Recall Frank's challenges as superintendent of River City and the long list of items on his reform agenda. Assuming that funds are perennially tight, and further assuming that the large numbers of political leaders with children in private schools would prevent large-scale tax increases from finding success at the ballot box, what are some creative ways that Frank could raise money for his pet projects? Are there sources of taxes or other contributions untapped in River City? Consider making a list of alternatives and sharing with your classmates.

"Free Riders." What about national defense costs? There is a different problem here: no individual operating only out of logical self-interest would pay taxes for a pure public good such as national defense, because there is no easy way for governments to defend citizens who pay for national defense without also defending those who do not pay. This is known as the **free-rider** problem. In addition, there is no rational way of calculating either individual benefits from or costs of national defense. Allocation of taxes on this basis is not feasible. Rather, the total budget is decided on a collective basis through congressional and executive branch actions, and resources are generated through taxes based on criteria other than benefits received.

Welfare costs present yet another problem. Here, individual benefits are clear—welfare payments to persons. However, the folly of charging individuals a tax equal to the amount of welfare benefits received is obvious. Welfare has income redistribution as its principal goal. Taxation based on benefit received would directly contradict this goal.

For these reasons, most taxes cannot be allocated on the basis of benefit received or contribution to cost. An alternative equity criterion must be found.

The Ability-to-Pay Principle. Another criterion for assessing the fairness of a tax is its impact on taxpayers' ability to pay. Proponents of progressive taxation policy hold that an individual's tax burden should be considered relative to that individual's wealth. The following sections will outline key concepts that inform the ability to pay principle.

Tax Burdens. An alternative method for determining if a tax is equitable is to examine the burden that a tax imposes on individuals. Besides determining that the tax system should treat equals equally (**horizontal equity**), it is also reasonable that those with greater means contribute more to the tax system than those with less means (**vertical equity**). The idea behind the ability-to-pay principle is that individuals should pay in proportion to the burden that the provision of the public good or service though taxes imposes, which is based on the individual's ability to pay the tax. When the tax system requires individuals with the same ability to pay to bear the same amount of taxes and requires individuals with less ability to pay to relinquish fewer taxes, then the tax system satisfies both horizontal and vertical equity.

Measuring Ability to Pay. The difficulty that arises from application of this principle is determining an individual's ability to pay. Potential indices to measure the ability to pay coincide with the four bases for levying a tax: income, consumption, wealth, and privilege.

Income-based measures are the most commonly used means to determine an individual's ability to pay. Some disadvantages of such measures are that income may not be easily measurable (in-kind income) or observable (gratuities) and that these measures could assign the same tax liability to a retired individual with low income but high wealth accumulation and a college student with low income and high debt. Further, although annual income is the more common measure, a construct of lifetime income might be a more complete measure of ability to pay. Regardless of the basis for levying a tax, taxes are paid mostly out of income, so current income-based measures most accurately reflect an individual's purchasing power at the time a tax is levied.

Progressive and Regressive Taxes

Taxes Relative to Income. In judging equity of a tax by the ability-to-pay principle, one must compare the amount of tax paid with the appropriate measure of an individual's ability to pay—most commonly, income. Suppose that for a given tax, people with incomes of $10,000 pay an average of $100 in tax, and people with incomes of $20,000 pay an average of $200 in tax. Each income group is therefore paying an average of 1% of its income in tax. This is said to be a **proportional tax**. Whether such a tax is a property tax, a sales tax, or an income tax, the comparison is the amount of tax paid with the **income** of the tax payer. A proportional tax would, on the surface, appear to meet the ability-to-pay standard, for each person pays the same percentage of his or her income in tax. Next, suppose that those with $10,000 in income continue to pay $100 in tax but those with $20,000 pay $150. Now the lower-income group is paying 1% of its income, but the higher-income group is paying only three-quarters of 1%. Note particularly that although the higher-income group is paying more dollars, it is paying a smaller percentage of its income than the lower-income group. A tax with this characteristic is called a **regressive tax** (see Figure 7.1).

Finally, suppose that the $10,000 group continues to pay $100 but the $20,000 group pays $400. Those with higher incomes are paying 2% of their income, those with lower incomes only 1%. Such a tax is called a **progressive tax** (because the rates progress toward higher percentages at higher incomes).

Research
Navigator.com

horizontal
equity

Research
Navigator.com

income

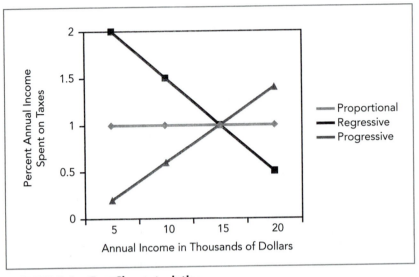

FIGURE 7.1   Tax Characteristics

This figure displays a proportional, regressive, and progressive tax imposed on four individuals that each generates the same amount of revenue.

Tax Equity.   Which of these types of tax (regressive, proportional, or progressive) comes closest to meeting the ability-to-pay criterion? In considering this, one must realize that there is a basic income amount that households need in order to maintain a minimum standard of living. Families whose incomes are at this subsistence level often spend all of their income for necessities and have little left to pay taxes. At the other end of the scale, extremely wealthy households find they are unable to spend all of their income on goods and services. They clearly have excess income, which could be used for investment or for paying taxes. Under these circumstances, it is evident that a regressive tax is not based on ability to pay. In actuality, a proportional tax is not either. A progressive tax, at least theoretically, leaves untouched the monies necessary for a minimum standard of living. However, there is no agreement on how progressive a tax must be in order to be equitable. If it is close to being proportional, it is probably unfair to poor people; if it is extremely progressive, it is probably inequitable to wealthy people. The broad band of disagreement between these extremes results partly from lack of consensus on how much life's necessities cost.

Another reason for belief in the equity of progressive taxation is an unwritten tenet in the American ethos that government should intervene to reduce extreme income inequalities. One way to do this is to tax a greater percentage of wealthy households' income than that of the poor. On the other hand, many political conservatives would point out that it is the rich who invest in businesses, create employment opportunities, and thus fuel the free enterprise system. Progressive taxes reduce the money available for such investment, decreasing general prosperity and incidentally the future income available to be taxed. An alternative way to redistribute income, used extensively in the United States, is to make payments to low-income people through programs such as Temporary Assistance to Needy

Families (TANF) and Medicaid. These **transfer payments** are discussed later in this chapter in connection with the incidence of taxation.

Liberty

The benefit principle of equity provides for the greatest freedom of the individual because individuals are taxed according to services that best fit their personal preferences. The ability-to-pay principle subjects individuals to taxation based not on their preferences, but (most commonly) on their income. Thus it is possible for a voter majority to increase the progressiveness of the tax system to force the high-income minority to provide services for the majority. This is known as **macro decoupling**. The converse, **micro decoupling,** will be explained in a subsequent section.

Federalism. In general, the lower the level of government enacting a tax, the greater the level of liberty for individuals in terms of the freedom to choose the tax schedule to which one is subject. This is the idea behind Charles Tiebout's hypothesis that individuals "vote with their feet" by moving to governmental jurisdictions that provide the closest level and type of services in accordance with their preferences (Tiebout, 1956). This implies that individuals live in the county or other local municipality that most satisfies their demand for a mix of government services and their willingness to pay for them through the tax system. Based on this theory, taxation at the local level achieves the greatest liberty because the individual chooses the local tax system, while taxation at the federal level provides the least amount of liberty.

Efficiency

The ability-to-pay principle of equity focuses on the burden that a tax imposes on individuals. However a tax often creates a burden on the economy that is greater than that felt by the individuals or businesses that directly pay the tax. This is referred to as the **excess burden** or **deadweight loss** of taxation. An **efficient tax system** is one in which the excess burden of taxation is minimized.

To understand the excess burden of taxation, look at Figure 7.2 which displays a demand and supply curve of a good with and without a tax on consumption that is a constant dollar amount (as is common with excise taxes).[4] The demand curve demonstrates that as the price of a good falls, individuals consume more of that good. The demand curve also represents the value that consumers place on a good and demonstrates that some individuals place a higher value on a good than others. The supply curve represents the price at which a company or producer is willing to sell a given quantity of the good or the marginal cost of producing the good. The intersection of these two curves represents the equilibrium price (P) and quantity (Q) of the good without a tax. At this equilibrium, some consumers would be willing to pay more for the good than the equilibrium price. The consumers' surplus represents this willingness to pay that exceeds the equilibrium price. This area is represented in Figure 7.2 by the regions ABFG. Similarly, at this equilibrium, some producers would be willing to sell their product for less than the equilibrium price. This is referred to as producers' surplus or economic profits and is represented by the area CDEH.

When an excise tax is imposed on producers of a good, the supply curve shifts up by the amount of the tax. Now there is a different price that the consumers pay for the good (P_C) and that the producers receive for the good (P_P). This difference is equal to the tax. The amount of revenue collected by the government by this tax is equal to the value of the tax per unit ($P_C - P_P$) multiplied by the quantity purchased or sold (Q_T), which is represented as the

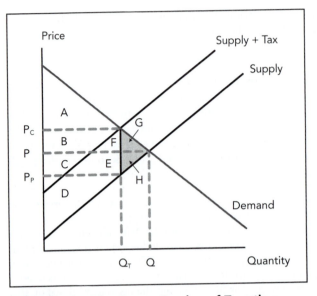

FIGURE 7.2   The Excess Burden of Taxation

The demand and supply curves of a good are drawn with a tax on the supply of the good. The tax is applied as a constant dollar amount as is common for excise taxes. The areas ABFG and CDEH represent the consumers' surplus and producers' surplus before the tax, respectively. After the tax is imposed, the area BCEF becomes tax revenue for the government. The consumers' surplus and producers' surplus change to the areas A and D, respectively. The area GH (the shaded area) represents the excess burden of this tax.

area BCEF. Because the tax causes the price that consumers pay to increase (from P to P$_C$), the consumers' surplus falls from the area ABFG to the area A. Similarly, the producers' surplus falls from the area CDEH to the area D. The excess burden of this tax is the original consumers' and producers' surplus minus the new consumers' and producers' surplus minus the tax revenue, which is the area GH. The excess burden demonstrates that the decrease in consumers' and producers' welfare exceeds benefits to government of this tax. The goal of efficiency is to reduce this excess burden.

The "Square Rule." Now consider a case when a good is sold at a fixed price for all quantities.[5] What happens to the excess burden when the tax doubles? Figure 7.3 demonstrates that when the tax doubles from t to t′ (read: "t-prime"), then excess burden quadruples. In general, size of the excess burden increases with the square of the tax. This is referred to as the square rule. An important efficiency consideration that arises from this rule is that taxes should not be levied on a single good or narrow class of goods, but instead should be imposed on a broad range of goods and services. It is more efficient to place a small tax on a large set of goods, than a large tax on a small set of goods.

Price Elasticity of Demand. The efficiency of a tax depends on the sensitivity of quantity consumed of a good to changes in its price. The price elasticity of demand for a good is defined as:

$$\varepsilon_D = \left| \frac{\text{percent change in quantity}}{\text{percent change in price}} \right|$$

If the price elasticity of demand exceeds 1 ($\varepsilon_D > 1$), so that the percent change in quantity exceeds (in absolute terms) the percent change in price, then the demand for that good is elastic. If the price elasticity of demand is less than 1 ($\varepsilon_D > 1$), then the demand for that good is inelastic. If the price of a good changes, but quantity that consumers purchase remains constant, then price elasticity of demand for that good is zero or perfectly inelastic.

Figure 7.4 demonstrates the effects of an excise tax on a good with a perfectly inelastic demand (again assuming that the price of the good is fixed or that the marginal cost is constant). Because demand is perfectly inelastic, the demand curve is a vertical line. When a tax is imposed, the supply curve shifts upwards. In this case, there is no excess burden of

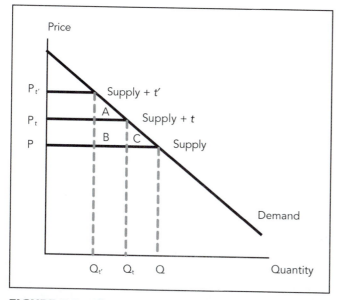

FIGURE 7.3   The Square Rule

When an excise tax or any tax of a constant value per quantity of t is levied, the excess burden of taxation is equal to the area C. When the tax is doubled from t to t′, the supply curve shifts to the top line in the figure. The excess burden then becomes the area ABC. This is four times as large as the area C because the area of the square B is twice the area of either of the triangles A and C. This demonstrates that doubling the tax quadruples (2^2) the excess burden.

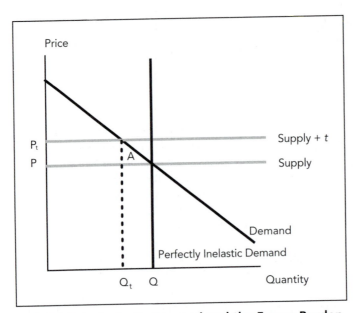

FIGURE 7.4 Inelastic Demand and the Excess Burden of Taxation

With a demand curve that is not perfectly inelastic, a tax results in the excess burden equal to the area A as the quantity purchased falls to Q_t and the price the consumers pay rises to P_t. When the demand curve is perfectly inelastic, a tax increases the price the consumers pay to P_t, but the quantity purchased does not change (Q). There is no excess burden of taxation for a good with perfectly inelastic demand.

taxation. In general, there is a smaller excess burden of taxation for goods with inelastic demands. Therefore, a second important efficiency consideration is that taxes should be levied on goods with inelastic demands.

Balancing Equity and Efficiency. Examples of goods with inelastic demands are goods that are necessities such as certain groceries, milk and bread. These are goods that individuals will continue to purchase at similar quantities regardless of price. An efficient tax would then be an excise tax on all grocery items. However, this would likely be a highly regressive tax because low-income families tend to spend a higher percentage of household budgets on these items, which would make this tax inequitable. This example highlights conflicts that often arise between equity and efficiency principles.

Impact and Incidence

The discussion thus far has implied that the burden of taxation rests on those who physically pay the tax. This is not necessarily true. Business firms of all kinds are taxed, but ultimately, of course, individuals bear the burden of taxation. To discover whether a tax is progressive or regressive, one must determine on whose shoulders the ultimate burden of the tax falls. The actual taxpayer—individual or firm—is said to bear the **impact** of the tax.[6]

Those individuals who ultimately experience the burden of a tax are said to bear its (economic) **incidence**. This is an important concept to grasp: those who bear the impact of the tax are not always the ones who bear the burden of the tax.

Tax Shifting. Discovering the tax impact is a trivial matter, for it is easy to record who actually pays. Discovering the tax incidence is much more difficult. There are no firm guidelines, and economists can only make reasonable assumptions. For example, suppose a federal excise tax is levied on cigarette production. On which individuals will the burden of this tax ultimately fall? There are three main possibilities. The tax may be shifted forward to cigarette purchasers in the form of higher prices. It may be shifted backward to the cigarette manufacturers' employees in the form of lower wages. Or it may not be shifted, but remain with the owners of the manufacturing corporation (its stockholders) in the form of lower dividends. In economists' language, the burden may be borne by **consumption, labor,** or **capital**. What will happen in individual cases depends on specific circumstances. Not **shifting the tax** is a corporation's last resort, to be used when other strategies fail. To some extent manufacturers may be able to shift a tax backward (probably not by reducing wages but by reducing the workforce, or by not granting a large increase the next time wages are negotiated). This may be possible where a tobacco company is the principal employer in a community, for workers are not apt to leave a company unless the difference between what they can earn there and what they can earn elsewhere is sufficient to offset the large economic and psychological costs of moving.

The chances of shifting a tax forward to the consumer are good. Demand for cigarettes is often assumed to be relatively inelastic: regardless of price, smokers will continue to purchase approximately the same amount. As a result, manufacturers will promptly increase product prices by an amount sufficient to cover the tax, which will have little effect on the number of cigarettes sold. It would be different in the case of a tax on peas or broccoli, for example, for the demand for peas and broccoli is highly elastic: faced with a higher pea price, many people would shift to beans or carrots. Under these circumstances, producers would be able to shift little of the tax forward, and the tax might ultimately be borne by owners in the form of a lower return on their investment.

Whether a tax is shifted backward or forward depends on individual circumstances. The main concern, however, is not with individual cases of shifting taxes, but with the overall effect of tax incidence—which determines whether a tax is progressive or regressive—and for this, there is no general agreement among economists. Assumptions must be made about what will happen on the average, and economists differ on which assumptions are the most reasonable. Economists have achieved modest levels of agreement, however, in their assessment of various specific taxes. This will be reported in the discussion of specific taxes later in this chapter.

There have been attempts to discover the progressiveness or regressiveness of the U.S. tax system as a whole. One example is a study by Joseph Pechman (Pechman, 1985: 48).[7] He calculates that for 1980, the sum of all federal, state, and local taxes in the United States had an incidence roughly proportional throughout a wide range of incomes, with most people paying approximately 25% of their income in taxes. Actual distribution of tax burdens depends on the assumptions about the extent to which certain taxes are borne by capital, labor, or consumption. Pechman computes tables based on a variety of assumptions, but there is surprisingly little difference among them. The table incorporating the most progressive assumptions indicates that the lowest income decile pays about 33% of its income in taxes. However, the second decile pays about 23% and the highest decile about 29%, with everyone else in between. The most regressive set of assumptions suggests that the lowest decile pays about 51% of its income in taxes, the second decile about 28%, the top decile about 26%, and everyone else between 25% and 27%. Regardless of assumptions, it does not appear that the wealthy manage to escape taxation. The top 1% of the population in income pays about 28% of its income in taxes under the most progressive assumptions, and about 22% under the most regressive assumptions. A brief summary of similar studies and the assumptions used is found in Fullerton and Metcalf (2002).

Transfer Payments. As pointed out, it is generally impossible to assign benefits of expenditures from tax monies to individuals. The exception is cash payments to people for welfare, unemployment compensation, Social Security, and so forth. Economists call these **transfer payments** for they represent neither income nor expenditure in the economy as a whole. They simply involve taking money out of the pockets of some individuals and putting it into the pockets of others without the provision of goods or services. Pechman finds, not surprisingly, that the lowest-income groups receive more in transfer payments than they pay in taxes. Analyzing the effect of transfer payments across all income levels, he finds that the U.S. tax system is progressive in the total range of incomes if one uses the most progressive assumptions. If one uses the least progressive assumptions, the tax system is progressive for the lowest 70% of incomes, roughly proportional for the next 29% of incomes, and slightly regressive for the top 1% of incomes. Based on these data, the U.S. tax system—as outlined in Table 7.1—may be considered on balance to be relatively equitable.

This is not to imply, however, that the system is equally equitable in every state or community, or among particular individuals. Tax laws in each state are different, with some states relying heavily on income taxes and others on sales taxes. The burden of the property tax varies substantially from one community to the next. Particular individuals must pay based on their liability for each tax, which may bear little relationship to their

(margin note:) Research Navigator.com — transfer payments

TABLE 7.1 **Transfers and Taxes as a Percentage of Adjusted Family Income Less Transfers under Two Incidence Assumptions**

Income Decile	Most Progressive Assumption			Most Regressive Assumption		
	Taxes	Transfers	Taxes Less Transfers	Taxes	Transfers	Taxes Less Transfers
Lowest	32.8%	98.3%	−65.5%	50.8%	101.3%	−50.5%
Second	22.6	58.3	−35.7	28.3	54.7	−26.4
Third	23.8	34.7	−10.9	28.3	34.8	−6.5
Fourth	25.1	23.7	1.4	28.4	23.7	4.7
Fifth	25.9	15.3	10.6	28.9	15.6	13.3
Sixth	26.1	10.9	15.2	28.6	10.5	18.1
Seventh	26.4	7.6	18.8	28.9	7.8	21.1
Eighth	27.4	5.7	21.7	29.8	5.5	24.3
Ninth	28.3	4.3	24.0	29.9	4.4	25.5
Highest	28.6	2.6	26.0	26.3	2.6	23.7
Top 5 %	28.5	2.1	26.4	25.0	2.1	22.9
Top 1 %	27.9	1.1	26.8	22.0	1.1	20.9
All Classes	27.5	10.0	17.5	28.5	9.9	18.6

The population is arrayed downward in ascending order of income for the income deciles.
Source: Joseph A. Pechman, *Who Paid the Taxes, 1966–1985*, p. 53.

income. One can speculate on progressivity and regressivity only in overall terms, not in individual ones.

Yield

The **yield** of a tax is its ability to generate revenue. In evaluating a tax, it is useful to compare its yield with those of alternative taxes and with costs of administering the tax. Some taxes are incapable of large yields. For example, the dollar volume of paper clip sales is so small that even a 100% excise tax on paper clips would yield relatively little revenue. On the other hand, the federal individual income tax yields an amount sufficient to cover more than half of federal operating costs. For the fiscal year ending in 2002, federal individual income taxes raised $858 billion. Federal expenditures, excluding Social Security, were $1,555 billion (U.S. Bureau of the Census, 2003). In general, the more broadly based a tax, the greater its potential yield. Thus, an excise tax is generally not capable of as great a yield as a general sales tax. The cost of administering a tax is discussed in the next section, and yield and administration costs are compared there.

Income Elasticity of Yield. A tax the yield of which increases at a greater rate than that of incomes is said to be elastic; one the yield of which increases at a slower rate is said to be inelastic. For example, suppose there is an excise tax on soap of 1¢ per bar. If individuals' average income increases, is the yield of this tax apt to increase, and if so, how rapidly? Soap demand changes only slightly with changes in income. Even if the incomes of all people doubled, people would probably use only a little more soap. Thus, one would expect tax yield on soap to increase less rapidly than incomes, defining the tax as inelastic.

The **income elasticity of yield** is defined as follows:

$$\varepsilon_1 = \frac{\text{percent change in tax yield}}{\text{percent change in personal incomes}}$$

If the percentage change in tax yield is equal to the percentage change in income, then income elasticity of yield will equal 1. An elastic tax has yield elasticity greater than 1; an inelastic tax has elasticity less than 1. Yield elasticity of a tax on soap of 1¢ per bar might be expected to be low, perhaps in the neighborhood of 0.2.

Contrastingly, the personal income tax is an elastic tax (Pechman, 1987). Elastic taxes are of significant advantage to governments in a period of expanding real income.[8] The reason is that government tax income increases more rapidly than income in general, whereas government expenses (given a constant level of services) tend to increase at about the same rate as that of incomes in general. This means that in an expansion period, the government has a continuing excess of income, which it may use to finance new programs or pay debt. Ramifications of this phenomenon are discussed shortly in connection with the political effects of taxes.

In general, a progressive tax is elastic and a regressive tax is inelastic. This follows from the definition of a progressive tax as one that collects a higher percentage of a wealthy person's income than of a less wealthy person's income. If incomes of all persons increase, a progressive tax will take a greater percentage of the incomes of all (as noted later in this discussion of the income tax). When average incomes increase, a progressive tax has an increased yield both from increases in income (assuming no indexation) and from increases in the percentage of that income that is taken. Thus, yield increases faster than increases in income. This connection should be clear in the case of the income tax. It is not as close and direct in the case of taxes not based directly on income, but it exists nevertheless.

Research
Navigator.com
income
elasticity
of yield

Research
Navigator.c✦m
compliance

Research
Navigator.c✦m
tax
compliance

Cost of Administration and Compliance

The cost of **administering** a tax is the cost to government of levying and collecting the tax. The cost of **compliance** is the cost to the taxpayer of complying with tax requirements. A federal tax of $1 a pack on cigarette manufacture would have a relatively low cost of administration. The reason is that there are only a few cigarette manufacturers. It is easy to require manufacturers to report monthly to the government the number of packs of cigarettes produced during the previous month. The number is multiplied by $1 per pack, and a check for the total accompanies the report. At a relatively low cost, the government can audit to ensure correct reporting of the number of packs produced.

The cost of **tax compliance** varies greatly. Usually it should be low. Perhaps the tax with the lowest compliance cost is the property tax. Individual property owners receive a tax bill yearly or semiannually, and write checks for the amount. No additional effort is required. The process may be made even easier if a mortgage lender requires property taxes be paid monthly as part of principal and interest payments. At the other extreme is the individual (or corporate) income tax. Careful sets of books must be kept, supporting evidence must be filed, accountants must often be hired to prepare tax returns, and occasionally time and expense are necessary in substantiating the return.

Economic and Social Effects

Tax Neutrality. If a tax is designed only to raise money, its economic and social effects should be as neutral. That is, imposition of a tax should not affect economic decisions made by people, nor should it affect social well-being. (Note that we are discussing the effects of tax imposition, not effects generated by spending tax proceeds for governmental purposes.)

Some taxes have more substantial economic effects than others. An excise tax on a particular commodity will serve to increase its price (if the incidence of the tax is passed forward) or decrease profit (if it is shifted backward). Either situation is apt to result in decreased consumption of the commodity—an economic effect. In the 1990s a "luxury tax" was imposed on costly personal sailing vessels and motor yachts. Consequently, dozens of boat manufacturers went out of business. These taxes, now rescinded, were not neutral; they shaped consumer behavior.

An important alleged social effect of the property tax has been abandonment of low-rent housing in cities because property taxes (on top of other expenses) exceed rental income. This can happen when the assessed value of a property is not changed to reflect reduced rentals obtainable on it. A result may be an increasing shortage of adequate housing for a city's poor.

Some states have higher taxes than others. New York consistently has had the highest total taxes, as a percentage of personal income, in the nation. Industries tend to move from highly taxed states. (This is, of course, only one reason industries move. Conversely, they are often held to their present location by investments in plants.)

Intended Tax Effects. Many economic effects of imposing taxes are unintended. Often, however, taxes have an intended social or economic effect. For example, an import tax is levied on foreign goods to protect a domestic industry. The fact is that most taxes have important social and economic effects. Insufficient federal taxation to cover federal expenditures leads to deficits and an increase in the national debt. If debt increases faster than economic expansion (as it did in the mid- and late 1980s and early years of the 21st century), borrowing necessary to service debt may result in higher interest rates. Higher interest rates, in turn, tend to discourage borrowing for expansion or capital construction. This can particularly affect an industry, such as housing, that is highly dependent on debt financing.

An excise tax on tobacco is intended, among other things, to discourage smoking, and an import tax on shoes is intended to protect a domestic industry. An income tax credit for installing home insulation is intended to encourage energy conservation. A problem with taxes designed for such specific effects is that they may, as a result, become less equitable. Balancing equity, efficiency, yield, and desired economic and social effects is a difficult task. Social and economic effects of specific taxes are discussed in subsequent sections.

Political Effects

Taxes are at once the nemesis and lifeblood of public officials. Without tax revenues, they are unable to provide governmental programs that attract votes. However, officials' votes to raise taxes can be politically fatal. Consequently, in a period of increasing incomes, such as the one the United States has had for the majority of years since World War II, an elastic tax is favored by elected officials. When incomes increase, tax yield increases even faster, providing money for new programs without necessitating higher tax rates. Public officials can have their cake and eat it. This has been generally true of the federal government's tax structure, which has had yield elasticity greater than 1. Many new federal programs have been undertaken in the last 40 years, financed mainly by federal tax structure elasticity.

Many states have had a combination of taxes that on the whole is inelastic, forcing frequent increases of tax rates.[9] This is a no-win proposition for public officials, and it is understandable that they have been attracted to state income taxes, which are generally elastic. Forty-one states plus the District of Columbia now have broad-based personal income taxes, compared with only thirty-three in 1960.[10]

Of course, elasticity is not a one-way road. An elasticity of greater than 1 implies that when income decreases, tax yield will decrease even faster. The U.S. economy has been blessed with more periods of expansion than of contraction, but a recession can be disastrous for a government that has based its operations on the expectation of ever-increasing tax revenues. An example is New York, where the halcyon days of the 1960s became the nightmare of the l970s. Governmental commitments to new and extended programs had been made with an expectation that tax revenues would increase to cover needs. When a recession hit, revenues were grossly insufficient. A state that had based much of its finances on borrowing against future revenues suddenly found its access to capital markets severely restricted. Some agencies and political divisions of the state were in even worse shape, with New York City seeking federal loan assurances and teetering on the brink of bankruptcy for years.

■ COMPARISON OF TAXES

This section compares an important tax from each of the three principal bases (income, consumption, and wealth) according to the characteristics described in the previous section. Because the property tax, rightly or wrongly, is the tax most closely connected with education,[11] it receives the most attention. Although important, the corporate income tax is not discussed separately.

Personal Income Tax

The federal personal income tax produces more revenue than any other U.S. tax. In addition, 43 states have income taxes, and 17 also allow local income taxes (U.S. Bureau of the Census, 2003). Although these state and local income taxes vary, they tend to be similar to the federal tax, and most of the remarks here will apply to them, too.

The basis of the income tax, of course, is income. Since income is what people mostly use to pay taxes, this is important. The income tax is more nearly based on ability to pay than any other tax. But, does the federal income tax treat equals equally? That depends on how one defines equals. If equals are people who have the same net income, deductions, marital status, and number of dependents, then their taxes will be equal. Similarly, one can say that of two persons who differ only in amount of taxable income, the higher-income person will pay a greater percentage of his or her income in tax. The income tax is thus a progressive tax. However, each of these qualifications is important, for they mask differences among individuals that many think are used as loopholes to avoid taxation. Two individuals with the same gross income will not necessarily have the same taxable income. Some expenses, such as tuition for higher education, can be deducted from income. Some income is not included at all, most notably interest on municipal bonds.

Two individuals may have quite different deductions. One can increase deductions (and thereby decrease taxable income) by having large medical bills, by paying taxes (since state and local income, sales, and property taxes are deductible), by mortgaging one's house and paying interest (since such interest is deductible), or by making charitable contributions.

There are, of course, many other deductions, exceptions, and adjustments to income, and all of them, at one time or another, have been referred to as loopholes. Whether they are in fact loopholes depends on one's perspective. A frequent complaint is that interest on municipal bonds is nontaxable. It is possible for a person to have an income of over $1 million a year, all of it in interest on municipal bonds, and pay no income tax at all. Although this seems grossly inequitable from an individual point of view, it is defended as a subsidy of state and local governments by the federal government; the former can sell their bonds at a lower interest rate because interest is nontaxable. If the decrease in interest received exactly balanced the tax that would have been paid, there would be no benefit to individuals. However, the decrease in interest received is equal to the taxes paid by the marginal purchaser. High-income taxpayers find that their reduction in income as a result of buying the bonds is substantially less than the tax they would have to pay if the money were invested elsewhere. For example, suppose it were possible to purchase a corporate bond paying 8% interest or a municipal bond at 7% interest. If the individual purchasing the bond had a top (marginal) tax rate of 25%, one fourth of the interest on the corporate bond would be taken away. The individual would be receiving the equivalent of a 6% return on the corporate bond, compared with 7% on the nontaxable municipal bond.

Most other adjustments to income, deductions, and exemptions are also defended as being desirable on some economic or social basis, or simply on the basis of equity to the individual. There is some justification for each. The result, however, is a law so complex that it is difficult to state that it treats equals equally. It has been proposed that all of these adjustments, deductions, and exemptions be abandoned, with people simply taxed a flat percentage of their gross incomes. This proposition solves only part of the problem, by eliminating itemized deductions and complicated tax tables. However, individuals who operate a small business at home should not report gross receipts as income, for they have expenses connected with the business. But defining which expenses are legally deductible revives several of the original complications. Other examples could be drawn. Even so, it is possible that the income tax could be further simplified, and it is clearly the most complicated tax.

Since the amount of one's income tax bill is largely determined by employment decisions, there is an incentive for taxpayers to reduce their labor supply and thus reduce the amount of tax owed. Although not without controversy, various estimates demonstrate that individuals do work less as a result of changes in the income tax (Elissa, 1995; Hausman, 1985). The result of the distortions of the income tax on individual behavior is a marginal excess burden of income taxation estimated to be between 16 and 38% (Ballard, Shoven, & Walley, 1985; Jorgensen & Yung, 1993). This implies that the actual cost to society of collecting an additional $100 in income tax revenue is between $116 and $138.

Since individual income taxes are paid by persons who are usually unable to shift the burden to others, its incidence and impact are essentially identical. Thus, its incidence can be measured more accurately than that of most other taxes. Based on the adjusted gross income of families (which is the usual basis for judging incidence), the income tax is a progressive tax. This is true not only because the first $4,850 of income per person is untaxed,[12] but also because the higher the income, the higher the tax rates. The personal income tax is generally conceded to be America's most progressive tax, and its progressiveness offsets the regressiveness of many other taxes. The result, as mentioned, is a total U.S. tax system that is remarkably proportional across the majority of incomes. Estimated effective rates of the federal individual income tax for 2004 for quintiles of population arrayed by income are shown in Table 7.2.[13]

Income tax yield is large and accounts for more than half of federal operating revenues. Many states also receive significant amounts of money from state income taxes. Nationally, the yield of state and local income taxes in 2002 was 2.2% of total personal income, or about 23% of the yield of the federal individual income tax.[14]

As noted, there is a direct connection between progressivity and income elasticity of yield, particularly in an income tax. Thus, the nation's most progressive tax is also its most

TABLE 7.2 Effective Rates of the Federal Individual Income Tax, 2004

The population is arrayed downward in ascending order of income for the income quintiles. The effective tax rates are the total tax divided by comprehensive household income, which includes pretax cash income and income from other sources such as in-kind benefits. These rates are based on the current tax law as of 2004 using 2001 incomes.

Income Quintile	Effective Tax Rate
Lowest Quintile	–5.7 %
Second Quintile	–0.1
Middle Quintile	3.5
Fourth Quintile	6.6
Highest Quintile	14.2
All	9.0

Source: Congressional Budget Office, *Effective Federal Tax Rates Under Current Law, 2001 to 2014*, August 2004, Table 1A.

Research
Navigator.com

indexation

elastic. When national (or state) incomes increase, income tax yield increases faster, because additional income is taxed at higher rates. This was formerly true (before 1985) even if income increases were caused by inflation. As understanding of this phenomenon increased, there came a demand for income tax **indexation**. The intent of indexation is to tie tax brackets to inflation rates so that inflation caused by income increases will not cause increases in the percentage of income taken by the tax. The tax would still be elastic when real incomes increase, but the inflation effects would be canceled out. President Reagan made indexation one of his goals in his first term, and the federal income tax was indexed starting in 1985.[15]

The cost of administering the income tax is high, for the tax is complicated. Many examiners, auditors, and computer operators are necessary to verify accuracy of returns and investigate questionable ones. However, yield of the tax is so great that cost of administration as a percentage of yield is acceptably low. It can be argued on economic grounds that the government should hire additional examiners, for each examiner currently returns far more than his or her salary each year in additional taxes. On an economic basis, government should hire examiners until the last one just covers his or her salary in taxes recovered. (In economic terms, the greatest yield is realized from the tax when marginal costs of hiring additional examiners equals marginal gains from hiring additional examiners.) The reason government does not do this is that the large number of additional examinations of income tax returns might generate political resistance.

Income tax compliance cost is also high, for the taxpayer must account for income and deductible expenses, keep accurate records, and either spend time preparing the tax return or pay someone else to do it. (The psychological costs are also high when one is audited.) High compliance cost is one of the reasons for calls to simplify the income tax.

Social and economic effects of the income tax are many and varied. Some are unintended, such as the tax shelter for the unusually wealthy provided by the nontaxability of municipal bond interest. Many of the effects, however, are intended. Deductibility of charitable contributions is intended to encourage charitable giving; churches, hospitals, and colleges would have a more difficult time raising funds if the deduction were repealed. Deduction of interest on residential mortgages is intended to encourage home ownership. Credits for expenses from higher education (such as tuition, books, and activity fees) are designed to promote college enrollment by decreasing the financial burden that this activity places on households.[16] In addition to such specific economic and social effects, the federal income tax is used to influence the overall business cycle. Several times, in periods of inflation, a surtax has been added to the tax to reduce the amount of money in circulation and thus to dampen inflation; at other times, most recently in 2002, there has been a tax reduction to speed recovery from recession.

The income tax has been an elected official's dream because of its elasticity, which provides ever-increasing revenues without the necessity of increasing taxes. Not since World War II has there been a significant increase in income tax rates. However, the percentage of income that an average person paid in income tax increased substantially over that period because inflation put everyone in a higher bracket. So-called **bracket creep** resulted in higher effective tax rates before 1985 even though almost all of the changes made in the income tax during that period reduced nominal rates. The indexation of the income tax is designed to reduce bracket creep.

Because it had not been necessary to increase nominal rates, there was little public outcry until the late l970s when the high rates of inflation created calls for tax reduction and indexation, as mentioned. Interestingly, during a recession the federal government does not experience the same problems as states with elastic tax structures. The federal government can budget for a larger deficit, and go into debt, rather than raising tax rates. States cannot usually run deficits.

A final policy issue confronting middle-class Americans is the alternative minimum tax, or AMT. Originally designed to ensure tax payments for wealthy citizens, the threshold for paying the AMT has held constant while the median individual income has been rising.[17] Taxpayers who fall under AMT face less friendly policies regarding deductions, and concomitantly higher tax bills. Experts warn of citizen tax revolts as were seen in the 1970s in California, if enough middle-class taxpayers fall under AMT.

General Sales Tax

Forty-five states plus the District of Columbia have **general sales taxes**, and for some it is the principal source of state income.[18] In addition, thirty-five states allow local governments (usually counties and municipalities) to "piggyback" a local sales tax on the state tax. The state collects both taxes simultaneously and rebates local proportions to appropriate government units. The basis of the sales tax, of course, is consumption. All retail sales are taxed at the point of sale. To avoid double taxation, states do not tax sales from wholesaler to retailer. The retailers pay the tax to the state.

Certain sales are usually exempted. Many states exempt food used for home preparation, on the basis that food is a necessity for poor people. Other states tax food at a lesser rate than other goods. Pharmaceutical drugs (prescription and nonprescription) are also exempted in many states because such taxes would unnecessarily burden the ill and infirm. In some states, services are not taxed, and in no state is there a tax on rent.

The sales tax treats equals equally, since people who spend the same amount pay the same amount of tax. (Actually, people who spend a greater part of their income on food and rent pay less tax in some states, which is presumably desirable.)

The general sales tax is broad-based, which ensures that consumers are not able to alter their consumption patterns to avoid taxation. This reduces the distortion to the economy caused by taxation and minimizes excess burden. Eliminating exemptions to the sales tax would increase efficiency of the tax, especially given that these exemptions are commonly placed on goods with inelastic demand; however this would conflict with the equity objectives of these exemptions. The marginal excess burden of the consumption tax has been estimated to range between 4 and 26 (Ballard, Shoven, & Walley, 1993). Thus the actual cost to society of collecting an additional $100 in sales tax revenue is between $104 and $126.

The impact of the sales tax is on retailers, for they pay the tax to government. However, the incidence is mostly on the purchaser. Because of the general nature of the tax, it is not apt to cause shifts in consumer purchasing patterns. Not only are all retailers of the same product subject to the same percentage of tax, but most other products to which individuals might shift are also subject to the same tax. This means that retailers are apt to be subject to the same competitive pressures after imposition of the tax as before, and they do not suffer by shifting the entire tax to consumers. (Again, exceptions would have to be made regarding food and rent.) To evaluate incidence of the sales tax, one can thus ask how individual expenditures compare with income. In general, poor people spend a greater percentage of their income than wealthy people. The sales tax is therefore regressive in spite of the exemptions for food, drugs, and rents, which constitute a large part of poor people's expenditures.[19] Table 7.3 shows sales tax incidence as a percentage of income for population quintiles.

Research Navigator.com
general sales tax

TABLE 7.3   Effective Rate of the General Sales Tax, 2002

Income Quintile	Effective Tax Rate
Lowest Quintile	3.6 %
Second Quintile	3.3
Middle Quintile	2.7
Fourth Quintile	2.3
Highest Quintile	
Next 15 %	1.8
Next 4 %	1.2
Top 1 %	0.6

The population is arrayed downward in ascending order of income for the income quintiles. Figures are based on the 2002 tax law using 2000 income levels for nonelderly taxpayers.
Source: McIntyre, Robert S., Robert Denk, Norton Francis, Matthew Gardner, Will Gomaa, Fiona Hsu, and Richard Sims, *Who Pays? A Distributional Analysis of the Tax Systems in All 50 States*, Second Edition (Washington, D.C.: Institute on Taxation and Economic Policy, 2003), p. 118.

The yield of state and local sales taxes is substantial. In 2003, general sales taxes produced $185 billion nationwide. This was 34% of total state and local taxes, making the sales tax the most important revenue source below the federal level (U.S. Bureau of Census, 2003).

The costs of administering and complying with the sales tax are low. Administration is less expensive than in the case of an income tax because it is easier to deal with a limited number of retailers than with a much larger number of individuals. The state must, of course, perform occasional audits to ensure that reported sales are correct. It is not necessary to keep the money paid for sales tax separate; firms simply total all sales at the end of the month, multiply by appropriate sales tax rates, and send a check to the state.

The economic and social effects of the tax may be rather small in most cases. The tax is paid in small amounts and on most products, and thus is not apt to exert much influence on purchases. There are geographic effects, though. The New York City sales tax is 4.375% (in addition to a state sales tax of 4.25%) (New York Department of Taxation and Finance, 2004). Although this does not cause casual shoppers to leave town to shop, major purchases may be made outside the city. Automobile dealerships have virtually been driven out of the city as a result of this tax. The total sales tax on a $20,000 car purchased in New York City would be $1,725, and it is possible to purchase the same vehicle only a few miles away in Connecticut or New Jersey, where the tax would be $1,200.[20] Similarly, residents of the Northwest are attracted to the north shore of the Columbia River, where they may live in Washington, with no income tax, and shop in Oregon, with no sales tax.

Sales tax elasticity has been estimated at around 1.0, which means that the yield of the tax rises at the same rate as personal income in a state. Since government expenditures have tended to rise faster than incomes, states that rely on the sales tax have occasionally been forced to raise sales tax rates, a politically unpopular step.

As the In the News box indicates, there is periodical political pressure for a national sales tax. After reading the article, evaluate the proposed national sales tax on the dimensions of equity, efficiency, compliance, and administration discussed above.

In the News

While immigration may be first and foremost on Rep. Mike Conaway's mind, it isn't the only issue he's passionate about. The freshman representative jokes readily about having to be able to delve a little into every topic that comes in front of Congress.

The trick, Conaway said, is picking issues where he wants to "dig 10 feet down."

As a Sunday story in the Odessa American showed, immigration is one of those areas Conaway is digging in on. There are others.

One ambitious goal Conaway supports is the complete revamping of how government collects money to fund operations. Instead of an income tax riddled with loopholes and exceptions, Conaway supports the idea of a national sales tax. He said a national sales tax is better than a flat tax system because a flat tax would lead to the same kind of loopholes the current system already has.

"My thought right now is that a national sales tax is the best way to collect the minimum amount of money to run this government," Conaway said, adding that a sales tax is a "fairer way to collect money to run the federal government." He said that studies show that the nation is split evenly between supporting the current tax system, supporting a flat tax and supporting a sales tax. For him, that means two-thirds of Americans don't like the way things are now. He said the concept of a national sales tax is gaining support and that now is the right time to debate the concept.

Current models show that a national sales tax would have to be in the range of 23 to 30% to collect the same amount of taxes as government collects now.

While spending a quarter in sales tax on every dollar seems a hefty price, Conaway argues that it is a fairer mechanism.

Eliminating an income tax means that businesses won't have to build in about 22% of cost to pay their own income taxes, he said. He said competition will force prices down, benefiting consumers.

Second, Conaway said American companies gain a competitive advantage in overseas markets because they can lower prices since they don't have to have as much profit to cover income taxes.

A national sales tax would also level the playing field and states wouldn't have to decide what to tax and what to exempt from taxes. Likewise, it would keep the federal government from building in loopholes and tax breaks.

"It will be tougher to create special exemptions and loopholes and other kinds of exemptions in the sales tax," Conaway said. "That isn't the case in the current code."

Conaway acknowledges that the pure concept of a sales tax draws criticism as being regressive. Critics claim that sales taxes hit the poorest people hardest.

"To address that, you put in place something that says none of us pays sales tax on the essentials of life," Conaway said, bringing up the idea of rebates on things like food and other necessities. "Guys who make more money buy more things and pay more taxes."

From Powell, G. (2006). "U.S. Rep. Conaway backs conversion to national sales tax." *Odessa (TX) American.* February 27, 2006: http://www.oaoa.com/news/nw022706c.htm.

Research
Navigator.com
real property
tax

Property Tax

The property tax is a principal financial support of the public schools in almost every state.[21] Just as the income tax is the principal revenue source for the federal government and the sales tax for the state governments, the property tax has been the mainstay of local government.

Basis. The property tax is the most important example of a tax on the ownership of wealth. The only other significant example is the estate tax. However, the property tax does not tax all wealth. Wealth can be divided into **real property**,[22] **tangible personal property**, and **intangible personal property**. Real property consists of land and improvements firmly attached to the land. Such improvements are mostly buildings, but also include fences, power lines, and landscaping. Tangible personal property includes items of intrinsic value not attached to the land. Automobiles, clothing and furniture, and business inventories and machinery are examples. Intangible personal property consists of evidences of wealth having no intrinsic value of their own, such as bank deposits, stocks and bonds, and mortgages. Most real property is taxed, some tangible personal property is taxed, and almost no intangible personal property is taxed.

The Assessment Process. Before property can be taxed, its owner must be located and the value of the property established. This is the duty of the **assessor**, an elected or appointed official of the town, city, or county. Assessors prepare area maps of their jurisdictions, displaying separate land parcels. Dimensions of the land, a description of its boundaries, and the owner's name are easy to obtain because all states require that any transfer of ownership of real property be recorded, usually by an official known as a **recorder**. These maps enable an assessor to account for every piece of real property in his or her jurisdiction. Each piece of property is given an identifying number, and its owner of record is determined from the recorder's files.

The next challenge is to assign a value to property. This is an extremely difficult process and the source of many complaints. Usually only property subject to taxation will be valued. This means that streets, public buildings, and other governmental properties will not be valued, nor will the property of churches and other tax-exempt private institutions. Tax-exempt property can be a large part of the total: in New York City approximately half of all property is tax-exempt (New York State Office of Real Property, 2002).

The usual standard is **fair market value**. This is generally defined as a sale price that would be agreed on by a buyer and a seller, both of whom were informed and were not in collusion. The assessor's problem is to assign such a value to each piece of property. The easiest place to do this is a subdivision of similar houses where there are a number of sales during the year. It is easy to average these sale prices and assign the rest of the houses in the subdivision the same value, with minor adjustments for differences such as installation of a swimming pool. It is more difficult to assess the value of an older home in an area of homes of widely differing styles and sizes.

More difficult yet is assessing a small business. Valued as a going concern, the business may be worth much more than if one were to sell the property for a different use. However, the assessor is to value property at its "highest and best" use, and this would normally be the present business use. Since small businesses change hands infrequently and tend to be quite different from one another, basing the valuation on a comparison of property sales may not be feasible. Frequently, an assessor will **capitalize** a business's **income**. That is, on assuming, for example, that a 10% profit on investment is reasonable, the assessor multiplies profit figures by 10 to determine the assumed value of the business as an investment. The assessor may estimate profit figures using sales tax data: if the sales tax is 5%, sales are 20 times the amount of sales tax paid. If profit is normally 2% of sales (e.g., in a supermarket), the 2% is used to estimate profit.

Valuation of a large factory is even more complicated. The factory may be only one of many properties of a large corporation, and it may be impossible to obtain an accurate estimate of the profit of this one property. A third basis of valuation is frequently used in such cases—**replacement value less depreciation (RVLD)**. Each part of the factory (land, buildings, machinery, and inventories) is appraised for an estimate of the cost to replace it at today's prices. Appraisals are then reduced by depreciation based on an assumed useful life of each item. Machinery might have a useful life of only 10 years, whereas a building might have a useful life of 50 years. Land is never depreciated, for its useful life has no limit (although a depletion allowance is made in the case of a mine, oil well, or quarry). The depreciated replacement values for various parts of the property are added to obtain a total property value.

Utilities present yet another problem, because of their extensive distribution networks. An electric utility's power lines are of no value (other than salvage) except as they are parts of an overall distribution system. If the entire property of a utility in an assessor's jurisdiction consists of a few miles of high-tension line, it is difficult to value. For this reason, many states assess utilities themselves. Some states use a combination of capitalized earnings and RVLD to assess utilities. A utility system's total value is determined by the system's capitalized earnings. The parts of the system are valued on the basis of RVLD. The RVLD of the part of the system within each assessor's jurisdiction is expressed as a percentage of the RVLD of the entire system, and the total value of the utility based on capitalized earnings is multiplied by this percentage to determine the value of the portion of the utility in each assessor's jurisdiction.

Another type of property that is difficult to value is farmland. Farmers who live some distance from centers of population may find that their farmland, based on its income-producing ability, has a value of only $500 an acre. Farmers on the outskirts of an expanding metropolitan area may find that their farmland, with exactly the same crop-producing ability, is valued by the assessor at $5,000 an acre. This is because the assessor must value the land at its **highest and best use** (the use for which one could realize the highest sale price), and this is its use as subdivision land. The resulting taxes may be so high that the farmer is driven to sell the land to developers. In effect, the assessor has constructed a self-fulfilling prophecy. This appears unfair to a farmer who wishes to continue farming, but it is not unfair at all to the farmer who is only waiting for the best offer from developers. A solution to this problem has been adopted in a number of states. Farmers in these states can place their land in an **agricultural reserve**. They guarantee that the land will not be used for purposes other than agriculture for a specified number of years, in return for which the assessor must value the land based solely on its value for farming. If the land is sold during the agreement period for a different use, the owner is subject to back taxes based on the difference in assessment between that for farmland and that for its highest and best use.

Effects of Assessment. This farmland example illustrates that the assessment process has important economic and social consequences. In the case of the highly taxed farmer, the economic consequence is that land near cities and suburbs is forced into housing developments sooner than it would be otherwise. Small farmers are forced out of businesses they expected to leave to their children. Land on the fringes of the city becomes less expensive to the developer than land closer to the city, encouraging sprawling development and involving considerable expense in terms of longer sewer and water lines, utility lines, roads, and travel time for residents. Of course, the economic and social consequences do not occur evenly, as is evident from developers' readiness to fight such special exemptions as that for farmland.

In California, golf courses were subject to the same kind of assessment adjustment described for farmland. They, too, are usually located near populated areas, and assessing them for their value as subdivision land was forcing them out of existence. However, there was no provision for paying back taxes if the land were converted from golf course use, and a large number of golf courses suddenly came into being as developers realized that this was a way of avoiding taxes on land they were holding for future development.

One of the greatest concerns about the economic and social impact of the property tax has been the adverse effect of the tax on poor people, who pay a larger share of their income in housing costs than do the wealthy. One way of remedying this is the **homestead exemption**, which is a deduction of a fixed amount from the assessed value of the property before determining the taxable assessed value. In Florida, for example, the first $25,000 of assessed valuation of an owner-occupied house is exempt from taxes (Florida Department of Revenue, 2004). This clearly favors individual ownership over rental housing. It is also a subsidy available only to those financially able to own a house, and not to those who must rent. The circuit breaker (discussed later) is another way of accomplishing the same purpose.

Assessing Personal Property.   The discussion to this point has concentrated on processes by which a value is attached to all real property by an assessor. The assessor may also assess personal property, but the extent to which this is done varies widely from one state to another.[23] One problem with assessment of personal property is discovering it in the first place. Real property transfers must be recorded, and construction of buildings usually requires a permit. Personal property, though, may be acquired and sold without public notice. Most assessors make little attempt to accurately assess homeowners' tangible personal property. If they assess it at all, they simply use a percentage of the value of the residence as the presumed value of the personal property in it. Of more importance is the **assessment of machinery and business inventories**, for the amounts involved are large.[24] This can lead to bizarre behavior. For example, in California, the value of inventories used to be assessed as of the first Monday in March each year. In February, therefore, businesses attempted to reduce inventories to a minimum. Retail businesses held inventory sales. Oil companies ceased pumping oil from the ground and allowed their tanks to go dry. In general, each business attempted to sell as much inventory as possible and to buy as little as possible. On the day following assessment day, everyone scrambled to rebuild inventories.

Intangible personal property is an even greater problem, for stocks and bonds (which, along with bank deposits, constitute most intangible personal property) can be easily hidden in safety deposit boxes or stored outside an assessor's jurisdiction. The result is that, with the exception of bank deposits in a few states, little intangible personal property is assessed. In some states all personal property is exempt from assessment. An interesting consequence of this occurred in New York. In-ground swimming pools were assessed and taxed as real property; they are vastly outnumbered by above-ground pools, which are personal property and not assessed.

Determining Actual Assessments. Having attached a value, which is presumed to be a fair market value, to each piece of property, the assessor must assign an **assessed value**. The assessed value is, in most cases, a fraction of the fair market value. This is true even in those 24 states where constitutions or statutes require assessors to assess real residential property at full market value.[25] The reason for **fractional assessment** is a practical one. Assessment, by its nature, is inexact. Because it affects their pocketbooks, people will protest if they believe that their assessments are too high. An assessment at **full market value** is much more open to public scrutiny than an assessment at some unknown fraction of market value. In addition, taxpayers who complain that their fractional assessment is higher than their neighbor's may be told by the assessor that the law requires a full market value assessment and may be asked if they wish their property valued at that. Courts in some states have supported assessors in this practice. There are more insidious reasons for fractional assessments. As pointed out, assessment of large properties (factories, for example) is extremely complicated. An assessor frequently does not have sufficient expertise to assess such properties accurately. In such a case, the assessed value of the property is frequently negotiated between assessor and property owner. Large property owners find it more difficult to convince a number of boards and councils to minimize taxes than to arrange privately with an assessor to set low assessments. There are clearly opportunities for illegal agreements.

The law usually requires all **classes** of property to be assessed either at full value or at the same percentage of full value. Again, this requirement is followed more in the breach than in the observance. Assessors know that individuals vote and businesses do not, for example. In San Francisco for many years, residences were assessed at less than 10% of full value while businesses were assessed at 50% of full value. In a few states fractional assessment at different rates for different classes of property is permitted or required. In Arizona in 1991, for example, telecommunications utilities were assessed at 30%, commercial and industrial property at 25%, and residential property at 10% of full value. However, in many states these interclass differences exist in defiance of the law, which usually requires that assessments be at 100% of full value, or that all property be assessed at the same fraction of full value. In the state of New York, many towns are reassessing as a result of a successful challenge of inter- and intraclass differences, the state's highest court having required that all property be assessed at full market value. The problem is that in many cities, commercial and industrial property was previously assessed at a much higher fraction of its full value than was residential property (an **interclass** difference). When assessed values are elevated to full value, the result is a massive shifting of property taxes from commerce and industry to residences. To neutralize this transfer, cities in some states are levying taxes at different **rates** for industry than for residences. This is often known as **splitting the rate** or **splitting the role**.

Calculating the Tax Rate. After an assessed value has been attached to each piece of property, an assessor's obligation is complete. The responsibility for adopting budgets then falls to general governments, such as cities and counties; special governments, such as school districts and mosquito abatement districts; and enterprise districts, such as port authorities and other taxing entities. The budget of a governmental unit less its income from other sources leaves an amount to be raised by property taxes. This amount, divided by the assessed valuation of the property within the geographical boundaries of the unit, provides the tax rate to be applied to that property. For example:

Budget	$15 million
Other income	$10 million
To be raised by taxes	$5 million
Assessed valuation	$250 million
Tax rate	0.020

This tax rate is customarily expressed in one of several ways, depending on the state: 20 mills (a **mill** is one-tenth of one cent, and this means 20 mills—2¢—per dollar of assessed valuation), $20 per $1,000 of assessed valuation, $2 per $100, or 2%.

It is not possible, however, simply to add the tax rates for each of the governmental units within the assessor's jurisdiction to obtain the total tax rate for that jurisdiction. Each unit usually covers a different geographical area, but there is overlap. Overlapping boundaries create areas in which the total tax rate differs from that of adjoining areas. Within each area, however, the tax rate is the same for all property. Each of these areas with a uniform tax rate is known as a **tax code area**. A typical county in some parts of the United States may have hundreds of tax code areas. On the other hand, there are a few places, mostly in the South, where all government functions have been consolidated under a single county government, with the same tax rate countywide.

Fractional assessment creates a number of problems. First, of course, if different properties (or different classes of property) are valued by an assessor at different percentages of market value, they will be unevenly subject to the property tax. If, however, an assessor values *all* property within the jurisdiction at the same percentage of market value, there appears to be no difficulty. A low total assessed value would simply mean a higher tax rate, since the tax rate is obtained by dividing budgeted tax needs by assessed valuation. In reality, however, there are two main problems. First, in many states school districts have statutory maximum tax rates. By assessing property at less than market value, an assessor is limiting the access of school districts to the full tax amount they would otherwise be able to levy. Second, states allocate aid to school districts based on the wealth of the district. An underassessed district creates an illusion of a poor district entitled to more state aid. In the past, this has led to **competitive underassessment** among districts in some states. A solution to the intergovernmental aid problem is a state **board of equalization**, which determines for each school district and other government units the ratio of assessed to full value, enabling state aid to be based on full value. Although this is now done in most states, it does not solve the problem of differences in assessment ratios *within* a district.

In addition to fractional assessment of all property and different assessment rates for property of different classes, there is the problem of *intraclass* discrepancies. Identical properties are often assessed quite differently. This results in part from the subjectivity inherent in appraisal. Part of the problem, though, is that many assessors revalue property infrequently. Assessors are understaffed and revalue only that property that comes to their attention, either because of a sale or because a building permit has been issued. This means that the new owner of an old home may find the assessment roughly equal to 90% of the home's value, whereas the long-time owner of an identical home next door, not reassessed for 30 years, may have an assessment less than 50% of the home's market value. These kinds of intraclass differences are particularly visible and trigger disgruntlement over the property tax.

Equity. The first concern of equity is whether equals are treated equally. The property tax is probably weaker in this respect than most taxes. The problem, of course, lies in assessment practices. The inter- and intraclass discrepancies in assessments previously described mean that owners of properties of equal value in the same tax code area may pay quite different taxes. In addition to these assessment problems, tax exemptions diminish the equity of the property tax as well as its revenue-raising capacity.

Incidence. Consideration of whether the property tax treats unequals equitably and the efficiency of the property tax involve the tax's incidence. It is a trivial matter to discover the impact of the tax, for tax bills are individually addressed, but analyzing incidence is another matter.

One school of economists views property taxes as an excise tax (the traditional view). Another group believes the property tax is a capital tax (the new view). A third group sees the property tax as a user fee (the benefit view). The first group finds the tax to be regressive, perhaps the most regressive of the major taxes. The second group believes the property tax is progressive. The third group argues that the property tax is not a tax at all and thus views the determination of incidence as inappropriate. The arguments will be summarized only briefly here. Those interested in further discussion should consult the literature in the field.[26]

Most economists agree that property taxes on land fall on the owner of the land at the time the tax is initially levied or increased. The tax cannot be shifted because under equilibrium conditions the only way to increase price is to increase demand or decrease supply. The landowner has no control over demand, and there is no way that supply can be decreased in the aggregate because the supply of land is almost perfectly inelastic.

Wealthy persons, who have more disposable income than poor people, own proportionately more land. Since the incidence of property taxes on land falls entirely on landowners, this portion of the tax is presumably progressive. However, property taxes paid are deductible items on the income tax, and wealthy property owners benefit more from this provision than do poor property owners because they have higher **marginal tax rates**. Thus, the net effect is not as progressive as might appear at first.

Taxes on improvements (and on personal property) can be divided into three categories. The first is owner-occupied housing. Again, all agree that the burden of this tax falls entirely on the owner-occupant, who is both capitalist and consumer; there is no one to whom to pass the tax liability. Since this was already true for the land on which owner-occupied houses stand, the incidence of the property tax on these properties is exactly the same as the impact. (One should not be confused by the existence of mortgages into thinking that banks own much housing stock. The individual who owns the house, and has merely borrowed money with which to purchase it, must pay the taxes, not the bank.) The incidence of the property tax on single-family owner-occupied housing tends to be regressive because wealthy people spend a smaller proportion of their incomes for housing than do poor people.

The analysis is more difficult in the case of rental housing, for it is not clear to what extent the burden of the tax can be conveyed to the tenant in the form of higher rents, and to what extent it must be absorbed by landlords in the form of a diminished return on investment. One view has all of the property tax on rental *housing* (not land) passed forward to the renter. Since poor renters pay a greater proportion of income in rent than do rich renters (and assuming for the moment that property taxes are a relatively constant percentage of rents), the incidence of the property tax on rental housing must also be regressive. The other view is that in the short run the supply of housing is almost as inelastic as the supply of land. This means that it will be impossible in the short run for landlords to pass the property tax forward to renters.

This second group of economists (the new view) notes in addition that even if the property tax on rental housing is passed forward to the renter, it may not be regressive because property taxes are not a constant percentage of rents, as the first group assumes. The proportion of rent that represents a return to capital in low-rent housing is considerably smaller than it is in high-cost housing. Most of the rent in inexpensive housing pays for current costs of the housing, including taxes.

Research
Navigator.com
marginal tax
rates

Third, the second group points out that it is an illusion that truly poor families pay high property taxes. Among those with unusually low incomes are a disproportionate number who have low incomes only temporarily. Examples are young couples who can reasonably expect to increase their incomes rapidly, retired persons who have accumulated substantial wealth even though their current income is low, and individuals who have been able to offset income against business expenses or otherwise reduce their adjusted gross income. This group of economists argues that one should not use current income as the measure in judging regressivity, but **permanent income**. They define permanent income as that income that individuals expect to earn on the average over the long term. They argue that when permanent income is used, even the tax burden on owner-occupied housing is progressive.

Finally, the more regressive view of the incidence of the property tax on commercial and industrial buildings and business machinery and inventories is that the tax is passed on to consumers in the form of higher prices for goods purchased. The more progressive view is that these taxes are borne by owners of capital.

It is not at all clear which group of economists is more correct. Anyone who reads the analyses of both sides carefully is struck by the number of assumptions that must be made because of lack of data. Economists are fond of making assumptions; doing so simplifies conditions and renders them more amenable to analysis. Unfortunately, it also abstracts from reality, and often it is difficult to determine the extent to which an assumption is justified, or how it will upset the conclusion if it is not correct. Pechman's analysis of the incidence of the property tax is presented in Table 7.4. It is clear that the two views display a different picture of the burden of the tax.

Progressive assumptions present a property tax that is clearly progressive. Regressive assumptions display a property tax that is regressive for the lowest 20% of the population in income, but proportional for all other deciles. It appears that the most one can say at present is that it is by no means certain that the tax is onerously regressive. It should not be condemned solely on that account.

If the property tax is regressive, its greatest burden is on poor people. The **circuit breaker**, a way of selectively reducing this burden, has been adopted in one form or another

TABLE 7.4   Effective Property Tax Rates as a Percentage of Income, 1985

| Population Decile | Tax Rates | |
	Progressive Assumptions	Regressive Assumptions
Lowest	0.7 %	3.3 %
Second	0.7	2.5
Third	0.9	2.1
Fourth	0.9	2.1
Fifth	1.0	2.1
Sixth	1.2	2.1
Seventh	1.3	2.1
Eighth	1.3	2.2
Ninth	1.7	2.3
Highest	3.3	2.3

The population is arrayed downward in ascending order of income for the income deciles.
Source: Joseph A. Pechman, *Who Paid the Taxes, 1966–1985*, p. 80, Table A-4.

by many states. The circuit breaker excuses all or a portion of the property taxes a family pays on its residence above a specified percentage of its income. For example, the law might provide that 60% of the excess of taxes over 3.5% of family income will be forgiven. Suppose a family has an income of $20,000 and pays property taxes of $1,000. Three and a half percent of its income is $700, and the excess of property tax is $300. Sixty percent of the latter is $180. The family would report this fact on its state income tax return and deduct the $180 from the income tax. If the deduction exceeded the tax, the state would refund the difference. The circuit breaker is applied to rental property also; it is assumed that between 8.5 and 35% of rental payments constitute property taxes paid, depending on the state (Advisory Commission on Intergovernmental Relations, 1995, Table 35). The circuit breaker has been adopted in one form or another by 36 states since its appearance in Wisconsin in 1964. The reason for its popularity is that it is a tax exemption tailored to the income of the taxpayer. Thus it is less costly to the state than a homestead exemption, which benefits rich and poor homeowners alike in dollar terms.

The circuit breaker has drawbacks, however. It tends to benefit the most those who spend a high proportion of income on their homes, including those with higher incomes who choose to invest in extravagant homes. Another problem is the assumption that a uniform percentage of rent is property tax, for this is patently false even if we agree that landlords pass the entire burden of the property tax on to tenants. Yet this notion too—that the incidence of the property tax is on renters—has come under challenge, as indicated in the previous section.

Efficiency. Determination of the efficiency of the property tax rests on one's view regarding the tax as an excise tax, capital tax, or user fee. If the property tax is a user fee that individuals pay in response to the services provided by the local government in the localities that they choose to live in, then there is no excess burden of the property tax. In this case, the property tax does not result in any distortions of individuals' behavior and is simply a payment for services similar to payment for any other type of service. If the property tax is an excise tax or a capital tax, then this method of taxation changes individuals' decisions regarding the consumption and investment in real estate, which results in the excess burden of taxation. The marginal excess burden of the property tax has been estimated at 18%, which is generally less than the excess burden of the income or sales tax (Jorgenson & Yung, 1993). This implies that the actual cost to society of generating an additional $100 in revenue from property tax is $118.

Yield. The property tax is a potent generator of revenue. In 2002, property taxes were 37% of combined state and local taxes and 73% of local taxes. Almost $280 billion is raised each year in property taxes nationwide.[27] However, property taxes have trended downward after hitting a high point in 1970. Much publicity has been given to tax limitation initiatives such as Proposition 13 in California and Proposition $2\frac{1}{2}$ in Massachusetts (for a review of Proposition 13 in California, see Fischel, 2004). But many other states have also lowered their effective property tax rates.

The property tax has usually been thought of as an inelastic tax. The reasoning is that assessed values do not tend to increase as rapidly as personal incomes, mainly because assessments are not constantly updated. The result is that a constant tax rate will produce revenues that do not increase as rapidly as incomes. However, the analysis is not that simple. It is not necessary to assume a constant tax rate. Government demands for money have increased faster than incomes. Those governments that depend heavily on the

TABLE 7.5 Federal, State, and Local Taxes as Percentages of Gross National Product, Selected Years, 1902–1990

Year	Federal Taxes	State and Local Taxes	
		Total	Property Taxes Only
1902	2.1%	3.6%	2.9%
1913	1.6	4.0	3.3
1922	4.6	5.4	4.5
1932	3.1	10.6	7.7
1940	4.9	7.8	4.4
1948	15.4	5.4	2.4
1956	15.9	6.4	2.8
1964	14.7	7.8	3.3
1970	15.2	9.0	3.4
1978	12.2	8.6	2.8
1981	13.3	8.0	2.4
1984	11.0	8.5	2.5
1987	11.9	9.0	2.6
1990	11.6	9.2	2.7

Sources: 1902–1940: Advisory Commission on Intergovernmental Relations, *Financing Schools and Property Tax Relief: A State Responsibility* (Washington, D.C.: Government Printing Office, 1973), p. 16; 1948–1970: Advisory Commission on Intergovernmental Relations, *Significant Features of Fiscal Federalism, 1985–86*, p. 43, Table 31; 1978–1990: Advisory Commission on Intergovernmental Relations, *Significant Features of Fiscal Federalism, 1992*, p. 130, Table 67.

property tax (that is, almost all local governments) have been forced to increase property tax rates, and they have been surprisingly successful in doing so, as shown in Table 7.5. From 1902 to 1922, property tax receipts increased from 2.9% of GNP to 4.5%. From 1932 to 1948, property taxes remained remarkably constant in dollars, generating between $4 billion and $5 billion per year. They jumped to 7.7% of GNP in 1932 as the depression hit while tax receipts remained almost the same. A long period of prosperity (interrupted by several minor recessions) began in 1946 and continued for 25 years. During this time, property tax yields in dollars increased eightfold and yield as a percentage of GNP rose steadily from 2.4% to 3.4%. The yield declined to about 2.4% of GNP in 1981, reflecting property tax limitation measures adopted by some states, and has remained at about that level since. The property tax, then, has shown a remarkable characteristic in this century: it is elastic in periods of prosperity, increasing in yield faster than the economy, yet inelastic during depression, decreasing in yield scarcely at all even when the economy takes a terrible beating. From the point of view of governments that depend on the property tax, this **revenue resilience** is the best of all possible worlds. From the point of view of the taxpayer, particularly the one with no children in school, the picture is, of course, not as rosy, and this is undoubtedly the reason for some of the tax limitation movements.

Costs of Administration and Compliance. The administrative cost of the property tax is usually low when expressed as a percentage of yield. Part of the reason for this, however, is that in most states assessments are poorly carried out. Proper assessments might double or triple administration costs. The general effect of this would be to improve the equity of the tax (by reducing inter- and intraclass discrepancies), but it would probably not improve the yield in most cases. The reason is that property tax yield is determined by local government revenue needs, which are translated into a tax rate. Evasion of formally levied property taxes is rare, for governments can collect unpaid back taxes by seizing the property and selling it. There is significant evasion of taxes through abandonment of property in a few cities, but it can be argued that the assessed value of the property was too high in such cases, for the property was obviously abandoned as worthless.

The cost of compliance is probably lower for the property tax than for any other major tax. Property owners receive a tax bill and pay it in one or more installments. The time and effort involved in doing so are nil. However, the dollar amounts of such payments render the property tax highly visible, which is responsible in part for its low public popularity or acceptance.

Economic and Social Effects. As should be evident from the foregoing discussion, the economic and social effects of property taxes are important. There is no general agreement among economists on overall or specific effects of the tax, but many would agree with the following ideas.

First, the property tax is, according to some researchers, an excise tax on consumption of housing, as noted by Netzer (1971). In other words, although it is a tax on ownership of a particular kind of wealth (primarily real property), to the extent that it is levied on residential housing it has an effect similar to that of a sales tax on expenditures associated with home ownership. If the average property tax, expressed as a percentage of average expenditures for housing, is greater than the general sales tax rates, the result will be to discourage consumption of housing—that is, people will choose to live in smaller, less expensive houses. This is not necessarily bad. Americans are the best-housed people in the world, and it may not be necessary or desirable to encourage overall increases in housing consumption. There may be specific instances where high taxes discourage housing, primarily in city ghettos, but this is a result mostly of assessed values that are unreasonably high considering the returns on landlord investment. Proper assessment can correct these abuses.

Second, that property taxes are higher in some places than in others has an effect on the value of property. An interesting example occurred in Rochester, New York, in the mid-1970s. Several small "free" school districts existed there, the result of an agreement many years before that brought some valuable industrial property from these districts into the city, in exchange for which the city agreed to educate students of the small districts at no cost in perpetuity. As a result, free-district residents paid no school taxes. A house in a free school district would sell for about $10,000 more than its identical counterpart across the street in the city school district. The cost of borrowing the money needed to make this additional $10,000 investment was approximately equal to the school taxes paid by the owner of the house in the city. When the legislature abolished these districts by annexing them to others, the free-district homeowners suffered a loss of roughly $10,000 in the value of their homes. This is an example of what is called **capitalization theory**. The effect of the property tax is incorporated (capitalized) into the value of the house (Gurwitz, 1980).

This problem is not confined to such unusual situations, however. In most states there are **tax islands**—school districts with large concentrations of industrial or commercial property and few students. The burden of school expenses is low and the total assessed value of the property in the district high, resulting in a low tax rate. This encourages location of more industry, exacerbating the situation. Perhaps the most egregious example is Teterboro, New Jersey, with an assessed value in 1986 of $195 million and only one pupil. Businesses locating in these tax islands effectively escape most school property taxation, which is typically more than half of the total property tax bill.

It has been proposed by many that commercial and industrial property be taxed by the state for schools at a uniform rate, thus leaving only the residential tax base available for local discretion. Presumably this would have several desirable results. Businesses would not be able to escape taxation by locating in tax islands. Decisions on business location would be made on bases other than the avoidance of taxes. Furthermore, local taxes would be paid only by those who decide on rates: local voters.

In spite of its attractiveness, this proposal has not yet been adopted by any state. This is partly because of the political power of industries situated in tax islands. Also, the short-range problems attending the proposal seem to outweigh its long-range benefits. For one thing, the necessary statewide tax rate would in many cases be more than industry is currently paying in large cities. In other words, large cities, whatever their other problems, are to some extent tax islands with regard to schools. That industry could relocate in suburbs without incurring a tax penalty might hasten the exodus of industry and commerce from the city, decreasing employment opportunities and increasing urban decay.

Research Navigator.com

tax
exemption

A third effect of property taxes springs from the **exemption** of certain types of property, such as government buildings, streets, churches, hospitals, private schools, and other nonprofit agencies. Exemption seems desirable since there is no point in government taxing itself, and encouragement of religious and charitable institutions is considered important by most people. However, exemption can result in a serious problem for cities (especially state capitals) and school districts having large concentrations of these properties.

There are a number of other economic effects, but it is possible that to some extent they merely balance the effects of other taxes. Netzer (1966, p. 69) has noted, for example, that the federal income tax encourages consumption of housing because it allows deductions of property taxes and of interest paid on mortgages. Sales taxes are never applied to rents. Both of these taxes, then, tend to encourage spending on private housing, although property taxes may act as a deterrent to home buyers.

The social effects of the property tax are also important, although it is often difficult to differentiate these effects precisely. A combination of factors, among them lower taxes at the time suburban land was being developed, have contributed to the urban sprawl that has rendered the United States a nation of commuters. Resistance to property taxes has affected schools more than other arms of government; the long-range effects of possible poorer education for many children are yet to be felt.

Liberty. If the property tax is simply a user fee for the provision of local services, then households choose their location based on their preferences for local services. Under this scenario, individuals have the greatest amount of liberty. Even if this is not the case, individuals have a greater amount of liberty regarding the tax rate imposed at a local level than at the state or federal level. This is because there is a smaller population at the local level, so each individual has a greater say. And in general, individuals do not prefer the property tax. This mainly results because, as opposed to the income and sales tax, the property tax is highly visible. It is directly paid by the individual in large payments. This is in contrast to smaller amounts withheld from each paycheck or added to the sales price of a product. Additionally the collection of the property tax can be perceived as unfair. This has lead voters to seek relief from property taxation.

■ TAX LIMITATION

Property tax relief generally falls into five categories: property tax limitation, property tax relief such as circuit breakers and homestead exemptions, state aid to local governments, a state takeover of local responsibility, and a change in the rules of the local tax system (Duncombe & Yinger, 2001). This section examines the first category. In June 1978, California enacted Proposition 13. This state constitutional amendment was placed on the ballot through a voter initiative and overwhelmingly approved by two-thirds of California's voters. It specified total property taxes for all purposes were limited to 1% of a property's assessed value. The assessed value of a piece of property could not be increased more than 2% per year unless the property was sold; it could then be increased to reflect the selling price. No property tax could be levied above the 1% limit, and other taxes could be levied or increased only by a two-thirds vote of the people. The effect was to drastically limit the ability of the state of California and its political divisions to raise money through taxes. The state was forced to "bail out" local governments. In general, each government was given a budget that was 90% of the previous year's budget. Property tax proceeds were divided among local entities, and differences between property tax receipts (and other revenues) and their approved budget were subsidized by the state. The effect was the same as it would have been if the state had levied a 1% property tax and then provided full support for all local governments. California schools are now, in effect, fully state-supported; the effects of this are discussed in Chapter 8.[28] Here, the concern is with the effect of the tax limitation movement that Proposition 13 exemplifies.[29]

Tax or **expenditure limitations** have been adopted in 22 states. All but two adopted these limitations between 1976 and 1982 (Advisory Commission on Intergovernmental Relations, 1995, pp. 14–17). Additionally, 43 states have adopted limitations on the powers of local governments. For most of these states, these limitations include property tax rate limits.

There are other kinds of tax limitation. Indexation of the income tax, mentioned earlier, is a way of limiting tax elasticity in response to inflation. Elected officials who want to spend a greater share of the national (or state) income must vote for higher tax rates when indexation is in effect, instead of waiting for inflation to provide the boost.

There are positive and negative features of tax limitations. On the positive side, limitations stem governments' gradual tendency to absorb a larger share of personal income. That government takes a particular share of income is not, in itself, bad. The problem is merely to decide how much and which services to furnish privately and which publicly. Tax rates in rural communities are often low because many services furnished by government in a city (street cleaning, fire protection, garbage collection) are provided by individuals or volunteers in rural areas. However, services furnished by government are available whether or not an individual wants them. Decisions on what is to be furnished are made collectively. Those who dislike this complain of creeping socialism.

There is also serious concern, both in the United States and abroad, about the effect of high taxes and broad provision of governmental services on incentives for individuals to work. Western European nations generally have higher tax rates than the United States. These same nations, in the post-World War II period, have had substantially slower rates of economic growth and are routinely willing to tolerate far higher unemployment rates than are voters in the United States.

On the negative side, tax limitations are by their nature general and often ignore the special needs of certain governmental jurisdictions. In California, where a second-wave tax limitation statute limits the amount that school districts may spend, rapidly expanding districts experience only limited funds available for new facility construction.[30]

Alternatives to Taxation for Education

Research
Navigator.com

tuition

In states with strong tax limitation statutes, citizens have examined the possibility of supplementing financing for schools from sources other than taxation. There are modest possibilities.

One alternative is **tuition**. However, this is not possible for school-age children under the constitutions of most states. State constitutions usually specify all children of the state shall receive a "free" education. It is usually possible to charge tuition for adult courses, but these, generally small in number, are often eliminated under a stringent tax limitation statute. In some states, it may be possible to charge schoolchildren for textbooks (a common practice at the high school level a few generations ago), but current laws in most states prohibit this also.

It is possible in most states to charge for a limited number of specific services not considered part of the normal educational process, such as transportation to out-of-town football games and provision of certain after-school activities. Another tactic is to deed school grounds to the city for joint use by schools and the community, making the city responsible for maintenance. The city may not be suffering as much from a tax limitation statute as the school district because it has other sources of income.

A district with surplus buildings and property can rent space or lease land to others. Of course, it can also sell surplus property. Large school districts can perform functions for smaller surrounding districts for less than it would cost smaller districts themselves, but a fee for performing those functions would be a greater than marginal additional cost to the large district. Examples are the furnishing of computer, purchasing, and warehousing services. These services could also be furnished to private schools in the area, which would increase the efficiency of operation of the schools.

A possibility in some high-income districts is to form a private, nonprofit foundation. The foundation solicits contributions from parents of schoolchildren and community residents and then distributes the money to the school district. In the city of Piedmont, California (a high-income community completely surrounded by Oakland), such a foundation provides approximately 10% of the district's total annual operating revenues.[31] At the school level, parent teacher associations (PTAs), parent teacher organizations (PTOs), and booster clubs are able to raise voluntary contributions from parents. Another possibility, tried in a number of communities, is to persuade a business firm to "adopt" a school as a special project, furnishing money for needed items and encouraging its employees to volunteer services for the school.[32]

In states where the population is increasing rapidly, legislation may permit districts to tax housing starts. The state legislature permits local school boards to levy a fee on developers for each house built, with the receipts used to construct schools.

International Comparisons of Tax Systems

Research
Navigator.com

value-added
tax (VAT)

Most industrialized and developing countries also have an individual income, general sales, and property tax. The **value-added tax (VAT)** used in many European countries is simply a general sales tax collected by a different method. Instead of all businesses involved in the manufacture and distribution of a product being exempt from the tax except the retailer, each business in the chain pays a portion of the tax. A wholesaler, for example, buys products from a manufacturer and pays the manufacturer a VAT based on the stated percentage of the sales price (that percentage approximates 20% or more in many countries, significantly higher than U.S. sales taxes). The wholesaler sells products to retailers at a higher price, and collects from those retailers VAT at the same rate. The wholesaler must then remit to the government the difference between the taxes collected from retailers and the taxes paid manufacturers. Thus, wholesalers pay a net tax based only on the value they add to products by performing wholesaling functions. VAT is similarly collected from each link in the chain of production and distribution. The total collected is equal to what would have been collected from a retail sales tax at the same rate.

Table 7.6 demonstrates the variation across nations in reliance on different forms of taxation. While the United States generates less tax revenue as a percentage of GDP than the OECD average, it generates relatively more revenue from the property tax and personal income tax than the average OECD member nation. Although the United States draws less revenue from a general consumption tax (relative to GDP) than the average OECD country, expenditures on education are not adversely affected.

TABLE 7.6   International Comparisons of Tax Revenues and Expenditure on Educational Institutions as a Percent of GDP

	Personal Income	General Consumption	Property	Total Tax Revenue	Education Expenditure
Austria	10.4%	8.2%	0.6%	45.4%	3.7%
Australia	12.3	4.0	2.7	30.1	3.7
Belgium	14.5	7.2	1.5	45.8	3.4
Canada	13.0	5.1	3.5	35.1	3.3
Czech Republic	4.8	6.9	0.5	38.4	2.8
Denmark	26.3	9.7	1.7	49.8	4.1
Finland	14.1	8.5	1.1	46.1	3.5
France	8.0	7.5	3.1	45.0	4.0
Germany	10.0	6.7	0.8	36.8	2.9
Greece	5.4	8.6	1.8	36.9	2.7
Hungary	7.6	9.9	0.7	39.0	2.8
Iceland	14.5	10.1	2.6	36.5	4.6
Ireland	8.9	6.9	1.7	29.9	2.9
Italy	10.9	6.2	2.0	42.0	3.2
Japan	5.5	2.4	2.8	27.3	2.7
Korea	3.8	4.7	3.1	27.2	3.3
Luxembourg	7.2	6.1	3.9	40.7	–
Mexico	–	3.6	0.3	18.9	3.3
Netherlands	6.5	7.4	2.0	39.5	3.0
New Zealand	14.5	8.7	1.8	33.8	4.6
Norway	10.5	8.1	1.0	43.3	3.6

continued

continued

	Personal Income	General Consumption	Property	Total Tax Revenue	Education Expenditure
Poland	7.9	7.3	1.3	33.6	3.7
Portugal	6.0	8.1	1.0	33.5	4.1
Slovak Republic	3.5	7.4	0.5	32.3	2.7
Spain	6.9	6.0	2.2	35.2	3.1
Sweden	16.4	9.1	1.6	51.4	4.4
Switzerland	9.8	4.1	2.8	30.6	3.8
Turkey	7.7	8.1	0.9	36.5	2.4
United Kingdom	11.3	6.8	4.3	37.3	3.4
United States	**12.2**	**2.2**	**3.1**	**28.9**	**3.5**
OECD Average	10.0	6.9	1.9	36.9	3.4

The OECD average is unweighted. OECD classifications: the personal income tax is no. 1100; the general consumption tax is no. 5110; and the property tax is no. 4000. Property tax includes taxes on immovable property, inheritance and gift taxes, and taxes on financial and capital transactions. Total tax revenue includes social security. The taxation statistics are based on 2001; the education expenditure statistics are based on 2000. Expenditures on educational institutions are from public sources for primary, secondary, and post-secondary non-tertiary institutions.

Source: Swiss Federal Tax Administration, Division Tax Statistics and Documentation, *Tax Burden 2003: International Comparison*, Tables 13, 17, 18, and 20. Organisation for Economic Co-operation and Development, Directorate for Education, *Education at a Glance 2003*, Table B1.2.

⎘ CASE 3 REVISITED ─────────────

Trial Judge Complexities

Assume that Judge Manheim has decided that additional funds are necessary for schools in her state to be successful. Further assume that Judge Manheim places the state under court scrutiny while raising additional funds. As a lawyer for the state, what approach would you advocate to generate revenue while avoiding an undue burden on taxpayers and meeting the judge's expectations?

Summary

Taxation is the main method of revenue generation for public services, especially education. General taxation for education occurs because it is generally believed that a community as a whole benefits from a well-educated citizenry and workforce. There exist multiple dimensions of taxation, as well as separate theories of taxation. All taxation has one of four bases: wealth, income, consumption, or privilege. Taxes can be assessed proportionally, progressively or regressively. Each tax assessed has a different level of yield and a different elasticity, that is, a different rate of response to changes in the greater economy. Three main categories of tax are income, sales, and property. Each tax has its own strengths and weakness in generating revenue. Each tax can also be differentially assessed. Businesses sometimes pay taxes at different rates than residents or citizens. This is intended to bring vertical equity into the tax system by taxing different classes of producers at different levels. Proponents of flat or proportional taxes advocate horizontal equity, whereby everyone is taxed the same. All taxes can be reduced through the political process. Tax limitation is the term used when growth rate of taxes is held constant for citizens and consumers.

Discussion Questions

1. Taxation is complicated because taxes affect citizens repeatedly and differentially. Imagine that you are a small business owner who also owns a home and has children. Create for yourself an optimal basket of taxation that addresses levels and limitations of property, income, and sales taxation. How would this optimal basket be different for a single professional just out of college and living in a rented apartment?

2. Discuss the tax limitation movements represented by Proposition 13 and Proposition $2\frac{1}{2}$. What steps could leaders have taken to avoid such constraints by the citizenry?

3. Describe the benefits of a value added tax over a general sales tax. Which tax is most fair to consumers? Which would be more stable for school funding purposes?

4. For a simulation associated with this chapter, visit this text's companion website, www.ablongman.com/guthrie1e/. Through the simulation exercise, you will be able to observe the relative power of property versus income taxes in generating funds on a per-pupil basis. Although income taxation is not used to generate educational funds, the exercise is instructive.

Web Resources

National Tax Association: http://www.ntanet.org/

National Conference of State Legislatures Budget and Tax Center:
http://www.ncsl.org/programs/fiscal/index.htm

Notes

1. A sales tax commonly takes the form of an *ad valorem* tax, which is a tax on a percentage of the price of the good. Alternatively a *unit* tax is a fixed dollar amount per unit of the good. Many excise taxes are examples of a unit tax.

2. Forty states plus the District of Columbia had lotteries as of 2006. Total lottery revenues in 2002 were $39.3 billion. The tax (the total revenue minus the prizes minus the cost of administration) equaled 34% or $13 billion. In all of the states (except Delaware), the lottery proceeds constituted less than 5% of total state revenue. U.S. Bureau of the Census, Governments Division, *State Government Finances: 2002* (Washington, D.C.: Government Printing Office, 2004; Education Commission of the States, 2006). In 2004, Tennessee implemented a state lottery, and North Carolina enacted a lottery in 2005. Some states, including Georgia and Tennessee, use the lottery proceeds to fund specific education programs or provide higher education scholarships.

3. Revenue raised by license fees totaled $35 billion nationwide in 2002 or about 3.2% of total state revenues. (U.S. Bureau of the Census, 2002).

4. For the discussion of efficiency, a tax on consumption and its effects on the price and quantity of goods and services are described. Similar arguments can be made for a tax on income where the service is an individual's labor, the quantity is the amount of labor supplied, and the price is the wage. Analogous arguments can be made for taxes on the other bases as well. Students new to economics will notice that the demand and supply curves in these examples do not curve. This is for the sake of simplicity.

5. This is equivalent to a constant marginal cost for all quantities. This is done for ease of exposition to understand the basic principles that can be seen by focusing on the consumers' side of the market. Similar arguments apply to the producers' side.

6. This is also referred to as the statutory or legal incidence.

7. Table 4–4. The most progressive assumption is Pechman's Variant 1c; the most regressive is his Variant 3b.

8. In 1985 the federal income tax began indexing for inflation. Prior to 1985, expanding nominal incomes caused by inflation resulted in increases in government tax income without increases in the tax rates.

9. For 1970, the Advisory Commission on Intergovernmental Relations listed 18 states with tax structures of low elasticity (0.80 to 0.99) and 23 states with medium elasticity (1.00 to 1.19). Only 9 states had tax structures with high elasticity (above 1.20). The lowest was Ohio, with an elasticity of 0.80; the highest was Alaska, at 1.47, followed by Wisconsin, at 1.41 (1977).

10. In 2004, Alaska, Florida, Nevada, South Dakota, Texas, Washington, and Wyoming had no individual income tax. New Hampshire and Tennessee had limited income taxes (Federation of Tax Administrators, 2004).

11. For higher education, which is financed from the states' general revenues, state income and sales taxes are most relevant.

12. This amount is the standard deduction for an individual filing their 2004 income tax return as a single person under age 65 who is not blind.

13. Note that the effective rate is obtained by dividing total tax by comprehensive household income, and is thus less than the marginal rate.

14. Authors' calculations based on data from U.S. Bureau of the Census, *Statistical Abstract of the United States: 2003*, p. 445, table 668; p. 325, table 481; and p. 284, table 440.

15. As of 1998, 13 states explicitly index their income tax in some form. Other states implicitly index their income tax by relating their rates to the federal tax structure. (Government of the District of Columbia, 2002.)

16. The difference between a credit and a deduction for the income tax is that deductions reduce your adjusted gross income (which is the value that the amount of tax that you owe is derived from), while credits reduce the amount of tax that you owe. In general, a credit reduces your tax bill by more than a deduction.

17. Policymakers neglected to pin the AMT threshold to inflation, thereby causing more and more taxpayers to fall under AMT.

18. Only Alaska, Delaware, Montana, New Hampshire, and Oregon did not have a general sales tax as of January 2004; however, Alaskan cities and boroughs were able to levy local sales taxes. (Federation of Tax Administrators, 2004).

19. The sales tax is found to be a regressive tax when the amount of tax paid is compared to annual incomes and when it is assumed that the incidence of the sales tax falls com-

pletely on the customer. Alternatively, when the amount of tax paid is compared to lifetime (permanent) incomes, the sales tax is found to be progressive (Metcalf, 1993).

20. Both states have a sales tax rate of 6% and no additional local tax as of January 2004 (Federation of Tax Administrators, 2004).

21. The local property tax is largest source of local revenue for public education in 40 states (U.S. Bureau of the Census, 2002).

22. The term *real* comes from *royal*, for all land originally belonged to the king in England, whence many of our legal terms come.

23. As of 1991, nine states did not tax personal property (U.S. Bureau of the Census, 1994.)

24. Forty-three states taxed business inventories and/or other commercial and industrial property as of 1981 (Advisory Commission on Intergovernmental Relations, 1984). By 1991, business inventories were exempt in 32 states, while commercial and industrial property was taxable in 41 states (U.S. Bureau of the Census, 1994).

25. The 24 states are listed in Advisory Commission on Intergovernmental Relations (1992), table 43.

26. A summary of the controversy is contained in Pechman and Okner (1974). Book-length presentations are Netzer (1966) and Aaron (1975). Netzer's book presents the regressive (traditional) view; Aaron's the progressive (new). The third view, that the local property tax is a benefit tax (simply a user charge for individuals who choose to locate within a jurisdiction because of capitalization) with no effect on the income distribution, is described in Hamilton (1976). These views are brought together in Zodrow (2001). The discussion in this section regarding incidence focuses on the first two views.

27. Calculated from data in U.S. Bureau of the Census, *State and Local Government Finances by Level of Government and by State: 2001–02.*

28. Interestingly, after a decade of Proposition 13's effects, a few school districts in California had experienced such high turnover of expensive properties that their property tax revenues enabled them to support their schools without the state subsidy, even though their property tax rate did not exceed the constitutional limit of 1%.

29. William Fischel, a Dartmouth economist, has argued that the court's decision in *Serrano v. Priest* established a voter mindset that, eventually, triggered Proposition 13. In effect, he contents that Proposition 13's tax limiting effects were a backlash from *Serrano.*

30. This second wave resulted from the 1979 Gann Initiative, which limits government spending to an amount determined by changes in population and personal income.

31. The LEFs, or local education foundations, sometimes leverage resources for policy change.

32. Over 2,000 nonprofit organizations raised $238 million for California public schools in 2001. These contributions tend to be concentrated in small, wealthy schools, but do not have an adverse effect on the distribution of school inputs across schools. These contributions were used to purchase computers, hire teacher's aides, and create smaller classes (Brunner & Imazeki, 2003).

CHAPTER EIGHT

Distributing State Education Funds

■ INTRODUCTION

This chapter concentrates on state revenue distribution. It assumes knowledge regarding revenue generation, covered in Chapter 7, and focuses on the policy mechanisms by which states allocate educational funds to districts, and the implications of those methods.

LEARNING OBJECTIVES

By the end of this chapter, you should be able to:

- Describe historical methods for allocating state funds to school districts, as well as any shortcomings of these methods.
- Describe current policies for distributing state educational funds to districts, as well as each approach's strengths and weaknesses.
- Manipulate data in a simulated exercise to determine effective ways to distribute educational funds.

When financing public schools, states are concerned with equity, adequate provision, and efficiency of education. They are also concerned with liberty or choice. Modern education finance has also begun to ask important questions about adequacy, including the levels to which students should be expected to perform. The emphasis on these values has shifted over time. However, there has been more formal attention in education finance paid to equity, the dimension with which this chapter begins.

■ EQUITY

The goal of school finance that is labeled **equity** is more commonly expressed as **equality of educational opportunity**. This expression recognizes that it is not reasonable to expect, and perhaps not possible, to educate all students to the same level. They and their parents have different preferences and students themselves have different innate abilities.

There are many possible definitions of equal educational opportunity, but in practice the concept has been defined most often as assuring equal dollars per student or assuring sufficient resources to provide comparable programs for students when their different individual needs and costs of providing them have been taken into account. The first goal, identical resources—**horizontal equity**—for each student, is technically easy to construct. It may not be politically easy to achieve.

Accomplishing the second goal, ensuring "adequate" resources tailored to the needs of each student—**vertical equity**—is difficult to achieve both conceptually and politically. To meet this goal, one must take into account three separate kinds of inequalities among school districts—differences in **wealth**, in student **educational need**, and in **educational costs**. Separate remedies are appropriate for each, and the three must be combined in constructing a school finance program that is truly equitable. Each will be discussed in turn.

Wealth Equalization

As shown in Chapter 7, the United States relies heavily on property taxes to support public schools. Although this is equitable among local taxpayers (ownership of property, at one time, was an accurate measure of ability to pay taxes), it is inequitable among communities. A property-rich community with a lower tax rate can finance a better education than could a property-poor community with a higher tax rate.

The situation is illustrated in Figure 8.1. The horizontal axis of the chart represents community wealth expressed in dollars of property value per pupil. The vertical axis represents dollars of expenditure per student. The numbers on this scale are purely arbitrary, used to illustrate the concept.

Assume that communities of the state differ in wealth per pupil, but that they all decide to make an equal sacrifice in providing education, by levying a property tax at a rate of 15 mills.[1] There is no other revenue available to schools besides receipts from this tax.

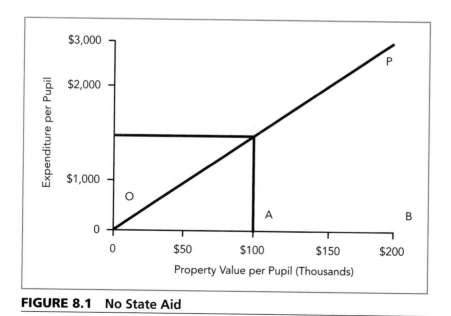

FIGURE 8.1   No State Aid

The line OP extending diagonally upward from the origin represents receipts from this tax for districts of different wealth. For example, at a tax rate of 15 mills, district A with $100,000 of property value per pupil will raise $1,500 per pupil (15 mills = $0.015 per dollar of property value; $100,000 × .015 = $1,500). District B, with property value of $200,000 per pupil, will raise $3,000 per pupil at the same tax rate. In other words, the amount raised is directly related to community wealth, and when there are variations in wealth, districts that levy the same tax rate raise widely differing sums per pupil.

Several points are of note here. One is that the range in value of property per pupil among districts within a state is usually much wider than illustrated in this figure. It might range from approximately $10,000 per pupil to over $500,000 per pupil. Thus, the range in amounts raised per pupil by the property tax is great. At a tax rate of 15 mills, the $10,000 district raises $150 per pupil and the $500,000 district raises $7,500 per pupil. On the other hand, the range can be deceptive. The vast majority of districts in the state might typically have property values per pupil ranging from, say, $50,000 to $200,000. Even so, this means a range of 4 to 1 in ability to raise money through taxes. (See Chapter 12 for additional information about such disparities.)

The concept of tax rate representing equal sacrifice is abstract. If houses are worth $100,000 on average in district A, and $200,000 in district B, a tax rate of 15 mills will mean that householders in district A will pay $1,500 in school taxes and those in district B will pay $3,000. Presumably, differences in home values represent differences in homeowners' wealth, and in their ability to pay taxes, although it is not that straightforward. Homeowners in district B do pay more money in taxes, although their tax rate and presumably their sacrifice is the same.

These are averages. In district A there may be two homeowners, each with two children in school, one of whom owns a home with a value of $40,000 and the other with a home valued at $100,000. The first pays $600 in taxes at a 15 mill tax rate; the second pays $1,500, yet the children of both receive the same education. And, of course, the homeowner who has no children also pays taxes, even though he receives no direct benefit from the schools. The principle involved here might be expressed as "from each according to his ability; to each according to his needs" (Marx, 1848).[2]

Finally, others besides homeowners pay taxes. Commercial and industrial enterprises also pay, usually at the same rate. This means that our two communities, A and B, (with property values of $100,000 and $200,000 per pupil) might actually have houses of equal value. The difference might result from a substantial industrial base in the second town. In that case, homeowners in both towns would pay the same amount in taxes but the school district in the second town would have twice as much to spend per pupil. This would seem to be particularly egregious, although it could be argued that the presence of industries in a town makes it a less desirable place to live.

There are three implicit philosophies behind the variety of wealth equalization strategies used by states. That they are seldom made explicit has rendered discussion of their pros and cons less clear than it should be.

The first of these philosophies might be called the **minimum provision philosophy**. Its proponents assert that there is an interest by the state as a whole in seeing that every child is provided with at least a minimum of education. This could be thought of, perhaps, as the amount necessary to make young people employable and to make them capable of intelligently making choices in a democracy. This minimum education should be guaranteed by the state, through some mechanism, to all students, regardless of the school district in which they live. Any additional education is thought of as a benefit to the individual student, or to the community. This additional level of education may be provided as a local luxury by the community, to the extent it sees fit, unsubsidized by the state.

The second philosophy might be called the **equal access philosophy**. Its advocates contend that there is an interest on the part of the state in ensuring that all school districts have equal access to money for education, but that each community should have a right to decide the amount of education to provide. Whereas the first philosophy emphasizes equality of provision, this philosophy puts its emphasis on equality of access to funds.

The third philosophy is more comprehensive, and might be called the **equal total provision philosophy**. Its supporters claim that all public education must be provided to all students in the state on an equal basis, regardless of geography or a community's ability to pay. A question within this camp concerns whether the provision of education is measured traditionally, by fiscal inputs, or by academic or social outcomes.

Minimum Provision Programs

Flat Grant Program. When states began to appropriate money to local communities to assist with schooling costs, intergovernmental grants took the form of equal amounts of money to each community, regardless of number of children or ability to raise money locally. Subsequently, funds were distributed on the basis of equal dollars per pupil to each district. At the turn of the 20th century, 38 states distributed so-called flat grants using a school census as a basis for apportionment. Other states used enrollment or average daily attendance (Cubberley, 1906, p. 100). Since the school census basis (a count of all school-age children in a district) provided districts with state money whether or not children attended school, it provided no incentive for districts to retain children in school.

Ellwood P. Cubberley, in 1906, was the first to write persuasively of the problems of school finance. He was concerned with the manner in which flat grant formulas favored cities, where school districts could afford to operate schools longer, and where larger class sizes were possible. School costs were higher in rural areas, where it was frequently necessary to employ a teacher to instruct ten or fewer children. Cubberley's solution was to allocate to each district an amount for each teacher employed. This, of course, still did not equalize wealth. Cubberley's plan can best be described as another variety of flat grant, with the teacher as the unit of distribution, instead of the student. Today, no state depends primarily on flat grants as a means of financing its share of educational cost. The last state to rely on such a method, Connecticut, adopted an equalizing plan in 1975. Equalizing plans will be discussed below.

Figure 8.2 illustrates the operation of a flat grant program. The graphic is similar to Figure 8.1. The only difference is that the state provides a flat grant of $1,000 per pupil. A horizontal line at $1,000 shows this. Each district receives this much regardless of its wealth or the rate at which it decides to tax. Now assume that each district decides, nevertheless, to levy a tax at a rate of 15 mills. The result is the total amount of money available per student shown by the sloping line. District A now has $2,500 per pupil to spend; district B has $4,000. The amount district B has is shown by the vertical line BOP to consist of the portion BO, which is the $1,000 flat grant, and the portion OP, which is the $3,000 raised by taxes. The absolute difference in expenditures is exactly the same as before: $1,500 per student. However, the ratio of expenditures has lessened. Without the flat grant, district B spends twice as much as district A. With the flat grant, it spends 60% more ($4,000/$1,500 = 1.60).

The flat grant approach adheres to the first philosophy in assuming that a specific minimum of schooling should be guaranteed to every citizen. It assumes further that the

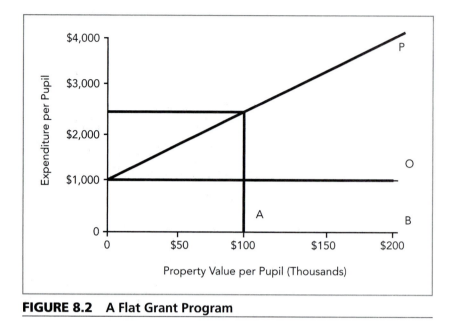

FIGURE 8.2   A Flat Grant Program

state, in its wisdom, can determine the costs of this minimum education and will allocate that dollar amount as a flat grant. Schooling in excess of this minimum is held to benefit only the individual recipient or the community in which he or she resides. It is therefore a local luxury to be indulged in as each community sees fit, but not to be subsidized by the state. Under this philosophy, the flat grant is a satisfactory wealth equalizer. It does not equalize for differences in need or cost, but that is a different matter, to be discussed later. Since the amount of the flat grant is presumed to be sufficient to cover the education level the state believes to be minimally necessary, and, furthermore, since it is provided to all students equally and is raised by taxes levied at a uniform rate on all residents of the state, there is nothing inherently unequal about it.

Foundation Program. One practical problem with flat grants is that states seldom have sufficient revenue to provide an adequate amount per student. For example, Connecticut, in the last year in which it used the flat grant (1975), provided $235 per student (plus some categorical aids); average expenditure per student in Connecticut at the time was $1,507 (Harris, 1975). The reason states typically cannot find the necessary money is that they have allocated use of the property tax exclusively to local communities. It is rare to find a statewide property tax. George D. Strayer and Robert M. Haig described a solution to this problem in 1923. In a report to the Educational Finance Inquiry Commission, based on a study of New York State, they proposed a system that has the effect of capturing a portion of the local property tax for state purposes, without that being openly evident. Their proposal has since become known as the **foundation program**, or the Strayer-Haig plan. Just as with a flat grant, the state specifies a dollar amount per student to which each school district is entitled. Presumptively, this is the amount of money per pupil necessary to guarantee a minimally adequate education. At the time of the foundation plan's invention or conception, there were few systematic efforts to ensure that the dollar amount prescribed was in fact sufficient to provide a foundational level of schooling. More

Research
Navigator.com
foundation
program

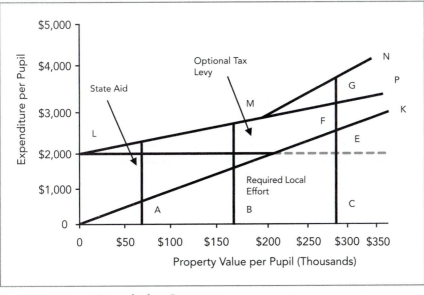

FIGURE 8.3   A Foundation Program

often than not, the foundation dollar amount was a political product. Knowing what it was willing to tax or what level of revenue was available, state legislatures would first establish the revenue pool and then, through division, determine the per-pupil amount of the foundation. More will be said regarding this situation when the topic of adequacy is raised in Chapter 9.

The state requires each district to levy a property tax at a fixed rate (called required local effort) and provides only the difference between the amount raised by that tax and the guaranteed expenditure level. Thus, a property-poor district will generate little with the tax at the specified rate, and the state will provide generously. A district richer in property will generate almost as much as the dollar guarantee and will receive little equalization aid from the state. A very rich district will generate more than the guarantee and will receive no subsidy from the state.

If the state requires each district to levy a property tax at a specified rate in order to receive state money, and counts proceeds of that local tax as part of the guarantee, the required property tax is, in effect, a state tax. If the required local tax rate is relatively high, a substantial amount of money will be raised. This, combined with state money, enables the legislature to establish a guarantee level sufficient for what is assumed to be a minimal education. Some states do not require the district to actually levy the tax at the specified rate, calling it instead a computational tax. It is then a device used only in determining the dollar amount of state aid to a district. A few property-poor districts may then levy a lower tax than this, raising less money per child than the guarantee and subverting the intent of the foundation concept.

Foundation program operation is illustrated in Figure 8.3. The horizontal line LE depicts the dollar amount of the foundation guarantee, supposedly representing the cost of a minimal program. The section labeled Required Local Effort is the amount raised by the local property tax at a required rate of 10 mills. The section labeled State Aid is supplied by the state, at a foundation level of $2,000. For district A, the required local effort (RLE) raises little money, and the state contribution is high. District B raises most of the guarantee locally, and district C raises more than the guarantee and receives nothing from the state. The solid sloping line at the top is the total amount that would be raised if all districts chose to levy an optional local tax at the rate of 5 mills, in addition to the required tax. District B can raise more than district A, and district C can raise more than district B. The line becomes steeper at point M because districts beyond that point already raise more than the guarantee by using only the required rate, thus making the total amount they collect that much higher. That is, the slope of the line OK is 10 mills, the slope of the line LM is 5 mills, and the slope of the line MN is the sum of those, or 15 mills.

It may be argued that it is unfair that some districts, because they happen to be rich in property, have more money to spend from levying the required tax rates than do property-poor districts. If the required tax is indeed a state tax, then the amounts raised above the guarantee should be returned to the state to be used elsewhere. This concept is called **recapture**, and its effect is shown by the dashed line in Figure 8.3. District C would raise, at the required rate, the amount shown by the line CF. It would return to the state the amount EF, leaving it exactly as much as every other district. Because of this, if it levied an additional optional tax at the same rate as the other districts, it would raise the amount EG. With recapture on the 10 mills of RLE, the line LMGP shows the amount generated by districts at a 15 mill tax rate.

The underlying philosophy of the foundation plan is the same as that of the flat grant: the state should provide for an adequate minimum educational program, defined as a specified number of dollars per student, and districts may raise money above that guarantee if they wish, as a local luxury, without help from the state.

A state education financing system such as this, including recapture, would provide complete wealth equalization if the underlying philosophy were accepted. States, however, have been unwilling to employ the recapture concept. To do so is to admit publicly that the required property tax is a state tax rather than a mechanism open to local option. In addition, the amount of taxes exported from a local district is highly visible. Recapture has been attempted in only a few states, and repealed in some of those. For example, in 2004, in the trial court decision in *West Orange Cove Independent School District v. Nelson*, Texas's statewide recapture and redistribution plan was declared a statewide property tax (prohibited constitutionally in Texas) and voided.

An alternative, of course, would be to simply levy a statewide property tax at the RLE rate, and use proceeds to finance a flat grant system. Looked at this way, one can see that the flat grant is simply a special case of the foundation program, in which the required local tax rate is zero.

As with the flat grant (and indeed with all school finance schemes), there are practical problems with the foundation plan. The plan assumes that the foundation amount is the amount necessary for a minimally adequate education, although there is no way of determining this with accuracy. Because of the additional money made available through required local effort, at least this guarantee may be set higher than it would be with the flat grant.

Another problem is the minimum grant that usually accompanies a foundation program. The reason for this grant is that it is not only unpopular to recapture excess tax money generated by districts; it is even unpopular to grant them nothing. As a result, each district receives at least a minimum dollar amount of state aid per pupil regardless of its wealth. Since this minimum aid flows only to the wealthy districts, it is obviously disequalizing.

Research
Navigator.com

recapture

Equal Access Programs

Percentage Equalizing. Flat grants and foundation plans have a similar philosophical underpinning: the state has an interest in seeing that each student receives a minimum education, and it undertakes to guarantee this on an equal basis. Percentage equalizing has a different philosophy. Essentially, it defines equity as equal access to money for education, and it also holds that the amount of education to be purchased by a community should be determined by that community.

With percentage equalizing, each district determines the size of its own budget, and the state pays a share of that budget determined by the district's aid ratio. The aid ratio is defined by means of a formula usually written in the form

$$AidRatio = 1 - f(y_i \div \bar{y}) \tag{1}$$

where

y_i is the assessed valuation per pupil of the district,
$\bar{y}$ is assessed valuation per student of the state as a whole, and
f is a scaling factor that is usually set somewhere between 0 and 1.

For example, if property value per pupil of the district were $20,000 and that of the state $80,000, and the scaling factor were 0.5, the aid ratio for the district would be

$$1 - .5 \times (20,000 \div 80,000) = .875 \tag{2}$$

This means the state would provide 87.5% of the budget of the district, with the district expected to raise the remaining 12.5% from local taxes. If the district instead had an assessed valuation of $80,000 per pupil (the state average), the aid ratio would have been 0.5, and the state would have provided half of the district's budget. It is easy to see that with this particular scaling factor, when a district's assessed valuation becomes twice that of the state, the aid ratio becomes zero. Above that point it becomes negative, the implication being that the district should instead send some tax money to the state. This is recapture, as discussed in connection with foundation plans, and it has proved no more popular in percentage equalizing states than in foundation states.

Just as the flat grant is a special case of the foundation plan, the foundation plan can be thought of as a special case of the percentage equalizing plan in which the budget to be participated in by the state is set at a particular figure instead of being allowed to fluctuate.

Adoption of percentage equalizing was first urged by Harlan Updegraff and Leroy A. King in 1922, about the same time Strayer and Haig were recommending the foundation plan (Updegraff & King, 1922). However, Charles S. Benson popularized it in 1961, and most of the eight states that enacted it did so shortly thereafter (Benson, 1961). It is interesting that the Strayer-Haig plan became part of the school finance plan of the majority of states, whereas percentage equalizing was never widely adopted. However, a plan with a new name but an identical purpose—power equalizing—evolved in 1970, and its concepts were adopted by many states.

Power Equalizing. Power equalization is a wealth equalization concept described by John E. Coons, William H. Clune, and Stephen D. Sugarman in their book *Private Wealth and Public Education* (1970). The authors concern themselves not with equalizing expenditures per pupil, but with equalizing ability of local districts to support schools. They argue

Research
Navigator.com
subsidiary

strongly for the virtues of **subsidiary**, by which they mean making decisions at the lowest appropriate level of government feasible. This implies that the local district should make decisions on school expenditures. (Indeed, the three authors argue that the individual family should even make these decisions, leading to a concept called family power equalizing.) Coons, Clune, and Sugarman put forth their Proposition 1, which states:

> *Public education expenditures should not be a function of wealth, other than the wealth of the state as a whole.*

This argument formed a substantial part of the legal reasoning exhibited in *Serrano* and other school finance equal protection cases.[3]

The philosophy behind power equalizing is the same as that behind percentage equalizing: the ability to raise money should be equalized, but the decision as to how much money to raise should be left to the local district. Under power equalizing, the state establishes a schedule of tax rates, with an amount per pupil guaranteed to a district for each level of tax. Such a schedule might look like this (the guarantee at other intermediate tax rates is obtained by interpolation):

Tax Rate (Mills)	Guaranteed Revenue Per Pupil
5	$1,000
10	$2,000
15	$3,000
20	$4,000

This schedule is the simplest power equalizing schedule, and amounts to a guarantee of a specified number of dollars per pupil per mill levied.

However, power equalizing is more general than percentage equalizing because it is not necessary to have the linear schedule implied by the guarantee of an amount per mill per student. For example, it would be possible to have a large guarantee per mill for the first 10 mills, and a much smaller guarantee for mills in excess of 10. This would tend to move districts toward a levy of 10 mills, where the high marginal increase in revenue per student would suddenly decrease. A few states (Michigan is an example) have done this, but most states enacting power equalizing have adopted the simple linear schedule.

The power equalizing ideas of Coons, Clune, and Sugarman were influential. By 1984, 18 states had adopted some form of power equalizing as an important feature of their school finance system (Education Commission of the States, 1984).

Guaranteed Tax Base. A third name for plans based on the equal access philosophy is the guaranteed tax base, or GTB. The state guarantees each district the same assessed valuation per student. The district calculates the tax rate necessary to raise its budget, using as an assessed value for the purposes of calculation the guaranteed valuation per pupil times the number of pupils. It then levies this calculated rate against the actual assessed valuation. The state compensates for differences between the amount actually raised and the amount that would be raised at the guaranteed valuation.

At this point it should be emphasized that percentage equalizing, power equalizing (with a linear schedule), and GTB plans are mathematically identical.[4] They are simply different ways of saying the same thing, emphasizing different facets of a general idea of equal access to funds. They are illustrated in Figure 8.4.

This graphic represents a percentage equalizing plan with a factor f of 0.5 and an average state assessed valuation of $100,000. Alternatively, it could represent a power

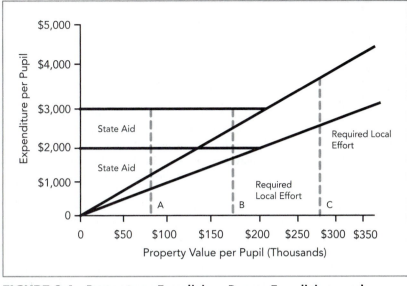

FIGURE 8.4   Percentage Equalizing, Power Equalizing, and Guaranteed Tax Base Plans

equalizing plan with a guarantee of $200 per pupil per mill of tax. Finally, it could represent a GTB plan with a guarantee of $200,000 assessed valuation per pupil. There is no difference in operation among the three plans. Figure 8.4 shows the results of two different tax rates. The solid lines and upright type show a tax rate of 10 mills; the dashed lines reflect a tax rate of 15 mills. The actual tax rate of a particular district, of course, could be any amount, but the principle is the same. Note that in each of the two instances, lines representing state aid and required local effort are graphically the same as those previously provided in Figure 8.3 for the foundation plan. District A receives $2,000 per pupil at a 10 mill tax rate, and $3,000 per pupil at a 15 mill rate. At the 10 mill rate, it provides $750 from local taxes and the state provides $1,250. At the 15 mill rate, the district raises $1,125 and the state provides $1,875. District B provides much more from its own taxes, and the state aid is much less, but it receives the same total amount per pupil at each tax rate as does district A. District C raises more money from its own taxes than is guaranteed by the state, and receives no state aid.

Like previously described state financing plans, these plans have suffered from practical problems. One is that since the emphasis is on a school district deciding the size of its own budget, there should be no restriction on the size of this budget. However, to guarantee that the state will share in any budget, no matter how large, is a frightening prospect for lawmakers and state officials, who fear wholesale raids on the state treasury. Consequently, the state usually limits the expenditure per student that will be equalized by the state. As long as this limit is substantially above the average expenditure, there is little cause for concern. Frequently it is set much lower. Then most districts simply are guaranteed the maximum state guarantee per student. This is the equivalent of a foundation plan with a guarantee at that level and a required local tax rate equal to the tax rate associated with that guarantee under the plan in use.

A second problem with equal access plans, one that they share with foundation plans, is that some districts might receive no equalization money at all (or, worse, be forced to contribute to the state instead). This has proven politically unpalatable, and the remedy has been to see that all districts receive some state aid, either by specifying a minimum amount per pupil to which each district will be entitled, or by specifying a minimum aid ratio.

Equal Total Provision Philosophy: Full State Funding

Henry C. Morrison first espoused the third philosophical position on equalization in 1930 (Morrison, 1930). It was brought forward again in 1967 by Arthur C. Wise as a legal position from which to argue for increased wealth equalization within a state (Wise, 1976). Charles Benson recommended it in a widely publicized revision of education finance for the state of New York (New York State Commission on the Quality, Cost, and Financing of Elementary and Secondary Education, 1973).

According to this position, education is a state responsibility and must be made available to all the state's children on an equal basis. There would be no geographical variation in school expenditure. It does not, however, preclude adjustments for differing educational needs or differences in the cost of producing education of equivalent quality. It does mean that, other things being equal, students will be recipients of equal monetary provision. The only means by which this can be accomplished operationally is for the state to mandate the expenditure level, and equity demands that the expenditures be supported by statewide taxation. Therefore, this method of financing the schools has become known as full state funding, or full state assumption.

Full state funding does not necessarily imply state operation of the schools, but merely a state guarantee of equal amounts of money per pupil to each district. However, it has been clear in states that have *de facto* or *de jure* full state funding that the result is substantially greater state control.

Only one state—Hawaii—has *de jure* full state funding. Education has been operated by the state since statehood, and there are no local districts. However, other states have approached full state funding as a *de facto* position, even though their school finance system is nominally quite different. New Mexico and Florida have foundation plans with low required local effort. Almost all of the districts in the state generate less than the state guarantee through the required local effort, and thus receive state equalization aid. Both states have rigid restrictions on optional extra millage. The result is a system in which all of the schools in the state are funded on the same basis, as if there were a full state funding scheme in effect.

California is an interesting case, which will be discussed in more detail later. As noted in Chapter 7, California's Proposition 13, passed in 1978, limits property taxes to 1% of property value for all purposes. With few exceptions, each school district's share of these taxes is less than is necessary to operate the district, and the state makes up the difference. There is little possibility of an optional local levy. However, the state does not guarantee districts the same amount of money per student. Rather, guaranteed revenue per student for each district is based on what a district actually spent in 1977–1978, adjusted for inflation. The effect is full state assumption without equalization (although, as will be shown later, there have been significant advances toward equalization in California).

An interesting way of distributing money in a full state assumption scheme has been suggested by Thomas Parish and Jay Chambers (1984). This is a precursor to "adequacy" solutions. They developed a resource cost model, which separates education into homogeneous programs. For each program, experts determine required inputs: teachers, aides, supplies, and so forth. For each district, a cost is developed for each kind of input. The state then provides the districts with the amount of money necessary to buy inputs for the programs required for its students. This is, then, a method for providing equitably for educational provision within a system of full state funding, taking into account differences in needs and costs.

Management Analysis and Planning Inc. (MAP) devised a similar system for Wyoming. Here, a variation was employed by which panels of education experts designed instructional programs intended to deliver state-specified objectives. Thereafter, funding is guaranteed by the state.[5] This system is described in greater detail in Chapter 13.

Full state assumption would appear to solve most of the problems previously discussed in connection with the other formulas. The marks of a true full state funding plan are that all educational funds are raised by statewide taxes (which could include property taxes) and that the money is spent equally on similarly situated students. Disallowing any local supplementary aid eliminates the tax and expenditure discrepancies that haunt practical application of the other plans. However, such a high degree of equity has a price. The legislature, having provided all education revenues from state sources, will want to see that the money is spent judiciously. It is almost inevitable that full state assumption will bring increased state control over education.

In Florida, for example, where *de facto* full state assumption was enacted in 1973, the state at the same time enacted a requirement that most of the funds generated by the presence of students in a school be spent on those students in that school. Since students in different programs (the mentally retarded, the physically handicapped, those pursuing career education, etc.) generated different amounts of state money, this requirement mandated a school-by-school, program-by-program accounting system, with auditing by state officials. The result is a dilution of local school officials' initiative.

Which Philosophy Is Best?

Read the In the News story about the manner in which exploding growth affects school districts in Pennsylvania. Educators there allege that rapid growth is not accounted for in the state's school finance distribution formula. They seek legislative action to remedy the situation. This illustares the point that every distribution formula has a "blind spot"—an area of interest to a few educators that is not adequately accounted for in the funding scheme. This should not come as a surprise. As previously shown, social and political factors have great influence on decisions about public matters, specifically education finance. Below is a consideration of the pros and cons of the various methods described above. These are theoretical considerations; each state will have peculiar legal, social, cultural, and economic contexts that may make one approach more palatable than others.

In the News

The Penn-Trafford School District has cited shortfalls in state subsidies in passing recent tax increases.

District officials have claimed Penn-Trafford is growing at a faster rate than the funding increases received from the state.

State Sen. Bob Regola, R-Hempfield

Township, has introduced legislation he hopes will help.

Under his "extraordinary growth supplement" proposal, an additional $12 million in state funding would be divided among 27 school districts in 14 counties.

"I became interested in this issue after the Penn-Trafford School District approached me with a concern they had with the state's education funding formula," Regola said. "Currently, school districts are funded by the state according to their previous year's enrollment. Therefore school districts that grow at a rapid rate may be left with funding shortfalls."

To receive the "extraordinary growth supplement," school districts must meet specific qualifications, including a growth in average daily student membership of more than 450 students, and a growth in average daily student membership of more than 10 percent between fiscal years 1994–95 and 2004–05.

Greater Latrobe joins Penn-Trafford on the list of 27 school districts—a list with many schools from eastern Pennsylvania.

"This is our response," said Tom Hower, Regola's policy director. "We've received tons of form letters from Penn-Trafford residents. There certainly is an inadequacy at the state level, and this is one way of helping."

Deborah Kolonay, Penn-Trafford superintendent, has spearheaded efforts to plead the district's case for the subsidies. Trips have been made to Harrisburg, and letters have been written to legislators.

"We are being heard," Kolonay said. "We have received numerous letters from our representatives. Yes, they do understand."

Obviously, she's pleased with Regola's proposal.

"I am totally delighted," Kolonay said. "He told us in December to be anticipating some legislation, something he would try to do to help school districts like Penn-Trafford and us as well."

Greater Latrobe has had a slight increase in enrollment in recent years, but expenses have risen, according to Assistant Superintendent Anne Simmons.

"We are spending additional funds on special education students and students attending charter schools," Simmons said.

Carl Baumeister, Greater Latrobe business manager, said the district spent $2.8 million last year on special education, and the price tag increases greatly each year.

Districts such as Greater Latrobe have to pay tuition for students enrolling in cyber charter schools. That's an expense that continues to grow. "It's taken off almost exponentially," Baumeister said.

Regola said while this legislation would help if approved, it's not the cure-all.

"Pennsylvania's public schools are funded through a mix of state and local revenues and thus local efforts to balance needs against available revenue must continue," Regola said. "This certainly doesn't preclude the need for effective local control on finances. In short, local officials must work to develop a tax structure to achieve the goals of their constituency."

From Paterra, P. (2006). "Fast-growing school systems eye quick financial relief." (Pittsburgh) *Tribune-Review*. February 21, 2006: http://pittsburghlive.com/x/tribune-review/trib/regional/s_425887.html.

The philosophy of equal total provision—that the state should furnish on an equal basis all public education in the state—is the most egalitarian. Not only is all funding equal, but taxation is also equal, since the source of funds is statewide taxes. The minimum provision philosophy equalizes expenditures and taxation only for that portion of expenditures deemed necessary for a minimum adequate program. Expenditures for other purposes are unequalized. The difference between minimal provision and equal total provision is actually one of degree. Full state funding does not equalize any educational services furnished outside the public schools, whether by private schools or by individual tutors. However, there is a great difference between equalizing all of the many things that the public schools offer and equalizing only a minimum program.

The equal access philosophy is quite different. Power equalizing, percentage equalizing, and the GTB make no attempt to equalize expenditures on education. They simply equalize access to those expenditures. One could think of the equalizing of expenditures as student equity, and the equalizing of access to funds as taxpayer equity. Full state funding does both, the foundation plan does both (but to a limited extent), and power equalizing is concerned only with taxpayer equity. The distinction is important. Most of the school finance equity lawsuits have raised the constitutional issue of education as a state function that must be furnished on an equal basis to all. It seems much easier to find a plan providing student equity that meets this criterion than one that provides only taxpayer equity.[6]

▮ NEED EQUALIZATION

The foregoing discussion of wealth equalization contains the "other things being equal" assumption—that all students are alike in their need for education. This is manifestly untrue. Many students have unusual learning problems that require costly special teaching methods. The mentally retarded, emotionally disturbed, blind, and deaf are only a few such categories. In addition, many normal children can benefit from a program that is more expensive. This is particularly true in the area of career or vocational education. Fortunately, these differences in needs can be incorporated into a wealth-equalizing scheme as part of a comprehensive state aid plan. The ways in which this is done can be categorized as entitlement, reimbursement, and organizational schemes.

Entitlement

These schemes entitle a school district to an amount of aid that is specified in advance, independent of the actual costs to the district of operating programs for students with special needs. (Of course, the amount is presumably related to the costs of such programs.) A number of approaches fall into this category, including:

Weighting Systems. Imagine a foundation plan that guarantees a given number of dollars per student. Implicit in such a plan is that all students should have the same basic amount spent on them. If one wishes to spend different amounts on students with special needs, a state can do this by counting each such person as more than one student. For example, educable mentally retarded students might be weighted 1.5 compared with the 1.0 weighting of so-called normal students. Weighting presumably represents the ratio of the cost of providing a basic special program to that of providing a basic normal program. Usually, the normal student in the middle elementary grades is weighted 1.0 and all other weights are related to this standard. The sum of all weighted students is obtained, and this weighted student count is used as the basis for calculating state aid. Simply by substituting weighted students for actual students, a state can use this method with any of the wealth equalizing plans that have been discussed. This means that practically, as well as conceptually, it is possible to separate need equalization from wealth equalization.

Research Navigator.com

entitlement

Weighting schemes assume that the cost of a special program bears a fixed cost relationship to the cost of a normal program. This is assumed to be true both within districts and among districts. The state compensates districts on this basis, but without otherwise dictating the content of programs.

If a weighting plan for need equalization is to be equitable, it is necessary to have an accurate determination of the program costs for special categories of students relative to the program costs for normal students. This constitutes a major difficulty in using weighting plans. Because there is not yet an agreed on technology for educating each category of student, it is difficult to agree on the extra cost involved. Even if it were possible to agree on the technology, local district cost accounting methods are undeveloped. However, research economists are beginning to approximate such costs with increasing accuracy by relying on an econometric technique known as "cost function analysis" (Duncombe & Yinger, 2001; Schwartz, Steifel, & Steifel, 2005). Even here, though, the above-mentioned caveat regarding accurate local level cost accounting as a base for such analyses still applies.

Another difficulty with pupil or program weights is that they need frequent revision in order to remain consistent with actual cost differences. But this is where circular reasoning enters the argument, for this year's weights will depend on the amount spent last year. However, the amount spent this year will depend on the money available, and therefore on the weights used.

If the specified weight allocates a state aid amount more than the per-pupil cost of a special program, school districts will tend to misclassify students into special programs, and then use the extra funds for other programs, including those for normal students. This happened in Florida, where several small rural districts placed the majority of their students into either mentally retarded or vocational programs. The remedy for such abuses is a state quota, which can be unfair if it prevents enrollment in special programs of students who actually need special assistance. Another remedy is state auditing of student placements.

Approximately 22 states use weighting schemes in their state aid programs. In Florida, there are 33 separate programs, with weights that vary widely. A few examples are as follows:

Program	Weight
Grades 1–3	1.234
Grades 4–9	1.00
Grades 9–12	1.116
Educable mentally retarded	2.30
Deaf	4.00
Hospital and homebound, part-time	10.00
Vocational education	1.17 to 4.26

Flat Grants for Special Programs. About 10 states fund one or more special programs through a flat grant of a specified number of dollars per pupil in the program. The implicit philosophy is that the excess cost of educating a child in such a program is that specified number of dollars in every district.

Individually Calculated Entitlements. The imprecision of weighting and flat grant schemes means that some districts receive more and others receive much less than they need for special programs. Computers have made it possible to calculate an entitlement for each program for each district in a state. For example, in California, such a system operates for special education. Each student who may be entitled to a special education program is examined and an individual education program (IEP) is established for him or her. The program, in other words, is tailored to the student. Special education and related services are provided by a local plan area, which may consist of a single district or a group of districts that have agreed to cooperate to provide the required full range of services. By summing the IEP requirements of all children in the local plan area, the district(s) can establish a need for personnel and other services. Entitlement for instructional personnel is based on the number required and the average costs of their salaries and benefits in the local plan area. To this is added an entitlement for support services (including administration, supplies, maintenance, and so on), based on a ratio of such costs to the costs of instructional personnel in the local plan area. The result is a total entitlement for special education. From this is subtracted any federal aid to which the local plan area is entitled. The remainder is provided by the state. (Remember that California is a state that has *de facto* full state assumption of educational costs.)

■ REIMBURSEMENT

Reimbursement schemes compensate districts for the actual costs of providing for special needs. Districts account for special program expenditures, deduct state-defined costs of educating normal students, and receive state reimbursement for all or a portion of the extra costs. Approximately 17 states have excess cost reimbursements for instructional programs.

A major advantage of this approach is that districts are reimbursed only for the actual excess cost of programs; this eliminates the previously mentioned misclassification incentive. Another advantage, particularly from the legislature's view, is that money is restricted to categories for which grants are provided. This necessitates state definition of types of reimbursable expenditures, a cost-accounting system, and a reliable state audit, all of which restrict district freedom. Another advantage of the excess cost system is that the amount granted is tailored to a district's expenditure pattern. This is better than the assumption, as in a weighting system, that costs in all districts constitute the same proportion of normal costs.

A disadvantage of the excess cost system, if the state pays all or most costs, is that there is little incentive for districts to operate an efficient program. This often forces the state to specify a maximum dollar limit on the amount of aid per student to be granted. This may be unfair to high-cost districts, while providing no brakes on the expenditures of a low-cost district. Another disadvantage is that districts are not reimbursed until expenditures have been made, reports submitted to the state, and expenditures audited. Often a district is hard-pressed to find money to start a new program because of this delay.

■ ORGANIZATION ARRANGEMENTS

A third manner of providing services for special students is to assign special program responsibility to an intermediate education district. The main advantage of the larger district is organizational. Because of economies of scale, intermediate districts can afford to provide programs for handicapped students that individual districts might find too costly because of the few students in the district with that handicap. A disadvantage is that it is not practical to use this approach for all special programs. Students must be transported from their usual schools, which inhibits mainstreaming. Also, additional transportation costs may outweigh the economies of scale gained by concentrating handicapped children in one place. Finally, local district authorities may fear loss of control over an important part of the education of their children.

▪ OVERVIEW

There is a place in a well-designed school finance system for each of these methods of need equalization. Weighting is heavily dependent on arbitrary cost factors, inviting misclassification of students or a failure to offer specific programs. It is probably best used where there is little or no possibility of either type of subversion—for example, when weights are used for various levels of education. That weights are arbitrary (e.g., high school students may be weighted 1.25) is not important from an equity standpoint (as it would be for special programs), because all students experience each level of schooling.

Certain special programs, such as those for the multiple handicapped or severely mentally retarded, are probably best handled by an intermediate education district, state schools, a consortium of school districts, or private contracting. These services usually require a large investment in tools and equipment, and such an arrangement can spread these costs over a large pupil population.

Districts should also be allowed to contract with intermediate education districts for special programs. Such services will then be offered by an intermediate district only if it can convince local officials that it can offer better services or operate at lower cost than they can. The state would offer aid through weighting or other entitlement methods to local districts for special students who are, for example, blind. The district would use this money either in operating its own program or in contracting with the intermediate district, whichever it found more effective or less expensive.

Most special needs should be handled through programs providing reimbursement for excess costs. Such programs offer little incentive to misclassify students into programs or not to offer the programs, as there is with weighting. Districts can spend different amounts to meet needs without being rewarded or penalized. The biggest problem is that the state must establish a maximum allowable reimbursement to prevent districts from operating needlessly expensive programs. An alternative is to reimburse only a percentage of the excess cost, which gives the district a stake in how much is spent.

Alternatively, these special needs can be handled through an individually calculated entitlement program. Such a system appears to provide reasonably adequate safeguards against improper classification of students, and there is an incentive toward efficiency in that the district does not receive more money if it spends more, or less money if it economizes.

Finally, there can well be special needs that the state will simply ignore in its financial scheme, or for which it will perhaps pay a small fixed amount per pupil, allowing districts to provide for them out of money to which they are entitled for regular students. This would be the case for experimental or inexpensive programs.

Cost Equalization

Equalization may be needed to balance differences among districts in the cost of providing educational services of similar quality and kind. There are several reasons for cost differences. They divide rather well into two categories: (1) differences in the amount and cost per unit of supplies and services that must be purchased by the school district, and (2) differences in the amounts districts must pay to attract and retain employees of comparable quality.

Supplies and services may differ in cost for various reasons. The school district in a mountain area may have to pay a large annual bill for snow clearance. The mountain district may also use more fuel for heating and find that its unit cost for fuel is higher. A sparsely settled rural area may be unable to avoid small classes and high busing costs. Land cost for school sites is much higher in cities, as is the cost of vandalism. In general, extra costs tend to be higher in rural and highly urbanized districts, and lower in suburban districts.[7]

Salaries constitute 70 to 80% of the average school district's budget. Thus differences in the costs of hiring and retaining employees of equivalent quality are even more important than differences in the cost of supplies. There may be differences in the cost of living among districts, resulting from variation in rents or housing prices, food, and so on. More important, however, are differences in the attractiveness of a school as a place to teach and a community as a place to live.

It is easier to recognize cost differences than it is to measure and subsequently compensate districts for them. All states compensate districts for costs of necessary bus transportation in some manner. This is because such costs vary so widely. Usually compensation is on a cost reimbursement basis. A district records the transportation cost of eligible students. Record keeping for such purposes is usually complicated. In fact, accounting for the transportation reimbursement—a small part of total state payments—is frequently more complicated than all the rest of the district's cost accounting combined. The state then reimburses the district for a portion of these transportation costs. In New York, state reimbursement is 90% of costs. There is clearly little incentive for New York districts to economize on transportation costs. In Florida, on the other hand, each district's transportation costs are estimated by means of a regression equation, with density of population used to predict a district's transportation expenditure. The district is paid this estimated cost. If it manages to transport students for less than the estimate, it may use the extra funds for other purposes. If it spends more than the estimate, it must make up the difference from its own sources. This approach encourages efficiency in operating transportation systems. Florida's is an entitlement approach, whereas New York uses a reimbursement system.

States also subsidize cost differences for necessary small schools—schools that must exist because transportation distances to larger schools would be too great. Students may be weighted, with those in the smallest schools given the highest weightings. These students are counted like those weighted for need differences. Alternatively, small-school students may be treated separately, with a formula specifically for them.

As previously noted, the major cost variation is in salaries necessary to attract teachers and other employees of equivalent quality. Some states have dealt with this challenge by using a state salary schedule, not for paying teachers individually but for placing the teachers of a district in order to determine the amount of state aid to be received. Teachers are each placed in the column and step of the schedule appropriate to training and experience, the total teacher salaries that would be paid if the teachers had been on the state salary schedule is determined, and this amount is used in making an adjustment to the amount of state aid to be received by the district. In effect, this compensates a district that has more teachers near the high end of the schedule for that fact, while not compensating it for paying higher salaries than the state schedule.

Whether this is an equalizing measure or not depends on whether one views placement of teachers on a salary schedule as something under district control. The general principle of cost equalization is that districts should be compensated for differences in cost that they cannot control, but not compensated for discretionary differences. If a district has declining enrollment, it cannot hire new teachers (except to replace some of those who retire or leave), and the teaching staff each year tends to move farther up the salary schedule. The district has little current control over this. On the other hand, if there is expanding enrollment, the district hires teachers, and it has a good deal of control over whether it hires experienced teachers or those near the beginning steps of the schedule. State aid confers greater help on districts that hire experienced teachers. Since wealthy districts are more able to hire expensive teachers in the first place, this kind of state aid may be anti-equalizing.

Florida adjusts a district's state aid entitlement by cost-of-living differences. Each district's foundation aid level is adjusted by a cost-of-living index. Districts with lower costs of living have lower foundation levels. A cost-of-living index is a poor indicator of actual cost differences in hiring employees of comparable quality, for differences in the attractiveness of the district as a place to work and live are also important to teachers. Nevertheless, it is generally considered to be a more effective way to compensate for differences in cost than the state salary schedule approach.

The most complicated attempt to adjust for differences in cost has been Jay Chambers' cost-of-education index (1998). This approach involves gathering information on all items resulting in cost differences among districts. Some of these items would be the result of conscious choices made by the district, such as the choice to have fewer pupils per classroom. Others would be outside the control of the district, such as amounts of snow that must be cleared. A schedule is prepared in which those items of cost not under the control of the district are shown at their actual cost to the district, and those under "district control" are shown at the state average cost. The total cost of operation of the district is computed on this basis. This would be the total cost if the district were in its current situation but made average decisions. State aid is based on this.

One of the principal problems with the Chambers approach is that many costs represent items that are not completely under district control. Although the district cannot control the amount of snow that falls, it can decide the extent and frequency of snow clearance. The major item, of course, is teacher salaries, and the extent to which the district controls this depends, among other things, on the rate at which it can hire new teachers. Some districts have little control over teacher costs; others have a great deal. Collective bargaining brings other problems. It is not clear how much control a district has over collectively bargained salary costs and this probably varies greatly from district to district.

A second problem with the Chambers approach is that it requires massive amounts of data from each district in the state. The procedure itself is sufficiently complicated that it is difficult to explain to legislators and laypeople.

◻ CASE 4 REVISITED ─────────────────────────

An Elected Official's Dilemma

Walter Romero has decided that schools need additional funds. He knows how to raise the revenue—he just does not know how to distribute it. Outline three ways to equitably distribute funds to address Walter's top education priorities.

Another area of frequent attempts at cost equalization is that of declining enrollment. Here, the problem is short-term. Typically, such declines result in one or two fewer students in each class; this makes consolidation of classes difficult. A district continues to use the same number of teachers and classrooms, resulting in an increase in per-student cost. Over time, a district can make reductions, remedying the short-term problem. In economists' terms, this is the result of marginal costs being substantially less than average costs. This works on the up side too, with a few additional students not increasing district costs very much, but state aid formulas have always given districts as much help for additional students as for existing ones. However, there are cries for help when enrollment declines.

Approximately half the states have tried to provide additional aid to districts suffering enrollment declines. One alternative is to permit a district to choose either the previous year's or the current year's enrollment as a basis for claiming state aid. Growing districts use the current year's enrollment figure; districts with decreasing enrollments use the previous year's figure. A variation allows districts to use either current enrollment or a moving average of the previous three, four, or five years. Either method provides temporary relief for a district faced with enrollment declines, but does not put off the day of reckoning indefinitely.

A different approach, used in a few states, is to offer a hold-harmless provision, which guarantees the district no less total state aid than it received the year before. If the district has declining enrollment, this could be thought of as the equivalent of counting "phantom students." If the hold-harmless provision disappears after a short time, the effect is similar to that of the plans just discussed. If it continues indefinitely, as it has in New York, it can result in districts being paid on the basis of enrollment many years before, even though current enrollment is less than that.

Adequate Provision and Cost Adjustments

Modern education finance concerns itself with this issue through a different set of mechanisms than historically has been the case. Indeed, adequacy is now a challenge of sufficient proportions to justify its own section in this book, Chapter 13. However, it was dealt with in past times chiefly through added programs. Here is a historical glimpse.

From 1950 to 1970, the major concern of state school finance officials was to provide resources necessary to meet rapidly increasing demands on schools. Not only were enrollments burgeoning, but also the public was demanding more services. Programs such as vocational education increased the average cost per student at the same time that the number of students was increasing rapidly. The result was that state governments were under persistent pressure for new money. There was also concern with efficiency and equality during this time, but those goals often had to be subordinated to a continuing need to finance expansion.

This post-World War II period of growth was accompanied by a labor shortage as well as a money shortage. Teachers were in short supply, and the economic system responded, as is typical, by increasing the price, thus encouraging more people to enter the profession. Teacher salaries increased faster than salaries of workers in general. Some saw this as an increase from grossly inadequate salaries to a decent living wage, while others believed the new salary levels were exorbitant.

Increased labor costs were added to other costs incurred from growing numbers of students and expanding program demands. Average cost per student increased tenfold, from $100 in 1940 to $1,000 in 1970; total elementary and secondary public education costs increased eighteenfold, from $2.26 billion to $40.27 billion during the same period.

Large increments of state monies were injected into education in the 1950s and 1960s, and this was generally matched or exceeded by increases in local revenues. Most of the state money and almost all of the local money were in the form of additional general aid—money that could be used for any district purpose (as opposed to categorical aid, which can be used only for specified purposes). From 1950 to 1970, expenditure restrictions were relaxed or eliminated, either by the legislature or by direct vote of the people. For example, many states had tax rate limitations, but local elections to permit school districts to tax above this limit regularly passed by large margins.

Post-World War II legislation increasing costs seldom increased equality. Although most states had equalization programs—and most were spending more on education than ever before—these higher disbursements did not lessen expenditure inequalities within states.

In addition to general aid, states provided categorical aid for a variety of special programs, such as education of mentally retarded and physically handicapped children. Several states even attempted to alleviate environmental handicaps such as poorly educated parents or poverty and ghetto living conditions. Other categorical aids went for construction of many badly needed new schools, particularly in suburbs in the fast-growing states. These suburbs frequently were unable to raise enough money locally, and state assistance became crucial.

During the late 1960s and the 1970s, there was considerably less emphasis on adequate provision. The strongly felt need to improve the U.S. educational system that arose with Sputnik in 1957 had spent itself as the United States achieved its goal in 1969 of putting a man on the moon. The concern was instead with equity—with seeing that all pupils had an equal chance to acquire an appropriate education. Even so, expenditures per pupil rose more rapidly than the economy grew.

Between 1965 and 1980, expenditures per pupil rose from $515 to $2,291—a 345% increase including inflation, and a 70% increase in constant dollars (U.S. Bureau of Census, 1985). During this same period, the national income per capita went up 42% in constant dollars. One reason for the rapid increase in expenditures per pupil was the rapid decline in the number of pupils during this decade and a half. Marginal cost in education is considerably less than average cost, because an additional student or two does not require an additional teacher. For this reason, a decline in pupils translated into an increase in cost per student. In addition, attempts to improve equity were usually accomplished by leveling up—increasing money for the low-spending districts while taking nothing away from the high-spending ones. Thus, a rapid increase in expenditures per pupil accompanied attempts to improve equity. However, it is not clear that the increase in expenditures per student resulted in a more adequate education. In many cases, teachers taught smaller classes but continued to use the same techniques.

With the early 1980s came an increasing concern with adequate provision. The realization that test scores had been declining for some time pervaded the national consciousness, increasing demands for school improvement. A series of reports in 1983 highlighted the problem and provided a rallying point.[8] The new push for more adequate schools did not manifest itself in the form of additional general aid for the schools. Instead, there were attempts to deal directly with the problems of improving schools, by increasing "time on task," lengthening the school day and the school year, improving the curriculum, providing special assistance to teachers, reducing class size in the early grades, and employing a wide variety of other tactics. These changes were claimed to cost money, and the money was usually provided in the form of categorical grants money that could be used only for specified purposes. In some cases, the new programs were mandated by the state, whereas in others, the categorical money was offered as an incentive for districts to institute specified new programs.

▪ OTHER GOALS OF DISTRIBUTION SYSTEMS: EFFICIENCY

Efficiency has long been a goal of those who finance education. It is expressed as a desire to obtain adequate education for as little money as possible. The goal is laudable, but difficult to attain. The problem is that there is little agreement on what education is to accomplish, how it is to be accomplished, and how accomplishments are to be measured. In the past, those concerned with school efficiency merely advocated imposing spending limits, theorizing that if educators had a restricted amount of money, they would use it more wisely. During the post-World War II period of rapid school expansion, the goal of efficiency was muted, but enrollment declines in the 1970s, coupled with a continued rapid rise in expenditures per student, prompted reinstitution of limits. In the 1980s, legislatures adopted a more active role by providing categorical money as an incentive for school improvement. Districts were often required to apply for the money, supplying detailed plans to the state education department for spending it.

📁 CASE 3 REVISITED ───────────────────────

Trial Judge Complexities

It seems as if Glenda Manheim, hearing a school finance case from the bench, will be asked to do more than to rule on the meaning of constitutional provisions. Both plaintiffs and defendants seem to want her to outline a better manner of funding schools. Were you to advise Judge Manheim, what are your preferred methods of distributing education funds? Defend your answer.

Political Pressures on Distribution Systems: Spending Limits

Spending limits have usually taken the form either of restricting amounts of money available to a district or of making money available in the form of categorical aid, which must be spent on programs considered desirable by the legislature rather than leaving expenditures to local discretion. Restrictions on amounts of money have taken the form of tax rate limits, annual budget votes, or expenditure or revenue limits.

Political Pressures on Distribution Systems: Tax Rate Limits

The most common form of restriction is the tax rate limit. Until recently, most states outside the Northeast (where budget votes are the norm) had such limits. The tax rate limit is a maximum rate that may be applied to a district's assessed valuation to raise money for school purposes.

These limits have numerous flaws. If a uniform limit is applied across a state (the usual situation), districts that have the same full valuation of property per pupil but different assessment ratios (see Chapter 7 for a discussion of the assessment process) will raise different amounts of money per pupil. These differences have led to state boards of equalization, which adjust local assessed values to a uniform assessment rate for school purposes.

Even if the tax rate limit is based on full valuation rather than assessed valuation, there are vast differences in the amount of money per pupil that can be raised by different districts levying the tax at the allowed limit. This is because there are great differences in the amount of property value per pupil among districts. Even though general state aid programs are designed to alleviate these differences, they are sometimes inadequate for this purpose. The result is that districts must levy taxes at a rate above the limit. States usually provide for districts to raise their tax rate limit by a vote of the people in the district. In addition, for certain special purposes they may provide for a school board to levy taxes above the tax rate limit without a vote of the people. Such *override* taxes are often used for special education, for free or subsidized meals for needy children, and for community services.

Political Pressures on Distribution Systems: Annual Budget Votes

Annual votes on the school district budgets have long been a custom in northeastern states. The school board proposes a budget, indicating total estimated expenditures, revenues expected from all sources other than local taxes, and (by subtraction) the amount to be raised from local taxes. Theoretically, this direct vote should be a useful mechanism for adjusting expenditures to voters' preferences. However, it sometimes does not work, partly by design of the school board. Even voters who want to inform themselves thoroughly before voting usually find it extremely difficult and thus may not be able to vote intelligently. The information furnished to the voters typically does not compare the coming year's proposed expenditures with the current year's actual expenditures, does not put expenditures in per-pupil terms, and does not adequately explain proposed changes.

Also, elections are sometimes delayed until autumn, which threatens voters with a delayed school opening if they do not pass the budget. New York law provides that a district that fails to pass a budget election can operate on an "austerity" budget. This budget is austere only in excluding auxiliary programs of particular interest to parents: interscholastic athletics, nonrequired transportation, and school lunches. On the other hand, whatever the district agrees to pay the teachers as a result of collective bargaining is automatically included in the budget, and taxes are raised to pay these salaries. Thus the budget is austere for the public but not necessarily for educators.

Political Pressures on Distribution Systems: Direct Revenue or Expenditure Limitations

Failure of tax rate limits or budget votes to provide meaningful limitations on school district expenditures has led some states to adopt more direct controls. Typically, the state limits the amount each district can spend per student. This is the most direct form of control and, if established uniformly on a statewide basis, would result in equal expenditures per pupil statewide. However, it is neither politically possible nor desirable to establish such uniform limits. Some districts have higher costs per student for providing the same amount of educational services, for reasons that are beyond their control. These include high costs for transporting pupils, for heating and snow removal, and for salaries of personnel in high-wage areas. Such districts would have insufficient money if the limit were uniform statewide.

The political justification for permitting disparity is as follows. Establishing a uniform limitation would either result in some districts being forced to reduce their expenditures drastically (if the limit were established only slightly above the median expenditure), or constitute no real limitation (if established near the level of the highest-spending district). As a result, when legislatures institute such limitations, they usually set each district's current rate of expenditures as its ceiling and provide for a yearly increase to allow for inflation. There may be a provision that allows low-spending districts a greater inflationary increase than high-spending districts, thus gradually squeezing the expenditures of the districts together. Such a provision is made for purposes of equity, however, rather than efficiency.

Political Pressures on Distribution Systems: Categorical Aid

The limits discussed above have represented a confession by the legislature that it does not know how to make the schools efficient, but that it hopes school professionals will find ways to do so if sufficiently motivated. It is unlikely that these limits will promote efficiency. The bureaucratic imperative is toward expenditure expansion, not cost containment. Faced with a shortage of funds, school professionals will often make decisions designed to encourage citizens to open their pockets (such as curtailing interscholastic athletics) rather than trying to find ways to operate more efficiently.

Recognizing revenue or expenditure limitation flaws, many legislatures have opted to decide which are the priority areas for spending money on education, and then to provide funds for these specific purposes. Much of the recent increase in school funds has been provided through this mechanism. Such categorical programs take away local discretion and substitute decision making at the state level. It is difficult to establish regulations at the state level that accommodate all the various local situations. Whether categorical aid, with its accompanying restrictions, contributes to efficiency is open to question, but at least it forces districts to concentrate more on areas considered high priority by the legislature.

Political Pressures on Distribution Systems: Choice

The three main values affecting public school policy noted in Chapter 2 are equity, efficiency, and liberty or choice. Most of the history of public education has been one of narrowing choice. By delegating local communities, or school districts, responsibility for education, states initially gave these communities wide latitude to choose the kind, amount, and quality of education to be provided. The first compulsory attendance laws began to circumscribe this freedom of choice. No one argues that this restriction of choice was bad. As noted, these three goals tend to conflict with one another, and each must be balanced against the others. Compulsory attendance is a restriction of freedom in favor of equity and adequacy.

However, as states have given more aid to local school districts, they have tended to exercise more control. Nowhere has this been clearer than in California, which in 1978 escalated from a local contribution of more than half of the total expenditure to a situation where the state in essence funds all education. School boards have found that their freedom to make decisions about most matters has been greatly circumscribed. It is clear that the legislatures have not necessarily been cavalier. They believe that they must exercise a prudent concern for the public funds they are granting to school districts. But the result has been a movement of control to the state as the proportion of school expenditures furnished by the state increased during the 1970s and 1980s.

Local school districts have also restricted the freedom of choice of parents and children. Most school districts tell parents what school their child will attend, which teacher he or she will be taught by, which subjects will be taught, and which textbooks will be used. In the elementary schools in particular, parents have little choice regarding the education of their children.

It need not necessarily be this way. Some school districts allow parents to send their children to any school in the district, or to one of several others besides that in their attendance area (subject, of course, to the availability of space). It is not clear, aside from bureaucratic convenience, why all school districts do not do this. But this is only a beginning. There have been a number of proposals to increase choice in the public schools.

■ VOUCHERS AND TUITION TAX CREDITS

This is an idea of sufficient significance that it is discussed both here and in Chapter 15.

Nobel laureate economist Milton Friedman first proposed the voucher plan in 1955. It is a radical concept in that it proposes dismantling the present system of publicly operated schools. It is conservative in an economic sense in relying on the private market rather than on government. Friedman described his plan thus:

> Governments could require a minimum level of education that they could finance by giving parents vouchers redeemable for a specified maximum sum per child per year if spent on "approved" educational service. Parents would then be free to spend this sum and any additional sum on purchasing educational services from an "approved" institution of their own choice. The educational services could be rendered by private enterprises operated for profit, or by nonprofit institutions of various kinds. The role of the government would be limited to assuring that the schools met certain minimum standards such as the inclusion of a minimum common content in their program, as it now inspects restaurants to assure that they maintain minimum sanitary standards (127–128).

Voucher proponents assert that the plan has a number of advantages. Parents would be allowed to place their children in schools of their choice, instead of being forced to use schools and teachers for which they might have no enthusiasm. The injection of a greater amount of private enterprise would make schools more efficient and promote a healthy variety. Salaries of teachers would become more responsive to market forces. On the other hand, there might be more segregation by economic class.

In fact, an equivalent of the voucher plan operated in higher education for more than 30 years. The "G.I. Bill," more formally, The Service Man's Readjustment Act, PL 78-346, enacted immediately after World War II, provided a higher education subsidy for any veteran who could gain entrance to a postsecondary program. It paid full tuition, regardless of tuition level being charged by the institution, and subsistence for the veteran and his family. It has been widely regarded as one of the most successful federal programs in the field of education, and many veterans who otherwise would not have gotten additional education became college graduates.

On the other hand, there were serious problems with the G.I. Bill, as it formerly operated. A number of private for-profit schools opened just to educate veterans. Audits showed that their curricula were inadequate and their instructors incompetent, and that they granted degrees without requiring the veterans to complete prescribed courses. Fortunately, the majority of veterans selected established schools that furnished a reasonable education. Nevertheless, the potential for abuse is present when the free market is allowed to operate unfettered.

In any case, voucher plans have not been widely accepted in United States elementary or secondary education. For several years during the 1960s and early 1970s, the Office of Economic Opportunity and the U.S. Office of Education attempted to promote a trial of a voucher system somewhere in the United States. The closest they came was a limited experiment in the Alum Rock School District, near San Jose, California, involving no private schools. Results were inconclusive.

The late 1900s saw added attention to vouchers—Wisconsin and Ohio approved voucher plans in Milwaukee and Cleveland. Privately funded voucher plans have existed in New York and in San Antonio, Texas. Also, the U.S. Supreme Court has approved public funding of private schooling in the landmark *Zelman v. Simmons-Harris* case in Ohio. None of these are large endeavors, but they may still prove to be historically important. The research literature regarding these programs is reviewed in Chapter 15.

Tuition tax credits constitute another proposal for subsidizing private schools. The family sending its children to private school is allowed a credit equal to their tuition on its federal income tax return. Note that this is a deduction from the tax, not from income, and is thus of more value to the family. The notion is more fully discussed in Chapter 7.

■ FAMILY POWER EQUALIZING

Coons, Clune, and Sugarman recognized a problem with their proposed system of power equalizing. Although it met their criterion that the amount spent on a child's education should not depend on neighbors' wealth, expenditures might still depend on neighbors' decisions. A rural family desiring and willing to pay for an excellent education for its children might find its neighbors preferring low taxes and low school expenditures. To remedy such forced inequity, Coons, Clune, and Sugarman proposed family power equalizing (1970). In this modified voucher plan, several levels of educational quality would be available in a community's schools. Each family would then be free to choose the quality level it preferred for its children, and would be taxed accordingly. Children would attend the school whose per-pupil expenditures were linked to their parents' choice of tax rate. Family power equalizing has had no warmer political reception than Friedman's voucher plan.

■ MAGNET SCHOOLS

Public schools advocates have been understandably reluctant to forego control over education, as is implied in the Friedman voucher plan. There has also been no observable inclination to adopt a scheme of differential taxation as suggested by Coons and colleagues. However, many districts (particularly those in large cities) have allowed and encouraged an option within public schools. They have established magnet schools. Each such school emphasizes a different feature of education. One may concentrate on the arts, another on science and mathematics, a third on "basics" and firm discipline. Parents are allowed to apply to these schools for their children. The concept has been widely discussed in districts faced with the alternative of busing to promote racial desegregation (Goldring & Smrekar, 2000; Smrekar & Goldring, 1999).

Magnet schools have much to recommend them if they are operated well. A major problem is that they tend to be feasible only in large districts containing a large number of schools. The usual balkanization of school districts in the suburbs makes such schemes difficult. Private schools envisioned in the voucher plans would not suffer from this problem because they draw pupils without regard for district boundaries. In rural areas, however, all of these plans to increase choice are limited by population sparsity, which makes it difficult to establish special schools, public or private. Telecommunications may alleviate this difficulty in the future, allowing instruction of pupils in widely scattered locations.

■ COMPREHENSIVE STATE SCHOOL FINANCE PLANS

Each of the plans described above is only a part of a general school finance plan for a state. The overall plan should foster adequacy, equity, efficiency, and choice. Because these goals tend to conflict with one another, each is usually compromised to some extent in order to foster the others. In addition, school finance plans are designed in the political arena, resulting in accommodations to powerful actors, whether they are school districts or elected officials. Finally, there is usually a wide variety of districts in the state—in size, special needs, and unusual situations—and the plan needs to make reasonable accommodation to these dimensions. The result is an overall school finance plan of fearsome complexity. It is not at all unusual to find no more than a handful of individuals in a state who understand the entire plan, and most of these are in the state education department. Such complexity makes it easy for inequity and inefficiency to insinuate itself into the system, generally unrecognized.

Summary

There are a number of ways a state can distribute education funds to school districts. Three philosophical orientations to the issue of disbursement are: minimum provision, equal access, and equal total provision philosophies. Minimum provision plans, such as flat grant or foundation level programs, are designed to provide a similar base level of funds to districts with an option for local supplementation. Equal access plans attempt to make taxation more equitable by using the power of the state to equalize either total funds or tax bases. Plans such as the guaranteed tax base formulae fall into this category. Finally, total provision adherents advocate for total state control of the entire education enterprise with no district involvement. These last two categories raise the issue of recapture, where money raised by a district is taken by the state and used to support other districts.

Discussion Questions

1. Discuss the seeming relationship between local community wealth and educational quality. Do you share the assessment of some cited in this chapter that the issues can be resolved through policy making?
2. Discuss the relative merits of foundation programs, flat grants, and other revenue distribution methods explained in this chapter.
3. For a simulation associated with this chapter, visit this text's companion website www.ablongman.com/Peabody. It allows you to:

   • Calculate per-pupil funds generated by various distribution formulae; and,
   • Observe how these amounts change when parameters are altered.

   Pay attention to the questions about state recapture. Given the nature of the politics of state governance, would you be tempted to recapture money for districts? Defend your answer.

Web Resources

National Conference of State Legislatures National Center on School Finance:
http://www.ncsl.org/programs/educ/NCEF.htm

Education Finance Statistics Center: http://nces.ed.gov/edfin/

Public School Finance Programs of the United States and Canada:
http://nces.ed.gov/edfin/state_finance/StateFinancing.asp

Notes

1. A mill is an old English coin, no longer in use, the value of which is a tenth of a cent, or $0.001. A tax rate of fifteen mills ($0.015) is a tax of 1.5 cents per dollar of assessed valuation. This is equivalent to a rate of $15 per $1000 of assessed valuation, $1.50 per $100 of assessed valuation, or 1.5 percent.
2. We discuss property value here without distinguishing between full value and assessed value. Although taxes are levied on assessed value, our illustrations assume uniform assessment rates—that is, the assessment of all properties at full value.
3. See the discussions of *Serrano* and other equal-protection suits in Chapters 5 and 12.
4. A proof of the equivalence of percentage equalizing and a guaranteed valuation per pupil is given in Walter I. Garms, Guthrie, and Pierce (1978: 194–195).
5. A follow up to the Wyoming study which updates the model can be found at http://www.edconsultants.com/documents/2001-02%20WY%20reports/ WYFinal.pdf.
6. See Chapter 5 for a more detailed discussion of the legal positions involved in these lawsuits.
7. See Garms, Guthrie and Pierce, *School Finance*, chap. 15, for a description of city schools' financial problems.
8. At least 15 reports critical of U.S. education were issued within a year. Prominent among them were Adler (1982), Boyer (1983), Goodlad (1983), and National Commission on Excellence (1983).

CHAPTER NINE

Federal Governance and Education Finance

■ INTRODUCTION

As discussed in Chapter 4, the federal government has limited or no powers over education enumerated in the Constitution. Yet, the federal government is deeply involved in matters of education in all 50 states. How did such a situation come to be? This chapter will trace historical federal involvement in education issues, define general responsibilities the federal government is meeting when it involves itself in education issues, and review the manner in which federal legislation becomes law.

LEARNING OBJECTIVES

By the end of this chapter, you should be able to:

- Review constitutional language that gives the federal government entrée into education issues.
- Describe current and historical acts and legislation that mark federal involvement in education.
- Articulate the manner in which legislation is crafted and enacted at the federal level.

In December of 2001, President George W. Bush signed the No Child Left Behind Act.[1] This legislation reinforced a 12-year long federal government educational reform drive initiated by his father, President George H. W. Bush. The senior Bush's efforts began with the 1989 National Governor's Summit in Charlottesville, Virginia, and evolved thereafter through three presidential administrations.[2] The 1989 Charlottesville Summit was only the third time in U.S. history that all state governors had been formally convened. The meeting resulted in the United States agreeing to its first ever set of national education goals. These goals, however symbolic, contributed to the enactment 12 years later of the No Child Left Behind Act. This piece of federal legislation marks a significant transition in American education:

- For the first time in American history, virtually all public schools are judged on students' academic performance. Until No Child Left Behind school systems were expected only to demonstrate *how* federal funds were used, and not *whether* use of funds resulted in elevated academic achievement.

- For the first time in American governmental history, academic performance was formally measured for a spectrum of student subgroups, which included African American, Hispanic, Asian/Pacific Islander students, as well as students living in poverty and students with other documented special needs. Although federal education legislation and funds previously targeted populations of poor and minority students, no legislation had ever before specified so clearly that a school or school system was successful only when it raised academic performance for all students.

- Finally, for the first time in American history, schools are held accountable for underperformance in student learning through a graduated series of incentives and sanctions that ultimately allow students to transfer from one school to another if their regularly assigned school continues to underperform. Until No Child Left Behind, school systems were sanctioned for failures of accounting and reporting on use of funds, not students' lack of achievement or academic improvement.

No Child Left Behind illustrates several long-standing themes permeating federal legislative impulses in public education. It reflects a commitment to equal opportunity, a connection between education and economic performance and social mobility of citizens, and a distinct American pragmatism that focuses on results more than inputs or processes. It represents a fundamental change in the way the federal government supports public education.

Few endeavors of this significance escape controversy. Opinion regarding No Child Left Behind and the federal role in education reflects two opposing perspectives:

1. A sense of relief that the federal government is *fulfilling a responsibility* to ensure that all students have access to a high-quality education after years of side stepping what had become a crucial issue for American's civil and economic rights.

2. A sense that the federal government has *overstepped its bounds* by becoming involved in a sphere conventionally reserved for state and local governments.

Proponents of each perspective claim the backing of the Constitution and legal precedent (Karp, 2003; West & Peterson, 2003). In the In the News box, Ann McColl reviews the need to find Constitutional authority for federal activity in education policy and reviews the authority used to make No Child Let Behind a reality. Still, how can genuine observers of public education history and policy and legitimate advocates for children so variously construe the federal role in education? This is a key question in this chapter. Other related questions include:

- What is the federal role in American public education, especially regarding finance?
- From where is Constitutional authority for federal action in public education derived?
- What policies and legislation have shaped federal educational policy throughout U.S. history?

Answers to these and similar questions are rooted in prior policy pursuit of equality, efficiency, and liberty. Federal government historic commitment to each of these ideals has shaped public education's modern policy context. This chapter explores this history. In addition, this chapter explains the constitutional foundations for federal involvement and the political dynamics behind federal policy making.

In the News

Is There Constitutional Authority for NCLB?

There is little dispute over whether NCLB represents an unprecedented level of federal involvement in the affairs of our public schools. However, there is disagreement between the law's supporters, who hail this federal intrusion into state and local education as effective national reform, and its detractors, who argue that the intrusion consists of a set of politically motivated mandates that are detrimental to our schools. The language of NCLB speaks to the sweeping authority intended by its passage: "The purpose of the title is to ensure that all children have a fair, equal, and significant opportunity to obtain a high-quality education and reach, at a minimum, proficiency on challenging state academic achievement standards and state academic assessments." To accomplish this, NCLB sets extensive requirements for states, including establishing an accountability system and staffing schools with high-quality professionals.

This level of federal intrusion into a domain typically under state control raises legal questions because Congress must act within the limits of federal authority established by the U.S. Constitution. The Constitution reflects a careful balance between the powers of the federal government and those of the states. James Madison argued, "The powers delegated by the proposed Constitution to the federal government are few and defined. Those which are to remain in the State governments are numerous and indefinite." The Constitution defines this balance in the 10th Amendment: "The powers not delegated to the

United States by the Constitution, nor prohibited by it to the States, are reserved to the States respectively, or to the people."

Past court decisions, most notably *San Antonio* v. *Rodriguez* (1973), have declared that the Constitution does not establish, either explicitly or implicitly, education as a right or delegate the authority over schools to the federal government. Instead, education is within the domain of state and local governments. As the U.S. Supreme Court said in the celebrated 1954 *Brown* v. *Board of Education* opinion, "Education is perhaps the most important function of state and local governments."

If the federal government is not specifically authorized by the Constitution to delve into matters of education, what other grounds could there be that would satisfy the 10th Amendment's conditions for the assignment of powers? For the authority to legislate as broadly as it has in NCLB, Congress relied on a provision in the Constitution that provides power unlike any other defined in that document: the spending clause. In archaic-sounding language, the spending clause (Art. I, sec. 8, cl. 1) states: "The Congress shall have Power To lay and collect Taxes, Duties, Imposts and Excises, to pay the Debts and provide for the common Defence and general Welfare of the United States. . . . " The spending clause is the basis not only for NCLB but also for most federal education policies, including those that prohibit discrimination—Title VI (race, ethnicity, and national origin), Title IX (gender), and the Individuals with Disabilities Education (IDEA)

Act and Section 504 of the Rehabilitation Act (disability)—and those, like the Family Education Rights and Privacy Act, that protect student privacy. Any future federal education reforms, including a national curriculum, national tests, or national licensure standards, will almost certainly have to be crafted as spending clause legislation.

From: McColl, A. "Tough Call: Is No Child Left Behind Constitutional?" *Phi Delta Kappan*, 86:8, April 2005. pp. 604–610.

▓ ALL OF THIS CONTROVERSY FOR SEVEN PERCENT?

Federal educational expenditures have ebbed and flowed. Enactment of the 1917 Smith Hughes Act authorized federal appropriations that eventually amounted to 1% of U.S. total K–12 revenues. The Elementary and Secondary Education Act (ESEA), toward the end of the 1960s, expanded federal spending to approximately 8% of the K–12 total. Since the Vietnam War, however, federal spending has generally comprised 7% of K–12 school system budgets (NCES, 2002). Put another way, 93¢ out of every dollar spent on U.S. public education comes from state and local governments. Why, then, is there such controversy regarding federal policies when their impact is financially negligible?

State officials have asked this question as well. During the Clinton administration, both Kansas and Oklahoma considered opting out of federal education programs over a concern with federal intrusion into states' rights (Pitsch, 1996; Zehr, 1998). The issue of federal involvement was so intense that in 1995, Oklahoma Senator James Inhofe publicly requested that the state's entrant into the Miss America competition, Shawntel Smith, stop giving the impression she supported federal education reform efforts, citing the erosion of local control triggered by standards-based reform (Schmidt, 1995). Despite such controversy, federal education funds—as well as accompanying rules shaping use of those funds—are important for a number of reasons.

Guaranteeing Opportunity

Federal funds support specialized students with unusual instructional needs. Antipoverty efforts and other targeted programs can be costly and expensive, and may not meet full approval of local electorates. Left to their own preferences, some local communities might underinvest in educating selected students or in the pursuit of selected subject or skill categories. Therefore, federal policymakers intervene to ensure that all students have opportunities for educational access.

Countering Underinvestment

Federal education funds support approaches and ideas that state or local governments may not have sufficient economic incentives to attempt. Imagine, for example, that the nation's supply of highly skilled scientists or individuals with a keen ability to speak languages other than English was so short as to jeopardize national defense or the nation's balance of international trade. It is unlikely that individual states would enact programs to meet such shortages. These are national needs, and on several occasions Congress has enacted and funded programs to solve such problems.

Capturing Scale Economies

The federal government acts in areas where states may not have sufficient capacity to address issues of concern. Some functions risk diseconomies of scale if performed by smaller units and beg to be undertaken more efficiently by a central authority. Data collection and research and development activities are good examples. Congressional action establishing the Department of Education in 1867 made prominent mention of the agency's role in collecting useful statistics for sustaining and improving the nation's schools. This task, though performed unevenly over time by the federal education authority, nevertheless falls naturally to a central government. States and smaller units of government are ill positioned to gather and analyze information from across the nation. Hence, the present-day cabinet-level Department of Education systematically collects, analyzes, and publishes information on education in the United States.

Underlying each of these federal government endeavors is the fact that, although 7% is a low percentage, it adds up to a great many real dollars. Figures 9.1 and 9.2 illustrate increased federal spending on education in billions of dollars. Since 1965, federal investment in elementary and secondary education has increased by over $60 billion. Some will argue, as noted in other chapters, that increased federal investment has not yielded elevated academic achievement. Another perspective argues that increases in education

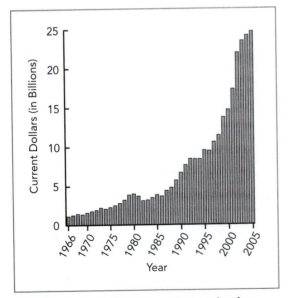

FIGURE 9.1   Federal Investment in the Elementary and Secondary Education Act

Source: 2005 U.S. Budget, Historical Tables

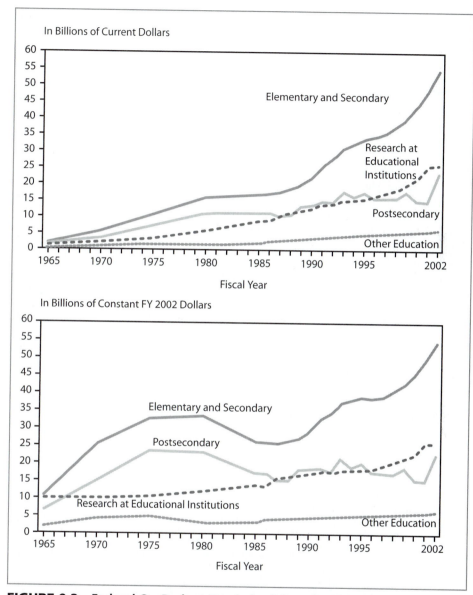

FIGURE 9.2   Federal On-Budget Funds for Education, by Level or Other Educational Purpose: 1965 to 2002

Source: U.S. Department of Education, National Center for Education Statistics; U.S. Office of Management and Budget, *Budget of the U.S. Government,* fiscal years 1967 to 2003; National Science Foundation, *Federal Funds for Research and Development,* fiscal years 1965 to 2002; and unpublished data.

spending in general have gone to teacher salaries, maintenance, inflation, and other costs not specifically related to student academic achievement (see, for example, Hanusheck, 1996; Hanushek & Rivkin, 1997).

■ CONSTITUTIONAL FOUNDATIONS OF FEDERAL EDUCATION POLICY

The United States Constitution does not explicitly grant citizens a right to an education, nor does it establish a national system of schools. Rather than a glaring omission, the absence of any provision explicitly concerned with education or schooling appears to have been a conscious choice by 18th-century Constitutional framers. Notes compiled by James Madison during the Philadelphia Constitutional Convention suggest that members discussed establishing a national university but made no formal proposal to provide the federal government with a role in lower education.

Others in attendance considered formal learning to be important, and several luminaries of the period, such as Thomas Jefferson and Benjamin Franklin, expressed favorable views on education in other settings (Franklin, 1749; Jefferson, 1779). Thus, omission of the words *schooling* and *education* from the Constitution might not have been a casual act or oversight.

Nevertheless, it was only in the mid-19th century that state-enacted compulsory attendance laws triggered present models of public schooling (Guthrie et al., 1975). Thus, those attending the 1787 Constitutional Convention had little experience with government provision of education, and their negative disposition toward King George III and the strong British monarchy prejudiced them further against granting a national authority the right to control such a potentially influential undertaking as schooling.

Given this context, exactly how did the founding fathers express a preference for a limited federal government? Mention was made of this dynamic in Chapter 4. Thus, this is an abbreviated explanation.

The U.S. Constitution's 10th Amendment specifies ". . . powers not delegated to the United States by the Constitution, nor prohibited by it to the States, are reserved to the States respectively, or to the people." This provision reflects social contract theories of government that were intensely important to Constitutional framers (Baker, 1947). The right to individual self-determination was held to be an inalienable quality of each human being, one that should be ceded to representative governing bodies only with strict limitations. Hence, the 10th Amendment explicitly asserts that national government is to be imbued only with powers expressly granted to it. All other authority is to be held by states or by individuals, unless specifically denied by the Constitution. The 10th Amendment's ending, "or the people," makes clear that the citizenry is the ultimate source of governing authority.[3]

The effect of the absence in the Constitution of a proclamation of express national responsibility for education and schooling, when coupled with language of the 10th Amendment, is to cede *plenary* (ultimate) legal authority for public education to state government. As a result, each state constitution, as a condition of entry into the union, contains an education clause explicitly acknowledging state authority over education and schooling. As will be evident later, it is these clauses that have become the focus of a series of school finance litigation cases.

Because of these federal and state constitutional arrangements, the federal government has no widespread specific responsibility for operating education programs. (Direct federal administration of institutions such as the armed service academies, Gallaudet College for the Deaf in Washington, D.C., and the Overseas Dependent Schools are limited exceptions.)

The federal government's Constitutional authority to finance and regulate education programs is derived from *implied powers* contained in several sections of the U.S. Constitution. Over the centuries since ratification, numerous judicial interpretations of Constitutional provisions have expanded the scope of the federal government's education authority. These implied powers have been reinforced by court decisions regarding the general welfare clause and other parts of the 1st Amendment and both the due process and the equal protection clauses of the 14th Amendment.

The 1st Amendment—General Welfare Clause

Article 1, Section 8, Clause 1, of the Constitution is commonly referred to as the general welfare clause. It states, "The Congress shall have power to levy and collect taxes, duties, imposts and excises, to pay the debts and provide for the common defense and general welfare of the United States." For a century or more following adoption of the Constitution, this was a controversial provision. Proponents of a limited national government, such as James Madison, desired a narrow interpretation, whereas advocates of a strong central government, such as Alexander Hamilton, argued for a broad view of the clause. In the 1930s, U.S. Supreme Court decisions substantially altered the nature of the debate. In a case involving New Deal legislation sponsored by the Roosevelt administration, the nation's highest court ruled that Congress had authority to interpret the general welfare clause as long as it did not act arbitrarily (United States v. Butler, 1936).

The U.S. Supreme Court also held that the clause could be interpreted differently from time to time as conditions necessitate redefinition of the nation's general welfare (Helvering v. Davis, 1937). Debate has since shifted to whether or not a particular policy proposal is useful, instead of whether Congress possesses authority to implement it. Consequently, federal education programs are viewed as falling within the implied Constitutional authority of Congress. This is not to assert that everybody always agrees on the wisdom of a particular legislative proposal or a new federal education program. Contemporary education initiatives can still provoke heated debate at the federal level.

The 1st Amendment—Contractual Obligations

Article 1, Section 10, of the Constitution has been judicially interpreted to allow the federal government to restrict ability of states and local boards of education to impair contractual obligations. The Supreme Court has held that "a legislative enactment may contain provisions which, when accepted as a basis of action by individuals, become contracts between them and the state or its subdivision" (State ex rel Anderson v. Brand, 1938). The constitutional provision regarding contractual obligations and legal principles derived from it have also been applied to controversies between teachers' unions and school boards over tenure rights and retirement agreements.

The 1st Amendment—Church and State Relations

The Supreme Court has held that the 1st Amendment was intended to create a wall of separation between church and state. Consistent with this view, both state and federal courts have repeatedly struck down state efforts to provide direct financial subsidies to religious schools. The U.S. Supreme Court evolved a three-pronged test to determine whether a sectarian school aid plan violates the wall of separation: (1) the statute must have a secular legislative purpose; (2) the statute's primary effect must neither advance nor inhibit religion; and (3) the statute and its administration must avoid excessive government entanglement with religion (Lemon v. Kurtzman, 1972).

Application of these principles served, until the last decade of the 20th century, to discourage state aid to church-related elementary and secondary schools. However, with the 1983 Supreme Court decision in *Mueller v. Allen*, matters began to evolve in a different direction. The Mueller decision approved a Minnesota statute providing state income tax deductions for school fees, both public and nonpublic. Advocates of federal aid to religious schools took this to be a signal that the Court was increasingly disposed toward their cause. A 1985 decision in a New York case, *Aguilar v. Felton*, counseled caution. Provision to church-related schools of federally funded compensatory instructional services authorized by Chapter One of the Education Consolidation and Improvement Act was restricted by this decision. However, at the opening of the 21st century, the nation's highest court seemed more disposed toward use of public funds for private and religious schools. In the 2001 case of *Zelman v. Simmons-Harris*, the court ruled that publicly funded education vouchers provided to students might be redeemed at religious schools, saying:

> We believe that the program challenged here is a program of true private choice, consistent with *Mueller*, *Witters*, and *Zobrest*, and thus constitutional. As was true in those cases, the Ohio program is neutral in all respects toward religion. It is part of a general and multifaceted undertaking by the State of Ohio to provide educational opportunities to the children of a failed school district.

The 14th Amendment—Equal Protection

The 14th Amendment adopted in 1868 was one of three Constitutional amendments intended to free slaves. It stretched the mantle of the first 10 amendments to protect the civil liberties of citizens from state encroachment (LaMorte, 1974). The 14th Amendment contains two clauses of particular importance to federal authority over education—the so-called due process clause and the equal protection clause.

The *equal protection clause* served as the basis for one of the most significant reforms ever undertaken in American public education—the overturning of dual school systems for whites and blacks, which evolved from slavery and were supported statutorily in 17 southern states and the District of Columbia. In 1954, the U.S. Supreme Court issued a school desegregation decision that overturned the "separate but equal" doctrine, which had dominated U.S. race relations since the 1896 decision in *Plessy v. Ferguson*. In *Plessy*, the Court had let stand an 1890 Louisiana statute segregating races on railway cars as long as, presumably, facilities were equal. In *Brown v. Board of Education*, by far the most noted of the desegregation cases, the Court stated:

> We conclude that in the field of public education the doctrine of "separate but equal" has no place. Separate educational facilities are inherently unequal. Therefore, we hold that the plaintiffs and others similarly situated for whom the actions are brought are, by reason of the segregation complained of, deprived of the equal protection of the laws guaranteed by the Fourteenth Amendment.

The *Brown* decision, in conjunction with implementation decrees and numerous lower-court decisions, was resisted, sometimes violently. The eventual result, however, was a dismantling of the *de jure* racially segregated school systems that had long characterized public schooling in the South. More subtle discriminatory mechanisms that contribute to *de facto* segregation have not lent themselves so easily to legal remedy (Kirp, 1982; Orfield, 1978; Walters, 1984; Wilkinson, 1976).

The equal protection clause has also been used as basis for a Constitutional challenge to school finance arrangements in many of the 50 states. Chapters 5 and 12 explain the legal logic and practical consequences connected with this judicial reform strategy. Suffice it to say that the practical outcome, though not wholly unsatisfactory, has been nowhere near the legal success of the school desegregation suits. Indeed, reform efforts in racial desegregation and school finance simultaneously display the power and limits of the federal government's ability to influence public education. Because of the complexity of the United States' multitiered and many-faceted system of government, the results of these efforts have not been nearly as successful as advocates had hoped, or as devastating socially as opponents had feared.

The 14th Amendment—Due Process

The 14th Amendment's due process clause states, "nor shall any State deprive any person of life, liberty, or property, without due process of law." This clause also provides a major legal vehicle through which the federal government can influence public education. Generally, the due process clause must be weighed against society's need to protect itself.

Though continually being redefined judicially, so-called police powers are inherently within the authority of government at all levels. For example, teachers and other school employees are not free to do or teach whatever they would like if such actions jeopardize society's need to protect itself. Courts have generally enforced the Smith Act, which makes it a crime punishable by fine and imprisonment to advocate forceful overthrow of the government. These rulings have established a limitation regarding what can be taught in public, as well as private, schools. As Morphet, Johns, and Reller (1982) stated,

> . . . those who insist that the federal government should have no control whatsoever over the curriculum of public schools seem to be unaware of the inherent police powers of the federal government relating to matters of national concern.

The federal government's ability to influence America's system of schooling is not limited to its legal authority. Influence is also possible through means such as financial inducement, demonstration projects, dissemination of information and research findings, evaluation efforts, and moral persuasion. These are discussed in subsequent sections of this chapter.

Despite its limited authority, the federal government has had a history of influence in education. In the mid-20th century, federal authorities inaugurated numerous education programs that presently provide services throughout all 50 states, trust territories, thousands of local school districts, and schools. It is these programs that are usually included when one considers the "federal role" in the provision and support of education. In actuality, the federal government has assumed a considerable role in matters of public education since the earliest days of the republic. It is unlikely that even a single American public school is presently untouched by federal education policy. Sections below review federal involvement in issues of equity, efficiency, and liberty that have had financial implications for American public schools.

▪ THREE PILLARS OF SCHOOL FINANCE AND FEDERAL INVOLVEMENT

Policy making at all levels—including the federal government—involves combining practical ideas with ideals in order both to solve problems and to convince the public that a solution is consistent with their idea of "America." Viewed in this light, the three value streams of equality, efficiency, and liberty can be articulated in this manner:

- *Equity*: A federal value of equal opportunity is expressed in U.S. foundational documents. In public education, equity is usually referred to in terms of opportunity; that is, every student should be assured a right to educational opportunity, but not a right to any specific level of personal educational attainment or academic achievement. This means that students should have access to schools and colleges and not be deterred from educational opportunities by race, creed, wealth, or selected other markers. Federal equity policies have directed funds toward students living in poverty as well as students of color and other minority groups in order to ensure that educational opportunity is distributed equally throughout society.

- *Efficiency*: A federal value of efficiency recognizes that federal action is sometimes the most cost-effective and quickest way to accomplish a task. In education, efficiency impulses have focused on state institutions of higher education and students' financial aid to acquire educational services. Historically, federal actions to ensure equity have included providing land directly to states to support education, funds directly to students to subsidize college costs, and data and feedback to school systems to support more effective education. In addition, federal policies may reflect a view that preexisting government bureaucracy needs to be rescued from itself and simplified or streamlined to provide federal funds to local districts in a more efficient manner.

- *Liberty*: A federal predisposition toward liberty stresses the idea that citizens, as well as state and local governments, are free to make choices without coercion. In public education, the federal role in enhancing liberty has involved walking a tightrope and serving as an adjudicator between rights of governments and rights of individuals. The federal government has supported liberty by providing funds directly to students, litigating cases thought to limit state or school system autonomy, and providing results-oriented directives for systemic improvement while leaving states and systems free to innovate—what some have termed "top down support for bottom up reform."

Equity: Ensuring Access

Although many scholars think of federal involvement in equity issues along the lines of race, such as the 1896 *Plessy* or 1954 *Brown* Supreme Court decisions, the federal government has been striving to ensure educational access for almost the entire history of our nation. One of the federal government's first attempts to ensure access to educational opportunity was initiated before the U.S. Constitution was even ratified.

Land Ordinance and Northwest Ordinance—Using Land to Ensure Access to Schools.
In 1785, even before ratification of the Constitution by all original colonies, central government policy on education was being made. The Land Survey Ordinance of that year provided for several sections of land in each township within newly formed territories to be reserved for support of public schools (Campbell et al., 1980). Specifically, section

16 of each plot was to be reserved for schools and, in a symbolic commitment to separation of church and state, section 29 was reserved for religious purposes.

The 1787 Northwest Ordinance continued support of access to public education in what was to become Michigan, Indiana, Wisconsin, Ohio, and Illinois. These early ordinances signaled a federal commitment to public education that was to continue throughout American political history. This commitment is summed up best in a sentence from Article 3 of the Northwest Ordinance, which reads:

> Religion, morality and knowledge being necessary to good government and the happiness of mankind, schools and the means of education shall forever be encouraged.

These two ordinances demonstrate federal government's historical commitment to use its greatest resource (at that time, land), as a lever to ensure citizens would have access to schools and educational opportunities.

Morrill Act—Using Land Grants for Higher Education. Vast amounts of undeveloped land remained one of the federal government's greatest resources into the 1800s. In 1862, Congress passed the first Morrill Act, named after Senator Justin S. Morrill of Vermont, the bill's major proponent. This statute allocated 30,000 acres of federal land to each state for each of its two senators and each representative to which it was then entitled. Income from the sale or rental of these lands was to be used for establishing agricultural and mechanical arts colleges. These "A & M" colleges were to contribute to the new nation's supply of artisans and technicians. Such institutions were also to instruct students in military science and tactics.

Each state benefited from this program. Not all recipients have been public institutions, however. Cornell University in Ithaca, New York, and the Massachusetts Institute of Technology in Cambridge, Massachusetts, are both examples of prestigious private institutions that have received aid from Morrill Act proceeds. So-called land grant colleges received additional aid upon passage of the Second Morrill Act of 1892 and the Hatch Act of 1897.[4]

Head Start—A Popular Foray into Education Policy Making. Creation of Head Start—through President Lyndon Johnson's antipoverty legislation, The Economic Opportunity Act of 1964—represents a textbook example of the federal government creating legislation to fulfill needs that state and local governments ignored. Head Start was created as an independent agency to help prepare children disadvantaged for school. Head Start was aligned with the Johnson administration's commitment to equity, while acknowledging the meritocratic nature of public education. While results from Head Start have been mixed, the program has remained popular with legislators as well as the general public.[5] Results from evaluations of Head Start have noted both improved student performance in early grades, with a diminished impact in later grades.

Elementary and Secondary Education Act (ESEA)—A Federal Plan for Education Support. Another piece of landmark federal education policy was passed in 1965. Unlike Head Start, the Elementary and Secondary Education Act (ESEA) was specifically directed to supporting public education for low-income students. Like Head Start, ESEA revenue is distributed widely across the nation.

Historically, the bulk of ESEA funds have been dedicated to "Title I," which seeks to support students living in poverty. Since its 1965 passage, the ESEA has been the main avenue by which the federal government seeks to influence K–12 educational policy. Both Bill Clinton's Improving America's Schools Act of 1994 and George Bush's No Child Left Behind Act of 2001 were reauthorizations of ESEA in which specific new approaches to education were added—for example, use of standards and assessments to determine if schools receiving federal money were attaining concomitant student achievement gains, and a system of rewards and sanctions for states, districts, and schools that were receiving funds but could not demonstrate improved results. Currently, under No Child Left Behind, the federal government annually invests over $20 billion in America's schools because of ESEA.[6]

One ESEA legacy is research into the effects of remedial action and family background on student academic achievement.[7]

Emergency School Aid Act (ESAA)—Federal Money as Incentives for Desegregation.

From 1955 through the 1960s, judicial pressure was exerted on southern schools to dismantle dual school systems. Throughout much of this period, the Justice Department and the Office of Civil Rights, both within the executive branch, also attempted to pressure school districts to undertake racial desegregation. Beginning in 1968, the Nixon administration attempted to dilute judicial and executive branch mandatory desegregation pressures and proposed substituting more federal inducements for voluntary desegregation of local school districts. Proponents of racially integrated schools were skeptical of such a strategy; nevertheless, in 1972 Congress enacted the Emergency School Aid Act (ESAA). The intent of this legislation was to assist local school districts in racially integrating schools by providing federal funds for in-service training of teachers, employment of teacher aides and instructional specialists for desegregated classrooms, or whatever else local school officials reasonably contended would assist their districts in voluntarily desegregating schools. Appropriations for this statute reached their peak in the late 1970s, totaling approximately $300 million.

Impact Aid—Just Compensation for Military Communities.

At the outset of World War II and again in the early 1950s with the Korean War, local officials frequently found school districts faced with virtually unmanageable growth problems. Nearby military bases and other federal installations expanded quickly, and adjacent public schools often would have to absorb hundreds of additional pupils in a short period. Worse, federal installations were not subject to local taxation. To compensate for this condition, Congress enacted in 1940 and subsequently renewed the Lanham Act, PL 81-874. This **in lieu of tax** statute compensates local districts for loss of property tax revenue resulting from the "impact" of federal activity. Hence, these funds have come to be known as **impact aid**. Local school districts annually conduct a census among pupils to determine eligibility. Thereafter, they use funds they receive as though they were general revenues.

Public Law 94-142—Letting More Students through the Schoolhouse Door.

Throughout the 1960s and the early 1970s increasing political pressure was brought to bear on state legislatures to correct injustices to handicapped students. Many states were not providing school services for severely handicapped students, and other states were underfunding such programs. Following several important state court cases in which it was held that handicapped children deserved equal protection of the law, state legislatures, as well as Congress, enacted programs to ensure better schooling for the handicapped (Mills v. Board of Education, 1972; PARC v. Commonwealth, 1971).

Public Law 94-142, the Education for All Handicapped Children Act (EHCA) of 1975, was one result. This federal statute distributes funds to states and ultimately to local districts for education services to various categories of handicapped schoolchildren. In accepting funds, states and districts must agree to follow a rigorous set of federal regulations in educating eligible students. One of the policies in place today because of PL 94-142 is that every identified student's instructional program be guided by collaborative development of an IEP or **individual education plan**. These plans ensure that each student's special circumstances are considered when making educational decisions. Many local school officials express annoyance at the high level of distrust implied by the unusually legalistic procedures, such as the paperwork required to initiate, implement, and assess an individual student's IEP. Advocates for the handicapped reply that past abuses speak poorly for the integrity of local education officials and contend that firm federal regulations are altogether necessary to ensure that handicapped students are treated fairly. Nevertheless, PL 94-142 brought many more students into the classrooms of American public schools, guaranteeing that access to educational opportunity was now distributed more widely than ever. In addition, the spirit of PL 94-142—that students should be placed in the "least restrictive educational environment," also known as "mainstreaming"—is reinforced by provisions of No Child Left Behind, which make academic improvement of special needs students a precursor for school and school system success.

Bilingual Education—Access for Non-English Speakers. Increasing immigration, particularly from Spanish-speaking and Asian nations, began to challenge the resources of selected local school districts after mid-century. Children of many new Americans had only limited, if any, ability to speak and read English. Ironically, these youngsters were compelled by statute to attend schools whose medium of instruction, English, was for them unintelligible. In San Francisco, the site of a heavy influx of non-English-speaking Asians, students and their parents filed suit against the school district in order to receive language assistance in school. The case, *Lau v. Nichols*, eventually was decided in favor of the plaintiffs. Based on Section 601 of the 1964 Civil Rights Act, the U.S. Supreme Court found that non-English-speaking students were discriminated against and mandated that the school district provide multilingual instructors and other educational assistance to these children.

The legal precedent became established that school districts were responsible for assisting limited- and non-English-speaking students. To defray the added costs of such services, several state legislatures enacted categorical school aid programs and Congress added Title VII to the Elementary and Secondary Education Act. The latter provision allocates funds, through states, to local school districts for bilingual instruction. Federal appropriations were never large, to the point that many state and local officials consider bilingual education to be an "unfunded mandate" from the federal government. Again, however, this commitment to non-native English speakers is reinforced through provisions of No Child Left Behind, that make the academic success of (what are now termed) English Language Learners a precursor for school and school system success.

Efficiency: Ensuring Best Use of Public Resources

A second pillar of education finance is that of efficiency. Some federal initiatives to improve efficiency of public schools are as follows.

Research Navigator.com

individual education plan

Vocational Education—Making Public Schools Work for American Business. In the early 20th century, as the United States moved toward World War I, Congress, concerned about availability of skilled workers to supply both American industry and the war effort, passed the Smith-Hughes Act of 1917. The statute authorized federal funds to states to establish secondary school programs in agricultural and industrial trades and homemaking. States were required to match federal funds. This act established a precedent for matching grants that has become a major lever used by federal officials to induce program cooperation by state and local agencies.[8]

The Smith-Hughes Act was controversial. John Dewey observed in 1917, on passage of Smith-Hughes, "It settles no problem; it merely symbolizes inauguration of a conflict between irreconcilable opposed educational and industrial ideals" (quoted in Killiebard, 1999, 335). Indeed, the tension in education policy between providing both academic and vocational courses and the practice of "tracking" students based on their perceived abilities is still present today.

The federal government's initial concern for vocational education has been strongly sustained. Congress enacted the George-Reed Act in 1929, the George-Ellzey Act in 1935, the George-Dean Act in 1937, and the George-Barden Act in 1946. The 1963 Vocational Education Act, promoted by President John F. Kennedy, established a different direction for vocational education, one that has been pursued with systematic reauthorizations. The Clinton administration's School-to-Work Act reflected a commitment to vocational education as well as the policy innovation of required matching funds.

During the Great Depression of the 1930s, Congress established several antipoverty programs containing significant educational components. Frequently, vocational training was a prominent feature of these undertakings. For example, the Civilian Conservation Corps (CCC) and the National Youth Authority (NYA) both provided vocational training for unemployed Depression youth. In 1965, as part of the Johnson administration's War on Poverty, the Federal Job Corps was established to enable out-of-school and out-of-work youth to gain job skills. Depression-era education programs were operated directly by federal agencies such as the War Department (now the Defense Department) and the Federal Security Agency, an ancestor of the present-day Department of Education. The Job Corps was operated by a variety of private organizations under direct contract to the now-defunct Office of Economic Opportunity. Compared with programs in surrounding local school districts, these federally funded and operated vocational training endeavors were unusually expensive, costing up to 20 times as much per enrollee as public school vocational training. Local and state public school officials insisted they could perform the same function more efficiently. Such complaints, along with changing economic conditions, eventually terminated these poverty-relief efforts, and virtually nothing of them remains today.

National Assessment of Educational Progress (NAEP)—Developing the Nation's Report Card. In 1966, the federal government funded an effort to assess the national performance of students and school graduates—the National Assessment of Educational Progress (NAEP). Initially, this undertaking was contracted by the Department of Education to the Education Commission of the States (ECS), in Denver, Colorado. At that time, appraisers of performance were prohibited from making state-by-state comparisons. In 1983, the NAEP was moved to the Educational Testing Service (ETS) in Princeton, New Jersey. In 1987, a highly visible national study panel chaired by Tennessee governor Lamar Alexander and Spencer Foundation president H. Thomas James issued *The Nation's Report Card*, a report that recommended massive changes in governance and procedures for the NAEP. The panel proposed, for example, that state-by-state test score comparisons be undertaken (Alexander & James, 1987).

This massive achievement-assessment program tests thousands of students throughout the nation. It is not an endeavor that individual states could easily organize or afford to operate for the entire nation. It falls more naturally to the federal government to conduct such an undertaking.

Data Collection and Dissemination—Making Innovation Available to All. There is less financial incentive to engage in research when potential results may create an advantage for a host of others besides the initiating agency. Under such conditions, a tempting strategy is to wait and hope to piggyback on the research funded by another agency. Educational research and development can be viewed in this light. Why should one state expend its scarce resources on basic research on, for example, human learning when there is no reasonable way to restrict useful results to its boundaries? Under such circumstances, there is likely to be an underinvestment in an activity that might otherwise enhance educational efficiency and the productivity of the entire economy. To avoid such a condition, the federal government has long supported educational research and development.

In 1954, Congress passed the Cooperative Research Act, which authorized federal funds for educational research in institutions of higher education. The U.S. Office of Education—one of several agencies constituting what was then known as the Department of Health, Education and Welfare (HEW)—administered this statute. In 1965, main features of the Cooperative Research Act were incorporated into Title IV of the Elementary and Secondary Education Act (ESEA). The latter act substantially expanded the amount of federal money available for education research. Additionally, it established 20 regional educational laboratories and 12 university-based research and development centers. The aim was for new ideas to be developed in the R & D centers and transformed into practical applications and distributed to school districts by the regional educational laboratories. This research, development, and dissemination strategy was patterned after a highly effective model utilized by U.S. agriculture.

In 1975, federal education research functions were transferred to the new National Institute of Education (NIE), then within HEW and subsequently a part of the Department of Education. By the late 1970s, however, federal expenses accrued from the war in Vietnam, large outlays for domestic social programs, and diminished political affection for public schools had reduced education research appropriations. Several of the R & D centers and regional laboratories were closed, and funding for the remainder was insufficient to support large-scale research projects. Though the NIE continued to be the major funding source for education research throughout the 1970s and early 1980s, its institutional impact was minimal in many areas, and there were even serious suggestions for its dissolution (Finn, 1983). By 1985, the NIE had been folded back into the Department of Education and was known as the Office of Educational Research and Improvement (OERI). With No Child Left Behind, OERI was reconstituted into the Institute of Education Sciences (IES).

National Defense Education Act (NDEA)—Funding for National Needs and Priorities. In 1957, the Soviet Union launched the first successful earth-orbiting satellite, Sputnik. The event rocked America's sense of technological superiority. U.S. public education served as a convenient scapegoat for popular frustration and disappointment. The nation subsequently regained its poise and launched a massive federal program that resulted in moon landings and other space successes of the 1960s and 1970s. Education also benefited, with enactment of the 1958 National Defense Education Act (NDEA). This statute utilized federal matching funds as an incentive for local school districts to upgrade instruction in science, mathematics, and foreign language. Higher-education institutions also participated, through expanded financial support for college students entering the fields of science and math teaching. The NDEA was successful in helping schools meet intensified public expectations for American scientific and technological supremacy.

In the 1960s the National Science Foundation (NSF) funded fellowships and advanced training programs for science and math teachers at many colleges and universities. The NSF also funded a number of science and math curriculum revision projects that substantially influenced secondary school instruction (Marsh & Ross, 1967).

In the early 1980s, the mass media and professional periodicals began reporting increasing shortages of qualified secondary school math and science teachers (Guthrie & Zusman, 1982). Fear of losing a competitive economic position in international sales of high-technology products and techniques motivated President Reagan in 1985 to propose and Congress to enact the Education for Economic Security Act, embodying many of the same purposes as the 1958 NDEA.

In 1966, Congress passed a Sea Grant program providing colleges and universities with added federal funding to expand marine research. In 1987, the Reagan administration proposed to provide land-grant institutions with added funding to conduct research in electronics and other high-technology areas.

Education Consolidation and Improvement Act (ECIA)—Reforming the Reforms. Sometimes, the federal government uses its role in education policy to attempt to improve its own efforts. In 1981, Congress accepted a Reagan administration recommendation and consolidated many existing education programs into two major statutes of the ECIA. Chapter One of this act continues the major feature of the 1965 ESEA—federal funds for compensatory education for students from low-income families into a limited number of the so-called block grants, wherein states and districts would be permitted greater discretion over spending. Interest groups comprising the educators and others who were benefiting most directly from the categorical aid resisted consolidation for fear their particular programs would lose ground to local spending priorities under a block grant (Kirst, 1986).[9]

In 1981, when the Reagan administration initially proposed deregulation and consolidation, several major programs were discussed for inclusion, among them special education and compensatory education. The eventual compromise was to preserve the categorical integrity of major programs and to combine many smaller authorities. ECIA Chapter Two was the result. This foray into more innovative federal funding for education programs called back to the tradition of local control in public education. Although the ECIA was eventually reformulated into the more recognizable categorical aid of ESEA, the precedent of using federal funds in more creative ways to spur change continues in No Child Left Behind. The failure of ECIA was due more to a lack of capacity of state and local officials to handle the massive change in the federal paradigm than to any specific problem with the policies proposed by ECIA.

A Nation at Risk—*The Bully Pulpit Changes the Course of Education Research.* In 1983, Terrell Bell, then Secretary of Education, and the National Education Excellence

Commission released a report. Titled *A Nation at Risk*, the report decried declining performance in American public schools and the seeming lack of will for substantive education reform. Although the report proved controversial and did little or nothing to change education legislation, it had an electrifying effect on the education research community. The report kicked off an era of research into excellent and effective schools that continues to this day. With hindsight, one can see that A *Nation at Risk* spawned the research base that undergirds federal policy today, such as No Child Left Behind. *A Nation at Risk* is an object lesson in the ability of the executive branch of government to use the bully pulpit to alter the course of education policy.

New American Schools and Comprehensive Schools Demonstration Project— Creating a Context for Innovation. During the administration of George H. W. Bush, education policy focused on the implementation of a standards and assessment paradigm. Part of this effort was the creation in 1991 of the New American Schools Development Corporation (NASDC), an organization intended as an incubator for education innovation.[10] NASDC was to transition from being federally funded to becoming an independent organization. Its task was to create and support models that created whole school change, or Comprehensive School Reform (CSR), as opposed to simply reforming schools through the categorical programs found in ESEA.

Federal legislation enacting the Comprehensive School Reform Demonstration Project supported NASDC by offering schools and school systems block grants for adopting one of NASDC's Comprehensive School Reform (CSR) models. In this manner, the federal government provided a laboratory for a new approach to school reform (Education Commission of the States, 2005). This strategy has generally been found wanting. Few school boards and central office administrators are in a position to adopt a radical reform. Public education is woven so tightly into the fabric of American politics that dramatic, rather than incremental, change is almost always the only change that can occur. New American Schools has repeatedly reinvented itself, but has not been, and probably cannot be, a major factor in changing American education. The federal government's measurement of outcomes and provision of rewards and sanctions for results strategy, embedded in No Child Left Behind, provides a brighter promise of provoking change.

America/Goals 2000—Using ESEA to Implement a New Education Paradigm. Both the Bush and Clinton administrations relied on the ESEA to bring a new reform strategy to pubic schools. Using the funding from the ESEA as an incentive, both administrations sought to implement federal legislation that demanded state standards and assessments for all states, with a system of rewards and sanctions for performance attached to the assessments.

Liberty

Confronted with large numbers of returning soldiers after World War II, Congress enacted the Serviceman's Readjustment Act, PL 78-346, which provided financial assistance to veterans to acquire post-secondary schooling. This statute, the G.I. Bill (described in detail in Chapter 6), was a forerunner of voucher plans in that federal funds flowed to the individual and he or she chose an institution to attend. Although aid was for post-secondary schooling, and therefore did not provoke intense questions of aid to non-public schools, the G.I. Bill set a precedent for the federal government to use the individual as a unit of assistance and not just an institution. Prior to this, educational funds for post-secondary education went directly to the college or university a student decided to attend. Afterward, the student held the power of the purse in using post-secondary support. This precedent was acted on in the 1975 Higher Education Act, which made a radical policy shift in providing federal student aid for higher education directly to students. Previously, federal student assistance had been funneled through institutions. This change enabled students to use their aid dollars in a more portable manner, thus giving them more control of their higher education decisions.

In the 1980s the Reagan administration proposed a tuition tax credit plan, which would benefit elementary and secondary as well as post-secondary institutions (Catteral, 1983; Jacobs, 1990; Mazzoni, 1987). Controversy over such an arrangement has been more intense than that concerning the G.I. Bill. Tuition tax credits expand choice by permitting households to deduct all or a portion of nonpublic tuition payments from federal income taxes. The allowable dollar amount is a credit against federal income taxes owed, not simply a deduction from income. Many private school officials and parents of private school children favor such a plan. Conversely, many public school advocates oppose the plan. Opponents fear that federal private school subsidies will undermine public schools, and they allege that the plan will violate 1st Amendment prohibitions of aid to religious schools (Longanecker, 1983).

Prior to 1983, tuition tax credit proposals had passed in the U.S. Senate on six separate occasions. In 1979, the House of Representatives enacted a tuition tax credit plan by a narrow margin, but President Jimmy Carter's threat of a veto, given Democratic control of the Senate at the time, was sufficient to stifle the bill. President Reagan's administration again proposed such a plan, but the prospect of huge federal budget deficits in the 1980s dampened prospects for congressional approval (Whitt, Clark, & Astuto, 1986). Aside from economics and politics, however, the constitutionality of such a plan is perhaps enhanced by the U.S. Supreme Court's decision in the previously mentioned cases of *Mueller v. Allen* and *Zelman* v. *Simmons-Harris*.

Another mechanism for enhancing choice in education is the use of vouchers. Voucher plans are described at greater length in Chapter 15. Suffice it here to mention that people have been advocating federal vouchers for several decades, and there was even a small federally funded voucher experiment in the 1970s. Reagan administration voucher proponents repeatedly proposed that Chapter One of the ECIA be revised to allow compensatory education funds to be allocated to households of low-income students so that they could decide as consumers how best to remedy their education deficit (McEwan, 2004).

▪ NO CHILD LEFT BEHIND—A POLICY SHIFT ON THREE LEVELS

No Child Left Behind's focus on results represents a commitment to efficiency in federal education policy. Sanctions for underperforming schools reflect a (relatively new) federal understanding that schools must be changed wholesale, rather than one program at a time. No Child Left Behind makes provisions for educational choice for students if a school demonstrates a failure to improve. In this way, No Child Left Behind connects to impulses toward liberty outlined in legislation such as the Higher Education Act, Regan-era initiatives, and present-day privately supported voucher programs.

■ MAKING AND IMPLEMENTING MODERN EDUCATION POLICY

Conventional wisdom holds that federal policy for almost any endeavor, not simply education, is a consequence of political interactions among the three components of the so-called "iron triangle"—the education agencies of the executive branch, congressional committees, and interest groups. The idea for a new piece of legislation may arise from any of these groups or from a large number of other sources, such as a new book, a study supported by a philanthropic foundation, a journalist's article, or an academic research project. This process is termed **agenda setting**, and there are a number of theories that discuss how to approach this from a theoretical perspective. Once an executive branch agency or a member of Congress is interested in sponsoring an idea, drafting the concept in bill form is relatively easy, either by counsel in an executive branch agency or by the Legislative Drafting Service in the House or Senate.

Research Navigator.c⊕m

agenda setting

Identifying potential supporters of an idea and then negotiating compromises may be necessary before important factions agree to support a bill. The more important a bill, the more groups likely to be affected, and the larger the federal appropriation involved, the greater the likelihood of controversy. Many more bills are defeated than enacted. In many cases, an idea must be submitted repeatedly over a number of years before eventually proving sufficiently understood and popular to be adopted. Also, whereas an idea may stem from many sources and be initiated by any one component of the triangle, conventional wisdom holds that eventually the other two components must also agree before passage will occur. Brokering the multifaceted agreements necessary to ensure enactment of a bill is an art form seldom fully appreciated by the public.

Making a Bill into Law

Conventional high school civics textbooks explain that policy is made by the legislative branch and implemented by a politically sanitized executive branch agency. This is but another form of the frequently promulgated myth that a clear distinction can be made between policy making and policy administration. In fact, political conflicts left unresolved in the enactment process are almost inevitably reflected in efforts to implement legislation. Consequently, administering federal education policy is far from a mechanically simple, politically sterile, technocratic undertaking (Bailey & Mosher, 1967; Jones, 1984).

Once an education bill has been approved by both houses of Congress, it is often necessary to convene a conference committee, composed of members from both House and Senate, to resolve differences between the two houses' versions of the bill. Assuming presidential approval, the bill then becomes a public law and is numbered as such. For example, Public Law 94-142 denotes the 142nd bill to become a statute in the 94th session of Congress, thereafter, the specified administering agency within the executive branch is responsible for drafting regulations to implement the new statute.

Implementation and Administration

Regulations are necessary because it is not generally possible in the enactment phase to write a statute so that it will cover every practical contingency connected with implementation and administration. Also, the political dynamics of enactment frequently necessitate a degree of ambiguity and vagueness. The higher the abstraction, the greater the probability that political agreement can be reached. "Accomplish good and avoid evil" is an admonition so vague as to be vapid. However, few oppose the principle. As soon as legislation becomes specific, detailing which groups will receive how much money for what purposes, the prospect of political conflict increases. Thus, to dampen controversy and attract a greater number of supporting votes, authors of legislation sometimes leave legislative wording deliberately vague, and it is up to those who draft regulation to tidy up the rules of administration. If the statute is ambiguous, interest groups may lobby as assiduously to influence regulations as they did to influence the initial legislation itself.

An education bill is likely to fall within the administrative province of the Department of Education. This cabinet-level department was created in 1978 on the recommendation of President Jimmy Carter. Previously, the U.S. Office of Education (USOE) as well as the National Institute of Education (now the Institute of Education Sciences—IES) were agencies within the Department of Health, Education and Welfare (HEW). The latter is now the Department of Health and Human Services (HH5), reflecting the separation of Education.

Department of Education legal counsel is responsible for drafting regulations. In this process, they pay particular attention to the legislative history of a bill. This is derived from the committee hearing recording and committee reports in both the House and the Senate. Whatever debate accompanied passage of a bill on the floor of each house also becomes part of the legislative history, as does the conference committee report, if any. From such records the intent of the bill is more fully deduced and prescriptions for administration are drafted that are intended to guide the actions of state and local officials as they implement legislation. Regulations specify purposes for which federal funds can be used, state and local plans that may be required by the Department of Education, and rules by which local projects will be audited.

Regulations, once drafted, are submitted to appropriate congressional committees for approval. Also, they are published and distributed in the *Federal Register* to ascertain the reaction of educators and others in the field. When the approval process is complete, regulations are inserted in the Federal Administrative Code and carry the weight of law. Often, guidelines are provided to assist state and local officials in interpreting regulations and the statute itself. Federal guidelines are typically written in straightforward language and provide examples of procedures and programs to assist local administrators (Kirp & Jensen, 1987).

Appropriation

To this point, explanations have focused on procedures concerned with enacting and implementing authorizing legislation, the substantive bill that specifies purposes of the federal education program and authorizes funds to be spent. The actual dollar amount Congress will allocate to purposes for which spending is authorized is established through an "appropriations" process. This endeavor is a virtually separate legislative track involving interaction with executive branch budget officials and relying heavily on the Congressional Budget Office and appropriations committees and subcommittees in both the House and the Senate. It is not sufficient for policymakers, professional educators, and members of the public merely to have a sophisticated understanding of the dynamics of authorization politics. Knowledge of appropriation politics, which is characterized by a separate political culture, is also necessary. A thorough reading of a book such as *The Politics of the Budgetary Process* is useful in gaining a comprehensive view of this important area (Wildavsky & Caiden, 2003).

Gaining Administrative Compliance

Federal officials are eager that education funds be spent in compliance with statutes and regulations. Inducing compliance is a topic that has been addressed by experts in public administration (Berman & McLaughlin, 1978; Knapp, 1983). A few of the strategies utilized by the federal government are listed here. Keep in mind that the United States bureaucracy is multitiered, with each layer wanting to guard its historically evolved prerogatives.

The major strategy pursued with education programs is to require state and local agencies to submit in advance a plan for the use of federal funds. The plan must comply with guidelines for the legislation involved. Thereafter, it is assumed that local administrators will operate in a manner consistent with a submitted plan. Periodically, state officials may audit a local or state agency—either the Auditor General of the Department of Education or the General Accounting Office (GAO) of Congress. The purpose of an audit is to ensure that program spending is consistent with locally submitted plans and federal regulations.

CASE 1 REVISITED

River City Blues

As Frank Farley reviews his options for fomenting school change, he realizes the federal government may be able to play a role in bringing additional funds to the district. What flexibility could Frank now have regarding the use of his federal funds? How could Frank use that flexibility creatively to bring about districtwide reform?

Another stratagem is to require local or state matching of federal funds. The reasoning is that a requirement of a mix of monies will commit local officials to the success of the federally subsidized endeavor as if it were wholly their own. Yet another strategy is to empower local clients or program recipients to pressure local districts to ensure compliance. There are at least two expressions of this strategy. One is to be found in PL 94-142, wherein parents of handicapped youngsters can request a "fair hearing" with local officials and even be represented by an attorney in the process. Such an adversarial process is intended to protect clients' statutory rights and to provide them with leverage for gaining local district compliance. Somewhat more subtle is the creation of school-site advisory councils and parent advisory councils, as recommended or required by a number of federal and state program regulations. The idea here is that parents—presumed program benefactors—will advise and appropriately oversee the actions of local education officials. No Child Left Behind's empowerment of parents to transfer children when confronted by a persistently failing local school is another strategy intended to gain administrative compliance with policy purposes.

Summary

Federal involvement in education policy making has increased substantially over the last 200 years, as has federal investment in educational programs. Federal investment in education rests at around 7% of total investment for education. Federal involvement usually addresses one of the following issues: promoting opportunity, ameliorating underinvestment, and capturing economies of scale. Within each of these motivating ideas, issues of equity, efficiency, and liberty can be found. The No Child Left Behind Legislation of 2001 represents a culmination of a number of federal efforts to spur educational reform. NCLB's accountability structure is well in tune with the language and structure of the standards-based reform movement in education that began to emerge in 1989. The sanctions outlined in NCLB (which include intradistrict school choice, school reconstitution, etc.) are in line with market-based reform ideas that have emerged since the publication of *A Nation at Risk* in 1983. In this sense, NCLB represents a culmination of other education reform impulses rather than a radical new direction in education policy. The process of enacting federal education legislation involves a number of players in the executive and legislative levels to design, pass, implement, and fund education policy.

Discussion Questions

1. From your reading of this and other chapters, craft an argument of federal involvement in public educational policy making. Base your argument in legal cases and Constitutional arguments. Determine your level of comfort detailing a rationale for federal involvement, and assess the strengths of your argument with classmates. Conversely, craft an argument for states to control educational policy making. Share this rationale with others and assess its strengths and weaknesses.
2. Assess No Child Left Behind from a federal perspective. How does this legislation complete the arc of legislation that came before it pertaining to education?
3. Determine a time line and a path for federalizing American curriculum. How would such a curriculum be crafted? What special interests would advocate for the defeat of such legislation? Under what authority could such legislation be crafted?

Web Resources

No Child Left Behind: http://www.ed.gov/nclb/

The Federal Register: http://www.gpoaccess.gov/fr/index.html

New American Schools: http://www.naschools.org/

Institute of Education Sciences: http://www.ed.gov/about/offices/list/ies/index.html

Head Start: http://www.acf.hhs.gov/programs/hsb/

Notes

1. Throughout this chapter and throughout this book, federal statutes will be referenced. Federal enactments are systematically numbered with the term Public Law (PL) and two digit sets. The first set of digits refers to the Congress in which the statute was enacted. The second set of digits refers to the sequence in which the bill became law in that Congress. Hence, No Child Left Behind is PL 107-110.
2. President George H. W. Bush's education legislation, America 2000, as well as President Clinton's Goals 2000 legislation were each built on a policy foundation that included standards, testing, rewards, and sanctions. For an academic perspective on this, see Smith and O'Day (1991). See also Pitsch (1995).

3. Contemporary Americans assume the Supreme Court to be the final arbiter when the executive branch and legislative branch reach an impasse or when there is another form of policy system gridlock. Interestingly, Baker (1947) asserted that Constitutional framers did not view the Supreme Court in this overarching role. Rather, the final arbiter of decision making was seen to be citizens, not institutions.

4. Congress passed Morrill's first effort in 1858, only to have it vetoed by President Buchanan. Morrill's "reply to President's veto of Land Grant Bill" is an articulate justification of federal encouragement of education.

5. See http://www.heritage.org/Research/Education/bg1755.cfm for a summary of research. Most researchers agree at this point that Head Start imparts initial gains to poor children, but there is controversy about whether those gains continue into late elementary or middle school. See also Zigler and Muenchow (1992).

6. http://www.ed.gov/about/overview/fed/10facts/index.html.

7. For an early example of this work, see Jencks and Smith (1972). For a more recent treatment, see Burtless (1996).

8. "Debate on the Smith-Hughes Vocational Education Act" (1917). Reprinted in Background Readings, pp. 47–49.

9. NASDC history can be found at http://www.naschools.org/contentViewer.asp?highlightID=6&catID=105.

10. There is a wide body of research on what is termed "agenda setting" at the federal level. For one overview, see Sabatier (1999). For alternatives to the iron triangle, see Kirst and Meister (1983).

CHAPTER TEN

Budget Planning and Administration

■ INTRODUCTION

Budgeting is a process by which an organization has an opportunity to rationally align resources and purposes.

An effective budget process has the potential to improve an organization's productivity and accountability. When used as a strategic tool, the budget process can focus the efforts of an organization's personnel on educational priorities in order to maximize student learning. Conversely, a poorly managed budget process can be a constant drain on educational stakeholders' time and energy, thus diverting attention from instructional activities (Hartman, 1988).

This chapter provides an overview of the budgetary process: planning, budgeting, and evaluation. It outlines how budgets are properly constructed and describes relationships between planning and resource allocation. Only a limited explanation of program evaluation is included, although it is an important component of a school district's budgetary process. Evaluation is a technical field in itself that is beyond the scope of this chapter.

LEARNING OBJECTIVES

By the end of this chapter you should be able to:

- Articulate and discuss a standard budgeting cycle.
- Discuss the merits of various theoretical overlays to budgeting—bureaucratic versus rational models, and others.
- Discuss the impact of politics on the budgeting cycle.

■ A PRODUCTIVITY PROBLEM PREAMBLE

Organizations should deploy resources so as to maximize effectiveness in pursuing goals and minimize consumption of resources in the process. Maximizing goal attainment while minimizing resource consumption is known as "productivity." In education, productivity

Crisis in the Chorus Room: The Budgetary Politics of Mission Statements

There is a new principal at Holly High School, and as a consequence, another round of meetings to determine the school's (or the principal's) new mission statement. The requisite rounds of meeting and secret ballots have been held, and the new principal calls a staff meeting in the chorus room (the only room on campus big enough to hold all 122 faculty and staff) to decide between two choices. The social studies department head presents choice one:

Holly High School aspires to enable every student to reach his or her maximum potential as a scholar and a citizen.

There are murmurs of support and discussion. The math department chair presents choice two:

Holly High School strives to ensure all graduating students be able to read and count at an eighth-grade level.

The faculty seems less enthused with choice two. After little debate, choice one wins and Holly High has a new mission statement. Which mission statement seems more appropriate to you? Given our discussion of precision versus abstraction, which mission statement would you most like to have your job performance measured by?

is a function of purposes achieved divided by resources consumed. That is easy to write or read. However, in education, particularly public education, it is difficult to pursue productivity and almost impossible to measure it precisely. It is difficult to gain agreement on specific organizational purposes, to reduce goals to measurable objectives, and to record resources in a manner that allows them to be linked systematically to objectives.

Consider the example given in the box above about Holly High's new mission statement: *aspires to enable every student to reach his or her maximum potential as a scholar and a citizen.* This is a noble goal, and it may well be that Holly High officials, teachers, and other employees routinely strive to fulfill it. The problem is that such a mission statement, however desirable from a political standpoint, does not easily lend itself to quantification. How would one know, other than through sheaves of self-reports and virtually unverifiable personal testimony, that Holly High was fulfilling its announced purposes?

Now consider the mission statement proposed by the math department chair: *Holly High School strives to ensure all graduating students be able to read and count at an eighth-grade level.* This goal is measurable technically. It may be far too restrictive to be acceptable politically. This is a public agency's dilemma. Political acceptance often demands abstraction. Technical accuracy requires practical precision.

However, even overlooking monumental measurement problems, it is difficult to know how to expend resources to maximize an inclusive and politically acceptable goal such as maximizing students' scholarly and civic potential. Does one do it through one or a combination of activities such as classroom instruction of mathematics and reading, striving to enhance students' self-esteem, field trips to city council meetings, athletics, student government, and so on? In effect, there is little known regarding production functions for meeting lofty aspirational purposes.

To make matters worse, major data and accounting challenges impede the process of determining production functions. In order to know accurately the most cost-effective means of teaching reading, for example, we need not simply know what reading materials are used, but also how reading teachers, and perhaps other teachers, allocate their time. If we know how teachers allocate their time, and how they use it to teach reading, then we have some chance of determining the best ways to teach reading and how much these "best ways" cost. We could then compare reading teaching costs and select from an array of possible instructional activities those that are most cost-effective.

School districts cannot easily specify what they spend on reading or mathematics instruction, or most any other kind of instructional activity, because they do not record the manner in which teachers allocate time. Hence, when one receives an estimate of reading instruction costs, it is likely to include amounts spent on instructional supplies or professional development costs for reading teachers. Such estimates, however well intended, miss the major cost element—teachers' instructional time.

Matters of mission and measurement imprecision presently render education an unusually soft undertaking, which will be discussed in detail in Chapter 14 devoted to issues of efficiency. Meanwhile, it is sufficient here to note such challenges. They explain why school budgeting will not have the rigor of resource allocation decisions in many other sectors. Still, education involves literally hundreds of billions of dollars annually. Even if these resources cannot be targeted with optimum precision, they should be allocated with as much rationality as possible.

■ BUDGETARY PROCESSES

The budgetary process gives an organization the opportunity to systematically establish educational goals and determine how to allocate resources so as to achieve them. The budgetary process comprises three major phases in a cycle of events aimed at enhancing an educational organization's ability to educate students: planning, budgeting, and evaluation. Table 10.1 illustrates the relationships among these three phases. The budget itself should not be seen as the starting point or ending point, or as a separate activity from planning and evaluation processes. *Budgeting is a practical bridge between planning and evaluation.*

Developing an effective budget requires educational stakeholders to plan in detail programs, services, and activities they intend to operate for an upcoming academic year. Budgets represent the financial crystallization of an organization's intentions by placing priorities identified in the planning phase into a financial context. This means that both the objectives of the budget and the means of attaining them should be explicitly stated in a financial plan. Ideally, resources are expended consistent with a school district's overall educational plan, and evaluations of programs and activities subsequently inform the next cycle of planning and budgeting.

The planning and budgeting process does not stop with development of a budget. In order to ensure that plans are correctly implemented, that progress is being made in reaching organizational targets, and that information is reported and monitored, an organization's actual performance must be assessed regularly.

Like many other processes, the budgetary *process* is as important as the final result of the printed budget document. It is clear when observing various budget development stages that participatory decision making is valuable also (Kratz, Scott, & Zechman, 2001).

TABLE 10.1 Budget Development Calendar

Date	Event	Participants
1/15 3 hours	Preliminary budget development discussion with Board	Superintendent Business Office
1/24 1.5 hours	General orientation meeting: preliminary budget development discussions	Budget Committee Principals Union reps
1/26 4 hours	Workshop to review base budget parameters (revenue, expenditures, staffing, etc.); begin to develop and balance preliminary budget	Budget Committee
1/28 3.5 hours	Continuation of 1/26 session	Budget Committee
2/7 4 hours	Review and discuss preliminary budget recommendations	Budget Committee Principals
2/8 4 hours	Review and discuss preliminary budget recommendations	Budget Committee Union reps
2/16 3 hours	Presentation of preliminary budget to Board	Board Superintendent
2/23 3 hours	Continuation of 2/16 meeting (NOTE: last day of action for layoffs, to meet legally requited notice to employees by 3/15)	Board Superintendent
March–April	General Group and Board workshop discussion sessions on program budget planning: special education, elementary and secondary instruction, operations and maintenance, instructional support services, etc. Dates and specific budgets for review to be determined	Board Superintendent Superintendent's cabinet
If Layoff Action Taken, Follow Up Includes		
4/7 6 hours	Refine preliminary budget, develop tentative budget. Review layoff recommendations	Budget Committee
4/11 4 hours	Review and discuss refined preliminary budget	Budget Committee Principals
4/12 4 hours	Review and discuss preliminary budget	Budget Committee Union reps
4/20 3 hours	Board action on final layoff notification	Board Superintendent
4/27	Final date for board action on layoffs	Board Superintendent
If No Layoff Action Taken, Process Continues		
5/17 6 hours	Tentative budget workshop: complete education plan and tentative budget recommendations for Board approval	Budget Committee
5/24 6 hours	Continuation of tentative budget workshop: complete education plan and tentative budget recommendations for Board approval	Budget Committee

continued

continued

Date	Event	Participants
6/2 4 hours	Review and discuss tentative budget recommendations	Budget Committee Union reps
6/6 4 hours	Review and discuss tentative budget recommendations	Budget Committee Principals
6/8 3 hours	Board workshop and discussion of tentative budget recommendations	Board Superintendent
6/15 3 hours	Board to adopt tentative budget	Board Superintendent
7/1	Last date to file adopted tentative budget with county (must indicate date, time, and location of public hearing on final budget)	School system business office
7/7 5 hours	Review, discuss, and complete final budget recommendation	Budget Committee Principals Union reps
7/13 3 hours	Board workshop and discussion on final budget recommendations	Board Superintendent
7/27 3 hours	Continuation of board workshop and discussion on final budget recommendations	Board Superintendent
8/1	County to have reviewed and returned filed tentative budget	School system business office
8/3 3 hours	Board to hold public hearing and adopt final budget	Board Superintendent
9/7	Last date to hold public hearing, adopt final budget	Board Superintendent School system business office

In gaining an understanding of the planning-budgeting-evaluation cycle, educational leaders and stakeholders are in a better position to translate educational objectives into reality through accomplishment of budgetary goals.

■ PLANNING

Planning is a management function that involves systematic determination of future resource allocation. The specification of educational goals, objectives, and priorities is the guiding compass of the budget around which both planned expenditures and anticipated revenue are determined. It is an integral part of the budgetary process that should occur at all levels within an educational system.

Even as decentralized as education is in the United States, federal officials should concern themselves with broad trends and provision of incentives for states and local districts to act in the national interest. Enactment of the previously mentioned No Child Left Behind Act draws federal programs ever more forcefully into the web of local district activities. Hence, an interaction between federal and state officials regarding budgets and priorities would be useful.

State officials should be concerned with matters such as enrollment projections, teacher supply and demand, and capital needs. In addition to these state concerns, local officials are regularly engaged in planning new buildings, alterations in curriculum, changes in attendance boundaries or bus routes, implementation of new student grading policies, or launching of school-site parent advisory committees.

Education decision makers often neglect formal discussion of such important topics. Under such circumstances, decisions are made by default and inertia prevails. When decisions regarding important preconditions are not included in the planning process, the budget fails to reflect a strategic mindset that seeks to optimize allocation of resources for improving student outcomes.

Basic Planning Concepts: Approaches, Philosophies, and Techniques

The purpose of planning is not simply to institute change. Change will occur whether or not there is a plan. Rather, a prime purpose of planning is to reduce uncertainty and focus organizational activities to use resources efficiently. Through systematic long-range planning, it may be possible for an educational organization to reduce inefficiencies involved in the administration of a school district, produce greater pupil achievement or parent satisfaction, induce parent participation, and so on.

Planning for the budget is not simply a technocratic process that is always rational and devoid of political considerations. The political side of planning is, of course, the amount of money governments are willing to provide for education. The "In the News . . ." section has a story about proposed California legislation that would impact the manner in which funds are provided to schools. There is no one comprehensive planning tactic that universally guarantees efficiency and effectiveness in the planning process. As the importance of planning for the school budget has dramatically increased, several planning approaches, philosophies, and techniques have evolved. The various choices regarding the way planning is conceived, and thus the way it is used in forming the budget, help planners to distill the purposes, goals, and priorities of an educational endeavor.

Which type of planning approach, philosophy, or technique is appropriate during the planning process depends on the goals sought and the organization's structure. The question is which of these planning approaches, philosophies, and techniques best serves an individual school or school district. The question is not planning versus no planning.

Planning Lens: Rational, Bureaucratic, or Political. As shown in Chapter 5, there are differing organizational perspectives on planning, budgeting, and evaluation. The three contrasting perspectives on the budgetary process are helpful for understanding how decision making is conducted. The first, a *rational* model, assumes that educational stakeholders involved in the planning process act in a logical fashion to improve student outcomes.

A second perspective assumes that budget planning is based on standard patterns of behaviors generated by the rules and regulations of a "top-down" hierarchy. This is known as a *bureaucratic* or *organizational* approach.

A third approach is a *political* perspective that assumes budgeting is a power play among actors seeking organizational rewards. These three perspectives to planning provide unique explanations of the objectives and motives of those planning for a school budget.

Rational. A fundamental assumption of the rational perspective is that those formulating an educational plan and developing a school or school district budget act in a logical

In the News

Since California's property tax revolt more than 25 years ago, teachers, parents and school supporters have honed their battle skills arguing with politicians in Sacramento for more education money every year.

They haven't always gotten their way, but since 1988 they have been able to count on a minimum funding level established by Proposition 98, the voter-approved ballot measure enshrined in the state constitution that says schools would be given first priority in the budget.

"It's a very profound statement," said Dan Kelly, a physician who has served on the San Francisco Board of Education since 1991. "It says that the public thinks that investing in children is the highest priority for the stability and the prosperity of California, not only now, but for the future."

Prop. 98 is again the hands of the voters now that Gov. Arnold Schwarzenegger has called a special election to decide his "Live Within Our Means Act," a measure that would dramatically reshape how the state draws up its spending priorities.

At its most basic, the special election ballot measure pits those who believe schools should have a steady, guaranteed source of funding against those who say the amount should be determined anew every year.

While the Live Within Our Means Act would not overturn Prop. 98, it would eliminate its central principle: that schools always get at least as much money as they got the year before.

Under Prop. 98, school funding rises with enrollment and the cost of living to create the legal minimum owed to schools each year. Schools can also receive more than the required minimum, and when that happens, the additional money increases the minimum schools get the next year.

For example, the state gave schools more than the legal minimum in the dot-com boom years between 1999 and 2001. For that reason, schools received $7.2 billion more in the fiscal year that just ended than they would have received if they had been getting only the minimum all along.

Passage of Schwarzenegger's ballot measure would end that practice.

The ballot measure would also eliminate a provision of Prop. 98 used in tough economic times that lets lawmakers use a less generous formula to decide the education budget. In its place, Schwarzenegger's measure would give governors the power to unilaterally cut portions of the budget up to four times a year in deficit years if the Legislature did not do it first.

The governor is selling his ballot measure with the help of public educators' prime nemesis: Supporters of the property tax cap known as Proposition 13, which educators blame for drying up the schools' best source of funding when it passed in 1978.

In fact, it was the shriveling of property tax money for schools that led voters to approve Prop. 98 as a counter-measure 10 years later—after the quality of public education had noticeably deteriorated.

Many parents and teachers believe there is still an imbalance under current law between what schools get and what they need. Bill Honig, the former state schools chief who pushed for passage of Prop. 98, agrees with that but said the measure has done a good job of protecting the vulnerable school budget.

"It's working just the way it's supposed to work," he said. "School funding is too big a target, there's too much money there, so people wanted to raid it.

Proposition 98 puts pressure on lawmakers and the governor not to do that."

But to fiscal reformers on the governor's side, Prop. 98's current spending formula feeds an already bloated system at the expense of good fiscal health for everyone else.

They say it's an example of the kind of laws that can create budget uncertainty in the state each year because they set aside general fund money for specific purposes—such as education—and then provide automatic increases based on a formula.

State Chamber of Commerce leaders and tax-cap advocates say that most such automatic spending needs to end. They say that governors should have the authority to make mid-year cuts in tough economic times if the Legislature won't, a new power that Schwarzenegger's ballot initiative would grant.

"We don't believe that the amount of money (for education) should be driven by an arbitrary formula that guarantees significant increases every year," said Jon Coupal, president of the Howard Jarvis Taxpayers Association, a group named for the author of Prop. 13. "While recognizing that education is a top priority, the amount of money should be driven by need, and showing that (school) programs are having a positive impact."

Without relatively predictable funding guarantees, the amount of money for schools would vary with the state's economy, said Brad Williams, an economist with the legislative analyst's office who is studying the impact of the measure.

"The long-term impact is that more and more school funding becomes discretionary, it would be determined by annual decisions by the governor and the Legislature," Williams said.

From Asimov et al. (2005). The Battle over How to Pay for Schools. *San Francisco Chronicle*, July 5: http://sfgate.com/cgi-bin/article.cgi?file=/c/a/2005/07/05/MNGEQDJ4A81.DTL

fashion to improve student outcomes (Drake & Roe, 1998). Acting in a logical fashion implies that planners have appropriate knowledge and authority to develop a plan centered on student outcomes as a primary criterion. Decisions and planning based on other criterion, such as political agendas, are irrational in the sense that they may not be aligned with elevated student learning.

An additional assumption of the rational approach is that a systematic plan seeks to operate with what is called technical efficiency. Technical efficiency requires that persons involved in the planning process strive to produce a maximum level of student outcomes with a set of given financial, organizational, and legal constraints (Satori, 1998).

Bureaucratic/Organizational. In the bureaucratic perspective, schools are regarded as complex, hierarchical organizations nested in a larger school system. Planning and decision making are constrained not only by school district policies and rules but also by state and federal statues and regulations. Consequently, according to Hartman, school personnel develop a set of "standard operating procedures" to guide their planning (Hartman, 1998).

The assumption of the bureaucratic approach is that planning focuses on sustaining or increasing last year's spending base and the school or school district's educational goals and objectives are secondary. The criterion around which educational stakeholders formulate an educational plan and the budget to support it are existing organizational processes. This translates into a tendency to maintain the status quo from planning one academic year to the next (Hymes, 1982).

Political Economy. The basic guidelines for a political perspective suggest that budgeting is, at its root, bargaining among self-interested individuals and groups (Hartman, 1998). Formulation of the educational plan and the budget must be understood as a political activity. Depending on their value orientation—for example, equality, efficiency, or liberty—various school constituencies may desire different organizational outcomes. Parents may prefer smaller classes, and teachers may reasonably prefer higher salaries. Science cannot easily be invoked to resolve such conflict.

Conflict is seen as normal or customary in budgeting characterized as political. A political perspective on decision making and budget formation assumes that when preferences conflict, the "political power" of various actors determines decision process outcomes. Power is used to overcome others' resistance and obtain one's preferences in the organization. Often, planned educational goals do not reflect a priority for student learning but instead reflect the personal goals of persuasive, powerful school personnel or groups external to the school, such as voters or businesses. Some of the planned goals and objectives may indeed be self-serving and status enhancing for individuals involved; others, particularly those concerning curriculum, pedagogy, or staffing, may represent beliefs that certain decision will be better than others for student learning (Hartman, 1998). Regardless of whether educational plans are altruistic or self-serving, they are largely subjective and intuitive and seldom use formal measures of student outcomes as criterion for planning.

Planning Philosophies. Planning can be conceived of as strategic or managerial. The distinction is one of abstraction. A strategic plan for one level of operation may be regarded as managerial for another. A strategy is a plan for achieving a large-scale objective. A tactic is one of several steps in a strategy. Managerial plans comprise tactics. The general meaning of these terms can be illustrated.

Strategic Planning. A nonprofit hospital increasingly loses patients. Rising medical costs and competition from outpatient clinics and neighborhood surgeries have reduced revenues. The board of directors requests top-level administrators to prepare a strategic plan for recapturing the hospital's share of the medical market. After examining available demographic and medical service information, the administrators conclude that several patient populations in the hospital's region are underserved. The hospital's board of directors adopts a strategic plan to enhance its client population and increase its market share by providing new services to the elderly as well as opening new programs in weight loss and sports medicine. Having settled on such a strategy for becoming more competitive, the board instructs management to undertake the detailed tactical planning necessary to implement this strategy.

Managerial Planning. A school board becomes uncomfortably aware that an increasing proportion of district students are scoring low on standardized tests. The board directs the superintendent to assess the situation and develop a plan for elevating pupil achievement.

An analysis of student performance throughout the district reveals two major problems. One is that the district's secondary school curriculum is no longer appropriately "aligned." What the district expects to be taught, so-called *standards of achievement*, what teachers are conveying in their classes, what is covered by tests, and what district criterion-referenced tests are measuring are not coinciding sufficiently. (Chapter 14 contains a more extensive explanation of *curriculum alignment*.) Second, low student performance is concentrated at a few schools where teachers' absenteeism, turnover, and formal grievances have increased over the last several years. In these schools, low employee morale and inadequate administrative leadership have compounded curriculum problems.

The superintendent and staff explain these findings to the board and recommend a two-pronged plan in which (1) a major realignment of the district's secondary school curriculum is proposed for the following summer (a project that should proceed in stages, subject matter area by area, and that may well take several years), and (2) a systemic assessment of low-performing schools' leadership and, where necessary, a buttressing or replacement of principals. The board agrees with the two procedural objectives—curriculum alignment and strong school-site leadership—and turns to the central administration for the managerial planning and operational procedures necessary to implement them.

Whether strategic or managerial, whether done by a school district or another organization, planning processes are remarkably similar. First, problem must be identified. In the two examples above, it is the loss of clientele, or market share, and lowered output. Subsequent analysis must be undertaken to identify possible causes of the problem. Efforts must then be made to generate possible solutions. An assessment of likely costs and effects of solutions should be made. Where a solution depends on events or actions outside an organization's immediate control, an effort should be made to judge the probability of such events taking place.

Finally, having assessed alternatives and associated probabilities, planners should rank solutions in order of priority and feasibility. Having agreed on a solution, they can proceed to the detailed planning necessary for implementation. Planning follows a paradigm similar to problem solving or decision making. Planning techniques can help rationalize the process and reduce uncertainty.

Planning Techniques. There are many useful planning techniques, such as *PERT*, *linear programming*, *queuing theory*, and *computer simulation*. It is uncommon for average and smaller sized school districts to employ these planning techniques, as they are most useful in large organizations with complicated scenarios of inputs and outputs, and require considerable effort and investment on the part of a school district to carry out. For this reason, only brief attention is devoted here to these planning techniques. Still, it is good for a school leader, public official, or finance expert to be familiar with such techniques.

PERT (Planning, Evaluation, and Review Technique). PERT was initially developed for use with the military's Polaris missile program in the 1950s as a technique for managing large-scale multistage defense projects. The process is particularly useful if stages of a large project are interdependent; for example, completion of step B may require prior completion of step A. Development of a PERT chart requires an analysis of each of the steps necessary to carry out the budgetary process, charting those steps to illustrate their sequence and relationships, and estimating the time required to accomplish each step (Hartman, 1998). It is also useful in assessing the resources needed for each step. Resources translate into three things: money, knowledge, and time. An important component of PERT is the *critical path*. This is the sequence of activities that allows the least room for delay and requires special attention. The critical path determines the minimum amount of time necessary for project completion.

Linear Programming. This technique is used in planning resource allocation where one factor is to be optimized (made as large or small as possible) while others are held constant or maintained within specified limits. It is a useful technique mostly where there is a single clear goal, where technology for achieving the goal is agreed on, and where all factors and constraints involved in goal achievement can be quantified. Some manufacturing processes exhibit these characteristics, but education seldom does.

Queuing Theory. A queue is a waiting line made up of either people or things. Queuing theory addresses the question of whether lines are too long or waiting periods are too excessive. It provides information on the value of the waiting time in quantitative terms. Queuing theory applies to a number of situations in a school setting, but it has limitations. Perhaps the most serious drawback is that it deals only in averages. It cannot determine expected waiting times in individual cases, or even maximum waiting times, which may be more important in some cases. For example, queuing theory may specify that the *average* wait in a school cafeteria line is 10 minutes. This may seem fine until experience shows that the *maximum* wait time is 25 minutes, giving some students virtually no time to eat if we assume a 35 minute lunch period. As queuing theory yields more precise information on the relationship between the number of cafeteria terminals and student waiting, decision makers can make fairly accurate estimates of the cost of reducing waiting time. In this case, queuing theory assists in identifying the value of reducing students' waiting time or savings made by lengthening it.

Computer Simulation. Models impute order to reality by positing relationships between things and events. Computer simulation attempts to accrue information about a process or phenomenon through the use of models. A model may be representative, in which case it reflects reality and allows a user to learn about and understand phenomena under study. Other models may be predictive. These must also be representative, in the sense that they resemble actual processes, but they are programmed to provide users with information regarding possible outcomes given different circumstances. A predictive computer simulation in the educational system might involve trying different bus routes in order to determine which route requires the least amount of fuel.

Because computer simulation models typically incorporate large numbers of variables and relationships, simulations cannot be described in terms of simple formulas and processes, and their complexities are beyond the scope of this chapter. Local level educational stakeholders rarely rely on sophisticated planning techniques to inform decision making. Most district personnel have mental models that allow them to give meaning to everyday experiences, to make predictions about future events, or to estimate the costs of waiting times on the educational process. In negotiating a teacher pay scale with a school board, one might use a mental model of school board characteristics, past behavior, and current budget constraints to predict the achievable, and to plot strategy accordingly.

The Planning Phase: Development of the Educational Plan.

What should be the first step in planning a budget? The planning process itself needs to be planned. Before the planning process starts, it is necessary to clarify which persons perform which functions when and for what period of time (Drake & Roe, 1994). The timeframe for which the plan is to be used can be long-range or short-range and the planning process can be either centralized or decentralized.

Determination of a timeframe for planning is often influenced by many factors: legislation, political pressures, past practice, attrition of key managerial employees such as the superintendent, or changes in members of a school board. Contemporary educational standards dictate the need for school districts to develop a strategic plan for a period of 3 to 5 years. Patterned after a planning strategy used in business, a strategic plan represents the school district's goals through a mission statement and a plan of action for achieving the mission.

A key to adhering to a strategic plan is to build in flexibility and adaptability so that the organization can change when needed. Upcoming legislation, an unexpected natural disaster, or unanticipated economic fluctuations are examples of changes that may modify a strategic plan and, consequently, the budget. If the educational plan is long-range, for example, 5 years, checkpoints along the way for adjusting the plan and budget are essential. These checkpoints are conventionally called benchmarks or targets. Long-range educational plans must also be accompanied by short-range plans that guide the budgeting process during the current school year.

The planning process can be either centralized or decentralized, depending on leadership style, relationships between the superintendent and the school board, relationships between the school district and the community, and organizational history (Hartman, 1988).

A centralized planning process is normally a top-down approach dominated by district administrators. There is little opportunity for involvement by school personnel and community or other educational stakeholders. Frequently, centralized planning coincides with centralization of budgeting, but this is not always the case. School district administrators may solicit suggestions for an educational plan in a participatory fashion and then autocratically develop the budget for implementing the plan. In a sense, this is practical as the budget can be too technical for those not familiar with budgeting to participate in the development of the budget. However, participatory involvement in both the educational plan and the budget by various educational stakeholders other than district administrators has gained momentum in the age of accountability.

In a decentralized planning process, decision making is participatory, with involvement from the school-site level. It envisions the principal, teachers, and community members cooperating to create an educational plan that stresses the unique needs of an individual school. The overall educational plan is coordinated by the district office to ensure that it meets legal mandates and federal and state requirements and restrictions, and reflects the educational goals of the larger community to which the school district is accountable.

The next step in the planning process is to identify the pervading philosophy and specific objectives around which the budget will be formed. The educational plan must identify in concrete terms the goals and priorities of the school district. These should be written in terms that avoid professional jargon so that the educational plan and budget can be understood not only by school personnel but also by the community (Drake & Roe, 1994).

Clear communication is crucial not only when conveying the educational plan to stakeholders but also in the planning process. An educational plan that reflects school district goals and priorities requires clear communication concerning issues such as legal limitations; political implications; regional, state, and national educational problems; and results of the evaluation of prior educational plans (Drake & Roe, 1994). Federal and state minimum requirements are increasingly becoming integral parts of the planning phase that must be communicated and considered when creating the school district's educational plan. Without clear communication, no matter how adroitly or attentively planners toil, their educational plan is likely to be ineffectual in meeting the needs of the student population.

■ BUDGETING

It is through budgeting that a school district aligns its resources with its purposes as determined in the planning process (see, for example, Wildavsky & Caiden, 2003). Budgeting is a concrete, practical link between *planning*, the forward-looking portion of an organization's budgetary process, and *evaluation*, which focuses systematically on past performance to inform future planning and budgeting developments.

School finance and administration textbooks commonly describe budgeting in the context of business practices. This book abandons such a convention for three reasons. First, as mentioned in the preceding paragraph, budgeting is more usefully viewed as a component of management's planning and evaluation activities. In addition, a budget should represent a plan for direction of an organization's total discretionary resources—such as time, personnel, and physical resources—not just money.

Like the development of an educational plan, formulation of the budget is a give and take process that must be understood as a political activity. Resource allocation is not simply a technocratic task. Once resource decisions have been made in alignment with the educational plan regarding matters such as personnel, salary levels, and supplies, the technical feature of the budget is limited to keeping accurate records, an activity that is by no means simple. However, prior to that point, budget decisions may reasonably involve bargaining.

Bargaining, ideally conducted in good faith with an organization's purposes and welfare in mind, is often a mechanism for resolving differences between constituencies. Even if the educational plan spells out a particular program, decisions must be made as to the amount of funds allotted to the program. Once a bargain has been struck, its fiscal consequences should be represented in the budget. In this sense, the budget is a political document. It is the concrete representation of the political compromises that have been made concerning allocation of funds as outlined in the educational plan.

Basic Budgeting Concepts: Assumptions, Power, and Methods

To the uninformed observer, it may seem that budgeting is a simple process of calculating the costs of operating a school district and then applying federal, state, and local government legal provisions to determine revenue sources. Such hit or miss notions of the budget fail to appreciate the complexity of the budgeting process. Traditionally, the school district budget has been viewed as an instrument of control rather than a strategic tool for optimizing educational outcomes for all students. In order to effectively develop a budget, those charged with the process need to consider budgeting assumptions, how the budget translates into power and control, and various budgeting methods that reflect an organization's objectives and goals.

Fundamental Budgeting Assumptions. For budgeting to be most effective, three critical conditions should exist—*annularity, comprehensiveness,* and *balance*.[1]

Annularity. A budget, an organization's resource allocation plan, is intended to cover a fixed period, generally a year. This need not be a calendar year, beginning January 1 and ending the subsequent December 31. Indeed, few school districts use a calendar year. The budget year is generally known as a *fiscal year*. The fiscal year for the majority of U.S. school districts begins July 1 and concludes at the end of the following June, in the next calendar year. However, some districts use a fiscal year that coincides with the academic year or with their state's legislative appropriations cycle.[2] The fiscal year for school districts is usually specified by the state.

Regardless of the precise period, or even if it is a 2-year period, the important principle is that there is a previously agreed-on span of time over which resource allocation and financial administration occur. Also, in order to be maximally useful, the fiscal year should not be altered frequently. It is important to select a fiscal year and stay with the decision. Otherwise, public confidence, record keeping, and fiscal analyses are jeopardized.

Comprehensiveness. An organization's budget should encompass all fiscally related activity, on both the resource and expenditure sides. A budget may contain a variety of funds and accounts, such as instruction, administration, maintenance, and transportation. It may well keep track of expenditures in more than one way—that is, by function, such as physical education, as well as by object of expenditure, such as instructional salaries. What is important is that the budget and the budgetary process encompass all revenues received by an organization, regardless of source or purpose, and all that an organization spends, regardless of source or purpose. If a budget is not comprehensive, organizational resources may be accrued or used for purposes outside the educational plan. This is certainly inefficient and impedes the path toward productivity and accountability.

Balance. This is the third critical budget assumption. What is spent must not exceed what is received by way of resources. This is not to assert that all organizations must always live within their immediately available resources. Certainly resources can be borrowed and paid back later. Borrowing money to construct a long-lasting building makes good sense (as illustrated in Chapter 11). The point is that a budget assumes explicit organizational acknowledgment of resources and obligations, and the two must match. If they are out of balance, again an organization is out of control.

📁 CASE 1 REVISITED ────────────────

River City Blues

Recall the case of Frank Farley, who wants to bring wholesale reform to a large urban district. Farley has specific priorities to address. Let's pick one: implementing a pay-for-performance program whereby teachers would earn bonuses for improved student performance. Such a policy would need to be researched, piloted, evaluated, and implemented. How would Frank budget for this process? Assuming no growth in revenue, where could Frank obtain these funds? What items of his budget could he cut? Where could he look for external funding?

Budgeting and Power. Individuals who are empowered to make decisions regarding resource allocation can determine an organization's direction. Frankly, budget control is organizational control; budget control is power. The appropriate conventional phrase is "power of the purse." The budgetary process can be used to concentrate power in the hands of a relatively small number of individuals or to distribute it to an expanded number of participants.

As with the planning phase, the budgeting phase is either centralized or decentralized. There are many possible degrees of decentralization or centralization that range from highly centralized to highly decentralized. Where on the continuum the individuals involved in the budgeting phase, as well as in the planning and evaluation phases, choose to locate themselves is affected greatly by the district and site administrators' underlying views regarding power and control.

A centralized budgeting process has budgeting decisions occurring predominantly in the district office. This is a hierarchical, top-down approach with a superintendent and a few key district personnel having the power and the control of the budgeting process. Schools within the district are given specific dollar amounts for each budget category and are required to report to the district office how funds were spent (Hartman, 1988). This is evidenced by all students at a grade level tending to be treated the same by the budget.

In decentralized budgeting, also known as site-based budgeting or participatory budgeting, budgeting decisions are made at the individual school level. In some cases, site councils that can include parents and other noneducator members of a community influence budgeting decisions (Kratz, Scott, & Zechman, 2001). In decentralized budgeting, a lump sum of money is sent to the school site for allocation according to a site-developed plan. In contrast to centralized budgeting, decentralized budgeting has students at the same grade in different school sites treated according to each school's educational plan.

Planning, budgeting, and evaluation methods in a school or school district must mesh smoothly to ensure coordinated and effective results. Trying to impose a centralized budget on a decentralized plan or, conversely, a decentralized budget on a centralized plan is feasible under certain circumstances. If all those involved understand beforehand their role in the process, the limitations of the process, and the expected outcomes, it is possible to effectively develop and execute planning, budgeting, and evaluating processes that are both centralized and decentralized. For example, carefully conceived centralized budgeting can involve school personnel and citizens in planning, and reap practically the same benefits as decentralized budgeting coupled with decentralized planning. However, if the degree of centralization or decentralization is extreme, it is unlikely that an effective plan, budget, and evaluation will result.

Budgeting Methods. The school budget is often characterized as being so complicated that few individuals outside of those who developed it understand its contents and intentions. The endless columns of figures that compose the traditional line-item budget are so confusing and complex that it is impossible to fathom how each item relates to schools' educational objectives. A number of alternate budgeting methods have surfaced in response to the public's demand for clarity in reporting how their educational dollars are spent.

Many factors must be considered when choosing which budgeting method to use: legal restrictions, size of the district, changes in enrollment, district financial condition, and school governance structure (Hymes, 1982). However, given the fact that the states have widely varying systems of funding and regulations for public education, there is no one method that can be described as superior to others. Conventionally, school districts determine the most workable budgeting methods for their unique situations and modify it as experience and circumstances dictate.

The budgeting method chosen by a school district provides the particular structure for the development of budget estimates and preparation of the budget document. A brief review of the most common budget methods helps in understanding various management objectives sought through the budget: cost control, organizational responsibility, program planning, output measurement and evaluation, political control, setting priorities, and reallocation of resources toward more efficient or desired areas (Hartman, 1988). Pure examples of any of these methods are rarely seen in practice and most budgeting involves a variation or combination of one or more of these.

Incremental Budgeting. Budgeting in most organizations is said to be incremental. This is particularly the case in public sector institutions such as schools. Historically, incremental budgeting is one of the most common approaches to school budgeting, as it is simple to understand and execute.

The beginning point for developing an incremental budget for this year is the previous year's budget. In this context "incremental" refers to the assumption that a previous year's budget expenditures are an adequate base for building next year's budget. The vast bulk of expenditures continues year after year, budget cycle after budget cycle. The term **incremental budgeting** is derived from the practice of adjusting each budget line the same "increment" as the percentage increase or decrease during each budget cycle (Thompson & Wood, 2001). A result of incremental adjustments to the base is that each line of the budget receives the same increase or decrease. Some school districts believe that incremental budgeting is fair in that no area of the budget can be said to receive less than another area. Adherence to the expenditure base gives little consideration to how the budget object fits into the educational objective, and the focus of the budget is not on outputs but rather on inputs.

Line-Item Budgeting. **Line-item budgeting** is a by-product of incremental budgeting. In line-item budgeting, the "line item," such as personnel and supplies, is considered the proper base for expenditure. As a result, budgets are planned around each line and the new budget is constructed on workload and inflationary increases to each line's base, usually last year's expenditure. Little attention is given to how the line-item object fits into the educational objectives. Thus, the focus of the budget is on the status quo and on inputs rather than outputs.

There are several benefits of line-item budgeting that make it one of the most common approaches to school budgeting. The line-item categorization of objects for which resources are allocated make the budget easily understood and controlled. Additionally, each line of the budget is taken into consideration for increases or decreases, making it more specific than incremental budgeting.

Formula Funding. This too is a variant of incremental and line-item budgeting. It is also the manner in which most school systems operate, particularly large school districts.

A number of functions are budgeted centrally. These include activities such as food service, transportation, central office management, and school board operation. Then, individual school operation is budgeted based on formulaic indices. Individual schools receive teaching positions based on anticipated enrollment (e.g., one position for every 25 students at the elementary level and one teaching position for each 20 students at the secondary level). Further, schools receive administrative assistants, psychologists, clerical workers, and so on based on enrollments.

Formulaic distributions give an impression of fairness and equity. Every school is resourced the same way, depending only on enrollment variations. In fact, this is deceptive and probably inefficient. It is inefficient if the principal has no control over how money is to be spent. In many heavily centralized systems, principals are but inert managers having little or no discretion over spending. They must accept and expend resources as budgeted. In effect, under such heavy-handed and centralized arrangements, principals are held responsible for successful operation of schools when, in fact, they are deprived of one of management's most powerful tools—financial discretion.

Formulaic arrangements can also be deceptively unfair. Usually it is teacher and other functional positions that are budgeted, not actual teacher salaries. In fact, particularly where teachers have contracted transfer privileges based on seniority in the district, higher salaried teachers may congregate in selected schools, taking their higher salaries with them. Under such arrangements it is entirely possible to have individual schools in which actual budgeted expenditures are twice as high as at another school, simply because the teaching staff at school "A" is vastly more senior than that at school "B."

Formula funding would be fine—that is, both efficient and equitable—if enrollment indices were used to determine overall school resource levels (a lump sum of operating funds, including all teacher salaries) and then principals were granted discretion over how to use the funds.

Research
Navigator.com
Program-
ming, plan-
ning, and
budgeting
systems
(PPBS)

Programming, Planning, and Budgeting Systems. **Programming, planning, and budgeting systems (PPBS)**, or its refined extension—programming, planning, budgeting, and evaluation systems (PPBES)—center on building a budget to support execution of the educational plan. Each element of the budget is built around educational objectives (outputs) rather than inputs. The cost of each educational objective is estimated, alternatives are considered, and the budget is developed around groups of corresponding objectives. Consequently, resource allocation is more complex than in incremental and line-item budgeting. Most school districts that use PPBS or PPBES are large in size with more resources and personnel dedicated to executing this often cumbersome budgeting method.

Research
Navigator.com
zero-based
budgeting

Zero-Based Budgeting. The basic concept of **zero-based budgeting (ZBB)** is to build an entire budget from cycle to cycle with little consideration of a previous year's budget. It is the opposite of incremental budgeting, in which an existing budget base is unchallenged and attention is focused only on new increases or decreases. The fact that a program or object was budgeted for in an existing or past year does not guarantee that it will be funded next year. All programs enter the budget development process with a resource allocation of zero dollars. The continuation or initiation of each program must be justified in accordance with the educational plan.

Zero-based budgeting forces careful consideration of priorities and goals, with the highest priority programs receiving funding. However, justifying every facet of a budget every year is a time-consuming, expensive process. Although most educational stakeholders believe ZBB to be conceptually appealing, the complexity of its process has led many school districts to abandon it (Thompson & Wood, 2001). Also, zero-based budgeting is unrealistic when there are multi-year labor and vendor contracts. An area in which ZBB is still considered to be quite useful is in the justification of new programs. New programs quite logically need to be reviewed annually for their educational contribution and requisite expenditures.

School-Site Budgeting. **School-site budgeting**, or site-based budgeting (SBB), is the concept of developing a school district budget through involvement of various school personnel and possibly the local school community (Brimley & Garfield, 2005). It is a decentralized budgeting process that has gained popularity with the advent of the notion of increasing productivity and accountability by actively involving those most directly able to effect results.

The budgeting committee or a school-site CEO or principal is responsible for developing a budget within the constraints set by federal, state, and district regulations and the limits of total resources allocated to an individual site. Typically, the scope of the school site's budgeting decision-making power is limited to supplies, activities, equipment, and, depending on the collective bargaining agreement, salaries. Budgeting for administration, capital projects, and maintenance remains within the domain of a district office or other central authority By involving a wider representation of educational stakeholders in the budgeting process, SBB seeks to foster better understanding of the educational plan and to provide a more inclusive view of education (Thompson & Wood, 2001).

School-site budgeting also is more consistent than any other budgeting strategy with the contemporary nature of research knowledge regarding instruction. Where there is uncertainty, as is true regarding instructional methods, a productive strategy is to permit a wide array of approaches. Innovation and variety are essential to experimentation. Schools, permitted to follow their own paths, but being held accountable for the results, are more likely to find useful new approaches. The dead hand of centralized, tightly drawn decision making often stifles innovation and results in a one-size-fits-all instructional mentality. Of course, permitting local school innovation assumes confidence in a centrally determined set of outcome measures by which progress can systematically be appraised.

All of these methods are evident to some degree, often in combination with each other, at state and local levels. Variation and mergers of methods occur from one district to another. This is as it should be given the differing needs, traditions, and goals of each school district.

The Budgeting Phase: Development of the Budget

Budgeting involves four important, sequential, and recurring components or activities. The first, **budget development**, is oriented toward the future; it embodies a concern for what will be or should be. **Budget administration** is concerned with the present and focuses on proper financial procedures and approvals. **Accounting** is oriented toward the immediate past; toward what happened and to what degree it was consistent with projections and plans. The fourth component, **cost analysis**, takes a longer view of the past; it involves an assessment of past actions and an appraisal of their effectiveness relative to costs. The first component, developing the budget, should be aligned with an organization's planning phase. The fourth, cost analysis should be aligned first with the evaluation portion of the budgetary cycle and, subsequently, with the planning phase of the cycle.

Budget activities are cyclical—beginning, ending, and beginning again. The four components of the budget—development, administration, accounting, and analysis—are arrayed sequentially, but they overlap. All four activities may be, and indeed should be, occurring simultaneously, though each may be focused on a different fiscal year.

For example, in August or September of any particular year, a school district's staff might well be engaged in current fiscal-year budget administration activities, such as preparing payrolls and approving purchase orders for the forthcoming spring semester's instructional supplies. This is budget administration. Accounting staff might well be closing record books on the recently completed school year. They would be summing expenditures for different categories and getting records in order for the annual audit. This is bookkeeping. Evaluation staff

Research Navigator.c●m
budget development

Research Navigator.c●m
Budget administration

members might well be engaged in data collection and analytic procedures involved in appraising the results of an instructional innovation that was tried during the just-ended school year. They might be undertaking these cost analyses in order to inform the superintendent whether or not the innovation should be continued or terminated. Last, officials may be engaged in developing the budget for the school year beginning the following September.

Budget Development. This is the forward-looking phase of budgeting, the time when decision makers consider the financial implications of the educational plan developed during the planning phase of the budgetary process. Decision makers must consider information crucial to budgeting—for example, what will district revenues be from federal, state, and local sources; what expenditures are required for funding the educational plan; and will revenues and expenditures balance?

Ideally, as mentioned in the discussion of the planning process, a school district's educational goals and objectives are identified and agreed on prior to discussion of revenues and expenditures. In reality, a typical budgetary process begins with a focus on revenues, followed by creation of the educational plan and determination of expenditures. Although this should be resisted the focus should be kept on the school district's educational priorities as the driving force of the budget, educational stakeholders know that more often than not the budgetary process begins with an estimation of revenue and, thereafter, a shoehorning of planned spending into estimated resources (Thompson & Wood, 2001).

Other decisions that must be made involve determining which educational objectives will not be funded. No matter how well a district plans and develops the budget, it probably will not get all the money it would like to have. With continuing expansion of programs and services coupled with reductions in federal and state aid, this could mean an actual cut. These and dozens of related decisions must be made prior to final production of the budget document.

To facilitate budget development, schools generally design a so-called **budget development calendar** (Table 10.1). The process of constructing a budget calendar and getting it approved by the superintendent and school board is typically the responsibility of a district's budget officer. Thereafter, the budget officer is responsible for ensuring that factual items and necessary analyses are supplied sufficiently early to mesh with appropriate calendar target dates.

A complete budget development calendar is guided by chronological events, such as state-legislated approval dates, actions by the legislature on appropriations, expiration of collective bargaining agreements with employees, and the school academic calendar. Such important dates are specified in the left-hand column of the calendar in Table 10.1. In addition to critical dates, a complete budget development schedule makes clear crucial items of information, or assumptions about crucial information. For example, budget participants need to know what projected enrollments are for the forthcoming year, what revenues are expected to be, what salary increases, if any, are to result for employees as a consequence of bargaining, and what the size of the teacher workforce is to be. Often this information will also be contained in a **budget assumption letter**. The budget assumption letter describes important preconditions of the school district that need to be considered when developing the budget. This document is distributed to appropriate budget development participants and informs the framing of their budget proposals.

The budget development calendar should also specify participants in the decision process. These are listed in the right-hand column of Table 10.1. The district illustrated here has a highly centralized budget development process. To be sure, principals and other employees participate in budget decisions. Indeed, the committee frequently

Research
Navigator.com
budget
development
calendar

referred to on the calendar comprises representative employees. However, even though employees participate in developing the budget, the result is still a centralized school district plan. It is possible to allocate substantially greater budgetary discretion to school sites—to have a decentralized budget.

It is during budget development that results of prior analyses should be taken into account. Planning techniques such as those illustrated earlier in this chapter can inform this part of the budget formulation.

Also, it is at this point in planning next year's resources that a decision should be reached regarding expansion of what has been appraised and found effective and termination of what has been judged ineffective. For example, if an instructional innovation has been shown to be cost-effective, it might well be inserted into the operational budget at this juncture. Of course, this suggests that what has not been demonstrated to be cost-effective should simultaneously be deleted from a budget at this juncture. Here one encounters a major deficiency in the operation of U.S. school districts. There is a tendency to add, but a reluctance to withdraw a program, even in the absence of evidence regarding its effectiveness. This is where the evaluation portion of the cycle begins to inform planning and budgeting.

Budget Administration. Once the various components of an organization have agreed on planned resource allocations for the forthcoming fiscal year, it becomes crucial to ensure that resources are indeed allocated in accord with the agreement, and that expenditures are consistent with the budget. This is the function of the organizational members responsible for budget administration, such as the comptroller, bursar, or business manager. Regardless of their title, their overall responsibility is to approve or to see that approval has been obtained for requests for spending from school personnel. The purpose of this is to ensure that spending requests are consistent with agreed-on educational and budget plans. For example, payroll departments, purchasing officers, maintenance supervisors, and shipping and receiving departments, as well as line administrators, all have a role to play in seeing that resources are received and distributed in keeping with a district's overall resource allocation plan—its budget.

Accounting. Assuming that resources are allocated in an approved manner, it is still necessary to maintain records of transactions. This is done for three reasons. The first is to ensure that over time particular functions do not receive more resources than intended. Accounting procedures can keep track of accrued actual expenditures by budget category, as well as **encumbrances**—resources that have already been obligated though not yet spent (for additional information, see Gross & Warshauer, 2000).

The second reason records are kept is to enable an organization, after the fact, to ensure compliance with the spending plan. To this end, auditors—people who review spending actions to report compliance, or lack thereof, with a budget—use bookkeeping records. An organization, if sufficiently large, may have both internal and external auditors. At least annually, most states require school districts to have an external audit of their books to ensure compliance not only with district budgets, but also with state and federal regulations.

The third reason for financial record keeping is that the organization can subsequently use the information as a basis for financial analyses, such as cost-effectiveness analysis or appraisals of equity. Records kept accurately and in a useful form are crucial to these analytic endeavors. Generally, the more abstract the level of aggregation, the less useful the data. For example, a single entry such as "Salaries" typically is of little use to analysts. How many individuals were being paid? How were they paid? To do what? For how long? These questions imply the kinds of bookkeeping categories more likely to permit studies of goals such as productivity, accountability, equity, or efficiency.

School districts generally adhere to a uniform accounting code. In 1957, the United States Office of Education published *Financial Accounting for Local and State School Systems: Standard Receipt and Expenditure Accounts* (Reason, Alpheus, & White, 1957). This was intended as a guide to state and local education agencies in keeping their financial records and continues to influence and form education accounting and bookkeeping procedures. This document and its successors (Roberts & Lichtenberger, 1973; Samuelson & Tankard, 1962) have been widely beneficial. By encouraging local and state agencies to adopt a standard form of record keeping, they have facilitated research across geographic boundaries as well as over time. Each state now has a uniform accounting manual patterned after the federal model.

Budget approval and accounting are typically considered together as budget administration. They are separated here simply for purposes of explanation. However, each differs from the fourth component of the budget process, cost analysis.

Cost-Analysis. Cost-effectiveness analysis and cost-benefit analysis are similar methods of examining the economic value of one or more alternatives. In cost-benefit analysis, the dollar amount of all benefits flowing from an alternative is compared with the dollar value of all costs associated with that alternative. A major problem with cost-benefit analysis is that it is often difficult to assign monetary values to benefits. (How much is it worth in dollars for a child to learn to read faster?) In cost-effectiveness analysis, two or more alternatives are examined, each of which is presumed to offer the same benefit; the intent is to discover the least costly alternative. This eliminates the problem of assigning monetary values to benefits (Greene, 1996; Levin, 1970; Verstegen & King, 1998; Wolfe, 1977).

It may seem unnecessary to provide a special name for a procedure as seemingly easy as adding up costs. However, the procedure is not as simple as it appears. The problem is that costs often occur at widely different times, and $1 in 5 years is not worth the same as $1 now, *even* if there is no inflation. An intelligent person, given the choice of $1 now or $1 in 5 years would choose $1 now, for this individual is more certain of getting it now and can invest it so as to have more than $1 in 5 years.

Suppose that $1 is invested at 10% and one can be just as sure of getting $1 5 years from now as now. Then, if it were invested, at the end of 5 years, there would be $1.61. Under these conditions, the *future value* of a $1 5 years from now is $1.61. Alternatively, the *present value* of $1 5 years from now would be only 62¢ ($1.00/1.61). To compare costs that occur at different times, it is necessary to convert all costs to present values and then compare these values.

Comparing two ways of providing beginning foreign language instruction illustrates an application of cost-effectiveness analysis. Both alternatives are assumed to result in 200 students per year being educated to the same level in a foreign language. Thus, the benefits are identical.

Alternative 1 uses two teachers. Each teaches five classes of 20 students for a full academic year. Teacher salaries are $20,000 the first year, and increase $1,000 per year thereafter. Each classroom costs $3,000 per year for light, heat, and custodial services. Textbooks cost $20 per student per year. (All other costs are ignored for this example.)

Alternative 2 uses a language laboratory, and only one teacher. Because the laboratory is a more efficient way of teaching, it is possible for a single teacher to bring 100 students (20 per period for a five-period day) to the same level of competency in one semester that the conventional method was able to do in a full academic year. Thus, one teacher is able to teach, with the aid of the laboratory, 200 students in an academic year. The teacher's salary is the same as in Alternative 1, as are room and textbook costs. Of course, it is necessary to purchase and install the language laboratory. The laboratory costs $95,000 and $4,000 per year is required for supplies and maintenance. At the end of 5 years it will be obsolete and have no salvage value.

The present value of the costs of the two alternatives can be compared using a *discount rate* of 10% (Table 10.2). The discount rate is the interest rate used in making the present-value comparisons. There is no agreed-on rate that should be used for cost-effectiveness

TABLE 10.2 Simulated Costs for Two Language Programs over 5 Years

		5-Year Total		Present Value	
	Budget Category	Alternative 1	Alternative 2	Alternative 1	Alternative 2
Year 1	Salary	40,000.00	20,000.00	40,000.00	20,000.00
	Books	2,000.00	2,000.00	2,000.00	2,000.00
	Classroom	3,000.00	0.00	3,000.00	0.00
	Laboratory	0.00	95,000.00	0.00	95,000.00
	Lab upkeep	0.00	0.00	0.00	0.00
Totals		**45,000.00**	**117,000.00**	**45,000.00**	**117,000.00**
Year 2	Salary	42,000.00	21,000.00	38,181.82	19,090.91
	Books	2,000.00	2,000.00	1,818.18	1,818.18
	Classroom	3,000.00	0.00	2,727.27	0.00
	Laboratory	0.00	0.00	0.00	0.00
	Lab upkeep	0.00	4,000.00	0.00	3,636.36
Cumulative Totals		**92,000.00**	**144,000.00**	**87,727.27**	**141,545.45**
Year 3	Salary	44,000.00	22,000.00	36,363.64	18,181.82
	Books	2,000.00	2,000.00	1,652.89	1,652.89
	Classroom	3,000.00	0.00	2,479.34	0.00
	Laboratory	0.00	0.00	0.00	0.00
	Lab upkeep	0.00	4,000.00	0.00	3,305.79
Cumulative Totals		**141,000.00**	**172,000.00**	**128,223.14**	**164,685.95**
Year 4	Salary	46,000.00	23,000.00	34,560.48	17,280.24
	Books	2,000.00	2,000.00	1,502.63	1,502.63
	Classroom	3,000.00	0.00	2,253.94	0.00
	Laboratory	0.00	0.00	0.00	0.00
	Lab upkeep	0.00	4,000.00	0.00	3,005.26
Cumulative Totals		**192,000.00**	**201,000.00**	**166,540.19**	**186,474.08**
Year 5	Salary	48,000.00	24,000.00	32,784.65	16,392.32
	Books	2,000.00	2,000.00	1,366.03	1,366.03
	Classroom	3,000.00	0.00	2,049.04	0.00
	Laboratory	0.00	0.00	0.00	0.00
	Lab upkeep	0.00	4,000.00	0.00	2,732.05
Cumulative Totals		**245,000.00**	**231,000.00**	**202,739.91**	**206,964.48**
Difference			−14,000.00		4,224.57

analysis. A reasonable rate is the rate the district would pay if it borrowed the money. Costs for each year are assumed for this illustration to be spent at the beginning of the year. As such, the present value of the first year's costs is identical to their nominal dollar value. However, the present value of costs in future years is less than their nominal dollar value.

Note in Table 10.2 that the costs for one teacher are the same in both alternatives, and thus need not be included in the analysis. Similarly, the service cost for one room and textbooks costs are the same in both alternatives. It is necessary to compare, for Alternative 1, the cost of one teacher and one room with, for Alternative 2, the cost of the laboratory and its maintenance.

If we are concerned only with the undiscounted costs, it appears that the purchase of a language laboratory will save $14,000 over five years. However, if one correctly assesses discounted costs (present values), the language laboratory actually costs $4,225 more! The reason is that most of the costs for Alternative 2 must be assumed in the first year, whereas those for Alternative 1 are spread over 5 years.

Evaluation

Evaluation of programs involves the systemic assessment of an endeavor in order to determine its effects. Once the effects on several selected dimensions are known, evaluation usually entails a judgment of the endeavor's relative success or failure. Such judgment may involve measuring project results against a predetermined goal. Did reading achievement scores increase? Were student absenteeism and vandalism reduced? Was parent satisfaction enhanced? These are the types of questions evaluators pose. Their objective is to determine whether or not or to what degree a desired outcome occurred, to suggest how the undertaking might be rendered more effective, and to influence the allocation of organizational resources as a result.

Summary

Although often considered a concrete activity, budgeting is an area of school finance that is heavily influenced by the values and philosophies with which one approaches the endeavor. A common method of understanding the budgeting process is to think of the budgeting cycle. This cycle includes planning. Approaches to planning a budget may rest in the rational, bureaucratic or political models of organizational theory. Actual budgeting also presents a range of choices: incremental or zero-based, school-based or program-based. Each of these choices will determine the manner in which the budget is developed, as well as the budget amounts that result. Planning, development, administration, and accounting are key components of the budget process. Finally, determining cost-effectiveness or overall productivity enables policymakers to judge the worth of a program in relationship to its costs. These methods allow for value to be placed on the budgets in question.

Discussion Questions

1. Assume that you are the administrator of a key educational intervention such as a reading program. Discuss whether incremental or zero-based budgeting works more in your favor from year to year. Elaborate on your preference.

2. How do the rational, bureaucratic, and political models fit the budgeting process in public education? What assumptions about budgeting does one make with each of these three models?
3. Imagine yourself to be a high school principal. Try your hand at overlaying the budgeting process on top of a traditional 9-month school calendar with testing, breaks, sports, workdays, and so on. When would be the best time to work on budgetary issues?
4. Review the In the News article. What are creative ways to link California's need for additional finding to the budgeting processes discussed in this chapter?
5. Included on the companion web site, www.ablongman.com/Peabody is a spreadsheet with a school-based budget simulation. Instructions provided on the spreadsheet will guide you through a school budgeting simulation.

Web Resources

The Wake Education Partnership publishes an annual guide to school funding issues: http://www.wakeedpartnership.org/Research&Reports/QM05Updates.html

The Milwaukee Public Schools have a comprehensive budget webpage:

http://mpsportal.milwaukee.k12.wi.us/portal/server.pt?space=Opener&control= OpenObject&cached=true&parentname=CommunityPage&parentid=2&in_hi_Class ID=514&in_hi_userid=2&in_hi_ObjectID=444&in_hi_OpenerMode=2&

Notes

1. The authors are grateful for Aaron Wildavsky's explanation of these assumptions.
2. The federal government's fiscal year begins October 1 and concludes September 30 of the subsequent year.

CHAPTER ELEVEN

Managing Capital Projects and Fiscal Resources

■ INTRODUCTION

The term *school finance* connotes processes by which money for support of schools is raised and distributed. However, once these monies are in the hands of individual school districts, "business administration" captures more accurately the processes of exactly how those monies are spent. This book is primarily about education finance, not business administration; nevertheless, there is a certain amount of overlap, and this chapter discusses facets of business management that impinge directly on the conservation and effective use of fiscal resources.

LEARNING OBJECTIVES

After reading this chapter, you should be able to:

- Describe the process of siting, funding, and constructing school facilities.
- Assess the different ways in which a school system can accumulate debt.
- Articulate the ways in which growth can present fiscal and physical challenges to school systems.

■ CAPITAL CONSTRUCTION

Capital construction can make enormous demands on a school district's fiscal resources, yet much of it is outside the normal current expenditures budget and tends to be ignored in school finance discussions. The ebb and flow of school construction is directly related to demographic trends, which are outside the immediate control of school personnel. Additionally, projecting and planning for this growth is beyond the capacity of local school districts and is placed in the hands of other city or county officials. As a result, projecting growth becomes a process that is prone both to error and misinterpretation.

Demography and School Construction

From World War II to the end of the 1960s, an unprecedented number of new schools were built in America. Rapid increases in student population, combined with migration from farm to city and suburb, necessitated construction of thousands of new elementary and secondary schools. Financing this construction placed a heavy burden on capital markets. Moreover, not all resulting schools were well constructed. Even now, at the beginning of the 21st century, school superintendents are facing renovation and repairs to hastily built post-World War II facilities.

Decreasing birth rates in the 1970s resulted in substantial reductions in school construction. Although some areas, primarily in the Sun Belt, continued to expand in school-age population, most districts in the North and upper Midwest witnessed a decrease in number of students. This was particularly true in older cities and close-in suburbs. How to close unneeded schools became a primary problem for superintendents and school boards. Invariably, parents agreed that for economic reasons schools should be closed, but "not in my neighborhood."

The school enrollment cycle is once again on the upswing. In some ways, the dynamics are much the same as after World War II. Instead of baby boomers, school planners are faced with the Baby Boom echo as the children of baby boomers fill school rolls. School planners also face other demographic pressures related to increased enrollment. One of these pressures is migration into the United States as immigrants and their children gain access to public schools. Finally, another big population shift is occurring as many Americans move away from locations in the American industrial Northeast to southern and western states.[1] School enrollments grew by about 5 1/2% between 1985 and 1992. Today, public schools enroll approximately 48.3 million pupils. This is the highest point in our nation's history, and is expected to increase to 50 million by 2014 (NCES, 2005) (Figure 11.1).

If a district is facing enrollment surges after enrollment declines, accommodating new students may be as "easy" as filling currently underused schools to capacity, or by reactivating mothballed schools. In other cases, however, new students are enrolling in communities that must create schools to hold them. Some school districts have established schools that operate year round with four staggered tracks of students to increase the capacity of school buildings. Plans have even been adopted to create schools composed entirely of modular building units (or, "portables") that can be established quickly in rapidly expanding subdivisions.

Dollars spent for school construction, land purchase, and major repair and renovation are capital expenses, and are normally budgeted and accounted for separately from current operating expenses. Figure 11.2 displays a one-time snapshot of governmental contributions to facility construction.

Unevenness in capital outlay has important implications. Because construction of a new school is such a large investment, it is worth spending the time and effort necessary to be sure it is done properly. Borrowing is frequently used for capital outlays. Financing capital expenditures completely out of current revenues would mean large fluctuations in tax rates. In many communities, capital costs are raised through the issuance of bonds, which must be passed through referenda. In rapidly growing communities, the ever-present "school bond construction referendum" tries the public's patience and politicizes even operating expenses. The mechanism of bonds is discussed in greater detail below.

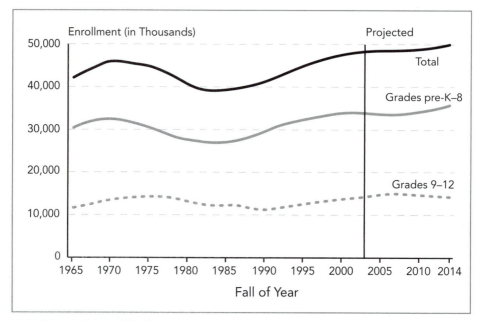

FIGURE 11.1   Public Elementary and Secondary School Enrollment in Prekindergarten through Grade 12, by Grade Level, with Projections: Fall 1965–2014

Note: Includes kindergarten and most prekindergarten enrollment.

Source: Hussar, W. (forthcoming). *Projections of Education Statistics to 2014* (NCES 2005–065), tables 1 and 4 and U.S. Department of Education, National Center for Education Statistics (NCES) (2005) *Digest of Education Statistics 2004* (NCES 2005–079), table 37. Data from U.S. Department of Education, National Center for Education Statistics, Common Core of Data (CCD), "State Nonfiscal Survey of Public Elementary/Secondary Education," 1986–2002 and "Statistics of Public Elementary and Secondary School Systems," various years.

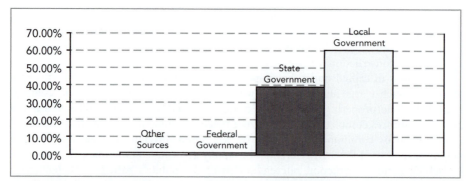

FIGURE 11.2   Percentage of Capital Outlay, 2002 (NCES)

An important characteristic of capital expense is unevenness of expenditure. Construction of a school in one year may cost millions of dollars, with expenditures in succeeding years being almost zero. Only the largest districts, such as New York and Chicago, can manage to smooth out these capital expenditures and spend about the same amount each year.

Building a New School

Land purchase and new school construction are major financial and planning undertakings. Large districts often do enough of this to have a special staff for the purpose; small districts must usually rely on the business manager to initiate the action. There are a number of books on the subject of construction, and an extended treatment is out of place here. Nevertheless, a brief outline of the steps in a construction project is useful.

Determining Need. The first step is determining the extent of the need. Projections of numbers of students to be served by a district for at least the following 5 years are essential. These projections, combined with careful analyses of present building capacity, verify the need for new facilities. Projections should be carefully examined before a decision to build a new school is made.

Below are listed alternatives to consider prior to constructing new facilities:

1. Space that is presently underused because of inconvenient arrangement of facilities could be remodeled.
2. It may be possible to use space in non-school buildings nearby. This is particularly true for classroom uses that are not part of K–12 instruction, such as day care. Nearby church school classrooms have often been used for this purpose.
3. It may be possible to consolidate selected operations with a neighboring school district that has space. An example would be special education classes that are smaller than necessary in each district.
4. It may be possible to increase the number of periods in a normal day at the high school level, thus increasing classroom use.
5. Multitrack year-round schooling, using selected models, can increase the capacity of a building by 20–25%.
6. Students may be reassigned to fill in underused classroom space.
7. Mobile classroom units (MCUs) may be used at schools to increase capacity. Some districts have constructed entire schools out of MCUs.

See the press release "In the News" from the Raleigh, NC–based John Locke Foundation listing many of these alternatives in opposition to bonds for construction in Charlotte, NC. How would you imagine educators would respond to these suggestions? Are these suggestions valid within the context of capital construction campaigns?

Determining Location. If, after a survey of options, it is decided that construction is the most appropriate solution to actual or potential overcrowding, the next step is to determine the new building's likely location.

Additions to present schools may be the least expensive alternative if space is available on a site and if shared facilities (multipurpose room, playgrounds, etc.) are adequate for the additional student load. However, this lower cost may be balanced by higher transportation costs if a sufficient number of students reside in a part of the district where there are no

In the News

RALEIGH—The proposed $427 million school bond in Charlotte-Mecklenburg would fund facilities that are far more expensive than in comparable districts and ignores alternative ways to build schools at a lower cost to taxpayers, according to the findings of a report published Wednesday by the John Locke Foundation.

Terry Stoops, author of the Raleigh-based think tank's *Building for the Future* report, used five different methods to evaluate the per-foot construction costs for Charlotte-Mecklenburg's planned new schools, including comparisons to planned schools in Wake and Guilford counties. Stoops found that Charlotte-Mecklenburg's costs were consistently higher—28 percent higher than in a comparable North Carolina school district, in the case of the planned CMS high school, for example.

"The Charlotte-Mecklenburg plan would spend many millions of taxpayer dollars in ways unrelated to providing a good education to students," Stoops said at a Sept. 28 press conference releasing the report in Charlotte. "Without innovative approaches to school construction, the planned series of bonds will exert a crippling tax burden on local residents."

The $427 million school bond to be voted on in November is the first of four issues that CMS officials have planned through 2011 to finance a 10-year, $2 billion capital plan for the school district. The plan would build 47 new schools, add classrooms at 22 existing schools, acquire additional school sites, and fund various support facilities and renovation projects.

John Hood, president of the John Locke Foundation, spoke at the press conference about the fiscal implica-tions of the CMS capital plan. While some bond supporters appear to believe that the passage of a state-run lottery will significantly defray the cost of school construction in Mecklenburg County, Hood said that lottery proceeds will in reality play only a small role. A JLF assessment found that the planned CMS school bonds would cost more than $200 million a year to finance, while lottery revenues would likely remain below $20 million a year.

Noting that Charlotte-Mecklenburg is already one of the highest-taxed urban communities in North Carolina, Hood said that enacting the district's capital plan would likely increase the tax rate by 22 percent or more when all the planned bonds are sold.

"The $427 million bond in 2005 is merely the opening bid on a massive construction project," Hood said. "Can taxpayers really afford a new $2 billion debt?"

In *Building for the Future*, Stoops discussed a range of options available to public-school districts to build needed school facilities more rapidly and at lower cost. These include:

- Forming public-private partnerships that give developers incentives to build schools and lease them to districts for a fixed term.
- Rethinking design standards and non-educational amenities at new school sites.
- Raising private dollars to help fund stadiums and other sports facilities.
- Using modular construction for many school-building needs.
- Operating some educational programs through virtual, Internet-based schools.
- Adapting and reissuing existing buildings.

> • Allowing more choice of schools to alleviate enrollment pressures and to model new approaches to building schools more efficiently.
>
> Excerpted from a press release by the John Locke Foundation, a conservative North Carolina think tank, on 2005 school bonds proposed in Charlotte, NC.

schools. Thus, it is vital that an enrollment projection include not only how many students are to be served but also where they live and will likely live in the future. Necessary data may often be obtained from city or county planning departments; electric, telephone, and other utility companies; and major residential builders and commercial developers.

Land Acquisition. Assuming that it is desirable to build a school at a new site, a district must proceed to purchase land. The simplest solution is to find a parcel of land in the middle of an area about to become a subdivision and agree with the owner on a price. Where large subdivisions are being built, a district often does this well before it will be necessary to construct a school. The district may be able to negotiate a good price for the land by cooperating with the developer, who should realize the increased value that closeness to schools brings to houses.[2] California is a case where state government and other local governments foster this cooperation. Each developer is required by state law to file an Environmental Impact Statement (EIS). This statement must be accepted by the city or county, which may require developers to deed a school site to the school district (or pay the district a specified number of dollars per house) before the EIS will be approved.

However, it is more likely that a suitable site must be assembled from parcels owned by a number of individual owners. A developer ordinarily does this by secretly obtaining options on each necessary parcel before making any purchases, to prevent owners from discovering what is occurring and holding out for a high price. It is difficult for school districts to deal in secrecy, particularly in states with open meeting laws. However, the district has an ultimate weapon not possessed by the private developer—power of condemnation, also called *eminent domain*.

Districts proceed in different ways on land purchases, some doing all purchasing through negotiation and others using condemnation exclusively. Condemnation has one advantage: the price is set by a court, relieving a district of allegations of overpayment. Negotiation, however, is often more appropriate when establishing cooperative arrangements with developers of a large area, or where special concessions important to the owner and unimportant to the district (such as payments spread over a number of years) would result in a lower price. Each situation must be approached on its own merits. In any case, the district's legal counsel must be involved at every transaction step.

Architectural Planning

Having selected a site, the district must begin architectural planning. A good architect can plan imaginatively and save the district money; a poor one can be a catastrophe and ill consequences can last for the life of the building. Architects should not be selected on a bid basis. Most architects' fees are standard (indeed, state law may specify what they shall be), and any architect who promises to charge a lesser fee should be viewed skeptically. Rather, an architect should be selected on the basis of past performance in other situations.

The firm (for it is seldom an individual architect) certainly should have built schools before. Stories abound of the famous architect who builds his first hospital, which is beautiful on the outside and absolutely unworkable on the inside. Firms should be invited to present sample photographs of their work, along with descriptions of the size of the firm and the kinds of expertise it offers.

After a preliminary screening, district personnel should visit schools designed by firms under consideration and talk with administrators, teachers, and maintenance personnel. This will narrow the choice to a few architects, who should then be interviewed on preferred work method, current office workload, and particular employees to be assigned to the project. It is important that these individuals' personalities be compatible with those of the district personnel who are to be most closely involved in the project.

The school district should next develop educational specifications—the number of students to be housed and the kind of educational programs to be offered. The more careful and complete such specifications, the more likely it is that an architect will be able to design the kind of school a district prefers. Avoid an architect who says, "Tell me how many students you want to house, and I will design a school for you with no further worry on your part." *Development of educational specifications is one of the most important parts of designing a school and should involve teachers, supervisors, and administrators.* It should not be rushed, for time must be allowed for reconciling differing views. Often, square foot per student figures will be used in political debate; school districts with square foot specifications greater than the state average will be tagged as extravagant, while districts with lower than state average figures will be tagged as unsympathetic.

With educational specifications in hand, an architect confers with district representatives to develop preliminary ideas. At this point it is desirable to keep the district delegation small so that it can reach tentative agreement on many facets of the plan in a reasonable time. However, a number of sessions may be necessary, and the district may need to gather additional data or refine its educational specifications. At some point the architect presents preliminary plans, usually consisting of plan view and elevations. When these have been sufficiently modified they will be ready for formal approval by the school board.

The architect now can develop detailed drawings and specifications. It is important from this point forward that the district's maintenance supervisor be involved, for the decisions made here can save or cost the district many thousands of dollars over the life of the building. District representatives should carefully review detailed final drawings. Errors found at this point are easy to correct. Found during construction, errors result in costly change orders; if not found until after the building is completed, they are even more costly to correct.

Bidding

The district then advertises for bids. Contractors interesting in bidding will obtain building plans from the architect, estimate labor and materials necessary, and obtain commitments from subcontractors. Typically, the general contractor does all carpentry, performs some of the other work, and supervises and coordinates all construction. Subcontractors are usually obtained for electrical work, plumbing, site grading, mechanical work, and a number of other jobs.

At the date and time advertised, general contractors' bids are opened and read. The district is generally required by law to accept the bid of the lowest qualified bidder, but this need not necessarily be the lowest bid. The architect should be present, and should carefully review the two or three lowest bids. The financial status of the general contractor should be determined, if possible, and the contractor's performance on other projects ascertained. The same is true of each subcontractor, who must be listed in the bid. Many other items must be assessed by an architect before recommendation of the bid award. (If recommending someone other than the lowest bidder, the architect should present good reasons, for there will probably be a challenge from the lowest bidder before the school board.) The board need not award the bid to anyone, although it usually will if the lowest acceptable bid is at or below the architect's estimate. Frequently an architect will specify alternatives, with a separate bid on each alternative, in order to be able to adjust total contract size to the funds available in case a bid exceeds the estimate. This complicates the selection of a bidder, for the lowest bidder on the base contract may be high on some alternative additions.

Construction

Construction now begins, under supervision of an architect, who visits the project site several times a week to ensure plans are followed and to resolve problems in interpretation of drawings or specifications, and to develop change orders where necessary. However, it is difficult for an architect to be on the site at all times, and shoddy workmanship can be covered up by subsequent construction before the next visit. Thus, it is essential for the district to hire a full-time inspector. This should be a person thoroughly experienced in all facets of building. He or she should be on the job anytime work is under way, and should insist on inspecting all work before it is covered. This is a crucial role; opportunities for concealing poor workmanship or perpetrating outright fraud are great, and the potential cost to the district is much more than what will be paid to the inspector in salary.

Design-Build Construction. Private and nonprofit organizations rely increasingly on design-build (or managed) construction for large buildings or projects such as industrial plants, commercial developments, or hospitals. This involves the services of a project architect and a prime contractor. However, the architect in this instance is not charged with both overall design and detailed drawing and specifications for the entire structure. Rather, once the functions to be performed within the proposed building are clearly known, the architect prepares requests for bids for various packages or components of the project: excavation, foundations, structural steel, heating and ventilation, interior finishes, and so on.

Bidders are provided with functional specifications, but not with detailed design drawings other than significant dimensions of the overall undertaking. Rather than simply expressing a dollar amount for which they will complete the component, a subcontractor also submits an overall plan with construction specifications for the component. In effect, the detailed work of an architect and structural engineer is completed by bidding subcontractors.

The design-build format has at least two advantages. It expedites construction of the overall project. Construction can begin early without being impeded just because the architect has not completed all drawings for every phase. More important, the managing contractor and architect have the advantage of subcontractor experience. By issuing overall performance specifications, but not detailed drawings, potential bidders can take advantage of their practical experience and offer better designs than might otherwise be the case, designs that often are less expensive to implement.

Design-build construction for public schools may not be possible in states that need to review detailed plans. Under such arrangements, whatever time was saved by the design-build mode would be lost by state review procedures. However, should managed construction become more widely adopted in the private sector, a means may be found to permit wider public sector use of similar techniques.

Completion and Preparation for Use

The final construction step is formal acceptance of a building after the architect has certified to the school board that construction is complete and satisfactory. Final payment may be made soon thereafter, although a percentage may be withheld for a legally specified period against the possibility of liens filed by employees or subcontractors for nonpayment by the general contractor.

This is not the final step in preparing a new school for students. The most important remaining activity (begun well before completion of construction) is purchase of equipment for the building. This involves careful planning to ensure that everything will be delivered in time. Lists of items must be compiled and cross-checked. Detailed specifications are drawn, based both on the educational needs expressed by principal and teachers and on the desires of the maintenance supervisor. These frequently conflict, for maintenance personnel prefer standardized equipment so as to minimize the problem of spare parts and of training mechanics, whereas teachers frequently want something unique, believing it will be more convenient or provide for better instruction. Equipment for a new building is a capital expense, usually paid for from the proceeds of the bond funds used in building construction. Equipment other than that for a new building (such as additional desks for an existing school) is also a capital expense, but is usually purchased from current revenues instead of from bond funds. These capital expenditures from current revenues are usually minor compared with those from bond funds.

Surplus Facilities. Many districts, because of previous enrollment declines or population shifts, have underused or unused buildings and properties. This is a smaller problem currently than in the 1970s, for school enrollments nationwide are trending upward again. However, in older sections of the nation, and particularly in older cities of those sections, enrollments may still be declining. Surplus schools and property are a fiscal problem primarily because they are a political problem. Everyone is for more efficiency, but not for closing a school in the neighborhood. The result is often underused schools and small class sizes. The most difficult problem facing a school board and superintendent is often that of deciding to close a school.

Assuming that a decision has been made to close a school, what is to be done with it? Sometimes the district itself can use the building and site for administrative offices or for special programs. However, unless the activities involved are being moved from rented facilities, this may simply mean shifting the surplus space to another spot in the district. (That may be good, if one part of the district is growing.)

In some cases, it is possible to convert surplus facilities to other community uses. A community hall, playground, library, or park are examples. The city, county, or state may need office space. In many states, law requires the district to offer the surplus property to other governmental agencies before it may market it publicly, and it may sell the property to another agency at lower than market value. This is often advantageous to the taxpayer, who supports both governmental entities, but that is scant comfort to the school district, which receives less cash than it might if it sold the property on the open market.

Unfortunately, nonschool uses for a surplus school may be limited, rendering sale difficult. Often the site is abandoned for school purposes because the clientele has moved away as the area becomes commercial or industrial. Even so, it is some times possible to find uses that make it possible to sell the property for a reasonable sum. Near Rochester, New York, Xerox Corporation bought a surplus school for warehousing purposes. In a number of cases, surplus schools in inner cities have been redeveloped into attractive apartments.

The list above is comprehensive. However, it assumes that funds are available for the siting and construction of new schools. This is not an easy or automatic assumption. Providing funds for school construction involves taking on debt, much as one would apply for a loan to purchase housing. Because it involves funding, debt, and often public referenda, funding capital construction is only slightly less charged and political a process than school board elections themselves. The next section examines in greater detail the ways in which school systems can manage debt.

■ SCHOOL DEBT AND ITS MANAGEMENT

There are three categories of debt, and they apply equally to individuals, school districts, and corporations. The first category is the amount owed for items recently purchased and received but for which payment has not yet been made. For an individual, examples are a charge account at a department store or an amount owed for current purchases on a credit card. For school districts, this category of debt is known as accounts payable and is normally paid out of current revenues within a month or two of receipt of goods and invoice. Thus it need not be considered further as part of debt management. Of course, if a district should be unable to pay its accounts on time, it might try to stall creditors (which is dangerous if you want to deal with them again), or borrow from a bank. Borrowing converts this debt into the second type.

This second type of debt is the sort that individuals incur when they borrow on a short-term basis to pay for purchases, or pay less than the full balance on their monthly credit card statement. This is short-term debt. One can think of this kind of borrowing as meeting a cash flow problem, whereby money comes in too slowly at one time of year and more rapidly at another time. This is particularly apt to happen with school districts, where tax receipts or tax-supported credits often arrive in school accounts from a county or municipal treasurer in large sums once or twice a year while expenses continue on a more uniform basis throughout the year. Districts faced with this problem usually borrow from a bank or other lending institution on a short-term basis, repaying loans when tax receipts arrive. The district guarantees to pay interest at a stated rate. Such loans must typically be repaid within twelve months, and this period constitutes the dividing line between short-term and long-term debt.

Finally, long-term debt is incurred almost exclusively for purchase or construction of capital assets. An individual incurs such debt when borrowing from a bank to buy a house or an automobile, giving the bank a mortgage. School districts borrow also, but special circumstances dictate the use of a different evidence of indebtedness, called a bond. A bond is simply an acknowledgment that money has been borrowed. The district promises to pay a specified rate of interest on the debt, and to repay the principal amount at a stated time. However, there is not just one loan. Rather, bonds are issued in multiples of $1,000 or $5,000. Since the amount borrowed at one time may be several million dollars, there will be many bonds, and many individuals or corporations can own them. In addition, bonds can be sold by one person to another. The school district owes interest and principal to whoever owns the bonds at the time payment becomes due.

Another difference between a bond and a loan to an individual is that an individual typically pledges property as security. If payments are not made, the bank can seize the property, automobile, or other physical asset and sell it, keeping what it is owed plus expenses and returning the remainder to the owner. School land and buildings are public property and cannot be seized for sale. Thus, the bond usually pledges the full faith and credit of the district. This means that the district is legally bound to tax its property owners a sufficient amount to pay principal and interest on the bonds, and it can be compelled to do so through court action. Because of this call on the taxes of property owners, school district bonds are relatively safe investments. However, it is possible that local conditions could cause a district to default on its bonds. In 1983, as a result of complications related to Proposition 13 and collective bargaining contracts, the San Jose, California, school district declared bankruptcy. The decision of the bankruptcy judge preserved bondholders' rights (employees forfeited negotiated pay increases), but until his decision there was serious concern among the district's creditors. The risk of default by a district is estimated by bond buyers and is reflected in the credit ratings and interest rates districts must pay when they borrow.

Reasons for Borrowing

Should a school district borrow? Some people believe any form of borrowing is wrong. However, there are several good reasons for borrowing under appropriate circumstances.

First, it is sometimes simply good business. Frequently, a vendor will give a cash discount for prompt payment. A typical bill might state, "Discount 1.5% 10 days, net 30 days." By paying 20 days sooner than required, the district can save 1.5% of the purchase price. Figured on the basis of 360 days per year, this is equivalent to an interest rate of 27% per year charged by the vendor. If the school district can pay the bill promptly, it should do so. Even if it does not have the money to pay promptly, it can probably borrow funds for less than 27% and it will save money in the process. Of course, this type of borrowing must be monitored carefully, for if more is borrowed than is necessary, extra interest costs may negate the savings.

Districts could eliminate the need to engage in short-term borrowing to ease cash-flow problems by levying a higher tax than is currently needed and amassing a reserve fund to meet cash needs during the year. In most states, however, this is illegal. The law requires that property tax rates each year be sufficient only to make up difference between budgeted expenditures and receipts, with receipts including all cash available at the beginning of the year. The reason for this is the basic principle of taxation that a government should not have tax revenues available until it is ready to spend money. In general, it is believed that individuals should have the right to use or invest cash themselves rather than giving it to government sooner than needed.

Of course, short-term borrowing can be abused. New York State provided a prime example during the 1970s. As a result of political pressure, the legislature voted a one-time large increase in school funding, hoping it would find the revenue to continue this in future years. However, there was insufficient money in the state's coffers to pay for the increase even in the year in which it was voted. The state solved the problem by a stratagem based on the difference between the fiscal years of the state and the school districts. This enabled the state to pay districts one year out of the following year's receipts.

However, the strategy also necessitated borrowing by districts until they received the state money, and borrowing by the state to pay districts before it actually had tax receipts in hand. All this borrowing was a bonanza for banks and increased the cost of doing business for school districts and the state. Nevertheless, not much thought was given to it until normal state receipts fell short of meeting state obligations to local school districts. In the spring of 1976, at the last possible moment, the state was able to borrow the necessary $4 billion, part of it from state employee retirement funds. If the state had been unable to borrow this money, many school districts would have defaulted on their short-term loans, something that did not happen even during the Great Depression of the 1930s.

Management of Short-Term Debt

Short-term debt, usually incurred to solve cash-flow problems, may be a loan from a local bank, as is usual when needs are small or for a limited period. Where needs are more substantial, districts may sell notes. These are similar to bonds, for they are promises to pay, but they have a short life (typically no more than twelve months) and do not pledge the full faith and credit of the district. Because they do not commit the district to tax itself for repayment, electoral approval is not necessary and borrowing is not subject to bonding limits. As security, notes pledge the revenue to be obtained from some future assured source. If they are secured by a promise to repay from taxes to be received at a later time, they are known as tax anticipation notes. Those secured by future state aid payments are called revenue anticipation notes, and those secured by revenue to be obtained from sale of bonds are called bond anticipation notes. Although notes are transferable, they are not usually bought by a dealer for resale, as are bonds. Rather, they are bought by the bidder who quotes interest cost, usually a bank. In addition to notes, which solve cash shortages expected to last for several months, a district may borrow directly from a bank for periods of one day to several weeks.

The other side of the cash flow coin is that at certain times of year a district may have substantial cash surpluses. Usually, keeping the money in bank savings is the least profitable way of investing it (with the exception of leaving it in a checking account, where it may draw no interest at all). Large districts typically have an employee whose duty is investment of idle funds (and usually also short-term borrowing as part of the cash flow problem). This investment specialist estimates the cash position for each day several months in advance, taking into account anticipated revenues and expenditures. Then he or she makes investments in such a way that the necessary amount of money, and not too much more, will be available to meet the district's day-to-day needs. The specialist makes only short-term investments—those less than a year in maturity—typically in certificates of deposit, bankers' acceptances, treasury bills, and so forth. To earn the most from funds, the specialist may even invest any cash left at the end of the business day overnight, and have it back again the next day. This is done through repurchase agreements with banks. Banks are required by law to have a specified percentage of assets available at all times in cash. However, they strive also to be as fully invested as possible. At the end of a business day they may find that their cash position is below requirement. Because government auditors always appear after business hours and without warning, the bank must borrow money overnight to cover its requirement, and it does so by means of repurchase agreements.

There are other types of repurchase agreements, all involving short-term borrowing. As with many other transactions, one must be careful to deal with reputable companies and take reasonable precautions. The city of San Jose, California, lost $60 million when two New York securities dealers went bankrupt and the securities San Jose presumably owned as a result of lending them money were never found.

Small districts usually cannot afford a specialist in short-term investment. However, even these districts can improve their cash flow management. School district revenues and expenditures are more predictable than those of a private business, both in timing and in amount. A business manager can therefore easily construct a calendar displaying predicted revenues and expenditures for each day of the school year, and from these projections, estimate the excess or shortage of funds in the district's possession for each day. Using this information, the manager can plan to invest idle cash during periods of excess for appropriate periods in, for example, certificates of deposit that earn more than bank savings, and to borrow on a short-term basis only the amounts needed for the minimum period necessary to keep money in the district's accounts. Most small districts do not do this, or do it poorly, and as a result, they operate less efficiently than necessary.

Long-Term Debt

Because long-term debt commits a school district to repayments over many years, it usually must be approved by a vote of the people, frequently by a super majority (votes of 60% or two-thirds are common). In addition, there are usually state restrictions on the total debt incurred. This limit is typically 5 or 10% of the value of assessed real property in the district. The intent is to prevent present district residents from saddling future residents with too large a debt, and to ensure that ability to repay present bonds is not overly diluted by future issues. Long-term debt may usually be incurred only for purchase of land and construction and initial equipping of buildings.

One reason for long-term borrowing is that school building construction is costly. To tax property owners sufficiently to pay for the entire construction cost during the year it is accomplished would usually mean prohibitively high tax rates, and in any case would result in extreme fluctuations of tax rates from year to year. By borrowing, the school district spreads costs over a period of years, giving more stability to tax rates. An alternative, possible in some states, is to pass a special tax levy that will be in effect for a specified number of years. The trouble with this method for major construction programs is that construction will not be possible until some years after the initiation of such a levy. School districts are seldom able to convince the public to pass such a levy sufficiently in advance of the need (and may in fact not be able themselves to project the need sufficiently). The idea is enticing to some because no money is borrowed and thus no interest need be paid. However, presumed savings are illusory. Taking money away from taxpayers prematurely means they are prevented from using the assets for their own ends, which might include earning interest on it.

Long-term borrowing is also defended as a reasonable way of spreading costs among generations. A school building will last many years, typically from 30 to well over 60. It seems unfair to force the present generation to pay the entire cost of buildings that will be used by future generations too. If people always lived in the same place, this kind of generational inequity could be excused on the same basis whereby we defend parents paying for the education of their children. However, since individuals move while school buildings stay, it is more equitable to allow a school district's future residents to pay part of the building's costs. Thus, bonds are the most frequently used method of financing new school construction.

Authorizing Bonds

Steps involved in authorizing, approving, and issuing bonds are numerous and complex. Each step must be conducted with complete legality; otherwise the bonds will not be salable. For this purpose, a district should engage a financial consultant specializing in bonding. Such a consultant:

(1) Surveys the issuer's debt structure and financial resources to determine borrowing capacity for future capital financing requirements;

(2) Gathers all pertinent financial statistics and economic data, such as debt-retirement schedule, tax rates, overlapping debt, and so forth, that would affect or reflect on the issuer's ability and willingness to repay its obligations;

(3) Advises on the timing and method of marketing—the terms of bond issues, including maturity schedule, interest payment dates, call features, and bidding limitations;

(4) Prepares an overall financing plan specifying a recommended approach and probable timetable;

(5) Prepares, in cooperation with bond counsel, an official statement, notice of sale, and bid form and distributes same to all prospective underwriters and investors;

(6) Assists the issuer in obtaining local public assistance and support of proposed financing;

(7) Keeps in constant contact with rating services to ensure that they have all the information and data they require to evaluate credit properly;

(8) Is present when sealed bids are opened and stands ready to advise on the acceptability of bids;

(9) Supervises bond printing, signing, and delivery; and

(10) Advises on investment of bond proceeds.

In addition to a financial consultant, it is necessary to engage bond counsel. This is a specialized law firm that reviews the legal details of bonding procedures to ensure that bonds are indeed a legal obligation of the district. Each purchaser of a bond expects to find attached to it an opinion by bond counsel (often printed on the back of the bond) that there can be no reasonable legal challenge to the indebtedness represented by the bond. This function cannot be served by the school board's attorney, for purchasers will want an opinion signed by an independent law firm. Indeed, sophisticated purchasers may insist that the opinion be written by one of a very small number of recognized bond counsels. The same firm may serve the functions of both financial adviser and bond counsel, if it has marketing as well as legal skills.

The bond election is the moment of truth when the district determines whether it will be possible to borrow money. District officials will, of course, have done all they can to ensure a successful outcome. From 1940 to 1960 over 80% of school district bond elections passed with the required majority, but since then passage has become increasingly difficult. The percentage of bond elections that have passed declined from 75% in 1960 to 35% in 1986 (Wirt & Kirst, 2005). Interestingly, the percentage of dollars approved has risen almost 80% over the same time period.

Fortunately, the need also decreased; there were fewer children to be educated. However, the demographic pendulum is now swinging the other way, and with increases in the number of school-age children, one can expect schools to issue more bonds and to be better able to convince the electorate to pass them. In any case, the need must be justified and documented, and then presented to voters in a convincing manner.

Selling Bonds

Assuming that district voters approve a bond issue, the next step is to find a purchaser. School districts do not sell bonds directly to individuals. Rather, they sell an entire issue to a dealer, usually a bank, brokerage firm, or syndicate composed of several banks or brokers. Availability of bonds is advertised and bids are received. The bid resulting in the lowest net interest rate to the district is accepted. Frequently, bids will differ only in the second or third decimal place (7.244% versus 7.235%, for example), but this difference of 0.009% on a $10 million bond issue amounts to a difference of over $13,000 in interest paid over 20 years.

To obtain the best bid, the district needs at least two things—a rating of its credit by one of the bond rating agencies and a bond brochure describing an issue. Both have the goal of assuring prospective purchasers that interest and principal will be paid in full and on time. There are two important bond rating agencies—Moody's and Standard & Poor's.

Moody's and Standard & Poor's. Although they use different codes to express the risk of a bond issue, both agencies rate issues on a scale from highest quality to extremely risky. If a district has sold more than $1 million in bonds fairly recently, it is probably already rated by one or both agencies. If it has not, or if the district's fiscal condition has changed markedly since it was last rated, the financial adviser will ask the agencies to review the rating. A small improvement in the rating can result in markedly lower interest costs over the life of the bonds, and is well worth pursuing. In making a rating, the bond analyst tends to look beyond the issue itself to the aggregated local economy and its burden of debt. He or she is interested in the *debt capacity* of the issuer (the maximum amount of debt that can legally be issued by the governmental unit) and in the untapped margin of debt capacity still available. The analyst is also interested in a quantification of indirect debt, composed of bond issues for which the issuer may be a guarantor, and overlapping debt, the sum of all debt issued by all local governments in an area. Usually expressed in per capita terms, overlapping debt includes the individual citizen's proportionate share of city, county, school district, and other special district debts outstanding.

Preparation of the bond brochure is the financial consultant's responsibility. The district should not attempt to do it unaided. Nonprofessional brochures are immediately apparent to purchasers, and tend to alienate sophisticated buyers. A professional knows what information prospective purchasers need, and knows how to emphasize the most positive facets. A properly prepared brochure may also result in lower interest costs, which will repay many times the cost of preparing the brochure.

Economies of scale are immediately apparent in bonding. The cost of an election, of bond brochure preparation, and of printing bonds is almost the same regardless of issue size. The cost to bidders of the analysis necessary to make a bid (again reflected in the bid) is also almost independent of the size of the issue. The larger the issue, the lower the cost of all these fixed items per dollar of indebtedness. In addition, it is extremely rare for a small district to receive a high rating by agencies, and frequently they will not rate such a district's issue at all. A low rating will result in higher interest, and no rating may even mean no bidders. In this case, the issue is usually privately placed with a local bank at a higher interest cost.

There is an alternative for small districts—the Municipal Bond Insurance Association. A school district can secure a commitment from the association. The wording of the commitment would be similar to this: "guarantee unconditionally and irrevocably the full and prompt payment of the principal and interest to the paying agent of the bonds," with the result that rating agencies will give the issue a higher rating than otherwise. Districts pay a premium to the association for this guarantee, with the amount based on the association's estimate of the issue's riskiness. It might seem that the premium would not be much less than the cost of higher interest rates if the issue went to market at the lower rating. The association, however, by specializing in small, fiscally sound districts, has been able to charge a premium that is sufficiently low to save money for these districts.

As with all other steps in the bonding process, care must be taken in the printing. The financial consultant assists in this. If the bonds are not correct in every detail, purchasing banks or brokers will discover the error and bonds will have to be printed again. The bonds are then sold by the bank or broker to individuals or other institutions. The bonds may either be coupon bonds, whose coupons bondholders clip and return each six months to receive their interest payment, or registered bonds, with the interest paid to the registered owner at the time each payment becomes due. A majority of bonds have been registered for a number of years (see, for example, Rabbinowitz, 1969).

Interest and Principal Payments

A school district could borrow, say, $5 million for 20 years through the sale of bonds, with interest payable semiannually and the entire principal falling due 20 years hence. Such a bond is called a term bond. This places a large repayment burden on the district at that future time. To meet its commitment to redeem the bonds, the district would have to establish a sinking fund into which it annually placed sufficient money (including interest on the fund) to add up to $5 million by the end of the 20 years. Bonds are not repaid, as are mortgages where each monthly payment is partly principal and partly interest. Instead, each individual bond is a term bond, with only interest paid on it until maturity. Typically, however, not all bonds of an issue will have the same maturity date. Instead, bonds are scheduled for sequential maturity dates: some may be only 5-year bonds while others are 20-year bonds. Maturities are scheduled so that the sum of principal and interest payments for the district is about the same each year. These are called serial bonds. An example is given in Table 11.1 for $5 million borrowed at 6% interest, with the first payment at the end of the present year, the last payment at the end of 20 years, and annual interest payments on the balance immediately prior to each principal repayment. Note that the sums of principal and interest are not precisely the same each year, for this would require paying a fraction of a thousand dollars in principal each year, but the schedule created here assumes that principal payments are in multiples of $5,000. A given number of bonds mature each year, as shown by the schedule and as stated on the face of each bond. Owners of bonds that mature in a given year present them for redemption and are paid face amounts. Except in the last year, annual payments are between $433,000 and $439,000.

The entire issue of bonds schematized in Table 11.1 has a 6% coupon rate. This means that the school district will pay 6% annually on the principal amount of each bond. The bank or broker, however, will make an independent decision on the effective interest rate for each maturity date that will be necessary to attract buyers. The broker will establish this effective interest rate by selling at a higher or lower price than the par value (face value) of the bond. In the case of a discount, for instance, the buyer may buy a $1,000 bond for $960. Nevertheless, interest of $60 per year is paid by the school district (6% of $1,000), and this amounts to 6.25% interest on the purchase price. In addition, when the bond matures, the owner will receive the full $1,000, or $40 more than was paid. This further increases the effective interest rate. If the bond matures in 10 years, the effective yield

TABLE 11.1 Schedule of Principal and Interest Payments on a $5 Million 20-Year Bond Issued at 6% Interest

Year	Interest Payment	Principal Payment	Total Payment	Principal Remaining, End of Period
1	$300,000	$135,000	$435,000	$4,865,000
2	$291,900	$145,000	$436,900	$4,720,000
3	$283,200	$155,000	$438,200	$4,565,000
4	$273,900	$165,000	$438,900	$4,400,000
5	$264,000	$175,000	$439,000	$4,225,000
6	$253,500	$185,000	$438,500	$4,040,000
7	$242,400	$195,000	$437,400	$3,845,000
8	$230,700	$205,000	$435,700	$3,640,000
9	$218,400	$215,000	$433,400	$3,425,000
10	$205,500	$230,000	$435,500	$3,195,000
11	$191,700	$245,000	$436,700	$2,950,000
12	$177,000	$260,000	$437,000	$2,690,000
13	$161,400	$275,000	$436,400	$2,415,000
14	$144,900	$290,000	$434,900	$2,125,000
15	$127,500	$310,000	$437,500	$1,815,000
16	$108,900	$330,000	$438,900	$1,485,000
17	$89,100	$345,000	$434,100	$1,140,000
18	$68,400	$365,000	$433,400	$775,000
19	$46,500	$390,000	$436,500	$385,000
20	$23,100	$385,000	$408,100	$0

to maturity of the bond will be 6.55%; if it matures in 20 years, the yield to maturity will be 6.36%. The bank will make these calculations for each maturity date, setting a price on the bonds maturing in each year that will yield the effective interest rate it believes necessary to attract buyers. The sum of these will be the anticipated receipt from sale of the entire issue. The amount bid by the dealer may be more or less than the par value of the bonds, and the difference between anticipated receipts and amount bid is the dealer's gross profit. The award of the bid is based on net interest cost to the district.

It is also common for dealers to adjust bond coupon rates (within limits stipulated by the school district) as another way to establish a yield to maturity that will be attractive to investors. Table 11.2 displays a 10-year bond with different coupon rates. Table 11.2 also displays calculations made to determine net interest cost to the district, bond offering price to individual investors, yield to maturity based on offering price, and calculations necessary to determine dealer profit. A brief explanation should clarify details of the table.

Principal and interest payments are assumed to be made at the end of each year (actually, interest payments are usually made semiannually, but for simplicity annual payments have been assumed). The principal amount due at the end of each year is shown in column 2, with the total amount of the issue being $5,000,000. Column 3 shows a separate coupon rate (the rate of interest paid by the district on the bond's par value) for bonds that mature in different years, ranging from 5.50% to 6.30%. In column 4, the principal amount is multiplied by the number of years to maturity. Column 5 multiplies the coupon rate by bond years to provide the total interest paid during the life of the bonds at each maturity date. Column 5 is the total interest paid during the life of the bond issue. This amount,

TABLE 11.2 A 10-Year Bond at Differing Coupon Rates

Year	Principal Amount	Rate	Bond Years (1 × 2)	Interest Cost (3 × 4)	Offering Price	Production (2 × 6)	Yield to Maturity
(1)	(2)	(3)	(4)	(5)	(6)	(7)	(8)
1	$350,000	6.00%	$350,000	$21,000	$10.04	$3,513,300	5.60
2	$400,000	6.00%	$800,000	$48,000	$10.07	$4,026,000	5.65
3	$450,000	5.90%	$1,350,000	$79,650	$10.05	$4,524,300	5.70
4	$450,000	5.85%	$1,800,000	$105,300	$10.04	$4,515,750	5.75
5	$500,000	5.90%	$2,500,000	$147,500	$10.06	$5,032,000	5.75
6	$550,000	6.00%	$3,300,000	$198,000	$10.10	$5,555,000	5.80
7	$600,000	6.10%	$4,200,000	$256,200	$10.11	$6,066,000	5.90
8	$650,000	6.20%	$5,200,000	$322,400	$10.16	$6,604,000	5.95
9	$700,000	6.30%	$6,300,000	$396,900	$10.21	$7,144,200	6.00
10	$350,000	5.50%	$3,500,000	$192,500	$9.59	$3,357,200	6.05
	$5,000,000		$29,300,000	$1,767,450		$50,337,750	

$$\text{Net Interest Cost} = \frac{\text{Total Interest Cost} - \text{Premium}}{\text{Bond Years}}$$

$$= \frac{1,767,450 - 1,000}{29,300,000}$$

$$= .060288, \text{ or } 6.0288\%$$

$$\text{Profit} = \text{Production} - \text{Amount paid for issue}$$

$$= 5,033,760 - 5,001,000$$

$$= \$32,760$$

less any premium paid by the dealer on the purchase, divided by total bond years, results in the net interest cost to the school district. In this case, the dealer offered to buy the bonds for $5,001,000, thus paying a premium of $1,000. The calculations at the bottom of the table show that the net interest cost to the district is 6.0288%.

The dealer decides what yield to maturity must be offered to attract buyers. In general, the longer the maturity, the higher the yield to maturity must be. The dealer will decide what offering price will be attractive. Knowing the offering price, desired yield to maturity, and actual years to maturity makes it possible, using a bond table or a special calculator, to calculate the coupon rate necessary for the bond. This rough calculation usually produces an uneven interest rate. For example, the dealer may decide to sell bonds maturing in 3 years at an offering price of 100.50. (The price of a bond is always expressed in terms of the percentage of par value at which the bond is priced. Thus, a $1,000 bond priced at 100.50 will cost $1,005.00.) Based on this calculation, the coupon rate would be 5.8837%. This rate is then rounded off to 5.90% and the offering price recalculated to 100.54.

Production, the money gained through the sale of bonds at each maturity, is shown in column 7. It is a product of the principal amount and the offering price (divided by 100). The total of column 7 is the total anticipated by the dealer from the sale of the bonds, and this, less the amount paid for the bonds, is the dealer's gross profit.

Note that the dealer plans to sell most of the bonds at a premium. However, those with a 10-year maturity have been tailored for a particular customer, who for tax reasons prefers to buy a low-coupon bond at a discount rather than a higher-coupon bond at a premium. This customer still receives a higher yield to maturity than any other purchaser.

Money to pay principal and interest on bonds is usually set aside by the district in a special bond interest and redemption fund. Each year a tax is levied sufficient (along with any balance in the fund) to pay the interest on all outstanding bonds and to redeem all bonds that mature during the year. Bonds are a legal obligation of the district, and neither the school board nor voters can refuse to levy the tax necessary to pay them. The decision made at the time the bond issue was approved by voters binds the district as long as any bonds of the issue are outstanding.

Money from the sale of bonds is received almost immediately (usually within three weeks of the bid date), but is spent over a period of perhaps two or more years as construction progresses. Meanwhile, it is invested in whatever ways are allowed under state statute. Typically, it may be put into other government securities. It is interesting that it is frequently possible to invest idle funds at a higher interest rate than it is necessary to pay on them. Doing this is called *arbitrage*. Investment must be carefully planned, of course, so that portions can be liquidated as necessary to make payments on construction contracts.

Ways of Financing Capital Improvements

The way most school construction is financed presents several problems, one of which is the increased difficulty in passing bond elections. As mentioned, the rate of approval of bonds by the public plummeted in the 1970s and early 1980s. People may be reacting to the general taxation level by rejecting new taxes on which they have an opportunity to vote. That a number of states have passed laws or constitutional amendments restricting tax increases testifies to this (Fischel, 1998). Another problem is that the cost of borrowing has increased substantially. Shortly after World War II, interest rates on municipal bonds averaged only 1.3%; by 1967 the rate was 4%, in 1976 it was 6.8%, and by 1985 it was about 9.5%. Part of this upsurge reflects a general increase in the interest cost of all money, for reasons that have to do with the national and world economies. Part of the increase, however, has been the result of a narrowing of the gap between the interest rates of municipal bonds and those of taxable bonds. Interest on municipal bonds is not even reported as income to the IRS, and is thus completely untaxed. Such income is of great benefit to highly taxed individuals, who are thus willing to buy such bonds at an interest rate lower than they would pay for a taxable bond. However, some of the major money sources are now eligible for tax breaks on ordinary interest, among them life insurance companies, mutual savings banks, and pension funds. Nontaxability of municipal bonds thus becomes unimportant to them, and lower yields then make them unattractive. The clientele for municipal bonds is now limited chiefly to commercial banks and highly taxed individuals. But even to these buyers, the reduction of maximum tax rates accompanying the federal income tax reform of 1986 reduced the attractiveness of municipal bonds. Both of these occurrences have narrowed the difference in interest rates, and thus the subsidy conferred by the federal government on local governments.

Another problem with the usual way of financing school construction is the limit set by all states on the amounts a school district can borrow, usually expressed as a percentage of assessed valuation. The intent is to prevent present voters from saddling future residents with unmanageable debt. Rapidly growing school districts have found themselves reaching this borrowing limit with no way to satisfy the needs of unhoused students. Then too, many states do not aid districts with construction, but force them to do it on their own. The property-poor district, perhaps able to have a good instructional program because of aid provided by an equitable state system for current expenditures, may find it cannot afford to build schools to house the program. Although this may seem as inequitable as the current expenditure inequities attacked in *Serrano* and its progeny, it is far less often litigated, and facilities inequities remain in many states.

📂 CASE STUDY 4 REVISITED

An Elected Official's Dilemma

Assemblyman Walter Romero is confronted with a budget surplus and a number of alternatives for the use of these funds. One of his options is to address school overcrowding through a school construction initiative. Walter is interested in breaking the cycle whereby poorer districts are unable to build schools in the same manner as wealthier districts. If you were advising Walter, what part of the school construction/debt cycle represents the easiest place for state intervention—and what type of intervention would you recommend? Would it be wise to recommend that the state assume all responsibility for facility construction?

The most complete answer to the problem of equity is for the state to assume total responsibility for school construction, an experiment that has been tried with varying success in California, Florida, and Maryland. In California, the 1978 passage of Proposition 13 made it impossible for school districts (or any other level of government) to increase the property tax rate, which was frozen at 1% for all governmental purposes. Thus, bond elections could not be held, and districts could not borrow money through that mechanism. Prior to Proposition 13, the state had had an aid mechanism for helping property-poor or fast-growing school districts. It called for state loans to those districts, to be paid back over 30 years by a specified tax levy, with the unpaid balance at the end of that time forgiven. After the passage of Proposition 13, the loan program became a grant program. The state provided all of the money for construction. The whole process became highly centralized. A district's need for school housing is determined by enrollment projections overseen by the state. The district must submit detailed plans of each school in the district, so the state may determine, through its square footage guidelines, how many students present schools will accommodate. The difference between capacity and need is what the district is entitled to from the state. However, the state also supervises every detail of planning and construction. The whole process generates an enormous amount of paperwork, which has overwhelmed the state agency. Construction authorizations and grants of construction funds have fallen far behind actual needs, particularly in fast-growing school districts.[3]

There are, of course, alternatives for financing school construction that reside between extremes of full state assumption on the one hand and complete local effort on the other. New York provides state funds on a percentage equalizing basis. The district decides what it wants to build and how much it wishes to spend. The state shares the cost of construction, with the percentage share depending upon district wealth. This system allows much more local discretion in school construction, but is of little comfort to the district that is unable to pass a bond election or has reached its legal bonding limit.

Summary

In addition to day-to-day operations, school systems are responsible for siting, planning, building, and maintaining schools. The process for doing this is intricate, influenced by the open and public nature of government. Accurately planning school sites to match projected enrollments presents a particular challenge to school systems and local governments. The construction of facilities usually requires the accumulation of debt. Most often, this is done through municipal and local bonds. As a result, school construction relies heavily on local wealth and capacity to fund school construction.

Discussion Questions

1. Describe the school construction process. With reference to the politics of education discussed in previous chapters, define the ways in which local politics can enter into the process of school construction.
2. Bonds are now harder to pass than previously. What tactics would you take for passing a bond referendum at the local level? Who would be members of your coalition? By what mechanisms would you hold these coalitions together?
3. What are the advantages of design-build approaches when compared to conventional school construction methods?

Web Resources

National Clearinghouse for Educational Facilities: http://www.edfacilities.org/

North Carolina School Design Prototype Clearinghouse:
http://www.schoolclearinghouse.org/

Great Schools by Design: http://www.archfoundation.org/aaf/gsbd/index.htm

What Schools Cost—An American School Board Journal Special Report:
http://www.asbj.com/specialreports/0603Special%20Reports/0603index.html

Moody's: http://www.moodys.com/cust/default.asp

Standard & Poor's: http://www.standardandpoors.com

Notes

1. Some have noted that this represents a reversal of the population shift known in the 1920s and 1930s as the Great Migration, where large numbers of African American citizens moved from the American South to the industrial cities of the Northeast and Midwest, both to find employment and to escape Jim Crow legislation.
2. In Cary, NC, developers offered a free school in exchange for preferential student assignment patterns that would keep the school as a neighborhood school for the subdivision in question. See Lee (2004).
3. Capital outlay was declared unconstitutional by an Arizona court in *Hollins v. Shofstall*, Civil No. C-253652 (Arizona Superior Court, June 1, 1972) rev'd 110 Ariz 88, 515 P.2d 590 (1973), but the decision was overturned by the Arizona Supreme Court.

CHAPTER TWELVE

Equality/Equity

■ INTRODUCTION

It is significant for policy purposes to define what is meant by equality and equity and to develop ways of measuring the extent to which such conditions exist, have been achieved, or are absent within school finance systems. Before beginning this discussion, however, it is important to emphasize a point of view. Defining and measuring equality or equity in education, for all of the challenges involved, is much easier than correcting inequalities. Much about school operation and policy is steeped in custom and entrapped by inertia. American public education has a long and proud history. It is a huge public system involving tens of millions of clients, millions of employees, billions of dollars, thousands of units of government, endless apologists, and seemingly an infinite range of opinions. What operationally exists now is the compilation of practical and policy compromises that have been hammered out over hundreds of years. It is not easy to change this system, even when it is found to be deficient.

LEARNING OBJECTIVES _____

By the end of this chapter you should be able to:

- Distinguish between horizontal and vertical equity, and the tools for measuring and assessing each.
- Discuss equity within an applied framework, using both input and outcome measurements.
- Work in a spreadsheet to manipulate school finance data to determine levels of equity.

■ DECIDING WHAT TO MEASURE

Important questions in addressing equity issues are (1) what to measure, (2) at what operational level or unit of analysis to measure it, and (3) with what metrics? Is the interest in outcomes, such as test scores, remediation or retention rates, percentage of graduates who go to college, employment or graduation rates, or lifetime earning streams of graduates? Is the interest in process measures, such as number of advanced placement classes offered, extent to which computers are used, or amount of emphasis on basic subjects? Or, is the concern for input measures, such as dollars spent per student, average teacher salary, or pupil-teacher ratio?

Ideally, schooling outputs are of greatest interests to measure. These encompass the purposes of education. As a practical matter, however, some outputs are difficult to appraise. Knowing how successful students are later in life is important, but it takes a long time to determine. Moreover, there are many other variables affecting the result. Research suggests that community and family effects are quite strong, for example. Those who measure outputs usually use test scores, not because they are the optimal output measure, but because they are available when results are of more than historical interest, and because they are quantified and thus amenable to analysis. Some researchers have had success measuring college going, attendance, disciplinary incidents, or promotion rates.

Process variables are also difficult to use in many cases, primarily because they are not usually measured consistently among school districts in a state. For example most states collect data that specify the number of professionals employed by a district. This number includes teachers and administrators. Seldom, however, do districts calculate actual class sizes or student-teacher ratios, which would be of much greater interest to researchers and policymakers.

For better or worse, most measurement of school finance equity has focused on input variables. By far the most frequent of these has been dollar inputs such as revenues or expenditures per student. Even though there is mixed evidence regarding a linear statistical relationship between dollar inputs and educational outputs, officials who must generate taxes believe that resources are important, and many of them want tax dollars spent equitably.

However, it is not simply what to measure that matters. One also has to determine a proper or useful unit of analysis. In an ideal world, one might even consider measuring resource levels available to each individual student. This would be difficult because we cannot easily know how much time Johnny's teacher, or how much time the teacher's aide spends on Johnny. Physicians, psychologists, attorneys, engineers, and other professionals often keep track of their work as billable time on a client-by-client, case-by-case, or project-by-project basis. Teachers are usually responsible for a collective of students and apportioning resources, such as instructor time, per student is, therefore, difficult.

If the analytic unit is not teachers, perhaps it could be classrooms? This could be done, but school districts seldom keep track of resources in such a fine-grained manner. The best that usually can be done (and even then it cannot always be accomplished) is to keep track of resources by school. In many districts and states this is not possible because districts do not readily assign specific teacher salaries to a school. Salaries are aggregated only at the district level. It is possible—through a laborious case-by-case, line-by-line, effort—to assign teachers to schools and then determine their salaries and fringe benefits. This is seldom done. In a more ideal world, every state would require that accounting be undertaken at least on a school-by-school basis.

Thus, in the absence of easily available information, most equity studies are undertaken with school districts as the aggregate unit of analysis.

▪ STRATEGIC APPROACHES TO EQUALIZATION

Chapter 8 makes clear that most school finance systems are concerned with disparities caused by three different categories of conditions. The first is that school districts differ in their local wealth, and, hence, their ability to raise money through taxes. Accommodating this issue is the province of **wealth equalization**. Review the op-ed piece published by two South Carolina state senators in the In the News box. Notice the specific definition of equity

In the News

Throughout the whole property tax debate, many have argued that property tax relief and school funding reform are inextricably intertwined. Past studies have found that our rising property tax rates are caused by our school funding problems. To provide real and permanent property tax relief, we must reform our antiquated system of paying for public education in South Carolina.

Senate Democrats have proposed a better plan—a plan that will offer real tax relief to property owners and a plan to equitably fund our public schools. Our plan would substantially reduce property taxes while making school funding equitable across the state. Under our proposal, voters would decide this November whether they want the state to pay for school operating expenses instead of relying on local property taxes, as South Carolina has for more than a century.

Our goals are clear and concise: Establish a state-funded system of education that no longer relies on local property taxes for school operating expenses, and provide an equal opportunity for every child to learn no matter what county he or she lives in.

If this constitutional change is approved by the voters this November, all property owners in South Carolina would have the school operating portions of their local tax bills removed, slashing their tax rates by up to 60 percent. This reduction would include all classes of property: homes, cars, land and boats—business, industrial, rental and residential. This reform would have the effect of leveling the playing field for South Carolina property owners. A 1992 Ford F-150 pickup truck in Hampton County will be taxed at the same reduced rate as a 1992 Ford F-150 pickup truck in Charleston County.

In addition to leveling the playing field for property owners, funding for our children's schools would finally have a chance to move into the 21st century. To offset the inequities of the state's current education funding structure, poor counties are often forced to raise property tax rates. These high property tax rates act in turn as a disincentive for economic development in those counties, helping to ensure that they will stay poor and unable to fund their education systems. The inadequate education funding of many of our poorer counties acts as a drag on our entire state. South Carolina will only move forward economically and educationally when we ensure that all our children have top-rate educational opportunities.

Many political leaders are afraid of serious reform of our taxation and education systems, but the time has come to make drastic changes for the better. It's time for your elected officials to have the courage and the fortitude to finally do what's right. The only sure thing is that doing nothing will leave South Carolina in the position it has occupied for too long—stuck with increasing property tax rates and inequitable school funding.

The only fair way to cut property taxes and end the current inequities is to adopt a state-funded system of education and end our reliance on local property taxes for school operations. We must take bold action to move South Carolina into the 21st century. And we must do it now. Our taxpayers and our children deserve it!

From Hutto, B., & Sheheen, V. (2006). "Paying for Schools." *The (Columbia, SC) State.* February 21, 2006: http://www.thestate .com/mld/state/news/opinion/13921868.htm.

that is used. What are some consequences of the senators' plan to "equitably" finance all school districts by removing local taxation from the funding equation?

Need equalization is necessary because some students require more expensive instructional techniques as a result of various conditions—mental, physical, contextual, linguistic, or emotional.

Cost equalization is designed to compensate for the fact that it costs more in some school districts to deliver the same quality and quantity of education than it does in others. These environmental differences result in differing needs for transportation, differing amounts of snow removal, and differing pay scales to attract high-quality employees.

If all students were completely the same in terms of physical well-being, intellect, and social circumstances; if all districts had identical revenue-raising ability per student; and if there were no environmental or contextual differences, there would be no need to use state money for equalization. Still, it might be of policy interest to define what is meant by equity, and to establish rules to see that it is attained or sustained.

There are two general schools of thought on the topic of equity. The first is that it is the state's duty to ensure that all children are equally provided a basic education. Basic education is variously defined, but it is usually conceived as that level of schooling necessary for students to become productive members of society rather than public charges. Education above basic requirements can be conceived of as a locally preferred luxury. Localities may tax themselves to pay for it, but they will receive no additional assistance from the state in providing it. As emphasized in Chapter 8, **flat grant** and **foundation** programs are based on this philosophy.

A second philosophy asserts that whatever services state schools provide should be provided equally, whether it be reading or driver training. This philosophy is divided further into two schools. One is that the education provided should be identical in all districts, resulting in complete state financing and provision of education. The other school of thought maintains that it is sufficient to make it equally possible for districts to raise money for education while not specifying how much they will generate. This is the philosophical underpinning of **percentage equalizing, power equalizing,** and **guaranteed yield** or **guaranteed tax base** plans.

All of these wealth-equalizing plans are concerned with equal treatment of equals. Similarly, plans that compensate districts for differences in cost of providing equivalent education are also concerned with providing equal treatment to equals. On the other hand, special provision for handicapping conditions or other children's debilities are concerned with unequal treatment of those who are not equal.

■ EQUITY MEASURES

As discussed in Chapter 8, **horizontal equity** applies to equal treatment of equals. **Vertical equity** involves unequal treatment of unequals to an end that is theoretically equitable. Horizontal equity is easier to measure by far, and devising measures of horizontal equity has attracted far more attention from scholars. The reason it is easier to measure, of course, is that it is relatively simple to determine whether two or more things are equal. It is much more difficult to determine whether an unequal distribution is equitable.

TABLE 12.1 Expenditure Data for Two Sample States

A Districts	State A	B Districts	State B
1	1,000	1	1,000
2	1,100	2	2,300
3	1,200	3	2,350
4	1,300	4	2,400
5	1,400	5	2,450
6	4,600	6	2,500
7	4,700	7	2,550
8	4,800	8	2,600
9	4,900	9	2,650
10	5,000	10	5,000

Horizontal Equity

Range. The most frequently used equity measure is the "range." This is simply the magnitude of difference between the lowest and highest numbers in a series. An item of data, typically expenditures per student, is arrayed for each school district in a state, and a comparison is made between the highest and lowest expenditures. For example, it might be noted that per-student expenditures in a particular state range from $5,000 to $10,000, a range of $5,000. This clearly appears to be inequitable, and such comparisons have often persuaded legislators and the general public in many states to alter their financial system.

However, the range measure has severe drawbacks. To assess problems with this and other measures, Table 12.1 presents two expenditure-per-student ($/PP) distributions. Each distribution displays data for 10 districts, constituting an illustrative, if overly simplified, state. Each school district has 1,000 students. Inspection of the data for the two states reveals that state A has five districts that are low-spending (between $1,000 and $1,400), and five that are high-spending (between $4,600 and $5,000). State B has one low-spending district, one high-spending district, and eight districts that spend similar amounts somewhere in the middle range of expenditures. To most observers, from the point of view of horizontal equity, state B has the more equitable system. With the exception of two districts, all districts are spending about the same amount. However, the distributional range is exactly the same for both states—$4,000 (the dollar difference between the highest-spending and lowest-spending districts). A major problem with the range as a measure is that it employs data for only two districts, ignoring all other districts. Also, because the two extreme spending districts are the highest- and lowest-spending, they are apt to be unrepresentative of the state as a whole.

Why, then, has the range been used so frequently? Aside from naivety, on the part of those quoting the figure, the most acceptable reason is that it is easily understood by non-specialists and is usually large and therefore alarming. Thus, the range has its political uses for those challenging the system, but it is perhaps the least accurate measure available.

Restricted Range. In an attempt to retain ease of understanding while improving measurement, the restricted range was devised. The idea is that one should eliminate the highest- and lowest-spending districts and examine the range among districts that are more representative. For example, it could be agreed that the lowest-spending 10% and the highest-spending 10% of districts will be eliminated, restricting the range to the middle 80%. In the case of the two sample states in Table 12.1, if the highest- and lowest-spending districts in each are deleted, then the restricted range is $3,800 ($4,900 – $1,100) for state A, and $350 ($2,650 – $2,300) for state B. The restricted range for B is less than one-tenth that for A. It would appear that the restricted range has accomplished its goal of distinguishing between these two distributions.

Federal Range Ratio. There are still other problems with the range as an equity measure. For example, in either of the above-illustrated sample states, the range (unrestricted) is $4,000. Now suppose that the nation experiences serious inflation, and the dollar declines 50% in its purchasing value. In order to obtain the same amount of labor and supplies, each school district must now spend twice as much as before. The lowest-spending district now spends $2,000, the highest-spending $10,000. The range is now $8,000, or twice as large. Does that mean that the distribution is only half as good as before? No. The only thing that has changed is the value of the dollar. Goods and services being purchased by districts are exactly the same as before. In other words, the range is sensitive to **changes in scale**. It is as though two persons measured the same distance, one with a foot ruler and one with a yardstick.

Research
Navigator.c✦m

changes in
scale

The "federal range ratio" was designed to address this problem. It is a restricted range in which the top and bottom 5% of arrayed districts are dropped. (Actually, it is the top and bottom 5% of arrayed students enrolled in however many districts necessary to encompass these enrollment proportions.) This restricted range is then divided by per-pupil expenditure at the 5th percentile.[1] Because there are only 10 districts in the illustrative sample constructed here, there is no way to delete only 5% of the districts from each end. In order, then, to illustrate the federal range ratio, we drop instead the upper and lower 10% of the districts, take the ratio, and divide by the expenditure at the 10th percentile. For state A, the federal range ratio is ($4,900 – $1,100)/$1,100 = 3.45. For state B, the federal range ratio is ($2,650 – $2,300)/$2,300 = 0.15. Exactly equal expenditures would give a federal range ratio of zero. These results clearly reveal that state A is less equitable than state B. Some researchers take the natural logarithm of the federal range ratio as a measure of inequity. The logarithmic transformation can be interpreted in terms of percentages gain or loss.[2]

Now, suppose that the same 100% inflation occurs. All numbers will double. But because both the restricted range and expenditures at the 10th percentile double, the ratio stays exactly the same. The federal range ratio thus accommodates the problem of sensitivity to changes in scale. This would also be true, of course, if one were comparing two states, one of which spends much more per student than the other.

Research
Navigator.c✦m

impact aid

The federal range ratio was devised for a specific purpose. Revenues from one flow of authorized federal funds, known as **impact aid**, are provided to school districts affected by a federal presence, such as a large army base. The money is given in lieu of local property taxes, since federal property cannot be taxed (see Chapter 7). Kansas decided that this money was like revenue generated by local taxes, and counted federally appropriated impact aid funds as part of the required local contribution to the school finance system. This, in effect, converted impact aid into general aid to the state rather than aid to particular school districts. Since impact aid goes to districts in most congressional constituencies, legislators were not pleased. Congress directed that only states with equal finance systems could be allowed to do this. Hence, the federal range ratio was devised as a way to measure equality of state systems.

Standard Deviation. It should be clear that a measure that encompasses all data instead of only two items is preferable. One such measure is the standard deviation. This is a measure of the extent to which data are dispersed about the mean.[3] In a normal, bell-shaped distribution, approximately two-thirds of cases will fall within plus or minus one standard deviation from the mean, approximately 95% of cases within plus or minus two standard deviations, and more than 99% of cases within plus or minus three standard deviations. State A has a standard deviation of $1,903, state B a standard deviation of $974. On the basis of this, it would appear that B has a system in which dispersion from the mean is only half as great as that in A.

Coefficient of Variation. It should be clear that the standard deviation suffers from the range's problem of being overly sensitive to changes in scale. The solution is similar to that adopted for the federal range ratio. Here, one divides the standard deviation by the mean. The resulting ratio is known as the coefficient of variation. For the two illustrative states, coefficients of variation are as follows:

$$\text{State A: } 1,903 \div 3,000 = 0.63$$
$$\text{State B: } 974 \div 2,580 = 0.38$$

The lower the coefficient of variation, the greater the equity. If all districts spent exactly the same amount per student, the coefficient of variation would be zero. This measure, like the standard deviation, is not well understood by laypersons, but it is otherwise a good measure. It is a favorite of those who analyze school finance systems.

Lorenz Curves and Gini Coefficients. Economists have long relied on the Lorenz curve and an associated statistic, the Gini coefficient, to display inequalities of income. For Figure 12.1, the horizontal axis measures percentage of the population (in, say, a state), and the vertical axis measures percentage of total personal income in the state. All individuals in the state are ranked in order of increasing income. Then, for each percentage of population, a dot is plotted displaying percentage of total personal income possessed by all persons below that point. If all persons had exactly the same income, the first 25% of the people would have 25% of the income, the first 50% would have 50% of

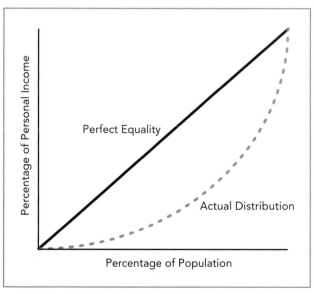

FIGURE 12.1 **Lorenz Curve of Income**

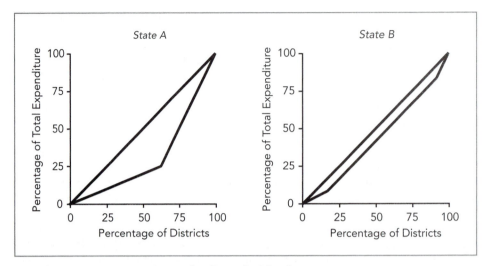

FIGURE 12.2 **Lorenz Curve for Sample Districts**

income, and so forth. Drawing this on the graph results in a straight diagonal line. However, since incomes are not equal, the lowest 10% of the population will have less than 10% of the income, the lowest 50% will have less than 50% of the income, and so on. A line connecting the dots will sag below the diagonal line. The more unequal the incomes, the more the line will sag. The curve this line makes is known as a Lorenz curve.

It is also possible to construct Lorenz curves for a state's school districts using percentage of districts (or percentage of pupils, as discussed later) on the horizontal scale and percentage of total expenditure on the vertical scale. If Lorenz curves are constructed for the two illustrative states, they will look like Figure 12.2. It is clear that the line for state B sags less than the line for state A, substantiating the subjective assessment that state B has the more equitable distribution of expenditures.

The Lorenz curve is one of the few graphic modes of measuring equity, and graphics are often helpful in visualizing information. However, graphs are time-consuming to construct, open to subjective interpretation, and use space. There is a natural desire to condense the information into a single number. This can be accomplished by considering the area between the diagonal line and the line of actual expenditures. This area can be expressed as a proportion of the total triangular area between the diagonal line and the bottom and right sides of the graph. If there were perfect equality, the area between the diagonal and the curve would not exist. If one district had all of the expenditures and none of the rest had any, the area would occupy all of the triangle. The ratio of area between diagonal and curve to the triangular area is called the Gini coefficient. It can range from 0.00 to 1.00, and the smaller the coefficient, the greater the equity. Calculating the Gini is time-consuming, and is best done with a statistical program such as SAS or Stata.[4] For the sample states, the Gini coefficient is .31 for A and .16 for B.

Theil Index. The Theil index is similar to the Gini coefficient in that it is sensitive to changes at the ends of a distribution and provides a snapshot of equity across a system. The Theil index represents equity at zero (denoting that every district has equal funding) and represents inequity at 1 (denoting that only one district has all of the money).[5]

Theil's measure of inequality, based on information theory, equates per-pupil objects with per-capita income, to assess horizontal equity. The Theil calculations are more complex than the calculations for other horizontal inequity measures; however, the Theil coefficient is similar to the Gini coefficient in both its level of rigor and stability across a distribution. An additional advantage is that Theil's measure can be decomposed; that is, it can be used to calculate the inequality within and between units of the distribution. Researchers have used this feature, for example, to calculate the amount of inequity present both within and between states (See Murray, Evans, & Schwab, 1997).

McLoone Index. At this point, it is important to make explicit the criteria by which each equity measure judges a distribution. The range is concerned only with the total span of distribution; it is utterly unconcerned with what happens between extremes. The restricted range does the same thing within its boundaries, ignoring not only the distribution between its two end points but also any data outside its boundaries. The federal range ratio is the same.

The standard deviation is concerned with distribution of all data, as are the coefficient of variation, Lorenz curve, and Gini coefficient. All of these measures would be appropriate for those who say that whatever education is provided publicly must be provided equally to all. However, those who believe that the state is obligated only to provide a basic education equally would find these measures inappropriate, unless the only expenditures measured are those used to provide a basic education.

In the absence of data on this dimension, some have decided that the important objective is to elevate districts that are in the lower half of the distribution. In their view, it is unnecessary to lower those in the upper half of the distribution, or to do anything with them. Presumptively in such thinking, the mean per-pupil expenditure is taken as sufficient to provide a basic education, and expenditures above this point are taken to be locally preferred luxuries.

The McLoone index is designed to measure the extent to which this goal of placing all at the median is achieved. The measure is a ratio of actual expenditure in all districts below or at the median expenditure to what the expenditures would be if all of those districts spent at exactly the median expenditure.[6] For state A, the median expenditure is $3,000 (halfway between $1,400 and $4,600). The five districts that spend below the median have a total expenditure of $6 million. (Remember that each district has exactly 1,000 students. District 5, then, with expenditures of $1,400 per student, spends $1,400,000.) If all of these districts spent exactly at the median expenditure, the total expenditure would be 5,000 students × $3,000 = $15,000,000. The McLoone index, then, is $6,000,000 ÷ $15,000,000 = 0.4. For state B, the McLoone index would be 0.85.

The McLoone index has a maximum of 1.00, representing exact equality of expenditures for all districts below the median. This is unfortunate, because all of the other equity measures have a value of zero with perfect equity. The resulting difficulty of comparison has led us to develop an adjustment we label the Springer index. It is the amount of money necessary to bring expenditure in all districts below the median to the median, divided by what expenditures would be if all districts spent at the median expenditure. Mathematically, the Springer index equals 1 minus the McLoone index. For state A it is 0.6; for state B, 0.15. Now, the closer to zero, the greater the horizontal equity.

Vertical Equity

All equity measures thus far have been univariate. That is, they measure dispersion of only one distribution, that of expenditures. This is appropriate if the goal of the school finance system is to equalize expenditures. This is usually the goal of foundation programs and full state funding.

On the other hand, percentage equalizing and power equalizing are not concerned with equalizing expenditures, but only with equalizing district access to resources, that is, money. Two districts that levy the same tax rate should have the same amount of money to spend per pupil, but one that levies a higher tax rate than another should have more to spend per pupil. In assessing the extent to which this is accomplished, the appropriate methodology is to compare tax bases (value within the community) with expenditures per student. If there is a perfect correspondence between them, the system is equitable by the criteria of those who believe in power equalizing. If there is no relationship between them, the opposite is true. This begins to measure concepts of vertical equity, or the unequal treatment of unequals. Vertical equity analysis will tell us, for example, whether poor districts are treated differently than wealthy districts by the state. If districts can raise their own funds, then it stands to reason that wealthy districts will use their wealth to generate more money for schools. A state financing plan that funds all districts equally under the banner of fairness may, in fact, be discriminating against poorer districts who cannot raise additional local dollars.

Correlation. The appropriate measure for such correspondence is the Pearson correlation coefficient. This coefficient is a measure with a maximum of 1.00, indicating perfect correspondence between two distributions, and a minimum of 0.00, indicating no relationship between them. It is usually more instructive to assess the square of the correlation coefficient (which also varies between 0 and 1), for it indicates the proportion of variation in one variable that is associated with variation in another variable. Thus, a correlation coefficient of 0.70 would have a square of 0.49, indicating that 49% of the variation in one variable is associated with variation in the other variable. The remaining 51% of variation in one variable is unrelated to variation in the other.[7]

The correlation coefficient encompasses all data, conveys a number that is easily understood subjectively by laymen (although, as stated previously, the square of the correlation coefficient is more easily understood), and it is unaffected by changes in scale of the data. Although there may be a high correlation between tax rate and expenditures per pupil, the amount of change in expenditure with tax rate may nevertheless be small. The idea is illustrated in Figure 12.3. Both graphs display data for districts plotted as points: a line is drawn through the points to provide the best fit to the dots. In both of the graphs, the points tend to be rather close to the line, and the squared correlation coefficient in both cases is about 0.90. However, in state C a 10-mill tax rate increase results in an increase of $300 per pupil in spending, whereas in state D a 10-mill increase results in an addition of only $50 per pupil in spending. Clearly, changes in tax rate are much more important in determining spending per pupil in state C than in state D.

Regression Coefficient. The extent to which changes in expenditure are affected by changes in tax rate can be measured with the regression coefficient. The regression coefficient measures the slope of the line of regression, which is the line of best fit through the data points (see Figure 12.3). The slope is defined as the ratio of the vertical component of the line to its horizontal component. For state C, the slope would be represented by the small triangle, the ratio being $a \div b$. There, a represents an increase of $600 in expenditure, and b an increase of 20 mills in the tax rate. The ratio is $30 per mill. For state D, of course, the slope, or regression coefficient, is $5 per mill.[8]

Both the correlation coefficient and regression coefficient are helpful statistics in assessing a state's school finance system based on percentage equalizing or power equalizing

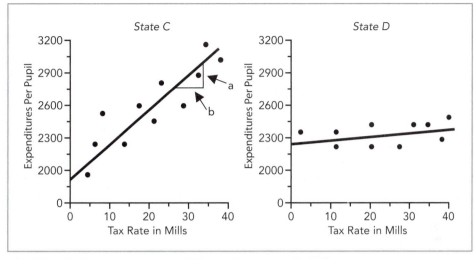

FIGURE 12.3   Regressions of Expenditures on Tax Rate

concepts. The correlation coefficient conveys the extent to which there is a relationship between tax rate and expenditures. The regression coefficient communicates the strength of that relationship. In Figure 12.3, there is a strong relationship between tax rate and expenditures for both states, but in state C the relationship is much more important in that a change in tax rate can make a much greater difference in expenditures.

Another strength of both correlation and regression coefficients is *directionality*. These measures will show a positive sign for relationships in which both variables move up together, and a negative sign for relationships in which the variables move in opposite directions. For example, horizontal equity statistics may tell us that state A does not spend money equally across all districts. However, if the correlation coefficient between district wealth and state spending is negative, we might infer that vertical equity is in place, since the state spends more on districts that are poorer and less on wealthier districts.

A final strength of correlation and regression analysis is that statistical programs provide additional calculations that inform researchers as to the significance of their figures. A finding is statistically significant when the probability of making an error in one's conclusions based on statistical output is very small, less than 5%. A large correlation or regression coefficient that is not statistically significant is rejected as untrustworthy, whereas statistically significant findings are used for research and policymaking.[9]

The correlation coefficient and regression coefficient are also frequently used to measure the relationship between expenditures and property value. In addition, other independent variables such as poverty, racial composition, and even performance metrics such as test scores or graduation rates can be used in examinations of vertical equity.

The Unit of Measurement

The discussion to this point has been about school districts rather than pupils. This chapter's illustrations have assumed for sake of simplicity that all districts in states A and B have exactly 1,000 students. Typically, however, a few districts in a state have many students and many districts have only a few students. Treating all districts alike may distort the picture.

Consider, for example, the situation in state B in two cases. In the first case, district 5 has 100,000 students, and each of the remaining districts only 100 students. In the second case, districts 1 and 10 each have 50,000 students while each of the remaining districts enrolls 100 students. Subjectively, it would appear that the first case represents greater equity, for more than 99% of the pupils reside in one district, where the expenditure is a uniform $2,450. In the second case, almost half of the students reside in a district where the expenditure is $1,000, and almost half reside in a district where the expenditure is $5,000. Yet, the district-based statistics just described would suggest the same results for both cases.

The solution to this problem is to base calculations on students rather than on districts. In this way, a weight is given to each district based on the number of students it has. Although an implicit assumption is made that within any district the expenditure on each child is exactly the same, this often is not the case. However, in most states there are few data allowing an analyst to penetrate below the district level in examining expenditures.

Until now, we have focused on vertical equity for unequal districts, but we can also focus on unequal students within districts. All equity measures described thus far contain an implicit assumption that all students in a state are the same, and that it is therefore equitable to spend exactly the same amount on each. This assumption is clearly spurious. Not only do school districts spend more on certain children (those who are handicapped or those who must be transported to school, for example), but often state school finance systems specifically take these needs into account and provide extra funds on their behalf. This confounds efforts to measure horizontal equity. Suppose half the districts in a state have large expenditures for transportation and the remainder have no expenditures for that purpose. Suppose further that except for this condition, all districts spend exactly the same amount of money per pupil. All mathematical measures would show less-than-perfect horizontal equity for the state, since half of the districts would be spending substantially more than the other half. However, it could be argued that the system has perfect horizontal and vertical equity, for money is spent on transportation only to facilitate children getting to school who live a long distance away, and once at school all students have the same amount spent on them.

There are two major points here. The first is that the obvious way to examine horizontal and vertical equity is to separate expenditures on normal pupils from those on exceptional pupils. (Measures explained thus far assess expenditures on normal pupils for horizontal equity.) The main problem is making the separation accurately. It is easy to do for transportation. Districts in almost all states maintain accounts for transportation separate from those for other purposes. It is a completely different matter for handicapped pupils, pupils who have only a limited capacity to speak English, or students from economically disadvantaged homes or neighborhoods, particularly those who are mainstreamed. Typically, separate records are not kept, or are not kept in a way that easily permits sufficient separation for purposes of an equity analysis.

The second point is that it is easy to establish criteria for judging horizontal equity (for example, that the range be 0, or that the correlation between tax rate and expenditures be 1), but there are no agreed-on criteria for vertical equity. How much more should be spent on an educable mentally retarded pupil than on a normal pupil? The answer often depends on unspoken or unverified notions of fairness, and on the technology available for education. It is clear that an educable mentally retarded child can seldom acquire the amount of learning possible for a normal child. Those in the business of educating disabled students speak of allowing each child to achieve to the limit of his or her ability. Though this is a laudable abstract goal, it is not subject to easy quantification.

Even supposing that it were, if it cost 20 times as much to develop a mentally retarded child to the limit of his ability as it did for a normal child, would society be willing to spend that much? Would it be fair to the normal children if expenditures on them were reduced by half so that more money could be spent on handicapped children? Questions such as these would be difficult to answer even if one knew how much more ought to be spent. For this reason, often the best policy analysts can do is to indicate how much is being spent on specific groups or proportionately how much more is being spent on them than on nonhandicapped children, and leave it to a political consensus to decide whether this is appropriate.

A different problem is posed by cost equalization. Does the fact that a mountain district spends more per pupil for snow removal mean that it has a better program? There is no answer unless the extra expenses that result from its location can be separated out. To do this, given the kinds of school spending records that are typically maintained, is almost impossible. However, if a state attempts to equalize for such differences in costs, it is probably appropriate to deduct funding provided for special purposes from revenues or expenditures being measured for equity.

▌ MULTIVARIATE METHODS

Almost all of those who have analyzed school finance systems quantitatively have used univariate or bivariate statistics such as those described previously. The result is that at best they can measure only horizontal equity. At worst, the statistics provide a misleading picture because of distortions introduced by attempts to introduce vertical equity into the system. In addition, there are two possible approaches to horizontal equity: equality of expenditures and equality of access to revenue. The measures to be used for the two are different. However, many states have elements of both in their school finance system.

A set of measures has been developed that attempts to capture the complexity of entire school finance systems (Ganns, 1979). The method relies on multiple regression techniques in which expenditure per pupil is the dependent variable; the independent variables measure dimensions such as assessed valuation, tax rate, number of handicapped pupils, number of pupils from poor families, number of bilingual pupils, and two district size measures that attempt to capture diseconomies of scale in unusually small and unusually large school districts. The results display the extent to which variations in expenditures are associated with variations in each of the independent variables. These measures enable one to compare the profile of the system with the legislative intent in establishing it.

For example, a system that is highly equalized, relying on power equalizing and special aids for the handicapped, would display a high multiple correlation, with a large percentage of variation accounted for by tax rate and percentage handicapped, and low percentages by variables such as assessed valuation and district size. A state system that is not well equalized but relies exclusively on a foundation program for what equalization it has would show a moderate multiple correlation, and the major proportion of variation would be associated with assessed valuation.

This is the only attempt made thus far to capture most of the value dimensions on which legislators attempt to achieve horizontal and vertical equity. It suffers from the problem that multiple regression is even more difficult for nonspecialists to understand than simple regression. Advances in computing technology and software development have meant that multivariate regression has been the standard method for discussing equity in school finance research. Researchers have also begun to criticize multivariate regression because it can only focus on one outcome at a time and because it assumes that any relationships between variables must be linear (Rolle, 2004). Newer methods such as multiple output regression, quantile regression, hierarchical linear modeling, data envelopment analysis, and stochastic frontier analysis have all been used to examine school finance questions with equity implications. These methods, however are usually used more in efficiency research than in equity research (see Chapter 14).

■ STATUS OF EQUITY

Comparisons among States

Most of the studies undertaken on the equity of school finance systems are of a single state at a single point in time. Such analyses are of limited use. Individual studies usually cannot be compared with one another because of differing definitions of the dimensions to be measured. Usually there are measures of expenditures or revenue per student, but analysts often define these differently. In 1978, however, the School Finance Cooperative was formed to develop measures of equity for a large number of states based on consistent definitions of revenues and students (Berne & Stiefel, 1978). Group members had access, among them, to data on 28 states for selected years from 1970 to 1977. They computed all of the equity appraisal measures described previously, as well as some that are more exotic. However, the fact that the measures are for some years for some states and other years for other states renders the data of limited use for comparisons.

The 1978 amendments to the Federal Education Act mandated the Department of Health, Education and Welfare to publish biennial profiles of each state displaying the degree to which financial resource equalization had been attained among the state's school districts.[10] Although these profiles were never officially published, the National Center for Education Statistics did analyze data and issue a draft report in December 1979 (NCES, 1979). It contained measures for 48 states for the years 1969 and 1976.

◁▽⁊ CASE STUDY 3 REVISITED ─────────────

Trial Judge Complexities

Judge Glenda Manning is confronted with a simple choice: What metric will give her the best gauge of school funding inequity across her state? If she uses multiple measures, how can she interpret them in a comprehensive fashion? Use the coefficient of variation, federal range ratio, and McLoone index to demonstrate theoretically how the three measures can be used to support each other's interpretation of inequity.

In 1987 the U.S. Department of Education commissioned a study of equity measures for 31 states for 1983 and 1984 using the same data definitions used in 1969 and 1977. Results of these studies, covering three selected years from a 14-year time span, are shown in Table 12.2. The mean for all three of the measures increased over the period, whether concentrating on 48 states between 1969 and 1976 or on 31 states from 1969 to 1983. In other words, on average, the equity of the school finance systems in these states, as measured

TABLE 12.2 State Equity Measurements over Time

State	Coefficient of Variation			Federal Range Ratio			Gini Index	
	1969	1976	1983	1969	1976	1983	1969	1976
Alabama	.087	.122	–	.30	.50	–	.053	.068
Alaska	.141	.230	.469	.40	.80	1.17	.075	.111
Arizona	.088	.140	–	.20	.40	–	.044	.064
Arkansas	.174	.181	–	.70	.80	–	.091	.100
California	.200	.140	.130	.60	.50	.42	.089	.071
Colorado	.163	.176	–	.50	.70	–	.087	.094
Connecticut	.237	.186	.210	1.20	.80	.81	.129	.103
Delaware	.162	.226	.166	.70	1.0	.54	.093	.117
Florida	.123	.121	.096	.50	.40	.32	.069	.067
Georgia	.165	.194	–	.70	.90	–	.088	.108
Idaho	.115	.147	.154	.50	.50	.58	.062	.077
Illinois	.180	.174	.244	.60	.60	1.14	.092	.097
Indiana	.166	.157	–	.60	.60	–	.087	.088
Iowa	.192	.073	.069	.90	.30	.23	.083	.040
Kansas	.151	.144	.156	.50	.50	.55	.072	.074
Kentucky	.170	.210	–	.70	.80	–	.088	.111
Louisiana	.093	.120	.143	.40	.50	.52	.051	.068
Maine	.181	.150	.188	.60	.60	.64	.093	.082
Maryland	.133	.147	.175	.60	.60	.65	.068	.080
Massachusetts	.172	.249	.248	.60	1.2	.91	.094	.125
Michigan	.186	.205	.195	.80	.80	.80	.102	.106
Minnesota	.127	.186	.162	.50	.90	.66	.071	.099
Mississippi	.152	.146	–	.60	.70	–	.069	.080
Missouri	.264	.234	.441	.80	.90	.82	.114	.122
Nebraska	.166	.181	.224	.70	.70	.89	.082	.087
Nevada	.076	.075	–	.10	.10	–	.028	.020
New Hampshire	.116	.139	.343	.60	.60	1.01	.063	.077
New Jersey	.149	.151	–	.70	.70	–	.080	.084
New Mexico	.129	.132	–	.50	.50	–	.056	.059
New York	.149	.198	.236	.80	.80	.85	.075	.106
North Carolina	.101	.121	.095	.40	.40	.33	.057	.066
North Dakota	.142	.162	.277	.60	.60	1.08	.075	.083
Ohio	.217	.229	.292	.90	.90	1.20	.121	.128
Oklahoma	.197	.172	–	.50	.50	–	.093	.079
Oregon	.089	.114	.126	.40	.40	.37	.048	.064
Pennsylvania	.216	.209	.195	.80	.80	.89	.112	.117
Rhode Island	.188	.136	.110	.50	.50	.35	.102	.077
South Carolina	.087	.136	–	.60	.60	–	.048	.074
South Dakota	.141	.180	–	.90	.90	–	.068	.091
Tennessee	.182	.227	.190	.90	.90	.74	.103	.128
Texas	.159	.181	.203	.70	.70	.79	.080	.093
Utah	.088	.097	–	.30	.30	–	.041	.047
Vermont	.226	.165	–	.80	.80	–	.118	.092
Virginia	.246	.243	.228	.80	.80	.91	.128	.127
Washington	.160	.184	.148	.80	.80	.51	.090	.102
West Virginia	.105	.097	–	.30	.30	–	.059	.055
Wisconsin	.118	.144	.146	.50	.50	.52	.065	.081
Wyoming	.190	.150	.234	.50	.50	.93	.085	.081
Number of States	48	48	31	48	48	31	48	48
Maximum	.264	.249	.469	1.2	1.2	1.2	.129	.128
Minimum	.076	.073	.069	.1	.1	.23	.028	.020
Mean	.155	.164	.203	.6	.6	.71	.080	.087

Source: School Finance Equity: A Profile of the States (1969, 1976); DRC, Inc. (1983).

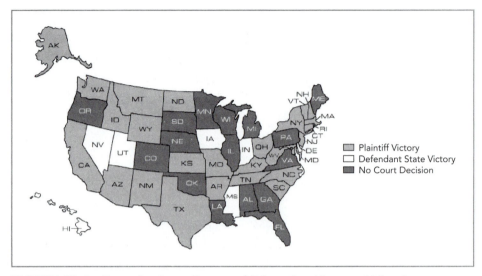

FIGURE 12.4   State-by-State Status of Education Finance Litigation

Source: ACCESS—Campaign for Fiscal Equity
http://www.schoolfunding.info/states/state_by_state.php3

by these statistics, was worsening. However, depending on the measure and the span of years selected, between one-fourth and one-half of states improved in equity. Since in a steady state with random variation one would expect half of states to improve over any period, the fact that fewer than half did reinforces the impression that school finance equality was being further diluted.

These historical data are interesting because they reflect conditions before the equal protection litigation movement got fully underway. In the three decades since these measures, virtually every state has been the scene of an equal protection suit. Figure 12.4 displays this condition.

In 1998, Murray, Evans, and Schwab undertook a time series analysis of state and education finance equity. They generated a nationwide panel dataset with more than 16,000 districts and estimated a series of econometric models to assess whether funding disequilibrium had decreased within and between states between 1972 and 1992. Key among a host of findings, Murray, Evans, and Schwab concluded that as a result of court-mandated reform, intrastate inequality was dampened to the point that disparities between states were greater than disparities within states; spending rose in the lowest- and median-spending school districts and remained constant in the highest-spending districts; and increased spending was a result of higher taxes and not a reallocation of resources from other government expenditure categories such as hospitals, health care, and highways (Table 12.3).

More recently, Springer, Liu, and Guthrie (2005) conducted a study to unravel the differential impact of equity- versus adequacy-based reform on resource distribution. While contrasting equity and adequacy reforms is beyond the purview of the present discussion, their work is particularly relevant considering that they traced national inequality trends in resource distribution by three horizontal equity measures from 1972 to 2002. Figure 12.5 contains a graphic representation for these analysis. The shaded data point

TABLE 12.3

	1972	1977	1982	1987	1992
Funding per Student (1991$)					
Local	1,923	1,881	1,799	2,163	2,621
State	1,394	1,708	1,900	2,451	2,587
Federal	325	346	297	315	368
Total	3,642	3,935	3,909	4,929	5,576
Measures of Inequality					
95/5 Ratio	2.72	2.37	2.22	2.53	2.40
Coefficient of Variation	30.8	28.1	25.6	29.6	29.9
Gini Index	16.3	15.0	13.8	15.8	15.5
Variance Decomposition					
Within States	32.2	41.5	47.5	32.8	35.3
Between States	67.8	58.5	52.5	67.2	64.7
National	100	100	100	100	100
Household Income					
Median (1992$)	30,642	30,129	29,602	32,186	30,386
Gini	40.1	40.2	41.2	42.6	43.3

Source: Adapted from Murray, Evans, & Schwab (1997).

depicts the average level of inequality in the United States for each year, while the corresponding trend line is used to represent change. Each graphic further contains "whiskers" that show the range of values for the 46 states included in the study.

Figure 12.5 illustrates a relatively constant level of mean national inequality from 1972 to 1982 with a sizable spike in the range in 1977. For example, the range in the coefficient of variation increased from 17.47 to 21.11. Although not presented graphically, the standard deviation increased 17% from 3.53 to 4.14. Inequality dampened from 1982 to 1987, during which it remained relatively static until a precipitous drop during the 1990s. Although average inequality remained constant, the range marks intensified variability in inequality. Indeed, the standard deviation for the coefficient of variations increased 18.9% and the range of values for the measures of inequality closely resembled those of the mid-1970s.

The 1990s signified change as legislators and governors, egalitarians and education advocates, sought finance equality and adequacy (Guthrie, 2004). During this time, social inequalities garnered increasing national attention as technological improvements and e-generation[11] growth marked the single longest period of continuous economic expansion in U.S. history. Not only did the range of values decrease following this recessionary period, but also the variability of inequality reached the sample low for all three measures of inequality. Furthermore, the mean coefficient of variation, Theil Index, and Log 95th/5th values decreased by 15.36, 34.97, and 16.8% from 1972 to 2002 and 15.89, 42.85, and 20.19% from 1990 to 2000, respectively.

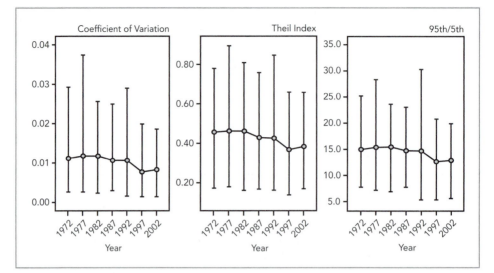

FIGURE 12.5   **National Trends in Inequality by Measure of Inequality, 1972–2002**

Intradistrict Equity. Education finance as a field of scholarly study has begun to shift focus away from large scale national comparisons and toward microlevel analysis of resource distribution to determine how individual schools within a district compare in terms of resources. Whereas it is likely that equal protection litigation has dampened interdistrict spending inequities, it is less clear that intradistrict inequities have been decreased. The "evil" here is not differences in wealth per pupil or uneven taxation charters—all schools within a district should have equal access to appropriate levels of revenue. Examine Case 5, Intradistrict Equity, for an example of the ways in which intradistrict inequities play out across schools within the same district.

📁 CASE 6 ───────────────────────────────────────

Intradistrict Equity

Todd Achilles was a community organizer in a big city. He had graduated from college, gone to divinity school, served in Africa in the Peace Corps, and had decided that conditions in his big city hometown were as deserving of his efforts at civic reform, democratic empowerment, and community development as were people overseas. He was an unreconstructed "liberal" in the sense that he was idealistic and proudly so.

Todd had thought of running for public office, and that idea was still attractive to him. However, in the short run, he had a mission. A local charity and a local church supported him financially, and he worked to organize the community around issues of child welfare. He was not paid much, and his wife worked, too. Between them they had all they wanted. Also, they had each other, and their values were truly synchronous. He loved her, loved his work, and loved the children he was committed to helping.

Todd knew that the children about whom he cared so much, and in whom he saw so much of himself, needed a good education to have a good chance in life. He was dedicated to ensuring they had good schools. However, the deeper he dug, the clearer it was to him that they did not have good schools.

Todd saw himself as an advocate for the poor people who lived in his neighborhood. When he attempted to bridge the community with schooling he began to see that there were troubling conditions regarding his neighborhood's public schools. Teachers seemed inexperienced and they seemed to come and go quickly. He sometimes had to learn the names of several new classroom teachers each month. They did not even last an entire school year. Principals assured him that all the newly employed teachers were appropriately credentialed; still, they seemed inexperienced and naive.

Todd decided he would get to the bottom of the teacher turnover matter. He was sure that there was some kind of pattern to these teacher turnover rates, a pattern that somehow, even if not consciously, was discriminating against the children he wanted to help. Why else would so many teachers come and go with such frequency, always leaving his children with inexperienced new teachers.

Todd went to school board meetings, made inquiries of city officials, examined the school district budget, and talked with teachers in whom he had confidence. Each conversation led him back to the formal collective bargaining agreement between the district and the teachers' union.

It seemed that in Todd's school district, teachers were free to apply for teaching position openings and were given first choice of being selected for a vacancy based on their seniority in the district. If they wanted to transfer out of one of the schools in Todd's neighborhood and go to a school where students had fewer learning problems or language deficiencies, then they had the right to do so.

When Todd began to examine the transfers with greater intensity, he began to see that teachers moved from his neighborhood to middle-class neighborhoods. This struck him as strange. It seemed to Todd that the most experienced teachers should be placed where the learning challenges were highest. Why did the district permit the most experienced, and often the best-educated, teachers to transfer to schools where the students were arguably the easiest to teach?

As Todd dug deeper, he began to see that the schools in his neighborhood were also underfinanced. Schools on the periphery of the city seemed to have more money spent on their enrollees. Assuredly, the school district's internal distribution formulae did not discriminate against minority and low-income children, did they? Not in the 21st century. How could his school have less spent on it per pupil than schools in middle-class neighborhoods? How could the district let this happen? It seemed unfair.

Todd began to see that the transferring teachers, because of their seniority and college credits, took a higher per-pupil amount to their new, receiving schools than their replacements at the schools in Todd's neighborhood brought with them as beginning teachers. The totality of this dynamic districtwide left schools in low-income neighborhoods with less money per pupil than their middle-class counterparts. In addition, parent organizations in Todd's district worked hard to raise additional outside funds to support the schools. Obviously, parents in Todd's neighborhood had less to contribute than parents in wealthier neighborhoods.

Todd came to see this pattern of fiscal discrimination as a kind of institutional racism. He wondered what opportunities for redress were available to him. Should he seek a political redress or a judicial redress of the problem.[2] Perhaps it could be solved as easily as simply moving the school system into school-by-school budgeting, a technical solution.

Intradistrict inequity typically occurs when districts permit, or have otherwise bargained away, the administration's ability to assign teachers to schools. For example, teachers' union collective bargaining demands often permit teachers to apply for instructional assignments based on seniority. Since select schools in a district are often perceived as more desirable, usually in keeping with the socioeconomic (SES) character of the students who attend these schools, more senior teachers (who are paid the most) shift to more advantaged schools.

Recent research by Paul Hill and colleagues displays substantial between-school spending disparities based on this arrangement (Roza & Hill, 2004). Over a 5-year period, Hill's research team reconstructed school-level budgets by identifying which teachers and administrators were assigned to which schools and then computing the cost of employing these individuals based on their actual salaries and benefit rates. Among a host of research findings, these researchers conclude that significant differences in actual salary costs existed from one school to the next in a single district; uneven spending patterns resulting from teacher salaries are not captured by current budgeting practices; and high-poverty, low-performing schools had smaller salary budgets than the district average.

Intradistrict revenue inequities were found to be an "evil" in a Los Angeles lawsuit, leading to a court-issued consent decree. This case, *Rodriguez v. Los Angeles Unified School District* led to an equalization reform within the district by which schools, effectively, are allocated equal amounts of revenue, in keeping with student-weighted distribution formulae. How these funds are spent at a school depends in part on the tradeoff school officials wish to make between having higher paid teachers, and thus, larger class sizes, or lower paid (presumably less senior) teachers and smaller class sizes.

Intradistrict expenditure differences are seldom recognized or publicized. However, they are one of the greatest sources of inequality in American public school education.

Summary

Measuring the equal distribution of education variables remains an important part of school finance analysis. The distribution of input, process, and outcome variables can all be accomplished with equity analysis. The first steps of equity analysis involve determining what is to be measured, and at what level of analysis. The next steps involve deciding whether to measure horizontal or vertical equity. Horizontal equity measures typically take the form of a ratio. Vertical equity measures make use of univariate and multivariate statistics to examine relationship between two variables of interest, say, wealth and per-pupil spending. Equity analysis generally suggests that inequity is decreasing within states but is maintaining or increasing slightly between states. Equity analysis within districts between schools is an emerging area of research. Early studies suggest disparities between funding per school, but little analysis has been done to determine if this is due to vertical equity or inequity.

Discussion Questions

1. Discuss the value of horizontal equity within the current policy environment, especially regarding No Child Left Behind (NCLB). Has NCLB made horizontal equity analysis untenable?
2. Discuss the implications of measuring the equitable distribution of outcomes. Should outcome variables such as test scores be distributed equitably across all students? Should states enforce policies to ensure this distribution?
3. Review the equity worksheet on the companion website, www.ablongman.com/Peabody. Describe the manner in which horizontal and vertical equity analyses allow you to assess the overall health of a state's school finance system.
4. Read the case study of Todd Achilles. Todd is learning that many mechanisms promote the unequal distribution of funds between schools within the same district. What are two sources of these disparities? Design a study plan to measure these disparities. Then, determine what policy changes would serve to lessen the inequitable distribution of funds across schools.
5. In what situations is inequitable funding across schools a positive policy? Even though positive, would such a policy be fair?

Web Resources

A group in Texas advocating for equity in funding: http://www.equitycenter.org/

A group in Ohio advocating for equity in funding: http://www.ohiocoalition.org/

A 1996 Government Accounting Office (GAO) report on equity in three states: http://www.gao.gov/archive/1996/he96039.pdf.

Notes

1. The formula is $(X_{95th} - X_{5th})/X_{5th}$.
2. This is sometimes referred to as the log95/5 measure.
3. As this is a nontechnical book, we make no effort to go into the derivation of the standard deviation. See any standard text on statistics. The formula is:

$$\sigma = \sqrt{\frac{\sum_{1}^{n}(x - \bar{x})^2}{n - 1}}$$

4. Stata now has an easily downloadable module ("inequal") that will calculate a Gini coefficient.
5. The Theil index can be written as:

$$T'_g = \frac{p_i}{p} \sum_{i=1}^{m} \frac{y_i}{\mu_i} \log\left(\frac{y_i}{\mu_i}\right)$$

where i indexes the groups, n_i is the number of individuals in group i, μ_i is the average income in group i, p_i is the population of group i, and P is the total population. T'_g is bounded above by log $(P/p_i(min))$, the logarithm of the total population divided by the size of the smallest group.

6. The median expenditure is the expenditure in the middle district when districts are arrayed in order of expenditure. If there is an even number of districts, the median expenditure is halfway between the two districts in the middle.

7. See any statistics text on the derivation of the correlation coefficient and the line of regression. The formula for the correlation coefficient is:

$$r = \frac{n \sum_{1}^{n} xy - \sum_{1}^{n} x \sum_{1}^{n} y}{\sqrt{\left[n \sum_{1}^{n} x^2 - \left(\sum_{1}^{n} x \right)^2 \right]\left[n \sum_{1}^{n} y^2 - \left(\sum_{1}^{n} y \right)^2 \right]}}$$

8. The formula for the line of regression is $Y = B_0 + B_1 x + \varepsilon$, where B_0 is the point at which the line intercepts the y axis (where $x = 0$), and B_1 is the slope of the line and ε represents an error term. For state C, B_0 is \$2,000 and B_1 is \$30. The formulas for calculating B_0 and B_1 are as follows (for ease of reading, we will assume that every summation function holds for the series from 1 to n):

$$A = \frac{\sum y \sum x^2 - \left(\sum x \right)^2}{n \sum x^2 - \left(\sum x \right)^2} \quad \text{and} \quad B = \frac{n \sum xy - \sum x \sum y}{n \sum x^2 - \left(\sum x \right)^2}$$

9. Again, a statistics textbook will provide all formulas need to perform these calculations. See Glass (1996) or Agresti and Finley (1997) for helpful guides.

10. Shortly thereafter divided during the Carter Administration into two cabinet departments, the Department of Education and the Department of Health and Human Services.

11. Generation that has grown up with the Internet as a common and necessary facet of life, particularly in terms of communication and the expenditure of disposable income.

CHAPTER THIRTEEN

Equity II (Adequacy)

■ INTRODUCTION[1]

Two decades of states-promulgated achievement standards and high-stakes testing—reinforced by the No Child Left Behind Act's (NCLB) "adequate yearly progress" achievement expectations and performance sanctions—have intensified a policy system quest to determine how much money is enough. Moreover, children's advocates and professional educator organizations have constructed an artful "equal protection" argument that relies on state learning standards as a means for propelling questions of financial adequacy before courts as a constitutional issue. Thus, officials in all three branches of federal, state, and local government are continually faced with the question of how much money is needed for an education system to be deemed adequate.

LEARNING OBJECTIVES _____

By the end of this chapter you should be able to:

- Discuss the connections between equity as a concept and adequacy as a concept.
- Discuss historic and modern cost modeling strategies, along with the strengths and weaknesses of each.
- Discuss the role of the courts in determining levels of adequacy for public education.

However significant the query, there is a regrettable lack of analytic capacity to construct credible answers to questions about adequacy.[2] The principal research approach pursued by economists is precise but impractical. Conversely, a costing out strategy devised by education policy analysts appears understandable and valid but lacks precision. This chapter describes currently employed economic and policy analytic procedures for determining adequacy, poses a sevenfold set of criteria by which to weigh their merits, and suggests an intermediate and longer range strategy for countering uncertainty.

■ EVOLVING POLICY SYSTEM DEMANDS FOR DETERMINING SCHOOLING COSTS

For most of the 20th century, an individual could complete elementary school, forego high school and college, and still aspire to the material components of the American Dream—a house, a car, and recreation. In the last two decades, however, many high-paying, lower-skilled jobs have become automated or moved overseas (Feentra & Hanson, 1999). To prepare for the issues to be discussed in this chapter, see the case study below for an example of the problematic questions raised within an adequacy framework.

CASE 3 REVISITED

Trial Judge Complexities

Glenda Manheim has deliberated and come to a startling conclusion: Her state is only providing a constitutional education system when all students can pass the state end-of-grade tests in math and reading. Judge Manheim feels like she has moved the debate about school finance in her state away from dollars and cents and into the realm of results that are good for students, as well as the state economy. School leaders across the state are concerned and confused. Their main questions include:

1. Is a test appropriate if everyone can pass it?
2. Can school leaders regulate and change student motivation?
3. Does this ruling imply they will receive more funding or less?
4. Are the tests used valid and reliable instruments?
5. How, then, can anyone determine how much money to invest in schools?

How would you respond to these issues? Are there other issues you would add to this list?

Public perceptions of education's significance in preserving or obtaining economic advantage have been fueled by these economic and technological conditions and have, in turn, provoked political system expectations for heightened academic performance. Prior to this modern era, K–12 schooling's financial resources were established at whatever levels legislatures and governors deemed the public purse could bear. Principal decision-making criteria were resource availability, competition between public sector endeavors, and political expedience. Certainly this continues to be true today in an overall sense. However, the emergence of a standards-based or systemic reform movement in education followed the 1989 education summit of state governors in Charlottesville, Virginia, convened by President George H. W. Bush. The summit launched a wave of state learning objective enactments. Throughout the 1990s, more rigorous and more codified state student achievement expectations and testing programs proliferated and the new performance era—a political system response to intensified public concern for better schooling—emerged as a dominant policy system concern.

Learning standards now serve as a basis for statewide performance appraisals of student academic achievement. Pairing learning standards with tests, particularly high-stakes tests, offers a ripe opportunity to attach consequences for low and high performance, and to monitor student, teacher, school, and district progress. Learning standards, statewide tests, and performance consequences began to be linked in what policy analysts have labeled **accountability systems**. To varying degrees, every state now has a version of an education accountability system for its public schools. Some, such as Florida, measure and reward, or punish, not only performance, but also value-added performance and academic return on public dollars investment.

Congressional enactment in December of 2001 of NCLB intensified academic achievement expectations and performance level consequences for states. Failure to employ accountability mechanisms, and eventually to meet performance expectations, jeopardizes state and school district eligibility for federal funding and triggers escape clauses for parents and students who may be able to leave failing schools for public or private alternatives.

Mounting pressure for higher student performance and a prospect of higher stakes for failure triggered debate over **opportunity to learn**. If there are now to be consequences for poor performance, whether for students, teachers, or education organizations, then does not the polity have an obligation to provide resources sufficient to ensure opportunity to acquire expected knowledge?

The notion of sufficient opportunity to learn is the foundation of contemporary policy system demands by child advocates and professional educators for "adequate" resources. Elected officials have been subjected to substantial political pressure to elevate education resources to ensure revenue adequacy. Where legislatures and governors have been reluctant or slow to act on such political demands, education advocates have been quick to seek legal redress. So-called "adequacy suits" have been filed in multiple states,[3] relying on an extrapolation of equal protection reasoning.

Demands for added resources, linked to an adequate opportunity, have not been restricted to state arenas. Teachers' unions have been among the most active organizations seeking elevated federal education appropriations, contending that added revenues are needed to ensure an opportunity to comply with intensified federal performance expectations. The National Education Association filed a suit against the federal government, and a coalition of education organizations has organized grassroots campaigns seeking to reduce federal accountability expectations, obtain added federal education appropriations, or both (NEA, 2005).

Trial courts have emerged as major policy system actors in the arena of school costs controversy. According to National Conference of State Legislature compilations, at least 30 states have been involved in some variant of an adequacy suit since 2000 (National Center on Education Statistics, 2005).

Conventional wisdom contends that judicial influence is a function of appellate decisions establishing precedent for trial courts within their jurisdiction. In a 2004 article, David Zaring points to a recent dynamic by which trial court decisions, rather than shaping legal views through vertical appeal processes, are ever more influential through horizontal networks and lateral decision-borrowing across judicial jurisdictions. It is in this manner, for example, that a trial court opinion regarding school finance in New York shapes a trial court judgment in Arkansas.

It is against this political and judicial backdrop that modern policymakers seek added information regarding the costs of offering services geared toward elevated performance

Research Navigator.com
accountability systems

Research Navigator.com
opportunity to learn

expectations. The quest for knowledge is particularly acute in regard to students at risk of failure from circumstances of household or community poverty, language deficiency, disability, and so on. Here, even less is known. Many students, probably mostly middle class, are already meeting heightened academic expectations and little or no added resources seem necessary for them to receive and take advantage of the educational opportunities available to them. It is with disadvantaged populations that the greatest gaps in technical and instructional knowledge exist, and these knowledge gaps contribute to an uncertainty regarding how much should be spent on such students in order to ensure that they have an adequate educational opportunity.

This is not the first time in American education finance history that questions regarding costs have been elevated. Indeed, there is a substantial precedent for today's search for balance in opportunity/cost relationships.

■ HISTORIC QUESTS FOR DETERMINING THE RIGHT AMOUNT TO SPEND

Under the auspices of the Educational Finance Inquiry Commission of 1923, George D. Strayer and Robert M. Haig developed a financial conceptualization of equalization of educational opportunity (EEO), thereby marking historical antecedents for today's search for cost relationships and giving rise to the normative foundations of modern day foundation aid programs and pupil weighting procedures in particular. Interpreting EEO in its "most extreme form," Strayer and Haig wrote:

1. The state should insure equal educational facilities to every child within its borders at a uniform effort throughout the state in terms of the burden of taxation; and
2. The tax burden of education should throughout the state be uniform in relation to tax-paying ability, and the provision for schools should be uniform in relation to the educable population desiring education. (171–175)

Within this context, Strayer and Haig devised a tripartite model for formulating a plan of state support to realize equal educational opportunity. The plan advocated:

1. Establishing schools or making other arrangements sufficient to furnish children in every locality within the state with equal educational opportunities up to some prescribed minimum;

2. Raising funds necessary for this purpose by local or state taxation adjusting in such manner as to bear upon people in all localities at the same rate in relation to their tax-paying ability; and

3. Providing adequately either for supervision and control of all schools, or for their direct administration by a state department of education. (Strayer & Haig, 1923, p. 74)

Strayer and Haig's plan suggested that states recapture a proportion of property taxes reserved for local support of education and repurpose these funds to property-poor districts to assure them sufficient revenue to provide an adequate amount of resources per student. However, this was only one part of their plan.

Less than a year later, in his doctoral dissertation entitled, *The Measurement of Educational Need*, Paul R. Mort, a student of Strayer's at Teachers College, Columbia University, advanced Strayer and Haig's framework. Mort hypothesized that, in addition to the diversity of students enrolled in districts, the location of districts within a state was not homogeneous, thus necessitating differential degrees of financial support within a state to provide each district with a sufficient educational program. That is, even if District A and District B had identical student and teacher demographics, the "harshness" of District B's external environment might necessitate additional resources to provide a like educational opportunity.

For his time, Mort employed "remarkably innovative regression techniques" constructed around average daily attendance, average teachers per pupil, and average district size statistics to confirm his supposition (Johns, 1971; Mort, 1924). Mort's analyses culminated in a pupil weighting system that espoused compensatory education for disadvantaged students, sparsity-of-population indices, and other cost variations to enhance state foundation aid equity.

By the 1930s and 1940s, even more intricate pupil weighting measures were devised for the recapture component of state foundation aid funding formulas. For instance, I. R. Waterman proposed adjusting formulas to compensate for cost variations in size of school and current expenditures that were unassociated with funding of teachers' salaries (Waterman, 1932). Whereas researchers such as Waterman were developing more equitable funding schemes, Mort, through his efforts as Director of the National Survey of School Finance, began to evaluate state use of equalizing components in their funding mechanisms (Mort, 1933). Mort evaluated states' treatment of variations in school and district size, differential costs of elementary and high schools, resident and nonresident tuition fees, cost of living expenses, cost of transportation, cost of rehousing rural schools, pupil/teacher ratios, and consideration of capital outlays.

Investigations of similar magnitude and purpose persisted throughout the 21st century. Duncombe and Yinger note, for example, that, "The idea that educational costs depend on student characteristics can be traced back to the famous article by Bradford, Malt, and Oates (1969), which showed that the cost of providing public services depends on the environment in which the services are delivered" (p. 2). Additionally, they acknowledge 14 more articles applying a similar notion between 1984 and 2004. While Bradford, Malt, and Oates examined the growth of public sector budgets in 1969, finding that technological innovation had neither increased nor decreased the costs of providing public services, including teaching, other researchers developed methodologies for including ideas of efficiency in examining school costs, and assessing whether state aid was being distributed to those districts in the greatest need (Bradbury et al., 1984; Downes & Pogue, 1994; Ratcliffe, Riddle, & Yinger, 1990). Through a use of econometric methods including multivariate regression, Duncombe and Yinger, using New York state data, estimated additional funding weights for poverty and disability that were larger than similar weights computed using district averages. A summary of their findings appears in Table 13.1 (Duncombe, 2002).

Politically, adequacy has become a source of litigation across the nation. Read the press release by the Consortium for Adequate School funding in Georgia in the In the News box. Reflect on the politics of adequacy cases and the constitutional authority for

TABLE 13.1 Pupil Weights for New York State, 2001

Characteristic	Simple Average	Estimated	Difference
Poverty	1.415	1.667	0.252
Limited-English-Proficient	1.007	1.308	0.301

In the News

ATLANTA—The Consortium for Adequate School Funding in Georgia filed a lawsuit against the State of Georgia in Fulton County Superior Court today to seek additional funding for Georgia's schools. This lawsuit is based on the State's obligation under the Georgia Constitution (Article VIII, Section 1) to provide an adequate education for all of its children.

The Consortium is a coalition of 51 local school systems, which was formed in 2001, in response to the financial crisis facing Georgia's schools. The Consortium is joined in the lawsuit by five individual school systems, which are examples of the financial crisis facing Georgia's schools, along with parents of students in these systems.

The parties bringing the lawsuit contend the State has chronically underfunded its schools. As a direct result, many students in Georgia are not receiving an adequate education. The lawsuit explains the problems in the method of financing used by the State and describes the harmful consequences for Georgia's children, including the tragic reality that four out of every ten students in Georgia are not graduating from high school.

"The purpose of the lawsuit is to ask the courts of Georgia to resolve a constitutional issue," said Joe Martin, Executive Director of the Consortium. "The under-funding of Georgia's schools has become so severe—and the prospects for a legislative solution are so remote—that the Consortium has no choice but to take this action."

The goal of the lawsuit is to ensure an adequate education for every student. The intent is not to help the members of the Consortium at the expense of other systems. If the State provides additional funding for the basic instructional program through the existing formula, all students and systems would benefit, according to Martin.

Dr. William A. Hunter, Superintendent of the Brantley County Schools and President of the Consortium, stressed the importance of the lawsuit. "The level of State funding has dropped below the minimum amount needed to provide an adequate education for every child in Georgia," he said. "Despite the best efforts of our teachers, the lack of resources prevents our schools from meeting the needs of all students, especially those who are disadvantaged."

The Consortium is asking the State to proceed with the plan previously announced by Governor Sonny Perdue to conduct an objective study on the cost of an adequate education, with this study being performed by an independent firm with expertise in school finance. Dr. Hunter explained that this study will be very helpful in any event, because it is likely that the courts will leave the task of designing a specific remedy to the General Assembly.

Mr. Martin noted that the State has shifted much of the cost of the basic program to local school systems. This problem affects all systems in Georgia, but is especially harmful to those systems that do not have a large amount of commercial property. Nevertheless, the Consortium is seeking a solution that would benefit all students and systems.

Dr. Hunter summarized the challenge as follows. "This lawsuit is about the future of Georgia. We cannot achieve our aspirations as a state if we continue to deprive our schools of the resources they need to provide an adequate education for all of our students."

He added, "The members of the Consortium are standing up for our children. We applaud the Governor for his leadership in addressing this issue, and we will work closely with the General Assembly. At the same time, the Consortium is calling on the State to fulfill its clear obligation under Georgia's constitution to all of our children."

Despite the filing of the initial complaint in this lawsuit, Dr. Hunter emphasized the willingness of the Consor-

tium to cooperate with the State in developing both short-term and long-term plans and to allow enough time for the necessary steps in this process.

A wave of similar litigation has occurred across the country, with most of these cases leading to increased financial support for education.

From a press release by the Consortium for Adequate School Funding in Georgia, September 14, 2004.

such cases. As you read, reflect on how you would organize a study to determine the cost of an adequate Georgia education.

▪ A FRAMEWORK FOR APPRAISING COSTING-OUT STRATEGIES' STRENGTHS AND WEAKNESSES

The following section is intended to offer a shorthand comparison of the strengths and weaknesses of the two principal costing-out domains that have dominated policy and legal decision making—the econometric approach, the resource cost model approach, and (a third, more minor approach) the market dynamics approach—and the principal means encompassed within these domains for determining costs. Table 13.2 offers seven criteria to frame

TABLE 13.2 Comparison of Cost-Modeling Strategies and Features

Criteria	Econometric Modeling		Resource Cost Modeling		Market Dynamics
	Successful Schools	Cost Function	Research Imputation	Professional Judgment	Education Management Organizations
Goal Inclusion	Narrow	Narrow	Broad	Broad	Broad
Validity	Limited	Limited	Full	Full	Full
Model Specification	Partial	Partial	Full	Full	Full
Method Transparency	High	Moderate	High	High	High
Reliability	High	Potentially High	Limited	Potentially High	Potentially High
Time Orientation	Static	Static	Dynamic	Dynamic	Dynamic
Data Dependency	High	High	Low	Low	Low

this appraisal: (1) goal inclusion, (2) validity, (3) model specification, (4) method transparency, (5) reliability, (6) time orientation, and (7) data dependency.[4]

Goal Inclusion

Goal inclusion is used to assess the capacity of a costing-out strategy to embrace a full spectrum of education expectations and objectives desired by an individual state. Outcome measurement deficiencies constitute the principal threat or limitation to the overall strength of any costing-out strategy. If a strategy cannot adequately encompass what an education system is expected to accomplish, then a strategy's ability to accurately project costs is severely jeopardized.

To date, econometric modeling studies have been limited to examining student performance dimensions such as standardized test scores and easily measured factors such as drop out rates (see Table 13.3). This reality is restrictive for several reasons. First, standardized test scores are "potentially noisy and unstable measures" (Ballou, 2002, p. 12). As Ballou established, student performance is not only due in part to ability, but is also subject to random influences such as emotional state on the day of the test, distractions during the test, and random selection of test questions.

Second, most state statutes list literally tens of other desired cognitive and noncognitive outcomes. These include such performance dimensions as citizenship, music, art, physical fitness, patriotism, personal honesty, and punctuality. In New York State alone, the Department of Education lists 28 learning standards divided into seven categories: (1) Health, Physical Education, and Family and Consumer Sciences; (2) Mathematics, Science, and Technology; (3) English Language Arts; (4) Languages Other Than

TABLE 13.3 Econometric Studies

Author(s) and Year	Type of Econometric Study	State Studied	Student Performance Measure
Gronberg et al. (2004)	Cost Function Approach	Texas	TAAS exam scores; % passing ACT/SAT; % completing at least one AP course
Duncombe & Yinger (1998)	Cost Function Approach	New York	% above reference point on 3rd- and 6th-grade PEP Math and Reading; % receive Regents diploma; graduation rate
Reshovsky & Imazeki (1998)	Cost Function Approach	Wisconsin	10th- and 8th-grade exam scores
Augenblick et al. (2002)	Successful Schools Approach	Kansas	5th-, 8th-, and 11th-grade reading scores; 4th-, 7th-, and 10th-grade math scores
Augenblick et al. (1998)	Successful Schools Approach	New Hampshire	Attendance rate; dropout rate; student performance

English; (5) The Arts; (6) Career Development and Occupational Studies; and (7) Social Studies.

While these other outcomes are seldom measured by state-directed data systems, their policy relevance is of crucial importance to parents, educators, elected officials, and courts. For example, in 2003, an annual ranking of state accountability systems noted that states such as New York, Massachusetts, and Virginia "continued to be roiled by protests and boycotts" to instituting test-based accountability as a means of defining and measuring the education system's multiproduct purposes (Princeton Review, 2003).

Research Validity

Research validity is used to judge a costing-out technique's ability to actually measure what it purports to measure. Research validity encompasses both external and internal properties of a study. External validity refers to "generalizability" (capacity to make causal inferences) of a study. Internal validity refers to confounding influences. This occurs when two potentially effective variables interact in such a way that it is nearly impossible to determine which variable is responsible for changes in outcome measures.

Model Specification

Model specification assesses the extent to which a cost strategy accurately specifies and measures an adequate educational cost. The focus of cost studies under consideration is to project the cost of an instructional delivery system that provides students an adequate educational opportunity to meet predetermined outcomes. Formal characterization of instructional and operating components is one of the most difficult and controversial issues in the development of cost models since the policy utility of cost strategy findings is severely dampened if a sound educational delivery system is absent.

Methodological Transparency

Methodological transparency is used to assess the ease with which technical complexity and presentation of a cost strategy can be conveyed to relevant constituents. A cost-modeling strategy, to approach a level of science, should possess research procedures that are describable in predetermined detail.

The evolution of debates around issues of transparency provides a good example. Guthrie and Rothstein (1999) argued that the current state of econometric modeling did not present "intuitively reasonable" calculations, thus it cannot be the sole means for measuring the cost of education. More recently, however, Duncombe argued that, "the onus is on the researcher using the cost function approach to explain the method in an intuitive fashion, and to convince policymakers and other policy analysts that the statistical decisions he or she made are reasonable" (Duncombe, 2002, p. 13).

Reliability

Reliability, in a technical sense, simply means that repeated uses of a methodology will yield the same results. This is different from the concept of validity, which means that an instrument is measuring that which it purports to measure. An instrument may be reliable but not valid. A scale for measuring weight provides *reliable* results over time. However, if one were interested in measuring height, a scale would not be a *valid* instrument. Methods for costing-out adequacy are the same. Often they are accurate and even reliable. However, seldom are they valid.

Time Orientation

Time orientation (or, temporality) is used to assess the extent to which a cost estimation procedure can accommodate anticipated changes in policy or practice. A cost estimation based on historical data might not be valid in newer contexts. Since education in particular (and public policy in general) is constantly changing, an instrument for costing-out adequacy must be flexible enough to adapt to changing contexts and policy environments.

Temporality may be an even more important element when dealing directly with school finance policy. Hanushek (2002) put forth that, "a change in school funding by a state would set in motion a pattern of changed housing values, altered residential and school choices, and adjusted spending and performance patterns of schools. The resulting equilibrium outcomes in terms of the distribution of expenditure and performance patterns across the population are not easy to project" (p. 2123).

Data Dependency

Data dependency assesses the degree to which a cost-modeling procedure is based on complete and accurate data. Data availability is crucial to cost models since data needed to answer questions under the new education finance paradigm, when contrasted with its conventional finance predecessor, differ on five critical dimensions—(1) unit of analysis and level of needed detail, (2) knowledge of production components such as instructional, operational, and organizational strategies, (3) outcome measures, (4) knowledge of education market dynamics, and (5) ability to link knowledge of all parts of the system together systematically (Guthrie & Springer, 2004b). Guthrie and Springer further note that not until institutions alter data collection processes will data-dependent cost models more sufficiently answer new education finance's relevant questions.

If data systems are altered to meet changing conceptions of schooling, cost-function analysis may prove to be the most powerful cost-modeling strategy. Cost function analyses, unlike other cost methods, rely on actual data.

▪ CONTEMPORARY COST-MODELING STRATEGIES[5]

There are two principal and one minor cost-modeling strategies: the econometric approach, the resource cost model approach, and the market dynamics approach. These are analytic means by which education program and service costs are approximated in an attempt to specify adequate educational opportunity. No one of these methods constitutes a "scientific" approach. All that can be claimed for them, pragmatically, is that they are better than guessing and better than uninformed political judgment.

We will use the framework developed above to assess the strengths and weaknesses of each approach, and then use it to provide some perspective on and to critique each of the methods for determining educational adequacy.

Econometric Approaches

There are at least two major variations within the econometric modeling domain: a cost function approach and a successful schools approach.

Cost Function Analysis. Cost functions grow out of research in economics. A cost function is the obverse of the production function (Henderson & Quandt, 1980). It is a useful technique when existing production procedures at least approximate a desired product, but a full or optimum production model is unknown. Cost functions use a range of independent variables to predict, or estimate, a per-pupil cost. This cost can be total expenditures per pupil, instructional expenditures per pupil, teacher salary per pupil, or a range of other costs associated with educational processes (Stiefel, Schwartz, & Amor, 2005). Cost functions are desirable because they can accommodate many outcome measures simultaneously and provide an assumption of exogeneity (or externality) for all independent variables.

In adequacy-based cost function analysis, researchers specify a desired student performance level of outcome and then seek variables or components such as student household and community characteristics that are statistically associated with that outcome. Once conditions associated with a specified student or school performance outcome are known—even if these conditions are remote from the actual production processes—it is possible to approximate costs associated with a desired outcome level or condition. There are even means for determining the *lowest* costs at which the highest correlated resource mix associated with a preferred outcome can be produced (e.g., data envelopment analysis and stochastic frontier estimation).

Cost function analyses remain in vogue today because they can, in a single model, predict costs associated with a predetermined pupil or school outcome standard.

The generic cost function equation is as follows:

$$C(y) = f(y, p, x)$$

where C represents costs, y represent an educational outcome (single output cost function) or a vector of educational outcomes (multiple-output cost function); p is a vector of price inputs; x is a vector of inputs used to produce y outputs; and f is a functional operator which specifies production function shape.

However, a function analysis that avoids high levels of abstraction and is useful in a policy environment depends crucially on the following presumptions:

1. A quantifiable variable or proxy variable closely approximating and encompassing characteristics embodied in a desired production outcome (i.e., a way to measure output reliably, with validity, consistently, over time.);
2. A definable, controllable, comprehensive, coherent, and empirically verified set of production components (i.e., discrete knowledge of what mechanisms produce output, and how); and
3. Accurate cost data or an ability to accurately impute cost to production components.

Inability to meet any one of these three threshold conditions compromises the validity of analytic outcomes and the usefulness of policy extrapolations.

The problems inherent in constructing a valid education cost and production functions are rooted in their genesis. Scholars have repurposed cost and production function attributes from the private manufacturing sector—where known ratios of inputs to outputs exist—into a public sector enterprise, where these relationships are less well known (Betts, 1990; Monk and Rice, 1999). That is, education is a multiproduct enterprise that must balance several outcomes (i.e., test scores, attendance rates, and graduation rates), whereas private manufacturing's purpose is to optimize revenues at minimum costs (Cohn, Elchanan, & Geske, 1990). Over time, economists have developed more and more intricate models for determining the cost thresholds for specific levels of educational output.

One case in point is in Texas, where two cost function studies came to very different conclusions based on differing assumptions built into econometric models. While one study found Texas funding to be sufficient, another study determined Texas schools to be underfunded to the tune of $2 billion (Gronberg et al., 2004; Imazeki and Rechovsky, 2004a; Imazeki and Reshovsky, 2005).

The complexity of "real" education production and cost functions is a consequence of the spectrum of characteristics embedded in the "raw material" (students) available to "producers" (schools). Whereas manufacturers specify requisite quality of their raw materials and suppliers bid to fulfill orders, schools, with the exception of highly selective private or independent institutions,[6] can seldom exercise such control over production inputs. Despite commonly holding a monopoly in their geographic region, public schools generally must accept raw material supplied to them by households highly diverse in makeup.

To assess cost functions then, we review Table 13.2. Cost functions rely on narrow and clearly designed goals that may not accurately reflect the education policy landscape. As a result, cost functions have questionable validity, although well-specified cost functions can be highly reliable. Cost functions present a partially specified model, and have the potential to leave out a number of highly important variables. Another limitation of cost functions is that they require large amounts of well-calibrated data. Furthermore, because they base future projections on historical data, adequacy cost functions are rooted in a static time orientation. Finally, cost functions are transparent to only a few well-trained researchers and econometricians, and may provide answers that are difficult to describe to educators, policymakers, and the general public.

Successful Schools Approach. The "successful schools" approach, also known as the empirical approach, was first employed by John Augenblick, Kern Alexander, and James W. Guthrie and was subsequently advanced by Augenblick for the State of Ohio (Augenblick, 1997; Augenblick, Alexander, & Guthrie, 1995). Based on a spectrum of desired student outcomes (i.e., standardized test scores and graduation rates) identified by districts as vital criteria for an adequate education system, the "successful schools" approach identifies schools or districts that effectively meet these criteria. These schools or districts are then used as models to construct base funding levels for target schools or districts.

For example, a district with high test scores and low dropout rates may serve as a model. If the district spends $1,000 per pupil on data-driven leadership development, the successful schools model would use this as a baseline and extrapolate to other district funding formulae.

The successful schools approach is an econometric strategy that relies on whatever schooling performance measures are available for a state and on relatively simple techniques for considering factors related to production. In its maiden voyage to assist the Ohio legislature in complying with a court decision, for example, the successful schools approach used state-administered high school exit examinations as a criterion for success. Augenblick then traced backward to discern spending levels by schools achieving specified levels of student passage. He further eliminated unusually high-spending and unusually low-spending schools to mitigate extraordinary influences and then calculated a mean per-pupil spending level for the remaining units in his sample.

The Ohio Supreme Court eventually found this procedure to be unsatisfactory. The narrow selection of school performance criteria and arbitrary removal of high- and low-spending schools gave an appearance of too great a level of researcher control over results. Ohio's highest court eventually washed its hands of the issue, despairing that any reliable means existed for objectively specifying "adequate" spending (DeRolph v. Ohio, 1997).

The successful schools approach is further compromised by not taking into account school or district inefficiencies. It is possible that schools selected might, in fact, spend more than is necessary to achieve outcomes on which selection relies, thus flirting with overfunding of education.

Although this method played a pivotal role in adequacy suits in Ohio and New Hampshire and is a transparent way to measure adequacy, it risks internal inconsistencies, it may lead to small numbers of homogenous schools being identified as models, and it does not adjust for cost differences from one region to another.

We assess the successful schools model as follows: Like cost functions, the successful schools method only provides for narrow goal definition. Like cost functions, the method has limited validity but high reliability. The method only provides for partial model specification and, like cost functions, is static in time and highly dependent on the availability of accurate data.

Resource Cost Model Approach

The resource cost model approach was pioneered by Chambers and first employed by Chambers and Parish as a means to determine cost adjustments for education funding structures in Illinois and Alaska (Chambers, 1978; Chambers & Parrish, 1982). However, there are now two major contemporary variations of these scholars' initial conceptualization that rely on somewhat different analytical techniques. One is the research imputation model and the other is the professional judgment model.

Research Imputation. This strategy involves compiling research-validated conditions and services and assembling them in a coherent instructional program. It is technically possible to assign costs to program components such as class size, professional development, or technology. Thus, costs associated with research-validated conditions and services are presumed to provide an adequate educational opportunity.

Research imputations' evidentiary deficiencies compromise external validity. Moreover, professional judgment panels conducted by less-informed designers could be susceptible to political compromise. Notwithstanding researchers' concern for, and systematic steps taken to negate, such invalidities, the potential for internal invalidity is highest within an econometric modeling strategy due to deficient data and theoretical conceptualizations.

This procedure recently has been modified by Odden, Fermanich, and Picus (2003a). These researchers provide selected research results to a panel of professional educators who, in turn, construct instructional packages and operating systems. Once prototype instructional and operating systems are identified, costs are imputed to the final product. These researchers contend that this model draws from cutting-edge findings and "craft wisdom," addresses student needs as a collective unit, and can be tailored to areas yielding inadequate results. This strategy presently suffers from a severe shortage of research-validated program components.

Take, for example, optimal class size. Tennessee's Student Teacher Achievement Ratio (STAR) study, after approval from the Tennessee state legislature, conducted a randomized field trial that provided additional appropriations to kindergarten through 3rd-grade classes to create smaller class sizes. STAR revealed that smaller class sizes significantly enhanced student achievement. Subsequent papers and investigation, however, asserted that

Tennessee's research results do not fully withstand scientific scrutiny (see Mischel & Rothstein, 2002).

Does this mean STAR was wrong? No one knows for sure. The only certainty is that highly contentious debate rages in nearly every facet of social science research (e.g., potential program elements such as teacher training or certification levels, professional development, teacher aides, instructional technology, and use of guidance counselors), further polarizing public and professional opinions. Without substantive empirical research findings, such research imputation techniques, no matter how useful and perhaps desirable, will not be ready for policy "prime time" until an empirical research base is solidified.

The research imputation method can be assessed as follows: It addresses a wide range of goals. It is a valid, although not often reliable method of determining educational costs. Its reliance on published research makes it highly transparent. It is not dependent on local data, and it can operate dynamically through time.

Professional Judgment Model. This strategy, with or without insertion of above-referenced research findings, offers another means for estimating educational adequacy. This strategy has been employed in approximately ten states, either to advise a legislature regarding adequate revenue levels in a distribution formula or as evidence for either plaintiffs or defendants in a court case regarding existing spending levels. States involved include Arkansas, Kentucky, Massachusetts, Minnesota, South Carolina, Texas, and Wyoming.

State standards or expectations for what students should know and be able to do are critical to professional judgment. Be they learning standards intended to guide state standardized tests of student academic achievement, high school graduation standards, college admission standards, or state-promulgated school accreditation standards, or any combination of the above, it is important that they be an accurate reflection of that which a state specifies in statute or regulation.

The professional judgment strategy presumes the ability of professional educators to exercise craft knowledge, that is, knowledge of teaching and schools, in the design of instructional programs. Panel selection is not intended to result in a representative sample of educators. Rather, participant selection strives for a mix of unusually successful classroom teachers, principals, and district officials. One criterion is that participants have professional experience in successful schools. The number of professional panels employed is proportionate to the complexity and size of the state in question.

Once formed, professional judgment panels are convened and charged with designing instructional programs and auxiliary services sufficient to ensure an adequate opportunity for students of all capacities to learn state-promulgated knowledge and skill expectations.

On panel completion of instructional program design, steps are taken by economic and finance experts to accurately impute current market prices (e.g., personnel salaries, fringe benefits, and supplies) to create a final per-pupil block grant. Additionally, panel participants are polled at the conclusion of the process to determine individual levels of confidence that a collectively designed program will in fact ensure an opportunity for students to learn state-specified knowledge and skills. Table 13.4 illustrates results of spending estimates derived from a series of professional judgment activities in Texas.

By convening a diverse number of experienced educator participants, professional judgment modeling can calm political tumult while remaining transparent and understandable to a layperson. However, expert judgments on "adequacy of what" and "how much is adequate" are based on individual professional opinions that do not guarantee

TABLE 13.4   Descriptive Statistics from Texas Panel Observations (School-Level Only)

School Level	Sample Size	Mean	Minimum	Maximum
Elementary School	35	$5,045	$4,127	$6,206
Middle School	35	$4,394	$2,821	$6,577
High School	35	$4,109	$3,306	$5,452

Note: Professional judgment panel was conducted by Management Analysis & Planning, Inc. (MAP) located in Davis, California, in preparation for *West Orange-Cove Consolidated ISD v. Nelson* (Texas).

success, that lack replication, that might over- or underestimate cost adequacy, and that might falter under political compromise. Moreover, when undertaken under the auspices of the unethical or inexperienced researcher or policy analyst, professional judgment efforts become little more than a facade for the political or self-interested manipulation of education finance specification of "adequate."

The professional judgment's perceived strengths have also been perceived as weaknesses. The use of professional judgment panels and the process of coming to consensus around issues of funding has been decried as bad science by critics. Critics also fault the professional judgment approach for an overreliance on self-interested parties and an open invitation for politicizing the educational finance process (Hanushek, 2005).

Defenders of the professional judgment approach note that the politicizing of educational finance is a historical fact and further find that, compared to the other approaches described, professional judgment models often come in with the lowest of all estimates (Smith & Guthrie, 2005).

The professional judgment approach acknowledges the inherently political and participatory nature of American public education and harnesses this dynamic to forge a consensus for funding. Convening teachers, superintendents, principals, policymakers, and education experts to identify instructional components required in fostering state-of-the-art educational opportunity identifies a "basket of educational goods and services." Economic and finance experts then engineer current market prices to create a final per-pupil block grant figure necessary to finance that basket. Guthrie et al.'s use (1997) of this approach in response to the Wyoming Supreme Court decision in *Campbell v. Wyoming* made the state "better able to address crucial structural components of the state's education system and point it in a direction that will better serve the needs of the schoolchildren and state for the remainder of this century as well as the century that awaits" (Heise, 1998).

The professional judgment approach is capable of addressing a broad range of goals. It is a valid and potentially reliable method for determining the services necessary for an adequate education. The broad participation of educational experts yields both a fully specified model and a very transparent protocol.

Market Dynamics Approach

A surprisingly large proportion of school-age children in the United States receive instruction under circumstances influenced, at least partially, by market conditions.

For example, 11% of school-age children attend a private or independent school. Approximately 4% are homeschooled. Another 4% are enrolled in charter schools or open enrollment schools (e.g., magnet schools) in public school districts. Finally, competitively selected outsourcing firms and management contractors, often called educational management organizations (EMO), operate approximately 500 public schools nationwide.

This latter category has potential to offer useful insights into costs. Competitively awarded and negotiated cost reimbursements suggest an operational definition of an adequate resource amount. The assumption here is that a school board contracting with an EMO (e.g., Robert Slavin's Roots and Wings, James Comer's School Development Program, Hudson Institute's Modern Red School House, or Chris Whittle's Edison Schools, Inc.) has specified instructional offerings sufficient to ensure students an opportunity to meet state learning objectives.

The market dynamics approach's recent evolution indicates that it may hold promise for future developments within education's new performance paradigm. For example, early reform movements reminiscent of market dynamics, such as comprehensive school reform, were often adopted without holding providers accountable for performance. However, today's service providers are expected not only to meet specified outcome standards, but also to coalesce with community expectations, operations, and values (Wong, 2003). To date, however, evidence from market dynamics has not been introduced in a trial and little has been written professionally or empirically regarding the approach.

An Overview of Cost-Modeling Strategies. An overall assessment of methods for costing-out educational expenditures within an adequacy framework yields a contested, confusing, and shifting ground. Leaving aside the new strategies of market dynamics approaches, policymakers are faced with a choice between an econometric or resource cost model. Econometric models tend to be data driven, highly reliable, and based on a more objective set of assumptions than resource cost models. Resource models, however, are much more transparent and, because they are responsive to local context, more valid in action than econometric models. They are also more dynamic temporally, allowing policymakers to make adjustments as policy contexts and situations change.

Next Steps. Determining how much of which funds will result in improved student performance is a laudable and necessary research goal. However, each method presented above for determining costs has philosophical or methodological flaws. The following actions are proposed to help more clearly define a basis for judging adequacy and costing-out education production.

■ LONG-TERM ACTIONS

What is eventually needed is a multidisciplinary effort at probing the instructional "black box" in order to identify more accurate and valid variables for both constructing a policy-permissible production function and guiding data design and collection. These initiatives may well involve matters such as identifying behaviors and tracing time allocations of effective instructors, fostering knowledge of curricular materials and interaction between instructors and students, and capturing cognitive patterns of effective learners and backward mapping to understand their origins and processes. Observation, interview, and perhaps even neural scanning may eventually come into play. The process will not be quick or inexpensive. However, there will be no valid production function until research of this nature is successfully undertaken.

■ INTERMEDIATE-TERM ACTIONS

While awaiting results of more intense and scientific inquiries regarding instruction, researchers can seek existing settings displaying a spectrum of instructional arrangements and probe their relative effectiveness. Organizational and instructional comparisons of private and independent schools with public schools display only small variation in patterns. Private and public, elite and conventional schools appear to rely on the same labor-intensive instructional procedures. However, these studies were undertaken in an earlier environment where few performance consequences existed. As accountability systems intensify sanctions, it may be that educators will explore a wider range of means for instructing conventionally difficult-to-teach students. Exploration in settings where success is taking place, confirming that identified behaviors or conditions are indeed unique to success, and converting these behaviors to variables that are definable and measurable may, eventually, lead to a "production function."

Duncombe and Yinger noted a 15 to 20% discrepancy between pupil weights using simple means and their estimated equations. If this 15% were accurate, and assuming the United States now spends $500 billion annually on the operation of K–12 schooling these researchers will have missed the mark on pupil weighting by $75 billion.

Summary

Convergence of society's shifting social, political, and economic contexts and the education system's responses have been marked by considerable ferment as schools, researchers, analysts, and policymakers struggle to locate themselves within the new performance paradigm. Scholars fervently seeking remedies for much needed systemic change are beginning to concede that attainment of elevated and enhanced outcomes will continue to prove treacherous in the face of knowledge and data deficiencies. Until the deeply ingrained modalities of thought on education on which we have relied for most of our history are reconsidered, the quest for a new, adequate center that effectively provides enhanced educational opportunities will not be realized. Given this, a twofold research objective to acquire greater understanding of schooling processes that contribute to student learning and to define and obtain data that accurately reflect those processes is detailed in intermediate and long-term actions.

Discussion Questions

1. To better understand the complexities of costing-out adequacy, work with a group of your peers to do the following: First, arrive at consensus on an appropriate measure of academic achievement for high school students to reach before they graduate. Next, brainstorm all of the possible resources that a school could use to aid students in achieving the agreed-on goal, such as tutors or extra teacher time. None but an expert could cost-out all of these resources, but examining the list will give an indication of the difficulty of the task.

2. Next, complete the steps of question 1 above, but choose a social outcome such as dropout or graduation rates as the focus of your work. Notice how the level of complexity increases dramatically.

3. With which costing-out strategy are you most comfortable? How does the strategy you have chosen align with your educational perspectives and philosophies?

Notes

1. This chapter is labeled "Equity II," after the suggestion of a National Research Council (1999) report entitled *Making Money Matter*. Here, authors, Helen F. Ladd and Janet S. Hansen traced the formative legal roots of the contemporary "adequacy" movement, making it clear that it is a legal successor to the horizontal equity efforts launched by Coons, Clune, and Sugarman (1970) and Arthur Wise (1968).

2. *Black's Law Dictionary* specifies that "adequate" pertains to that which is "[s]ufficient . . . equal to what is required; suitable to the case or occasion."

3. In 2004 alone, adequacy-based school finance cases were filed in four states (Kentucky, Louisiana, Missouri, and North Dakota) and states' highest courts ruled in favor of the plaintiffs in two more (Kansas and Montana).

4. These criteria represent conventional views important for appraising social science.

5. Little is new in the development of alternative costing-out strategies that was not previously explained by Guthrie and Rothstein (1999). However, in the intervening years since publication, many more adequacy cost studies have been undertaken for policy purposes. The quality of these studies serves only as added evidence to the need for quality data and enhanced theoretical conceptualizations to alleviate weaknesses of many of these various techniques.

6. The high value of social capital embodied in upper-income students, which they bring to a selective school and which is readily available to benefit classroom peers, is itself an element of production function.

CHAPTER FOURTEEN

Efficiency

■ INTRODUCTION

The purpose of this chapter is to clearly define the concept of efficiency in the field of education, to review key studies and findings in the field of educational efficiency and productivity, and to further discuss conceptual and policy-related issues involved in reforming schools with an eye toward achieving greater educational productivity and efficiency.

LEARNING OBJECTIVES _____

By the end of this chapter you should be able to:

- Define educational efficiency.
- List current methods of measuring educational efficiency.
- Discuss emerging and alternative measures of efficiency.
- List policy changes that would provide a "zero cost" boost to educational efficiency.

From a layperson's point of view, American education appears unusually inefficient. Figures 14.1 and 14.2 display two types of trends. One is a century of inflation-adjusted public school per-pupil expenditures and the other is a longitudinal set of scores on the National Assessment of Educational Progress (NAEP, 2005). What one sees here is that while school spending has increased dramatically over time, academic achievement appears stable.

This is an overly simple display. National Assessment of Educational Progress test results do not fully capture U.S. citizens' expectations for schooling. Moreover, much more is expected of American schools now than was true 100 or even 50 years ago (Rothstein, 1998). For example, high school graduation and college attendance are now the norm. Neither outcome was typical 50 years ago. Also, today, most disabled students are enrolled in school. This was not the case 50 years ago, prior to a stream of post-World War II equal protection court cases brought successfully on behalf of disabled students. Changes such as these, and dozens of others, have added to schooling's operating costs.

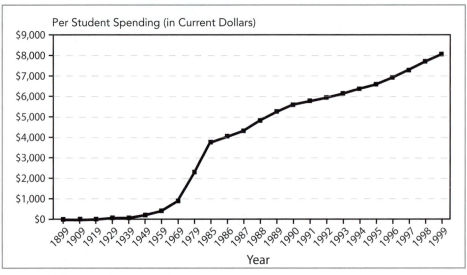

FIGURE 14.1   U.S. Per-Student Spending in Current Dollars in Public Schools

Source: Compiled from U.S. Department of Education, National Center for Education Statistics, *Digest of Education Statistics, 2004.*

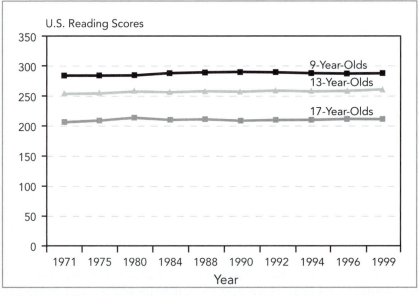

FIGURE 14.2   U.S. Reading Scores of 17–, 13–, and 9-Year-Olds

Source: Compiled from U.S. Department of Education, National Center for Education Statistics, *Digest of Education Statistics, 2004.*

Still, K–12 schooling costs approximately $3 billion for each operating day, more than the cost of the nation's military defense. Public education accounts for a large and growing share of the value of all goods and services produced in the nation (Gross Domestic Product—GDP) and absorbs a huge proportion of the nation's public sector spending. Any endeavor this costly inevitably provokes questions regarding its efficiency. Policymakers repeatedly wonder why it is apparently so difficult to gain greater academic achievement from the large resource outlays being appropriated for public school support. They point to remarkable productivity gains characterizing sectors such as agriculture, financial services, communication, and transportation and wonder why education cannot be equally efficient.

▓ DEFINING EDUCATIONAL EFFICIENCY

Almost everyone knows what efficiency means. If one wants something to be more efficient one generally wants it to perform more quickly, be less complicated, have more useful features, be of higher quality, and all at the same or a lower price. However, efficiency has other components for economists. One dimension is allocative efficiency. Another dimension is technical efficiency. Each has a quite different outcome, even though they have several common roots.

Allocative Efficiency

If a person went to the store to buy bread and the only available starch was spaghetti, he or she would probably be disappointed. At least in this instance, producers had not correctly anticipated individual preference. Even if the store had loaves of bread but did not have the whole-wheat bread the person sought specifically, he or she might be dissatisfied. This exemplifies a problem in allocative efficiency. Producers have not accurately anticipated consumers' preferences. Regardless of how efficiently manufacturers were making spaghetti or white bread, even though they might be offering them at exceedingly low prices, if it was not the product the person wanted, then the system was not efficient from the consumer's perspective.

How does allocative efficiency apply to education? At the extreme, imagine a school system that provides training only in fashion design. Potential clients wanting training in electronics, agriculture, foreign languages, journalism, or music would be disappointed. Decision makers for such a system would have misjudged the demand for other kinds of services, and potential clients or consumers would be unhappy. Similarly, an elementary school that stresses social skills and interpersonal relations might disappoint parents preferring greater emphasis on academic preparation and basic skills. In such a situation, school decision makers—the "producers" of educational services—have misjudged the "market." They are allocatively inefficient.

This explanation suggests that providers are allocatively inefficient unless every consumer's product or service preferences are satisfied. Clearly there is no economic system that can completely meet such a stringent test. There is seldom a sufficient array to meet all demands. However, allocative efficiency is enhanced when providers are free to enter the marketplace with new ideas, products, or services, and when consumers are free to select from what is available. In education, under present conditions, the near monopoly of the public schools may restrict choice more than is necessary to protect the public welfare.

If education providers could accommodate a greater range of choices, allocative efficiency would be enhanced. A few means for enhancing allocative efficiency are described in this chapter. However, a major illustration of strategies for encouraging greater choice is provided in Chapter 15.

Technical Efficiency

This term refers to efforts to maximize output at any given level of resource input, or to minimize input for a desired level of output (the more frequent goal). Technical efficiency encompasses attempts to reduce unit costs of producing any particular good or service, or producing a higher-quality unit for the same cost. In the private sector this kind of efficiency is motivated strongly by a desire for company and personal profit. The less expensively a good or service can be produced, all other things being equal, the greater the financial return to the owner or owners of the means of production. (Another means of maximizing profit is to eliminate all competition, create a monopoly, and charge as much as consumers will tolerate before exhausting elasticity of demand. Actions such as these, a natural tendency in capitalism, are disadvantageous to consumers. Hence, there are numerous government agencies charged with regulating business to dampen the tendency to seek monopolistic standing in a sector.)

In the public sector, profit is typically not possible and a monopoly may exist. Public education, enrolling 90% of school-age pupils, in the United States is a practical monopoly. Under such conditions, incentives for seeking technical efficiency are weak. (This explains why most gains in economic productivity are pioneered in the private sector.) The relative absence of public sector efficiency incentives is often used as a justification for imposing regulations, price ceilings, and revenue limits on public sector agencies and so-called natural monopolies, such as utilities.

Technical efficiency can apply to educational services. Those desiring that schools be more efficient or productive are, at one level, asking that educational output be maximized relative to a given level of resource input. Definitional difficulties immediately become evident. What will be taken as measures of output? Is student achievement the measure? If so, then on what dimension—average SAT scores or Advanced Placement Test scores? If a school sought to enhance average SAT scores for all its secondary students, it might have substantially different resource allocation implications than if it chose simply to elevate the number of its most able students taking Advanced Placement exams and their scores on those exams. The production function—the technically most efficient means of maximizing a school's output—may well depend on the output measure selected. Relative lack of agreement regarding desired outputs, at least in public schools, renders technical efficiency in education difficult to achieve. Even when there is agreement on desired outputs, much of education continues to be more of an art and a craft than a science. Be that as it may, there exist four major strategies for enhancing school efficiency.

■ MEASURING EDUCATIONAL EFFICIENCY

Although William T. Harris ushered in the notion that school districts should produce uniform outcomes across all students through his work with the St. Louis school system in the late 1800s, it was not until the early 1900s that researchers began to show interest in the specific relationships between inputs (specifically, money) and educational outcomes

(Cubberly, 1906; Strayer & Haig, 1923; Updegraff, 1922). The modern era of school efficiency inquiry began in the mid-1960s. The publication of *Equality of Educational Opportunity* (also known as *The Coleman report*) and *A Nation at Risk* raised important questions about the efficacy of America's public education system and launched parallel lines of research into the excellence and efficiency of American public schools (Coleman, 1966; National Commission on Excellence in Education, 1983). Advocates for what has come to be termed the "educational excellence movement" argued for increased efficiency through the reduction of perceived administrative bloat in public school systems. Advocates of this general approach believe that increased efficiency can be gleaned by streamlining the bureaucratic systems currently in place in public education (Finn, 1983; Hanushek, 1981, 1986; Kirst, 1986; Mann & Inman, 1984; Walberg & Fowler, 1987; Walberg & Walberg, 1994). One method of determining efficiency is through statistical analysis. Linear regression equations can be used to determine if any relationship exists between spending and performance. Beginning in the 1980s, Eric Hanushek's regression analyses, which indicated no relationships between educational inputs and educational outcomes, were particularly persuasive in supporting the idea that educational reform need not necessarily equate to increased educational funding. Continued research in this area includes findings of statistically insignificant relationships between expenditures and student achievement in Florida schools (Nyhan & Alkadry, 1999; Santin, Delgado, & Valino, 2004).

Another strain of educational effectiveness research includes those who believe that schools do produce educational outcomes efficiently and that efficiency can be increased with additional financial inputs. Researchers have reexamined Hanushek's work and determined that there were significant relationships between educational inputs and outcomes (Hedges, Laine, & Greenwald, 1994; Laine, Greenwald, & Hedges, 1996). Others have pointed to the restrictions in traditional education production function analysis in accounting for nonlinear relationships (Figlio, 1999).

More recently, a movement rooted in standards, assessment, and accountability policies seeks a middle ground in asserting that additional funding may help achievement once school systems have policies and procedures aligned with state-level curriculum. The systemic reformers seek to support a core of district, school, and teacher characteristics through the application of curriculum standards, assessment, and rewards and sanctions for school performance (King & MacPhail-Wilcox, 1994; Odden & Picus, 1999; Smith & O'Day, 1991a; Verstegen & King, 1998).

A Critique of the Normative Approach

Much of the efficiency research in education is based on private sector econometric models that rely on assumptions of cost minimization and profit maximization. As such, these models measure efficiency in two ways. Technical efficiency is achieved when maximum output is obtained for set amounts of input, and allocative efficiency is achieved when all inputs are exhausted in pursuit of stated outputs. These measures of efficiency yield a great deal of information about the ways in which school systems produce results. However, the normative focus does not allow for consideration of the wider sociopolitical and contextual factors that may affect school and school system performance and production. The manifold influences suggest that schools and districts are faced with the task of producing *multiple outcomes*, which at times may come into conflict with each other (Rolle, 2004a). Tracing the intersection and influence of these simultaneous processes is difficult within the confines of a traditional education production function. In addition, the following factors may lead to underestimated statistical relationships in traditional production functions:

- Production functions assume optimal effort on the part of students and teachers, yet there is no way to measure this effort;
- There is no clearly defined educational production process; and,
- There is little consensus on how to account for the myriad family, community, and social factors that affect student performance and school operations (Deller & Rudnicki, 1993).

A Relative Solution to a Normative Problem

One way to avoid the difficulties facing the multiple output nature of education production research is to examine relative efficiency among similar units. Relative measures of efficiency will allow researchers to explore nonlinear relationships and isolate factors that may differentially affect school systems. Much of the work in this area grows out of public choice economic theory. This theory holds that schools (and other public institutions) do not produce profit in the traditional economic sense. Research suggests that school administrators act more like public sector bureaucrats than private sector managers by seeking to maximize their budgets regardless of performance (Boyd & Hartman, 1988; Hughes, Moon, & Barnett, 1993). These critiques are addressed within the field of public choice theory, which acknowledges these differences between public and private sector organizations and provides an alternative framework to traditional economic analyses (Buchanan & Tollison, 1984; Peacock, 1992). Along with public choice theories come new ideas about measuring educational productivity. Such methods include the data envelopment analysis, stochastic frontier analysis, total factor productivity, and modified quadriform analysis.

The modified quadriform is a method of classifying data based on a pair of multiple regression formulas. The method then plots the residuals of those regressions against each other to provide a visual heuristic for comparison. Rolle used the modified quadriform to examine the efficiency of Indiana school districts from 1974 until 1994. Through this analysis, Rolle found that—over multiple outputs and for multiple years—approximately 30% of Indiana school districts produced outcomes "efficiently" and that 15% of Indiana school districts produced "inefficiently" (Hickrod, 1999; Rolle, 2000).

Another model used is the process of data envelopment analysis (DEA) (Thanassoulis & Silva-Portela, 2002). DEA examines the degree to which school inefficiency can be attributed to student behaviors and characteristics. The process aggregates multiple input and output streams into single "virtual input" and "virtual output" variables, and it is the ratio of the variables that provides a school's efficiency measure (Madden, Savage, & Kemp, 1997). DEA is helpful because it can account for the production of multiple outcomes instead of only one. In addition, DEA estimates are created based on the performance of a known group of subunits and finds the hypothetical highest level of multiple outputs available. Grosskopf and Moutray (2001) used DEA to examine the productivity of decentralized Chicago schools.

Another method of measuring relative efficiency is that of stochastic frontier analysis (SFA). Like DEA, this method uses statistics to create an efficiency *frontier* for a group of organizations and measures each member of that group against the performance frontier.

Although similar in nature, SFA relies on statistical techniques that are more robust than those of DEA (Rolle, 2005).

Researchers are also beginning to experiment with methods such as total factor productivity (TFP) to determine the relative efficiency of public sector organizations, particularly ones that produce multiple outcomes. One drawback is that TFP relies on price information, which is difficult to construct in public sector analyses (Madden, Savage, & Kemp, 1997). Although highly complex and technical in nature, the measurement of educational efficiency is beginning to give researchers better ideas about exactly how schools take financial inputs and create academic and social outcomes.

Larger questions, however, remain. Once researchers have determined at what level of efficiency a system functions, it remains to be determined how to make the system more efficient. The following section reviews key policy initiatives and movements designed to increase school system efficiency.

■ WRINGING EFFICIENCY FROM THE SYSTEM: POLICY INTERVENTIONS TO IMPROVE EFFICIENCY IN SCHOOLS

Means exist by which schooling in America can be rendered more productive in terms of elevating academic achievement. However, for many other purposes—for example, social, economic, and civic instruction—schooling is a weak or uncertain instrument and there is little that can be done to render it more effective in these endeavors.

Assuredly, schools can effectively instruct students in matters such as reading and mathematics, and higher-order academic tasks. However, it is far less clear that schools are an effective instrument for pursuing a spectrum of other societal challenges. Ensuring racial harmony, elevating citizen participation in government, reducing societal violence, enhancing public health, and redistributing income are social objectives that, even if strongly held by a majority of voters, schools cannot effectively accomplish. *The wider the spectrum of purposes a community or society expects schools to accomplish, unrelated to the fundamental academic instructional purposes for which the institution was established, the less likely it is that schools will be effective at anything, even their core academic functions.*

Closing the Academic Achievement Gap

Even staying with the historically derived and relatively simplified purpose of instilling student academic understanding, there are selected circumstances in which schools are a weak instrument. For example, for more than half a century, the United States has lamented the gap in academic achievement between middle- and low-income students. Because household and individual income is unevenly distributed among racial components of the American population, this achievement gap also frequently appears as a gap in achievement between white and minority students. Virtually every thinking person would like this gap to be vastly narrowed or totally eliminated.

However, the challenge is monumental. The inverse relationship between poverty and academic achievement is one of the most strongly proven of all social science findings. Prominent scholars from James S. Coleman (1966), to David Armor (1972), and Richard Rothstein (2004) have steadfastly documented the powerful connection between household and community income levels and academic achievement. See Figure 14.3 for a sample of Armor's analysis for the 2004 Abbeville (South Carolina) adequacy trial. Here one

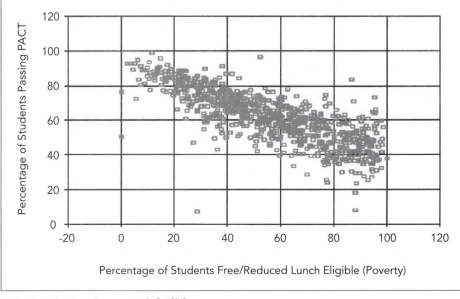

FIGURE 14.3   Armor Trial Slide

can see the classic and lamentable statistical relationship between student poverty and academic achievement.

Indeed, Rothstein asserts, following an unusually thorough review and analysis of all research bearing on the topic, that the most optimistic reading of social science results grants schooling the capacity to influence only one-third of a student's academic achievement. The converse implies that a student's social background influences two-thirds of what is acquired in school as measured by standardized examinations.

Given the impact of out-of-school conditions, it is unrealistic to expect that schools by themselves can totally overcome the effects of poverty on academic achievement. Thus, when considering matters of school productivity, one must take into consideration that, in the absence of neuroscience breakthroughs, there are some objectives for which schools may never be dramatically successful engines, regardless of how much money is poured into them.

📁 CASE 2 REVISITED

Bay Point Principal's Performance Pressures

Sandra Howard is tasked with improving test scores among her students. She needs to perform this feat without benefit of additional resources and with very little control over crucial aspects of her operation, such as teacher quality. Reflect on the ways in which Sandra could make her school more efficient. In addition to policy changes, consider how the use of data could facilitate efficiency among teachers.

■ ZERO-COST AND LOW-COST TACTICS FOR RENDERING SCHOOLING MORE PRODUCTIVE

In their original work on equity, Berne and Stiefel (1984) noted that equity considerations apply for the objects of education (students) as well as the providers of education (taxpayers). Review Case 6, Efficiency Considerations, for an example. Given this, finding methods to render the education function more efficient is an important policy consideration.

CASE 7 ———————————————————————————————————————

Efficiency Considerations

James Lykens was the executive secretary of the Metropolitan Taxpayers Association. His principal function was to monitor municipal budget processes and ensure that taxpayers got their money's worth from government. He was not opposed to taxes or, generally, to higher taxes. He just thought that those who paid taxes should be ensured a good return.

Lykens viewed taxes as investments. The money that businesses, homeowners, and consumers paid were amounts of money that they otherwise could spend somewhere else, whatever their personal priorities. Therefore, if that money was taken from their pockets by government, there had to be some clear-cut rationale for doing so. He understood the need for government, and was eager to ensure safe streets, efficient municipal services, and good schools. He understood that all of those came together to create an environment that was good for business, good for creating jobs, and good for maintaining a pleasant place to live.

Few budget activities were as frustrating to Lykens as overseeing the local school district. The district was fiscally dependent. That is, it submitted its annual proposed spending plan to the mayor who then forwarded it with his recommendations to the city council for final approval. Even though there was a locally elected school board and they hired a superintendent of schools, the school district budget and tax rates were approved and levied by the city council. This complexity kept Lykens busy. He had to attend school board budget meetings, mayoral budget hearings, and city council budget hearings. All had different sets of technicalities and personalities associated with them.

Among Lykens' frustrations was the low level of understanding on the part of the public, even sophisticated taxpayers and business operators. The multiple and fragmented levels of government involved, the reciprocal finger pointing when problems arose, and the overall lack of accountability were, in his view, unnecessary. It could all be made more simple if the mayor was charged with operating schools and selected a school commissioner as part of his cabinet, and the school board went away. The city council could just as well serve as the democratic or representative arm of government. Why a school board, too?

Under his simplified scenario, Lykens thought, he would have to participate only in the mayor's budget development processes, as he had to do anyway, and the interaction with the city council. His job would be easier and the public's sense of accountability would be greater.

Lykens was particularly frustrated this year. The school district had been given a 10% budget increase the prior year, and now it was asking for a similar level of new money again this year. This was despite the fact that the Consumer Price Index had gone up only 3% over the past year, and superintendent and board had proclaimed that they could live within their means, if they simply could have a one-time catch-up.

Now, here they were again asking for more money and their principal argument was "built-in cost increases." As far as Lykens could tell, what built-in cost increases meant was that teachers were to continue to benefit from the single salary schedule wherein every teacher in the district would be paid relative to his or her seniority in the district and the number of college credits he or she had. In addition, although the school system constructed schools through issuing bonds, the resulting schools were heated, cooled, and maintained with annual money. Since the school system had added five schools, the incremental cost of maintaining those schools was shifted to the operating budget. A similar scenario presented itself regarding technology: Although computers and infrastructure were considered capital expenses, the costs of maintenance and software were deferred to the annual budget.

Lykens kept looking for the scientific evidence that linked either of these conditions, seniority and college course taking, to student learning. He could not find anything persuasive. Still, the superintendent and board insisted that these step and column increments were built-in costs and unavoidable increases and must be funded. Lykens searched for methods of finance in the business world that accounted for capital and technological expenses in this manner—and none were to be found. Apparently, "living within their means" to the school board, meant living with annual budget increases.

Finally, the metrics for determining how the school system was performing were shifty. Increased student achievement became a cry for additional funds to "finish the job." Depressed student achievement outcomes resulted in cries for increased funding to "get the scores up." Although a businessperson by nature, even Lykens sometimes wondered if test scores were the true outcome measures to use to assess the degree to which the school system operated efficiently.

Lykens was wondering what to do. He was pro-school but anti-waste.

Within the one-third of student academic performance apparently within the purview of schools to influence, there are a variety of strategies by which educational institutions might be made more effective. These changes in schooling tactics need not involve enlarged education budgets. Whatever, if any, additional costs might be involved in implementing these illustrative changes can be absorbed by reallocating existing costs—costs of presently unproductive schooling practices (e.g., relying too heavily on teacher aides). A number of zero- or low-cost efficiency-enhancing ideas are illustrated below. There is no claim here, however, that these examples are the only way to enhance school productivity.

These zero- and low-cost productivity enhancement illustrations are arrayed on an action and policy continuum ranging from classroom, to school, to district, to state, and to the polity. The point in supplying such a continuum of change is to emphasize that there are productivity levers to be pulled at every operating and policy stage of schooling.

These illustrative efficiencies involve replacing, reinforcing, motivating, or otherwise taking advantage of human capital. The strategies involve: (1) improved schooling tactics, (2) "production" incentives for education personnel, (3) enhancing students' out-of-school and before-school well-being, (4) empowering principals in a manner that facilitates school improvement, and (5) privatizing school services and enfranchising clients.

These strategies are not mutually exclusive; they can be employed in combination. All can be used simultaneously, though it is not evident that this has ever occurred. Most of these paths to greater productivity have met and will likely continue to meet intense political opposition.

Two Final Caveats. First, it should be understood that these likely methods for improving school efficiency do not necessarily enhance other important value dimensions of equality or choice. On occasion, the latter two values will be elevated by one or more efficiency strategies. However, should this occur, it is a secondary outcome. Second, these illustrative efficiency tactics, while rooted in logic and experience, have seldom been subjected to the rigorous randomized field trial research scenarios that likely could provide greater assuredness of their productive consequences.

Intensifying and Extending Learning Tactics in Classrooms and Schools

Illustrative instructional efficiencies included in this discussion are (1) school learning climate, (2) pupil assignment policies, (3) pupil time allocations, (4) school and class size, (5) subject-matter requirements, curriculum alignment, and mastery learning, (6) altering the mix of personnel in a school, and (7) student performance data use.

School Learning Climate. What emerges from research and practical experience is that the "tone" of a school does matter for student learning: reasoned discipline policies are important, high expectations for pupil performance can influence student academic outcomes, and school effectiveness is enhanced when a strong sense of academic purpose is shared by a school's faculty members and communicated clearly to a school's parents and students.

It falls primarily to a school's chief executive and faculty members to agree on and establish a positive sense of purpose. Effective schools have been found to concentrate on academic outcomes. If too many additional objectives are established, schools' energies appear to become diluted.

Similarly, the disciplinary tone of a school, while not oppressive, must reinforce educational purposes. Students must feel physically safe and the learning environment must be free from frequent interruption from student misbehavior or administrators' overuse of classroom public address systems. An effective school is one in which the general academic climate is suffused by the high standards that instructors hold for student achievement and student conduct.

While it may be obvious, the crucial role of leadership in organizing and sustaining these important characteristics should not be overlooked. Educational research at times searches so diligently for procedural and structural variables associated with student achievement that time-honored understandings such as the significance of overall leadership is overlooked.

It is also worthy of note that identifying effective leadership, establishing high performance expectations, maintaining safe and orderly environments, and suffusing a school with academic purpose do not usually entail significant added costs.

Pupil Assignment Policies. School leaders should be acutely aware that students learn from each other and that a critical mass of high-performing students can establish a productive tone for a school. Hence, when opportunities present themselves, usually through attendance area alterations, pupil assignment policies should be used to create such conditions.

The socioeconomic status (SES) of a student's household and neighborhood can influence his or her school performance. Also, student socioeconomic composition, when taken as a collective, can influence academic achievement in an entire classroom or school. Figure 14.3 displays the regrettable but tenacious relationship between SES and student achievement.

The precise dynamics by which SES influences academic achievement are not fully known. One overarching model is as follows. Various hypotheses exist to explain SES effects. For example, it may be that teachers expect higher learning of upper-SES students, and thus pitch their instruction at a higher level. If this hypothesis is accurate, such a dynamic creates a self-fulfilling academic prophecy. Another hypothesis involves more direct peer influence. Higher-SES students may contribute to higher teacher expectations, and may influence each other's learning, both by direct peer instruction and by contributing to a classroom and school environment that is conducive to learning.

Cost-effectiveness analyses conducted by Levin, Glass, and Meister (1984) suggest yet another important instructional component of student assignment composition. Cross-age tutoring—older students assisting in the instruction of younger students—was found to be several times more cost-effective than three other instructional improvement strategies, including reduced class size.

School (and Class) Size. Whether considered as a variable of school climate or of pupil assignment, the enrollment size of schools may influence achievement. It may be possible for a school to become either too large or too small. At least to some extent, a larger school and more pupils may be accompanied by scale economies. It may also be that beyond a certain point, large numbers of pupils under a single roof trigger alienation, anomie, lack of institutional identification, and an unfavorable disciplinary environment.

Schools with fewer pupils may generally be more conducive to higher levels of student achievement, but the relationship is far from linear. An elementary school that is extremely small, having, for example, fewer than two classrooms per grade level, certainly restricts choice, or allocative efficiency, for parents. If a substantial personality conflict develops between student and teacher under such circumstances, there is often no recourse. A school containing at least two classrooms per grade level permits alternative placements. Similarly, extremely small secondary schools may have too few students to justify specialized academic courses. Students, especially advanced placement students, may suffer as a consequence.

Class size is also worthy of comment. It is conventional education wisdom that students learn more in smaller classes, presumably where each student receives added instructional attention from the teacher. With an important exception for primary school grades, the so-called Tennessee STAR study, no research evidence suggests that reducing numbers of students in a class increases student academic learning. These research results also suggest that whatever benefits of class size reduction may accrue do not justify the awesome added costs involved. Despite the absence of evidence favoring class size reduc-tions, it remains a favorite policy reform lever for parents and teachers. This probably ex-plains why class size reduction is attractive politically, even if unsupported technically.

Student Time. Beginning in the 1970s, school-related research began to demonstrate the significance of time allocation for student achievement. Several research studies quan-tified support for the conventional wisdom that the more a student studies a topic, the more he or she learns. What became evident was that time per se is not crucial. More im-portant was how available time is used by both learner and instructor. However, greater research precision and better problem definition eventually resulted in concepts such as academic learning time (ALT), time on task, and engaged time.

Studies of instructional time reveal the importance of instructors' allocating sufficient time for learning, ensuring that learning environments are relatively free from interrup-tion, and gaining the attention of students so that they are actually engaged with the task at hand. Teaching skills necessary to attract and retain student attention are complicated and beyond the scope of this text. What is of particular note is that pedagogy has progressed to the point where it is now quite possible to train teachers to be effective in this undertaking.

Subject-Matter Arrangements, Curriculum Alignment, and Mastery Learning. Students learn best those school subjects to which they are systematically exposed. This appears so obvious as to justify a reader's cynicism. However, throughout the 1960s and 1970s, this truism appeared to have been neglected. The subject-matter curriculum in many secondary schools lost its cohesion. Students were permitted to select from among a wide range of electives, and analyses of student transcripts revealed wide gaps in sequential courses. Scores on standardized achievement tests dropped during this time and the de-cline, though complicated, almost certainly was related to dilution of academic expecta-tions and the laissez-faire nature of the high school curriculum. Contemporary instruc-tional tactics focus added attention on the utility of having an integrated set of subjects ascending in intellectual complexity. Expectations of high performance are essential to ef-fective schooling, and the expectations should focus on learning important material. The curriculum cannot be forgotten in any effort to render schooling more effective.

For a school or classroom to be an effective instructional setting, expectations for stu-dent achievement, standards of achievement, content of classroom instruction, textbooks and other instructional materials, and evaluation procedures or tests must all be consis-tently focused. This is known technically as curriculum alignment (see Figure 14-4). As common-sensical as such a procedure may appear, misalignment can substantially impede achievement. If at any point on this continuum misalignment exists, achievement test re-sults may be lower than they ought to be (Spillane, 2005).

A second technical component of curriculum to be kept in mind is mastery learning. Standards of achievement for any particular grade level or course should be sufficiently specified to facilitate careful assessment of student progress. A student generally should not be permitted to progress to the next grade level or next course in a subject sequence until he or she has mastered the content in the present learning module.

If policies such as these are followed, student failure will not be routinely conveyed from level to level. Also, if an accurate student performance information system exists in a school or school district, it becomes possible over time to identify those teachers in whose classes students frequently fail to master subject matter. Appropriate supervisory steps can then be taken to enable that instructor to overcome his or her weaknesses (Celio & Harvey, 2005).

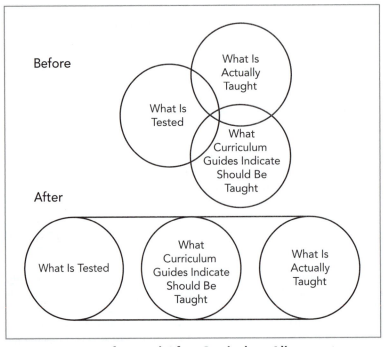

FIGURE 14.4   Before and After Curriculum Alignment

Mastery learning is particularly important when applied to basic skills at the elementary school level. It may also apply to fundamental understandings in science, mathematics, foreign language, and English at the secondary level. The important principle is that fundamental understandings be identified and that students be assisted in mastering them. To a reasonable degree, then, progress to the next level of schooling or the next course in the subject-matter sequence should depend on accomplishing these tasks.

Altering Personnel Mix. A component of technical efficiency is holding outcomes equal while reducing production costs. The labor-intense nature of instruction has usually militated against reductions. For most local education agencies, 85 to 90% of expenditures are devoted to personnel, salaries, and wages. There certainly are ways to eliminate waste in the remaining 10 to 15% of an annual budget. For example, increases in petroleum costs have motivated many school districts to implement dramatically effective energy conservation programs.

However, significant savings in the cost of schooling will have to come from more efficient deployment of personnel. History on this dimension is not encouraging. The mean number of pupils per teacher in 1930 was 30. By 1983, this figure had declined to fewer than 18 pupils per teacher. If the pupil/teacher ratio had remained at the 1930 level, the United States would be spending much less today for each year of schooling.

In order to counter past and prospective increases in labor costs, various proposals have been made to redeploy instructional personnel. A key ingredient in any of these cost-saving proposals is altering the mix of expensive and inexpensive instructors by increasing class sizes, using less expensive labor, or substituting capital for labor. It appears, however, that the United States has yet to undertake a serious effort to reduce personnel costs, for example, through widespread use of television or computers for instruction.

Creating a cadre of master teachers and relying more on cross-age tutoring are illustrations of cost savings that can result from personnel redeployments. Professional career-ladder proposals have been in existence since the 1970s, when they were deployed extensively as Tennessee state policy. However, the idea, while worthwhile, has never been widely adopted. It has even disappeared in Tennessee. Such proposals are generally justified on the grounds of professionalizing teaching and thus rendering instruction more effective. However, at least in the abstract, they could also be construed to reduce labor costs.

The presumption is that an unusually well-trained and effective teacher is capable of supervising a cadre of less-prepared, less-experienced, and hence less costly junior instructors. Assuming an overly simplified situation in which a cohort of 200 elementary students was grouped in classes averaging 25, and mean teacher salaries were $50,000, instructional salaries under the conventional system would total $400,000. Under a master teacher/apprentice configuration, a senior professional might well be paid $100,000 in 2005 dollars. However, eight junior professionals would each be paid only $30,000, for a total instructional salary cost of $340,000. Cost savings would be a substantial 15% under this scenario, class sizes would not have been increased, and the ability of a superior teacher is distributed over a larger number of students.

The so-called Lancastrian system of instruction, initially developed in Lancaster, England, during the industrial revolution, minimized labor costs. This system called on a teacher to instruct students, presumably the most able or oldest, in the day's lesson and then depend on them to act as monitors to instruct literally dozens of other pupils. Classroom seating was constructed in ascending tiers to facilitate such tutorial arrangements and maintain the entire student body under direct line-of-sight supervision of a senior teacher.

The contemporary version of Lancastrian teaching is known as cross-age tutoring, and the previously cited research by Levin, Glass, and Meister suggests that, appropriately used, it is a cost-effective means of enhancing student academic achievement.

Pupil Evaluation. Appropriate feedback regarding instruction can enhance learning. Two kinds of tests, criterion-referenced and norm-referenced, are needed. The former are keyed to school or classroom standards of achievement. Often, these are teacher-constructed tests. Regardless of their origin, criterion-referenced examinations assess student comprehension of the basic skills conveyed in classes. It is with these tests that decisions on student mastery learning can be made.

Norm-referenced tests, allowing comparison of an individual student's performance relative to that of a group of students, are also an important part of instructional technology. Such tests enable judgments to be made on the effectiveness of one school relative to another or on the degree to which one SES ethnic or racial group is achieving relative to another. These latter measures are important in assessing equity outcomes, a topic discussed extensively in prior chapters.

Value-added testing, relying on means for determining how much more a student learned over a given time period relative to a beginning point, is crucial for identifying particularly productive classrooms, schools, and districts. Value-added tests, when appropriately constructed to account for the SES of students are a vital link to the idea discussed below—paying teachers and schools for student performance.

Paying for Pupil Performance

A second means for educational institutions to increase productivity, or technical efficiency, is the use of effective extrinsic incentives. One might ask, "incentives for whom?" Should inducements be offered to the learner; to those who influence the learner, such as parents, siblings, or peers; or to those who directly deliver educational services, such as teachers and administrators? Should rewards be directed at individuals or at groups? What should be the nature of the rewards—simple recognition, symbolic displays, money? Who should decide rewards, and what criteria for rewards should be employed?

These are neither simple nor rhetorical questions. Education, being labor-intensive, is fraught with complex human interactions. This complexity, when coupled with the difficulty in agreeing on desired outcomes of schooling, suggests that any payment-by-results strategy should be approached with substantial caution. Otherwise, the risk of goal displacement is extraordinary. An example dramatizes the point.

Unanticipated Outcomes. If a school district decided to reward teachers for elevating student academic achievement and took as the performance criterion increases in class average scores on a standardized test, teachers might pursue multiple strategies in response. An ideal teacher response strategy might be to focus on each student in an effort to elevate scores individually and thus to achieve a higher aggregate class average. Under such a scenario, arguably, everyone would benefit.

However, imagine a wily instructor who calculates that for the time invested, it was the intellectually most able students in the class who were capable of the greatest individual test score gains. This hypothetical teacher then proceeds to ignore less-than-average students and concentrates only on those from whom the greatest achievement "payoff" is possible. Subsequent test administration reveals an elevated class average, and the teacher receives a salary bonus. Below-average students' test scores in the class actually decline, perhaps because of teacher neglect. It is unlikely that the school board desired such an outcome. Inappropriately structured incentives can displace legitimate organizational goals.

Assumptions. Paying for results, regardless of the actual form of the incentive or reward, assumes the utility of extrinsic sanctions. Do humans beings respond to such incentives, and, if so, under what circumstances?

McGregor et al. (1968) constructed an interesting set of principles based on assumptions about internal and external motivation. Space prohibits full explanation of this theory here. Suffice it to say that inappropriately applied organizational inducements can misfire. If individuals have been socialized to a strict professional standard—that is, if they have internalized the view that high performance and attention to client welfare is expected of one correctly performing his or her duties, regardless of external rewards—then application of payment for results can undermine professionalism, contribute to deteriorating performance, and simply be seen as insulting by employees. The point here is not that external rewards are bad or ineffective but that such a system must be carefully considered and implemented.

Another assumption embedded in education payment-for-results schemes is that a desired performance outcome has social utility: the outcome benefits not simply the individual learner but the larger society as well. It seems wasteful to allocate public resources to a result that benefits only the learner.

Incentives for Individual Pupils. Some learning apparently has its own rewards. Simply stated, acquiring new knowledge or a new skill can be pleasurable in and of itself. Additionally, behavioral psychology posits that learning can be enhanced through appropriate use of external rewards—positive reinforcement. Such reinforcement, to be effective, need be no more complicated than praise or commendation from the instructor. (Indeed, recognition need not necessarily even stem from a human being. Many computer-assisted instruction [CAI] programs depend on praise embedded in the program when a correct response is made by the learner.) Positive sanctions, such as rewards, are said to be substantially more effective in inducing learning than are negative sanctions, such as criticism.

What about paying pupils for learning—not simply giving praise or small candies when they display correct performance, but actually paying money for academic achievement? However crass or corrupting of the culture of education, this idea has actually been tried, albeit on an extraordinarily limited basis. In the 1960s, under President Lyndon Johnson's War on Poverty, a number of pay-for-results education "experiments" were sponsored by the now-defunct executive branch Office of Economic Opportunity (OEO). Among these was an attempt to induce higher levels of achievement by paying individual students for higher test scores. The experiment was small, involved only a few classroom settings, was not enthusiastically endorsed by teachers, and had ambiguous results. Numerous individual psychology research studies have been built around this strategy. However, the limited OEO experiment was the only recorded public policy trial.

Enhancing Productivity through Peers. Pupil achievement is known to be influenced significantly by peers and peer group composition. This influence occurs through the social mechanisms for which hypotheses are offered in this chapter's prior discussion of instruction. In addition, there is another potential dynamic operating in schools, a dynamic that appears too often overlooked by professional educators as a useful means for enhancing achievement.

Pioneering research on adolescent student culture conducted by sociologist James S. Coleman suggests the existence in most secondary schools of a set of peer group-related learning disincentives. Coleman contends that the secondary school student culture esteems social popularity and athletic prowess more than academic achievement. A student is more likely to gain peers' respect and friendship through competitive sports or social savoir-faire than through sustained scholarship.

Schools in part reflect the larger society. Professional football players make more money than many physicians or attorneys. Schools cannot be expected to cure all society's ills, and it is unlikely that any pay-for-results scheme will eliminate this condition. However, proposals have been made to establish greater amounts of interscholastic academic competition in order to create scholarly as well as athletic heroes. Aside from tactics, the principle involved is to reward a major purpose of schooling—academic achievement—with a level of recognition at least equal to that accorded by sports achievement.

Paying Producers. This is the external incentive dimension to which the greatest policy attention has been devoted. There exist such a wide variety of pay-for-results proposals regarding teachers and other "producers" that space permits no more than a selective description here. Among the more interesting policy suggestions have been performance contracting, merit pay for teachers, and merit schools.

Performance Contracting. Another much-publicized OEO pay-for-results experiment was conducted with performance contracting. In exchange for a specified educational service, such as operating an entire elementary school or a remedial reading program within a school, a qualified educational contractor would be paid an agreed-on base amount plus bonuses tied to increases in student achievement. The more students learned, the greater the payoff to the contractor. Contractors were free, within reason, to offer whatever incentives they wanted to students. Some offered trinkets such as transistor radios to students who increased their test scores.

However effective the results, or noble the concept, performance contracting in the 1960s came to an ignominious conclusion with press accusations of widespread contractor misfeasance. It was alleged that instructors employed by contracting companies were leaking test items to students before formal examinations. Students previously supplied with test questions increased their scores, but by a means judged fraudulent. A scandal involving a company under contract to the Texarkana schools was intensely publicized, and school officials lost what little enthusiasm they once had for added experimentation. Teachers' union officials said "We told you so!" and a number of private sector corporations dropped plans for expanding into the provision of public schools services under contract.

Teachers' unions, or any appropriately chartered group of teachers, could have become contractual providers under the OEO experiment. Such an idea presaged 1980s visions of teacher-managed schools. However, no sustained effort at teacher-operated performance contracting resulted. Indeed, as with so many education reforms, performance contracting was a fad that endeared itself to virtually no one and left little legacy for contemporary educational policy or practice.

In the 1990s, performance contracting, under a new label, "charter schools," had a resurgence. Now, the concept is broader, involving household choice. Chapter 15 explains charter schools as an avenue for provision of greater choice or "liberty." However, a reader should understand that with attachment of appropriate performance incentives, charter schooling can rapidly evolve into a pay-for-performance scheme.

Merit Pay. Merit pay, or educator pay for pupil performance, proposals for teachers and administrators are a continuing, or at least cyclically recurring, policy proposal. Merit pay is an external reward scheme that offers classroom instructors and principals added financial remuneration for better student performance.

A few school districts operate merit pay schemes; some have done so for a sustained period. However, the idea is intensely controversial and traditionally opposed by the National Education Association. This organization frequently asserts that the idea is fine in the abstract but bogs down in the details of implementation. On what bases will student performance be assessed? How much added reward is appropriate to motivate teachers to try harder? How can a merit pay system adequately control for students' SES backgrounds so that teachers with students from low-income households are not unfairly judged? Who will decide if a teacher is meritorious? Is the idea subject to collective bargaining as a term of employment? It is on questions such as these that the proposal usually founders.

Aside from difficulties in determining outcome measures, such as those illustrated by the pay-for-performance scheme hypothesized at the beginning of this section, teachers' unions offer other criticisms of merit pay. Of great concern is the prospect of administrative favoritism. If criteria for merit pay are broader than test scores alone, then will they be fairly applied by principals? If not, teachers' unions contend, then merit pay risks being divisive. Teachers not selected for a merit reward or bonus will resent those who are. In that a successful school depends on a cooperative atmosphere, merit pay might erode, not enhance, productivity.

Merit pay advocates contend that all of the above criticisms can be met by modern testing methods. For example, value-added testing, with its capacity to control for students' SES, offers an opportunity to discern the relatively unique contributions of a classroom teacher over the course of a school year. Performance pay proponents also contend that performance rewards have to be substantial in order to provoke added motivation. Many merit pay efforts have only offered teachers $1,000 or $2,000 more for a year of effort. Potential recipients do not view this remuneration level, in the range of 2 or 4% annually, as significant or motivating. However, amounts of $20,000 or more might be.

Merit Schools. This is a pay-for-results proposal in which an entire school is assumed to be the unit of production. Whatever the rewards, such as added money from the district or the state, they are accorded the whole school. Agreement on output measures is still crucial to such a plan. However, assuming agreement on assessment procedures and reasonable cooperation on the part of the faculty, schools judged to merit rewards would have added resources. This money could be distributed evenly to faculty in the form of pay bonuses or divided between faculty bonuses and added resources for the school itself, such as more field trips, library books, or instructional materials. Florida has adopted such a policy, though it is too early to judge its advantages and disadvantages. California used another version applicable only to secondary schools. The output measure was narrowly defined as increased test scores for graduating seniors. The program was enacted in 1983 and abandoned in 1986. When these plans have been tried to date, the potential reward has not generally been of a magnitude that provokes motivation. Also, the "free rider" problem is significant. A few teachers appear additionally motivated, and if they succeed through their efforts in elevating overall school performance, others who worked less hard are still rewarded. This often engenders cynicism and a subsequent reluctance to work hard on the part of high-performing teachers.

Empowering Students

Given the powerful influence of out-of-school conditions on academic achievement, it is foolish to believe that students' performance, or at least low-income students' performance, will be significantly elevated by schooling activities alone. Hence, advocates such as Richard Rothstein and Whitney Allgood make it clear that there are a host of out-of-school strategies that lend themselves to social policy and that, if undertaken, would have a high prospect of elevating students' school performance.

Allgood and Rothstein (2000) have undertaken extensive research regarding the returns to investing in a spectrum of out-of-school vectors. These include community development, parent income subsidies, parent job training, health and mental healthcare, housing, and family counseling. Not all of these possible vectors are cost-effective, but many are. It is not within the purview of this book to review this evidence in detail. However, it is important that readers and policymakers realize that academic achievement for low-income children may be more a function of out-of-school empowerments than in-school operations.

Empowering Principals

Among the inconsistencies and ironies of American public schooling is a view that a school's principal can be held accountable for the performance of students. In the abstract this is a reasonable idea. In virtually every other sector—public, non-profit, and private—the CEO is thought to be the individual in charge and it is his or her job and reputation that are at stake when it comes to the performance of the organization. School principals are frequently lumped into a similar category. After all, a modern school is an extremely complex, and often unusually costly, operation. Thus, why not hold principals accountable for student performance and parent satisfaction? It altogether makes sense.

Here is the problem, however. Most principals in America's public schools are not empowered to operate their schools. Thus, it is not fair to hold them accountable for performance results. Central office officials, not principals, make most important decisions. This includes, but is not restricted to decisions regarding personnel assigned to a school and discretion over most of the budget allocated to a school. The curriculum, teachers, class size, school attendance zone boundaries, textbooks, professional staff to student ratios, hours of school operation, annual school calendar, transportation arrangements, custodial supervision, food service, and plant maintenance and renovation are decision vectors generally managed centrally by school district officials.

Until principals are further empowered on these important dimensions, it is unlikely that America's schools will become more productive. Only by aligning resources appropriately with authority can accountability be rendered effective. Such reforms are a tall order. Most superintendents are reluctant to cede such authority to subordinates for fear that somehow something will go wrong. Of course, if school boards would appraise superintendents' performance more by the academic achievement of students, then superintendents might adopt a different management style than that which pervades most of America's school districts today (Hill & Harvey, 2004).

Privatization and Enfranchising Clients

Some critics of the current system contend that public schooling suffers primarily from being oppressively bureaucratic and overly insulated from clients' preferences. Historic developments such as the 1920s Progressive Era efforts to depoliticize public schooling, school district consolidation, growth of professional school managers, and educational administrators' efforts to ape the scientific management movement in the industrial sector, when coupled with the post–World War II development of collective bargaining, are said to have rendered schools' decision making the domain of education professionals, a domain from which the public generally and school clients specifically are isolated.

The logic underlying this set of criticisms suggests that schools would become more productive (more allocatively efficient) if client, parent, and pupil preferences could effectively be expressed in a manner that attracted the attention of professional educators. Proposals to facilitate expression of client preferences span a wide spectrum, from those that simply necessitate administrative reorganization of the current system to more radical recommendations that portend alterations of the basic decision-making unit in education. These proposals are described in three major classifications: (1) client opinion polling, (2) organizational restructuring, and (3) decision-unit reforms.

Client Opinion Polling. Popular studies of effective private companies stress the tight linkages that profitable firms often maintain between themselves and customers. Repeated sampling of customer opinion apparently aids both technical and allocative efficiency. Consumer views on new or contemplated products and services can prove useful to a firm trying to decide how to alter its product array. Also, customer views regarding recently purchased products offer "quality-control" feedback. Complaints, if acted on quickly, can stanch the spread of negative rumors and help remedy whatever flaws are reported.

Educators seldom engage in such monitoring. Administrator preparation programs lack a component on opinion sampling. A view frequently held by educators is that such marketing efforts are at once counterprofessional and technically beyond their comprehension. Neither is correct.

Advocates of greater marketing in education assert that new techniques render survey research quite reliable with relatively small samples. District-level client surveys can be useful in matters such as bond and tax referenda, boundary alterations, location of a proposed new school, or districtwide curriculum alterations. The school site population—parents and, above some grade level, pupils—is the one from which feedback is particularly desirable. Schools, not districts, are the typical unit of production in education. Thus, it is from the most immediate clients that opinions on course offerings, quality of instructional service, and preferred changes should be sought. When surveying school-level clients, one may not necessarily have to "sample." Modern web-based survey procedures enable organizations to design and administer online surveys to clients at remarkably low costs, in the range of 5¢ per respondent.

Although the school may be an appropriate unit of survey analysis, it need not be an individual school that is responsible for conducting the survey research. This is a function that can most appropriately be undertaken for all schools, unit by unit, by a district central office planning and evaluation division. Such a central management policy unit ought to report directly to the chief executive officer. Client survey results can be considered in much the same manner as internal audit reports in a large organization. Such reports, and client surveys, should not be the exclusive property of, or accessible to manipulation by, line administrators other than the chief executive and policymakers. Such results are necessary for evaluation and policy planning purposes.

Organizational Restructuring. Seeking client views is easily accomplished and, if conducted appropriately, can contribute to allocative efficiency. However, public school critics sometimes assert that the insensitive bureaucratic nature of schools will not easily succumb to expressions of consumer preference. At a minimum, some contend, the system needs structural revision. Toward such an end, four post-World War II reform surges have taken place. They have all proven feckless. However, in hopes of preventing readers from repeating history, a short description of each is provided here. These include: (1) the so-called community control movement, (2) efforts to establish "alternative schools," (3) administrative decentralization, and (4) school site management and parent advisory councils.

Community Control. In the early 1970s, the Ford Foundation sponsored a study of New York City schools. The report recommended that steps be taken to disaggregate the huge New York City public school district into presumably more manageable units. Three experimental community control districts emerged and rapidly became a focus for intense political conflict. Eventually, the New York legislature enacted a bill that divided the city's schools into 31 elementary districts with elected boards subject to the overall authority of the city's central school board. Each of these subdistricts contained more pupils than the overwhelming majority of school districts throughout the United States. Community control proponents were dismayed that the new sub-bureaucracies would be touted as a way to re-turn schools to the "people." Moreover, early political analyses asserted that newly elected local boards were heavily dominated by citizens supported by teachers' unions. Much dis-cussion was devoted to similar disaggregating proposals in other city districts, but little came of it. A 1980s expression of this spirit was the return in several large cities to district- or ward-elected central city school boards. This early 1980s phenomenon, a return to the arrangements of the early 1900s, was also intended to render elected officials more re-sponsive to their constituents. Almost predictably, by the late 1980s, critics were asserting that decentralization had realized the worst predictions of corruption and inefficiency. They called for yet another cycle of reform.

Alternative Schools. This concept, much like accountability, has continued to be a se-mantic umbrella of sufficient breadth to encompass numerous schooling ideas, some of them antithetical. In the 1960s, several notable authors wrote stinging critiques of public schools, asserting that they were debilitatingly uniform, repressive, stifling, and mindlessly administered. "Alternative education" was proposed as a reform. British infant schools, fre-quently cited as a model for students' early years, easily assisted in the transition from home to scholarly activities. Many parents removed their children from public schools to place them in private "alternative schools." Public school systems themselves, unwilling to forego their market share easily, established public alternative school experiments. By the end of the 1970s, the movement had run its course and several of its major ideologues had revised their opinions, confessed to a change of heart, and advocated more structured schools.

Administrative Decentralization. Large city school districts underwent a wave of de-centralization during the 1960s and 1970s. The general justification was that organiza-tional disaggregation would permit schools to be more responsive to clients and employ-ees. The typical pattern was to divide a district into several administrative units, each with an executive officer nominally in charge of all subdistrict schools. Districts varied in de-gree of decision-making discretion permitted these units. In most instances, fiscal author-ity continued to be centralized. Personnel administration also typically remained a central office function. Curriculum planning and instructional emphasis were often permitted to vary in accord with the tastes of subdistrict administrators. Only in New York City was disaggregation accompanied by political reform, namely, election of subdistrict school boards. In other cities, the central school board continued to be the policy-making body for the entire district. Consequently, critics contended that decentralization accomplished little more than added costs and insertion of yet another bureaucratic layer between local schools and "downtown" decision makers. It was difficult, outside of city school central of-fices and subdistrict administrators, to identify those favoring the reform.

School Site Management. The relative failure of community control, alternative schools, and administrative decentralization encouraged yet a fourth effort to infuse schools with greater citizen participation. This additional reform was described in detail initially by a New York state reform commission, using the label school site management.

The plan was intended both to gain a greater measure of lay control and to provide more accountability by using the school, rather than the district, as the basic decision-making unit for personnel and curriculum. School district central offices would continue to handle fiscal and business matters and serve as planning, coordinating, and record-keeping bodies. A parent advisory council (PAC) at each school would be responsible for principal selection and evaluation and for advising that officer on curriculum, instructional, and personnel matters. Principals were envisioned as being on multiyear contracts, renewal of which was subject to PAC approval. Within specified boundaries, the principal and parent advisory council would have discretion over funds budgeted for the school by the central office. Each school's budget allocation was to be determined by a set of uniform decision rules, including criteria such as number, grade level, and achievement records of pupils assigned to the school. The parent advisory council would issue an annual evaluation report including plans for the subsequent year.

Several states adopted PAC components for their state categorical aid programs. Portions of the idea also were favorably received by federal authorities, which began in the 1970s to include PAC requirements for schools receiving categorical aid funds. The idea became so pervasive that school administrators soon asked that parent advisory councils undergo consolidation lest principals' nights consist of one council meeting after another.

Aside from widespread adoption in form, there is slight evidence regarding the idea's effectiveness. In many instances, little budget discretion is ceded to parents, collective bargaining agreements with teachers continued to render most decisions a central office matter, some parents claim they are too easily co-opted by administrators, and few principals are attracted to the idea of having their job security tied to parental approval.

Decision-Unit Reform. The relative lack of success of 1960s and 1970s structural revisions stimulated proposals for more radical reforms, alterations that would not simply change the bureaucratic layering of American education but would more dramatically shift fundamental decision-making processes. The two most prominent of these radical reform proposals are vouchers and tuition tax credits. Vouchers permit a greater amount of public regulation of education than do tuition tax credits, and in this sense are the less radical of the two reforms.

Vouchers

Regardless of operational details, voucher plans possess a common fundamental principle. Their intent is to enfranchise households as the basic educational decision-making unit. Vouchers do not eliminate government interest in education. Rather, voucher plans retain the prospect of government responsibility for financing and otherwise maintaining a marketplace of education providers, which would require regulation.

This plan, should any state adopt it, would not only alter school financing but would also dramatically change the pattern of school governance. A voucher plan was enacted by Congress following World War II to help returning veterans pay for their higher education. A complete lower education voucher plan has never been enacted by any state. Efforts were made by the now-defunct federal Office of Economic Opportunity in the 1970s to induce school districts to experiment with the idea. Only one, Alum Rock, near San Jose, California, accepted the offer. Alum Rock dropped the plan within three years. The idea, usually espoused by fiscal conservatives and political libertarians, and sometimes by those who view it as a means of empowering school choice among the poor, has not yet proved attractive to a political majority either nationally or in a particular state. The principal discussion of this idea is provided in the Chapter 15.

Substituting Capital for Labor

The history of education is filled with predictions and promises of an imminent revolution in instructional technology. In fact, despite the advent of motion pictures, television, and computers, American education has simply become ever more dependent on labor. The wide availability of computers in homes, where parents can use them with children, might eventually alter this pattern. Perhaps enough students will eventually come to school already knowledgeable in computers to have a significant impact on classroom instruction. Meanwhile, it is clear that larger numbers of personal computers are to be found in schools. However, there is little consistent evidence to suggest that they are substituting for labor, that is, that they are replacing teachers.

Summary

Efficiency is concerned with increasing outcomes and decreasing cost. Whereas this paradigm is acceptable in the world of business and manufacturing, it is less of a good fit with the real world of education. Nevertheless, efficiency is an important component of school finance, for it is always better to have a more efficient school system than a less efficient one. Two types of efficiency confront educators and policymakers: allocative and technical efficiency. Measurements of efficiency are often regression based. Recently, new measures of efficiency, including data envelopment analysis and stochastic frontier analysis, have emerged to challenge the notion that there is one normative education production function for all situations and contexts. A number of policy reforms exist to increase efficiency at low or zero cost. The reforms include addressing class size, maximizing student and parental choice, and including more community members in the education governance process.

Discussion Questions

1. Discuss the outcomes educators are seeking to maximize under the NCLB legislation. Are these outcomes worthy of being maximized?
2. What other outcomes might educators look for in order to assess improvements in educational efficiency?
3. How would you feel about a teacher incentive plan that rewarded teachers for improved test scores?
4. Read the efficiency case study of James Lykens. From what we have reviewed about governance and efficiency, what recommendations would you make in order to boost the degree of efficiency within the Metropolitan school system?

CHAPTER FIFTEEN

Liberty

"Freedom is the right to choose, the right to create for oneself the alternatives of choice. Without the possiblity of choice and the exercise of choice, a man is not a man but a member, an instrument, a thing."

—*Thomas Jefferson*

▌ INTRODUCTION

Liberty and the associated freedom to choose among political, philosophical, and economic alternatives is at the heart of the American experience. However, when applied to schooling, "liberty" is often a controversial idea. There is a philosophical and policy tension between the notion of families or students having a choice in their schooling versus the idea of schools contributing to a uniform American culture and an idealized community of citizens. The fundamental question, one with which the United States continually wrestles through its courts and elective processes, is the extent to which the student is a creature of the family, the state, or the individual. Balancing the interests of these three agents is the sustained challenge facing the policy system. It is for this complex set of conditions that "liberty" is a controversial topic in education. Who has liberty to do what, at whose expense?

Before reviewing the technical and policy considerations of liberty, read Case 8, Cathy's Choice, for a more applied example of the manner in which educational choice might affect the lived reality of parents. Use this case study as a framework for reviewing the policy initiatives described below.

📁 CASE 8 ————————————————————————

Cathy's Choice

Cathy Corbis was a single mother raising two children. She worked two jobs, as a paralegal and an after hours pharmacy clerk, to support her family. Though far from wealthy, she was nevertheless well educated. She had graduated from college and had specialized training in law. In addition, she held high educational aspirations for her son and daughter.

Cathy could not afford to live in a nearby suburb the schools of which were to her liking. Instead, because of housing costs, she had to settle for buying a small home in a lower-middle-class district on the fringe of the big city where she worked. Here, her children had several school disadvantages. They often had to take classes with youngsters whose parents had nowhere near the same level of education expectations for their children as Cathy did. Until recently, children had opportunities to find remunerative factory work without a high school diploma. Discipline was also a problem and teachers had their hands full simply keeping order.

Second, both of Cathy's children wanted to go to college, and both wanted to enroll in Advanced Placement (AP) courses. In her district of residence, school spending per pupil was high. However, the district had a large number of very senior teachers who qualified for high salaries, and this inflated the district's per-pupil costs. Under policy pressure to boost the academic achievement of low-performing schools, the district had decided to operate small remedial classes, as a way of combating the discipline, English-language deficiency, and attendance problems of the students it served. The end result of this resource allocation pattern was that the school offered only a limited number of AP classes.

Cathy had visited the school and talked with the principal. He was sympathetic to her plea, but could offer no solution, except suggesting that she relocate within the attendance boundaries of another district. He said he had little control over how money was spent. The school board and central office made allocation decisions, and they had set a policy of high teacher pay and small introductory classes. Advanced electives were not a high priority for the district.

Cathy felt trapped. She could not afford to live in the district that met her education hopes. She could not influence the school to offer her children the educational opportunities she thought they needed. She believed that economic and political forces beyond her control were shaping her and her children's lives.

As a last resort, Cathy visited the Catholic high school in a nearby town. It would require a long two-way bus commute for her son and daughter. Still, it offered the advanced courses they needed. The tuition was not too high because the parish subsidized the school. Cathy liked the principal and liked the atmosphere of the school. She was not a Catholic, but she did not feel the school was a place where her children would be unduly proselytized.

Cathy's problem with the school was the $3,000 per student tuition. This was not high. Her public school district spent three times that, at least. Still, she would have to come up with $6,000 a year, on top of the residential property taxes she already paid for public schools.

To Cathy, it just did not seem fair. She paid her taxes, but could not get what her children needed. The attorneys for whom she worked simply purchased homes in districts that served their children's needs. They did not have to pay private school tuition to get the courses they wanted. She did not have that luxury.

LEARNING OBJECTIVES

By the end of this chapter you should be able to:

- Discuss positive and negative definitions of liberty.
- Define incremental policy changes to enhance liberty within education.
- Define more drastic policies to enhance liberty.
- Evaluate these policies within the context of current education legislation.

The notion of an American people united in their liberty and free to act as liberated agents in almost all arenas of life is deeply rooted in American education's history. Education leaders such as Horace Mann and William T. Harris in the 19th century fostered a vision of public education rooted in the community and the public's need for citizen workers and educated voters. To these historic public school advocates and activists, it was a collective responsibility to strengthen democracy not simply by publicly supporting but also by publicly providing educational opportunities for children. The idea of a common public school has become identified with America. Still, Americans are not completely comfortable with uniformity, and, as a consequence, the policy system routinely entertains proposals for expanding choice in public schooling or expanding choice between public and private schooling.

Calibrating the relative importance of efficient operations, equitable distributions of resources, a sense of community, and the degree of liberty that families prefer in making educational choices for their children is a difficult balancing act for educators, policymakers and parents. For example, efficient school operation may dictate that students attend a school closest to home to minimize transportation costs. Yet, this policy will more than likely result in an aggregation of poor or minority students in neighborhood schools. In addition, a neighborhood school may not be the choice of families in the neighborhood. Issues of this nature are the subjects of this chapter.

■ DIFFERING VIEWS OF LIBERTY

There exist two different philosophical notions related to liberty—*negative liberty* and *positive liberty*. Simply put, negative liberty seeks to free an agent, while positive liberty seeks barriers necessary to protect choice for a greater number of people, such as a community or a nation (Carter, 2003). For example, one may decry imposition of a speed limit as an affront to one's personal liberty to drive at high speed. Conversely, a police department or city government may argue that it is the very imposition of such limits that allows the greatest number of citizens to enjoy the liberty of driving safely throughout a community. Many agents such as state or local school districts rely on both definitions of liberty in conversations with constituencies.

The liberty debate is based on an assumption inherited from the founding fathers: the idea that government is best when it governs least and, if it governs at all, does so in a manner closest to the people. This idea privileges local control as the type of government closest to the public and, hence, most responsive to the public's needs. Some scholars resist, arguing instead that there is no inherent relationship between local government and liberty, especially in issues of education. These thinkers contend that for a more systemic form of public education, localities should be able to respond to federal standards and guidelines as they see fit (Bull, 2000). Still other scholars see no government role in the provision of education at all, and base their proposals on the economic primacy of the family.

Much of the debate regarding liberty in education and education finance policy revolves around the idea of negative liberty and seeks to remove barriers to action for any number of agents. Among these agents in educational policy are states, local school districts, and individual families. These three agents present differing variations of the liberty argument. When combined, a liberty argument may go something like this:

> Public provision of education contributes to bureaucratic organization and, thus, severely restricts choice. In many American communities, if a student does not attend a private school, he or she must attend an assigned public school. Once in the school, a student is assigned to a class taught by a teacher selected by a bureaucracy, with little or no counsel from student or parents. Even though there may be a severe clash of personalities, the student is often assigned to a teacher for an entire year. Professionals decide the curriculum with little influence from parents, and a student has little or no choice of courses in the elementary school, and only somewhat more in the secondary schools. Students are required to attend school for a specific number of hours per day, and the schedule is usually quite uniform, without recognition of individual parent or student needs. Students must attend a specific number of days per year, with school-specified vacations frequently having no necessary relation to parents' vacations. Students must attend until age 16 or 18, regardless of how much or little has been learned.

Overcoming enforced uniformity, adding choice, or liberty, to a public education system will, according to advocates, create a competitive market where pressures to compete among institutions will lead to increased instructional innovation and student achievement (Chubb & Moe, 1990; Hess, 2002; Hoxby, 2003). Adding to or dismantling the nation's current publicly supported schools that teach a vast majority of students could create an education market. Determining *if* additional liberty should be legislated into the U.S. system of schools, and *how* that liberty should be legislated are key questions for this chapter.

The liberty argument exists on a number of administrative levels. Many groups make the negative liberty argument to the administrative level that is directly above them in the American system of public education. Therefore, states see themselves as agents, and use negative liberty to argue that federal regulations hamper their educating children. Similarly, local school districts contend that states themselves impede district effectiveness with onerous regulations and oversight. Finally, families argue that school districts are not implementing policies in the interest of their specific children's needs. All levels of education use a liberty argument at some point in order to gain more traction to implement personal or collective preferences that they contend will lead to a better education for children.

State-Level Liberty and the Federal Role

According to Article 10 of the Bill of Rights, education, because it is not explicitly discussed, is a responsibility allocated to states. This is why many school finance cases are filed using state constitutions; they have explicit education clauses specifying state aspirations for educational systems. For most of U.S. history, the federal government was silent regarding state public education issues (although the federal government was more active in supporting higher education), leaving states and school districts to divide educational responsibility.

This condition changed in 1954 when the U.S. Supreme Court ruled in *Brown v. Board of Education of Topeka Kansas* that "separate educational facilities are inherently unequal." Using as a justification the equal protection clause of the 14th Amendment, the U.S. Supreme Court defined a federal role in state educational policy. Although the ruling was necessary to abolish unjust laws and practices in southern states, the *Brown* decision also influenced the freedom of states to locate, construct, and zone students into specific schools.

The federal government implemented its anti-poverty education programs such as Title I of the 1965 Elementary and Secondary Education Act (ESEA) using this same logic and argument. States receiving federal Title I funds to enhance educational opportunities for students in poverty (and that is all of the states) must also submit to federal regulations as to how those funds and the systems that support those funds are used. This is why, although the federal government only provides approximately 7% of total national education funding, it is able to pass sweeping education legislation such as the No Child Left Behind Act of 2001. Other clauses in the United States Constitution, such as the "commerce clause" found in Article I, Section 8, may also be used to justify federal involvement in public education policy, and thus decrease state liberty. At the same time, states also act in ways that impinge on the liberty of local school districts.

District-Level Liberty and the State Role

Local school districts also have a liberty interest. Review the In the News story. Consider the Durham Public Schools in Durham, North Carolina. Until 1992, students in Durham either attended predominantly African American Durham City public schools or the predominently white Durham County public schools. The county school system encircled the city school system. In 1992, the Durham County Board of Commissioners agreed to merge the Durham City and Durham County public schools. The State Board of Education approved the merger, which took place in 1995. Neither the Durham City school board nor the Durham County school board had a say in the merger decision; yet both were left to implement the policy (Cohen, 1992; Jones, 1991).

In the case of Durham, county commissions and state education officials made educational decisions. Although these bodies had reason for their action (they were striving to avoid federal intervention on school segregation issues), the actions of these bodies diminished the freedom of two elected school boards to determine their own future. Although the Durham example is a stark one, state policies routinely restrict the liberty of districts in many ways. Since most state constitutions place ultimate responsibility for public education at the state level, state educational agencies dictate a range of issues to districts— from curriculum to facilities to financial arrangements. Since state funding of public education approximates 60% nationally, states assume the right to make rules to ensure that funds are spent in an appropriate manner. Districts often cry foul over rules and regulations from the state level. Similarly, families often sense that districts present them with significant barriers to exercising their liberty regarding their child's schooling.

Family-Level Liberty: School Choice

Although both states and districts can make compelling liberty arguments using the negative liberty outlook, the notion of liberty most often discussed in the current education policy space is that of family liberty. Commonly referred to as school choice, family-level liberty is conceived of as an idea whereby the household, as the closest available unit of governance, has the most invested and greatest empowerment in educational choices for students.

In the News

DURHAM—A consulting firm hired by the Durham County Board of Commissioners has delivered its verdict: the Durham County and city school systems should merge.

The long-anticipated report by Stanton Leggett and Associates of Larchmont, N.Y., was delivered to county commissioners Thursday, in advance of a formal presentation Wednesday. Commissioners had hired the firm to study the merger question—one of Durham's most divisive issues—and make a recommendation.

The pro-merger recommendation was greeted gingerly by members of both school boards, who had not seen the report and said they wanted more details on how the merged school system would work.

"Our board has taken a stand opposed to merger, that at this time we don't see any educational benefit for our students from merger," said Joy B. Baldwin, chairman of the Durham County school board. "But obviously I'm interested in seeing for what reasons they recommend merger."

Betty M. Copeland, vice chairman of the city school board, said she had not decided whether to favor a merger. Durham city schools are predominantly black; the county system is mostly white.

Commissioners will consider next week whether to ask the consultants to develop a detailed merger plan.

The document lays out reasons for merger, with background on the county's demographics and economics and on student achievement in both school systems. It concludes that merger would have two chief benefits: improving education countywide and improving the overall social and economic health of the county.

The report also acknowledges that the Durham city schools, with a 92 percent black enrollment, are now essentially segregated, while the county schools are predominantly white but less lopsided. A merged school system would be 50.6 percent black, it predicts.

The study also suggests that a referendum, favored by the county commissioners, would be a "divisive and bitter battle, one the county might do well to avoid." Instead, it would be preferable for the state legislature to order merger, either on its own or at the request of the commissioners, the report suggests.

The report critiques the performance of both school systems, and says merger would make for better educational resources across the county. For instance, preschool, all-day and all-year programs would be better provided by one system, the report states.

"A merged school district is Durham's best—and perhaps only—opportunity to meet the needs of its children," it states.

Second, merger would help Durham economically, by improving the county's business and real estate climate, the report contends.

Split school systems and their respective weaknesses have hurt employee recruitment, home sales, the redevelopment of downtown Durham and business development, it concludes.

Saving money and increasing efficiency—particularly in school construction and administration—also are possible benefits of merger. But saving money should not be the impetus for merger, the report states, and merger would in fact be costly in its first years.

While it is not a detailed merger plan, the report does include some suggestions. For instance, magnet schools and school-based management techniques should be considered.

A merged system should also include a single school board; fewer administrative positions; equalized school facilities across the county; neighborhood elementary schools providing all-day, all-year instruction; and a "reordering of priorities so the emphasis is on education," the report states.

Finally, the report advises the commissioners to move quickly in pursuing the merger question. "A long drawn-out process will allow opposition to form," it states.

County commissioners contacted Thursday had not had a chance to review the document in detail. Commissioners may decide to ask for a more detailed merger plan as early as next week, said board chairman William V. Bell.

"Depending upon how the presentation goes, we possibly could make a decision that night," Mr. Bell said. "I don't want to delay it much longer than that if we're going to do it."

Despite the report's recommendation against a referendum, Mr. Bell, commissioner Ellen Reckhow and Rebecca M. Heron, the board's vice chairman, said Thursday they were unwilling to abandon the idea of a referendum.

"We have all said that there will be a referendum," Ms. Heron said.

Curtis J. Eshelman, a member of the Merger Issues Task Force—a citizens' committee that studied the merger question before the consultants were hired—said he was pleased to hear that the consultants had recommended merger.

Ms. Heron released the report late Thursday, after county officials refused to make the document public earlier in the day.

Gerald J. McPhail, special projects manager for the county, refused to release the document even after Ms. Reckhow had requested that he do so. So did Paul N. Warren, assistant county manager and finance director.

Both Ms. Reckhow and Ms. Heron said Thursday they were disturbed by Mr. McPhail's and Mr. Warren's actions.

"I don't understand what happened today, and it really troubles me," Ms. Reckhow said. "I consider it a public document. The press should have received it today when we did."

From Jones, A. (1991). "Consultants back Durham school merger." *Raleigh (NC) News and Observer*, January 11; A1.

Subsidiarity

The idea of the lowest decision unit, the decision unit closest to the client, be it the individual, family, school, district, county, state, or nation, having primary decision authority is known as *subsidiarity*. The libertarian argument on this dimension is that the burden of proof rests with those desirous of elevating any decision to a higher level, the assumption being that the decision should rest at the lowest or simplest possible level unless there is a compelling reason for elevating it to the next higher level. By such reasoning, fire protection for one's home should be elevated beyond the family, and perhaps higher. Similarly, national defense or homeland security can be seen as logically residing at levels beyond the individual or family. However, why should school decisions be taken to a higher level? Of course, communitarians contented that they should be elevated because of a need to create a uniform culture and common bond of citizenry. Libertarians do not easily submit to this contention, claiming that the need to reinforce the role of the family is a higher good than the need to use schools to create a common culture.

The idea of the family as a unit of governance is not new. Historians often thought of the Puritan-era family as "a little commonwealth" that reproduced all necessary government functions (Demos, 1971). Often, this idea of family liberty is expressed in terms of choice. The choice referred to most often is choice of where students attend school. The geographic configuration and organizational composition of many American communities and school districts influence a family's choice of where a student attends. However, school attendance can also be a choice about curriculum, instructors, and peer groups. It is here that one begins to see tensions between family choice and knowledge and skills of educators. Coons and Sugarman termed this the "family/professional dispute" (1978). Essentially, some school choice policies pit the will of parents against the expertise of professional educators. Determining which of these two groups—both well-intentioned—garners final say over decisions about school attendance is a thorny policy issue that school choice advocates allocate to parents.

The notion of school choice gained currency in United States policy parlance with the 1965 publication of Milton Friedman's voucher proposal. Scholars used these ideas to develop and articulate the first notions of family choice in the modern era. Although this impulse toward family choice was motivated by a deep concern for impoverished children and families, who were often trapped in low-performing urban public school systems, the resulting choice-oriented policy proposals were envisioned for all parents (Coons & Sugarman, 1971, 1978). The 1983 publication of *A Nation at Risk* spurred efforts to reform public education. The ensuing policy emphasis on efficiency and effectiveness came to dominate the debate, leading educators and policymakers away from a notion of a common schooling experience for all children (National Commission on Excellence in Education, 1983).

Educators and policymakers are faced with a spectrum of choice policies. These range from relatively timid open enrollment and magnet schools to bold proposals that use family choice as a basis for dismantling the entire current public education system. Each step along the continuum injects added choice into the public education system. Each step along the school choice continuum provides increased liberty for families. As may be expected, each step also brings along key policy questions for educators.

■ INCREMENTAL MEANS FOR ENHANCING SCHOOL CHOICE

There is a continuum of choice plans, stretching from the incremental to the radical. This section anchors the incremental end of the continuum.

Research
Navigator.c◆m

magnet
schools

Magnet Schools

Magnet schools—a term that emerged in the 1970s—are schools with specialized programs and curricula specifically designed to attract students into underutilized and racially homogenous facilities, usually in urban cores. Parents may choose to have their children attend these schools. In other instances, parents choose to place their child's name in a lottery for attendance in these schools. In either case, magnet schools offer parents slightly more choice than a standard residentially based attendance zone assignment.

Magnet schools often receive additional funding and other supplemental materials so their programs and curricula will appeal to parents and students. In effect, parents trade neighborhood location and the possible absence or diminution of transport for specialized curriculum, programs, and attention. Once a family has applied for a child to attend a magnet school, students are usually accepted by a lottery or a first-come basis. Some magnet schools, focusing on the arts or higher-level coursework, also rely on an application or even a competitive application process. For example, the specialized secondary schools in New York City, such as the Bronx High School of Science, are among the nation's most rigorous academic institutions. Admission to this magnet school is highly competitive.

Magnet school popularity received a boost in 1975, when the U.S. Supreme Court ruled, in *Morgan v. Kerrigan*, that magnet schools were an acceptable method of racially desegregating school districts. Recent data from the National Center for Education Statistics indicates that 12 to 14% of all public school students are enrolled in magnet schools or similar "public schools of choice" (NCES, 2003).

Intradistrict Choice

In this plan, parents are free to choose any public school within a specified attendance zone or school district. School districts provide varying degrees of transportation support. Advocates for this type of intradistrict choice claim that it creates a market within which district (public) schools compete—developing programs and practices that parents and students want in an attempt to lure them to a particular school. This type of choice can be supplemented with charter schools and even private schools through the use of vouchers.

After 40 years of racial desegregation rulings, federal circuit courts are declaring more school districts "unitary," meaning that the vestiges of separate but equal polices are in the past. This does not mean that school districts are unsegregated; it simply means that any present segregation is not a result of intentional or conscious policies.

One the more interesting unitary rulings occurred in 2002, when the 4th circuit court of appeals ruled that the Charlotte-Mecklenburg school system was unitary. Charlotte-Mecklenburg was the district highlighted in the U.S. Supreme Court's 1972 *Swann* decision, which ruled that cross-district busing of students to achieve racial integration was constitutional. For years after, Charlotte was known as "the city that made busing work." Charlotte-Mecklenburg schools now operate under a zone choice plan, where families are guaranteed attendance at a nearby school, but may apply to attend any school within their zone, transportation provided.[1] As of 2005, selected enclaves of middle-class parents were petitioning to break away from the larger district and form smaller school districts over which they contend they can have greater control.

Intradistrict choice plans significantly increase liberty for parents. Parents can make choices along any decision vector they prefer: a school's curriculum, school climate, or campus location. While some parents may be interested in the curriculum of a particular school, others may be more interested in the proximity of a school to their home or work. Other parents may choose a school for their child based on peer relationships or other intangible factors. In this sense, intradistrict choice allows parents to exercise preferences for a wide variety of reasons, not all of them good. In a 2000 study of parents using the Internet to research schools in Washington, D.C., researchers found that student body demographics and location were the school attributes parents looked at most, above test scores, programs, and faculty/staff information (Schneider & Buckley, 2002).

As with almost all policies, intradistrict choice has tradeoffs. First, some systems have resegregated racially when parents were free to make school choices (Mickelson, 2002). This resegregation may not be unconstitutional, but some researchers question whether the nation is ready for resegregated schools. Experiences from other nations, such as New Zealand, suggest that social stratification may come with such a choice model (Ladd & Fiske, 2000).

Second, intradistrict school choice benefits are dependent on the demographic composition of the district itself. An urban school district consisting entirely of poorly outfitted and ill-maintained schools presents parents with little variation and choice, whereas a revenue-rich suburban district may provide a host of options for parents. A related point is that, within an intradistrict choice model, only public schools are open to parental choice. If, as some argue, it is the bureaucracy of public school districts that represents an impediment to student learning, intradistrict choice does not address the problem (Walberg & Walberg, 1994). Finally, school choice policies can sometimes increase transportation costs, as districts committed to providing student transportation have to make logistical sense out of attendance patterns that can change annually. In this instance, increasing liberty decreases efficiency for school districts and their budgets.

Charter Schools

Research
Navigator.com

charter
schools

The charter school movement began legislatively in 1991 in Minneapolis, Minnesota, and has gained momentum ever since. A 2002 report specified 2,348 charter schools operating in the United States, enrolling 1.2% of all school students (NCES, 2003).

State charter school laws vary widely. Some states restrict the number of charters that can be in operation at any one time. Such restrictions are usually part of a legislative compromise in which charter advocates accept a limited number in order to obtain the right to open charter schools at all. Often, professional educators are intimidated by notions of choice, perhaps fearful that parents will not choose public schools. Consequently, their advocacy groups lobby intensely to restrict formation of charter schools. Other states stipulate that charters may operate only on behalf of at-risk students who already attend failing schools.

Despite wide variation, several common charter school elements emerge:

- An independent governance structure, where decisions are made at the school level without the intervening layer of the school district;
- Reduced or eliminated state regulations designed to acknowledge a charter's specific mission;
- Direct parental control over policies and procedures through planning teams or other means; and,
- A mandate to succeed with sanctions for failure. These include revocation of the school charter. (Adapted from Finn, Manno, & Vanourek, 2000)

A national survey of charter school parents revealed that the following characteristics were important in choosing a charter school:

- Small school and class size,
- Safe environment,
- Quality of academic program,
- High standards, and
- Specialized curricular focus. (SRI, 2002)

Since each state's charter law may differ significantly from others, it is difficult to determine exactly how charter schools are performing or which policies are most effective in ensuring charter school success. State-level studies present differing views on the effectiveness of charter schools. Academically, charters seem either to equal or outpace comparable public schools in subject matter achievement, although there is no large gap in academic performance either in favor of or against charter schools.[2] Although some charter schools score lower on state standardized tests than surrounding public schools, others perform much better. Additionally, many charter schools intentionally seek to serve students already in academic difficulty, such as poor or minority populations. In a few instances, these operating conditions may explain the relatively low level of their students' achievement.

Table 15.1 from the National Center for Education Statistics (NCES) describes the number and types of charter schools in America in the year 2000. The following points are of note:

- Three states—Arizona, California, and Michigan—account for 47% of all charter schools, and 52% of all students.
- 63% of all charter schools have minority populations that comprise 25% or more of the student body.

A 2003 report from the National Center for Education Statistics illustrates trends in school attendance over time. Table 15.2 delineates public schools to which students are assigned, public schools that children choose to attend, and private schools, both religious and secular. A charter school is considered a "chosen" public school. Note that assigned public school attendance and religious private school attendance dropped slightly between the years 1993 and 1999, while the percent of students enrolled in a school of choice increased from 11% in 1993 to 14% in 1999.

A 2004 study found, in a random selection of 50 charter schools, that 12 had either had their charters revoked or nonrenewed (Hassel & Batdorf, 2004). Charter schools fail for a range of reasons. A review of research suggests that many of those reasons have little to do with the curriculum or instructional program, and more to do with a lack of business acumen or management experience. Visionaries who start charter schools, a report notes, are not always skilled in meeting federal and state regulations, managing finances, or sharing leadership responsibilities with parents and governing boards. As more states implement charter laws, specialized organizations are emerging to assist charter school founders and boards in navigating these challenges.

Another measure of charter school success is whether or not they create the educational marketplaces envisioned by founders and supporters. Research suggests that charters inspire innovation in surrounding schools, but that a degree of political ill will toward them inhibits transfer of innovative practice from a charter school to surrounding schools (Hoxby, 2002; Teske, 2001).

■ VOUCHERS: A BOLD PATH TO CHOICE

Research
Navigator.com

vouchers

Modern proposals for vouchers are rooted in Milton Friedman's conception of liberty and its application to public education. Friedman's approach views the family as an economic unit and free markets as the best distributors of educational goods and services. Friedman conceives of vouchers as a mechanism to create a school market, in which each institution competes for family educational vouchers. Since education funds can

TABLE 15.1 Number and Percentage Distribution of Public Charter Schools and Students, and Percentage of Charter Schools and Students by School Origin Status, by Selected School Characteristics: 1999–2000

Selected School Characteristics	Schools and Students (Standard Errors)					School Origin Status (Percentage Distribution)		
	Number of Schools	Number of Students	Average Enrollment	Percent of Schools	Percent of Students	Newly Created	Pre-Existing Public School	Pre-Existing Private School
Total	1,010 (4.3)	266,721 (3,957)	264 (3.6)	100.0 (0.0)	100.0 (0.0)	73.6 (0.6)	16.5 (0.4)	9.9 (0.4)
State								
Arizona	207 (2.8)	39,860 (1,594)	193 (7.1)	20.5 (0.2)	14.9 (0.5)	78.3 (1.4)	5.3 (0.8)	16.4 (1.3)
California	133 (1.3)	64,152 (2,541)	482 (17.4)	13.2 (0.1)	24.1 (0.8)	55.7 (1.8)	43.4 (1.8)	0.9 (0.4)
Michigan	135 (0.6)	36,052 (699)	267 (5.1)	13.4 (0.1)	13.5 (0.3)	76.4 (1.2)	6.5 (0.6)	17.2 (1.0)
All Other States	535 (3.7)	126,656 (2,244)	237 (4.1)	53.0 (0.3)	47.5 (0.7)	75.6 (0.8)	16.7 (0.6)	7.8 (0.6)
Community Type								
Central City	537 (8.2)	139,307 (3,149)	260 (4.8)	53.1 (0.8)	52.2 (1.0)	76.3 (0.7)	11.9 (0.6)	11.8 (0.6)
Urban Fringe/Large Town	324 (6.9)	108,807 (3,273)	336 (8.3)	32.1 (0.7)	40.8 (1.0)	68.5 (0.9)	23.4 (0.8)	8.1 (0.6)
Rural/Small Town	150 (5.8)	18,607 (1,040)	124 (4.9)	14.8 (0.6)	7.0 (0.4)	75.4 (1.9)	17.8 (1.6)	6.9 (1.1)
School Level								
Elementary	586 (5.9)	158,801 (2,239)	271 (3.6)	58.0 (0.6)	59.5 (0.9)	72.2 (0.6)	17.3 (0.5)	10.5 (0.5)
Secondary	235 (6.4)	58,218 (2,952)	248 (9.7)	23.2 (0.6)	21.8 (0.9)	75.3 (1.5)	18.9 (1.3)	5.8 (0.6)
Combined	190 (5.0)	49,702 (2,192)	262 (10.7)	18.8 (0.5)	18.6 (0.7)	76.0 (1.4)	11.1 (1.0)	12.9 (1.2)

Enrollment								
Less than 300	730 (6.9)	94,271 (1,425)	129 (1.3)	72.3 (0.7)	35.4 (0.8)	78.9 (0.7)	9.2 (0.5)	11.9 (0.5)
300 to 999	251 (6.6)	130,683 (3,569)	520 (5.3)	24.9 (0.6)	49.0 (1.0)	64.4 (1.2)	30.5 (1.0)	5.2 (0.6)
1,000 or more	29 (2.1)	41,766 (3,090)	1,448 (38.4)	2.9 (0.2)	15.7 (1.0)	21.0 (4.0)	79.0 (4.0)	0.0 (0.0)
School Origin Status								
Newly Created	744 (6.6)	166,060 (3,483)	223 (4.1)	73.6 (0.6)	62.3 (0.9)	100.0 (0.0)	††	††
Pre-Existing Public	166 (4.4)	83,811 (2,760)	503 (14.6)	16.5 (0.4)	31.4 (0.9)	††	100.0 (0.0)	††
Pre-Existing Private	100 (4.0)	16,849 (871)	169 (5.5)	9.9 (0.4)	6.3 (0.4)	††	††	100.0 (0.0)
Percent Minority Enrollment								
Less than 10.0	180 (5.3)	41,115 (1,584)	228 (7.6)	17.8 (0.5)	15.4 (0.6)	72.9 (1.4)	17.7 (1.2)	9.4 (0.9)
10.0 to 24.9	197 (6.3)	45,279 (2,163)	230 (8.6)	19.5 (0.6)	17.0 (0.8)	71.7 (1.4)	18.3 (1.2)	10.0 (0.9)
25.0 to 49.9	147 (5.7)	43,462 (2,584)	295 (15.0)	14.6 (0.6)	16.3 (0.9)	74.3 (1.6)	14.8 (1.1)	10.9 (1.2)
50.0 to 75.0	136 (4.8)	36,986 (1,976)	272 (11.1)	13.5 (0.5)	13.9 (0.7)	70.2 (1.9)	22.0 (1.6)	7.8 (1.1)
More than 75.0	349 (7.2)	99,878 (2,939)	286 (6.2)	34.6 (0.7)	37.4 (1.0)	76.2 (0.9)	13.4 (0.7)	10.4 (0.8)

† Not applicable.

Note: This tabulation includes all public charter schools operating in the 1998–99 school year. Public charter schools that first opened in the 1999–2000 school year, or later, are not included in these data. Detail may not sum to totals due to rounding. Standard errors appear in parentheses.

Source: U.S. Department of Education, National Center for Education Statistics, Schools and Staffing Survey (SASS), "Public School Questionnaire," 1999–2000 and "Charter School Questionnaire," 1999–2000. (This table was prepared December 2002.)

TABLE 15.2 Percentage of Students Enrolled in Grades 1–12 by Public and Private School Types, and by Student and Household Characteristics: 1993, 1996, and 1999

Student and Household Characteristics	School Type																							
	Public Assigned						Public Chosen						Private Church-Related						Private Not Church-Related					
	1993		1996		1999		1993		1996		1999		1993		1996		1999		1993		1996		1999	
	%	s.e.	%	s.e.	%	s.e.	%	s.e.	%	s.e.	%	s.e.	%	s.e.	%	s.e.	%	s.e.	%	s.e.	%	s.e.	%	s.e.
Total	80	0.4	76	0.5	76	0.4	11	0.4	14	0.4	14	0.4	8	0.3	8	0.3	7	0.3	2	0.1	2	0.1	2	0.1
Grade Level																								
Grades 1–5	79	0.6	74	0.7	74	0.6	12	0.4	15	0.5	15	0.5	8	0.4	9	0.4	9	0.4	2	0.1	2	0.2	2	0.2
Grades 6–8	81	1.2	79	0.9	79	0.8	10	1.3	11	0.6	12	0.7	7	0.5	7	0.5	7	0.5	2	1.9	2	0.2	2	0.2
Grades 9–12	81	0.8	76	0.7	77	0.7	11	0.5	14	0.6	16	0.6	7	0.5	7	0.4	5	0.4	2	0.3	3	0.3	2	0.2
Race/Ethnicity																								
White, Non-Hispanic	81	0.5	77	0.6	77	0.5	9	0.4	11	0.4	11	0.4	9	0.4	9	0.4	9	0.4	2	0.2	3	0.2	3	0.2
Black, Non-Hispanic	77	1.0	73	1.4	71	1.2	19	0.8	22	1.3	23	1.2	3	0.4	4	0.4	4	0.5	1	0.2	1	0.3	2	0.3
Hispanic	79	1.1	76	1.1	77	1.0	14	1.0	16	0.9	18	1.0	6	0.5	6	0.7	4	0.4	1	0.2	1	0.3	1	0.2
Other, Non-Hispanic	73	2.8	69	1.8	73	2.2	15	2.9	19	1.8	17	2.0	9	1.4	10	1.2	7	1.1	3	0.7	2	0.6	3	0.6
Sex																								
Male	81	0.5	77	0.6	76	0.6	11	0.4	13	0.5	14	0.5	7	0.4	8	0.4	7	0.3	2	0.2	3	0.2	2	0.2
Female	79	0.6	76	0.7	75	0.6	11	0.5	14	0.6	15	0.5	8	0.4	8	0.3	8	0.4	2	0.2	2	0.2	2	0.2
Disability Status																								
Has a Disability	—	—	—	—	76	0.9	—	—	—	—	16	0.8	—	—	—	—	6	0.4	—	—	—	—	2	0.3
Does Not Have a Disability	—	—	—	—	76	0.5	—	—	—	—	14	0.4	—	—	—	—	8	0.3	—	—	—	—	2	0.2
Household Income																								
$10,000 or less	83	1.1	77	1.5	74	1.6	14	0.9	19	1.4	22	1.5	3	0.5	3	0.5	3	0.6	#	0.2	2	0.5	1	0.4
10,001–20,000	82	1.6	79	1.1	78	1.1	14	1.7	16	1.1	17	1.0	3	0.4	4	0.6	3	0.5	#	0.2	1	0.3	1	0.4
20,001–35,000	82	0.6	78	0.9	78	0.8	11	0.6	14	0.8	16	0.7	7	0.6	6	0.5	4	0.4	1	0.1	1	0.2	1	0.2
35,001–50,000	80	1.0	77	0.9	77	0.9	10	0.6	12	0.8	14	0.7	9	0.7	9	0.6	8	0.6	2	0.2	2	0.2	2	0.3
50,001–75,000	77	0.9	76	0.9	78	0.9	9	0.6	10	0.6	11	0.6	11	0.7	12	0.8	9	0.7	2	0.3	2	0.3	2	0.3
More than	73	1.4	68	1.1	70	0.9	8	0.6	11	0.7	10	0.6	14	1.1	15	0.9	14	0.7	6	0.9	6	0.5	5	0.5

travel with a particular student, each household can have ultimate educational control and can choose a school with preferred location, curriculum, and peer relationships. Because every family is presumed to be treated the same, Friedman's plan provides horizontal equity. Because the system as conceived would eliminate much education bureaucracy, Friedman's plan is also intended to be efficient. Finally, Freidman would rely on the market to ensure adequacy. If a school were not performing, it would go out of business (Friedman, 1965).

In the 1970s, Coons and Sugarman supported voucher plans (Coons & Sugarman, 1971). These authors drafted a statute for implementation of vouchers. In the 1980s, in *Politics, Market and America's Schools*, Chubb and Moe suggest that perhaps a voucher program was a panacea for what ailed American public education, because it was the only public school reform effort that was not "system preserving" (Chubb & Moe, 1990).

No matter what the reason for policy advocacy, voucher advocates have been carefully studying several programs that test the use of vouchers within existing education systems. The U.S. Supreme Court ruled vouchers programs constitutional in *Zelman v. Simmons-Harris*, ensuring that experimental voucher programs would continue to develop as both an educational alternative for students and families and an arena for experimentation and research by policymakers. Although the specific question revolved around the issue of public vouchers being used for students to attend private religious schools, the ruling, combined with freedoms set forth in *Pierce*, served to support the use of educational vouchers at private schools.

What exactly is a voucher plan? A voucher program relies on a transfer of funds, rather than direct public provision of services, in order to acquire access to an appropriate education. Under a full voucher plan, families receive government coupons (vouchers or chits) redeemable only at educational institutions or vendors for educational services. Families could choose to spend vouchers at a host of public or private educational institutions. Depending on a specific plan, the government would provide oversight and sanctioning of schools or not.

Why are voucher plans controversial? Many issues revolve around the effect voucher programs might have on the communitarian notion that most children in America attend a similar public school, receive a similar curriculum and, by attending school together, come to develop an appreciation for American diversity and democracy. Some argue that voucher programs will result in ethnic and socioeconomic balkanization, ultimately destroying the American ideal of the public school. Other critics note that elite schools will simply charge more than the available voucher amount, thus ensuring that voucher plans divide students economically. Still others note with alarm that private companies would be able to operate schools, and wonder about the implications of school managers having to choose between profit and the best interests of children. Finally, previously mentioned in the context of the *Zelman* decision, there are concerns that voucher programs violate church and state separation. Given such speculation, what is known empirically about voucher plans that might shed light on these questions?

Existing voucher plans are targeted at poor and minority populations in urban settings. Some are publicly funded and private foundations manage others. Studies attempting to discern voucher programs' effects have been filled with controversy. Recent research has reported substantive gains in the performance of African American students. Specifically, Howell and Peterson found increasing and cumulative positive effects of private school attendance for African American students. Over the course of three years of study, African Americans in public school scored .18, .28, and .3 standard deviations better than a comparable group in public schools. This represented a 33% decrease in the Black/White test score achievement gap (Howell & Peterson, 2002). Although this research has subsequently been criticized for methodological errors, creating a stir and debate among education finance researchers and economists,[3] the overall conclusion is that small-scale voucher programs seem particularly effective for certain types of students. Specifically, African American students seem to improve academically under voucher programs as they have been tried in America (McEwan, 2004).

Studies in other nations suggest that large-scale voucher implementation, when relying on notions of unrestricted choice, may result in talent skimming and in reduced achievement among remaining public school students.

■ TUITION TAX CREDITS

This mechanism, as with vouchers, enfranchises households as decision-making units regarding education services. However, tuition tax credits entail less government regulation of nonpublic schooling. Federal or state provisions would permit parents to deduct all or, as more commonly proposed, a portion of nonpublic school tuition payments as a credit against federal or state personal income tax obligations. Such tax credits can be graduated in terms of schooling level—for example, larger dollar tax credits for secondary school tuition than for elementary—or by taxpayer income bracket—for example, proportionally lower tuition payments allowed as a credit against the tax obligation of upper-income taxpayers. President Reagan espoused tuition tax credit plans early in his administration. The U.S. Senate has passed tuition credit bills six times, the House of Representatives once. This last case was in 1979, and the threat of President Carter's veto was then sufficient to discourage Senate approval. In 1985, Minnesota adopted a partial tuition tax credit plan. Early assessments suggest that the low tax forgiveness amounts involved did not greatly influence parent choice of nonpublic schooling. Indeed, parents reported that state provision of transportation was a greater determinant of nonpublic school choice than the small net tax deduction for private school tuition. Regardless, the idea is likely to be the topic of debate for years to come.

■ OTHER MARKET MECHANISMS

Proponents of added efficiency often suggest that schools would benefit from added use of market mechanisms. Sometimes these proposals are simple suggestions, such as permitting private providers to contract with schools for cafeteria services. Other proposals attempt to subject components of the school bureaucracy to greater accountability through the "invisible hand" of the marketplace. For example, a school district's central office budget for staff development and curriculum assistance might be decentralized and placed at school sites. Schools might then purchase central office services or they might buy such assistance elsewhere—from local universities, other districts, or the private sector. Whatever the choices, their selections would reflect local school personnel judgment about the utility of central office services. Failure to "buy" staff help from "downtown" would display a market judgment and bring about greater accountability.

▮ LIBERTY AS ASPIRATION AND POLICY: NCLB AND THE FUTURE OF SCHOOL CHOICE

Historically, liberty has been considered an *outcome* within the context of public education: well-educated students, it was thought, had greater liberty to pursue additional educational opportunities or remunerative employment while fulfilling a crucial role as informed citizens and advocates.

Only recently have educators and policymakers begun to consider liberty as an *input* in the schooling process; that is, viewing liberty and family choice as crucial facets of the process parents undertake to obtain educational excellence for their children.

Recently, viable choice options have become more and more a part of the education policy landscape. Florida, for example, has committed to providing vouchers to students in the state whose schools fail to meet performance requirements (Salisbury, 2003). No more clear example of this move can be seen than the NCLB legislation of 2001. NCLB provides choice options as sanctions for persistently low-performing schools and districts. This is the first time that a viable choice option has been provided as a part of the greater education policy continuum on a national scale.

What are the implications of greater liberty within a national education policy framework? Advocates of vouchers and other choice options have long advocated their alternatives as an ideological replacement to top-heavy and bureaucratic "government schools." The problem with this approach is that school systems vary widely in performance and efficiency by community. Many public school systems continue to provide high-level instruction and meet community demands for high quality and excellent service. Imposing market options on these communities may be perceived as a violation of their political will to fund schools for their community. Other school systems are dysfunctional and students and their parents may feel trapped within them.

The legislative impulse of NCLB points to a new conception of the relationship between choice-based education policies and the public education policy space generally, where choice options are brought into the policy space as available tools that can be used to sharpen and supplement failing public education systems.

Summary

As with many policy improvements to public education in the past, choice options represent an untried and, to some, dangerous idea. The introduction of the concept of choice in public education has set off a groundswell of empirical research that seeks to determine which facets of policy support or inhibit operation of effective schools. Findings from these studies continue to enlighten and inform educators, policymakers, and parents as to the costs and benefits associated with a move toward greater liberty in the public school realm. The idea of public education itself was once seen as dangerous. Students of education and education finance today have the opportunity to take part in a great policy debate that will shape the future of American education for years to come.

Discussion Questions

1. We learned in the previous chapter that assigning students to schools strategically could maximize school efficiency. Discuss the liberty implications of such a plan.

2. At what level of education governance—parental, local, or state—should the concept of liberty be maximized?

3. Review the In the News story of the Durham schools merger. Discuss the need to balance the policy priorities of liberty with equity. Explain how similar tensions occur at the individual (parental) level.

4. Read the case study of Cathy, the paralegal. Discuss the manner in which the choice issues described in this chapter pertain to Cathy's situation. What choice provisions—intradistrict choice, magnets, or vouchers—would influence Cathy's educational decisions for her childrens?

Notes

1. The current assignment plan for Charlotte-Mecklenburg schools can be found online at http://www.cms.k12.nc.us/studentassignment03-04/section4_Priorities.asp.

2. A 2004 report by the Goldwater Institute examined test scores of 60,000 students in Arizona—a state with the most liberal of charter school laws—and determined that charter schools accelerated academic growth, but only in certain grades. See Solomon and Goldschmidt (2004).

3. For a reply to Howell and Peterson, see Kreuger and Zhu (2002).

Court Cases and Significant Federal Legislation

Abbott v. Burke, 575 A. 2d 359 (N.J. 1990)

Abbott v. Burke, 693 A. 2d 417 (N.J. 1997)

Alabama Coalition for Equity v. Hunt, WL 204083 (Ala. 1993)

Bill for the More General Diffusion of Knowledge, Virginia Legislature, 1779

Board of Education of Levittown v. Nyquist, 408 N.Y.S. 2d 606 (N.Y. Sup. Ct. 1978)

Board of Education of Levittown v. Nyquist, 57 N.Y. 2d 27 (1982)

Brown v. Board of Education of Topeka, 347 U.S. 483, 74 S. Ct. 686, 98 L. Ed. 873 (U.S. 1954)

Busse v. Smith, 247 N.W. 2d 141 (Wis. 1976)

Campaign for Fiscal Equity v. State of New York, 100 N.Y. 2d 893 (N.Y. 2003)

Campaign for Fiscal Equity v. State of New York, 162 Misc. 2d 493 (N.Y.S. 1994)

Campaign for Fiscal Equity v. State of New York, 187 Misc. 2d 1 (N.Y.S. 2001)

Campbell County School District v. State of Wyoming, 907 P. 2d 1238 (Wyo. 1995). Hereafter *Campbell I*

Campbell County School District v. State of Wyoming, 907 P. 2d 1238, 1274 (Wyo. 1995)

Capacchione v. Charlotte-Mecklenburg Board of Education, 99-2389 (2001)

Claremont School District v. Governor, 147 N.H. 499 (N.H., Apr. 11, 2002)

Claremont School District v. Governor, 635 A. 2d 1375 (N.H. 1994)

Claremont School District v. Governor, 635 A.2d 1375 (N.H. 1993)

Columbia Falls Elementary School District No. 6 v. State of Montana, WL 648038 (Mont. 2005)

Connecticut Constitution, Article VIII, 1

Cooperative Research Act of 1954

DeRolph v. State of Ohio, 677 N.E. 2d 733 (Ohio 1997)

DeRolph v. State of Ohio, 728 N.E. 2d 99 (Ohio 2000)

Dupree v. Alma School District No. 30, 651 S.W. 2d 90 (Ark. 1983)

Edgewood Independent School District v. Kirby, 777 S.W. 2d 391 (Tex. 1989)

Eisenberg v. Montgomery County Schools, 197 F. 3d 123 (1999)

Emergency School Aid Act of 1972

George-Barden Act of 1946

George-Deen Act of 1936

George-Ellzey Act of 1934

George-Reed Act of 1929

Hancock v. Driscoll, No. 02-2978, Mass. Sup. Ct., 2004, WL 877984

Helena Elementary School District v. State of Montana, 769 P 2d 684 (1990)

Helvering v. Davis, 301 Dr. S. 619, 57 Sup. Ct. 904, 1937.

Higher Education Act of 1975

Horton v. Meskill, 332 A. 2d 113 (Conn. Sup. Ct. 1974)

Horton v. Meskill, 376 A. 2d 359 (Conn. 1977), hereafter *Horton II*

Kasayulie v. State, 3AN-97-3782 CIV (Alaska 1999)

Lake View School District, No. 25 v. Huckabee, 91 S.W.3d 472 (Ark. 2002)

Lake View School District, No. 25 v. Huckabee, No. 1992-5318 (Pulaski County Chancery Court, May 25, 2001)

Land Survey Ordinance of 1785

Lau v. Nichols (1973) 483 f2d (9OR., 1973); 94 S. C7 786 (1974). Sup. 866

Leeman v. Sloan, 340 f. Suppl. 1356, 1972

Lemon v. Kurtzman, 403 US 602, 91 Sup. Ct. 2105

Massachusetts Constitution, Part II, c.5, §2

McDuffy v. Secretary of the Executive Office of Education, 615 N.E. 2d 516 (Mass. 1993)

McInnis v. Ogilvie, 394 U.S. 322 (U.S. 1969)

Mills v. Board of Education (1972)

Morrill Act of 1862

Muellar v. Allen, 54 US LW 5050, 1958

National Defense Education Act of 1958

New Jersey Constitution, Article VII, Section 4

No Child Left Behind Act of 2001, P.L. No 107-110 (2001)

Northshore School District v. Kinnear, 530 P. 2d 178 (Wash. 1974)

Northwest Ordinance of 1787

Ordinance of 1802

Papasan v. Allain, 106 U.S. 2932 (S. Ct. 1986)

PARC v. Commonwealth, 834 F. Sup. Ct. 1257 (1971)

Parker v. Mandel, 344 F. Supp. 1068 (D. Md. 1972)

Pauley v. Bailey, 324 S.E. 2d 128 (W. Va. 1984)

Pauley v. Kelly, 255 S.E. 2d 859 (W. Va. 1979)

Robinson v. Cahill, 62 N.J. 473, 303 A. 3d 273 (N.J. 1973)

Roosevelt v. Bishop, 877 P. 2d 806 (1994)

Rose v. Council for Better Education, 790 S.W. 2d 186 (Ky. 1989)

San Antonio v. Rodriguez, 411 U.S. 1, 93 1278 (S. Ct. 1973)

Sawyer v. Gilmore, 109 Me. 169, 83 A. 673 (1912)

School-to-Work Opportunities Act (1994)

Seattle School District No. 1 of King County v. State, 585 P. 2d 71 (Wash. 1978)

Serrano v. Priest (1971)

Serrano v. Priest, 557 P. 2d 929 (Cal. 1976)

Serrano v. Priest, 557 P. 2d 929 (Cal. 1976). Hereafter *Serrano II*

Serrano v. Priest, 569 P. 2d 1303 (Cal. 1977). Hereafter *Serrano III*

Servicemen's Readjustment Act, PL 78-346, 1944

Shaffer v. Carter, 252 U.S. 37, 40 S. Ct. 221 (U.S. 1920)

Skeen v. State, 505 N.W. 2d 299 (Min. 1993)

Smith-Hughes Act of 1917

Springfield Township v. Quick, 63 U.S. 56 (U.S. 1859)

State ex rel Anderson v. Brand, 313 US 95, 1938

State v. Board of Commissioners of Elk County, (1899)

State v. Campbell County School District, 19 P. 3d 518 (Wyo. 2001)

Stuart v. School District No. 1 of Village of Kalamazoo, 30 Mich. 69 (1874)

Tennessee Small School System v. McWherter, 851 S.W. 2d 139 (Tenn. 1993)

Tennessee Small Schools Systems v. McWherter, WL 119824 (Tenn. Ct. App. 1992)

United States v. Butler, 297 US 1, 56 (Sup. Ct. 312), 1936

Vincent v. Voight, 614 N.W. 2d 388 (Wis. 2000)

Vocational Education Act of 1963

Washington Constitution, Article IX, Section 1

West Orange-Cove Cons. Indep. Sch. Dist. v. Neeley, No. GV-100528 (Tex. Dist. Ct. Nov. 30, 2004, pet. filed)

Williston Public School District v. State (ND pending)

Zelman v. Simmons-Harris, 00–1751 (S. Ct. 2001)

Glossary

Accounting Ensuring that anticipated and actual expenditures are consistent with an adopted budget and with legal requirements.

Accounts Payable What is owed by an organization to vendors for services performed or goods purchased.

Accrual Basis Accounting An accounting system by which transactions (expenses such as payroll, equipment purchases, contracts, etc., or revenues such as tax receipts) are formally recorded on the agency's books when they have been transformed into a legal or contractual right or obligation to receive or pay out cash or other resources.

Adequacy (Measurement) Attempting to determine the costs of providing a group of students with an opportunity to learn. Methods of determining adequacy, all incomplete or lacking in science, include cost function analysis, successful schools approach, resource cost model, research imputation, professional judgment model, and market dynamics approach.

ADA/ADM These are two ways by which state education distribution formulae measure students to be served by a school or a school district. ADA is an abbreviation for student average daily attendance, and ADM is an abbreviation for student average daily membership. The latter signifies the number of students enrolled. ADA is always less that ADM.

Administrative and Compliance Costs Concept acknowledging that oversight or implementation of a social program has costs attached, in addition to those directly connected with the delivery of services or goods.

Ad Valorem Taxes Taxes based on the value of property, such as the standard property tax. Taxes may be for the operation of an agency, for capital construction, or for debt service.

Agricultural Reserve Government tax inducements to retain land in agricultural production or at least not immediately subject to development other than agriculture.

Allocative Efficiency Market provision of goods or services consistent with consumer preferences.

Annularity Occurring each year. This is a characteristic of budgeting, as are "comprehensiveness" and "balance."

Apportionment Financial aid distributed by a higher level of government (county, state, or federal) to a school district, school, county office of education, or some other operating unit.

Appropriation The formal legislative authority or right to expend public funds. Several appropriations comprise a school budget and, except in the Capital Projects Fund, appropriations are valid for one calendar year.

Appropriation Bill A bill before the legislature authorizing expenditure of public money and stipulating the amount, manner, and purpose for the expenditure.

Assessment Ratios Relationship of the market value of property—what an owner might actually be able to obtain from the sale of a property—to the assessor's view of the value of the property parcel. The assessed valuation of property in most states is often less than the market value of a listed property.

Assessed Valuation Assessed valuation is the officially specified total value of property subject to the property tax in a government jurisdiction, including a school district. It is conventionally established by a local or county government officer known as an "assessor," who is frequently appointed but in some jurisdictions may be elected.

Assessed Valuation, Adjusted Because local assessing jurisdictions in a state usually have different actual assessment ratios, reported assessed valuations often need to be adjusted in order to compare them across school districts and other government jurisdictions within a state. These comparisons and adjustments for state aid distribution purposes are undertaken by a state agency, often known as a state board of equalization.

Assessed Valuation Per Pupil, Adjusted Adjusted assessed valuation per pupil is the state board of equalization's adjusted assessed valuation for a school district divided by a district's total ADA or ADM.

Attendance Reports Each school agency reports its attendance, usually three times during a school year.

Baby Boom Echo Demographic bulge resulting from the children of the World War II baby boom themselves having children. Resulted in late 1900s bulge in K–12 and postsecondary enrollments.

Basic Aid Many states, for example, California, have an anachronistic basic aid provision left over from the flat grant financing era in the early 1900s. The California constitution guarantees that each school district will receive a minimum amount of state aid, called "basic aid," equal to $120 per ADA or $2,400 per district, whichever is greater. "Basic aid school districts" are those eligible for the basic aid constitutional guarantee only, since all of the balance of the school districts' revenue limit is funded by local property taxes.

Bonded Indebtedness An obligation incurred by the sale of bonds for acquisition or construction of school facilities or other capital expenditures. Usually, such bonded indebtedness must be approved by a two-thirds vote of the electorate.

Brown v. Board A 1954 Supreme Court case declaring de jure racially separate schools inherently unequal and unconstitutional. It is the most important domestic policy court case of the 20th century in terms of moral and policy impact.

Budget Administration See Budget Development.

Budget Assumption Letter Communiqué issued by a central authority or deliberative body (school board) to operating agencies or units, distributed at the beginning of budget planning, regarding forthcoming fiscal year revenue assumptions and expenditure boundaries.

Budget Balance Legal requirement that state and local governments, including school districts, must adopt annual spending plans that are in balance with expected revenues. Budget balance can also refer to unexpended or unobligated revenues remaining in a budget.

Budget Development One-half of the budget cycle, the other half being budget administration.

Budget Development Calendar Predetermined dates by which various important segments of the budget process for an organization are anticipated to be completed.

Capitalization Theory Perceived value of schools thought to enhance the value of residential properties within the district.

Categorical Programs This term refers to state aid that is designated for specific programs. Examples would be transportation aid, special education aid, and aid for vocational education. Equalization formula aid is not an example of categorical aid. Formula funds provide general aid that can be used for purposes the local school board determines.

Certificated Personnel School employees who hold positions for which a state-issued certificate or credential is required: teachers, librarians, counselors, and most administrators.

Chapter 1 (Elementary and Secondary Education Act) Federal financial assistance to districts to meet the special needs of educationally deprived children, that is, children whose educational attainment is below the level appropriate for children of their age. Funding is to supplement services in reading, language arts, and mathematics to identified students. Chapter 1 now forms the legislative base for the No Child Left Behind Act (NCLB).

Chapter 2 (Elementary and Secondary Education Act) Federal financial assistance for schools under the Education Consolidation and Improvement Act, 20 U.S.C. Sec. 3811 et seq., which consolidated the provisions of Titles II, III, IV, VI, and VII, and part IX of the Elementary and Secondary Education Act of 1965. The law provides federal grants to develop and implement a comprehensive and coordinated program to improve elementary and secondary instruction in basic skills of reading, math, and language arts, as formerly authorized in Title II.

Classified Personnel School employees holding positions that do not require a professional credential, such as aides, custodians, clerical support, cafeteria workers, and bus drivers.

Class Size Penalties Penalties imposed on school districts that have classes in excess of state-specified maximum sizes. Class size penalties result in a reduction in ADA that, in turn, results in a loss in revenue limit income.

Competitive Underassessment Tendency of taxing jurisdictions to underassess property as an inducement for residential or industrial development.

Comprehensiveness (Budget Comprehensiveness) A condition, along with annularity and balance, that characterizes the budget process. Comprehensiveness refers to the necessity that a complete budget include all of an agency's anticipated revenues and planned expenditures.

Concurrently Enrolled Pupils who are enrolled both in a regular program for at least the minimum school day and also in a regional occupational center or other educational institution. By qualifying for both regular ADA and concurrently enrolled ADA, such a student can generate more than one unit of ADA.

Consumer Price Index (CPI) A measure of the annual cost-of-living fluctuation for consumers compiled by the U.S. Bureau of Labor Statistics. The CPI is one of several measures of inflation.

Consumption Good Item or condition principally benefiting an individual recipient.

Correlation A correlation coefficient indicates whether, in which direction, and how strongly two sets of data are related to each other.

Correlation Coefficient The correlation coefficient is a number indicating the degree of correlation between two variables. Because of the way a correlation coefficient is calculated, it will always have a value between -1.0 and $+1.0$. When the correlation coefficient is around $+0.5$ to $+1.0$, the two variables have a *positive relationship* or are *positively correlated*—when one variable measure enlarges, the other tends to enlarge. When the correlation coefficient is 0 or close to 0, two variables do not appear to have any relationship. When the correlation coefficient is between −0.5 and −1.0, the variables have a *negative relationship* or are *negatively correlated*—as one gets larger, the other tends to become smaller.

Cost-Effectiveness   Relationship of anticipated costs connected with an endeavor relative to the anticipated or actual effectiveness of the endeavor in achieving the specified operating objective.

Cost Equalization   Adjustments to a state funding distribution formula necessitated by differences in local district regional cost of living or cost of operating differences.

Cost-of-Living Adjustment (COLA)   An increase in funding for government programs or individual compensation, including revenue limits or categorical programs.

Credentialed Teacher   A credential is issued to those who have successfully completed all college training and courses required by the state, have graduated from an accredited college or university, and have met any other state requirements.

Current Operating Expenditures   Expenditures for the daily operation of the school program, such as expenditures for administration, instruction, attendance and health services, transportation, operation and maintenance of plant, and fixed charges.

Debt Service Fund   The debt service fund is used to budget and account for receipts and expenditures necessary to meet the annual debt obligations of a school corporation. Expenditures from this fund may be used to make bond and lease rental payments and state technology and construction loans. Interest on loans taken for the purpose of any other fund can be paid from the debt service fund. For taxation purposes, this fund is only used when there is a need to retire

debt. The tax rate must be sufficient to raise the amount necessary to meet the debt obligations during the year. Under most sets of state laws, debt service has priority over all other obligations.

Declining Enrollment Adjustment   A formula that cushions a prospective district revenue decline resulting from a declining student population.

De Facto   From fact.

Deficit Factor   When an appropriation to the State School Fund for revenue limits—or for any specific categorical program—is insufficient to pay all claims for state aid, a deficit factor is applied to reduce an agency's allocation of state aid proportionate to the amount actually appropriated.

De Jure   From law.

Demography   Study and accumulation of factual information and theoretical explanations regarding population dynamics.

Design-Build Construction   Proceeding with construction in the absence of detailed architectural and engineering renderings, designing a building more as the project flows from day to day. A technique used to expedite construction of a needed facility.

District Power Equalization   District power equalization (DPE) refers to a state aid program that "equalizes" the revenue-raising ability of each school district to generate resources for education. In a pure DPE program, a state guarantees to both property-poor and property-rich school districts the same dollar yield for the same property tax rate.

Easton's Political Systems Model   Paradigm displaying components and relative roles of structures and functions within a political system. Developed by political scientist David Easton.

Economics   Social science discipline concentrating on the theoretical and empirical study of the production and distribution of goods and services.

Economic Impact Aid (EIA) State categorical aid for districts with concentrations of children who are bilingual, transient, or from low-income families.

Education Policy Presumed to be such a decision rule, one especially affecting education, schooling, instruction, or something related to these activities.

Efficiency See **Allocative Efficiency** and **Technical Efficiency.**

Elasticity of Tax Revenues Term referring to responsiveness of tax revenues to changes in economic growth or decline in the state or nation.

Elementary and Secondary Education Act (ESEA) Initially enacted in 1965, part of the Johnson Administration's War on Poverty. Was the first ever major federal financial aid to education bill. Now serves as the statutory spine for the No Child Left Behind Act.

Encroachment Expenditure of school district general-purpose funds in support of a categorical program, that is, the categorical expense "encroaches" into the district's general fund for support.

Encumbrances Obligations in the form of purchase orders, contracts, salaries, and other commitments chargeable to an appropriation or for which a part of the appropriation is reserved.

Equilibrium Theory Tendency of social systems to achieve a balance, or *stasis*, between forces desirous of action and those desirous of stability resulting from conditions aligned with equality, liberty, or efficiency.

Equalization Formula Aid Equalization formula aid is financial assistance distributed by a higher-level government—the state—to a lower-level government—school districts—to equalize the fiscal resources of the lower-level government.

Equal Protection Clause 14th Amendment provision extending U.S. constitutional protections to individuals within states, ensuring that each citizen benefits from equal protection under the law.

Fact-Finding This is a step in conflict resolution in states that have collective bargaining laws.

Fiscal Capacity The ability of a local government agency, such as a school district, to generate tax revenues. It is usually measured by the size of the local tax base, usually property wealth per pupil in education.

Fiscal Neutrality Fiscal neutrality is the equity standard in education finance. It is a negative standard, stating that the current operating expenditures per pupil, or some resource, cannot be related to a school district's adjusted assessed valuation per pupil or some fiscal capacity measure. Differences in expenditures per pupil cannot be related to local school district wealth. This is related to Coons, Clune, and Sugarman's Principle One.

Fiscally Independent/Dependent Approximately 80% of U.S. school boards have taxing authority. They are said to be fiscally independent. The remainder cannot tax property. They must submit their annual operating budgets to municipal or county authorities for approval, for which they are said to be fiscally dependent.

Flat Grant Programs A flat grant program simply allocates an equal sum of dollars to each public school pupil in the state. A flat grant is not an equalization aid program because it allocates the same dollars per pupil regardless of the property or income wealth of the local school districts. If *no local* dollars are raised for education and all school dollars come from the state, a flat grant program becomes equivalent to full state assumption. (See **Basic Aid.**)

Forest Reserve Funds Where federal forest lands exist within a county, 25% of funds received from the U.S. government from rentals of forest reserve lands are apportioned among various districts in the county according to school population.

Formula Funding Operating revenue projected as due an organization as a consequence of the computation of a state, or federal, distributional formula.

Foundation Program A foundation program is a state equalization aid program that typically guarantees a specified dollar foundation expenditure for each student, together with a minimum tax rate that each school district must levy for education purposes. The difference between what a local school district raises at the minimum tax rate and the foundation expenditure is made up in state aid.

Fractional Assessments Partial assessment, or less than the full market value of a property.

Free Riders Those deriving benefits even if not participating to create the condition or product under consideration.

Full State Assumption Full state assumption (FSA) is a state school finance arrangement in which the state pays for all education costs and sets equal weighted per-pupil expenditures in all school districts. FSA would satisfy the expenditure per pupil "uniformity" standard of equity. Only in Hawaii has the state government fully assumed most of the costs of public education.

Full-Time Equivalent (FTE) A count of full-time and part-time employees (or students) where part-time employees (or students) are reported as an appropriate fraction of a full-time position. This fraction is equal to the ratio of time expended in a part-time position to that of a full-time position.

Fund A complete accounting component reflecting a set of specified financial transactions, both receipts and expenditures, of finances for a specific purpose. The fund concept also applies to budget activities.

Fundamental Right Constitutionally protected activities such as freedom of worship, speech, and right to assemble.

General Fund The general fund is used to budget and account for all receipts and expenditures for the basic operation of a school district. Capital and debt service funds may be outside the general fund.

General Obligation Bonds Bonds that are a "general obligation" of a government agency issuing them, that is, their repayment is not tied to a selected revenue stream. Bond elections in a school district often must be approved by a two-thirds vote of the electorate, but state bond measures may require only a majority vote.

General Welfare Clause Constitutional provision that has come to be interpreted judicially as authorizing government assistance for and regulation over selected federal government endeavors not specifically enumerated in the Constitution, including education activities. Undertaken for the general welfare of the nation.

George-Reed Act (1929) Precursor of the still-existing Vocational Education Act.

George-Ellzey Act (1935) Precursor of the still-existing Vocational Education Act.

George-Deen Act (1937) Precursor of the still-existing Vocational Education Act.

George-Barden Act (1946) Precursor of the still-existing Vocational Education Act.

Gifted and Talented Education (GATE) A program for students in grades 1 through 12 who are thought to display potential abilities of high performance, capability, and needing differentiated or accelerated education.

Guaranteed Tax Base Program (GTB) See **District Power Equalization.**

Guaranteed Yield Program See **District Power Equalization.**

Homestead Exemption A forgiveness of property taxes, or some portion thereof, for owners who, in fact, reside on the property.

Horizontal Equity Treating equals equally.

Implicit Price Deflator See **Cost-of-Living Adjustment.**

Income Elasticity of Yield

$$\varepsilon_I = \frac{\text{percent change in tax yield}}{\text{percent change in personal incomes}}$$

Incremental Budgeting Planning on adding, or subtracting, marginal amounts from the base year operating budget.

Indirect Expense and Overhead Those elements of indirect cost necessary for the operation of a district or in the performance of a service that are of such a nature that the amount applicable to each accounting unit cannot be separately identified. Indirect costs are allocated to all programs in a school agency as a percentage of direct and allocated costs for each program.

Individualized Education Program (IEP) A written agreement between a school agency and parents or guardians of a disabled child specifying an educational program tailored to the specific needs of the child, in accordance with federal PL 94-142 regulations.

Law Public sector decision rule (see **Policy**). Federal laws are numbered by the congress in which they were enacted and the sequence within that congress in which they became law. Hence Public Law 94-142 (The Education for All Handicapped Children Act) was enacted by the 94th congress and it was the 142nd statute officially enrolled in that congress.

Least Restrictive Environment Federal and state laws requiring that disabled students be placed in the least restrictive educational setting appropriate to their needs so that they can, to the extent appropriate, integrate and be educated with nondisabled students.

Leveling Down Lowering the revenue level of high-wealth or high-revenue districts to promote revenue equity among school districts.

Leveling Up Raising the revenue level of low-revenue districts to promote revenue equity among school districts.

Line-Item Budgeting Projecting operating expenditures object code line by line.

Local Control See **Ye Old Deluder Satan Act.**

Magnet Schools Means for attempting to reduce racial segregation by formulating a school, often a theme school, the attendance boundaries of which draw from wide geographic and, presumably, racially mixed areas.

Mandated Costs School district expenses that occur because of federal or state laws, decisions of state or federal courts, or federal or state administrative regulations. Costs that are mandated by state law or regulations must be reimbursed by the state, while costs mandated by federal law, a court, or an initiative do not need to be reimbursed by the state.

Measures of Education Finance Equity Range, restricted range, federal range ratio, coefficient of variation, Lorenz curves, Gini coefficients, and McLoone index.

Median Family Income Median family income usually is that reported in the decennial U.S. census. It reflects income for the year before the census was taken, that is, 1999 income for the 2000 census. If the income of all families in a school district were rank-ordered, the median income would be the income of the family midway between the lowest- and the highest-income families.

Mill Old English coin representing one-tenth of a penny.

Morrill Act of 1862 Congressional granting of public lands and perpetual funds to states to establish institutions of higher education capable of serving public needs, particularly in agriculture, mining, and military-related endeavors. Results in what today are known as "Land Grant Colleges," of which one institution in each state, either public or private, is so designated. Act named for member of Congress who championed the idea, Justin Morrill.

Multivariate Statistics   Involves observation and analysis of more than one variable simultaneously. Multivariate methods include factor analysis, multidimensional scaling, and cluster analysis as well as regression. The interpretation of any one coefficient is made in terms of holding values for all other coefficients constant (sometimes referred to as "controlling for" or "fixing" other effects).

Municipal Overburden   An abstraction that refers to the fiscal position of large cities. Municipal overburden is said to include noneducation services that central cities choose to provide and that many other jurisdictions do not have to provide, or at least do not have to provide in the same quantity, or through the public sector.

National Assessment of Educational Progress (NAEP)   An annually administered set of standardized academic subject achievement examinations, drawing on both a national sample and multiple student samples, from which generalizations can be made to the performance of students within a state. Known as the "nation's report card."

National Defense Education Act (NDEA)   Enacted in 1958 as a reaction to the Soviet Union's launching of the first space satellite, *Sputnik*. The Soviet act was taken as evidence of the loss of U.S. military and scientific supremacy. NDEA was intended to use schools to restore U.S. scientific and defense prowess. In following year, the United States launched manned space flight.

Necessary Small School   A school with a small or diseconomic number of enrollees but, possibly because of geographic remoteness or population sparsity, is necessary to operate.

Need Equalization   Adjustments to a state funding distribution formula necessitated by differences in local district pupil population characteristics (e.g., poverty, language proficiency, or student disability).

No Child Left Behind Act of 2001   Major federal statute linking the provision of federal education funding to the achievement of student learning targets by schools. It is actuated as an amendment to Title I of the Elementary and Secondary Education Act (ESEA).

Nonrevenue Receipt   Money borrowed that increases the debt of the school district or money received in exchange for some other asset in the school district.

Northwest Ordinance of 1787   Congressional granting of public land to states for initiation and support of public schooling.

Opportunity to Learn   Modern consideration that students are provided with the instruction and equipment thought necessary to learn that which is expected by state learning standards. Opportunity to learn serves as a foundation for the notion of financial adequacy.

Parcel Tax   A special tax that is a flat amount per parcel and not ad valorem-based (i.e., not according to the value of the property). Parcel taxes must be approved by a two-thirds vote of the electorate.

Percentage Equalizing Programs   See **District Power Equalization.**

PERT   Acronym standing for Program Evaluation and Review Technique. An early strategic planning tool.

PL 81-874   A federal program of "impact aid" that provides funds to school agencies that educate children whose families live or work on federal property, such as military bases. Also called "PL 874."

PL 94-142 Federal law that mandates a "free and appropriate" education for all disabled children.

Plenary Latin for ultimate. States, under the U.S. Constitution, are said to have plenary authority over education.

Policy A uniform decision rule, either formally or informally adopted, specifying action, resource distribution, or regulation, intended to guide an organization's internal actions or agency practice. Authority, either management in the private sector or representative individuals or institutions in the public sector, issues such rules. (See also **Education Policy** and **Public Policy**.)

Price Elasticity of Demand Price elasticity exists if consumption remains stable or increases when prices increase.

Prior Year's Taxes Tax revenues that had been delinquent in a prior year and that are received in the current fiscal year. These revenues offset state aid in the current year in the revenue limit formula.

Productivity Concept involving measurement of output of goods and services relative to inputs.

Programming, Planning, and Budgeting Systems (PPBS) Budgeting format in which projected operating expenditures are aligned with organizational purposes and specific programs.

Progressive Tax A progressive tax is one that increases proportionately more than income as the income level of the taxpayer increases. Under a progressive tax, a high-income taxpayer will pay a larger percentage of annual income than a low-income taxpayer.

Property Tax Circuit Breaker Program A tax relief program, usually financed by a state, that focuses property tax relief on particular households presumed to be overburdened by property taxes. That is, it is intended to reduce presumed regressivity of the property tax.

Property Tax Incidence or Impact Incidence refers to the individual or institution that ultimately pays the tax. Impact refers to the individual or institution that actually pays the tax. Incidence and impact can be the same. However, in some instances they differ, for example, property owners pay the tax (impact) but may, when occupancy rates are high, pass the actual economic consequence to renters in the form of higher rents (incidence).

Property Tax Levy The product of a specified tax rate and the assessed value.

Property Tax Rate A statement in dollars and cents, expressed per $100 of assessed value, that will yield a specific amount of money in property taxes. The yield is also referred to as the levy.

Proportional Tax A proportional tax is one that consumes the same percentage of individual or household income at all income levels.

Proposition One (Principle of Fiscal Neutrality) Specification of wealth neutrality. Used as standard for remedy in equal protection education finance cases. "The quality of a child's schooling should not be a function of wealth, other than the wealth of the state as a whole."

Proposition 13 One of the original late-20th-century state tax limitation plans. An initiative constitutional amendment passed in June 1978, adding Article XIII A to the California constitution. Under Proposition 13, tax rates on secured property are restricted to no more than 1% of full cash value. Proposition 13 also defined assessed value and required a two-thirds vote to increase existing taxes or levy new taxes.

Public Policy A product of government; draws on public resources for its implementation, operation, or oversight.

Pupil-Weighted System or Weighted-Pupil Programs A pupil-weighted system is a state aid distribution arrangement in which pupils are given different weights based on the estimated or assumed costs of their education program; aid is allocated on the basis of the total number of weighted students. Illustrative weightings include disabled, limited-English-proficient and low-income student classifications.

Rational Basis Test relied on by courts to determine legal acceptability or constitutionality of a statue.

Recapture Flow of revenues to central (state) government when a school district generates more per-pupil revenue at a specified tax rate than it is permitted statutorily to spend.

Reduction-in-Force (RIF) A process whereby employment is terminated because of a need to reduce staff rather than because of any performance inadequacies of an individual employee.

Regression Coefficient A predictor or additive constant in a regression equation. In linear regression, the regression coefficient represents the rate of change of the dependent variable as a function of changes in independent variables. Simply put, a regression coefficient is the straight line ("line of best fit") that most closely relates two correlated variables.

Regressive Tax A regressive tax is one that increases proportionately less than income as the income level of the taxpayer increases. Under a regressive tax, a low-income taxpayer will pay a larger percentage of income than a high-income taxpayer.

Reliability Technical term referring to the extent to which a specific judgment, action, or research result is repeatable over time or over various horizontal repetitions.

Reserves Funds set aside in a budget to provide for estimated future expenditures, to offset future losses, to cover contingencies, for working capital, or for other purposes.

Revenue Limit The amount of revenue that a district can collect annually for general purposes from local property taxes and state aid. The revenue limit is composed of a base revenue limit—a basic education amount per unit of ADA computed by formula each year from the previous year's base revenue limit—and any of the number of revenue limit adjustments computed anew each year.

Revolving Cash Funds A stated amount of revenue used primarily for emergency or small or sundry disbursements and reimbursed periodically through properly documented expenditures, which are summarized and charged to accounting classifications.

School Budget A financial plan considering both revenue and expenditures necessary to finance the educational program and related operations of a school district. The budget is valid for one year.

School District Tax Rate A term on which states rely to indicate the local school property tax rate. The tax rate is often stated as the amount of property tax dollars to be paid for each $100 of assessed valuation or, if given in mills, the rate indicates how much is raised for each $1,000 of assessed valuation. For example, a tax rate of $1.60 per $100 of assessed valuation means that a taxpayer pays $1.60 for each $100 of his total assessed valuation; a tax rate of 16 mills indicates that $16 must be paid for each $1,000 of assessed valuation.

School-Site Budgeting Places projected revenues for operating purposes at the school site for decision discretion by school-site officials, rather than central office officials.

Scope of Bargaining This refers, in a state in which collective bargaining is permitted, to the range of subjects that are negotiable between school agency officials and employee organizations during the collective bargaining process. Scope includes matters relating to wages, hours, and working conditions as defined in a state code.

Secured Roll That portion of the assessed value that is stationary—land and buildings. See also **Unsecured Roll.**

Serrano **Decision** One of the earliest equal protection cases. In 1974, the California Superior Court in Los Angeles County ruled in the *Serrano v. Priest* case that school district revenues in California depended so heavily on local property taxes that students in districts with a low assessed value per pupil were denied an equal educational opportunity, in violation of the equal protection clause of the California Constitution. This ruling established standards under which the school finance system would be constitutional and was upheld by the California Supreme Court in 1976. In 1983, the California Superior Court in Los Angeles County ruled that the system of school finance in effect at that time was in compliance with the earlier court order.

The Servicemen's Readjustment Act, PL 78-346 This is popularly known as the GI Bill. It was a remarkably successful public investment in human capital, the dividends of which continue to be reaped by the American economy. It served as the forerunner of subsequent benefit packages for those who serve in the military.

Slippage Savings in state school fund appropriations that are the result of property tax revenues growing faster than a district's cost of living and enrollment growth. When property tax growth is greater than the growth in a district's total revenue limit, state aid to the district declines, creating a "slippage" in state expense.

Smith Hughes Act of 1917 Initial vocational education act that has been continually reauthorized.

Social Contract Theory Concept underlying representative government. Authority to govern is assumed to reside within citizens who voluntarily cede such authority to elected representatives. Granting of authority to governing representatives is tentative, subject to revocation in the event of abuse.

Spending Limit A ceiling, or limit, on each year's appropriations of tax dollars by the state, cities, counties, school districts, and special districts.

Standard Deviation A measure of statistical dispersion. The standard deviation is the square root of the sum of a distribution's variation. The standard deviation describes how tightly all observations under consideration are clustered around the mean. One standard deviation away from the mean in either direction accounts for approximately 68% of the observations in a given group. Two standard deviations away from the mean account for roughly 95% of the observations, and three standard deviations account for approximately 99% of the observations. The more dispersed a group of observations, the larger the standard deviation needed to account for 68, 95, and 99% of observations.

State Aid for Current Operating Expense The sum of the equalization formula aid and categorical aid for vocational education, special education, bilingual education, transportation, and other categorical aid programs. (See **Categorical Programs.**)

State Allocation Board (SAB) In states where such exists, the regulatory agency that controls most state-aided capital outlay and deferred maintenance projects and distributes state-appropriated funds for them.

State School Fund Each year the state appropriates revenue to this fund, which is then used to make state aid payments to school districts.

Statute Formally adopted decision rule in the public sector (see **Policy**).

Strict Scrutiny Burden of proof demanded by courts when civil or criminal issues regarding fundamental interests are at stake.

Subsidiarity Decision principle by which the weight of an argument must favor elevating a decision to a higher level of government or management; otherwise, the presumption is that the decision should rest with those closest to the production of the good or service, or closest to the client.

Subventions Term used to describe assistance or financial support, usually from higher governmental units to local governments or school agencies. State aid to school agencies is a state subvention.

Sunset The termination of a categorical program. A schedule is in current law for the Legislature to consider the "sunset" of most state categorical programs. If a program sunsets under a schedule, funding for the program may continue, but the specific laws and regulations shall no longer apply, or both the program and funding may disappear altogether.

Supplemental Roll An additional property tax assessment for properties that are sold or newly constructed that reflect a higher market value than on their prior lien date. Taxing this increase in assessed value immediately—rather than waiting until the next lien date—generates additional property taxes.

Suspect Classification Judicial concept invoked when there is an issue of possible deprivation or equal protection to individuals based on race, geographic location, or economic status.

Tax Bases Wealth, income, consumption, and privilege.

Tax Burden (or sometimes Tax Incidence) Tax burden typically refers to the percentage of an individual's or family's income that is consumed by a tax or by a tax system.

Tax Code Area Geographically bounded area within which various property tax codes apply.

Tax Incidence See **Tax Burden.**

Tax Islands Geographically bounded areas in which taxes are low.

Tax Neutrality A revenue-generating mechanism for government that does not distort consumer or producer market behavior.

Tax Price The tax price is generally the tax rate a district must levy to purchase a given level and quality of school services. Poor districts generally have to levy a higher tax rate, and thus pay a higher tax price, to purchase a given bundle of school services than a wealthy district because, at a given tax rate, a property-poor district would raise fewer dollars per pupil than the wealthy district.

Technical Efficiency Production of goods or services at the lowest cost consistent with a specified level of quality.

Transfer Payments Occurs when wealth is transferred from one individual to another or one institution to another without any quid pro quo or added production of goods or services.

Tuition The price of or payment for instruction.

Unencumbered Balance That portion of an appropriation or allotment not yet expended or obligated.

Unsecured Roll That portion of assessed property that is movable, such as boats, planes, and so on.

Univariate Statistics Involves observation and analysis of a single variable. Univariate methods include measures of central tendency, mode, median, mean, dispersion, range, percentiles, standard deviation, variance, skew, and normal curve.

Value Added When applied to testing of student achievement or performance, the term connotes the increment of presumed new knowledge added by a specific teacher or school for a specified length of time or school year.

Validity The extent to which a measure or result is in fact gauging that which is purported or intended.

Value-Added Tax (VAT) Form of taxation on goods and services particularly popular in the European community whereby a tax is imposed at each stage of production consistent with the value added by that producer. In effect, it is a sales tax or consumption tax.

Vertical Equity Treating unequals equally.

Wealth Equalization Adjustments to the state funding distribution formula necessitated by differences in local property wealth.

Wealth Neutrality See **Proposition One (Principle of Fiscal Neutrality).**

Ye Olde Deluder Satan Act of 1642 Commonwealth of Massachusetts statute establishing local schools under the authority of a lay board specializing in school governance. The foundation of the American system for governing schools at the local level.

Zero-Base Budgeting Expenditure projection strategy wherein no assumptions are made regarding the maintenance of this year's programs for next year. Each program must rejustify itself each budget cycle.

Bibliography

Aaron, H. J. (1975). *Who pays the property tax?* Washington, DC: Brookings Institution Press.

Abbott v. Burke, 575 A. 2d 359 (N.J. 1990).

Abbott v. Burke, 693 A. 2d 417 (N.J. 1997).

Adams, J. E., Jr. (1991). *Kentucky case study: CPRE core state study, year 1.* Los Angeles: University of California, Consortium for Policy Research in Education (CPRE).

Addonizio, M. (2000). Class size and student performance: A framework for policy analysis. *Journal of Education Finance, 26*(2), 135–156.

Addonizio, M. (2003). From fiscal equity to educational adequacy: Lessons from Michigan. *Journal of Education Finance, 28*(4), 457–484.

Adler, M. J. (1982). *The Paideia proposal.* New York: Macmillan.

Advisory Commission on Intergovernmental Relations (1977). *Significant features of fiscal federalism, 1976–77* (Vol. II, p. 50). Washington, DC: Government Printing Office.

Advisory Commission on Intergovernmental Relations (1984). *Significant features of fiscal federalism, 1984*, pp. 122–123, Table 73.

Advisory Commission on Intergovernmental Relations (1995). *Significant features of fiscal federalism*, p. 131, Table 35.

Agresti, A., & Finley, B. (1997). *Statistical methods for the social sciences* (3rd ed.). New York: Prentice Hall.

Aguilar v. Felton, 473 U.S. 402 (1985).

Alabama Coalition for Equity v. Hunt, WL 204083 (Ala. 1993).

Alexander, L., & James, H. T. (1987). *The nation's report card.* Cambridge: National Academy of Education.

Alexander, N. A. (2003). Considering equity and adequacy: An examination of the distribution of student class time as an educational resource in New York state 1975–1995. *Journal of Education Finance, 28*(3), 357–382.

Allgood, W., & Rothstein, R. (2000, October 18). *Adequate education for at-risk youths* (Economic Policy Institute memo).

Ammar, S., Duncombe, W., Jump, B., & Wright, R. (2005). A financial condition indicator system for school districts: A case study of New York. *Journal of Education Finance, 30*(3), 231–258.

Armor, D. (1972). School and family effects on black and white achievement: A re-examination of the USOE data. In F. Mosteller & D. P. Moynihan, (Eds.), *On equality of educational opportunity.* New York: Vintage Books.

Augenblick, J. (1997). *Recommendations for a base figure and pupil-weighted adjustments to the base figure for use in a new school finance system in Ohio.* Report presented to the School Funding Task Force, Ohio Department of Education, July 17.

Augenblick, J., Alexander, K., & Guthrie, J. W. (1995). *Report of the panel of experts: Proposals for the elimination of wealth based disparities in education.* Report submitted by Ohio Chief State School Officer T. Sanders to the Ohio State Legislature.

Bailey, S. K., & Mosher, E. K. (1967). *The ESEA: The office of education administers a law.* Syracuse, NY: Syracuse University Press.

Baker, B. D. (2003). The influence of state policies on the internal allocation of school district resources: Evidence from the common core of data. *Journal of Education Finance, 29*(1), 1–24.

Baker, B. D. (2005). The emerging shape of educational adequacy: From theoretical assumptions to empirical evidence. *Journal of Education Finance, 30*(3), 259–287.

Baker, B. D., & Richards, C. E. (2002). Exploratory application of systems dynamics modeling to school finance policy analysis. *Journal of Education Finance, 27*(3), 857–884.

Baker, B. D., Taylor, L., & Vedlitz, A. (2004). *Measuring educational adequacy in public schools.* Austin, TX: Texas Select Joint Committee on Education Finance.

Baker, E. (Ed.). (1947). *Social contract: Essays by Locke, Hume and Rousseau.* Oxford, UK: Oxford University Press.

Ballard, C. L., Shoven, J. B., & Walley, J. (1985). General equilibrium computations of the marginal welfare costs of taxes in the United States. *American Economic Review, 75*(1), 128–135.

Ballou, D. (2002). Sizing up test scores. *Education Next, 2*(2), 10–15.

Ballou, D., & Podgursky, M. (2000). Reforming teacher preparation and licensing: What does the evidence show? *Teachers College Record, 101*(1), 5–26.

Barr, W. M. (1960). *American public school finance.* New York: American Book.

Barr, W. M., Jordan, K. F., Hudson, C. C., Peterson, W. J., & Wilkerson, W. R. (1970). *Financing public elementary and secondary school facilities in the United States* (National Educational Finance Project Special Study No. 7). Washington, DC.

Baumgartner, F. (1999) Punctuated-equilibrium theory. In P. A. Sabatier (Ed.), *Theories of the policy process* (pp. 97–116). New York: Westview.

Belfield, C., & Levin, H. (2003). The economics of education on judgment day. *Journal of Education Finance, 28*(2), 207–234.

Benson, C. S. (1961). *The economics of public education.* New York: Houghton Mifflin.

Benson, C. S. (1965). *The cheerful prospect: A statement of the future of American education.* Boston: Houghton Mifflin.

Berman, P., & McLaughlin, M. (1978). *Federal programs supporting educational change: Implementing and sustaining innovations, Vol. 8.* Santa Monica, CA: Rand Corporation.

Berne, R., & Stiefel, L. (1978). *A methodological assessment of education equality and wealth neutrality measures.* New York: Graduate School of Public Administration, New York University.

Berne, R., & Stiefel, L. (1983). *The measurement of equity in school finance: Conceptual, methodological, and empirical dimensions.* Baltimore: Johns Hopkins University Press.

Betts, J. R. (1995). Does school quality matter? Evidence from the national longitudinal survey of youth, *Review of Economics and Statistics, 77,* 231–247.

Betts, J. R. (1996). Is there a link between school inputs and earning? Fresh scrutiny of an old literature. In G. Burtless (Ed.), *Does money matter: The effect of school resources on student achievement and adult success.* Washington, DC: Brookings Institution Press.

Bill for the More General Diffusion of Knowledge 1779.

Board of Education of Levittown v. Nyquist, 408 N.Y.S. 2d 606 (N.Y. Sup. Ct. 1978).

Board of Education of Levittown v. Nyquist, 57 N.Y. 2d 27 (1982).

Boyd, W. L., & Hartman, W. T. (1988). The politics of educational productivity. In D. H. Monk & J. Underwood (Eds.), *Micro-level school finance: Issues and implications for policy* (pp. 271–310). Cambridge, MA: Ballinger.

Boyer, E. L. (1983). *High school: A report on secondary education* in *America.* New York: Harper & Row.

Bradbury, K. L., Ladd, H. F., Perrault, M., Reschovsky, A., & Yinger, J. (1984). State aid to offset fiscal disparities across communities. *National Tax Journal, 37,* 151–170.

Bradford, D. F., Malt, R. A., & Pates, W. E. (1969). The rising cost of local and public services: Some evidence and reflections. *National Tax Journal, 22*(2), 185–202.

Brent, B. O., Sipple, J. W., Killeen, K. M., & Wishnowski, M. W. (2004). Stalking cost-effectiveness practices in rural schools. *Journal of Education Finance, 29*(3), 237–256.

Brimley, V., & Garfield, R.R. (2002). *Financing education in a climate of change* (8th ed.). New York: Allyn & Bacon.

Brimley, V. Jr., & Garfield, R. R. (2005). *Financing education in a climate of change* (9th ed.). Boston: Pearson Education.

Brown v. Board of Education of Topeka, 347 U.S. 483, 74 S.Ct. 686, 98 L.Ed. 873 (U.S. 1954).

Brown, C. L. (1978). Adequate program for education in Georgia. *Journal of Education Finance, 3*(4), 402–411.

Brunner, E. J., & Imazeki, J. (2003). *Private contributions and public school resources* (Working Paper). San Diego: San Diego State University.

Buboltz, W. C., Jr., & Savickas, M. L. (1994). A 20-year retrospective of the career development quarterly. *The Career Development Quarterly, 42*(4), 367–392.

Buchanon, J. M., & Tollison, R. D. (1984). *The theory of public choice II*. Ann Arbor, MI: University of Michigan Press.

Bull, B. (2000). Political philosophy and the state-local power balance. In N. D. Theobald & B. Malen (Eds.), *Balancing local control and state responsibility for K–12 education*. Larchmont, NY: Eye On Education.

Burke, A. J. (1957). Financing public school in the United States. New York: Harper & Brothers.

Burke, S. M., & White, G. P. (2001). The influence of district characteristics on intra-district resource allocation. *Journal of Education Finance, 20*(3), 259–280.

Burtless, G. (1996). *Does money matter? The effect of school resources on student achievement and adult success*. Washington, DC: Brookings Institution Press.

Busse v. Smith, 247 N.W. 2d 141 (Wis. 1976).

Campaign for Fiscal Equity v. State, 100 N.Y. 2d 893 (N.Y. 2003).

Campaign for Fiscal Equity v. State, 162 Misc. 2d 493 (N.Y. 1994).

Campaign for Fiscal Equity v. State, 187 Misc. 2d 1 (N.Y.S. 2001).

Campbell County School District v. State, 907 P. 2d 1238 (Wyo. 1995).

Campbell, R., et al. (1980). *The organization and control of American schools* (pp. 26–27). Columbus, OH: Chas. E. Merrill.

Capacchione v. Charlotte-Mecklenburg Schools, 57 Supp. 2d 228 (1999).

C. D. Perkins Vocational and Applied Technology Education Act (1990).

Carter, I. (2003). Positive and negative liberty, *The Stanford encyclopedia of philosophy* (Spring 2003 ed.). E. N. Zalta (Ed.), http://plato.stanford.edu/archives/spr2003/entries/liberty-positive-negative/

Catterall, J. S. (1983a). Tuition tax credits: Issues of equity. In T. James & H. M. Levin (Eds.), *Public dollars for private schools*. Philadelphia: Temple University Press.

Catterall, J. S. (1983b). *Tuition tax credits: Fact and fiction*. Bloomington, IN: Phi Delta Kappan Educational Foundation.

Celio, M. B., & Harvey, J. (2005). *Buried treasure: Developing a management guide for mountains of school data*. Seattle: University of Washington, Daniel J. Evans School of Public Affairs.

Chambers, J. G. (1978). Educational cost differentials and the allocation of state aid for elementary/secondary education. *Journal of Human Resources, 13*(4), 459–481.

Chambers, J. G. (1998). The development of a cost of education index. *Journal of Education Finance, 5*(3).

Chambers, J., & Parish, T. (1982). *The development of a resource cost model funding base for education finance in Illinois*. Report prepared for the Illinois State Board of Education.

Charlotte-Mecklenburg v. Capacchione, 99–2389 (2001).

Chubb, J., & Moe, T. (1990). *Politics, markets and America's schools*. Washington, DC: Brookings Institution Press.

Claremont School District v. Governor, 147 N.H. 499 (N.H. 2002).

Claremont School District v. Governor, 635 A. 2d 1375 (N.H. 1994).

Claremont School District v. Governor, 635 A. 2d 1375 (NH 1993).

Clotfelter, C. (2004). Private schools, segregation, and the southern states. *Peabody Journal of Education, 79*, (2), 74–97.

Clune, W. H. (1995). Educational adequacy: A theory and its remedies. *University of Michigan Journal of Law Reform, 28*, 481.

Cochran, K. T. (2000). Comment, beyond school financing, defining the Constitutional right to an adequate education. *North Carolina Law Review, 78*, 399.

Cohen, M. (1992, August 22). As school bell rings, two systems become one. *Raleigh (NC) News and Observer*, B1.

Cohen, E., & Geske, T. (1990). *The economics of education* (3rd ed.). Oxford, UK: Pergamon Press.

Cohen, M. D., March, J. G., & Olsen, J. P. (1972). A garbage can model of organizational choice. *Administrative Science Quarterly, 17,* 1–25.

Cohen-Vogel, L. A., & Cohen-Vogel, D. R. (2001). School finance reform in Tennessee: Inching toward adequacy. *Journal of Education Finance, 26*(3), 297–318.

Cohn, E., & Morgan, J. M. (1978). Improving resource allocation within school districts: A goal-programming approach. *Journal of Education Finance, 4*(1), 89–104.

Coleman, J. S. (1966). *Equality of educational opportunity*. Washington, DC: U.S. Department of Health, Education, and Welfare, Office of Education.

Columbia Falls Elementary School District No. 6 v. State of Montana, WL 648038 (Mont. 2005).

Connecticut Constitution, Article VIII, 1.

Coons, J., & Sugarman, S. (1971). *Family choice in education: A model state system for vouchers*. Berkeley, CA: Institute of Governmental Studies.

Coons, J., & Sugarman, S. (1978). *Education by choice: The case for family control*. Los Angeles, University of California Press.

Coons, J. E., Clune, W. H., & Sugarman, S. D. (1970). *Private wealth and public education*. Cambridge, MA: Harvard University/Belknap Press.

Cooperative Research and Training Units Act, 16 U.S.C. § 753a–753b (1960).

Cremin, L. A. (1980). *American education: The national experience, 1783–1876*. New York: Harper and Row.

Cubberley, E. P. (1905). *Schools funds and their apportionment*. New York: Teachers College Press.

Cubberley, E. P. (1908). The salary question and the rural school. *Western Journal of Education, 15,* 3–10.

Cubberley, E. P. (1912, October). Taxation and distribution. *School and Home Education, 32,* 46.

Cubberley, E. P. (1915a). Report of a survey of the organizational scope and finances of the public school system in Oakland, California. *Board of Education Bulletin, 8,* 1–48.

Cubberley, E. P. (1915b). Desirable reorganization in American education. *School and Society, 2,* 397–402.

Cubberley, E. P. (1919a). *Public education in the United States: A study and interpretation of American educational history: An introductory textbook dealing with the largest problems of present-day education in the light of their historical development.* New York: Houghton Mifflin.

Cubberley, E. P. (1919b). *State and county school administration*. New York: Macmillan.

Cubberley, E. P., & Sears, J. B. (1924). *Education finance inquiry commission report VII.* New York: Macmillan.

Cubberley, E. P., & Strayer, G. D. (1913). Report of the committee of the national council of education on standards of tests for measuring the efficiency of schools or systems of schools. *United States Bureau of Education Bulletin, 13,* 3–9.

Darling, L., & Kirby, S. N. (1980). Public policy and private choice: The case of Minnesota. In T. James & H. M. Levin (Eds.), *Public dollars for private schools*. Philadelphia: Temple University Press.

Dayton, J. (2001). Serrano and its progeny: An analysis of 30 years of school funding litigation. *Education Law Reporter, 157,* 447–464.

Deller, S. C., & Rudnicki, E. (1993). Production efficiency in elementary education: The case of Maine public schools. *Economics of Education Review, 12*(2), 45–57.

Demos, J. (1971). *A little commonwealth: Family life in Plymouth Colony*. Oxford: Oxford University Press.

DeRolph v. Ohio, 677 N.E. 2d 733 (Ohio 1997).

DeRolph v. Ohio, 728 N.E. 2d 99 (Ohio 2000).

Dewey, J. (1917). Learning to earn: The place of vocational education in a comprehensive scheme of public education. *Schools and Society 5*(24), 335.

Downes, T. A., & Pogue, T. F. (1994). *Accounting for fiscal capacity and need in the design of school aid formulas*. Fiscal Equalization for State and Local Government Finance.

Drake, T., & Roe, W. (1994). *School business management: Supporting instructional effectiveness* (5th ed.). Needham Heights, MA: Allyn and Bacon.

Drake, T., & Roe, W. (1998). *School business management: Supporting instructional effectiveness* (6th ed.). Needham Heights, MA: Allyn and Bacon.

Duncombe, W. (2002). *Estimating the cost of an adequate education in New York* (Center for Policy Research Working Paper No. 44). Syracuse, NY: Syracuse University.

Duncombe, W., & Yinger, J. (1998). School finance reform aid formulas and equity objectives. *National Tax Journal, L1*(2), 239–262.

Duncombe, W., & Yinger, J. (2001). Alternative paths to property tax relief. In W. Oates (Ed.), *Property taxation and local government finance*. Cambridge, MA: Lincoln Institute of Land Policy.

Duncombe, W., & Yinger, J. (2005). How much does a disadvantaged student cost? *Economics of Education Review, 24*(5), 513–532.

Dupree v. Alma School District No. 30, 651 S.W. 2d 90 (Ark. 1983).

Edgewood Independent School District v. Kirby, 777 S.W. 2d 391 (Tex. 1989).

Education Commission of the States. (1983). *A Summary of Major Reports on Education.*

Education Commission of the States. (1984). *School Finance at a Glance*, 1983–84.

Education Commission of the States. (2005). Comprehensive School Reform. Retrieved June 15, 2006, from http://www.ecs.org/html/issue.asp?issueid=27

Eisenberg v. Montgomery County Schools, 197 F.3d 123 (1999).

Eissa, N. (1995). *Taxation and labor supply of married women: The tax reform act of 1986 as a natural experiment* (Working Paper No. 5023). Cambridge, MA: National Bureau of Economic Research.

Elchanan, C., & Geske, T. (1990). *The economics of education* (3rd ed.). New York: Macmillan/Pergamon.

Elementary and Secondary Education Act (ESEA), 20 U.S.C. § 6301 (1965).

Emergency School Aid Act of 1968, Pub. L. No. 92-318.

Federation of Tax Administrators. (2004). Comparison of State and Local Retail Sales Taxes, 2004. Retrieved June 15, 2006, from http://www.taxadmin.org/fta/rate/slsource.html

Federation of Tax Administrators. (2004). State Individual Income Taxes, 2004. Retrieved June 15, 2006, from http://www.taxadmin.org/fta/rate/slsource.html

Federation of Tax Administrators. (2004). 2004 State and Local Tax Collection by Source. Retrieved June 15, 2006, from http://www.taxadmin.org/fta/rate/slsource.html

Feentra, R. C., & Hanson, G. H. (1999). The impact of outsourcing and high technology capital on wages: Estimates for the United States, 1970–1990. *The Quarterly Journal of Economics, 114*(3), 907–940.

Figlio, D. N. (1999). Functional form and the estimated effects of school resources. *Economics of Education Review, 18*, 241–252.

Finn, C. E. (1983a). The drive for educational excellence: Moving toward a public consensus. *Change, 15*(3), 14–22.

Finn, C. (1983b). Why NIE cannot be. *Kappan, 64*(6), 407–410.

Finn, C., Manno, B., & Vanourek, G. (2000). *Charter Schools in Action: Renewing public education.* Princeton: Princeton University Press.

Fischel, W. (2004). Did John Serrano vote for Proposition 13: A reply to Stark and Zaaslof's "Tiebout and tax revolts; Did Serrano really cause Proposition 13?" *UCLA Law Review, 51*(4), 887–932.

Fischel, W. (1998). *School finance litigation and property tax revolts: How undermining local control turns voters away from public education.* Lincoln Institute of Land Policy Working Paper.

Florida Department of Revenue. (2004). Retrieved June 21, 2005, from http://www.myflorida.com/dor/property/exemptions.html

Franklin, B. (1749). Proposals relating to the education of youth in Pennsylvania. Retrieved August 15, 2004, from http://www.archives.upenn.edu/primdocs/1749proposals.html

Franklin, G., & Sparkman, W. E. (1978). The cost effectiveness of two program delivery systems for exceptional children. *Journal of Education Finance, 3*(3), 305–314.

Friedman, M. (1955). The role of government in education. In R. A. Solos (Ed.), *Economics and the public interest.* Rutgers, NJ: Rutgers University Press.

Friedman, M. (1965). *Capitalism and freedom.* Chicago: University of Chicago Press.

Fullerton, D., & Metcalf, G. E. (2002). Tax incidence. In A. J. Auerbach & M. Feldstein (Eds.), *Handbook of public economics, Vol. 4* (pp. 1787–1872). Amsterdam: Elsevier.

Ganns, W. L. (1979). Measuring the equity of school finance systems. *Journal of Education Finance, 4*(4), 415–35.

Garms, W. I., Guthrie, J. W., & Pierce, L. C. (1978). *School finance: The economics and politics of public education.* Englewood Cliffs, NJ: Prentice-Hall.

Garvue, R. J. (1969). *Modern public school finance.* New York: Macmillan.

George-Barden Act of 1946, Pub. L. No. 79-586.

George-Deen Act of 1937, Pub. L. No. 74-673.

George-Ellzey Act of 1935, Pub. L. No. 73-245.

George-Reed Act of 1929, Pub. L. No. 70-702.

Glass, G. (1996). *Statistical methods in education and psychology* (3rd ed.). Boston: Allyn and Bacon.

Goertz, M. E., & Hannigan, J. (1978). Delivering a thorough and efficient education in New Jersey. *Journal of Education Finance, 4*(1), 46–64.

Goldin, C., & Katz, L. F. (2003). *The virtues of the past: Education in the first hundred years of the republic* (Working Paper No. 9958). Cambridge, MA: National Bureau of Economic Research.

Goldring, E., & Smrekar, C. (2000). Magnet schools and the pursuit of racial balance. *Education and Urban Society, 33*(1), 17–35.

Goodlad, J. I. (1983). *A place called school: Prospects for the future.* St. Louis: McGraw-Hill.

Government of the District of Columbia (2002). *Tax rates and tax burdens in the District of Columbia—A nationwide comparison: 2002* (pp. 16–17). Washington, DC: Author.

Graham, H. D. (1984). *The uncertain triumph.* Chapel Hill: University of North Carolina Press.

Green, P. C. (1996). Equity, adequacy and efficiency in New York City school finance litigation. *Journal of Education Finance, 22*(Summer), 88–113.

Gronberg, T. J., Jansen, D.W., Taylor, L. L., & Booker, K. (2004). *School outcomes and school costs: The cost function approach* (Report prepared for the Texas Legislature Joint Committee on Public School Finance, The Texas School Finance Project). Retrieved October 25, 2004, from http://www.tlc.state.tx.us/roadmap/tsfp/Reports/school%20outcomes%20and%20school%20csts.doc2.pdf

Gross, M. J., & Warshaner, W. (2000). *Financial accounting guide for non-profit organizations* (5th ed.). New York: John Wiley.

Grosskopf, S., & Moutray, C. (2001). Evaluating performance in Chicago public high schools in the wake of decentralization. *Economics of Education Review, 20*, 1–14.

Gurwitz, A. S. (1980). The capitalization of school finance reform. *Journal of Education Finance, 5*(3), 297–319.

Guthrie, J. W. (Ed.). (1980). School finance policies and practices: The 1980s, a decade of conflict. *First Annual Yearbook of the American Education Finance Association.* Cambridge, MA: Ballinger.

Guthrie, J. W. (2004). Twenty-first century education finance: Equity, adequacy, and the emerging challenge of linking resources to performance. In K. K. Wong & K. DeMoss (Eds.), *Money, politics, and law: Intersections and conflicts in the provision of educational opportunity* (pp. 1–15). Poughkeepsie, NY: Eye on Education.

Guthrie, J. W., et al. (1975). The erosion of lay control. In *National Committee for Citizens in Education, public testimony on public schools.* Berkeley: McCutchan.

Guthrie, J. W., Garms, W. I., & Pierce, L. C. (1988). *Education finance and policy: Enhancing education equality, efficiency, and liberty* (2nd ed.). Boston: Allyn & Bacon.

Guthrie, J. W., & Rothstein, R. (1999). Enabling "adequacy" to achieve reality: Translating adequacy into state school finance distribution arrangements. In H. F. Ladd, R. Chalk, & J. S. Hansen (Eds.), *Equity and adequacy in education finance: Issues and perspectives* (pp. 209–259). Washington, DC: National Academy Press.

Guthrie, J. W., & Springer, M. G. (2004). *The "new" education finance policy paradigm, and its research and preparation implications* (Peabody Center Working Paper). Nashville, Tennessee: Vanderbilt University.

Guthrie, J. W., & Zusman, A. (1982). Teacher supply and demand in mathematics and science. *Kappan, 64*(1), 28–33.

Hamilton, B. W. (1976). Capitalization of Intrajurisdictional differences in local tax prices. *American Economic Review, 66,* 743–753.

Hancock v. Driscoll, S. Ct. Mass. 02–2978(2004), WL 877984 (Mass. S. Ct.).

Hanushek, E. A (1976). The economics of schooling. *Journal of Economic Literature, 24,* 1141–1177.

Hanushek, E. A. (1981). The impact of differential expenditures on school performance. *Educational Researcher, 18*(4), 45–62.

Hanushek, E. A. (1986) The economics of schooling: Production and efficiency in public schools. *Journal of Economic Literature, 24*(3), 1141–1177.

Hanushek, E. A. (1996). The quest for equalized mediocrity. In L. Picus & J. Wattenbarger (Eds.), *Where does the money go?* (pp. 20–43). Thousand Oaks, CA: Corwin Press.

Hanushek, E. A. (2002). Publicly provided education. In A. J. Auerbach & M. Feldstein (Eds.), *Handbook of public economics. Vol. 4* (pp. 2046–2141). New York: Elsevier.

Hanushek, E. A. (2005). Pseudo-science and a sound basic education: Voodoo statistics in New York. *Education Next,* Fall, 67–73.

Hanushek, E. A., Kain, J. F., O'Brien, D. M., & Rivkin, S. G. (2005). *The market for teacher quality* (Working Paper No. 11154). Cambridge, MA: National Bureau of Economic Research.

Hanushek, E. A., Kain, J. F., & Rivkin, S. G. (1998). *Teachers, schools, and academic achievement* (Working Paper No. 6691). Cambridge, MA: National Bureau of Economic Research.

Hanushek, E. A., & Rivkin, S. G. (1997). Understanding twentieth century growth in U.S. public school spending. *Journal of Human Resources, 32,* 35–68.

Hanushek, E. A., & Rivkin, S. G. (2004). *How to improve the supply of high quality teachers.* In D. Ravitch (Ed.), Brookings Papers on Educational Policy 2004 (pp. 7–25). Washington, DC: Brookings Institution Press.

Harris, M. A. (1975). *School Finance at a Glance.* Denver: Education Commission of the States.

Hartman, W. T. (1988). *School District Budgeting.* Englewood Cliffs, NJ: Prentice-Hall.

Hartman, W. T. (1998). Allocation and distribution of resources in high schools. In W. Hartman & W. Boyd (Eds.), *Resource allocation and productivity in education: Theory and practice.* Westport, CT: Greenwood Press.

Hassel, B. C., & Batdorf, M. (2004). *High stakes: Findings from a national study of life-or death decisions by charter school authorizers.* Retrieved May 15, 2004, from www.publicimpact.com/highstakes

Hausman, J. A. (1985). Taxes and the labor supply. In A. J. Auerbach & M. Feldstein (Eds.), *Handbook of public economics, vol. 1* (pp. 214–268). Amsterdam: Elsevier.

Hazlett, S. J. (1971). Financial support for schools. In L. C. Deighton (Ed.), *The encyclopedia of education, vol. 4* (pp. 30–37). New York: Macmillan & Free Press.

Hedges, L. V., Laine, R. D., & Greenwald, R. (1994). Does money matter? A meta-analysis of studies of the effects of differential school inputs on student outcomes. *Educational Researcher, 23*(3), 5–14.

Heise, M. (1998). Schoolhouses, courthouses, and statehouses: Educational finance, constitutional structure, and the separations of powers doctrine. *Land and Water Law Review, 33*(1), 282–327.

Helena Elementary School District v. State of Montana, 769 P 2d 684 (1990).

Helvering v. Davis, 301 Dr. S.619, 57 Sup. Ct. 904 (1937).

Henderson, J. M., & Quandt, R. E. (1980). *Microeconomic Theory: A Mathematical Approach* (3rd ed.). New York: McGraw-Hill.

Henderson, J. M., & Quandt, R. E. (2004). A multi-product cost functions for universities: Economies of scale and scope. In G. Johnes & J. Johnes (Eds.), *International handbook on the economics of education* (pp. 579–612). Cheltenham, UK and Brookfield, MA: Edward Elgar.

Hess, F. M. (2002). *Revolution at the margins: The impact of competition on urban school systems.* Washington, DC: Brookings Institution Press.

Hickrod, G. A., Liu, C. C., Arnold, R., Chaudhari, R., Frank, L., Franklin, D., et al. (1989). *The biggest bang for the buck: An initial report on technical economic efficiency in Illinois K–12 schools.* Normal, IL: Center for the Study of Educational Finance.

Hickrod, G. A., et al. (1990). *The biggest bang for the buck: A further investigation of economic efficiency in the public schools of Illinois.* Normal, IL: Center for the Study of Educational Finance.

Higher Education Act of 1972. Pub. L. No. 92-318.

Hill, P. T., & Harvey, J. (2004). *Making school reform work; New partnerships for real change.* Washington, DC: Brookings Institution Press.

Horton v. Meskill, 332 A. 2d 113 (Conn. Super. 1974).

Horton v. Meskill, 376 A. 2d 359 (Conn. 1977), hereinafter Horton II.

Howell, W. G., & Peterson, P. E. (2002). *The education gap: Vouchers and urban schools.* Washington, DC: Brookings Institution Press.

Hoxby, C. M. (2002). How school choice affects the achievement of public school students. In P. Hill (Ed.), *Choice with equity.* Stanford, CA: Hoover Institution Press.

Hoxby, C. M. (2003). School choice and school productivity: Could school choice be a tide that lifts all boats? In C. M. Hoxby (Ed.), *The economics of school choice. A National Bureau of Economic Research conference report.* Cambridge, MA: National Bureau of Economic Research.

Hughes J., Moon, C. G., & Barnett, W. S. (1993, September). *Revenue-driven costs: The case of resources allocation in public primary and secondary education.* Paper presented at the annual meeting of the Atlantic Economic Society, Philadelphia, PA.

Hymes, D. (1982). *School budgeting: Problems and solutions.* Sacramento, CA: American Association of School Administrators.

Imazeki, J. & Rechovsky, A. (1998). Measuring the cost of providing an adequate education in Texas. *Proceedings of the 91st Annual Conference on Taxation.* Washington, DC: National Tax Association.

Imazeki, J., & Reschovsky, A. (2003). Financing adequate education in rural settings. *Journal of Education Finance, 29*(2), 137–156.

Imazeki, J., & Reschovsky, A. (2004a). *Estimating the costs of meeting Texas education accountability standards.* Report submitted to the plaintiffs as evidence in *West Orange-Cove et al. v. Neeley et al.*, District Court of Travis County, Texas, Rev. July 8, 2004.

Imazeki, J., & Rechovsky, A. (2004b). School finance reform in Texas: A never ending story? In J. Yinger (Ed.), *Helping children left behind: State aid and the pursuit of educational equity* (pp. 251–281). Miami: MIT Press.

Imazeki, J., & Reschovsky, A. (2005). Assessing the use of econometric analysis in estimating the costs of meeting state education accountability standards: Lessons from Texas. *Peabody Journal of Education, 80*(3), 96–125

James, H. T. (1958). *Toward a unified concept of state finance systems.* Unpublished doctoral dissertation, Chicago, IL.

James, H. T. (1961). *School revenue systems in 5 states: Report of a pilot study.* Stanford, CA: Stanford University.

James, H. T. (1969). *The new cult of efficiency and education. Horace Mann lecture 1968.* Pittsburgh, PA: The University of Pittsburgh Press.

James, H. T., & Dyck, H. J. (1963). *Wealth, expenditure, and decision-making for education.* Stanford, CA: Stanford University.

James, H. T., Kelly, J. A., & Garms, W. I. (1966). *Determinants of educational expenditure in large cities of the United States (Cooperative research program of the United States Office of Education).* Stanford, CA: Stanford University.

Jefferson, T. (1976). Bill for the general diffusion of knowledge. Reprinted in J. S. Pancake (Ed.), *Thomas Jefferson, revolutionary philosopher: A selection of writings.* Rootberry, NY: Barron's.

Jencks, C., & Smith, M. (1972). *Inequality: A reassessment of the effect of family and schooling in America.* New York: Basic Books.

Johns, R. L. (1938). *An index of the financial ability of local school divisions to support public education.* Montgomery, AL: Alabama State Department of Education.

Johns, R. L. (1971). The development of state school support for the public schools. In R.L. Johns, K. Alexander, & D. H. Stollar (Eds.), *Status and impact of educational finance programs* (pp. 1–27). Gainesville, FL: National Educational Finance Project.

Johns, R. L. (1972). *Full state funding of education: Evolution and implication* (Horace Mann Lecture Series). Pittsburgh, PA: University of Pittsburgh.

Johns, R. L. (1977, spring). Analytic tools in school finance reform. *Journal of Education Finance, 2,* 499–511.

Johns, R. L., & Kimbrough, R. P. (1968). *The relationship of socioeconomic factors, educational leadership patterns, and elements of community power structure to local school fiscal policy.* Gainesville, FL: University of Florida.

Johns, R. L., & Morphet, E. L. (1972). *Planning school finance programs: A study guide.* Gainesville, FL: University of Florida.

Johns, R. L., & Morphet, E. L. (1975). *The economics and financing of education.* Englewood Cliffs, NJ: Prentice-Hall.

Johns, R. L., Morphet, E. L., & Alexander, K. (1983). *The economics and financing of education.* Englewood Cliffs, NJ: Prentice-Hall.

Jones, A. (1991, January 11). Consultants back Durham school merger. *Raleigh (NC) News and Observer,* A1.

Jones, J. R. (1984). The role of federal government in educational policy matters: Focus on finance. *Journal of Education Finance, 10*(2), 238–255.

Jorgenson, D. W., & Yung, K. (1993). The excess burden of taxation in the U.S. In A. Knoester (Ed.), *Taxation in the United States and Europe* (pp. 11–136). New York: St. Martin's Press.

Joseph, L. B. (2001). *Education policy for the 21st century: Challenges and opportunities for standards-based reform.* Chicago: University of Chicago.

Karoly, L. A., & Panis, C. (2004). *The 21st century at work: Forces shaping the future workforce and workplace in the United States.* RAND Labor and Population.

Karp, S. (2003, November 7). The No Child Left Behind hoax [Speech]. Retrieved August 15, 2004, from http://www.rethinkingschools.org/special_reports/bushplan/hoax.shtml

Kasayulie v. State, 3AN–97–3782 CIV (Ark. 1999).

Kaufman, B. (1991). *Up the down staircase.* New York: Harper Perennial.

Kelly, T. (forthcoming). *The WTO's impact on the environment, public health and sovereignty.* Cheltenham, UK and Northampton, MA: Edward Elgar.

Kershaw, J. A., & McKean, R. N. (1962). *Teacher shortages and salary schedules.* New York: McGraw-Hill.

King, R. A., & MacPhail-Wilcox, B. (1994). Unraveling the production equation. *Journal of Education Finance, 20*(1), 47–65.

King, R. A., Swanson, A. D., & Sweetland, S. R. (2002). *School financing: Achieving high standards with equity and efficiency.* Boston: Allyn & Bacon.

Kingdon, J. W. (1997). *Agendas, alternatives and public policies* (2nd ed.). New York: Longman.

Kingdon, J. (2003). *Agendas alternatives, and the policy process (Longman classics in political science).* New York: Longman.

Kirp, D. L. (1982). *Just schools.* Berkeley: University of California Press.

Kirp, D. L., & Jensen, D. N. (1987). *School days, rule days: The legalization and regulation of education.* New York: Falmer Press.

Kirst, M. W. (1983). A new school finance for a new era of fiscal constraint. In A. Odden & L. D. Webb (Eds.), *School finance and school improvement linkages for the 1980s* (pp. 1–15). Cambridge, MA: Ballinger.

Kirst, M. W. (1986). *The federal role and chapter I: Rethinking some basic assumptions.* Paper prepared for Research and Evaluation Associates, Washington, DC.

Kirst, M., & Meister, G. (1983). *The role of issue networks in state agenda setting* (Institute for Research on Educational Finance and Governance Project Report 83–80A1). Stanford, CT: Stanford University.

Kliebard, H. M. (1995). *The struggle for the American curriculum, 1893–1958* (2nd ed.). New York: Routledge.

Kliebard, H. M. (1999). *Schooled to work: Vocationalism and the American curriculum, 1876–1946* (p. 132). New York: Teachers College Press.

Knapp, M. S., et al. (1983). *Cumulative effects of federal education policies on schools and districts.* Menlo Park, CA: SRI International.

Koski, W. S. (2003). Of fuzzy standards and institutional constraints: A re-examination of the jurisprudential history of educational finance reform litigation. *Santa Clara Law Review, 43,* 1185.

Kratz, R. N., Scott, C. A., & Zechman, H. T. (1998). *A primer on school budgeting.* Lancaster, PA: Technomic Publishing.

Kreuger, A. B., & Zhu, P. (2002). *Another look at the New York City voucher experiment* (Working Paper No. 9418). Cambridge, MA: National Bureau of Economic Research.

Kubiszyn, T., & Borish, G. (2003). *Educational testing and measurement* (7th ed.). New York: John Wiley & Sons.

Kuhn, T. S. (1962). *The structure of scientific revolutions.* Chicago: University of Chicago Press.

Ladd, H., & Fiske, E. (2000). *When schools compete: A cautionary tale.* Washington, DC: Brookings Institutional Press.

Ladd, H. F., Chalk, R., & Hansen, J. S. (Eds.). (1999). *Equity and adequacy in education finance: Issues and perspectives.* Washington, DC: National Research Council.

Ladd, H. F., & Hansen, J. S. (1999). *Making money matter: Financing America's schools.* Washington, DC: National Academy Press.

Laine, R. D., Greenwald, R., & Hedges, L. V. (1996). Money does matter: A research synthesis of a new universe of education production function studies. In L. Picus & J. Wattenbarger (Eds.), *Where does the money go?* (pp. 44–70). Thousand Oaks, CA: Corwin Press.

Lake View School District, No. 25 v. Huckabee, 91 S.W.3d 472 (Ark. 2002).

Lake View School District, No. 25 v. Huckabee, 1992–5318, Pulaski Cty. Chancery Ct. (2001).

LaMorte, M. W. (1974). The Fourteenth Amendment: Its significance for public educators. *Educational Administration Quarterly, 10*(3).

Land Survey Ordinance of 1784.

Lau v. Nichols (1973) 483 f2d (9OR., 1973); 94 S. C7 786 (1974). Sup. 866.

Lee, D. (2004, February 21). Complications arise in funding of Cary school. *The (Raleigh) News and Observer,* B1.

Leeman v. Sloan, 340 f. Suppl. 1356, (1972).

Lehne, R. (1978). *The quest for justice: The politics of school finance reform.* New York: Longman.

Lemon v. Kurtzman, 403 US 602, 91 Sup. Ct. 2105 (1971).

Levin, H., Glass, G. V., & Meister, G. R. (1984). *Cost-effectiveness of four educational interventions.* Stanford, CA: Institute for Research on Educational Finance and Governance.

Levin, H. M. (1970). Cost-effectiveness analysis of teacher selection. *Journal of Human Resources, 5*(1), 37–52.

Lindblom, C. E. (1959). The science of muddling through. *Public Administration Review, 19,* 79–88.

Litigation. (2001, December 6). *West's Education Law Reporter.*

Longanecker, D. A. (1983). *Public costs of tuition tax credits.* Stanford, CT: Institute for Research on Educational Finance and Governance.

Madden, G., Savage, S., & Kemp, S. (1997). Measuring public sector efficiency: A study of economics departments at Australian universities. *Education Economics, 5*(2), 153–168.

Mann, D., & Inman, D. (1984). Improving education with existing resources: The instructionally effective schools' approach. *Journal of Education Finance, 10*(2), 259–269.

Mann, Horace (1848). *Twelfth Annual Report of the Secretary of Massachusetts Board of Education.* Boston, MA: Author.

March, J. G., & Simon, H. A. (1958). *Organizations.* New York: John Wiley Press.

Marion, R., & Flanigan, J. (2001). Evolution and punctuation of theories of educational expectation and student outcome. *Journal of Education Finance, 26*(3), 239–258.

Marriner, L. S. (1977). The cost of educating handicapped pupils in New York City. *Journal of Education Finance, 3*(1), 82–97.

Marsh, E., & Ross, A. (1963). *Federal aid to science education: Two programs*. Syracuse, NY: Syracuse University Press.

Martha, J. M. (1980). Tuition tax credits for elementary and secondary education: Some new evidence on who would benefit. *Journal of Education Finance, 5*(Winter), 233–245.

Marx, K., & Engels, F. (1848/2002). *The Communist manifesto*. New York: Penguin Classics.

Massachusetts Constitution, Part II, c.5, §2.

Mathis, W. J. (2003). Financial challenges, adequacy, and equity in rural schools and communities. *Journal of Education Finance, 29*(2), 119–138.

Mazzoni, T. (1987). *The politics of educational choice in Minnesota*. Paper presented at the annual conference of the American Education Research Association, Washington, DC.

McDuffy v. Secretary of the Executive Office of Education, 615 N.E. 2d 516 (Mass. 1993).

McEwan, P. (2004). The potential impact of vouchers. In Rolle, A. R., (Ed.), *Peabody journal of education, special issue: K–12 education finance: New directions for future research, 79*(3), 57–80.

McGregor, D., et al. (1968). *Leadership and motivation: Essays of Douglas McGregor*. Cambridge: MIT Press.

McInnis v. Ogilvie, 394 U.S.C. 322 (1969).

McUsic, M. (1991). The use of education clauses in school finance reform litigation. *Harvard Journal on Legislation, 28*(307), 311 n.5.

Menz, F. C., & Raphaelson, A. H. (1976). Some issues in equalizing educational spending. *Journal of Education Finance, 2*(1), 99–109.

Metcalf, G. E. (1993, January). *The lifetime incidence of state and local taxes: Measuring changes during the 1980s* (Working Paper No. 4252). Cambridge, MA: National Bureau of Economic Research.

Mickleson, R. (2002, August 30). *The academic consequences of desegregation and segregation: Evidence from the Charlotte-Mecklenburg schools*. Paper presented at the Resegregation of Southern Schools Conference, UNC-Chapel Hill School of Law, Chapel Hill, NC.

Mills v. Board of Education 348 F. Supp. 866 (D. DC 1972).

Minorini, P. A., & Sugarman, S. D. (1999a). Educational adequacy and the courts: The promise and problems of moving to a new paradigm. In H. F. Ladd, R. Chalk, & J. S. Hansen (Eds.), *Equity and adequacy in education finance: Issues and perspectives* (pp. 175–208). Washington, DC: National Academy Press.

Minorini, P. A., & Sugarman, S. D. (1999b). School finance litigation in the name of education equity: Its evolution, impact, and future. In H. F. Ladd, R. Chalk, & J. S. Hansen (Eds.), *Equity and adequacy in education finance: Issues and perspectives* (pp. 34–71). Washington, DC: National Academy Press.

Mishel, L. & Rothstein, R. (2002). *The class size debate*. New York: Economic Policy Institute.

Moelhman, A. B. (1922). Revision of school accounting report. *American School Board Journal, 64*, 24–25, 121–122, 125.

Moelhman, A. B. (1927). *Public school finance*. Chicago: Rand McNally.

Monk, D. H., Rice, J. K. (1999). Modern education productivity research: Emerging implications for financing education. In W. Fowler, Jr. (Ed.), *Selected papers in school finance: 1997–1999* (pp. 111–139). National Center for Education Statistics, Washington DC.

Morphet, E., Johns, R. L., & Reller, T. L. (1982). *Educational organization and administration*. Englewood Cliffs, NJ: Prentice-Hall.

Morrill Act of 1862, Pub. L. No. 97-98.

Morrison, H. C. (1924). *The financing of public schools in the state of Illinois. Report of the educational finance inquiry Commission IX*. New York: Macmillan.

Morrison, H. C. (1930). *School revenue*. Chicago: University of Chicago Press.

Morrison, H. C. (1932). *The management of the school money*. Chicago: The University of Chicago Press.

Mort, P. R. (1924). *The measurement of educational need*. New York: Columbia University Press.

Mort, P. R. (1926). *State support for education*. New York: Teachers College.

Mort, P. R. (1932). *State support for education*. Washington, DC: American Council on Education.

Mort, P. R. (1933). *State support for public education, A report by the National Survey of School*

Finance. Washington, DC: American Council on Education.

Mort, P. R. (1957). *The foundation program in state education policy*. Albany, NY: New York State Department of Education.

Mort, P. R., & Reusser, W. C. (1941). *Public school finance: Its background, structure, and operation*. New York: McGraw-Hill.

Mort, P. R., Reusser, W. C., & Polley, J. W. (1960). *Public school finance: Its background, structure, and operation* (3rd ed.). New York: McGraw-Hill.

Muellar v. Allen, 463 US 388 (1983).

Murray, S. E., Evans, W. N., Schwab, R. M. (1998). Education finance reform and the distribution of education resources. *American Economic Review, 88*(4), 789–812.

National Center for Educational Statistics. (1979). *School finance equity: A profile of the states, 1976–1977*. Washington, DC: NCES, U.S. Department of HEW.

National Center for Education Statistics. (2002). *Federal support for education: Fiscal years 1980–2002*. Washington, DC: U.S. Department of Education.

National Center for Educational Statistics (NCES). (2003). *National assessment of educational progress*. Washington, DC: U.S. Department of Education.

National Center for Educational Statistics. (2005). *Condition of education*. Washington, DC: U.S. Department of Education.

National Commission on Excellence in Education. (1983). *A nation at risk: The imperative for educational reform*. Washington, DC: United States Department of Education, http://www.ed.gov/pubs/NatAtRisk

National Defense Education Act of 1958, Pub. L. No. 85-864.

National Education Association. (1923, July). *Report of the salary committee of the National Education Association*. Washington, DC: Author.

Netzer, D. (1966). *Economics of the property tax*. Washington, DC: Brookings Institution Press.

Netzer, D. (1971). Property taxes. *Municipal Finance, 44*(2), 36.

New Jersey Constitution, Article VII, Section 4.

New York State Commission on the Quality, Cost, and Financing of Elementary and Secondary Education. (1973). *The Fleischmann report: On the quality, cost, and financing of elementary and secondary education in New York state*. New York: Viking Press.

New York State Department of Taxation and Finance. (2004). *New York state sales and use tax rates by jurisdiction* (Publication No. 718). Albany, NY: Author.

New York State Office of Real Property Service Municipal Profile. (2002). *New York City: Summary of exemptions by roll year, 2002 assessment rolls*. Albany, NY: Author.

No Child Left Behind Act of 2001, Pub. L. No. 107–110 (2001).

Northshore School District v. Kinnear, 530 P.2d 178 (Wash. 1974).

Northwest Ordinance of 1787.

Nyhan, R., & Alkadry, M. (1999). The impact of school resources on student achievement test scores. *Journal of Education Finance, 25*(2), 211–227.

Odden, A. R. (2000). The new school finance: Providing adequacy and improving equity. *Journal of Education Finance, 25*(4), 467–488.

Odden, A. R., & Archibald, S. (2000). Reallocating resources to support high student achievement: An empirical look at 5 states. *Journal of Education Finance, 25*(4) 545–564.

Odden, A., & Clune, W. (1998). School finance systems: Aging structures in need of renovation, *Educational Evaluation and Policy Analysis, 20*(3), 157–177.

Odden, A., & Picus, L. (1999). *School finance: A policy perspective*. San Francisco: Jossey-Bass.

Odden, A. R., & Picus, L. (2000). *School finance: A policy perspective*. Boston: McGraw-Hill.

Odden, A., Picus, L. O., & Fermanich, M. (2003a). *A state-of-the-art approach to school finance adequacy in Kentucky* (Paper prepared for the Kentucky Department of Education). Los Angeles: Picus and Associates,

Odden, A., Picus, L. O., & Fermanich, M. (2003b). *An evidence-based approach to school finance adequacy in Arkansas* (Report prepared for the Joint Committee on Educational Adequacy). Little Rock, AK: Author.

Odden, A. R., Archibald, S., Fermanich, M., & Gross, B. (2003). Defining school-level expenditure structures that reflect educational strategies. *Journal of Education Finance, 29*(3), 323–356.

Ordinance of 1802.

Orfield, G. (1978). *Must we bus?* Washington, DC: Brookings Institution Press.

Orfield, G., Frankenberg, E., & Lee, C. The resurgence of school segregation. *Educational Leadership, 60*(4),16–20.

Papasan v. Allain, 106 U.S. 2932 (S. Ct. 1986).

PARC v. Commonwealth, 834 F. Sup. Ct. 1257 (1971).

Parker v. Mandel, 344 F. Supp. 1068 (D. Md. 1972).

Parrish, T. B., & Chambers, J. G. (1984). *An overview of the resource cost model (RCM)*. Stanford, CA: Associates for Education Finance and Planning.

Patt, J. S. (1999). School finance battles: Survey says? It's all just a change in attitudes. *34 Harvard Civil Rights—Civil Liberties Law Review 547.*

Pauley v. Bailey, 324 S.E. 2d 128 (W.Va. 1984).

Pauley v. Kelly, 255 S.E. 2d 859 (W.Va. 1979).

Peacock, A. T. (1992). *Public choice analysis in historical perspective* (pp. 1–83). Cambridge, England: Press Syndicate of the University of Cambridge.

Pechman, J. (1987). *Federal tax policy* (5th ed., p.74). Washington, DC: Brookings Institution Press.

Pechman J. A., & Okner, B. A. (1974). *Who bears the tax burden?* (pp. 25–43). Washington, DC: Brookings Institution Press.

Pemberton, S. M. (1981). *The federal government and equality of educational opportunity*. Washington, DC: University Press of America.

Picus, L. O., Odden, A., & Fermanich, M. (2004). Assessing the equity of Kentucky's SEEK formula: A 10-year analysis. *Journal of Education Finance, 29*(4).

Pitsch, M. (1995, June 7). Goals 2000 fails to gain firm foothold. *Education Week*.

Pitsch, M. (1996, May 1). To placate conservatives, measure alters Goals 2000. *Education Week*, Retrieved August 10, 2004, from www.edweek.com

Plessy v. Fergeson, 163 US 537, 16 Sup. Ct. 1138 (1896).

Podgursky, M. (2004). Reforming the single teacher salary schedule in public schools. *Texas Education Review*, 2003–2004.

Porter, A. C. (2002). Measuring the content of instruction: Uses in research and practice. *Educational Researcher, 31*(7), 3–14.

Poterba, J. (1997). Demographic Structure and the Political Economy of Public Education. *Journal of Public Policy and Management, 16*, 48–66.

Princeton Review. (2003). Testing the Testers 2003: An Annual Ranking of State Accountability Systems, 6–36.

Rabinowitz, A. (1969). *Municipal bond finance and administration* (p. 35). New York: John Wiley/Interscience.

Radcliffe, K., Riddle B., & Yinger, J. (1990). The fiscal condition of school districts in Nebraska: Is small beautiful? *Economics of Education Review, 9*(1), pp. 81–99.

Ramirez, A. (2003). The shifting sands of school finance. *Educational Leadership, 60*(4), 54–57.

Ratner, G. M. (1985). A new legal duty for urban public schools: Effective education in basic skills. *Texas Legal Review 63*(777).

Ratvitch, D. (Ed.). (2001). *Brookings papers on education policy: 2001*. Washington, DC: Brookings Institution Press.

Ravitch, D., & Vinovskis, M. (1995). *Learning from the past: What history teaches us about school reform*. Baltimore: John Hopkins University Press.

Razin, A., Sadka, E., & Swagel, P. (2002). The aging population and the size of welfare. *Journal of Political Economy, 110*(4), 900–918.

Reason, P. L., & Alpheus L. White, A. L. (1957). *Financial accounting for local and state school systems: Standard receipt and expenditure accounts*. Washington, DC: Government Printing Office.

Reschovsky, A., & Imazeki, J. (2001). Achieving educational adequacy through school finance reform. *Journal of Education Finance, 26*(4), 373–396.

Roberts, C. T., & Lichtenberger, A. R. (1973). *Financial accounting: Classifications and standard terminology for local and state school systems.* Washington, DC: Government Printing Office.

Robinson v. Cahill, 62 N.J. 473, 303 A. 3d 273 (N.J. 1973).

Rolle, R. A. (2000). *Marching to the beat of a different drum: An empirical analysis of public school corporations as budget maximizing bureaus.* Unpublished doctoral dissertation, Indiana University.

Rolle, A. R. (2004a). An empirical discussion of public school districts as budget maximizing agencies. *Journal of Education Finance, 29*(4), 277–298.

Rolle, A. R. (2004b). Out with the old—in with the new: Thoughts on the future of educational productivity research. *Peabody Journal of Education, 29*(3), 31–56.

Rolle, A. R. (2005). Rethinking educational productivity and its measurement: A discussion of stochastic frontier analysis within a budget maximizing framework. In L. Steifel, et al., (Eds.) *Measuring school performance and efficiency: Implications for practice and research. 2005 yearbook of the American Educational Finance Association* (pp. 185–204). Larchmont, NY: Eye on Education.

Roosevelt v. Bishop, 877 P. 2d 806 (1994).

Rose v. Council for Better Education, 790 S.W. 2d 186 (Ky. 1989).

Rosen, H. S. (1997). The way we were (and are): Changes in public finance and its textbooks. *National Tax Journal, 50*(4), 719–730.

Rosenstengel, W. E., & Gastmond, J. N. (1957). *School finance: Its theory and practice.* New York: Ronald Press.

Rossmiller, R.A., & Geske, T.G. (1976). Toward more effective use of school resources. *Journal of Education Finance, 1*(4), 484–502.

Rothstein, R. (1998). *The way we were? The myths and realities of America's student achievement.* New York: Century Foundation.

Rothstein, R. (2004). *Class and schools. Using social, economic, and educational reform to close the black-white achievement gap.* Washington, DC: The Economic Policy Institute, and New York: Teachers College, Columbia University.

Roza, M., & Hill, P. (2004). How within-district spending inequities help some schools to fail. In Diane Ravitch, (Ed.), *Brookings papers on education policy 2004.* Washington, DC: Brookings Institution Press.

Sabatier, P. (Ed.). (1999). *Theories of the policy process.* Boulder, CO: Westview Press.

Salisbury, D. (2003). *Lessons from Florida: School choice gives increased opportunities to children with special needs* (Cato Institute Briefing Paper). Retrieved December 23, 2004, from http://www.cato.org/pubs/briefs/bp81.pdf

Samuelson, E. V., & Tankard, G. G. (1962). *Financial accounting for school activities.* Washington, DC: Government Printing Office.

San Antonio v. Rodriguez, 411 U.S. 1, 93 1278 (S. Ct. 1973).

Santin, D., & Delgado, F. J., & Valino, A. (2004). The measurement of technical efficiency: A neural network approach. *Applied Economics, 36*, 627–635.

Satori, M. B. (1998). Allocation and distribution of resources in high schools. In W. Hartman & W. Boyd (Eds.), *Resource allocation and productivity in education: Theory and practice* (pp. 155–172). Westport, CT: Greenwood Press.

Sawyer v. Gilmore, 109 Me. 169, 83 A. 673 (1912).

Schmidt, P. (1995, October 11). Miss America's platform ruffles partisan feathers. *Education Week,* Retrieved August 23, 2004, from www.edweek.com

Schnieder, M., & Buckley, J. (2002) What do parents want from schools? Evidence from the internet. *Educational Evaluation and Policy Analysis, 24*(2), 133–144.

School-to-Work Opportunities Act of 1994, Pub. L. No. 103-239.

Schwartz, A. E., Steifel, L., & Amor, H. B. (2005). Measuring school performance using cost functions. In L. Stiefel, et al. (Eds.), *Measuring school performance and efficiency: Implications for practice and research—2005 yearbook of the American Education Finance Association* (pp. 67–92). New York: Eye on Education.

Sears, J. B., & Henderson, A. D. (1957). *Cubberley of Stanford and his contribution to American education.* Stanford, CA: Stanford University Press.

Seattle School District No. 1 of King County v. State, 585 P.2d 71 (Wash. 1978).

Serrano v. Priest, 5 Cal. 3d 584 (1971). Hereinafter Serrano I.

Serrano v. Priest, 18 Cal. 3d 728 (1976). Hereinafter Serrano II.

Serrano v. Priest, 20 Cal. 3d 25 (1977). Hereinafter Serrano III.

Service Man's Readjustment Act, Pub. L. No. 78-346.

Shaffer v. Carter, 252 U.S. 37, 40 S.Ct. 221 (1920).

Skeen v. State, 505 N.W. 2d 299 (Min. 1993).

Smith, J., & Guthrie, J. W. (2005). *A rejoinder to Hanushek* (Working Paper No. 2005-08). Davis, CA: MAP.

Smith, M., & O'Day, J. (1991a). *Putting the pieces together: Systemic school reform* (CPRE Policy Brief). New Brunswick, NJ: Eagleton Institute of Politics.

Smith, M., & O'Day, J. (1991b). Systemic school reform. In S. H. Fuhrman & B. Malen (Eds.), *The politics of curriculum and testing* (pp. 233–268). Bristol, PA: Falmer Press.

Smith, M. J. (2004). How the apportionment of district money is associated with differences in the grade 8 mathematics and reading achievement scores in Minnesota students. *Journal of Education Finance, 29*(4), 299–314.

Smith-Hughes Act of 1917, Pub. L. No. 64-347.

Smrekar, C., & Goldring, E. (1999). *School Choice in Urban America: Magnet Schools and the Pursuit of Equity.* New York: Teachers College Press.

Solomon, L. C., & Goldschmidt, P. (2004). *Comparison of traditional public schools and charter schools on retention, school switching and achievement growth* (Goldwater Institute Policy Report No. 192). Retrieved July 4, 2004, from http://www.goldwaterinstitute.org/pdf/materials/431.pdf

Sparkman, W. E. (1990). School finance challenges in state courts. In J. K. Underwood & D. A. Verstegen (Eds.), *The impacts of litigation and legislation on public school finance: Adequacy, equity and excellence.* New York: Harper & Row.

Spillane, J. P. (2005). *Standards deviation; How schools misunderstand education policy.* Cambridge: Harvard University Press.

Springer, M. G., & Liu, K. (2005). *The impact of court mandated reform on resource distribution: Is there anything special about adequacy?* Paper presented at the 2005 Annual Meeting of the American Education Finance Association, Louisville, KY.

Springer, M. G., Liu, K., & Guthrie, J. W. (2005). *The impact of court-mandated reformn on resource distribution: Is there anything special about adequacy?* (Working Paper No. 12). Nashville, TN: Peabody Center for Education Policy.

Springfield Township v. Quick, 63 U.S. 56 (U.S. 1859).

SRI International. (2002). *A decade of public charter schools: Evaluation of the public charter schools program—2000–2001 evaluation report.* Washington, DC: United States Department of Education. Retrieved June 18, 2006, from http://www.sri.com/policy/cep/choice/yr2.pdf

State ex rel Anderson v. Brand 313 US 95 (1938).

State of Florida, Department of Revenue (2004). *Florida property tax exemptions,* 2004. Tallahassee: Author.

State v. Board of Commissioners of Elk County (1899).

State v. Campbell County School District, 19 P. 3d 518 (Wyo. 2001).

Stiefel, L., Schwartz, A. E., Portas, C., & Kim, D. Y. (2003). School budgeting and school performance: The impact on New York City's performance driven budgeting initiative. *Journal of Education Finance, 28*(3), 403–425.

Strayer, G., & Haig, R. (1923). *Financing of education in the state of New York.* New York: Macmillan; p. 173.

Stringer, K. (2002, October 31). How to have a pleasant trip: Eliminate human contact. *Wall Street Journal,* D1.

Stuart v. School District No. 1 of Village of Kalamazoo, 30 Mich. 69 (1874).

Swanson, A. D., & King, R. A. (1991). *School finance: Its economics and politics.* White Plains, NY: Longman.

Taylor, L., Chambers, J., & Robinson, J. P. (2004). A new geographic cost of education index for Alaska: Old approaches with some new twists. *Journal of Education Finance, 30*(1), 51–78.

Tennessee Small School System v. McWherter, 851 S.W. 2d 139 (Tenn. 1993).

Tennessee Small Schools Systems v. McWherter, WL 119824 (Tenn. Ct. App. 1992).

Teske, P., et al. (2001). Can charter schools change traditional public schools? In P. Peterson & D. Campbell, (Eds.), *Charters, vouchers and public education*. Washington, DC: Brookings Institution Press.

Thanassoulis, E., Portela, M., & Silva, A. (2002). School outcomes: Sharing the responsibility between pupil and school. *Education Economics, 10*(2), 183–207.

Thomas, J. A. (1961). *Efficiency in education: A study of the relationship between selection inputs and test score in sample of high schools.* Unpublished doctoral dissertation, Stanford, California.

Thomas, J. A. (1962, October). Efficiency in education: An empirical study. *Administration Notebook, 11*, 1–4.

Thomas, N. C. (1979). Equalizing education opportunity through school finance reform: A review assessment. *University of Cincinnati Law Review, 48*(255).

Thompson, D. C., & Wood, R. C. (2001). *Money & schools* (2nd ed.). Larchmont, New York: Eye on Education.

Thro, W. E. (1989). Note, to render them safe: The analysis of state constitutional provisions in public school finance reform litigation. *Virginia Law Review, 75*.

Thro, W. E. (1994). Judicial analysis during the third wave of school finance litigation: The Massachusetts decision as a model. *Boston College Law Review, 35*(4), 597, 598.

Tiebout, C. M. (1956). A pure theory of local expenditures. *Journal of Political Economy, 65*(5), 416–424.

U.S. Bureau of the Census. (1985). *Statistical abstract of the United States* (p. 131, Table 207, p. 475, Table 789, p. 433, Table 717, p. 6, Table 2). Washington, DC: Government Printing Office.

U.S. Bureau of the Census. (1994). *Census of governments: Assessed valuations for local general property taxation* (p. 8). Washington, DC: Government Printing Office.

U.S. Bureau of the Census (2003). *Statistical abstract of the United States: 2003* (p. 325, Table 481, p. 322, Table 476). Washington, DC: Government Printing Office.

U.S. Bureau of the Census. (2002). *Public elementary-secondary education finances: 2001–02* (Table 13). Washington, DC: Government Printing Office.

U.S. Bureau of the Census, Governments Division. (2002). *State and local government finances: 2001–02* (Table 2). Washington, DC: Government Printing Office.

U.S. Bureau of the Census, Governments Division. (2003). *State government finances: 2002* Washington, DC: Government Printing Office.

U.S. Bureau of the Census, Governments Division. (2004). *State government tax collections: 2003*. Washington, DC: Government Printing Office.

U.S. Bureau of Census. http://www.census.gov/main/www/popclock.html

Undergraff, H. (1919). Application of state funds to the aid of local schools. *University of Pennsylvania Bulletin*, (1).

Underwood, J. K. (1989). Changing equal protection analyses in finance equity litigation. *Journal of Education Finance, 14*, 415–416.

Underwood, J. K., & Sparkman, W. E. (1991). School finance litigation: A new wave of reform, *Harvard Journal of Law and Public Policy, 14*(517), 520–535.

U.S. Department of Education. (2003a). Commissioner's statement. Retrieved http://nces.ed.gov/programs/quarterly/vol_5/5_2/q7_1.asp

U.S. Department of Education. (2003b). *Overview of public elementary and secondary schools and districts: School year 2001–2002*. Washington, DC: National Center for Educational Statistics.

United States v. Butler, 297 US 1, 56 Sup. Ct. 312 (1936).

Updegraff, H. (1922). *Rural school survey of New York state*. Ithaca, NY.

Updegraff, H., & King, L. A. (1922). *Survey of the fiscal policies of the state of Pennsylvania in the field of education*. Philadelphia: University of Pennsylvania.

Verstegan, D. (2002). Financing the new adequacy: Towards new models of state education finance systems that support standards based report. *Journal of Education Finance, 27*(3), 749–782.

Verstegen, D. A., & King, R. A. (1998). The relationship between school spending and student achievement: a review and analysis of 35 years of production function research. *Journal of Education Finance, 24*(2), 243–262.

Vincent v. Voight, 614 N.W. 2d 388 (Wis. 2000).

Vinovskis, M. A. (1999). *History and educational policy making.* New Haven, CT: Yale University Press.

Vocational Education Act of 1963, Pub. L. No. 88-210.

Walberg, H. J., & Fowler, W. J. (1987). Expenditure and size efficiencies of public school districts. *Educational Researcher, 16*(7), 5–13.

Walberg, H. J., & Walberg, H. (1984). Losing local control. *Educational Researcher, 23*(5), 19–26.

Walters, R. (1984). *The burden of Brown: Thirty years of school desegregation.* Knoxville, TN: University of Tennessee Press.

Washington Constitution, Article IX, 1.

Waterman, I. R. (1932). Equalization of the burden of support for education. *University of California Publications in Education, 6*(5), 285–358.

Webb, L. D. (1976). Cost-benefit analysis: An accountability asset. *Journal of Education Finance, 2*(2), 209–223.

West Orange-Cove Cons. Independent School District v. Neely, No. GV–100528 (Tex. Dist. Ct. Nov. 30, 2004, pet. filed).

West, M. R., & Peterson, P. P. (2003). The politics and practice of accountability. In M. Peterson & M. West (Eds.), *No Child Left Behind? The politics and practice of accountability.* Washington, DC: Brookings Institution Press. Retrieved August 9, 2004, from http://www.brookings.edu/dybdocroot/press/books/chapter_1/nochildleftbehind.pdf

Whitt, E. J., Clark, D. L., & Astuto, T. A. (1986). *An analysis of public support for the educational policy preferences of the Reagan administration.* Charlottesville, VA: University Council for Educational Administration, University of Virginia.

Wiggins, G., & McTighe, J. (1998). *Understanding by design.* Washington, DC: Association for Supervision & Curriculum Development.

Wildavsky, A., & Caiden, N. (2003). *The new politics of the budgetary process* (5th ed.). New York: Longman.

Wilkinson, J. H. (1976). *From Brown to Baake.* Oxford: Oxford University Press.

Williston Public School District v. State (ND pending).

Wirt, F. M., & Kirst, M. W. (2005). *The political dynamics of American education.* Richmond, CA: McCutchen.

Wise, A. (1968). *Rich schools, poor schools.* Chicago: University of Chicago Press.

Wise, A. E. (1976). Minimum educational adequacy: Beyond school finance reform. *Journal of Education Finance, 1*(4) 468–483.

Wolfe, B. (1977). A cost-effectiveness analysis of reductions in school expenditures: An application of an educational production function. *Journal of Education Finance, 2*(4), 407–418.

Wong, K. K. (2003, November). *The changing landscape in school governance: Proposing a framework.* Paper presented at the Conference on Science and Sensationalism: The New Foundations of Educational Administration, Policy and Politics, University of California at Riverside.

Wood, R. C., & Thompson, D. C. (1996). *Educational finance law: Constitutional challenges to state aid plans—An analysis of strategies.* Topeka, KS: National Organization on Legal Problems of Education.

Young v. Williams, Franklin Cty. Cir. Ct. (2003).

Zarig, D. (2004). National rulemaking through trial courts: The big case and institutional reform. *UCLA Law Review, 51,* 887–1232.

Zehr, M. A. (1998, October 28). School to work opponents unable to block funding. *Education Week.* Retrieved August 7, 2004, from http://www.edweek.com

Zelman v. Simmons-Harris, 00 U.S. 1751 (2002).

Zigler, E., & Muenchow, S. (1992). *Head Start: The inside story of America's most successful experiment.* New York: Basic Books

Zodrow, G. R. (2001). The property tax as a capital tax: A room with three views. *National Tax Journal, 54*(1) 139–156.

Index

Page numbers followed by *f* and *t* represent figures and tables respectively.